Photoshop® 5&5.5 Artistry

A Master Class for Photographers, Artists, and Production Artists

▼▼▼▼▼▼▼▼▼▼▼▼▼▼▼

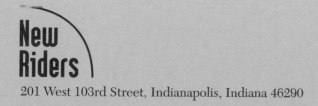

New Riders

201 West 103rd Street, Indianapolis, Indiana 46290

Barry Haynes
Wendy Crumpler

Photoshop® 5&5.5 Artistry

A Master Class for Photographers, Artists, and Production Artists

By Barry Haynes and Wendy Crumpler

Published by: New Riders Publishing
201 West 103rd Street
Indianapolis, IN 46290 USA

International Standard Book Number: 0-7357-0994-7

Library of Congress Catalog Card Number: 99-067434

Printed in the United States of America   2 3 4 5 6 7 8 9 0

First Printing: December 1999

TRADEMARKS

WARNING AND DISCLAIMER

EXECUTIVE EDITOR:
  Steve Weiss
DEVELOPMENT EDITOR
  Jennifer Eberhardt
PROJECT EDITOR
  Katie Purdum
COPY EDITOR
  San Dee Phillips
INDEXER
  Greg Pearson
TECHNICAL EDITORS
  J. Scott Hamlin
  Gary Kubicek
SOFTWARE DEVELOPMENT
 SPECIALIST
  Craig Atkins

COVER DESIGN
  Wendy Crumpler and
  Barry Haynes
COVER PRODUCTION
  Barry Haynes and
  Wendy Crumpler
COVER PHOTO
  Barry Haynes
BOOK DESIGN AND PRODUCTION
  Wendy Crumpler and
  Barry Haynes

A MESSAGE FROM NEW RIDERS

At New Riders, we work hard in building and maintaining valuable relationships—partnerships, really—with our authors. We consider ourselves quite fortunate to be associated with such talented, creative, detail-oriented, selfless and genuinely cool people as the authors of this book, Barry Haynes and Wendy Crumpler. Thanks, you two.

New Riders is proud of every title we publish. But some titles… some titles we keep in mind when we really want to show off. *Photoshop Artistry* is one such title.

Judging from the response that Barry and Wendy's previous editions of this book have earned from reviewers, students, and countless satisfied users, *Photoshop Artistry* may well be the best Photoshop book available anywhere, for any audience, for any price. It's a unique book, designed to bring out the uniqueness in you, the Photoshop user. Please let us know how you use the book and how the book works for you. Thanks…

HOW TO CONTACT US

As the reader of this book, *you* are our most important critic and commentator. We value your opinion and want to know what we're doing right, what we could do better, in what areas you'd like to see us publish, and any other words of wisdom you're willing to pass our way.

As the Executive Editor for the Graphics team at New Riders, I welcome your comments. You can fax, email, or write me directly to let me know what you did or didn't like about this book—as well as what we can do to make our books better.

Please note that I cannot help you with technical problems related to the topic of this book, and that due to the high volume of mail I receive, I might not be able to reply to every message.

When you write, please be sure to include this book's title, isbn and authors, as well as your name and phone or fax number. I will carefully review your comments and share them with the authors and editors who worked on the book.

For any issues directly related to this or other titles:

Email: steve.weiss@newriders.com
Mail: Steve Weiss
　　　　Executive Editor
　　　　Professional Graphics and Design Publishing team
　　　　New Riders Publishing
　　　　201 West 103rd Street
　　　　Indianapolis, IN 46290 USA

Call toll-free (800) 571-5840 + 9 + 3567. Ask for New Riders.
If outside the USA, please call 1-317-581-3500. Ask for New Riders.
Fax: 317-581-4663

VISIT OUR WEBSITE: www.newriders.com

On our website you'll find information about our other books, the authors we partner with, book updates and file downloads, promotions, discussion boards for online interaction with other users and with technology experts, and a calendar of trade shows and other professional events with which we'll be involved. Maybe we'll see you around.

ABOUT THIS VERSION OF *PHOTOSHOP ARTISTRY*

New Riders and the authors decided to update *Photoshop 5 Artistry* to include coverage of Photoshop 5.5 because it didn't seem appropriate to not have a version of *Photoshop Artistry* available to anyone new to Photoshop during the 5.5 rev cycle.

Suffice to say: If you already own a copy of *Photoshop 5 Artistry*, you may not need this upgrade version of the book, just as if you already own Photoshop 5, you probably already own ImageReady and haven't seen a huge need to go out and upgrade to 5.5. Of course, this all changes when Photoshop 6 releases: Look for *Photoshop 6 Artistry* to be rewritten from the ground up, the better to reflect the changes we're all expecting to see in the next gen version of Photoshop…

ABOUT THE AUTHORS

Barry Haynes uses digital technology to print, show, and sell his photography. In addition to his love for creating photographs, Barry teaches digital photography, creates commercial special effects, and does digital image consulting. His books, *Photoshop Artistry: A Master Class for Photographers and Artists*, and *Photoshop 4 Artistry: A Master Class for Photographers, Artists, and Production Artists* are available in bookstores around the world. He has been teaching Photoshop courses since 1990 to clients including Apple, Oracle, Kodak, Nikon, Pacific Bell, Sony, Tandem, SuperMac, *The San Jose Mercury News,* and many others. He teaches regular digital photography workshops for University of California Santa Cruz and UC Santa Barbara Extension programs, and AD Vantage Computers in Des Moines, Iowa. He has given talks or workshops for the Photoshop Conference, The Golden Gate School of Photography, Seybold Seminars, the MacSummit conference, MacWorld, the Center for Creative Imaging, the Digital Photography Conference, the American Society of Magazine Photographers, advertising agencies, design firms, and other organizations.

His articles have appeared in desktop publishing magazines, and his imaging effects can be seen in brochures, on the Web, and on magazine covers for companies including Apple, Netscape, and Tandem. Barry has a degree in computer science and spent 10 years, from 1980 to 1990, doing software development and research at Apple. There he did research involving desktop publishing, digital imaging, and high-speed networks, and before that he worked on Pascal and Object Oriented software development environments for Apple including Macintosh Smalltalk, MacApp, the Lisa Workshop, and Apple II Pascal.

Wendy Crumpler has been in advertising and design since 1980. She has worked in print, television, CD-Interactive, interactive television, and computer-based training. Prior to her discovery of the computer in 1981 and the Macintosh in 1986, she was an actress and teacher. Since her involvement in digital imaging, she has done production, illustration, design, and training for a variety of clients using Quark, PageMaker, Illustrator, Freehand, Photoshop, and other applications. She has worked for Angotti Thomas Hedge, Boardroom Reports, Deutsch Advertising, J. Walter Thompson, TBWA Advertising, Wechsler Design, Manhattan Transfer, Wells Rich Greene, Canon, Parke Davis, IBM, and AT&T.

SAY YES TO THE UNIVERSE

In three days, we fell in love. In three months, we were married. In four years of marriage, we've produced one remarkable son and three terrific books. A lot can happen when you say, "Yes!"

LET US KNOW WHAT YOU THINK

There's been a lot of student and reader involvement in the shaping of this book. Listening to people who use these techniques helps us to refine and dig deeper to find solutions to our clients' and students' problems. And, we get smarter in the process. We love what we do and invite you to become part of the digital revolution with us. Let us know what you think of the book, what was helpful, what confused you. We are committed to empowering people to use their computers and their software to advance their own artistic abilities and to make a difference on this planet.

TAKE ONE OF OUR IN-DEPTH WORKSHOPS

We recently moved to Corvallis, Oregon, an arts-oriented college town where we will be teaching week-long hands-on classes for small groups of students. These classes will be tailored to meet individual needs. Our next book project is a comparative guide to Photoshop, Painter, and Illustrator. We welcome insights you might have into using those three programs together, discussions of work you've done using them, or work that you need to accomplish that we can do for you using all three. Send information on this new project and check for the latest information about the times and locations for our digital imaging courses, as well as book updates, and other useful information on our Web site, www.maxart.com.

WE LOOK FORWARD TO HEARING FROM YOU!

Barry Haynes Photography
Wendy Crumpler Enterprises
2222 NW Brownly Heights Drive
Corvallis, OR 97330
541-754-2219
email: Barry@maxart.com, or Wendy@maxart.com

Please check our Web site http://www.maxart.com

DEDICATION

For those Tony left behind,
  live fully and do what you love.

ACKNOWLEDGMENTS

Each time we go through the amazing process of putting a book together, we worry. How will it be this time? Will we get the support we need, will people be competent, will they be fun? It's a difficult and daunting task to put so much effort into a book that will need to be updated again in a very short time. But, each time we write, we're blessed with people who ease the way, straighten us out, keep us going, and make us laugh.

So thank-yous to:

Jennifer Eberhardt, for being unbelievably organized, always pleasant, a joy to work with, everything we could ask for in an editor and more. Could we be a little more effusive? I don't think so. We loved working with you.

Beth Millett, for believing in us, for running a tight ship (we were very impressed), and for the 80lb-paper. You're the greatest.

Steve Weiss, for his enthusiasm about our books and for helping us get the 5.5 upgrade done right.

Chris Nelson, for his help in printing the 5.5 upgrade, for his encouragement and for being fun to have dinner with.

Seán Duggan, for helping to write sections of chapter 45 and for being a good instructor using our book.

Scott Hamlin and Gary Kubicek, whose comments were so good we often wrote them down verbatim, and whose questions made us work harder.

Katie Purdum for keeping a handle on where things were even in the midst of chaos, and for always being placid and pleasant.

San Dee Phillips, for her lovely mark-ups, her desire to get things right, for "agonizing" and telling us about it.

Craig Atkins, for working so hard to get the demo versions on our disk, and for remaining calm when we were nervous.

Brad Bunnin. We continue to rely on your advice and knowledge—you are such a gift. Thank you and Nenelle so much for visiting, it was as refreshing as a vacation.

Jim Rich, for all your help with color and calibration, for your friendship, and for being one helluva dancer.

Bill Atkinson, a generous and creative human being, whose fire to know and share and learn pulls us in and pushes us forward.

Bill Justin, for his comments about the color calibration issues and for keeping us in RAM.

Bruce Ashley for all his wonderful images, and for his help and advice, particularly in CMYK monitor calibration.

Bruce Hodge, who is not only a wonderful photographer, but the kind of friend who would drive your station wagon all night to your new home and then hop a flight so's not to miss his daughter's recital. Was there ever better?

Nancy White, for letting us sit in on her wonderful "Photoshop for Multimedia" course, for her great help in the multimedia chapter of this book, and for being excited and eager to assist.

Ed Velandria (one of the smartest artists we'll ever meet) for his help with the Web chapters, and to Rox and Sarah for opening their home to us and being patient, loving, and fun.

Charlie Cramer, a gifted artist, whose work continues to inspire us. Thank you so much for sharing your knowledge.

Adobe's Russell Brown, Chris Cox, Mark Hamburg, Andrei Herasimchuk, David Herman, and George Jardine, thanks for detailed information during the beta testing, inspired creativity, and for using our book.

Bruce Fraser, Joseph Holmes, and Jeff Schewe who continue to dig deeper into the possibilities of accurate color.

Our friends, Angelika and Ryan, Bob and Sandy, Steve and Sarah, Neil and Linda, Al and Mary, Bruce and Liz, the McNamaras, Victor, Diane, Luke, Susan Merrie, Karen, and Marcella.

All of the fabulous caregivers who help Max grow more fantastic every day.

Denise Haynes, a brave, wonderful, and supportive lady.

Our son, Max, for sharing his life this time with us.

Our readers, who continue to give meaning to our work.

From Wendy to Barry

If I were a better writer, a good and true writer, I would come up with some new and powerful way to tell you what you are to me. Perhaps in the future that will happen. For now, I say thank you for growing with me and changing with me, thank you for bringing me to Oregon, and thank you for bringing me to myself. I love you.

From Barry to Wendy

As it is with everything we do, we do it together and this book is just as much your creation as it is mine. Thanks, Wendy, for the chapters you updated and wrote and for all your design, illustration, and creative wonder. Thank you mostly, though, for being the best partner I could have in travel through life and love.

Finally, and most importantly, our thanks to the Divine Creator for the bounty of this life.

TABLE OF CONTENTS

A Photoshop book for photographers, artists, production artists, and people who deal with images. Here's what makes this book and CD different from all the rest. Read this section to decide if *Photoshop 5 Artistry* is the book for you.

An overview of the new Photoshop 5 features and some quick tips about using them. A reference guide to where the new features are documented within the rest of the book. An extensive chart of the new shortcut keys added to Photoshop 5. See chapters 42 through 46 for the new features in Photoshop 5.5 and ImageReady.

For those new to digital imaging, a brief glimpse of the different types of input and output devices that are possible and a discussion of where digital imaging and the digital world is headed. (More advanced users may find they are familiar with most things in this chapter.)

THINGS YOU NEED TO KNOW   XXXX

This section of the book contains overview information about Photoshop that all users should learn. Everyone should read the chapters, "How to Use This Book," "Using the Photoshop 5 Artistry CD," "Navigating in Photoshop," "Automating with Actions," "Setting System and Photoshop Preferences,"and "History Palette, History Brush, and Snapshots." More advanced users, or those who want to play first, should read the other chapters in this part of the book when they want to pick up extra information.

A guide to help you learn Photoshop and enjoy this book. A must-read for everyone. This chapter also summarizes the minor Photoshop differences between Mac and Windows users.

Using the images and steps on the CD to do all the step-by-step examples yourself and then compare your results with ours. Do the book's examples using the sample version of Photoshop 5, and try out Adobe ImageReady and other Adobe and third-party products on the CD.

Organizing your screen, windows, palettes, and working environment to access and use Photoshop's features most effectively. A must-read for new Photoshop users.

Using the Photoshop 5 Actions palette to automate your tasks. Creating, enhancing, and editing actions, including adding breakpoints and prompts, and getting user feedback during an action, making sets of Actions as well as batch processing large groups of files automatically. Loading the ArtistKeys set of predefined actions, which you'll use with this book to speed your Photoshop tasks.

Setting up your system and Photoshop's preferences for the most effective use of Photoshop; understanding and benefiting from the new Photoshop 5 color management features, a standard RGB or Lab workspace; and better RGB to CMYK conversions, and standardizing Photoshop preferences and systems within an organization.

Understanding the different file formats (Photoshop, TIFF, EPS, GIF, JPEG, and so on) and when, how, and why to use each. The options for image compression are also explored.

Overall color correction using Levels, Hue/Saturation, and Curves Adjustment layers on a problem image that has unbalanced colors and lacks a good highlight or shadow position. Using the new Photoshop 5 Hue/Saturation features along with the new Color Sampler tool to more accurately measure colors.

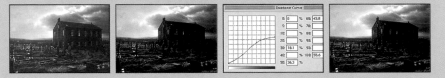

Using the Photoshop 5 enhanced Duotone features in Photoshop with custom curves, looking at separate duotone and tritone channels, printing duotones as EPS, and converting duotones and tritones to RGB and CMYK for final output.

IMPROVING COLOR AND MOOD WITH SELECTIONS, LAYERS, ADJUSTMENT LAYERS, AND LAYER MASKS

After you finish overall color correction, you will want to use selections, layers, Adjustment layers, and layer masks to isolate specific areas of your image and change their color, retouch them, or make them lighter or darker. Many of these techniques, including color matching different color objects, retouching to make fine black-and-white and color prints, using layers for specific color control, and color correcting in Lab color, demonstrate the finer artistic control that digital photography gives you.

Selecting a complex object within an image using the Magic Wand, Lasso, and Quick Mask and then changing its color with Hue/Saturation to create an advertising quality final hi-res image. Other Photoshop 5 approaches to this process are explored, including using the new Magnetic Lasso with the new Hue/Saturation Eyedroppers to simplify the selection and color change process.

Now that overall color correction is complete, fine-tune the GrandCanyon image using selections and Adjustment layers with Curves and the new Photoshop 5 Color Sampler to burn and dodge light and dark areas and remove the spots and scratches. Saving your Master RGB image then resampling and sharpening it separately for a CMYK print and a Web image.

Make final improvements to specific off-color and dark areas using manual and threshold selections, Adjustment layers and Hue/Saturation tricks, dealing with out-of-gamut colors when converting to CMYK, and the details of using the Unsharp Mask filter to sharpen an image.

Using Color Range and Replace Color to easily isolate all the yellow flowers and change their colors. Using Selective Color to fine-tune those colors after RGB to CMYK conversion. Moving Replace Color or Color Range results into an Adjustment Layer layer mask so you can soften or edit the mask, as well as change the color as many times as you like, without degrading the image.

Making a fine black-and-white print, using Color Samplers to assist with detailed dodging and burning, darkening the edges of the print using a Curves Adjustment layer with a feathered oval mask, doing detailed retouching to remove unwanted blemishes and facial objects, and colorizing the final image. Using the new Photoshop 5 History palette and History Brush to give you more control when retouching.

COMPOSITING MULTIPLE IMAGES WITH
LAYERS, ADJUSTMENT LAYERS, AND LAYER MASKS   214

The examples in this part of the book show you many possibilities for intricate effects and more accurate color correction by combining images using layers, Adjustment layers, and layer masks. These chapters also show you how layers can be a great prototyping tool.

After an introduction to the Pen tool and Paths, we use them to trace the outline of Bob, and then convert to a selection and layer mask to create a knock-out of Bob. We then use Free Transform to send Bob on journeys to Las Vegas, Miami, and other locations as we look into using Levels to create a hair mask and hand editing with the Paintbrush and Airbrush tools to fine-tune his layer mask.

Automatically creating a knock-out of the bicycle using Threshold on a channel and then editing that mask and adding a blend using the Gradient tool. Using this knock-out as a layer mask to place Bob behind the bicycle and seamlessly blend the two together.

Using layers and layer masks to seamlessly combine two different scans of the same high-contrast original (one to get shadow detail and the other to get highlight detail), color correcting this difficult, yet exciting image with multiple Adjustment layers and the new Curves and Color Sampler features; then finally, using several effects layers, each with its own opacity and filter effect, to achieve a dramatic result.

Combining images using gradient layer masks, blending color channels to correct a badly exposed image, color correcting after compositing with the new Photoshop 5 Curves features and the Color Sampler, and then using Adjustment layers to increase final color correction flexibilities.

Try the ultimate retouching and color correction challenge as you move six smiling heads from other exposures into this initially imperfect family portrait to end up with everyone smiling. Resizing and rotating the heads with Free Transform, blending them together using layer masks, and using Adjustment layers with the new Color Sampler so you can continue to tweak the color of each head and the original group shot until they all match.

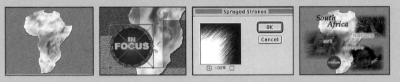

Using layers to set up your Photoshop files to show unlimited variations of a composite or effect quickly, without losing any of those variations. Using the Layers palette and Layer options, including Clipping Groups, Linking, layer masks, Blend modes, opacity, Layer effects and the new Text tool. Using the History Brush, History palette, and snapshots to mix effects. Filters for texture and edges. Using guides and zero origin to set safe areas. Actions to speed production tasks. Special considerations as you prepare images for eventual use in Premiere, Director, After Effects and the Web.

The examples in this section use Blend modes, filters, bitmaps, calculations, and layers in combination with each other to achieve a variety of special effects, including motion simulation, drop shadows , pattern creation, glowing text, text with shadows, placing images on a computer monitor, line drawings, and many others.

Detailed explanations and examples of using the Blend modes in all the tools (painting tools, the Fill command, Layers, Calculations, and Apply Image); the many variations and uses of the Apply Image and Calculations commands demonstrated and demystified.

Using the new Photoshop 5 Text editing, Layer effects, Bevel, Shadow, and transformation abilities. Combining positive and negative versions of the same image using Multiply, creating neon text with the Blend modes and placing it using Layer options, combining Illustrator text with Photoshop drop shadows, and saving as EPS from Illustrator for more creative control and higher-quality PostScript text output.

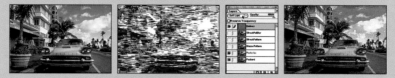

Creating texture and pattern effects using Posterize, Diffusion Dither bitmaps, layers, Layer options, Mezzotint, and Streak Patterns, and 3-D color embossed effects—cool stuff!

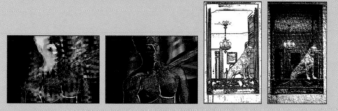

Getting the most from the standard Photoshop filters by combining filters and effects using layers, layer masks, opacity, Blend modes, levels, and other techniques to get many more combination effects. Demonstrating great uses of some more complex filters like Wave, Displace, Lighting Effects, Emboss, Find Edges, Minimum, Maximum, and others. Techniques to turn photographs into line drawings and get painterly effects, using a 50% gray layer for burning and dodging, the Fade command, and the Photoshop 5 Artistic, Brush Stroke, and Sketch filters.

Creating a color add for a portable computer from a black-and-white shot of the computer with nothing on the screen. Placing an Illustrator created cereal box, creating shadows and a textured background on the screen as well as screen grabs of a Tool palette and menu bar. The image is composited with layers in such a way that the background, color of the computer, and image on the computer screen can easily change as you show the ad and its variations to your clients. Here we use the new Measure tool to measure angles, move linked layers from one document to another, and then Free Transform them to fit within an angled window.

Using the new Photoshop 5 Drop Shadow options to create drop shadows. We also go into more traditional and flexible Photoshop techniques using layers, Blend modes, opacity, and the painting tools to create drop shadows and cast shadows against both white and colored backgrounds and to properly blend them into RGB and CMYK images.

Using Photoshop 5.5 and ImageReady 2 with their 4-Up Web Optimization dialogs as well as the GIF89a Export and the Photoshop 5 Web features to create the highest quality 8- and 24-bit GIF, JPEG, transparent GIF, Animation and Rollover images and HTML pages for Web sites and multimedia projects. Understanding 8-bit and smaller Color palettes and creating small fast images that look good on both the Mac and PC.

Understanding the differences in creating images for the Web and multimedia. Knowing why 8-bit color is important and understanding how it works. Working with JPEG, GIF, PNG-8 and PNG-24 files and knowing when to use each. Creating the images for your site so they look best to the users you care about most.

Using the ImageReady 2 and Photoshop 5-5 4-Up Dialogs or using Photoshop 5 to create GIF, JPEG and PNG files. Creating and comparing GIF, JPEG and PNG files and seeing how they look on 8-bit versus 24-bit systems. Looking at the Photoshop Versus ImageReady Web options to decide which ap to use for creating your Web images. Understanding all the JPEG options (Optimized, Progressive, ICC Profile, Blur and Matt) and the GIF Options (Lossy, Color Reduction Algorithum, Dither, Transparency, Interlaced, Matte and Web Snap).

Scanning images at a larger than Web size and then color correcting, sharpening, and creating knock-outs to composite a jacket with a separate collar image and create the "invisible man" look. Comparing Photoshop 5.5, ImageReady 2 and the Photoshop 5 GIF89a filter as we downsample the composite, sharpen again, create transparent GIFs, then test and correct them with various Web page backgrounds. Learning when to have aliased versus anti-aliased edges on transparent GIFs and how to convert between the two with either Photoshop 5, 5.5 or ImageReady.

Photoshop 5.5 and ImageReady color management and image display as well as the new type features. Jumping between Photoshop & ImageReady. In Photoshop 5.5... creating automated Contact Sheets, Picture Packages and Web Photo Galleries, the new Magic Eraser, Background Eraser and Extract Image tools; in ImageReady... using the Shape tools, Layer Effects and Layer Styles, opening and editing QuickTime movies as animations, saving animations as QuickTime movies, creating image maps and creating Master Palettes.

Making a Web page using ImageReady, setting up the page and guides, creating slices and optimizing each slice within a page, adding the text information to your page and animations, creating animations between different images and also image positions, adding rollover states to your slices, tweening between frames of an animation, cleaning up animation and rollover interactions.

FOREWORD

Ansel Adams, discussing the decision to make his original negatives available for future photographers to print, wrote in his autobiography that

> *"Photographers are, in a sense, composers and the negatives are their scores. ...In the electronic age, I am sure that scanning techniques will be developed to achieve prints of extraordinary subtlety from the original negative scores. If I could return in twenty years or so I would hope to see astounding interpretations of my most expressive images. It is true no one could print my negatives as I did, but they might well get more out of them by electronic means. Image quality is not the product of a machine, but of the person who directs the machine, and there are no limits to imagination and expression."*

Ansel Adams had a good vision for the future that we are now living. We hope this book will help you experience that vision in your photographic work.

Seeing an image on the computer screen is a beautiful thing. You bring it up from the scanner and you begin to think, "Now what do I really want this to look like?" If you know the Zone System, developed by Ansel Adams in traditional photography, you know the type of control you can have while taking a photo or printing it in the darkroom. On the computer screen, you can have this control and much more. You can try numerous variations, making extreme or subtle changes easily and quickly. The computer is a tool that enables the photographer to get precisely what he or she wants.

Many people think of using computer imaging for its proven capability to create special effects and image composites. It is very good at this, and we will show you how to create images that you cannot do optically in the darkroom, but I often use my computer darkroom to make a print of nature because it gives me much finer control in making that print. Realistic photography is another area in which we will show you things that you can do on the computer that you can't do easily or at all in the darkroom. Hey, I recently finally sold my darkroom!

This book has developed from Photoshop courses I started teaching in 1990. It's not an exhaustive book that goes through each menu bar and each feature, listing them in order. The examples in *Photoshop 5 Artistry* teach you how to use Photoshop 5 by working with typical situations that you encounter as a photographer, artist, or production artist. This is Photoshop for creating fine images that are sometimes high-quality reproductions of reality and sometimes fine renditions of composites and effects.

In this third edition, we have added all the information you will need to use the new Photoshop 5 features including Color Calibration and Color Management. We not only show you valuable techniques, but we give you a strategy for managing your digital images by creating an RGB or Lab master file for each image, which you can then use (automating using actions) to create different RGB files for color transparency, digital laser, dye-sub or inkjet printers, multimedia, or Web images and icons. These files, used with other actions, can create custom CMYK images for each of your printing situations.

For each situation, we spell out the detailed, step-by-step process. You can practice the technique yourself because the original images, masks, and progress steps, as well as the final images for each example, are included on the *Photoshop 5 Artistry* CD that accompanies the book. We have taught these examples over the past eight years to thousands of students across the country. Their feedback has helped us refine these exercises to make them easy to understand, concise, and full of special tips for more advanced users. All the the exercises have been updated and changed so that you can take advantage of the latest features, such as the new Photoshop 5 color capabilities, and deal with current trends like making images for the Web. In addition to student tested, step-by-step instructions, *Photoshop 5 Artistry* includes explanations of concepts like color correction, calibration, 24- and 8-bit file formats and compression, duotones, selections, masking, layers, layer masks, Adjustment layers, history, and channels, so you really understand what you are doing and are not just blindly following directions. Understanding allows you to expand the ideas in this book as you apply them to your own situations and creations without wasting your time on unnecessary issues.

We start with simple examples like cropping and color correcting a photograph. We cover color correction in great depth, and then move into things that you normally would do in the darkroom, like changing the contrast, burning and dodging, removing spots and scratches, and making a nice photographic print. Before we get into compositing and special effects, we talk about the importance of having absolute control over the colors in your photographs—which you can do more easily now with the new Photoshop 5 color management features. The masters of color photography have used contrast reduction masks, shadow, highlight, and color masks in the darkroom to make very fine Ilfochrome, C, and dye transfer art prints. Now many of them are switching to digital techniques and making LightJet 5000 prints. Using these techniques, you can make specific colors pop by increasing their saturation and changing their relationship to the rest of the photograph. *Photoshop 5 Artistry* shows you how to do all these things digitally using Adjustment layers, layer masks, and multiple layers of the same image, and how to generate art-quality output to LightJet 5000, Fugix, dye sublimation, color laser or inkjet printers, or to the Web. We also talk about enhancing an image for output back to 4x5 and 8x10 film as well as for output to separations for printing on a press. We also show you how to use the above techniques along with sharpening to get great quality prints from Photo CD and Pro Photo CD scans.

After we explain how to make a fine color print using Photoshop, we make extensive use of layers, layer masks, and image compositing techniques. You can do commercial compositing techniques easily using Photoshop, and we present step-by-step examples for some simple compositing jobs and then move on to some more complex examples that involve using hard- and soft-edge masks, as well as a variety of shadow and drop shadow effects and all the features of Layers, Adjustment Layers, and Layer Masks. The Apply Image and Calculations commands, as well as the Blend mode variations, are explained in detail along with examples of where to use them.

Photoshop 5 Artistry also includes many tips and techniques on getting the most from the Photoshop filters. We explain Layer options and also get into creating duotones and bitmaps, adding textures to images, and other fun things.

Photoshop is great fun! And the more you know, the better time you will have and the easier it will be to turn the images in your mind into reality. We hope *Photoshop 5 Artistry* helps you have more fun than ever before with photography and digital imaging.

Happy Photoshopping!

P.S. Those of you who already have *Photoshop Artistry* or *Photoshop 4 Artistry* will notice that the techniques in all the *Photoshop 5 Artistry* examples have been improved to take full advantage of the great features in this new version. You can compare this book to the Photoshop 3 or 4 versions and quickly see how to use the new features. Use our "Taking Advantage of Photoshop 5" chapter to get a quick overview of the new features and get through the transitions to the new Photoshop 5 command keys. At the end of "Taking Advantage of Photoshop 5," there is a table of the new command keys added for Photoshop 5. We also have added new chapters to help you learn about the new History Palette and Brush, all the new Free Transform and Transformation possibilities, the new Color Spaces, Preferences and Calibration, Spot Colors, the new Portable and Multimedia Composite examples, and the latest info about creating Web images. Many more new features and techniques are distributed throughout the book. The CD has updated ArtistKeys to set up your Actions palette and to give you a great set of function keys and automated sequences for bringing palettes up and down, converting file formats, and doing other useful but repetitive tasks.

TAKING ADVANTAGE OF PHOTOSHOP 5

*Easing the conversion from Photoshop 4 to 5;
making sure you are taking advantage of
the important new features in Photoshop 5.*

Photoshop 5 is a maturing of Photoshop in which some of the features we have always wanted, like multiple undo and full color and separation support, have finally arrived. This is a major release of Photoshop that daily users, especially photographers and digital imagemakers, will want to have. You will find it to be a much more complete and well integrated creative tool throughout. *Photoshop 5 Artistry* has been completely updated to take full advantage of the new Photoshop 5 features. The new features are described and used throughout the book. This chapter is a summary of the major new features and will point to the best chapters in the book for you to use to learn about each feature. In this chapter, we point out the features you are most likely to use. Each feature mentioned herein is explained in great detail in the appropriate chapter of *Photoshop 5 Artistry*. To find more detail about a feature, follow the references mentioned here or look it up in the index or table of contents. At the end of this chapter is a table of all the new Photoshop 5 shortcut keys. References in this book to the Option key should be translated to the Alt key on Windows systems, and the Command key here is the Control key in the Windows world.

BETTER SUPPORT OF CALIBRATION, COLOR MANAGEMENT, AND COLOR SEPARATIONS

Photoshop 5 has much more advanced support for Color Management of your files and workflow. Similar to the way that Photoshop 4 modified the appearance of CMYK files on the screen depending on your Printing Inks Setup settings, Photoshop 5 allows you use File/Color Settings/RGB Setup to set the preferences for how your RGB files appear on the screen. This more ideal situation allows you to choose an RGB space to work in that may encompass a wider gamut of colors than what your monitor can actually display. After using the new Adobe Gamma tool, or other hardware/software methods, to characterize your monitor with an ICC profile, Photoshop does its best to preview the images from the color workspace you have chosen onto the monitor you are working with. In theory, this allows people with different types of monitors to work on files within the same RGB workspace and have those files look as close as possible on those different monitors. For this to work correctly, the ICC profile for your monitor has to be accurately produced and you need to choose the correct RGB space for the type of color work you are doing.

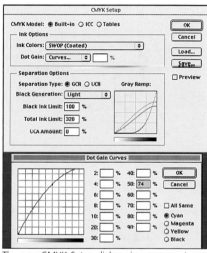

The new CMYK Setup dialog gives you exact control over all your Dot Gain curves when converting from RGB to CMYK. You can also select from different built-in CMYK models or use ICC profiles for CMYK conversion.

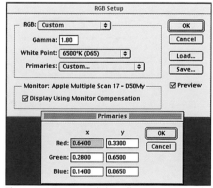

The new RGB setup dialog allows you to set the RGB color space for the type of files you use. Photoshop will then preview that workspace on your monitor using your monitor's ICC profile. This makes setting up for working in RGB more complicated but allows you to get more accurate monitor previews while not throwing out useful RGB data.

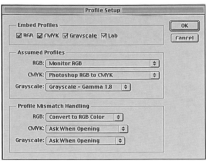

The new Profile Setup preferences dialog allows you to set up what Photoshop does when opening files with different color tags than your default configurations. You should probably set most of these options to Ask When Opening until you get used to the new color system. This way you'll be sure you know what is happening to your files as they are opened.

You can now define custom dot gain curves for all four colors in CMYK setup. Your CMYK space and color separations can also be defined using ICC profiles. The Custom Inks setup in CMYK Setup now also allows you to enter Lab coordinates.

ICC profiles are used with ColorSync on the Mac and probably ICM2.0 with Windows. Photoshop 5 does have its own engine for transforming from one profile to another, which Adobe claims is more accurate than the ColorSync 2.5 engine. You have the option to use either the Photoshop built-in engine or Color-Sync to do conversions.

It is very important that you read the "Color Spaces, Device Characterization, and Color Management" chapter and then the "Calibration" chapter to understand this new built-in color system. After reading these, use the "Setting System and Photoshop Preferences" chapter to set up your color settings. Do these things before doing serious color work with Photoshop 5, or you could be disappointed and confused with your color results!

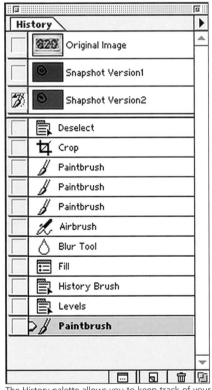

The History palette allows you to keep track of your changes. Command-Z still toggles between Undo and Redo of the last Photoshop command. Now Command-Option-Z marches back through the History palette, undoing one thing at a time, and Command-Shift-Z redoes things in the order that they appear in the History palette. When you save a file or quit, the History palette for that file goes away.

THE HISTORY PALETTE AND HISTORY BRUSH GIVE YOU MULTIPLE UNDO AND MUCH MORE

The new History palette keeps track of each step that you make, up to 100 steps, as you work on your image. Every time you do something, a new line is added to the History palette for that step in your process. This is better than multiple undo because by clicking one of these states in the palette, you can instantly return to that state in your image. If you then start editing again, the steps you made after that all disappear. You can also choose the History Options and turn on Allow Non-Linear History; then when you start editing again, your old steps stay in the History palette in case you later want to reuse them.

The History palette also allows you to take a snapshot of your image at any time. These snapshots stay around at the top of the palette and, at any point, you can click one of them to return to that state. The History Brush is a new painting tool that will paint on your current image from any previous snapshot or from any previous history step currently in the History palette. You can remember up to a maximum of 100 steps of history. The actual number you remember is a value you set in the History Options. The old Rubber Stamp or Fill From Saved options have now changed due to the History system. You now use the History Brush instead of the Rubber Stamp with either the From Snapshot or From Saved option. This gives you more flexibility because you can paint from the image at any previous step, or any snapshot, in the history. You can also fill from the state or snapshot specified in the History palette. The History palette and everything in it goes away when the file or Photoshop is closed. For more info about the History palette, see the new "History Palette, History Brush, and Snapshots" chapter on page 89.

FREE TRANSFORM OF SELECTIONS AND PATHS, PLUS A CENTER POINT FOR ROTATE TRANSFORMATIONS

The Free Transform of a layer that was added in Photoshop 4 has now been generalized and expanded to allow you to also do Free Transform of selections and paths. You can also do the rest of the transforms (Scale, Rotate, Skew, Distort, Perspective, Numeric, and so on) on selections and paths. Most of the Transform commands have been moved from the Layer menu to the Edit menu. When you have a path or point active, the name will change to Transform Path or Transform Points. When you have a selection, you can choose one of the Transform commands from the Edit menu and the area within the current layer that is selected will be transformed. With a selection, you can also choose Select/Transform Selection, which allows you to Free Transform the selection marquee itself! Very cool stuff indeed.

All transforms in Photoshop now also have a center point around which the Rotate transformation happens. Just click the center point and drag to move it to a new location. Command-T gives you Free Transform and now Command-Shift-T repeats the last transform. For more information on transforms of all kinds, see the new "Transformation of Images, Layers, Paths, and Selections" chapter.

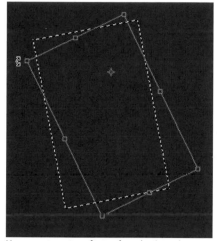

Here we see a transform of a selection where we are rotating around a center point that has been moved to the top-right of the box.

A MUCH BETTER BUILT-IN TYPE TOOL

Photoshop has finally improved its Type tool. There is now a vertical and horizontal Type tool, and selection versions of both of these. For regular type, not selection type, the type ends up in a special type layer than can now be edited after the fact. Within the type layer, you can double-click the layer name and go back to change the font, size or actually change the letters in the text. Type layers can also have Drop Shadows and the other new Layer Effects added to them, and then even later taken away or changed. It's a whole new world where you can even use the new command keys to align, resize, change leading, kerning/tracking, baseline shift, and other useful functions. However, you will still end up using Illustrator or another vector program if you want to set type on a curved path or do anything like that. See the "Tool Palette" chapter for a more complete description of the exciting new type functions. To get the new command keys for type, see the New Command Keys table at the end of this chapter.

The improved Type tool can be re-entered to edit type and change the font, size, kerning, tracking, baseline shift, or color, after the initial type creation. Way to go Photoshop, finally!

MAGNETIC LASSO AND PEN SELECTIONS, AS WELL AS THE FREEFORM PEN TOOL

The Magnetic Lasso and Pen tools are new for Photoshop 5. They will help you more easily make selections by doing the fine detail selection work along a contrasty edge as you simply move the mouse fairly closely to the edge of the area you want to select. You use the Lasso Width, Frequency, and Edge Contrast settings to hone in on the type of edge you are selecting this time. These seem to work quite well on contrasty edges. Adobe has also added the FreeForm Pen tool, which allows you to make a path by freehand drawing like you would with the Lasso tool. This seems to do a good job defining the path and does it in a way that makes the path easily editable after the initial drawing. For lots more about these new tools, see the "Tool Palette" chapter.

The Magnetic Lasso and Pen tools have this new set of options to help you automatically make a selection.

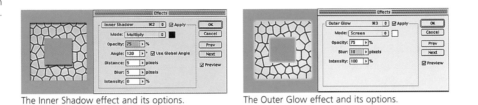

The shape surrounded by transparency with no effects applied.

The Drop Shadow effect and its options.

The Bevel and Emboss effect.

Inverted then Inner Glow.

The Inner Shadow effect and its options.

The Outer Glow effect and its options.

BUILT-IN LAYER SHADOW/EDGE EFFECTS AND ALIGNMENT OF LINKED LAYERS

Drop shadows are now as easy as pie! For any layer that has a transparent area around it or inside it, like text or a button for example, Photoshop 5 now has built-in Shadow and Edge effects. Above are some of their names and what they look like.

For more information on these new shadow and edge features, see the "Creating Shadows and Edge Effects" chapter.

Photoshop has also added some useful commands to align or distribute the layers linked to the current layer on the top, vertical center, bottom, left, horizontal center, or right. You can also align the active layer, and those linked to it, to a selection in the same six ways. These features will be very useful to those working on Web and multimedia projects. For more features on these new layer alignment features, see the "Layers, Layer Masks, and Adjustment Layers" chapter.

The options for the new Spot Color channels.

BUILT-IN SPOT COLOR SUPPORT WITH OUTPUT TO DCS 1.0 AND 2.0, FLASHPIX & PDF IMPORT/EXPORT

Photoshop 5 now has built-in spot color support, which will come in very handy for some people. When you add another channel to the Channels palette, it can be added as a Spot Color channel. You can then use the Custom Color picker to pick a Pantone or other spot color for that channel. The Spot Color channels can be output as separate channels in Photoshop, DCS 2.0, or TIFF format. When a Spot channel is active, you can also use the Merge Spot Channel command in the Channels palette to merge this channel and its effects into the current RGB or CMYK channels.

The new Hue/Saturation tool dialog. You can click in the image to specify the color range you want to modify. This makes the Hue/Saturation tool much more flexible because it can now modify any range of colors you select.

IMPROVED HUE/SATURATION AND CURVES TOOLS, AND THE NEW CHANNEL MIXER

The Hue/Saturation and Curves tools have been greatly enhanced for Photoshop 5. You will find that they now allow you to make much more accurate selections of color ranges. The Hue/Saturation tool allows you to use the Eyedropper on the screen to initially select and then, with the new Plus or Minus Eyedropper, tweak the color range you are going to modify with Hue, Saturation or Lightness changes. To add or delete colors, you can either click or click and drag a range within the image using the plus and minus droppers. You can also move the sliders on the color ramp at the bottom of the dialog to narrow or widen the part of the spectrum you are working with. At the bottom of the dialog, the topmost spectrum shows you the before colors and the bottom spectrum shows you the after colors.

The Curves tool also has some impressive improvements. The display of the points on the curve is easier to see with the active point being all black and the other points being small circles. You can create a point on the curve now by Command-clicking somewhere on your image (use Command-Shift-click to add individual points to each color curve); then you can move the active point one value at a time using the arrow keys (Shift-Arrow for 10 values at a time). You can also type in a new value for the active point. Command-Tab toggles the active point to the next one present and Command-Shift-Tab to the previous one. You can even use Shift-click to select multiple points on the curve and then move them all as a group. Far out! As in Select/Deselect, Command-D is used to deselect all points on the grid.

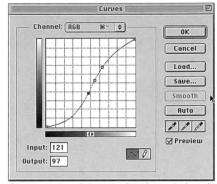

The new Curves dialog now has the vertical gradient to help people understand the output axis. You can now type in the location values of the current point or you can use the arrow keys to move the point by one value at a time (Shift-arrow for 10 values at a time). You can also add points to the curve by Command-clicking that point on the screen.

ON-THE-FLY PREVIEWS OF DUOTONES, COLOR MANAGEMENT, AND MORE

You will notice now that most of the color correction tools, even changing the curves in Duotone mode, give you on-the-fly preview of changes on the screen. For Duotones, you will find this allows you to try many more variations and be more creative while taking up much less time and effort. You will find this especially useful when deciding what color space to work in for your RGB and CMYK files. The preferences changes you make will be previewed on the screen as you are making them. Just make sure the Preview box is checked whenever you are working to be sure you see the changes as you make them.

Make sure the Preview option is checked to see the most accurate on-the-fly previews of many more changes now in Photoshop 5.

BETTER COLOR SAMPLING AND MORE 16-BIT CHANNEL SUPPORT

The new Color Sampler Eyedropper allows you to click on up to four points within your image whose values are added to the Info palette's

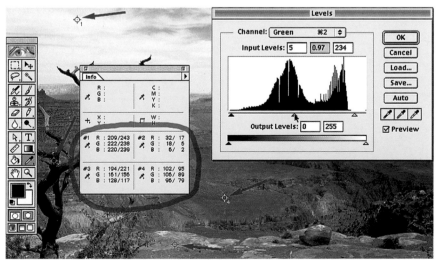

Here we have used the Color Sampler Eyedroppers to enter four locations whose values we want to keep track of while we are color correcting. As we make changes in Levels and other correction tools, we simultaneously see what these changes do to these four points. This is a color corrector's dream!

display. When you are making any color correction changes, those changes' effects on the four Color Sampler points are displayed within the Info palette. You still see the Info readouts for the current location of the cursor as you always have.

Photoshop 5 now supports 16-bit channel files in Levels, Curves, Hue/Saturation, Brightness/Contrast, Color Balance, Equalize, Invert and Channel Mixer. You can also Crop, Rubber Stamp, Image Size and Rotate Arbitrary as well as use the History Brush with 16-bit channel files. The advantage of these files (48 bits per pixel for RGB and 64 bits per pixel for CMYK) is that they allow one to save all the information obtained from a high end scanner, and then manipulate this information without having to throw away values converting to 8 bits per channel. Even though you can't see all the 16-bit color detail on the monitor, working in 16-bit color allows Photoshop's calculations to be done without losing information due to rounding and truncation errors. When the corrections are finished, the final files can be converted to 8-bit color for output and you should end up with a better final 8-bit result. The argument for doing this is similar to the reason you want to do all your Web color correcting in RGB until you get to the final step, and then you convert to a GIF file or save your Web version as a JPG. You still get better results doing all your manipulations within the larger color space. Now that memory is cheaper and hard disk space is larger, I believe we will start to see more people working with 16-bit files.

At the bottom of the dialog, you see the new Color Matching options for Index Color. These allow you to produce better 8-bit color files for your Web sites and multimedia documents.

Actions now support different sets of Actions. This gives you a way to organize your Actions. The function keys are global to all the sets, so you cannot reuse the same function key in two different sets. Besides Shift, Photoshop 5 allows you to also use the Command key as a Function Key modifier, and you can use both Shift and Command. This gives you twice as many function keys as you had available in Photoshop 4.

Photoshop 5 also gives you these three choices for your Action's playback speed.

BETTER SUPPORT FOR INDEX COLOR

Besides getting a preview in the Index Color Mode Change dialog, there are also improvements in the quality of the Index Color files created. Adaptive palette creation is touted as being better and you now have the options of choosing Faster or Best color matching. If you turn off Best, then dithering and conversion is a little lower quality but a lot faster. The Preserve Exact Colors option does not dither colors in your image that are an exact match for colors that are in the palette you use. This may do a better job of preserving detailed lines and text, depending on the prevalence of those colors within the image and palette. For more information about Index Color, see the "Differences in Creating for the Web and 8-Bit Color," as well as the "GIFs, JPEGs, and Color Palettes" chapters.

BETTER ACTIONS SUPPORT AND BATCH CONTROL

In addition to what Photoshop 4 Actions could do, in Photoshop 5, Actions can be organized into different sets. Now twice as many function keys are available and you can control the speed of Action playback. When in Batch mode, you have the option of stopping an Action upon an error, or just recording the error in a file and continuing. If you are running a Batch from a folder, you can decide whether to Include all Subfolders in the Action or not. Photoshop 5 Actions can now also record things from the Paths, Layers, and History palettes using the Gradient, Marquee, Crop, Lasso, Line, Move, Magic Wand, Paint Bucket, and Type tools; the Lighting Effects filter; and the Calculations, Apply Image, File Info, and Free Transform commands. Actions can also record switching and selecting documents. If you want to be able to record relative positions, set the ruler units to the new Percent option.

PLUG-IN CONTROL OF PHOTOSHOP FUNCTIONALITY

In the File/Automate menu, you will notice Conditional Mode Change, Contact Sheet, and Fit Image, which are implemented using Photoshop's new capability to control functions from within a Plug-In module. The Export Transparent Image and Resize Image commands in the Help menu are also implemented this way. You will probably be seeing some third party plug-ins that use this feature for a variety of purposes. It is a powerful addition to what can be done with Photoshop for sure. We'll just have to see what comes along to make use of this neat feature.

CHANGES TO THE RUBBER STAMP AND PEN TOOLS

Because the History Brush now enhances the old Rubber Stamp functionality of the From Saved and From Snapshot options, these options are no longer available in the Rubber Stamp tool. This tool has been further dissected by dividing it into two tools, the Rubber Stamp and the Pattern Stamp tools. Although we now have two tools, which are both selected from the Rubber Stamp pop-out in the Tool palette, there really is no additional functionality here. Is this a case of Adobe saying, "wow, a new tool," when they just added more user interface to the tool you used before? Well, the History Brush part of the Rubber Stamp's demise is certainly a new and much more powerful tool. The two separate Rubber Stamps that are left don't add anything new to what you had in Photoshop 4. The other changes in user interface are that you turn on the Aligned option to do Clone Aligned or Pattern Aligned, and, of course, you are doing Non-Aligned if this option is turned off; also the old Sample Merged option is now called Use All Layers. Still, both these things allow the same functionality as was available before.

Here is the "new" Rubber Stamp tool. Notice that Aligned is now a checkbox item instead of a different mode of the tool. The old Sample Merged is now called Use All Layers. This name is better!

Here is the "new" Pattern Stamp Tool!

OTHER NEW FEATURES OF NOTE

- Photoshop 5 now supports Postscript Level 3.
- Brush Sizes can now be up to 32000x32000 on the Mac.
- Tools now show the Cancel sign when they are unusable, due to the current situation. A single click on the Cancel sign will beep once; a double-click will tell why the tool can't currently be used.
- You now can use the Paths Palette only, not the Save As EPS dialog, to set the clipping path.

There are some new features that seem like token user interface changes that don't add much or any functionality. The most prevalent of these is the changing of sliders, like the Opacity slider in the Layers and Brushes palettes, to pop-down sliders. The only added functionality here is that you can always type in a value by selecting the number box and typing the number. I don't usually want to do this because I have to move the mouse and make a selection. The old way of just typing a number still works and is much faster. I'm finding the actual sliding of the slider a bit more awkward because the slider has to now pop down and out when you click the arrow. It seems like in a lot of cases it was faster before in Photoshop 4. Maybe this change was required by Mac or Windows User Interface Standards.

	Mac OS	*Windows 95/NT*
GENERAL SHORTCUTS:		
Fill from history	Cmd - Opt - Delete	Ctrl - Alt - Backspace
Scale using center point (free transform)	Opt - Drag corner handles	Alt - Drag corner handles
Skew using center point (free transform)	Cmd-Opt-Shift-Drag side handles	Ctrl-Alt-Shift-Drag side handles
Scroll left one screen	Cmd - page up	Ctrl - page up
Scroll left 10 units	Cmd - Shift - page up	Ctrl - Shift - page up
Scroll right one screen	Cmd - page down	Ctrl - page down
Scroll right 10 units	Cmd - Shift - page down	Ctrl - Shift - page down
Move view to upper-left corner	Home key	Home key
Move view to lower-right corner	End key	End key
Cancels out of pop-up slider in mouse up mode	Esc	Esc
Commits edit in pop-up slider in mouse up mode	Return	Return
Pop-up slider resets to prev in mouse down mode	Hold Opt outside of slider rectangle	Hold Alt outside of slider rectangle
Scroll forward through Blend modes	Shift - + (Plus)	Shift - + (Plus)
Scroll backward through Blend modes	Shift - – (Minus)	Shift - – (Minus)
Set layer to next Blend mode	Shift - + (Plus)	Shift - + (Plus)
Set layer to previous Blend mode	Shift - – (Minus)	Shift - – (Minus)
Set brush or layer to Normal	Opt - Shift - N	Alt - Shift - N
Set brush or layer to Dissolve	Opt - Shift - I	Alt - Shift - I
Set brush or layer to Multiply	Opt - Shift - M	Alt - Shift - M
Set brush or layer to Screen	Opt - Shift - S	Alt - Shift - S
Set brush or layer to Overlay	Opt - Shift - O	Alt - Shift - O
Set brush or layer to Soft Light	Opt - Shift - F	Alt - Shift - F
Set brush or layer to Hard Light	Opt - Shift - H	Alt - Shift - H
Set brush or layer to Color Dodge	Opt - Shift - D	Alt - Shift - D
Set brush or layer to Color Burn	Opt - Shift - B	Alt - Shift - B
Set brush or layer to Darken	Opt - Shift - K	Alt - Shift - K
Set brush or layer to Lighten	Opt - Shift - G	Alt - Shift - G
Set brush or layer to Difference	Opt - Shift - E	Alt - Shift - E
Set brush or layer to Exclusion	Opt - Shift - X	Alt - Shift - X
Set brush or layer to Hue	Opt - Shift - U	Alt - Shift - U
Set brush or layer to Saturation	Opt - Shift - T	Alt - Shift - T
Set brush or layer to Color	Opt - Shift - C	Alt - Shift - C
Set brush or layer to Luminosity	Opt - Shift - Y	Alt - Shift - Y
Set brush to Threshold	Opt - Shift - L	Alt - Shift - L
Set brush to Dissolve	Opt - Shift - I	Alt - Shift - I
Set brush to Behind	Opt - Shift - Q	Alt - Shift - Q
TOOLS PALETTE:		
Access Adobe Online	Click identifier icon	Click identifier icon
Airbrush tool	J	J
History Brush tool	Y	Y
Pencil tool	N	N
Add Anchor Point tool	+ (Plus)	+ (Plus)
Delete Anchor Point tool	– (Minus)	– (Minus)
Direct Select tool	A	A
Measure tool	U	U
Cycle through Marquee tools	Shift - M	Shift - M
Cycle through Lasso tools	Shift - L	Shift - L
Cycle through Rubber Stamp tools	Shift - S	Shift - S
Cycle through Blur, Sharpen, & Smudge tools	Shift - R	Shift - R
Cycle through Toning tools	Shift - O	Shift - O
Cycle through Pen tools	Shift - P	Shift - P
Cycle through Type tools	Shift - T	Shift - T
Cycle through Eyedropper tools	Shift - I	Shift - I
Cycle through above tools	Opt - Click in tool slot	Alt - Click in tool slot

LAYERS PALETTE:

Clear each Effect on layer one at a time	Opt-Double-Click effect icon	Alt - Double-Click effect icon
Edit Type Options	Double-Click Type icon	Double-Click Type icon
Edit Layer Effect Options (last edited)	Double-Click Layer Effect icon	Double-Click Layer Effect icon

CHANNELS PALETTE:

Create new spot color channel	Cmd - Click New Channel button	Ctrl - Click New Channel button

HISTORY PALETTE

Step forward	Shift - Cmd - Z	Shift - Ctrl+ Z
Step backward	Opt - Cmd - Z	Alt - Ctrl - Z
Duplicate history state (other than current)	Opt - Click state	Alt - Click state
Create new snapshot	Click New Snapshot button	Click New Snapshot button
Create new document from state snapshot	Click New Document button	Click New Document button

ACTIONS PALETTE

Selects multiple items of the same kind	Shift - Click	Shift - Click

MOVE TOOL

Link with top-most visible layer	Ctrl - Shift - Click	Right Mouse + Shift - Click

MAGNETIC LASSO TOOL

Add to selection	Shift - Click then draw	Shift - Click then draw
Delete from selection	Opt - Click then draw	Alt - Click then draw
Intersect with selection	Opt - Shift - Click then draw	Alt - Shift - Click then draw
Add point	single Click	single Click
Remove last point	Delete key	Delete key
Close path	Double-Click/Enter	Double-Click/Enter
Close path over start point	Click start point	Click start point
Close path using straight line segment	Opt - Double-Click	Alt - Double-Click
Cancel operation	Esc/Cmd - . (Period)	Esc/Ctrl - . (Period)
Switch to Lasso	Opt - Drag	Alt - Drag
Switch to Polygonal Lasso	Opt - Click	Alt - Click
Increase Magnetic Lasso width	[(Open Bracket)	[(Open Bracket)
Decreases Magnetic Lasso width	] (Close Bracket)	] (Close Bracket)

ERASER TOOL

Erase to History	Opt - Drag	Alt - Drag

DODGE TOOL

Set Dodge to Shadows	Opt - Shift - W	Alt - Shift - W
Set Dodge to Midtones	Opt - Shift - V	Alt - Shift - V
Set Dodge to Highlights	Opt - Shift - Z	Alt - Shift - Z

BURN TOOL

Set Burn to Shadows	Opt - Shift - W	Alt - Shift - W
Set Burn to Midtones	Opt - Shift - V	Alt - Shift - V
Set Burn to Highlights	Opt - Shift - Z	Alt - Shift - Z

SPONGE TOOL

Set Sponge to Desaturate	Opt - Shift - J	Alt - Shift - J
Set Sponge to Saturate	Opt - Shift - A	Alt - Shift - A

PEN TOOL

Toggle to Convert Direction tool	Opt	Alt
Add/delete anchor points	track over path/anchor points	track over path/anchor points

DIRECT SELECT TOOL

toggle to Convert Direction Tool	Cmd - Opt over anchor points	Ctrl - Alt over anchor points

MAGNETIC PEN TOOL

Add point	single Click	single Click
Remove last point	Delete key	Delete key
Close path	Double-Click/Enter	Double-Click/Enter
Close path over start point	Click start point	Click start point
Close path using straight line segment	Opt - Double-Click	Alt - Double-Click
Cancel operation	Esc/Cmd - . (Period)	Esc/Ctrl - . (Period)
Switch to Freeform Pen	Opt - Drag	Alt - Drag
Switch to Pen	Opt - Click	Alt - Click
Increase magnetic width	[(Open Bracket)	[(Open Bracket)
Decreases magnetic width	] (Close Bracket)	] (Close Bracket)

MEASURE TOOL

Measure constrained to 45 degree axis	Shift - Drag	Shift - Drag
Create protractor	Opt - Click + Drag on end point	Alt - Click + Drag on end point

SAMPLER TOOL

delete Sampler	Opt - Click sampler	Alt - Click sampler

LAYER MENU

New Layer…	Cmd - Shift - N	Ctrl - Shift - N

SELECT MENU

Reselect	Cmd - Shift - D	Ctrl - Shift - I

TYPE DIALOG

Zooms in of dialog preview	Cmd - + (Plus)	Ctrl - + (Plus)
Zooms out of dialog preview	Cmd - – (Minus)	Ctrl - – (Minus)
Cut copy and paste in the type dialog	Cmd - C, Cmd - X and Cmd - V	Ctrl - C, Ctrl - X and Ctrl - V
Left/Top text alignment	Cmd - Shift - L	Ctrl - Shift - L
Center text alignment	Cmd - Shift - C	Ctrl - Shift - C
Right/Bottom text alignment	Cmd - Shift - R	Ctrl - Shift - R
Increase text point size by 2 pt increments	Cmd - Shift - >	Ctrl - Shift - >
Decrease text point size by 2 pt increments	Cmd+ Shift - <	Ctrl - Shift - <
Increase text point size by 10 pt increments	Cmd - Opt - Shift - >	Ctrl - Alt - Shift - >
Decrease text point size by10 pt increments	Cmd - Opt - Shift - <	Ctrl - Alt - Shift - <
Increase leading in by 2 pt increments	Opt - Down Arrow	Alt - Down Arrow
Decrease leading by in 2 pt increments	Opt - Up Arrow	Alt - Up Arrow
Increase leading by10 pt increments	Cmd - Opt - Down Arrow	Ctrl - Alt - Down Arrow
Decrease leading by 2 pt increments	Cmd - Opt - Up Arrow	Ctrl - Alt - Up Arrow
Increase kerning/tracking by 20/1000 em space	Opt - Right Arrow	Alt - Right Arrow
Decrease kerning/tracking by 20/1000 em space	Opt - Left Arrow	Alt - Left Arrow
Increase kerning/tracking by 100/1000 em space	Cmd - Opt - Right Arrow	Ctrl - Alt - Right Arrow
Decrease kerning/tracking by 100/1000 em space	Cmd - Opt - Left Arrow	Ctrl - Alt - Left Arrow
Increase baseline shift by 2 pt increments	Opt - Shift - Up + Arrow	Opt - Shift - Up + Arrow
Decrease baseline shift by 2 pt increments	Opt - Shift - Down + Arrow	Opt - Shift - Down + Arrow
Increase baseline shift by 2 pt increments	Cmd - Opt - Shift - Up Arrow	Ctrl - Alt - Shift - Up Arrow
Decrease baseline shift by 2 pt increments	Cmd - Opt - Shift - Down Arrow	Ctrl - Alt - Shift - Down Arrow
Move to the right one character	Right arrow	Right Arrow
Move to the left one character	Left Arrow	Left Arrow
Move up one line	Up Arrow	Up Arrow
Move down one line	Down Arrow	Down Arrow
Move to the right one word	Cmd - Right Arrow	Cmd - Right Arrow
Move to the left one word	Cmd - Left Arrow	Cmd - Left Arrow
Select word	Double-Click	Double-Click
Select one character to the right	Shift - Right Arrow	Shift - Right Arrow

Select one character to the left	Shift - Left Arrow	Shift - Left Arrow
Select one word to the right	Cmd - Shift - Right Arrow	Ctrl - Shift - Right Arrow
Select one word to the left	Cmd - Shift - Left Arrow	Ctrl - Shift - Left Arrow
Select one line above	Shift - Up Arrow	Shift - Up Arrow
Select one line below	Shift - Down Arrow	Shift - Down Arrow
Select all characters	Cmd - A	Ctrl - A
Select characters from current insertion point	Shift - Click	Shift - Click
Position type	drag type in image	drag type in image

CURVES DIALOG

Add color as new point on curve	Cmd - Click in image	Ctrl - Click in image
Add color as individual points for each curve	Cmd - Shift - Click	Ctrl - Shift - Click
Move points	arrow keys	arrow keys
Move points in multiples of 10	Shift - arrow keys	Shift - arrow keys
Select next control point	Cmd - Tab	Ctrl - Tab
Select previous control point	Cmd - Shift - Tab	Cmd - Shift - Tab
Add point	Click in grid	Click in grid
Delete point	Cmd - Click point	Ctrl - Click point
Select multiple control points	Shift - Click	Shift - Click
Deselect all points	Cmd - D	Ctrl - D

HUE/SATURATION DIALOG

Move range to new location	Click in image	Click in image
Add to range	Shift - Click/Drag in image	Shift - Click/Drag in image
Subtract from range	Opt - Click/Drag in image	Alt - Click/Drag in image
Edit master	Cmd - tilde	Ctrl - tilde
Edit individual colors	Cmd - 1 - 6	Ctrl - 1 - 6
Slide color spectrum	Cmd - Drag on ramp	Ctrl - Drag on ramp

LAYER EFFECTS DIALOG

Toggle effects without dialog on or off	Opt - Menu Item	Alt - Menu Item
Move effect	Drag in image	Drag in Image
Move effect constrained to 45 degree axis	Shift - Drag in image	Shift - Drag in image
Drop shadow	Cmd - 1	Ctrl - 1
Inner shadow	Cmd - 2	Ctrl - 2
Outer glow	Cmd - 3	Ctrl - 3
Inner glow	Cmd - 4	Ctrl - 4
Bevel and emboss	Cmd - 5	Ctrl - 5

AN OVERVIEW OF DIGITAL IMAGING

For those of you new to the digital world, this is
a quick introduction to the possibilities.
More advanced users may find they are familiar
with many things in this chapter.

It's the year 2008 and you're on location in the Amazon jungle taking photos of a bambleberry plantation for tonight's issue of *Earth Survival News*. Since the discovery that the rain forest bambleberry cures AIDS and the teetee bush cures cancer, all countries have agreed to stop old-growth forest cutting. You're sitting high on top of a 90-foot bambleberry tree looking at the electronic layout of the article on the screen of your 17" color, 1024 by 768, fold-out, wristwatch Mac Decca. From the layout, you can see the home office needs a 5x7 still photo for the cover and a five-minute movie slot for the rest of the article on screen 10. Now you're taking the photo they need; gee, this is going to look great in the layout! The 20 megabyte file is transmitted directly from your Nikon F10 digital camera into the layout on the Mac Decca. Now you're using Photoshop 9.1 to crop and edit the photos for final transmission. It's now 4:50 P.M. in Manhattan, so you have only five minutes to finish working with the photo. It is transmitted via satellite from your Mac Decca directly into the page layout. This gives the editorial team five minutes to make final approvals and adjustments for the 5:00 P.M. transmission. Readers around the world now see *Earth Survival News* and get most of their news and information on their wristwatch Mac Deccas and PC communicators. Think of all the trees this digital transmission technology is now saving. With the street prices for entry-level Mac Deccas dropping to $100, newspapers, magazines, and catalog advertisers across the world have either converted to digital transmission or gone out of business. Paper is no longer the medium of choice. Aren't you glad you got into digital photography!

BACK FROM THE FUTURE

Now it's back to reality in 1998. Here I am with my $20,000 Macintosh digital photography system. When I set out on my own in 1990, after 10 years of doing software development and imaging research at Apple Computer, I wanted to return to my love for photography. I planned to set up a self-sufficient business that I could run from my home using my own equipment and without the need for partners or outside investors. It cost me under $10,000 to purchase a 4x5 camera system and a traditional color darkroom that can make professional-quality 16x20 color prints. This traditional color darkroom now sits idle most of the time because I'm in front of the computer screen playing with my *digital* darkroom. With Photoshop on the Mac or PC, you can do anything to an image that you can do in a traditional darkroom, only much more easily. It is easy and fast to try something, or to try 20 different variations, and pick the one you like most. With complete personal control and much more creative software on your own computer, you can do anything a high-end Scitex retouching station can do and much more. The possibilities for creativity in a digital darkroom are endless.

I'm sure that many of you have been wondering about digital photography. It is possible today to produce the highest-quality digital images using a desktop system. This includes going out to original-quality color transparency film or black-and-white negatives; making the highest-quality professional color laser, inkjet, and dye sublimation digital art prints; making 24- and 8-bit images for the Web and multimedia; and also converting to CMYK for print on a press.

THE OPTIONS FOR DIGITAL PHOTOGRAPHY

You may be wondering if digital photography is worth the cost and effort. In this introductory discussion, I divide digital photography into three functional areas:

- Capturing the image
- Adjusting and manipulating the image
- Outputting the image

CAPTURING THE IMAGE

In most cases, film is still the highest-quality medium for image capture, especially if you are talking about short exposures on 4x5 or larger film. There are certain situations in which using a digital camera makes sense, which we will discuss in later chapters. Once you capture an image on film, there are various ways to scan it into a digital version for your computer. You can take your original to a traditional color house and have it scanned with a quality drum scanner, or you can take your film to a desktop service bureau and have it scanned with a desktop scanner. With either of these alternatives, you often have little or no personal control over the quality of the scans. This book will help you learn what to look for in a good scan and how to make better scans yourself.

SCAN IT YOURSELF

A third alternative for scanning is to rent or purchase a desktop scanner and do the scans yourself, which is a great way to learn about scanning. There are desktop scanners that scan film and there are flatbed scanners to scan prints and artwork. Some flatbed scanners have optional attachments that allow you to scan film. Scanning original film gives you the best quality. If you can afford your own scanner, it makes it much easier to prototype image creations and publishing projects. Before you buy a scanner, you ought to read the latest articles comparing the newest scanners because they get better and cheaper all the time.

THE KODAK PHOTO CD SYSTEM

An exciting alternative for scanning is the Kodak Photo CD system, which allows the masses to get high-quality scans quickly and in bulk for very little expense—about $1 to $2 per scan in most places. With Photo CD, you bring your film to get it processed and, at the same time, the images can be scanned and placed on a digital Photo CD disc. You can also send in any 35mm original (positive, negative, color, or B&W) that has been previously taken and get it on Photo CD. The Photo CD discs can hold 100 images on the average. The quality of these images after color correction is high enough for most publishing output. What I have done is get over 600 of my best photographs put on Photo CD, which lets me use these images in brochures, this book, advertising, and other promotions. For publication at 150 line screen, regular Photo CD images usually are good for sizes of about 7x9 or smaller. Sometimes you can go bigger than this; it all depends on the image and the quality of the scan. I have some great-looking 11x17 dye sublimation prints from Photo CD scans. They also work great on the Epson inkjet printers. The maximum image size for a regular Photo CD scan is 18 megabytes. Photo CD Pro allows scans of up to 70 megabytes from originals that are 35mm, 2¼, or 4x5. These are a bit more expensive, about $20 each, but are still much cheaper than high-end drum scans. If you give the CD processor a high-quality original, and if the shop you choose knows what it is doing, the quality of these scans can be excellent. See the Chapter 16: Scanning, Resolution, Histograms, and Photo CD for more information on how to get great scans from any scanner and also get the most from your Photo CD scans.

THE DIRECT DIGITAL METHOD

For certain applications, it makes sense to capture your images using a direct digital method. This makes your work much simpler because you process no film and do no scanning. Several technologies are available for capturing images. One of the earliest offered, still video, uses a 35mm type camera that you load with a small, still video disk. You can also get a card for your computer, called a video digitizer, that allows you to get digital still frames from any video camera or player. The problem with video digitizing and still video is that the quality of the digital images is not high enough for most print production.

For significantly better than video quality in a compact filmless camera, you can use the Kodak Digital Camera System (DCS). DCS is a series of digital backs that attach to Nikon, Hasselblad, and other cameras. DCS comes in various models and prices. Nikon also makes a high-quality digital camera called the Nikon E2. For studio work, there is the Leaf Catchlight Digital Back and the Dicomed Camera Back system. These systems act as digital backs for 2¼ and 4x5 cameras. The quality of the digital files captured with these systems can be very good.

Digital cameras make a lot of sense for studio work because, while you are shooting the picture, you can bring the file directly into the Mac or PC and make sure it meets your needs. With digital cameras, you don't get the cost, time, and environmental problems associated with film processing. You also don't have the cost or time lag required to get scans done. For studios that do a lot of catalog work, especially with small to medium size images, digital cameras could save a lot of time and money and allow the photographer to shoot the images and provide digital separations.

Stephen Johnson, a well-known landscape photographer, uses the Dicomed digital camera insert on his 4x5 camera and is very happy with the results he is able to get. This digital back is not able to do fraction of a second exposures, but it produces very large accurate files, over 100 megabytes, and is great for still camera work where much detail and dynamic range is required. Steve has mentioned to me that in most lighting situations he can actually capture more detail using this setup than he could using even 4x5 film. His Dicomed prints are very beautiful. Using this type of camera setup, he actually sees the image on the computer screen of his Mac portable in the field, like on site in Yosemite.

Another advantage to direct digital capture with smaller images is that the images are in a form in which they can be easily compressed and transmitted over a phone line. Newspapers and magazines use this feature in highly time-sensitive situations. Pictures can be shot and sent compressed over the phone, and literally be on a press minutes later. If you use a digital camera and want to learn how to use it

An Overview of Digital Imaging

to create automatic knock-outs, see the Difference blend mode in Chapter 36: Blend Modes, Calculations, and Apply Image.

ADJUSTING AND MANIPULATING THE IMAGE

Once you have converted an image into digital format, you can more easily perform standard darkroom techniques like spotting, cropping, dodging, burning, changing the color balance, contrast, and so on. You can use a variety of adjustment layer, selection, and feather techniques to isolate portions of an image for change without affecting the rest of the image. You can do all these things in such a way that you can show many variations and always undo or change any effect. Not only are digital images easier to create, they are much easier to change and show variations in technique. Check out Chapter 23: Grand Canyon Tweaks, Chapter 28: Desert Al, and Chapter 29: Bryce Stone Woman.

In addition to standard darkroom techniques, there are thousands of special effects, like posterization, rotation, skew, solarization, stretching, perspective, edge effects, sharpening, distortions, applying patterns and textures, blending, and far too many others to even list. Take a look at "Photoshop Filters and Effects" and "Blend Modes, Calculation, and Apply Image."

You can use layers, adjustment layers, layer masks, channels, and other techniques to create knock-outs, drop shadows, and special lighting effects, as well as to combine images in any way you want. These changes are easy to set up so you can turn them on and off and show your client many variations. See Chapter 34: The McNamaras and Chapter 40: The Portable Computer Ad.

You can use Adobe Photoshop's painting tools to retouch, colorize, add to, and modify your images. The real-world examples in this book show you how to do all these things. Any manipulation or effect that you can do on a Scitex or other high-end imaging workstation, you can do in Photoshop more easily. You can actually do far more in Photoshop, and Photoshop is fun to use, too.

MAKING COLOR SEPARATIONS

If you are going to output your digital images to video, the Web, digital printers, or to color transparency film, the digital files need to be in RGB (Red, Green, Blue) format. Most desktop scanners currently scan in this format. If you are going to print your final images on a press, you need to convert the images into CMYK (Cyan, Magenta, Yellow, Black) format. Photoshop and many other desktop applications do the conversions from RGB into CMYK format. This conversion process, called *making color separations*, has many variations depending on the type of printer and paper you will be using.

CREATING YOUR OWN BOOKS

One of the advantages of using digital photography is that the computer equipment also gives you the required tools for doing your own publishing. If you want to create a brochure, poster, or even a book, you can learn the necessary skills to design and create the entire project yourself. Photographers and artists can publish their own books. This entire book—including the design, layout, color correction, compositing and effects, as well as the final color separations and the cover—was created by Wendy and me in our home studio in the Santa Cruz mountains using desktop equipment. The scans are mostly Photo CD, which we color corrected and separated using the techniques taught in this book. A few of the scans were done using the Leafscan-45 and several scans were done on a Howtek drum scanner, also attached to a Mac, at Robyn Color in San Francisco. Using this technology, you can create your own book like we did!

OUTPUTTING THE IMAGE

The choices available for output of your digital image are improving and getting cheaper on a month-to-month basis. Black and white laser printers now cost $\frac{1}{20}$ the price of 15 years ago. The same price drop is happening with color printers. There are many types of digital printers. Here, I am sticking to the ones that make prints of photographic quality or close to it.

DYE SUBLIMATION AND INKJET PRINTERS

A common type of digital printer is the dye sublimation or desktop inkjet printer. On images that are properly color corrected and sharpened, one can make prints with these printers that look close to or sometimes better than Ilfochrome quality. These printers can make prints of sizes up to 12x18 inches and larger. These prints are beautiful and also big enough to frame and hang on the wall. I have a Radius ProofPositive dye-sub and an Epson Stylist Photo Ink Jet and find that they make excellent prints. Most people cannot tell the difference between these and color photographs. I like these prints better than photographs because of the amazing control I have over color, effects, and sharpness using Photoshop. Many printers come with Level 2 PostScript so you can use them to prototype any publishing project up to tabloid size. Many companies make dye sublimation printers, including Kodak, Tektronics, Fargo, and 3M. Epson, Hewlitt Packard, and Tektronics, among others, make ink jet printers.

You can usually make digital prints at a service bureau, but having a photographic-quality digital printer in your studio is the final component that really makes a digital darkroom complete. Having it attached to your own computer allows you to work in the iterative way a photographer works in the darkroom. Make a print, tweak the colors and contrast a bit, make another print, and so on, until you get exactly what you want. I love it! Having your own printer in your studio gives you the control and ease of use that is essential for the artist and high-quality image maker. Dye sublimation printers that make prints from 8½x11 up to tabloid size from $1,500 to $15,000. Make sure you check out the market well before purchasing one. The ink jet printers are cheaper, costing from $250 to about $2,000 for desktop models, depending on the size and quality of the prints. There are new products every day, and to accurately compare them, you should print the same digital image on each printer you are considering purchasing. Different printers have various resolutions and quality; you need to carefully compare before you buy. For the best quality on most of these printers, you need a 300-360 dpi original. I use files of about 50 megabytes in size at 300 dpi to get the best quality 11x17 prints on my ProofPositive and files of about 25 megs and 360 dpi for my Epson Stylist Photo.

IRIS PRINTERS AND CANON COPIERS

Iris makes a series of printers that produce art-quality work from digital images, in sizes up to 30x40 inches. These Iris printers can print on many types of standard art paper, including parchment. Unfortunately, Iris printers are out of the price range that most individual photographers can afford. Many specialized service bureaus do quality Iris prints and provide high-quality duplications of color and control. Among these service bureaus are Digital Pond in San Francisco and Nash Editions in Los Angeles.

Another very interesting set of devices is the Canon full-color copiers. With PostScript controllers, like the EFI Fiery and the Xerox Splash, desktop computers can send color images directly to the copier. I have seen some impressive prints from these machines in sizes up to tabloid, which makes them very useful for prototyping print work. Because the copiers are quite fast, they also are useful for short-run color printing.

THE FUGI PICTROGRAPHY PRINTERS

The desktop size printer that appears to really have photographic quality is the Fugi Pictrography (Fugix) 3000 and 4000. This RGB printer actually prints on a paper with a photographic-type emulsion (based on RA4) and the maximum image area is 12x18 for the bigger 4000 model. The prints look like photographic prints even when you look at them with a loupe. These printers are worth checking out for final output and also for proofing devices for larger prints. Using color profiles, they can be calibrated to very closely match the LightJet 5000 output.

LARGE PRODUCTION COLOR LASER PRINTERS

The Durst Lambda 130 Digital Photo Printer and the Cymbolic Sciences' LightJet 5000 digital printer are both RGB devices that print on photographic-type papers and also transparent materials with prints up to 50 inches wide and with varying lengths. These things are in the quarter-million-dollar price range, so most of us will probably have to go to a color house or service bureau to get prints. Printed on Fuji FA5 type C matt paper, prints from the LightJet 5000 can have color permanence of up to 70 years! Just find a color house that is well calibrated and can give you repeatable results once you arrive at a final print. Two that I would recommend are Robyn Color (415-777-0580) in San Francisco, which has the LightJet 2000 film recorder and the LightJet 5000 digital printer, and Evercolor Fine Art (508-798-6612) in Worcester, Massachusetts, which also has the LightJet 5000. Several photographer friends and I have had great results with Evercolor.

PROTECTING YOUR PRINTS

One thing to watch out for when you make digital prints is that they may not have the color permanence of a Ilfochrome or C print. I mount my ProofPositive prints behind UV protective True-View glass and also UV protective plastics. I've had these prints for up to five years now and some of the older ones are fading and changing color from being out in the light all this time. You should contact Wilhelm Imaging Research, Inc. at www.wilhelm-research.com to get the latest independent test results on digital prints. Henry Wilhelm wrote the book, *The Permanence and Care of Color Photographs,* and is in the process of testing digital prints. The web site will be constantly updated to give you the latest information. A table of the latest information on permanence at the time of this printing is included at the back of this book.

OUTPUT TO FILM

Various companies make film recorders across a wide variety of prices and quality. These recorders take a digital file and output it back to an original piece of film. You can create original-quality film with the best of these. The film recorders I have seen that create the best-quality film are the Kodak LVT (Light Valve Technology) and the Cymbolic Sciences' Light Jet 2000. These are both very expensive devices, so output to film of original quality will probably have to be done at a service bureau for now. If you want to create a piece of film that has the same quality as an original, you need about 90 megabytes for a 4x5 transparency and much more for an 8x10. Some photographers who do successful commercial work use files in the 30Mb range for 4x5 film output. If you look at the film with a loupe, it won't be quite as sharp as a properly focused original, but it is good for many commercial purposes. You will have to run tests at your service bureau to determine the file size and image quality that works best for you.

PostScript Imagesetters

Imagesetters make halftone films for B&W and color printing. Imagesetters, and many of the other printers I have been talking about, use a computer language called PostScript. PostScript allows computer graphic data, like text and line drawings, to be represented generically within the computer and output in various sizes at the highest possible resolution that each printer or imagesetter allows. Some imagesetters print at over 3,000 dots per inch. Early PostScript imagesetters could not achieve the same quality halftones as their traditional counterparts. These problems have now been solved, so it is possible for PostScript imagesetters to make halftones and color separations of the best quality. It is also possible to print directly to a printing plate using a special type of imagesetter. This is now becoming very popular in the printing industry; this book was even printed direct to plate. When printing color to a PostScript imagesetter, you get better results if it has a Level 2 PostScript RIP. (RIP stands for Raster Image Processor, and *RIPping* is a computer process that converts a digital file from computer byte values into halftone screen dots and patterns.)

I have recently seem some amazing black-and-white darkroom prints by Huntington Witherill of Monterey, California. These were made as contact prints from large imagesetter output. These prints looked better than the traditional black-and-white prints he made from the original negatives and all of Huntington's prints are excellent. The technique used is described in the book *Making Digital Negatives for Contact Printing* by Dan Burkholder from Bladed Iris Press (bladediris@aol.com). Burkholder uses the technique to make platinum prints, whereas Witherill makes larger silver prints up to 20x24 in size. The advantage of this technique is that instead of spending hours burning, dodging, and spotting each print in the darkroom, you spend the time creating a dodged, burned, spotted, and corrected digital file that you then output as a series of very small black dots, about 3,600 per inch, onto the imagesetter film at the full size of the print. You can then use this film to make contact prints in the darkroom that are just exposed and processed the same way each time. Once you get the system down, you get a perfect print every time. One of the difficult parts, according to Witherill, is getting the imagesetter output to create perfect dots across the entire print area. The dot patterns used in this process are not halftone screens.

The Digital Deliverable

The day when most deliverables are digital is arriving. The Communications Superhighway that we keep hearing about is now reality in many places. From our home studio in the Santa Cruz mountains, which is 20 minutes by car from the nearest town, we can get 200 TV channels on a small radio dish pointed toward a satellite. One day we'll be able to transmit back. Over our phone lines we can receive ISDN digital services. The speeds of digital access to the home or business can be orders of magnitude faster than what we have. The technology exists in some areas to send hundreds of megabits per second over fiber-optic phone lines, called *broadband ISDN*.

The technology exists for a photographer to quickly send an entire book digitally over these high-speed broadband ISDN lines to a printer or, better yet, to a customer who wants to read and interact with a digital book on their computer screen. Although the technology exists, both the artists and their clients must have easy access to it before it can become usable.

For some photographers, it will still be easier to output a digital creation to film and deliver that to the client. Art directors are used to film, and using film frees the photographer from responsibility for color separations and other possible reproduction problems. More and more photographers I know are also delivering digital files and even separations to their clients, which gives them an extra billable service and also gives them more control over the final printed piece. More and more clients are seeing the advantage of this digital system. In creating this book, we sent digital files, mostly from corrected Photo CD scans, to our printer, Shepard Poorman, on removable 650Mb CDs we mastered in our studio. We sent a few JPEG compressed files over the phone line too. Maybe you will send your next book or art piece from your studio to your client or output center digitally. We are now in the digital era!

THINGS

SETTING PREFERENCES

AUTOMATING WITH ACTIONS

THE TOOL PALETTE

UNDERSTANDING FILE FORMATS AND CHOOSING COLORS

UNDERSTANDING PATHS, SELECTIONS, MASKS, CHANNELS, AND LAYERS

THE HISTORY BRUSH AND PALETTE

YOU NEED TO KNOW

This photo was taken high above Blacks Beach in La Jolla with a Canon F-1 and 50mm FD lens. I love the abstract wave patterns.

1 HOW TO USE THIS BOOK

*This chapter gives you a quick preview of
what you'll find in this book and gives you some
valuable tips on the best way to use it.*

We believe that *Photoshop 5 Artistry* can help both new and advanced Photoshop users. If you read this book from front to back and do the hands-on sessions in order, it is an in-depth, self-paced course in digital imaging. If you're new to Photoshop and digital imaging, going in order may be the best way to proceed. If you are a more advanced Photoshop user more interested in learning new techniques, you may want to read the sections and do the hands-on exercises that cover the skills you need to learn. Use the table of contents and index to find the areas you want to reference.

The book has two types of chapters: overview chapters, which contain information that everyone should learn, and hands-on chapters, where you learn by color correcting and creating images. The chapters are ordered beginning with the fundamentals and moving on to more advanced skills. All the chapters are in-depth, and we expect most users, even experienced Photoshoppers, to learn something from each chapter. Some of the chapters toward the end of the book are very detailed and assume you already have a lot of Photoshop knowledge. You need to know the foundation skills taught in the earlier chapters before you do the later, more advanced chapters.

The first part of the book, "Things You Need to Know," presents overview chapters that provide readers with a common base of knowledge. Everyone should read the chapters, "Setting System and Photoshop Preferences," "Calibration," "Scanning, Resolution, Histograms, and Photo CD," and "Steps to Create a Master Image," so you can set up your system and Photoshop correctly, and calibrate your monitor for working with the book and doing color output. The rest of these overview chapters go into a lot of detail. If you are anxious to get your hands into the program, you don't need to read all of them before you start the hands-on exercises. You should come back to these chapters later, however, to learn valuable information about the Zone System, picking colors, all the color correcting tools, and other matters. Before doing a hands-on chapter, it's a good idea to read any overview chapter in that part of the book.

The *Photoshop 5 Artistry* CD that comes with the book includes all the images you need (including the authors' before and after versions, Levels and Curves settings, masks, and so forth). Each hands-on chapter has a separate folder on the CD containing the original scan files you absolutely need for doing the hands-on exercise. The Extra Info Files subdirectory of each folder contains the authors' versions of the exercise, including masks, steps along the way, and Levels, Curves, Hue/Saturation, and other tool settings. Use these files to compare your results to the authors' or to recreate the authors' results. For more information about using the CD, see Chapter 2: Using the *Photoshop 5 Artistry* CD.

IMPORTANT DIFFERENCES FOR MAC AND WINDOWS USERS

Photoshop users, on both the Mac and the PC, will find this book beneficial. That's because in 99.9% of the cases everything in Photoshop is exactly the same for Mac and PC users. The contents of each of Photoshop's tool windows and menu bars are the same in a Mac window and a Windows window. Adobe has done an excellent job of making Photoshop cross-platform compatible in every way it can. Mac and PC users both have tested this book, and have found it valuable and easy to use. We have taught in classrooms where some of the computers are Macs and some are PCs and it works out fine.

The following sections discuss the few minor differences between Photoshop on the Mac and on the PC. I also point out any important differences that are relevant to the various topics I discuss.

MODIFIER KEYS

References in *Photoshop 5 Artistry* to keyboard modifier keys use the Option and Command keys, which are the main modifier keys on the Mac. *Windows users need to remember that whenever we mention the Option key, you use the Alt key, and whenever we mention the Command key, you use the Control key.* In those rare cases where we actually mention the Control key, you also use the Control key on the PC. To get the Fill dialog, Shift-Delete on the Mac, but Shift-Back Space on the PC.

FUNCTION KEYS

Most PCs only have 12 function keys on their keyboards where the Mac extended keyboards have 15. *Photoshop 5 Artistry* includes a predefined set of actions for using the function keys, called ArtistKeys, which we reference in the book. We have set these up so the ones used most often are within the first 12 keys. They will work the same for the Mac and the PC. We discuss this further in "Setting System and Photoshop Preferences."

STATUS BAR

Windows users also have a Status bar that tells you what tool you are using and gives you additional information about what you are doing.

MEMORY SETUP

For Photoshop to work most efficiently, you need to set up the computer's application memory correctly. The process for setting up memory on the Mac is a little different than on the PC. Setting up memory for both types of systems is explained in "Setting System and Photoshop Preferences."

VIDEO LUT ANIMATION

A few Macs and many more PCs don't have support for Video LUT Animation in their 24-bit video boards. If you don't have Video LUT Animation support, the way you use certain tools, like Levels and Curves, will change slightly. We explain this in "Setting System and Photoshop Preferences" and we also cover both uses throughout the book whenever Video LUT Animation becomes a major part of an exercise.

2 USING THE *PHOTOSHOP 5 ARTISTRY* CD

Using the Photoshop 5 Artistry *CD to create the examples in this book.*

When you insert your *Photoshop 5 Artistry* CD on the Mac or Windows systems, the Photoshop 5 Artistry folder contains the set of Photoshop 5 format images for doing the book's exercises. The Photoshop 5 Artistry CD also contains demo versions of Adobe Photoshop 5, Adobe ImageReady and other third-party software.

The *Photoshop 5 Artistry CD* that comes with this book contains all the images for doing the examples in the book yourself. You can use this as a self-paced course or you can use it to teach a course at the college or professional level. When you put the CD in a Mac CD player, it will come up with the name *Photoshop 5 Artistry CD*, and it will look like a Macintosh directory with folders, files, and icons, as well as filenames that are often longer than eight characters.

When you put the *Photoshop 5 Artistry CD* in a Windows machine, you will see a Windows directory named *Photoshop 5 Artistry CD* that contains files that have the same filenames as in the Mac directory and the appropriate three-character suffixes that the PC requires.

WHAT'S ON THE CD

The directory on the *Photoshop 5 Artistry CD* opens up to show you a folder for each chapter that is a hands-on exercise. It also contains folders with files and images that you can use to enhance your knowledge about some of the overview chapters. Green folders are for hands-on exercises and blue folders are for overview sections. The folders are numbered with the same numbers that the corresponding chapters have.

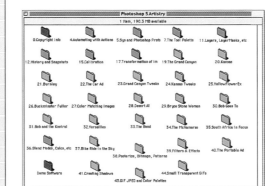

Each hands-on chapter's folder contains the images and other information you need to complete that hands-on exercise and a folder called Extra Info Files. The Extra Info Files folder contains the authors' intermediary and final versions of the images for that exercise, as well as masks, levels, and curves settings and other pieces of information that will help you learn more and also compare your results to the authors'. We have tried to make the images printed in this book look as much like those on the CD as possible. The digital files on the disc, however, are more accurate comparisons of the progress that happens on each creation.

To get the best results when viewing any of the CD files, you should calibrate your monitor and system as explained in Chapter 15: Calibration.

TO TEACH A COURSE

We certainly hope that other instructors will use this book to teach Photoshop courses around the world. Since 1990, Barry has used these examples to teach many Photoshop courses at the University of California Santa Cruz Extension, the Photoshop Conference, the Palm Beach Photographic Workshops in Florida, Ad Vantage Computers in Des Moines, and many other places around the country, including the famous but now defunct Center for Creative Imaging in Maine. Having a professional course where the students can take home the images and exercises to practice them again later has been a main factor in making Barry's Photoshop courses so well received. We hope that you can take advantage of his years developing these exercises by using this book as the text for your Photoshop courses.

If each student purchases the book, they will have copies of all the images and step-by-step exercises for each example. The main images on the CD, in the Photoshop 5 Artistry folder, along with the extra info files, are in Photoshop 5 format. Most images open to about 4 megabytes in size and will grow as the exercise progresses. For a professional course, I have discovered that using images large enough to see the kinds of details students will be working with when they are doing real projects for their art, magazines, film output, and publications works best. These 4Mb Photoshop files from the Photoshop 5 Artistry folder are the easiest to use and give the students the most information for doing the course. If your course machines each have CD players, each student should access the images directly from his or her own CD within the Photoshop 5 Artistry folder.

If you plan to use *Photoshop 5 Artistry* to teach a class, please contact the authors at www.maxart.com to find out about school discounts and also to get complete information regarding purchase and distribution of books and images. We also teach our own in-depth courses for people who want to use our materials to teach Photoshop as well as other fun and worthwhile courses. Check our site at www.maxart.com for the latest course info and schedules.

USING THE DEMO SOFTWARE ON THE CD

The *Photoshop 5 Artistry* CD now contains demo versions of Adobe Photoshop 5, and Adobe ImageReady, as well as other third-party software. You can use the demo version of Photoshop 5 to try out the examples in the book and learn Photoshop, but you can not save files with this demo version. Check out the new ImageReady that is customized to help you do more when creating Web images. Follow the installation directions on the CD to try out each of these packages.

USING THESE IMAGES WITHOUT A COPY OF THE BOOK

We do not mind if teaching institutions or individual users use a copy of the *Photoshop 5 Artistry* images from their hard disk or over a network, as long as they have a copy of the *Photoshop 5 Artistry* book. Each person or student who uses these images to learn about Photoshop should have a copy of the book. If a school, company, institution, or person gives out copies of these images to any person who has not purchased the book, that's copyright infringement. If a school,

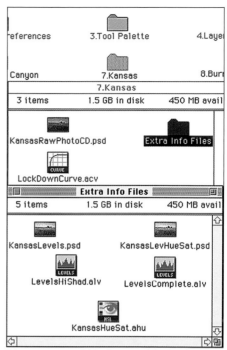

When you open a folder for one of the hands-on sessions, it contains the images and other files you need for completing the exercise. The Extra Info Files folder will contain things like the intermediate and final versions of the images and masks for that exercise, as well as levels and other settings we used along the way. You can compare these with your results if you have any questions about the way you are doing the exercise.

company, institution, or person copies the step-by-step instructions or copies paraphrased step-by-step instructions and hands either of those out in class, especially when using them with the *Photoshop 5 Artistry* images, that too is copyright infringement. Please don't do this! Thanks.

IF YOU HAVE PROBLEMS READING YOUR CD

When you get your book, please remove the CD from the holder in the back of the book and immediately transfer it to a solid plastic case for save storage. The CDs are too easily scratched or made dirty by leaving them in the holder at the back of the book. If your CD has problems opening a file, clean it with a CD cleaning wipe that you can get from a computer store. This will often solve the problem.

There are some files on the Photoshop 5 Artistry CD that don't contain the correct three character suffix to work on a PC. To open one of these files on a PC, just use Windows Explorer to copy the file to your hard disk then change the name of the file to include the correct suffix for the PC. The Mac does not use the three character suffix to figure out the file type so all the files should work on the Mac. We appologize for not noticing this before the CD was reproduced.

Here are all the files that have a missing suffix and the correct suffix to add to each of them: Folder 4.Automating with Actions: add .abr to BigBrushSet. Since the file "LightJet Actions 4/3/98" has slashes in it, you can't see it on a PC, so you can download it from www.maxart.com in the Latest Tips area. The other files within the BillsLightJetActionScripts folder are a text file and an ICC profile. I'm not sure of the correct suffix for each of those. Folder 5.Sys and Photoshop Prefs: You don't need the Paths, Prefs and Color Settings files, add .abr to BigBrushSet. Folder 15.Calibration: Inside the BillsColorCalibration folder, Create_SpectroChart is a Hypercard stack, which I don't believe will work on the PC; the Read-Me is a SimpleText file, all the files in the CMYK Targets and RGB Targets folders are Photoshop format files so add the .psd suffix and they should open. You need to scale these files up using Image/Image Size with the Nearest Neighbor setting in Resample Image. Folder 19.The Grand Canyon: add .ahu to the file MyInitialHueSaturationCHanges. Folder 20.Kansas: Extra Info Files: add .ahu to KansasHueSaturation and .alv to KansasLevels. Folder 24.Kansas Tweaks: Extra Info Files: add .acv to CMYK Tweak Curve. Folder 28.Desert Al: Extra Info Files: add .ahu to 5AlHSSettings, add .alv to 5AlLevels and 5FixedLevels. Folder 39.Filters & Effects: Since the file in the Extra Info Files folder called "Left/Right Flop.psd" has a slash in it, you can't see it on a PC, so you can download it from www.maxart.com in the Latest Tips area. Folder 40.The Portable Ad: add .ai to the file Wholly Os Outlines.

Here is the New Riders technical support information if you need it. Mailing Address: 201 W. 103rd Street Indianapolis, IN 46290. Tech Support Phone: (317) 581-3833. To email tech support: userservices@macmillanusa.com. You can also access our tech support website at http://www.mcp.com/product_support/mail_support.cfm.

3 NAVIGATING IN PHOTOSHOP

*How to most efficiently use the tools, palettes, and windows
that Photoshop provides; make the most of big and small
monitors; and use some general shortcut tips,
like the Actions palette, that make Photoshop more fun.*

Each digital image file you open into Photoshop has its own window. At the top of the window is the name of the file as it was last saved. This is a standard Macintosh or PC window with scroll bars and a grow box in the lower-right corner, and all the rest of the standard fare. If other windows cover the one you want, you can find it in the list of open files in the Window menu. You can view any of these windows in any of three modes, which the icons at the bottom of the Tool palette denote. The left icon denotes the standard window mode, shown here. The middle icon, which we call Full Screen mode, places the active, top window in the center of the screen in the middle of a field of gray.

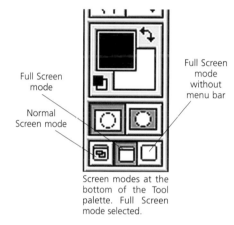

Full Screen mode

Normal Screen mode

Full Screen mode without menu bar

Screen modes at the bottom of the Tool palette. Full Screen mode selected.

WORKING IN FULL SCREEN MODE

Working in Full Screen mode offers many advantages. If you are working on a small monitor, Full Screen mode does not waste the space that scroll bars normally take up. Also, accidentally clicking down in the gray area while in Full Screen mode doesn't switch you to the Finder or some other application. This gray area is especially useful when making selections that need to include the pixels at the very edge of the window. Using any of the selection tools or the Cropping tool, you can actually start or end the selection in the gray area, which basically just ensures that you have selected all the pixels along that edge. When using a typical Mac or PC window, the cursor often fluctuates between displaying as the tool you are using and the arrow cursor for the scroll bar when you move the mouse ever so slightly while at the edge of the window. Even if you are not using Full Screen mode, if you are making an edit along the edge of the image, you may

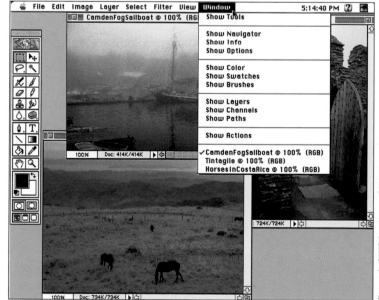

Here we see the Photoshop desktop with three windows open. The active window, CamdenFogSailboat, is the window on top with its title bar striped. You will see a check mark beside this window in the Window menu. You can bring any window to the top, even a hidden one, by choosing it from the bottom of the Window menu.

Here we see the Photoshop desktop in Standard Screen mode and how it can be cluttered by other applications in the background. It is easy to accidentally click outside a window and switch to another application on such a cluttered desktop.

Here we see Photoshop working in Full Screen mode with various palettes around the active window. We can still get to underlying windows by selecting them from the Window menu. A single press on the Tab key removes all these palettes and allows you to use the whole screen for your work. A second Tab press and all the same palettes are back in the same positions. This is a great way to see the big picture.

ZOOMING IN AND OUT

If you are inside Levels and you want to zoom in to see more detail, which I do all the time, you can't select the Zoom tool from the Tool palette the way you usually can. Holding down the Command key and the spacebar will show you the Zoom icon, which you can then click on to do a zoom in and see your image from closer up.

want to make the window a little bigger than the image. Doing so adds Photoshop gray space between the edge of the file and the window's scroll bars so you can more easily make these edge edits. As you can tell, I am very fond of Full Screen mode. It removes all other distractions from your screen and allows you to focus on your beautiful image surrounded by nondistracting neutral gray. On the PC, Photoshop has this advantage in any screen mode. That is, when Photoshop is maximized on the PC, it covers any other programs and the Windows 95 or NT user interface.

The right icon at the bottom of the Tool palette gives you a mode similar to Full Screen mode, but with the image surrounded by black instead of gray, and the menu bar removed. If you are a Photoshop power user, you can work without the menu bar by using command and function keys—but I generally use this mode only for presentations.

CONTROL KEYS FOR ZOOMING AND SCROLLING

There are certain keyboard shortcuts that I make everyone learn when I teach Photoshop. IT IS VERY IMPORTANT THAT YOU LEARN THESE THREE SHORTCUT KEYS! Even if you hate keyboard shortcuts and you don't want to be a power user, you have to learn these or you will find working in Photoshop a constant pain. I worked on the Lisa project at Apple. The Lisa was the predecessor to the Mac and much of the Mac's user interface actually was designed for the Lisa. Larry Tesler, who was head of applications software for the Lisa project, had a license plate on his car that read, "NO MODES." A mode is a place in the user interface of a program where you can't access the tools you normally use. Programs that have a lot of modes can be confusing, especially for the beginner. Photoshop is less modey than before, but it still has a lot of modes. Many tools in Photoshop come up in a modal dialog box; for example, Levels, Curves, Color Balance, and most of the color correction tools. When you use these tools, you are in a mode because you can't go to the Tool palette and switch to, for instance, the Zoom tool.

Command-Option-Spacebar-click will do a zoom out. When you zoom in and out using the Zoom tool or these control keys, Photoshop zooms by a known amount. If you are at 100%, where you see all the pixels, then you will zoom into 200% and then 300% and then 400%. You will find that the image is sharper at a factor of 2 from 100%. Fifty percent, 100%, 200%, or 400% are sharper than 66.6%, 33.3%, and so on. You can also use Command-+ and Command-- to zoom in and out. In Normal Screen mode on the Mac these keys change your window size while zooming, which the other spacebar options do not. On the PC you can hold down Control-Spacebar and right mouse click to get a pop-up menu with zoom in and zoom out. Don't forget that

Again in Full Screen mode, here we have used Command-Spacebar-click to zoom in and fill the screen with our image, a more inspiring way to work. Learn to use Command-Spacebar-click to zoom in, Option-Spacebar-click to zoom out, and the Spacebar with a mouse drag for scrolling. View/Fit on Screen (Command-0) will fill the screen with your image and it fills the entire screen if you first press Tab to remove your palettes. View/Actual Pixels (Command-Option-0) zooms to 100%. This is the most efficient way to move around the Photoshop screen, especially when in Full Screen mode or using a dialog box like Levels.

you can always zoom so the entire image fits in the screen by pressing Command-0 (zero). If you press Command-Option-0, the image zooms to 100%.

Scrolling with the Hand Icon

Just holding the spacebar down brings up the Hand icon, and clicking and dragging this icon scrolls your file.

Palette Management

Photoshop contains a lot of different palettes, each of which controls a different set of functions. The Tool palette is the main palette. Its functions are discussed in Chapter 7: The Tool Palette. The different color picking palettes are discussed in Chapter 8: Picking and Using Color. Palettes include the Channels, Layers, and Paths palettes, which are discussed in Chapter 10: Selections, Paths, Masks, and Channels, and Chapter 11: Layers, Layer Masks, and Adjustment Layers. What we discuss in this chapter is how to most efficiently use all the palettes on the Photoshop screen.

Accessing palettes

All palettes are accessed from the Window menu. You can use this menu to open or close a particular palette. We recommend using the Actions palette to define function keys to bring up and close the palettes you use most often. The chapter, "Setting System and Photoshop Preferences," explains how to do this. Pressing the Tab key makes the Tool palette—and all other visible palettes—disappear. Pressing Tab again brings all these palettes up in the same locations. Pressing Shift-Tab opens or closes the other palettes without changing the status of the Tool palette. You can close any of the palettes, except the Tool palette, by clicking the close box in the top-left corner of the palette on the Mac or the top-right corner in

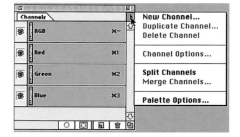

Here we see a typical palette with its Options menu on the top-right, accessible by clicking the black triangle icon. The Palette Options item shows you different ways to display the palette. You should check out the Palette Options on all the palettes that have them. Most Palettes have a close box on the top left and a similar box on the right for collapsing or opening the palette. The icons at the bottom of the palette are shortcuts for various functions associated with that palette. The name at the top is the palette's name tab. Here are some standard icons and what they mean:

Load Selection from Channel or Path

Save Selection to Channel or Path

New Channel, Layer, Path, Action or Snapshot

Throw Channel, Layer, Path, Action or Snapshot away

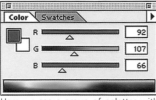

Here we see a group of palettes with the Color palette currently active. The Palette Options menu would now bring up the Color palette's options.

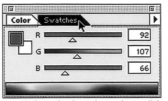

To switch to the Swatches palette, click its name tab and when you release the mouse, the palette group will look like the group to the right.

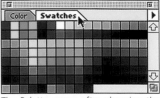

The Palette group after choosing the Swatches palette. Now the Swatches Palette options show in the Swatches Palette Options menu.

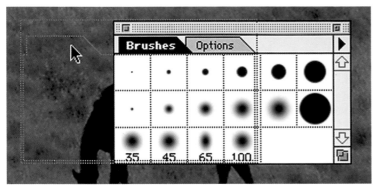

Click a palette's name tab and drag it outside the group window to put that palette within its own window.

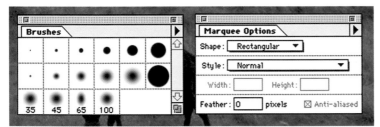

Here we see the Brushes palette after it has been removed from grouping with the Options palette. To regroup these palettes, click the name tab of one of them and drag it on top of the window of the other. The palette that is within a group window first has its name tab on the left. New palette tabs are added to the right.

Clicking the first time in the Grow box, at the top-right, resizes the palette so that it just holds the things within it, like the palette on the right. In Windows systems the rightmost box closes the palette and the box just to the left of it duplicates the behavior we describe here.

Clicking a second time in the Grow box resizes the palette to show just name tabs, like the palette on the right, and will also send it to the top or bottom of your monitor.

Clicking again in this palette's Grow box expands it to the size to the immediate left. The compacted size shown here can be left at the bottom or top of your monitor without taking up much screen real estate until you need it again later.

Windows. You can use the Tab key or define an action to open or close the Tool palette or any palette. We have done this for you as explained in "Automating with Actions." If the Tab key does not make the palettes go away and come back, the cursor is probably within a field on the current tool's Options menu. Just click the tool in the Tool palette again and the Tab key hides the palettes again.

PALETTE OPTIONS

Most palettes also have a menu that you can access by clicking the Menu icon at the top-right of the palette (see previous illustration). You can move palettes around on the screen by clicking the title bar at the top and moving the palette to a new location. Photoshop opens the palettes in the same location at which they were last used unless you turn off the Save Palette Positions option within Photoshop's Preferences (which you reach by choosing File/Preferences/General).

GROUPING AND SEPARATING PALETTES

In Photoshop, you can group several palettes in the same palette window. You then switch between palettes in the group by clicking the name tab of the palette you want or by choosing the palette from the Window menu. If you hide any of the palettes within the group, the whole group gets hidden. Therefore, you are better off grouping only palettes that are used together. Sometimes you want to see two palettes at the same time that are usually used within a group. I do this often with layers and channels. When I'm working on a complicated layer document that has a lot of mask channels, I separate them to see both at the same time. To do this, click the name tab of the palette you want to separate and then drag it out of the group window to a new location by itself. To move more palettes into a group, click the name tab of the palette you want to add and then drag it over the group window. New palettes in a group are added to the right. If you have a small monitor, you may want to group more of your palettes together to save screen space. You can also compact and collapse your palettes by clicking in the Grow box at the top right.

MORE THAN ONE WINDOW PER FILE

You can have more than one window open at a time for the same Photoshop document. To do this, first open a Photoshop file that gives you your first window. Next, go to the View/New View command to open a second window of the same file. Utilizing this capability, you can, for example, have one window of a section of the file up close and the other window showing the entire file. You can also use this technique to have one window display a particular channel or mask of the file, while another window shows the RGB or CMYK version. There are many uses of this feature.

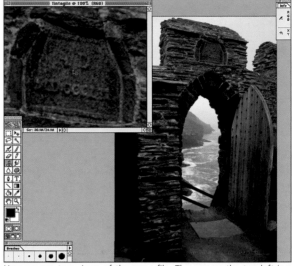

Here we see two views of the same file. The one on the top-left is a close-up of the inscription on the stone above the door at Tintagel Castle, England, the supposed castle of the Knights of the Round Table.

USING THE INFO PALETTE

The Info palette is one of the most useful tools in Photoshop. Not only does it measure colors like a densitometer (which we will do extensively in the color correction exercises in later chapters in this book), it also gives you important measurements any time you are scaling, rotating, making, or adjusting a selection. The top-right location, the size of the box you are drawing, the degree of rotation, and many other useful measurements are always present in the Info palette. This is a good one to keep up on the screen most of the time. See "Color Correction Tools" and "Color Correction for the Master Image" for a discussion of the new Color Sampler part of the Info Palette.

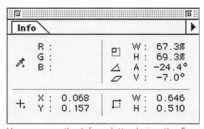

Here we see the Info palette during the Free Transform command. The contents of the right and bottom two sections change to show you information about your transformation.

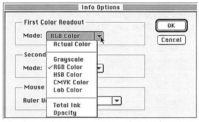

Check out the many options of the Info palette accessed from its Palette Options menu.

RULERS, GUIDES, AND GRIDS

Photoshop has always had rulers, but now version 5 also has guides and grids. Guides and grids are very helpful for creating composite images where you need to place objects in exact locations. They are also great for Web and multimedia projects to control the alignment of buttons and action objects. The controls for rulers, guides, and grids are all located on the View menu. As you can see in the diagram on the next page, there is a different command key to turn each of the rulers, grids, or guides on and off, as well as a different key to snap to each of grids or guides. You can also lock guides to prevent accidentally moving them.

Command-R turns your rulers on, at which point you can set the zero-zero location of the rulers (by default the top left of the image) by clicking in the top-left ruler box and then dragging to the point in your image that you want to be zero-zero. To return it to the top-left position again, just double-click in the top-left corner of the ruler display. You set up the ruler unit preferences in the File/Preferences/Units and Rulers.

You use File/Preferences/Units & Rulers to set up the types of rulers you have. Notice that Photoshop 5 has added percent. This displays the cursor, or object, location as a percentage of the total height and width. It is useful for recording Actions where you want the playback to do the same thing based on relative positions within a file.

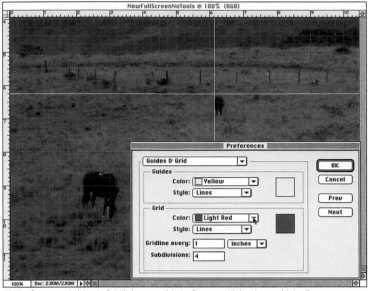

File/Preferences/Guides & Grid brings up this Preferences dialog box ,which allows you to set the color and appearance of your grids and your guides. You can also specify how often you have gridlines and subdivisions.

To create a guide, just click in the horizontal or vertical ruler and drag the guide to where you want it. Clicking the horizontal ruler will drag out a horizontal guide and clicking the vertical ruler will drag out a vertical guide. You can move a guide, if Lock Guides is not turned on, by using the Move tool (V or the Command key) and just dragging the guide to its new position. Option-dragging a guide toggles it from vertical to horizontal or vice versa. Another important keyboard option for guides is to hold down the Shift key while dragging out your guides. This forces the guides to even pixel boundaries, which is critical for multimedia and web work where precision is paramount. Take a few minutes to play with these options and you will find rulers, grids, and guides easy to learn.

When working on projects where I need to measure the sizes and placements, I usually have at least rulers on. When you are drawing a selection, you can actually see the starting location as well as the current location of the mouse by following the dotted lines that show you the current mouse location along each of the rulers. For faster positioning, turn on the grid as well as Snap To Grid; then you will know that things are exactly placed. To set your own specific locations, create guides anywhere you want. You can then line up objects along these guides. When I am just color correcting a photograph, I usually turn off Rulers, Guides, and Grids and put the image into Full Screen mode so that I can see it unobstructed.

THE NAVIGATOR PALETTE

Photoshop has a cool Navigator palette (Window/Show Navigator or Shift-F2 with ArtistKeys) that allows you to zoom in and out to quickly see where you are in an image and more efficiently move to a particular spot in that image. This palette contains a small thumbnail of your entire image with a red box, called the View box, on top of the thumbnail that shows you the part of the image you can currently see in your window. As you zoom in, you will notice this box getting smaller because you are seeing less and less of the image area. You can click and drag this box, in the Navigator palette, to a new location and then your window will display what's inside the box. This is much faster than doing large scrolls with the Hand tool on the actual image window, because in the Navigator palette you always see the entire image. You do not need to guess where you want to scroll to; just click the red box and move it there. It is even faster if you don't drag the box there, but instead just click down in the Navigator palette where you want the box to be; then the box instantly moves there. To change the size and location of the red box, just Command-drag a new box over the area you want to see. You can change the size of the Navigator palette and its thumbnail by clicking and dragging in the Grow box at the bottom-right corner of the palette on the Macintosh, or click and drag on any edge when using Windows. Making the

Here you see the choices you get for either Grid or Guide colors. Each can have a different color and choosing Custom brings up the Color Picker, where you can pick any color you want.

Using the View menu, you can use Command-R to turn rulers on and off, Command-; to turn Guides on and off and Command-" to turn the Grid on and off. To snap to the Grid or Guides, you use Command-Shift-" or Command-Shift-;.

Here you see the options for Grid styles. Guides can be in either the Lines or Dashed Lines styles.

palette bigger gives you more exact positioning within your file using the bigger thumbnail. You can use the slider on the bottom-right to drag the zoom factor smaller or bigger. You can also click the smaller or bigger icon on either side of the slider to zoom in a similar way to Command-Spacebar-clicking and Option-Spacebar-clicking. In the bottom-left of the Navigator palette is a numeric text box where you can type in the exact zoom factor that you need. If you hold down the Shift key while pressing Enter after typing in a new zoom factor here, you will zoom to the new factor, but the text percentage number remains highlighted so you can enter a new value without having to click the text box again. I have found that images are a little sharper on the screen when zoomed to an even multiple of 100% (25%, 50%, 100%, 200%, 400%, and so on). You can change the color of the View box from red to another color by choosing Palette Options from the Navigator Palette menu.

THE ACTIONS PALETTE

Check out the next chapter, "Automating with Actions," to learn how to use the Actions palette with my ArtistKeys command set to quickly set up function keys to show and hide any palette. You may notice, throughout the book, references like (F11 with ArtistKeys) or just (F11). These show you places where I have created shortcuts for you using the Actions feature. Actions can be used to automate a single menu choice, like bringing up a palette, or a whole sequence of events, like creating a drop shadow. Please check out actions; they are very powerful!

CONTROL KEY FOR CONTEXT-SENSITIVE MENUS

Photoshop has a great feature using the Control key and the mouse (just right mouse button on Windows)! At any time, you can hold down the Control key and then press the mouse button (just right mouse on Windows) to bring up a set of context-sensitive menus. What shows up in the menu at a particular time depends on the tool you are currently using and the location where you click. If you are in the Marquee tool, for example, you get one menu if there already is a selection and a different one if there is not. If you are in the Move tool, you'll get a menu showing all the layers that currently have pixels at the location where you click. These are a great set of time-saving features. To learn more, see "The Tool Palette" and the step-by-step examples.

Navigator palette and red View box when image is zoomed to 100% and all is visible in the image window.

Navigator palette and red View box when zoomed to 300%. Now only the area in the red View box is visible in the image window.

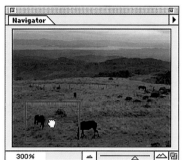

Dragging on the red View box to change what is visible in the image window.

Command-dragging a new box to view just the large horse at the bottom center. When the mouse button is released, we will zoom so this box fills the window.

Here is the small default size Navigator palette.

You can use the Grow box in the bottom-right corner to change the size of the Navigator palette. Here is a big Navigator palette.

4 AUTOMATING WITH ACTIONS

Using the Actions palette to add function keys for frequently used menu items and to add sequences of keys and events to automate your Photoshop production.

The Actions palette with Button mode turned off. This allows you to edit the actions in many ways. The Actions menu bar shows you all the things you can do with actions. We discuss each of these in this chapter and explain how they work. Notice the icons at the bottom of the palette that, from left to right, stop recording, start recording, play current action or command, make a new set of actions, create a new action or command, and allow you to throw an action or command into the trash.

Actions allow you to record and even edit single menu items or very complicated sequences of events. You can then run that menu item or series of events over an entire folder full of files. You can execute these events with the press of a function key on the keyboard or a click of a button onscreen. You choose Window/Show Actions (F11 with ArtistKeys) to bring up the Actions palette. To create new actions, you want to turn off Button mode from the Actions Palette menu. After you define all your actions, you can turn on Button mode, which turns the actions into buttons that you can play by clicking them.

ARTISTKEYS TO SET UP YOUR ACTIONS

In the Automating with Actions folder of the Photoshop 5 Artistry CD, we have given you a predefined set of actions, called ArtistKeys. You should add this set of Actions to your copy of Photoshop since we will show you how to use them in this book. Do this now by first choosing Save Actions, from the Actions palette menu, to save your existing actions. Now choose Replace Actions, to replace your existing actions with ArtistKeys. Replace Actions is not going to cause conflicts with your existing actions. What we did with ArtistKeys is go through all the menu items in Photoshop and set up as function keys the ones that you will use most often. For example, F9 through F12 will bring up and close down the palettes you use most often. We tried to do this logically, so F9 is the Info palette and Shift-F9 is the Color palette. Both of these palettes deal with measuring color. F10 is the Layers palette and Shift-F10 is the Channels palette. You often use these together. I use F2 through F12 to implement single menu items (and we do mention these quite often in the book, so you will find them quick to learn). I mention these keys in context as alternatives, so you don't have to learn them if you would rather not. I consider F1, as well as F13 through F15, optional, so you can use them to reprogram other actions. You can also program most of the Command key Actions as well as all the Shift-Command ones.

To Record a Single Menu Item Action

Create a new Action or Duplicate current Action or Command.

Stop Action Recording or Playback.

Play current Action or Command.

If you want to set up an action with a function key to perform any menu item, even the palette menus, here are the steps to take. Make sure the Actions palette is not in Button mode (Button Mode unchecked), by using the Actions Palette menu. Create a new action by clicking the New Action icon at the bottom of the Actions palette or by choosing New Action from the Actions menu. Either way, the Action Options palette opens, enabling you to name your action as well as pick a function key and color for it. You do not need to pick a function key or color. When you click the Record button, you can record a single menu item simply by choosing Insert Menu Item from the Actions menu. Doing so opens the Insert Menu Item dialog box shown here. Now just choose the menu that you want to automate and its name fills the text box. Choose OK and then click the Stop Recording icon at the bottom of the Actions palette or choose Stop Recording from the Actions menu. To play the action you just recorded, press the function key or click the action in the Actions palette and choose Play from the Actions menu, or click the Play icon at the bottom of the palette. In Button mode, clicking an action plays it. The good thing about Actions is that you can now record, and even edit, highly complicated sequences of events and then run them over an entire folder full of files.

Recording Actions with Multiple Commands

To record an action with a sequence of events, you start the same way, by choosing the New Action icon or menu item. Name your action, press the Record button, and then go through the sequence of events on the open file. Each recorded menu item in the sequence is now called a command. Because you want to run this sequence on many other files, you need to be aware of the state of the file when you start recording. All subsequent files will have to be in the same beginning state for the action to work properly. Actions are like computer programs; they have no intelligence to pick the right layer within the file or make sure the file was saved before you start. Take a look at the first multiple command action within ArtistKeys. It is called Drop Shad (Ob In Actv Lyr) and is meant to add a drop shadow to an object on its own layer surrounded by transparency. Open the file called Ball from the Actions folder on the Photoshop 5 Artistry CD. You will notice that the layer called Ball is currently the active, grayed layer and the ball within this layer is surrounded by transparency. Any file that you run the Drop Shad action on will have to first be in this state for the action to do the right thing. If you have programmed before, this will be obvious, but I know that many of you have not.

Why not get your feet wet now? Start out with a file in this state (you can use the Ball file, you have it open anyway) and then create the action as described above. Click the Record button and go through the simplest sequences of events to create a drop shadow. The Actions feature records these events as you do the work. If you have the Actions palette open, you can see the events recording as you work. Do absolutely nothing except this sequence of events; otherwise, you record that too. After you finish your sequence of events, choose Stop Recording from the Actions Palette menu or click the Stop Recording icon at the bottom of the Actions palette. You are not done! Now you need to look at the sequence of actions and edit it to

Actions	
Tool Palette	F2
Navigator Palette	⇧F2
Gif89Export	F3
Color Table	⇧F3
Unsharp Mask	F4
Gaussian Blur	⇧F4
Duplicate	F5
Replace Color	⇧F5
Apply Image	F6
Selective Color	⇧F6
Image Size	F7
Threshold	⇧F7
History Palette	F8
Color Range	⇧F8
Canvas Size	⌘F8
Info Palette	F9
Color Palette	⇧F9
Layers Palette	F10
Channels Palette	⇧F10
Actions Palette	F11
Paths Palette	⇧F11
Brushes Palette	F12
Options Palette	⇧F12
Flatten Image	F13
UpdateWorkChannel	F14
MakeWorkChannel	⇧F14
SharpEdgesShp	
Set Preferences	
Drop Shad (Ob In Actv Lyr)	
Drop Shad No Stopping	
Drop Shad w Insert Menu Item	
Drop Shad Before Editing	

The Actions palette with Button mode turned on. In Button mode, you can click an action to play it, even if it doesn't have a function key alternative.

New Action

Name: A New Action — Record

Set: Barry's Actions 1/3/98 — Cancel

Function Key: F1 ☑ Shift ☐ Command

Color: ☐ Green

The New Action command, or double-clicking an existing action, brings up the Actions Options dialog box, where you can name your action, choose a function key for it, and also a color that shows up in Button mode.

Insert Menu Item

Menu Item: None Selected — OK

Find: — Cancel

To record a menu item, select a menu item using the mouse, or type a partial name and press the Find button.

Use this to create an action that plays a single menu item. You can pick any menu item from anywhere within Photoshop. Also use this when you don't want the action to insert any values into the command for you.

Here we see the Drop Shadow action prior to editing. If you play this action, the Offset command always offsets your shadow by −10 horizontal and 10 vertical. The Gaussian Blur of your shadow will always have a Radius of 10. This will not create the correct drop shadow in most cases because the size of the object will be different and the light may be coming from a different direction. You need to edit this to make it user-friendly and object-specific.

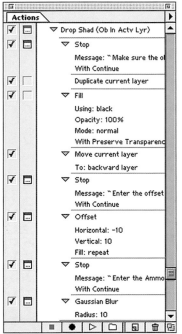

Here is the Drop Shadow action after editing to add the Stop commands as well as the breakpoints in the Offset and Gaussian Blur commands.

make sure it does the right thing when you play it back. Think about it; will you always want all the parameters to each command to be the same or will some things be slightly different for each instance? The great thing about actions is that you can customize them easily.

EDITING ACTIONS AFTER RECORDING

I wanted to create a Drop Shadow action that would work for most people most of the time. Photoshop 5 has Layer/Effects/Drop Shadow, but this is a different more editable way to create a drop shadow. I wanted people to figure out how to use it without any verbal directions, so I added a Stop message. The unedited Drop Shadow action is shown here to the left at the top of the page with the edited

Enter the message you want displayed to give the user information about the action that is playing. Turn on Allow Continue so the action will continue when the user clicks OK.

one below it. We added a Stop message by clicking the Drop Shad (Ob In Actv Lyr) line to activate it, and then clicking the arrow to the left of the name, which opens up the action and displays the list of commands in it. Now choose Insert Stop from the Actions menu to open the Record Stop dialog box. Enter the text of the message you want the user to see. The message I entered just explains that to use this action, you need to start with an active layer that has an object surrounded by transparency within it. The Stop command now happens before the action starts so that the user can click Cancel if the file he is running it on is not in the right state. If the user clicks Continue, the action then goes on to make a copy of the target layer, fill that copy with black using preserve transparency, and then move this new black layer below the original target layer. To turn this new black layer into a shadow, we need to now offset it from the original and then blur it to make its edges soft. I added another stop message before the Offset command, this one explaining that the user needs to adjust the offset numbers to fit the object in question. The direction and amount of the offset will depend on the lighting on the original. To allow the user to change these values, I put a break point on the Offset command by clicking in the column to the left of this command in the Actions palette. Finally, I added another stop to explain that the Gaussian Blur amount also requires editing to make sure the shadow looks right for this situation. Then I added a break point on the Gaussian Blur again by clicking in the column to its left.

FURTHER EDITING REFINEMENTS

The preceding exercise illustrates the types of editing you can do to actions. After you understand how this action works, you could turn off the Stop commands by clicking their check marks to turn off each check in the leftmost column next to each Stop command. You could also throw away the Stop commands as you can any command or action, by dragging it to the Trash icon at the bottom of the Actions palette. If you're using Batch mode to run the action on a bunch of items that all have the same offset and blur values, you can turn off the breakpoints on Offset and Blur by clicking in the middle column next to each of them. You can change the actual value of the default offset or blur by clicking that command line and then choosing Record Again from the Actions menu. It will play that one command line and allow you to change its default value within the action. If you want the user to always enter the values for a particular command when he uses the command, you need to use the Insert Menu Item option from the Actions menu when recording the

Chapter 4: Automating with Actions

command, and choose that command. It doesn't actually execute the command until the action is played, so the user has to enter the values at that time.

ADDING TO ACTIONS

After you record an action, you can add to it by selecting a particular command within the action and choosing the Start Recording menu from the Actions menu bar, or by clicking the Start Recording icon at the bottom of the Actions palette. New commands are recorded right after the command you select. You can click an existing command and drag it to the New Action/Command icon to make a copy of that command. You can then drag that copy, or any command, to another location in the current action or in another action. If you want to start playing an action in the middle, just click the command at the point at which you want to begin and choose Play from the Actions menu to play the action from that point forward. You can also play an action or command by clicking the Play icon at the bottom of the Actions palette.

THINGS THAT ACTIONS DON'T SUPPORT

Some menu items in Photoshop, like the Preference menus, don't do anything during the recording of an action. If, while recording, you choose a menu item or click a tool or do anything and a new command doesn't show up in the actions palette, then that thing is not recordable. Adobe probably didn't have time to include action support for those commands. If you want to include any of them as part of an action anyway, you can choose Insert Menu Item, which will play that menu item when the action plays. You can't put default values into these commands, but at least you can get the user to respond to them. Notice that the Set Preferences action is done this way. It brings up most of the preference items that I recommend you change from defaults. (You need to read "Setting System and Photoshop Preferences" for the values to enter.) I could not find any way to record certain things into an action, such as setting the Eyedropper preferences to read a 3 by 3 Average instead of a Point Sample—I decided to do it as a Stop message so that you know that it needs to be done.

You will also notice that the actual painting with any brush is not recordable, although switching to a painting tool is now recordable in version 5. Making selections and crops are now recordable and when you record something like this, you may want to set your Ruler Units (File/Preferences/Units & Rulers) to Percent so the locations of selections and the size of selections is proportional to the current file. On the other hand, if you want absolute sizes and locations, then leave the ruler units set to Inches or Pixels. Photoshop 5 Actions will record selections with the Selection tools (not the Pen tool), yet it won't record switching to a selection tool. It will record switching to a painting tool, yet it won't record paint brush strokes. This seems inconsistent at best and I'd call it a bug!

NEW ACTIONS FEATURES FOR PHOTOSHOP 5

In Photoshop 5, actions can be organized into different sets. To create a new set, choose New Set from the Actions palette menu or click the third icon from the right (looks like an empty folder with a tab) at the bottom of the Actions palette. Use Sets to organize your actions into different functional groups. The Function keys are global across all the sets so you can't use the same function key twice for two different things without loading different actions. There are now twice as many Action function keys available (60 on the Mac and 48 on Windows) and you can control the speed and mode of action playback.

Here we have the Drop Shadow action where the Offset and Gaussian Blur were created using Insert Menu Item. These will automatically stop and allow the user to specify the parameters each time. There are now default values if you do it this way.

Throw Action or Command away.

Start Recording.

Choose Playback Options from the Actions palette menu to bring up this dialog for your Playback options. If you have one of the new faster computers, you may have to put a Pause For several seconds between each action to have time to see them as individual steps on the screen.

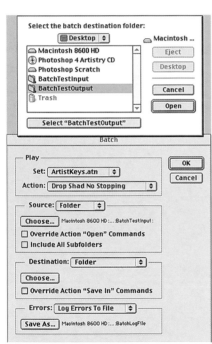

On the left we see the action that will break with each Stop command and also on the Offset and Gaussian Blur commands. On the right we have removed the Stop commands by clicking their check marks in the check mark column to the left, and we have taken away the break points on the Offset and Gaussian Blur by clicking them in the break column. This is the kind of thing you might want to do to an action to prepare it for automatically running in Batch mode over a lot of files.

Here is the dialog box for Batch where you can choose the Source, Action, and Destination for your Batch. Notice the new Photoshop 5 features let you choose the Action Set, let you Include All Subfolders, and also allow you to Log Errors To a File. When you use one of the Choose buttons that brings up the dialog box at the top here, the trick is to click the Select "Folder Name" button as shown above, rather than the Open button, when you find the folder you want.

Photoshop 5 actions can now also record creating selections from the Paths (although not actually making the path), doing things in the Layers and History palettes, using the Gradient, Marquee, Crop, Lasso, Line, Move, Magic Wand, Paint Bucket and Type tools, the Lighting Effects filter, as well as the Calculations, Apply Image, File Info and Free Transform commands. Actions can also record Switching and Selecting documents. If you want to be able to record relative positions, set the ruler units to the new Percent option. When in Batch mode, you now have the option of stopping an Action upon an error or just recording the error in a file and continuing. If you are running a Batch from a folder, you can decide whether to Include all Subfolders in the action.

One "new" feature of Photoshop 5 actions is that they won't do anything during a Modal dialog like Levels, Curves, Color Balance, and so on. In Photoshop 4, while in the middle of using Levels, you can press F9 and the Info Palette comes up. You often want to bring up or remove a palette while in a Modal dialog. With Photoshop 5, your normal ArtistKeys actions won't work, and even worse, you get different "default" behavior on some functions keys, which is different than your normal action behavior, while in a Modal dialog. Photoshop 5 will not play any actions while in a Modal dialog, even those that play dialog legal menu items. Too bad!

RUNNING THE SAME ACTION ON A WHOLE BATCH OF FILES

The File/Automate/Batch menu enables you to specify an action along with a source and destination folder for that action. If you specify a source folder and a destination folder, Photoshop opens each file in the source folder and runs the action on the file and then saves that modified file in the destination folder. If the source folder has sub-folders, you can choose to have Photoshop also process the files in the sub-folders. You do not have to put Open or Close commands in your action; the Batch command automatically adds these at the beginning and the end. If your action has any Open commands in it, the Override Action Open Commands check box in the Batch dialog box allows you to tell it to ignore those commands. Another check box lets you tell the Batch command to ignore any Save commands. You select the action you want to perform by using the Action pop-up menu in the Batch dialog box and you choose the Source and Destination folders by clicking their respective Choose buttons. If you choose None for Destination, Photoshop leaves the modified files open. If you choose Save and Close, they are saved back in the folder in which they started, under the same name. You can also create a Multi-Batch action that records more than one Batch command. You can then play this Multi-Batch action, which allows you to batch one action after another on the same set of files, or to batch the same action over and over again on different files in more than one folder.

Photoshop 5 added the capability to Log Errors to a file, whose name and location you choose. After the error is logged, the action continues. When running actions on a large group of files within a folder, this allows the action to process the other files even if there is an error with several of them. When an error comes up, you can also choose to have Photoshop stop the action and put an error message on the screen. Let's get some action into our lives!

5 SETTING SYSTEM AND PHOTOSHOP PREFERENCES

Setting up your system and Photoshop's preferences to make Photoshop run more efficiently and make your work easier.

If you are new to computers or Photoshop, some of the discussions and settings here may seem a bit confusing to you. You should still read this chapter and set up your preferences as it recommends. Your Photoshop will run more efficiently and give you better results with your color corrections and separations. Your understanding will grow as you do the exercises and read the rest of the book, especially the chapters, "Color Spaces, Device Characterization, and Color Management;" "Calibration;" "Scanning, Resolution, Histograms, and Photo CD;" and "Steps to Create a Master Image."

SETTING UP YOUR MAC

You may want to read this section with your Macintosh turned on so you can refer to your screen as you follow the steps outlined here. In the System 8 Finder, choose About This Computer from the Apple menu. An information window opens, giving you the total memory available on your Macintosh and how much memory each application currently running is using. If you check this when no applications are running, Largest Unused Block tells you the amount of space available for all your applications in megabytes. An abbreviation for 1,024 bytes is the expression One K. 1024K (1,024 x 1,024 bytes of memory) equals 1 megabyte (Mb) or 1,048,576 bytes of memory. If you had, like I do, 160Mb of Total Memory, and your system software used about 12Mb, the Largest Unused Block would display about 147Mb. Your system can use this 147Mb for the applications that you want to run concurrently.

If you are going to use only one application at a time, then you can let Photoshop have most of this remaining memory. You want to leave at least three to four megabytes of space free for desk accessories to run. I often use Photoshop and Quark at the same time, so I assign 128Mb to Photoshop and 6Mb to Quark, which leaves about 12Mb for other applications. If I were working on a really large Photoshop project, I would assign all available memory to Photoshop. Still, I would leave the three to four megabytes for desk accessories. If you don't leave enough room for the desk accessories, you can end up getting a message that there isn't enough memory to run a particular desk accessory. When the system barely has enough room to run a desk accessory, it becomes more prone to crashing.

To tell the system how much memory to assign an application, you first select the icon for the application from the Finder. You select an application icon by opening the folder that contains that application and then clicking (just once) on the application file. You need to do this when the application is not running, so don't click

The About This Computer window with only the system running. The spaces for System Software and Largest Unused Block don't add up to exactly Built-in Memory because the system constantly borrows small amounts of memory for various purposes.

About This Computer on my Mac with the system, Photoshop, and Quark running.

twice because that starts the application. Next, choose Get Info from the File menu in the Finder. An information window about that application appears. For every application, a suggested size and a preferred size appear at the bottom of the information window. Suggested size usually refers to the minimum size that the application developer recommends to allow the application to operate efficiently. Preferred size refers to the amount of memory this application is actually given when it runs. Some applications will still operate if you set preferred size to less than the suggested size and some will not. I would recommend an absolute minimum of at least 24Mb of memory for Photoshop 5.

You can always set Preferred size to more than Suggested size, and that usually improves the application's performance level. Photoshop usually requires three to five times the amount of temporary space as the size of the file(s) you currently have open. It is much faster if Photoshop can put all this temporary space into real memory. If Photoshop doesn't have enough real memory for the temp space, it allocates a temp file on the disk and uses it as virtual memory for its temp space needs. When this happens, Photoshop runs much slower than when everything is in real memory. Photoshop comes with its Preferred size set to a default of about 23Mb. If you try to work on large files with so little memory, Photoshop operates very slowly. If you increase Photoshop's memory on your Macintosh, you should notice a great improvement in performance.

Several settings in the Memory control panel (Apple menu/ Control Panels/Memory) are important to Photoshop's performance.

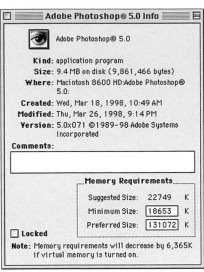

The Get Info window for Photoshop.

DISK CACHE

With OS versions before 8.5, Photoshop runs faster if you set the Disk Cache size to 96K—making it any larger just slows Photoshop down. Leave the Disk Cache set at the default value if using Mac OS 8.5 or newer.

VIRTUAL MEMORY

Photoshop has its own virtual memory system that is much more efficient for Photoshop than System 8's Virtual Memory. Therefore, you really need to turn off Virtual Memory in the Memory control panel. Power Mac owners get a message that system RAM requirements decrease by "x" if they use virtual memory. Still, Photoshop runs better on Power Macs with Virtual Memory turned *off*.

RAM DISK

Giving more memory to Photoshop using the Get Info procedure we just described makes Photoshop faster than allocating that same memory as a RAM Disk, so keep the RAM Disk off.

The Memory control panel and how it should be set for Photoshop.

SETTING UP YOUR PC

When using Photoshop on a Windows-based machine, setting up your Photoshop memory usage is less complicated than on the Mac. Choose File/Preferences/Memory & Image Cache from Photoshop and make sure that the Memory Usage setting is 75% (which should be the default). Next, click OK in the Memory Preferences dialog box. You need to quit Photoshop and then restart it for these changes to take effect. When Photoshop starts up, it calculates the amount of available RAM in your system. Photoshop measures this RAM by taking the amount of installed RAM and subtracting any that is used by disk caching software, RAM disks, and other software that permanently reserves RAM (including the Windows OS).

Chapter 5: Setting System and Photoshop Preferences

Photoshop will allocate 75 percent of the available RAM for its own use. You should have a minimum of 20Mb of RAM available for Photoshop to use on a standard PC and a minimum of 24Mb available for Photoshop on a Pentium-based machine. Check the Scratch Size and Efficiency box at the bottom-left of your open document to see how much RAM is available and how Photoshop is using it. See the "Plug-ins and Scratch Disk," section later in this chapter for more information on these.

Here is the Memory Preferences dialog box from the Windows version of Photoshop. Use it to set up how Photoshop uses memory on your PC.

SETTING UP THE PHOTOSHOP PREFERENCES

You access most Photoshop preferences from the File/Preferences or File/Color Settings menus. I go through the preferences in order and talk about the ones that are important for working efficiently with photographs. For a description of Photoshop preferences that I don't talk about, see the Photoshop 5 manual. If you are new to Photoshop, prepress, or photography, you may not know some of the concepts or Photoshop functions mentioned in this chapter. If so, just set the preferences as we recommend for now, and then reread this chapter after you study the rest of the book.

These are the different categories of general preferences. You can go to any one of them using this pop-up menu or by clicking the Next and Prev buttons. You can also use Command-1 through Command-8 to get to a particular dialog box. Command-K brings up the General dialog box and Command-Option-K brings up the last preferences dialog box you were working on.

GENERAL PREFERENCES (COMMAND-K)

COLOR PICKER

You usually want the Photoshop Color Picker, because it gives you more options than the Apple Color Picker. The Photoshop Color Picker is the default color picker.

INTERPOLATION

Interpolation chooses the algorithm used when making images bigger or smaller. This process is called resampling because you are taking the current image pixels and either adding more pixels or taking some away. Bicubic interpolation is the most accurate way to resample images, so select it for the best quality. If you are prototyping ideas and speed is more important than image quality, you might try one of the other choices. Nearest Neighbor is the fastest, and poorest quality.

These are our recommended settings in the General Controls dialog box.

ANTI-ALIAS POSTSCRIPT

Check Anti-alias PostScript if you are importing PostScript artwork from Illustrator or FreeHand; otherwise, your PostScript imports end up having jaggy diagonal and circular edges.

EXPORT CLIPBOARD

Have you ever seen the message "Converting Clipboard to Pict Format" while you impatiently waited to switch to the Finder or some other application? Turn off Export Clipboard to make switching between Photoshop and other applications much faster. You can still cut and paste inside Photoshop, just not between Photoshop and other applications.

SHORT PANTONE NAMES

Check Short PANTONE Names if you're exporting a PANTONE color as a Duotone EPS or in some other way to Quark, PageMaker, or Illustrator. Make sure those other applications use the exact PANTONE names you used in Photoshop.

Tool Tips show up in many places and can help you learn the program and the icons.

SHOW TOOL TIPS

When Tool Tips is on, you get a small yellow line of information that explains what each tool does when the cursor is on top of that tool. Displaying these tips, once you know the program, can slow Photoshop user response down. You can turn Tool Tips off here by unchecking this option.

BEEP WHEN DONE

Setting Beep When Tasks Finish is useful if you have a slow computer or are working on exceptionally large files. It lets you go cook dinner while Unsharp Mask finishes up, for example. I used this feature a lot back when I had a Mac IIx. With my 300 Mhz PowerPC, 160Mb of memory and fast hard disk, I don't need the beeps much anymore.

DYNAMIC SLIDERS IN PICKER

Dynamic Sliders in Picker allows the Color palette to show you all the possible colors, for future changes, on the fly, as you are changing one color. It is very useful to have this on when you're color correcting.

SAVE PALETTE LOCATIONS

Save Palette Locations remembers where you had all the palettes last time you shut down and restores them the next time you power up.

RESET PALETTE LOCATIONS TO DEFAULT

This button restores all the dialog box and palette locations to the default locations on your main monitor screen. It comes in handy if you cannot find a particular palette. Some bugs in older versions of Photoshop made the Tool and Color palettes partially disappear above the menu bar, so you couldn't move them down. Using this button is a good way to overcome such bugs in Photoshop. So far, though, I haven't encountered this problem in Photoshop 5.

SAVING FILES

IMAGE PREVIEWS

Here is the Windows Saving Files dialog box.

I like to decide whether to save an icon whenever I save a file. You also can choose to always save an icon or never save one. Icon refers to the icon picture of your image you see when you are in the Mac Finder. Thumbnail refers to the preview you see in the Open dialog box. Full Size saves a 72dpi full size preview for applications that are faster at opening files with such a preview. In the Windows version of Photoshop, icons are not an option, but you can create a Thumbnail when saving an image. When you work on files for the Web, it is best to set this to Never Save since any type of preview will increase your file size.

APPEND FILE EXTENSION

These are our recommendations for the Mac Saving Files Preferences dialog box.

If you turn this on (either Always or Ask When Saving), Photoshop appends the correct three-character file extensions to files so they can be understood and opened on the Windows platform. The Mac knows the type of file you have without the extension. On the PC, the extension tells the software the type of file. Before Windows 95, Windows format files could have only eight characters in their file names before the three-character file extension (often called the 8/3 file format). If you want to make sure your file will be recognized correctly on any platform, use the 8/3 file

Chapter 5: Setting System and Photoshop Preferences

name convention and use only lowercase letters without special characters; also make sure you turn on Always and the Use Lower Case option.

Include Composited Image With Layered Files

The now renamed 2.5 Format Compatibility allows applications that can read Photoshop 2.5 file format to open Photoshop files with layers. If you have layers in your Photoshop files, Photoshop 2.5 format applications cannot see the layers, but they can open a flattened version of the layers whose Eye icons were on when the file was last saved. There is a space cost for this convenience though. Every time the file is saved, Photoshop must save a flattened version of the file in addition to all the layers. Turning off Include Composited Image With Layered Files saves disk space and time when you are working on files that have more than one layer.

DISPLAYS AND CURSORS

CMYK COMPOSITES

If you are working in CMYK color, you should choose Faster for the CMYK Composites option. Smoother is a little more accurate, but it usually is very hard to see the difference. If you want or need to see CMYK gradients more accurately, especially if your CMYK gradients seem uneven, turn on the Smoother option.

COLOR CHANNELS IN COLOR

Turn off Color Channels in Color—it displays your Red, Green, and Blue, or CMYK channels, with a colored overlay that makes it very hard to see detail. Viewing individual channels in grayscale gives you a more accurate image.

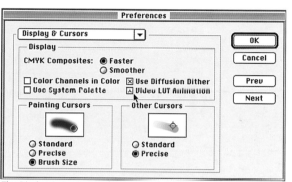

The Display & Cursors preferences. These are our recommended settings. Setting the Painting Cursors and Other Cursors settings to Brush Size and Precise is particularly important.

SYSTEM PALETTE

If you are working in 8-bit color, you don't usually want to use the System palette. You usually want a custom adaptive palette for each image. Having a custom palette for each image makes the image display more accurately, but also makes the screen flicker when you switch from one image to another in the 8-bit mode.

DIFFUSION DITHER

When working on an 8-bit system, the Diffusion Dither option makes smoother transitions on colors that are not in the current palette. I like the Use Diffusion Dither option to display 24-bit images on an 8-bit screen. I recommend leaving this option on.

VIDEO LUT ANIMATION

Unless you have a very old video board, you want to have Video LUT Animation on. It allows you to see many color and contrast changes instantly by tweaking the monitor display through the video card. A few old or poor video circuits don't support this, and you only want to turn this feature off if you have one of those displays. Video LUT Animation is not available on most PCs, because the PC-video cards don't support it. PC users should ask their video board supplier if Video LUT Animation is supported and turn it on only if it is. Another way you can see if your computer supports Video LUT Animation is to turn the option on and then go through the steps in the Chapter 19: Grand Canyon, which uses Video LUT Animation. If it is supported, leave the option on here. If not, turn this option off.

TOOL CURSORS

The Tool Cursors settings are important! If you set Painting Cursors to Brush Size, you will paint with a circle outline the size of your brush. This setting even takes into account the current zoom factor. I recommend Brush Size. Using the Precise option is like using the Caps Lock key, in that you paint with a cross-hair cursor. Standard uses the standard Photoshop cursors, a different cursor for each tool. I find that the standard cursors usually get in the way of seeing what I am painting. For the Other Tools option, I recommend the Precise setting.

PLUG-INS AND SCRATCH DISK

The Plug-ins preference tells Photoshop where to find its Plug-in filters. Usually these are in a folder called Plug-ins within the Photoshop folder. On the Mac, you can easily interpret this dialog box incorrectly, or click the wrong button. When you find the folder that contains the plug-ins, you need to click the Select "Plug-Ins" button at the bottom of the dialog box. Don't click the Open button at that point, like you would for most other uses of an Open dialog box or you'll just open the folder.

The Scratch Disk preference tells Photoshop where to store temporary files on disk. Even if you give Photoshop plenty of memory, it also stores things on a scratch disk. In fact, Photoshop requires more scratch disk space than the amount of memory you assign to it. Use the largest, fastest disk drive you can afford for your primary (First) scratch disk. If you purchase a Mac that has a built-in drive and then later go out and purchase a very large high-performance external drive or a disk array, you probably should specify that disk array as your primary (First) scratch disk because it may be faster than your built-in original drive. You can also specify Second, Third, and Fourth drives on which Photoshop can store temp files when it runs out of space on the First drive. Try to leave at least five times the scratch space for the size of the file you are working on and certainly leave much more space on the disk than the amount of memory you assign to Photoshop.

Photoshop has a scratch disk efficiency indicator. To access it, select the pop-up menu at the bottom-left of the image border and choose Efficiency. The efficiency rating changes depending on the amount of time Photoshop spends swapping image data in and out of RAM from the disk. If your efficiency rating is less than 100% for most operations, you are using the scratch disk instead of RAM. You might want to add more RAM to your system to get better performance.

If the "*" character follows the percent display, your primary (First) scratch disk is operating with asynchronous I/O working. That is good for better performance because Async I/O allows the disk to read or write while Photoshop does something else. If you don't see the "*," check the folder within the Adobe Photoshop® 5.0/Plug-Ins/Extensions folder called "¬ Enable Async I/O." If this folder *has* the character "¬" in front of it, remove that character and restart

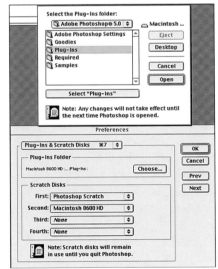

The Plug-ins & Scratch Disk preferences with the choosing Plug-ins dialog box above, which we accessed using the Choose button. Make sure you click the correct Plug-Ins folder and then click the Select "Plug-ins" button. Setting the First Scratch disk to your largest, fastest drive is also important for Photoshop performance. Also set the Second, Third, and Fourth choice if you have that many drives.

If the Efficiency is at 100%, Photoshop can do all its operations on this file without using the scratch disk. If Asynchronous I/O is working with your First scratch disk, you should see the * character to the right of the efficiency percentage, as shown here.

The Document Sizes option in this same pop-up shows you the flattened image size on the left (if you saved the file with no channels or layers) and the actual size including all the channels and layers on the right.

Photoshop. This turns on asynchronous I/O for Photoshop's primary scratch disk. If you still don't see the "*" character, read the About Enable Async I/O document in the Enable Async I/O folder in the Extensions folder in the Photoshop 5 Plug-Ins folder. that comes with Photoshop to learn how to set up the correct disk drivers for Async I/O.

The Document Sizes option in this same pop-up shows you the flattened image size on the left (if you saved the file with no channels or layers) and the actual size including all the channels and layers on the right.

The Scratch Sizes option gives you the amount of image data space Photoshop is using for all open images on the left and the amount of scratch memory space available to Photoshop on the right. If the number on the left exceeds the number on the right, you are using the hard disk for scratch space and likely are slowing Photoshop down. See the ReadMe file that comes with Photoshop for more information about improving Photoshop performance.

The Current Tool option just displays the name and info about the current tool selected in the Tool palette. This information can be useful when the Tool palette is not on the screen, although I find that I can usually remember what tool I'm using and would rather have this window set to one of the other settings.

TRANSPARENCY AND GAMUT

The Transparency and Gamut preferences settings allow you to change the way transparent areas of a layer look and also what color is used to display out-of-gamut colors. The default settings work fine for us, but check them out if you want to play around some. You might want to change the settings here for certain types of images, for example, line art work where the line art has similar colors to the transparent grid.

GUIDES & GRID

The Guides & Grid preferences allow you to change the way Photoshop guides and grids appear onscreen. You can change the color as well as the types of lines (you can choose between Lines, Dashed Lines, and Dots). You can also specify how often the gridlines occur and how many subdivisions each major gridline has. When working on Web and multimedia projects, I use the grid and guides to help place objects precisely. When you're in the Move tool (V or Command key), you can double-click a guide to bring up the Guides & Grid preferences, then easily change the colors and styles, and view these changes as you make them.

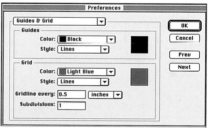

You should set the Guides & Grids preferences according to the colors of objects in the project files you are currently working on.

IMAGE CACHE

The Image Cache increases Photoshop's efficiency when working with larger files. When Cache Levels is greater than 1, Photoshop makes several copies of the file in different sizes and uses the smaller versions to update the screen quickly when working with layers and doing complex tasks. When working with smaller files, set the Cache to about 2 or 3, and when working with larger files, set it to 4 or higher. The larger the image cache setting, the more RAM and disk space Photoshop uses when you open a file. We recommend leaving the Use Cache for Histograms setting off; it sometimes gives you slightly inaccurate histograms. The histogram you get with Use Cache for Histograms on depends on the cur-

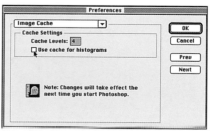

Turn off the Use cache for histograms check box to get more accurate Levels histograms. If you leave this on, the smaller cache image may be used to calculate the histograms. This will not be as accurate because the smaller file has fewer pixels being read. The default setting for Cache Levels is 4.

rent zoom ratio of your file. Leaving it off slows creating a histogram for a large file but ensures that your histograms always are completely accurate and consistent, regardless of your zoom ratio.

UNITS AND RULERS

The Ruler Units setting in the Units and Rulers Preferences dialog box controls the scale on Photoshop's rulers when you go to View/Show Rulers (Command-R). It also controls the dimension display settings in the Info palette and the initial dimension display when you enter the Canvas Size command. Changing the setting in the Info palette also changes it in Canvas Size. We usually leave it set at inches, but for very detailed measurements as well as for Web and multimedia projects, we change it to pixels. Photoshop 5 has added a Percent setting here which will display your scale, and also record your Actions using percentage of the total size. Turn this on when making Actions where proportional locations and sizes are more important than actual inches or pixels in a particular image.

COLOR SPACE SETTINGS

The File/Color Settings Photoshop preferences are the settings that affect how Photoshop displays images on the computer screen as well as how Photoshop does color separations. These have all changed in a major way between Photoshop 4 and Photoshop 5. Photoshop 5 is now much more compatible with ICC profiles for different input and output devices, and Photoshop 5 also allows you to work in a particular device-independent RGB color space that is different from your monitor's color space and also the color space of any particular input or output device. You need to set these preference settings correctly and should standardize your settings, especially if you have several people contributing Photoshop files to the same publication. To better understand the recommendations made in this chapter, you should read Chapters: 14: Color Spaces, Device Characterization, and Color Management, 15: Calibration, and 18: Steps to Create a Master Image. To get the best results when using Photoshop 5, you will probably want to use different preference settings depending on whether you are working on projects for the Web, for an RGB output device like the Lightjet 5000 color laser printer, or for a particular CMYK printing situation. The settings we give you here are recommended as a starting point, and we will explain how to change them if you want to develop your own custom settings. We used the CMYK settings described here under CMYK Setup Built-in to create the color separations in this book.

RGB SETUP

As explained in more detail in Chapter 14, with Photoshop 5 you can choose an RGB space to work with. This will determine the gamut of your RGB files and, when you have an ICC profile of your monitor, Photoshop will compensate for your monitor's gamut and give you a preview of what your file will look like within the space of your particular monitor. This allows you to choose a space, like Adobe RGB (SMPTE-240M) that has a larger gamut than your monitor or any one particular output device. When a file from a particular RGB space is displayed on different monitors, the monitor compensation will make that file look as similar as possible.

Choosing a wide gamut RGB space for your RGB workspace means that colors that you can't see on some monitors and also can't print to a CMYK press will not be

We usually leave the Ruler Units set to inches. When working on Web and multimedia projects, we change it to pixels to get very detailed measurements. The Units setting also controls the dimension display in the Info palette when selecting or drawing rectangles.

In Photoshop 5, you need to make sure that all four of these Color Settings areas are correctly set up for the type of work you are doing or you might get results other than what you want. This is no longer as simple as it was in previous versions of Photoshop, but if used properly, you can get much better results.

These are the RGB Setup values I used for creating most of the color separations in this book. For people who do mostly print work to a CMYK press and who have been using a Radius Pressview monitor, these settings will give you results similar to what you are used to and will probably allow you to open your legacy files, those created with older versions of Photoshop, without doing any conversions.

thrown away but left in your file so when you make a print to a higher gamut RGB device, like a film recorder or the Lightjet 5000 RGB laser printer, you will actually be able to use and see those colors. However, if your main output device is the CMYK print on a press or the Web, then you might want to choose an RGB workspace with a smaller gamut like ColorMatch RGB for print or sRGB, the Photoshop 5 default space, for the Web.

When you choose a RGB workspace from the RGB pop-up, Photoshop will automatically set the Gamma, White Point and Primaries for that space. This is because things that show up in the RGB pop-up are ICC profiles that specify this information. Not all ICC profiles show up in the pop-up, only ones that have a uniform gamma for all three colors, a white point and three x-y primary values. You can create your own RGB workspace with profile making software or by editing either the Gamma, White-Point, or Primary values within an existing space. You can then use the Save button to pass this space on to others who can also use it by using the Load button.

Photoshop assumes the ColorSync space that is set up for your System Profile is the correct space for your monitor. You can create a ColorSync (ICC) profile for your monitor by using the Adobe Gamma control panel that comes with Photoshop or by using a hardware monitor calibrator. The Adobe Gamma tool is good to use if you don't have a hardware calibrator, but if you have a Radius Pressview monitor, an AppleVision or Apple ColorSync monitor, or some other monitor with hardware calibration, you should use that calibration to create an ICC profile for your monitor and then set that profile to your System Profile so it shows up next to Monitor: at the bottom of this RGB Setup dialog. Then you want to turn on Display Using Monitor Compensation at the bottom of the dialog. If you have the Preview option checked in the dialog and a file open at the time, you can change from one RGB workspace to another to see how that will change the appearance of a particular file. Remember that after you set an RGB workspace, you will then be using that space to do your color corrections and you will adjust each file so it looks correct in that space. You should, therefore, be able to adjust a particular file to look good in its own RGB workspace even if it looks strange in another RGB workspace.

If you want to get every possible printable CMYK color, but also include a lot more colors that are not printable, or if you are printing to a Lightjet 5000 or a film recorder, you will probably want to choose the wider gamut Adobe RGB (SMPTE-240M) space as your RGB workspace. This space also has its Gamma set to 2.2 versus the Gamma 1.8 Color-Match RGB space. The higher gamma space gives you a wider range of contrast values and will show you more detail in the shadows when the file is adjusted to compensate for the extra darkness and contrast over the gamma 1.8 space. Unless you are working on images for the Web, multimedia or TV output, you should still calibrate your monitor itself to gamma 1.8.

CMYK SETUP

Photoshop 5 has a lot more options for controlling CMYK separations than previous versions of Photoshop did, and you should expect the built-in separations in Photoshop 5 to work a lot better than those in Photoshop 4 or previous versions. The display of CMYK images on the screen in Photoshop 5 should also be more accurate when you have your system set up correctly. There are three main choices for how to specify your CMYK Model in Photoshop 5: Built-in, ICC, and Tables. We will go through each of these and their subcategories and explain them in detail in this chapter.

Within the Built-in CMYK Model are most of the controls that can be changed using Photoshop itself. These might look similar to the controls in the old Photoshop separator but you will find the results better with Photoshop 5 separations—you also have much more control here too.

INK OPTIONS

INK COLORS: This setting tells Photoshop the types of inks you will be printing with on a press. You will notice that the number of preset values here has been changed from Photoshop 4 to those that really relate to press conditions. Because

Here are starting values for the Built-in CMYK Setup settings we recommend for output to coated stock. We are basing these settings more on the actual CMYK values we get when separating our gray Stepwedge file. Using the Info palette to measure what you actually get, after influence from Ink Colors, Dot Gain settings and Separation Options, when making a separation is more accurate than just looking at the limits and graphs shown in this dialog box. Change some of the settings and with the Preview option here checked, you can measure the differences on the fly using the Eyedropper or Color Sampler tools and Info palette within the Stepwedge file that comes in the Calibration folder on the Photoshop 5 Artistry CD.

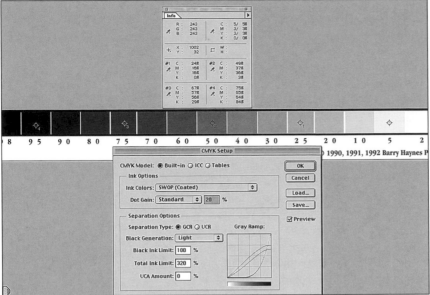

Here is the setup to use the Info palette to measure what you actually get, after influence from Ink Colors, Dot Gain settings, and Separation Options, when making a separation. Change some of the settings, and with the Preview option checked as you see here, you can measure the differences on-the-fly using the Eyedropper and Color Sampler tools, and Info palette. Here we have four Color Sampler settings to measure the values at 25%, 50%, 75%, and 95%, and we are using the Eyedropper to measure 5% within the Stepwedge file that comes in the Calibration folder on the Photoshop 5 Artistry CD. When we change any parameter seen here, including the Dot Gain curves, Black Ink Limit, Total Ink Limit, UCA Amount, and so on. we see what separation values those changes will actually give us in the five measured areas. You should be able to use this technique to tweak the Built-in separator to get very close to what your press person wants for a particular press. First though, I'd try the built-in Photoshop seps, and you might find that even if the numbers are different than what you normally get, the results are much better than they were in Photoshop 4. You can also use this measuring technique to compare the CMYK values you would get using different ICC or Tables CMYK model settings for your CMYK Setup.

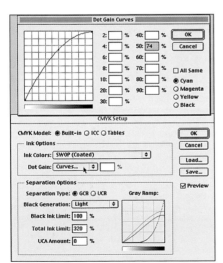

In Photoshop 5, you now have the option of setting the individual dot gain curves manually. To do this just set the Dot Gain pop-up to Curves and you will get the dialog at the top that allows you to set the dot gain for each color individually and in detail, or you can create one curve to use for all the colors by turning on the All Same check box.

printing inks are fairly standardized, you will probably find it unnecessary to change this setting after you pick the right ink. For printing this book on a sheet-fed press, I used the SWOP coated setting. You would want to choose the SWOP Newsprint for newspapers or the SWOP Uncoated for uncoated paper. If you are printing with Toyo inks, which I was impressed with the time I used them, you would pick one of those settings. You can also choose Custom and enter the xyY values or LAB values in the case of special custom inks. When you convert from RGB to CMYK, the actual CMYK values you get for a given RGB value depend on a combination of the preferences settings in RGB Setup, CMYK Setup, and also where and how you set your highlight and shadow values in Levels or Curves. For magazine-quality output to coated stock, you should start out using the SWOP Coated setting here.

DOT GAIN: The Dot Gain setting adjusts how dark Photoshop displays the CMYK image on the screen as well as how dense Photoshop makes each of the CMYK separation channels. The Dot Gain value represents how much the printing inks will spread when printed on certain papers. If you set the dot gain to 30%, Photoshop will separate each CMYK color with less density and display the colors on the screen darker than if the dot gain were set to 20%. As a general setting, you should start with a dot gain setting of 20% for coated stock. You should talk to the press expert at the printshop you will be using to find the exact dot gain settings for the press and paper combination you will be using. Most print shops are familiar with Photoshop settings these days, although the extra control that Photoshop 5 offers may be new to them. Photoshop 5 allows you to specify each of the Cyan, Magenta, Yellow, and Black dot gain curves separately instead of just picking one dot gain value to use for all three. Again, you should discuss the expected dot gain with your printer and set the Photoshop Standard single value or the new Dot Gain Curves accordingly.

SEPARATION OPTIONS

The Separation Options further control RGB to CMYK conversion values. The Gray Ramp is a curve diagram showing how Cyan, Magenta, Yellow, and Black are generated for neutral colors as the image goes from highlights on the left to shadows on the right. There is more ink used in the shadows, and black ink gets used only in the darker half of the color ranges. If you adjust the settings for Black Generation from Light to Medium, or Dark, you can see how the black setting effects the Cyan, Magenta, and Yellow curves. You can also choose Custom for the Black Generation curve, and this will bring up a curve dialog that allows you to manually modify the black curve. You cannot manually modify the Cyan, Magenta, or Yellow curves here, although you can now modify their dog gain curves. Changing the Black Ink Limit, Total Ink Limit, and UCA (Under Color Addition) also affect all the curves shown in the Gray Ramp. The Separation Type lets you choose between GCR (Gray Component Replacement) or UCR (Under Color Removal) separations. Our recommended settings for Separation Type are GCR (Gray Component Replacement) turned on; for Black Generation, Light; for Black Ink Limit, 100%; and for Total Ink Limit, 320%. These settings are based on the CMYK values we actually measured when separating a standard grayscale stepwedge and from comparing the numbers to known good CMYK values for neutral colors and coated stock on a sheet-fed press. If your were printing on a Web press, your total ink settings would probably be somewhat lower, around 280, and for a newspaper press, they would be lower still. Each newspaper press is a little different. We are leaving the UCA, Under Color Addition, amount set to 0, but you can increase the UCA value if you find that the GCR separations are removing too much colored ink in the nonneutral areas. Again, if you are not happy with the results you are getting, the best thing to do here is talk to your print shop and run some tests with different settings until you get the results you like. If the Built-in CMYK Setup controls don't allow you to get what you want, Photoshop 5 now allows you to get your CMYK Setup from ICC separation profiles or the Tables that we will explain next.

USING AN ICC PROFILE FOR SEPARATIONS

When you are using the ICC setting for CMYK Model, you will set the Profile to a special ICC profile for your press and paper conditions. There are standard profiles available for particular presses and inks, and you might want to ask your printer or service bureau if they have any of these to recommend. In theory though, the best thing to do is to make a custom profile for your particular press, paper, and ink condition. To do this, you have to choose the profile making software you are going to work with. An example of profile making software for this type of task is PrintOpen by Linotype-Hell. There are other profile-making software products on the market, and there are also service bureaus and other organizations in the business of creating color profiles for you.

The process would be to print a standard test target, made up of many swatches of color and neutral values, on your press using standard ink densities and printing conditions. This test target would then be measured with a spectrophotometer to see how these standard color swatches printed on this press with this paper and ink. Those measurements would be entered into a software package, like PrintOpen, which would then create the ICC profile with its best separations for that press, ink, and paper combination. That profile would then be chosen here in your ICC profile under ICC Options. When you printed those separations, it would be expected that you would get the best results when printing using the same standard ink densities and printing conditions that were used to make the test.

When you use a profile for your separations, your results will be based on three things. These are the accuracy of the printing test proof that was used to take the measurements from, the accuracy of the person and equipment making the measurements from that proof, and finally, the quality of the software making the ICC profile from those test results. If the persons running the test printing and making the profile do a good job, you might get the best possible results from this approach, however, if it doesn't work that well, you may have less control over any changes you need to make unless you actually own all the software, equipment, and knowledge to make further tests and correct the situation.

Using the ICC setting for CMYK Model allows you to create your color separations from an ICC profile of your output device. There are standard ICC profiles for particular types of presses and printing conditions that you can use. You can also print a profile-making test target on the press and paper you were going to use and then use profile-making software, like PrintOpen from Linotype-Hell, to make a custom ICC profile for that particular press/paper combination. That profile would then be selected here from the Profile pop-up.

When using an ICC profile to print photographic continuous tone images, you will probably get the best results by setting the Engine to Built-in, the Photoshop 5 profile processing engine, and the Intent to Perceptual, which are the best settings for continuous tone photographs. You can also choose the Apple ColorSync and LinoColor CMM profile processing engine. If you are using Apple ColorSync, make sure you have version 2.5 of ColorSync installed. This can be downloaded for free from Apple's Web site if you don't already have it. Version 2.5 is much more accurate than 2.1, but I have the word from Adobe that its built-in engine is even better.

USING THE TABLES CMYK MODEL

After setting up your CMYK Setup using either the Built-In or ICC settings, if you then click the tables setting, you will notice that under the From CMYK Table area and also under the To CMYK Table area in italics is a short description of your current settings. For our default settings. we see *SWOP (Coated), 20%* under the From CMYK Table and *SWOP (Coated), 20%, GCR, Light* under the To CMYK Table. The From CMYK table is telling you what Photoshop will currently use to convert CMYK values back to RGB for display on your monitor, and the To CMYK table is what Photoshop will use when converting RGB values to CMYK. You can now click on the Save button to Save this set of tables. To quickly get back to exactly this CMYK Setup configuration, you can then later go to the Tables option and click on the Load button that would load all these same settings. If you routinely have to change your CMYK Setup depending on the particular press and paper you will be printing on this time, you might want to save each of your CMYK Setups using the Tables area and then you go here and reload any setting using the Load button. You can use the Load and Save buttons in the Built-In mode for CMYK Setup to do a similar thing when using the Built-In settings; the Tables area just gives you a more generic way to quickly load or save any regularly used separation values.

Another thing you can do using the Tables area is Load your old separation tables from an older version of Photoshop. The process to make the loadable tables and then load them here is as follows:

1. Go to your old version of Photoshop, in this case Photoshop 4, and make sure your Monitor Setup, Printing Inks Setup, and Separation Setup settings are correct for the tables you want to move over to Photoshop 5.
2. Go to File/Color Settings/Separation Tables, and click the Save button to save your old tables.
3. Quit from your old Photoshop and start up Photoshop 5. Now go to File/Color Settings/CMYK Setup and set the CMYK Model to Tables; then click the Load button to load your old separation tables.
4. After you have these old tables loaded, click the Save button in the Tables area and resave them. This will save them as an ICC profile. If you put this ICC profile into the ColorSync Profiles folder within the System Folder (or where you put your ICC profiles on Windows), you will be able to use this as the source profile when opening and converting CMYK files created in an old Photoshop. When you add ICC profiles to the ColorSync Profiles folder, you need to quit from Photoshop 5 and then restart Photoshop 5 for those profiles to show up in within Photoshop 5.
5. If you were just doing this to create an ICC profile from your old separation tables, you should now put your Photoshop 5 CMYK Setup back to the standard settings you are using. In general, you should find the Photoshop 5 separations better than those from older versions of Photoshop, so I would not recommend

Use the Tables CMYK Model to save your current setting in a table that you can pass on to others and to also quickly switch from one set of CMYK settings to another when you are switching between different types of printing situations. You can also use this to load separation tables from old versions of Photoshop, although you are probably better off using the new separation engine.

Chapter 5: Setting System and Photoshop Preferences

just using your old tables. However, if you were happy with your old tables and you just got Photoshop 5 and need to do some work before having time to test the new Photoshop 5 separations, you can load your old tables and use them until you set up the new Photoshop 5 stuff the way you want. I do really encourage you to use the new Photoshop 5 separation engine, however, because it is much better when you get it set up correctly for your needs.

GRAYSCALE SETUP

Photoshop 5 now has a more understandable way to deal with grayscale images. You will want to go into Grayscale Setup and set your Grayscale Behavior to RGB if you are working on grayscale images to be used for the Web or any RGB output device. My recommendations would be to work on your master grayscale image using the RGB setting because this will give you the same monitor calibration that you will get for your RGB workspace. When you choose the Black Ink setting for Grayscale Behavior, the dot gain setting you have chosen in your CMYK Setup for the black ink will be used to change the appearance of grayscale images on the screen and also the measurements in the Info palette based on the expected dot gain when you print this grayscale image on a press. When I am working on a grayscale image, I usually don't want my monitor preview and digital values modified in this way. If you are going to print that grayscale image on a press, you might want to change the Grayscale Behavior to Black Ink to do any final adjustments using a preview of how this will print on the press. You may find, however, that you want to change the dot gain of the black ink curve in CMYK Setup, Built-in to more accurately reflect what you will get with just a single ink. This Black Ink setting does a similar thing as the Use Dot Gain for Grayscale Images check box at the bottom of Printing Inks Setup in the older versions of Photoshop.

PROFILE SETUP

The last menu item in the Color Settings menu is the Profile Setup choice. This brings up the Profile Setup dialog that makes various decisions about how Photoshop deals with files having current, different, and no ICC profiles.

We recommend that you have the Embed Profiles check boxes on for each of RGB, CMYK, Grayscale, and Lab files types so that when you save a file from Photoshop 5, it embeds the profile information from the current RGB Setup, CMYK Setup, Grayscale Setup, or Lab into that file. Embedding the profile will tell others, and yourself, who later have to use that file, what workspace that file was created in and therefore give others the chance to set up their system correctly in order to deal with a file from that workspace. One of the few times you don't want to embed a profile is when you are creating a test file that has values that you don't want to be modified by profile conversions, like for example, a standard IT8 target you are using to create profiles for different printers. If you turn off Embed Profiles for that type of file, RGB for example, then Photoshop actually tags that file with a tag that says you explicitly specified that the file was to remain untagged. When this file is later opened, Photoshop or other applications can then tell the difference between it and a file that never had a tag because it came from an earlier version of Photoshop or some other app.

The Assumed Profiles area tells Photoshop what profile to assume a file came from when it tries to open a file that has never been tagged. These files will mostly be files that came from older versions of Photoshop. The Profile Mismatch Handling

Set the monitor to the type of monitor you have. That also sets the phosphors for you. If your monitor is not listed, ask the monitor manufacturer what settings to use. Unless you have a hardware calibrator to accurately set your gamma and white point, leave them set at 1.8 and 6500. Set the ambient light based on the standard lighting in your room.

Until you get used to working with Photoshop 5, and maybe forever, we recommend setting your profile setup as you see above. This way whenever you open a file that was not set up for your current configuration you will be notified and given the chance to make the right decision.

After working with Photoshop for a while, you may find that you are always opening old files that always come from the same nontagged space, for example if you were using a Radius PressView monitor with Photoshop 4, you could probably assume your old RGB files came from the ColorMatch RGB space and your old Grayscale files were Gamma 1.8 files. In this case, you could set your Assumed RGB Profiles up to ColorMatch RGB and your Assumed Grayscale up to Grayscale-Gamma 1.8. If you wanted to automatically convert these into your current RGB and Grayscale spaces, you'd want to set RGB Profile Mismatch Handling to Convert to RGB Color and Grayscale to Convert to Grayscale. These old files would then automatically be converted to your current RGB Setup and Gray Setup space when they were opened. If you don't want to automatically convert, leave RGB and Grayscale set to Ask When Opening. Since there are so many ways to do CMYK separations and there are always different destinations for CMYK seps, we recommend you leave both the CMYK settings in this dialog set to Ask When Opening.

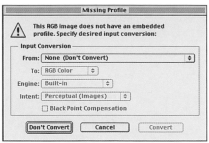

When you get this dialog upon opening a file, you have your Assumed Profile setting for this type of image set to Ask When Opening. If you want to convert the file, you need to use the From: pop-up to choose a profile; then the Convert option will highlight and you will usually choose the default To option because that will be your current workspace for that type of file, in this case the RGB workspace. If you are a service bureau or person that has to deal with files coming from a lot of different places, you should now ask people to let you know what type of space those files actually came from, or probably just don't convert the file if you don't know. You can also probably assume ColorMatch RGB if the file's owner had a PressView, or otherwise maybe assume Apple RGB for most of the other generic color monitors out there. If you have the same type of Monitor, like from a PressView to a PressView with the current ColorMatch RGB workspace, you might not need to convert the file.

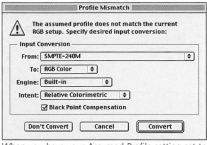

When you have your Assumed Profile setting set to something, like Adobe RGB (SMPTE-240M) in this case, and you have your Profile Mismatch handling set to Ask When Opening, you will get the dialog setup like this, and you can press Return if the file actually came from a Adobe RGB source and you want to convert it.

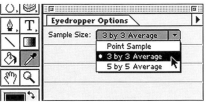

When the Embedded profile from an existing file is different than your current profile, you will get the same dialog as above except the word assumed will be replaced by embedded, and the From setting will be set to whatever profile is actually in the file.

area tells Photoshop what to do with files that either have no profile or a different profile than your current workspace when you are opening those files. If you choose Ask When Opening in either the Assumed Profiles or Profile Mismatch area, then Photoshop will put up the Missing Profile or Profile Mismatch dialog when you open a file that doesn't match your current RGB, CMYK or Grayscale workspace. We recommend that you initially set up each category in Assumed Profiles and Profile Mismatch Handling to Ask When Opening. This will get you familiar with what Photoshop is doing when it is opening old nontagged files. You can then be aware of the choices you and Photoshop are making instead of having Photoshop making choices you are unaware of and may later be unhappy with. When you later become more familiar with your workflow using Photoshop 5 and are more comfortable with working in an ICC-profiled environment, you may want to to set up default values for some of the Assumed Profile cases. This will allow you to deal with the most common case more quickly because it can tell Photoshop what profile most of your old nonprofiled files actually came from. I would still leave the Profile Mismatch Handling set to Ask When Opening. If you have the situation where all your old files always come from the same place with the same color setup information, you can set the Mismatch handling, at least for RGB or Grayscale, to either Ignore, if you don't want Photoshop to convert the file to the current workspace, or to Convert to RGB Color or Convert to Grayscale, if you want Photoshop to automatically convert old nontagged files into your current RGB or Grayscale workspace. I would recommend not converting CMYK images into a different space unless you really know what you are doing because the conversions for CMYK have a greater possibility for causing problems because there are so many different types of CMYK separation types, and they are really customized to a particular output device. Another possibly better choice for dealing with older CMYK files might be to convert them into your RGB workspace, clean them up, and correct them there, and then generate new CMYK separations customized to the current output situation.

OTHER PREFERENCES RELATING TO COLOR

EYEDROPPER TOOL SETUP

Usually when you measure digital image values in Photoshop, you want the Eyedropper set to measure a 3 by 3 rectangle of pixels. That gives you a more accurate measurement in a continuous tone image because most colors are made up of groups of different pixels. If

Usually you want the Eyedropper set to measure a 3 by 3 average when measuring continuous tone color. Setting either the Eyedropper Options or the Color Sampler Options to 3 by 3 Average will set both of them to the same setting.

you were to measure a Point Sample, the default, you might accidentally measure the single pixel that was much different in color from those around it. Double-click the Eyedropper tool and set its Sample Size to 3 by 3 Average. Setting the Eyedropper to 3 by 3 Average also sets up the new Photoshop 5 Color Sampler to read a 3 by 3 average, which is what you want.

HIGHLIGHT AND SHADOW PREFERENCES

The last preferences items that you need to set up for color separations are the Highlight and Shadow settings, which you can reach by choosing either Levels or Curves. Here, we show you how to get to them from Levels. Choose Image/Adjust/Levels, and double-click the Highlight Eyedropper (the right-most one). The Color

Picker opens. For CMYK print work, you want to set the CMYK values to 5, 3, 3, 0, which is a neutral color for highlights. If all your other preferences are set as in this book, after you enter 5, 3, 3, 0 for CMYK, you should see 242, 241, 242 as your initial RGB settings if your RGB workspace is ColorMatch RGB, and you will see 244, 244, 244 if your RGB workspace is Adobe RGB (SMPTE-240M) or sRGB. If this is not the case, double-check your RGB Setup and CMYK Setup values. For the Color-Match RGB case, also change the 241 Green value to 242. Even if you are using different settings than ours, if your final output space will be RGB, you should make sure your RGB values all equal each other so you get a neutral highlight color when setting the highlight with the Eyedropper in RGB. Click OK in the Color Picker to return to Levels, double-click the Shadow Eyedropper (the left-most one). Set the CMYK

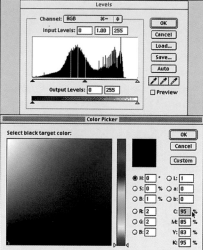

These are the shadow settings we recommend for CMYK coated stock, RGB output to film recorders, digital printers, and general overall color correction of a file. Double-click the Shadow Eyedropper in Levels or Curves to change these settings. The RGB values here should always be all the same, a neutral color will be 2, 2, 2 whether you choose Color-Match RGB, Adobe RGB, or sRGB as long as your CMYK Setup settings are the same as this book's settings.

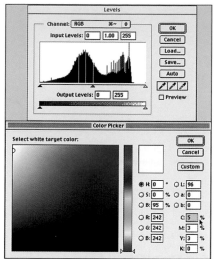

These 5, 3, 3, 0 settings are the highlight settings we recommend for CMYK coated stock. The corresponding values you get in RGB will depend on your chosen RGB workspace and also on your CMYK Setup settings. Initially, 242, 241, and 242 are the RGB values you get with your RGB workspace set to ColorMatch RGB and with the other settings we show in this chapter. If you are using ColorMatch RGB as your workspace, double-click the Green 241 value and change it to a 242; the 5, 3, 3, 0 values should stay the same. If we change the RGB workspace to Adobe RGB or sRGB, the RGB values will change to 244, 244, 244 with these same CMYK settings. For RGB output to the Web, film recorders, and digital printers, and general RGB overall color correction of a file, you should make sure the RGB values here are neutral and around 244, 244, 244. Double-click the Highlight Eyedropper in Levels or Curves to change these settings for different output devices or situations.

values in the Color Picker to 95, 85, 83, 95, and check to make sure the RGB values are 2, 2, 2. If not, double-check your RGB Setup and CMYK Setup. Click OK in the Color Picker and then click OK in Levels. To learn more about these Highlight and Shadow settings and how you use them, turn to Chapter 19: Grand Canyon, which takes you through all the basics of color correction.

SAVING AND STANDARDIZING YOUR PREFERENCES

After you make major changes to your standard Photoshop 5 preferences, you should quit from Photoshop immediately. When you leave Photoshop, it saves its current state (preferences, tool option choices, palette locations, and so on) to three files within the Adobe Photoshop Settings folder within the Adobe Photoshop 5.0 folder named Adobe Photoshop 5 Prefs, Actions Palette, and Color Settings. Quitting at this point ensures that Photoshop saves your preferences changes to these files. If you were to crash before quitting Photoshop, you would lose these latest preferences changes, and they would revert to the preferences you had when you last successfully quit from Photoshop.

It is a good idea for everyone in your company to standardize on a set of separation and workspace preferences, especially for the same publication, and vitally important to standardize separation and workspace preferences if you are doing color corrections and separations. You can copy a standard version of these files to the Photoshop Settings folders on everyone else's machines, or print up a standards document and have your systems administrator make sure that everyone is using those settings.

CREATING CUSTOM SEPARATION SETTINGS

If you want to calibrate Photoshop separation settings for a newspaper, a particular type of Web press, or other custom CMYK output, you can do this much more easily using Photoshop 5. First, you need to find out the correct CMYK values for the full range of neutral colors in a stepwedge file, like the one included in the Calibration folder on the Photoshop 5 Artistry CD. The press expert at your print shop should know this information. Next, you adjust CMYK Setup, as well as the way you set highlights and shadows, using the techniques described in the earlier CMYK Setup section of this chapter, until you get the CMYK values closest to the CMYK values from your press expert for neutral colors in the stepwedge file. Using those settings in Photoshop usually gets you very close to the separations that you want. That's basically what we did to get our settings using the following table of desired values for coated stock.

	Neutral RGB 0...255 values			Sample Target GCR type CMYK values to print these as neutrals			
	Red	*Green*	*Blue*	*Cyan*	*Magenta*	*Yellow*	*Black*
highlight	243	243	243	5%	3%	3%	0%
1/4 tone	192	192	192	25%	16%	16%	0%
midtone	128	128	128	50%	39%	38%	4%
3/4 tone	64	64	64	69%	58%	58%	30%
shadow	13	13	13	76%	66%	65%	85%

Actual CMYK values when separating the unmodified StepWedgeFile using our Photoshop Separation settings

	Cyan	*Magenta*	*Yellow*	*Black*
05% highlight	5%	3%	3%	0%
25% 1/4 tone	24%	16%	16%	0%
50% midtone	49%	37%	36%	3%
75% 3/4 tone	67%	57%	56%	29%
95% shadow	75%	65%	64%	84%

The preference settings we chose don't exactly match the values in the target CMYK table, but they give the closest overall settings to these values, which also are the most useful starting point settings. For more information on calibration, see Chapter 15: Calibration.

NEWSPAPERS AND OTHER CUSTOM SETTINGS

Our default highlight and shadow values usually are good for most RGB output purposes including output to film recorders and also for CMYK separations to coated stock. If they are not working for you, use this process to change them. Newspaper presses tend to vary much more than web or sheet-fed presses for coated stock. If you are doing output for newspapers or some other special process, first get a set of correct values for printing neutral colors from your press person. It should look like the preceding table but with different numbers. For newspapers, start out with CMYK Setup Built-In set to SWOP Newsprint with a Standard Dot Gain of 30%. Set the Separation Type to GCR, Black Generation to Medium, Black Ink Limit to around 85%, and Total Ink Limit to around 260%; again, get these values from your press person. Set the highlight and shadow preference values in Levels initially as your press person recommends for the brightest and darkest place that can still carry a dot or not be solid black on your press.

Bring up the StepWedgeFile, which starts out as a grayscale, and convert it to RGB. Bring up the Info palette and and use Color Samplers to measure the RGB and CMYK values you get at different density areas along your stepwedge. Compare the CMYK numbers with the ones you got from your press person. Change the Dot Gain (remember, you can now use the Curves setting to adjust each curve separately and exactly if needed), Black Ink Limit, and Total Ink limit settings in Separation Setup until you get values that are as close as possible to those your press person gave you. You can also change the Black Generation curve between Light, Medium, and Heavy as well as create a custom Black curve by choosing Custom. Photoshop doesn't give you direct control over the Cyan, Magenta, or Yellow curves, but you can affect them via changes you make to the Black curve.

You will have to play with all these settings until you get a feeling for the relationship they have with each other. The settings we have recommended for coated stock have worked quite well in producing this book and for other projects that I have done. We don't recommend particular settings for newspapers because they tend to vary from paper to paper. For more information on output to black-and-white halftones, you should get *Photoshop in Black-and-White: An Illustrated Guide to Producing Black-and-White Images with Adobe Photoshop Version 5.0* by Jim Rich and Sandy Bozek.

Using the ICC CMYK Model, you can also load a custom ICC profile to run your separations. This custom profile would decide for you how to convert from RGB to CMYK. There are companies that sell custom separation tables and ICC profiles for Photoshop. If you have another color separation system that you would like to import into Photoshop, like from Scitex or some other high-end system, you can do that also by converting that to an ICC profile.

6 FILE FORMATS AND IMAGE COMPRESSION

When and how to use each of the important file formats, and understanding Photoshop, TIFF, and JPEG image compression.

OVERVIEW OF FILE FORMAT ISSUES

OPENING AND SAVING FILES

When you read a file in Photoshop, no matter what format it was in when you read it, the file will be in Photoshop's built-in format while you are working on it. Photoshop creates a temporary work file in memory and also, depending on the size of the file you are working with, in the free space remaining on your disk. Photoshop doesn't touch the original file that you opened on the disk until you do a File/Save. As you work on a project in Photoshop, it's a good idea to save often. You should do another Save any time you have done enough work since your last save that you would be upset to lose that work in a computer crash. When you choose File/Save (Command-S) to save the file, Photoshop overwrites your original file on the disk. If you have just had a file scanned, or if you want to save the original before you change it in Photoshop, you should choose File/Save As to save the file you are about to modify with a different name. This leaves your original file unchanged. When you do a Save As, the name of your window changes from the your original file name to the new name you used when you did the Save As. Doing another Save later overwrites the file with the new name, not the original.

PHOTOSHOP 5 VERSUS OTHER FORMATS

While you are working on a project, you should normally save in Photoshop 5 format (just called Photoshop in the Save dialog box). When you first open a file in Photoshop, if you save it immediately before any modifications, Photoshop saves the file using the same format in which you opened it. If you open it as a TIFF, for example, Photoshop saves it as a TIFF. If you open it as a JPEG, Photoshop saves it as a JPEG. The first time you save the file, you should use Save As and change the format to Photoshop. Using the Photoshop format makes Photoshop operate more efficiently because it's Photoshop's internal format and it supports everything that Photoshop can do, including history, action, layers, adjustment layers, channels, and paths. None of the other file formats support all of these features. You especially should avoid resaving JPEG files over and over again because every time you save a JPEG file it loses some information; more about this later in this chapter. If you open a file in TIFF format and add a channel to it, Photoshop still saves it in TIFF format because TIFF supports extra channels. If you were to add a layer to the same file, however, Photoshop would save it in Photoshop format because TIFF doesn't support layers. If the format changes automatically to Photoshop, it means you added a feature to the file that the format you were working with before doesn't support.

DIFFERENCES BETWEEN FILE FORMATS

What are the differences between file formats? After you open the file in Photoshop, it always resides there in Photoshop's own internal format. Saving the file into a different format is like translating a book into a different language. In most cases, the raw data for the different formats is exactly the same; only how the data is stored or what additional information can go with the data changes. For example, an RGB file in format A may have all the red bytes stored together, then all the greens, and then all the blues. In format B, the storage might be a red, green, and blue byte for pixel 1, then a red, green, and blue byte for pixel 2, and so on. Some formats may use a simple type of compression called run length encoding, a lossless compression where, if there are say 50 bytes in a row that are exactly the same, these 50 bytes are stored using a special code so they take up only 4 bytes. Another format may specify a space at the beginning of the file where extra information can be stored. The EPS file format, for example, allows you to store clipping paths, preview picts, screen angles, and transfer function information within the file. In all these cases, the RGB or CMYK information in the file format remains the same. Only the packaging of the information changes from one format to another. If you save the file as a JPEG, this format does a "lossy" data compression. The lossy compression allows this format to save the file in much less space than in other formats. The lossy part means that when you read the file back in, or decompress the file, it will be the same size you started with, but the actual data won't be identical. You need to be careful when using lossy compression not to lose important image data. We talk about this in the second part of this chapter.

INFORMATION ABOUT EACH FORMAT

Now let's discuss each of the formats that most of you will be using and when using that format might be best. The file formats you are more likely to use with Photoshop are Photoshop 5, Photoshop 2, TIFF, Photoshop EPS, DCS1 and DCS2, JPEG, GIF89, PICT, Photoshop PDF, and Scitex CT. Photoshop supports other file formats too, but these are the ones we recommend for the type of work you will be doing. If you need to know about some other format, the Photoshop 5 manual discusses all the formats that Photoshop supports.

PHOTOSHOP 5 AND 2.0

When you work on the same file in Photoshop between shutdowns of your computer, you should usually work on that file in Photoshop 5 format (just called Photoshop in the version 5 Save dialog boxes and having the .psd suffix). It's the only format that supports all of Photoshop 5's features, such as history, adjustment layers, and actions. If you need to exchange files with others that are using Photoshop 4, 3, or 2.5, you can make sure every Photoshopper can open this file by saving it in Photoshop 2.0 format. Photoshop 2.0 and 2.5 formats do not support layers. Photoshop 3 format (which you get automatically by saving from Photoshop 3) does not support adjustment layers or guides and grids, but it does support regular layers, layer masks, and channels. Photoshop 4 supports adjustment layers and actions, but not some new Hue/Saturation and Curves features, editable type or layer effects. Photoshop 5 can open any Photoshop 4, or earlier format, but Photoshop 4 cannot read layer effects and other new features in a Photoshop 5 file and if you resave this file in Photoshop

4 format, from Photoshop 4, these features are stripped from the file. If you are working with Photoshop 5 and you have the "Include Composited Image with Layered Files" option set from File/Preferences/Saving Files, then people using older versions of Photoshop and other applications can open your layered files and see a composite of the layers for which the Eye icons were on when you saved the Photoshop 5 file. If the file has multiple layers, those users can't modify the file's different layers and the cost of this compatibility is an extra RGB layer the size of your Photoshop 5 canvas. You can save a lot of disk space by turning off the Composited Image with Layered Files option. Most page layout applications and many other programs can't read any Photoshop format. Some applications can read Photoshop 2.0 format but not the newer Photoshop formats; the main purpose for the this option is the capability to still open files into those applications.

Photoshop file formats do some compression, especially on mask channels. Consequently, files saved in Photoshop format are smaller than their corresponding TIFF files, especially those that have a lot of mask channels. Photoshop 5 does a great job of compressing simple masks; they are often in the same size ratio as JPEG. The RGB and CMYK components of Photoshop files are also compressed, although this compression does not make the file much smaller unless large areas in the file have the same color. The advantage of using the Photoshop 5 format to compress is that it's a fast, lossless compression.

TIFF

The most common file format that popular imaging applications support is TIFF. You can save both RGB and CMYK files in TIFF format and TIFF is supported on both the Mac and the PC. I often save grayscale and RGB files in TIFF format so I can go back and forth between Photoshop and my page layout application. TIFF format also saves your mask channels. If you want to save a TIFF file but not the mask channels, use File/Save a Copy and choose the Exclude Alpha Channels option. You can also specify a clipping path to include with a TIFF image, which some page layout programs will be able to read and/or edit.

The normal choices available for saving a TIFF image. To save TIFF without the mask channels, use File/Save a Copy and choose Don't Include Alpha Channels.

When working on the Mac, you should set the byte order to Macintosh. If you set the byte order to IBM PC, both Photoshop and Quark on the Mac can still open the TIFF file. Some applications on the PC probably can't open the Mac byte order TIFF files.

The TIFF dialog box lets you choose LZW compression. LZW compression is a standard TIFF form of compression that typically takes longer to open and close than JPEG or Photoshop compression. TIFF LZW compression is a lossless compression. When you use LZW, you usually get a file that falls somewhere between 1/3 to 2/3 as large as the original, depending on the image details in the original. If you run into problems with LZW compressed files, resave your TIFF file without compression.

ENCAPSULATED POSTSCRIPT (EPS) AND DESKTOP COLOR SEPARATION (DCS)

The EPS format, now called Photoshop EPS, is one of the most versatile formats. It's especially useful for communicating back and forth between Photoshop and Illustrator when you want to link your Photoshop file to Illustrator rather than embed it. You can also save a clipping path from Photoshop EPS format. You choose the path you want to use as a clipping path from the Paths palette pop-up menu. For more information on saving paths from Photoshop to page layout

The normal choices available for saving an EPS image. These are the most common options chosen.

programs and Illustrator, see Chapter 30: Bob Goes to… and Chapter 37: Bike Ride in the Sky!.

After converting your file into CMYK using the Mode menu, you can save it into EPS format in several ways. Photoshop 5 allows you to save your EPS in either a Photoshop EPS, DCS1, or DCS2 format. The Photoshop EPS format is the smallest of the three. DCS1 is the format that those of you who've been using DCS (Desktop Color Separation) are used to. It divides your EPS file into five smaller files: one file each for cyan, magenta, yellow, and black, and one preview file. The new format, DCS2, allows you a couple of additional options. With DCS2 you can now save alpha channels, which will allow you to save a special channel as a spot or varnish plate, and you can also choose whether to save your document as a single file, or multiple files, with or without previews. Placing just the one CMYK file directly into your page layout program is less error prone, although it does create very large files, because the same file that is placed is printed. Before you save any file for final output, make sure the dots per inch (dpi) setting is correct for that final output. For a 150 line screen, for example, the setting should be 300 dpi. If you set the dpi properly, the fifth preview EPS usually is small and can read very quickly into a page layout program. Be aware, however, that all five (or more if you choose the DCS2 format) of the files must be in the folder with the layout document for the image to print correctly.

The big advantage of DCS1 is that you need to transfer only the preview EPS over the network (or, on removable media, to the desk of the person placing and cropping the pictures in the page layout application). It's much faster than transferring the entire CMYK file, which you would have to do with the EPS composite or TIFF format. The tricky thing about DCS multiple file documents is that you need to be sure to include the other four CMYK files in the same folder as your layout document and preview file when you print your layout to the imagesetter; otherwise, you get a low-quality printout. Again, you should discuss this file format choice with your service bureau and printer. Also, the Photoshop manual offers more information about the EPS/DCS file formats.

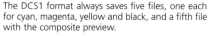

The DCS1 format always saves five files, one each for cyan, magenta, yellow and black, and a fifth file with the composite preview.

The DCS option with 72 dpi preview gives you five files. The cyan, magenta, yellow, and black files need to be in the same folder as your page layout document when you send the job to the imagesetter. The EPS preview file is used for placing and cropping in your page layout document.

GIF AND GIF89

The GIF format is used most often for images intended for use on the World Wide Web. The GIF format is a lossless compression format for images of up to 8-bit color. Photoshop can create GIF files from the Save dialog boxes if the file is in bitmap, grayscale, or index color format. Using File/Export/Gif89, you can create GIF format files from RGB Photoshop documents that have layers and transparent regions with much more flexibility and control. The GIF file format is discussed in great detail in the last section of this book, "Images for the Web and Multimedia."

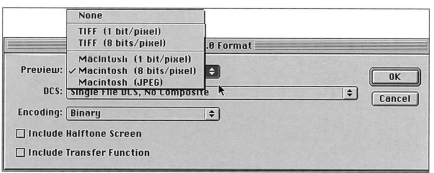

The different types of previews that can be saved with DCS1 or DCS2 format. Macintosh (JPEG) gives you a better looking preview, but older page layout applications may not be able to read the preview. Use TIFF if you need to transfer files between the Mac and a PC. Don't check Include Halftone Screens or Transfer Functions unless you are setting these things in Photoshop. Discuss all these settings with your service bureau before you send them any files.

With the new DCS2 format, you have lots of different options as to how to save your file.

PDF

You can use PDF format to send small versions of your files across networks or the Internet. These files can be RGB, CMYK, indexed color, Lab color, grayscale, or Bitmap format. In Photoshop 5, you're given the opportunity to compress your PDF files using either JPEG compression or ZIP compression for most formats, or CCITT Group 4 compression for Bitmap files. However, the real value of PDF may be the capability to open and print PDF files from other sources if, for whatever reason, you don't have a copy of Adobe Acrobat Reader. Photoshop 5 even speeds this conversion by an automate command (File/Automate/Multipage PDF to PSD). PDF files do not retain their alpha channels.

PNG

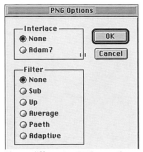

The different PNG options. Choosing Adam 7 as the Interlace method allows the file to be downloaded incrementally; the viewer sees a rough image and then increasing detail. The filters control how the file is compressed and decompressed. The Adobe Photoshop 5 manual explains how the filters prepare data for compression. Use Adaptive to let the program choose the filtering method for you.

The PNG (pronounced ping) format is another Web compression format that gives you some additional options over either JPEG or GIF compression. It's a lossless compression method that allows you to choose between saving your 24-bit color information or saving indexed color information. PNG can produce transparent areas without jagged edges by saving one (and only one) alpha channel to define the transparent areas. In addition, you can store the gamma setting of your system and use two-dimensional interlacing to help your file load even more quickly. It's a pretty recent addition to the Web-based image bag, so it's not supported by all browsers. Also, compressing large images takes a long time and the size savings are small, but PNG shows a great deal of promise.

PICT

PICT format is an Apple standard file format supported by automatic compression and decompression in QuickTime. I have found this format to cause some problems when placed in page layout documents and don't recommend it for that purpose. It is, however, a commonly used multimedia format, as well as the format that is used by the system between applications when you copy an image from one and paste it into another. When you save in PICT format, the QuickTime compression you automatically get is lossless, but if you choose one of the JPEG options, you get a compression that isn't lossless—so beware.

SCITEX CT

Scitex CT format is sometimes used when saving CMYK files that will be processed on a Scitex imaging system. These files are generally quite large and have very few problems with moiré patterns. You can also save RGB or grayscale files in Scitex CT format, but this format does not support alpha channels. Again, your service bureau will tell you if you need to save in this format.

DISK SPACE AND COMPRESSION FORMATS

After converting the JPEG low-compressed image to Lab color mode and looking at the A channel, you can see how JPEG compression breaks the image up into square areas and then tries to optimize each of these areas by representing it with fewer color and tone variations.

In today's world of color page creation, disk space is a commodity that can be used up quite quickly. Color photographs for print are the items that take up the most disk space. For the best quality, a color photograph has to be scanned at twice the dots per inch (dpi) as the line screen at which it will be printed. For a 5x7 color image in a 150-line screen publication, the required disk space would be: *(5x300) x (7x300) x 4 = 12,600,000 bytes for the CMYK version of the file* (over twelve megabytes for just one copy of the file). Usually, by the time you finish production, you may need two or three copies of each file. That could be close to 40 megabytes of storage for just one 5x7 photograph. You might want to consider using compression to reduce the size of your image files. You also use compression for sending files to a client or printer electronically and in placing images on Web pages. To find out more about GIF and JPEG compression for Web and multimedia use, please refer to "Images for the Web and Multimedia."

LZW Compression

When you save a file in TIFF format from Adobe Photoshop, you can choose LZW (Lempel-Ziv-Welch) compression. It saves the 9Mb uncompressed Victorians file in 5.5Mb. When you look at the amount of time LZW compression takes versus the minimum space savings you get, LZW compression often isn't worth the effort.

JPEG Compression

Using the Joint Photographic Experts Group (JPEG) compression software built into Photoshop with the quality setting on High, the 9Mb Victorians file is compressed to 640K. You can see a real savings in data space here—the compressed file is about 1/15 the size of the original! When you use JPEG compression, you can choose how much you want to compress a file. Using more compression gives you a smaller file but also more loss of image detail. A smaller amount of compression gives you less loss of image detail, but the compressed file doesn't save as much disk space. Depending on your publication quality requirements, you can choose a compression factor that compresses files without any visible detail loss on the final printed page.

JPEG is an industry standard file format for image compression. Many companies sell JPEG software and hardware compression products. The hardware compression boards that contain DSP chips can compress and decompress images much faster than they could without the DSP. DSP stands for Digital Signal Processor, which is a chip that speeds up the mathematical operations used in many image processing filters and effects, including JPEG compression and decompression.

Choosing a Compression Factor

To show you the kinds of problems to look for when choosing your compression factor with JPEG compression, we have printed the same file with different

The uncompressed TIFF version of the Victorians image: nine megabytes saved as TIFF and 6.5 megabytes saved in Photoshop format.

The JPEG high-compressed version of the Victorians image. This file is 640K.

Victorians new compressions		bytes	16.5 MB
40Victorians.jpg high	Today, 11:52 AM	421,920	448K
40Victorians.jpg high opt	Today, 12:03 PM	404,318	448K
40Victorians.jpg high prog 4	Today, 12:04 PM	402,486	416K
40Victorians.jpg high.prog	Today, 12:03 PM	405,602	448K
40Victorians.jpg max	Today, 11:51 AM	774,230	800K
40Victorians.jpg max opt	Today, 12:00 PM	764,759	800K
40Victorians.PDF high	Today, 11:57 AM	537,276	576K
40Victorians.PDF max	Today, 11:52 AM	984,451	992K
40Victorians.PDF zip	Today, 11:58 AM	5,480,158	5.2 MB
40VictoriansOrigPS	Today, 11:50 AM	6,778,333	6.5 MB

Some sizes of different compression methods. The jpg high and max files are set with the Baseline Standard setting. The jpg high.prog file uses three scans and the prog 4 file uses four scans. You can see that you start to get some savings as you use more scan passes. The PDF high and max files are using the JPEG compression method and don't give you quite the savings as a direct JPEG. The ZIP compression method gives you very little savings over the original Photoshop file. Because the Mac rounds out the file sizes, we've included the actual byte size in red.

degrees of compression. For printing on coated stock or for art prints, we would recommend not compressing your file at all unless you need to. If you do need to save space, use the Maximum Quality setting when possible, because it gives you the best image quality. If you can't see any data loss in your final printed image, then the loss may not be important to you. On the other hand, if you archive a digital file for use in future printed pieces, slide productions, or multimedia presentations, you need to be sure that compression data loss won't show up in one of those future applications.

Another JPEG compression issue is that compressed files take longer to open and process when printing at the service bureau. Before you compress, talk to your service bureau about whether to use JPEG compressed files. Unless the service bureau owns a Level 2 or Level 3 PostScript imagesetter, they cannot download JPEG files directly. They have to re-open the file in Photoshop and save it to another uncompressed format. They may charge you more for JPEG compressed files if it will take them longer to process them on output. Other lossless compression options are DiskDoubler and StuffIt. With these, you need to make sure the person on the other end who decompresses the file has the right version to do the decompression. Again, you should discuss any compression option with your service bureau before choosing one of them.

The original Victorians, 9Mb TIFF, uncompressed, is on the top left. Below that is the JPEG compression set to the maximum image quality, 1.2Mb. On the bottom right is the medium quality setting, 352K. Finally, on the top right you see the low-quality setting, 256K. All these JPEG compressions, except for the low quality, will work for printing. For printing, I would usually use the high or maximum quality to be safe, or better yet, not compress at all unless you really must. The Medium quality is good for sending a comp to a client over the Net, and for creating Web images. Avoid using the low setting. These files were compressed with the Baseline Optimized setting on in the JPEG dialog box, which should create higher color quality.

Chapter 6: File Formats and Image Compression

7 THE TOOL PALETTE

An explanation of each tool in the Tool palette with tips for usage and discussions of helpful, hidden features. General information about selections, cropping, painting tools, and other good stuff!

This is not an exhaustive tour of every tool with all its possibilities and applications. Several other very fine books, including the Photoshop manual, go into more detail. We try to give you all the information that you need for working with photographs. This is actually a lot of fun for us and we hope you enjoy it and take some time to play with these tools. As you begin to discover how the tools work, you can apply them to the type of images you have been creating and, perhaps, begin to discover new creative impulses. Open the CeramicFruit, Fish Art, Starry Night, and TheLeaf images in the Tool Palette folder on the CD and play with the Tool palette features as you work through this chapter.

Most of the tools have changeable options you can access through the menu bar from Window/Show Options or by double-clicking the tool itself. If you choose a tool by using its shortcut character, pressing Return brings up the Tool options for it. This lets you change a tool's options without moving the mouse from your work. Additionally, some of the tools can have different brush sizes, which are available through the Brushes palette (Window/Show Brushes). Some of the tools in the Tool palette have a little arrow in their bottom-right corners. Clicking it shows other tools that you can access from the same icon area.

Holding down the Control key (right mouse button on Windows) and clicking on the screen brings up a context sensitive menu of useful options you can do with the current tool. This is a very powerful feature because the items in this Control menu may actually come from several different regular menus in Photoshop and are chosen based on Photoshop's state when you click Control. We point

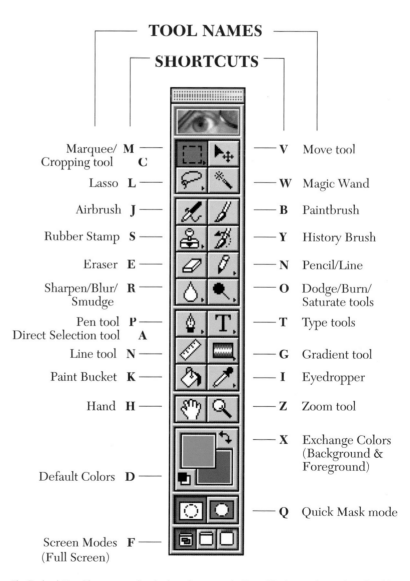

The Tool palette with corresponding keyboard commands. Copy this chart and paste it to the side of your monitor for a quick reference.

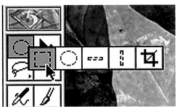

This is the menu that comes up when you Control-click and have no current selection loaded, but you do have selections saved in mask channels.

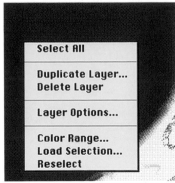

When you press down on an icon that contains an arrow in the lower-right corner, a flyout of additional tools appears. To select any of these tools, simply drag your mouse to the tool you want to select and then unclick.

Constrained aspect ratio of 4:5.

To compute size of selection in pixels, multiply the width or height in inches times the number of pixels per inch of resolution in your image.

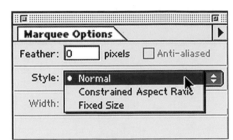

Styles available for Rectangular and Elliptical Marquees. Note that Anti-aliased is not available on rectangular because it is not needed on vertical and horizontal selection lines.

these context sensitive menus out as you go through this chapter.

THE SELECTION TOOLS

The first three tools in the Tool palette concern making selections. In conjunction with items from the Selection menu and the Pen tool (which we discuss later), you can isolate portions of your image for editing.

MARQUEE TOOL

KEYBOARD SHORTCUT: Type the letter M. Type Shift-M to make the tool cycle through its available options.

You can use the Marquee tool to make rectangular or oval selections or to select a single row or single column of pixels. The Cropping tool is also a pop-out of this item, but we talk about it in a later section.

CONSTRAINED ASPECT RATIO: The Style pop-up menu allows you to choose a constrained aspect ratio or a fixed size for either the rectangular or oval marquee. You would use a constrained aspect ratio if you were making a selection that you knew needed to have a 4:5 ratio, for example, or a 1:1 ratio for a perfect square or circle.

FIXED SIZE: A fixed size is useful when you know exactly the size in pixels of the print you want to make and want to crop to that size. Here, if you click down with the Marquee tool, you get a rectangular selection of the size that you specified. By keeping the mouse button down while moving the mouse, you can move the selection around the image to find exactly the crop you desire. Of course, you can also use this option simply to select and edit an area of a specific size.

FEATHER: The Feather option allows you to set the amount of blend on the edges of your selection. A larger feather radius gives you more of a vignette effect. The amount of feather is calculated in both directions from your selection border. For example, a 15-pixel feather measures both 15 pixels to the outside of your selection area and 15 pixels to the inside, giving you a total feather effect of 30 pixels. We rarely set a feather radius on our Marquee tool, preferring to make a selection and then use Select/Feather from the menu bar to set the feather. This way, we can change our radius if we are unhappy with the effect. Also, if you make a selection with the Rectangular Marquee and the feather is zero, you can later choose Image/Crop to crop to that selection. If you set the feather to a non-zero value, on the other hand, Image/Crop would be disabled.

ANTI-ALIASED: You may have noticed that the Elliptical Marquee has one other option, Anti-aliased. Anti-aliased subtly blends the edge of your selection with the surrounding area, so you usually want to leave it on. It's also available on the Lasso and Wand tools, but it is grayed out on the Rectangular, Single Row, and Single Column tools. Keep Anti-aliased on when you want your selection edge to blend with the surrounding area. Making selections with Anti-aliased off gives you hard edges that are jagged on diagonal lines and curves.

SINGLE ROW AND SINGLE COLUMN: Single Row and Single Column are just that. Single Row gives you a selection 1 pixel high all the way across your file; Single Column selects 1 pixel top to bottom. We rarely use these selection modes, but you can use them to draw straight lines or as a quick guide to make sure things are lined up.

Generally, though, the Line tool is easier to use for both purposes. This option also is useful for selecting single row or column artifacts introduced by scanners or bad media and then cloning into the selected area.

MODIFIER KEYS: Holding down the Shift key while using either of these tools constrains your selection to 1 to 1; that is, you get a perfect square or a perfect circle. Make sure you release the mouse button before you release the Shift key. If, however, you already have a selection, the action is different. The Shift key causes Photoshop to add a new, unconstrained selection to your original selection.

Holding down the Option key while drawing forces the selection to draw from the center where you first click down. This can be extremely useful, as you will see in "Buckminster Fuller" later in this book.

Holding down the Shift and Option keys while dragging gives you a perfect circle or perfect square drawn from the center.

Be careful how you click in a file with an active selection. If you click inside the selection, you may inadvertently move the selection slightly. If you click outside the selection, you lose the selection.

If you press the Spacebar after starting a selection, you can move the selection while making it and then release the Spacebar again to continue to change the selection.

LASSO, POLYGON, & MAGNETIC LASSO TOOLS

KEYBOARD SHORTCUT: Type the letter L. If you type Shift-L, the tool cycles through its various options.

You use the Lasso tool to make freehand selections. Although it's a little clunky to draw with a mouse, you'll find yourself using this tool a lot. You can always get a graphics tablet if you want to draw with a pen. Clicking and dragging gives you a line that follows the track of your mouse. After starting the selection, if you hold down the Option key and click, let go of the mouse button, and then click in a new spot, you can draw with straight lines between mouse clicks. Continue clicking this way to make geometric shapes, or you can hold down the mouse button and draw freehand again. When you let go of the mouse and the Option key, a straight line is drawn connecting the beginning and ending points of your selection, so be careful not to let go of the Option key until you finish your selection. Because the Option key in Photoshop 5 is used for deleting from a selection, you have to press Option after starting the selection to get the straight line behavior. If you prefer to use the Polygon Lasso tool, you can draw straight lines at every click, without using the Option key. In the Polygon Lasso tool, using the Option key after starting the selection enables you to draw in freehand. The Polygon Lasso tool requires you to click on the selection starting point again to complete a selection, as you also need to do in the Pen tool to complete a path. New to Photoshop 5 is the Magnetic Lasso tool. With this tool, you can set a contrast value for the edge that you're trying to capture, then draw freehand around that edge and let the lasso decide how to draw the selection. Click the artwork to set the first fastening point. As you move the mouse, the Lasso lays down more fastening points to define the edge. You can click down at any time to manually place a fastener or hold down the Option key and either drag to access the regular Lasso or click to access the Polygonal Lasso. Draw until you reach the starting point and you get an icon that looks like the one in the Tool palette. If you let go of the mouse, the selection is made. If you double-click or press Enter before you get to your starting point, a line is drawn from the current mouse position to the starting point to complete the selection. Hold down the Option key and double-click to draw a straight line segment between the mouse position and the starting point. Needless

Anti-aliased is available as an option for the Elliptical Marquee.

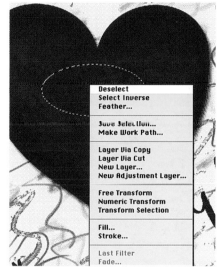

This is the menu that comes up when you Control-click when there is an existing selection.

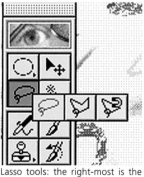

Lasso tools: the right-most is the Magnetic Lasso.

Lasso options.

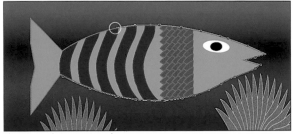

Magnetic Lasso options.

The Magnetic Lasso at work.

Magic Wand options.

SELECTION TOOL TIPS

ADDING TO YOUR SELECTION: After you make a selection using any of these selection tools, you can hold down the Shift key to add to that selection.

SUBTRACTING FROM A SELECTION: If you hold down the Option key after you make your initial selection, you can take away portions of the selection.

MOVING A SELECTION MARQUEE: After you have made a selection, you can move the selection marquee without affecting the underlying pixels by clicking within the selection using any selection tool and dragging.

to say, this tool works most easily where there is a good amount of contrast between the edges. But, with experimentation, you can get a pretty decent first selection using this tool, and then finesse the selection with some of the more sophisticated selection methods.

LASSO WIDTH: Set your lasso width wide enough to accommodate your drawing style but not so wide that you take in many additional areas around the edge you trying to select. The steadier your hand, the smaller the lasso width.

FREQUENCY: Frequency governs the number of "points" that the lasso automatically puts down to define the selection

EDGE CONTRAST: Edge Contrast is the minimum contrast that you want Photoshop to consider when trying to discern the edge. The lower the contrast between the edge you're outlining and the background, the lower you need to set the Edge Contrast.

See the chapter, "The Car Ad," for more information on how to use these Lasso features as well as other selection tools.

Magic Wand Tool

KEYBOARD SHORTCUT: Type the letter W.

Whereas the Marquee and Lasso tools make selections based on physical proximity of pixels, the Magic Wand makes selections based on color values of adjacent pixels.

TOLERANCE SETTINGS: The tolerance that you set determines how close in value pixels must be before they can be selected. The lower the tolerance, the more similar the colors must be, and the higher the tolerance, the greater the range of colors.

USE ALL LAYERS: The Use All Layers option makes its selection based on a merged version of all the currently visible layers. Whether you want this option on or off depends on the type of image you are working with and the kind of selection you wish to make. If another layer affects the colors of the object you want to select, you probably want this option on. If all the colors you want to select are on only one layer, leave it off. But remember: Regardless of whether your selection is based on one layer or on merged layers, the edits that you make affect only the currently active layer.

THE GROW AND SIMILAR COMMANDS: The tolerance value that you set on the Magic Wand also affects which pixels you select when you use the Grow and Similar commands from the Select menu. The Grow command selects adjacent pixels that fall within this tolerance, whereas the Similar command selects pixels throughout the entire image that fall within the tolerance range. You can also change the tolerance setting on the Magic Wand between uses of these two commands, to select a larger or smaller range of colors.

Move Tool

KEYBOARD SHORTCUT: Type the letter V or hold down the Command key.

You use the Move tool to move a selection or the contents of a layer. Click and drag a selection or layer to move it to a new location within your document. You can also use the Move tool to drag and drop a layer from one document to another. If you are using any other tool, you can hold down the Command key to access the Move tool without deselecting the currently active tool. The Pixel Doubling option in the Options palette makes moving selections more efficient. Auto Select Layer allows the Move tool to activate the layer of the object that you click. This can facilitate moving objects around if the boundaries of the object you're selecting are clear. If you're having trouble selecting the appropriate layer, hold down the Control key and choose the layer from the pop-up.

CROP TOOL

KEYBOARD SHORTCUT: Type the letter C.

The Crop tool is a subtool of the Marquee. You can access it by typing a C or using the arrow pop-out menu at the bottom-right of the Marquee icon area. Although we often use the Rectangular Marquee tool and the Image/Crop command to crop an image, the Crop tool is more powerful. To use the Crop tool, click and drag a box around the area you want to crop. Click and drag on one of the handles (little boxes in the selection corners and edges) to change the size of the crop area. To cancel the crop, press the Escape key, and to accept the crop, press Return or Enter.

MOVING AND ROTATING: Click in the middle of the selected area to move the crop boundary without changing its size. Click outside the crop box corners when you see the curved double arrow rotate icon and drag to rotate the crop boundary. Photoshop 5 now lets you move the "center point" around which you will rotate the selected area.

FIXED TARGET SIZE: With fixed target size on, click the Front Image button in Crop Tool Options to make the crop the exact dimensions and resolution of the currently active image, or you can set the width, height, and resolution of the crop manually. Whatever crop you make will be constrained to these proportions and it will be resampled to exactly these specs when you accept the crop by pressing Enter. Leave the resolution blank to maintain the specified aspect ratio. Photoshop resamples the file if necessary. For example, if you ask for your crop in inches, and the dimensions are larger than the area you selected, Photoshop lowers the resolution of the file after the crop but does not resample the crop area. However, if you ask for your crop in pixels and the crop is larger than the current file, it maintains the resolution of the image but adds pixels; in effect, it samples up the image. Make all entries blank, deselect Fixed Target Size, or choose Reset Tool from the Options triangle to restore the tool to normal, non-resampling cropping operation.

THE PEN/MAGNETIC PEN/FREEFORM PEN TOOLS

KEYBOARD SHORTCUT: Type the letter P. Type Shift-P to cycle through the three pens.

The Pen tool is one of the most powerful selection tools. Although it is located further down in the Tool palette, possibly because you can use it to fill or stroke paths that you build, we include it here because of its applications for making very exacting paths that can later be turned into selections. Remember that the selections you make with the Pen tool will all be hard-edged though—no subtlety, no shading.

When you begin to use the Pen tool, make sure you show the Paths palette. This is where you will name your path, fill or stroke your path, turn the path into a selection, or turn a selection into a path. You can also duplicate a path or delete a path. These options are available as icons on the bottom of the palette and from the pop-up menu. The pop-up menu is also where you can designate a path as a clipping path to be included with the file when it is placed in your page layout program (more on this later).

Move Tool options.

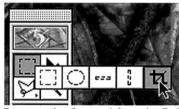

To access the Crop tool from the Tool palette, press down the arrow at the lower-right corner of the Marquee icon; then drag and choose the Cropping Tool icon. Or it is faster to just type a C.

Crop tool options.

Click the fish path to activate the path. The icons on the bottom of the palette are for fill, stroke, make a selection, turn the selection into a path, make a new path, and delete a path.

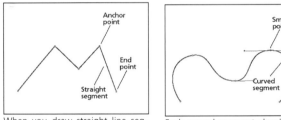

To take a look at a path, click the fish path in the Paths palette for Fish Art. Hold down the Command key as you near the path and you get the Direct Selection tool (white arrow). When you click the path with the arrow, you'll see where the points are located. Notice the "handlebars" for the curved points.

When you draw straight line segments, the anchor points and endpoints have no direction handles.

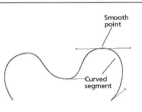

Each curved segment should have two direction points and handles associated with the curve, one at the beginning and one at the end.

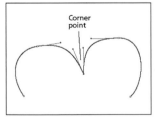

A corner point has two handles that work independently of one another.

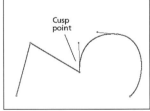

A cusp point that connects a straight line segment to a curve segment has one handle that helps define the curve.

If you've never used the Pen tool, either in Photoshop or a drawing program, you might find it a bit confusing at first. Oh, alright, you might find it absolutely one of the most frustrating experiences of your digital life. But, we promise if you just keep at it, one day you'll have that AHA! feeling that lets you know that your hand understands something that your brain cannot and somehow you're just able to draw a path. Till then, let's talk about the basics.

The Pen tool works by placing points and connecting those points with line segments. A segment can be either straight or curved. Each segment has two points associated with it, a begining point and an end point. (Are you with us so far?) Now the points that control the segments can have handles. Notice that we say can. A corner point (that is, a point that connects two straight line segments) has no handles. A smooth point connecting segments in a continuous curve has two handles that are dependent on each other. If you adjust the direction of one of the handles, you affect the other handle in an equal and opposite manner. Simple enough so far. However, a corner point can also join two curve segments that are noncontinuous and abut sharply as in the two curves forming the top of this lowercase m. In that case, the anchor point would have two handles that work independently of each other. And finally, a straight line segment that joins a curve segment does so by an anchor point that has only one handle, which controls the direction and height of the curve. This type of point is sometimes referred to as a cusp.

The beauty of the Pen tool is that once you make a path, it is infinitely editable. You can add points or delete points, change the height or direction of curves, and even turn a curve into a straight line segment or vice versa. It may seem hard to believe if you're a Pen tool novice, but we know many Photoshoppers who rarely use any of the other selection tools. When you do learn to use the Pen, you'll have an in to the major drawing programs, and you'll understand why page layout programs are now including tools that draw Bezier curves.

The Magnetic Pen tool has options almost identical to the Magnetic Lasso and functions accordingly. The Freeform Pen tool allows you to draw a freehand path and anchor points are placed for you automatically. Neither is as accurate as drawing with the Pen tool but both are faster and may help you get over the hump of learning how to use the tool.

The Direct Selection tool (Keyboard shortcut Command-A) is a subtool of the Pen tool. Use it to select one, some, or all of the points or segments of a path for editing. You can access the Direct Selection tool when using the Pen tool by holding down the Command key. It has no effect on any other part of your file than a path.

See the "Bob Goes to…" chapter for more on using the Pen tool.

THE PAINTING TOOLS

The Pencil, Paintbrush, and Airbrush tools are the regular painting tools. The Rubber Stamp, Smudge/Blur/Sharpen, Dodge/Burn/Sponge, and History Brush tools are more specialized painting tools. If you double-click any of these tools or go to Window/Show Options, you get the specific options for that tool. Note also that the

Tool Cursor options you set in your File/Preferences/Display and Cursors preferences control how your tool cursor appears. We use Brush Size for the Painting Cursors and Precise for the Other Cursors. Before we discuss each particular tool, we discuss the Brushes palette and some options that are pretty standard to all the tools.

THE BRUSHES PALETTE

All of the painting tools get their brush information from the Brushes palette. To see this window, choose Window/Show Brushes (F12 with ArtistKeys). The set of brushes is the same for all the tools except the Pencil tool, which has only hard-edged brushes. Each tool retains the brush and option set last used for that tool. You can add and save brushes or groups of brushes using the pop-up menu at the top-right of the Brushes palette.

SETTING BRUSH OPTIONS: If you double-click a particular brush, or an area where no brush is currently defined, you get the Brush Options window, in which you can change the diameter of the brush, up to 999 pixels, the hardness of the brush, and the spacing. When you set the hardness to 100%, you get very little or no blending between the color or image you are painting and the background. A hardness of 0 gives maximum blending with the background. Try the same large brush with different hardness settings to see how it can affect the stroke. The spacing affects how closely dabs of the paint tool are placed together on the screen (the default value for this is 25%, which causes a 75% overlap of each dab, so it looks like a continuous stroke). To learn about spacing, set it to 100% and then paint using the Paintbrush tool with a big, hard-edged brush. At 100%, the dabs are tangent to each other on the canvas. Now try turning the spacing off (uncheck the Spacing box). With spacing off, the spacing is controlled by how fast you move the brush. Try it!

You can change the angle and roundness of the brush by typing values in the dialog box or by using the handles and arrow on the brush definition area on the lower-left of the palette. The lower-right portion of the window illustrates what that brush will look like.

DEFINING A CUSTOM BRUSH: In addition, you can define a custom brush by drawing a rectangle around all or part of an image and pulling down the Brush Options to Define Brush. You can use a color or grayscale rectangular selection to define your brush, but the brush appears as grayscale in your palette. Consequently, if your brushes are built in grayscale with a white background, your results will be more predictable. When you paint with any brush, it uses the density of the gray in the brush to determine the amount of foreground color to lay down. After you have defined your custom brushes, you can use Save Brushes from the Brushes menu to give your new brushes distinctive names. You can save the brushes wherever you like, but if you've hit on something you think you're going to use again, save your brushes in the Photoshop folder inside the Goodies/Brushes and Patterns folder.

Photoshop includes several custom brush palettes inside this folder already. You can load these palettes or any palette you create by using Load Brushes from the pull-down options, or if you want to add those brushes to the current palette, choose Append Brushes. Reset Brushes restores the default Brushes palette.

THE OPTIONS PALETTE

The following options work primarily the same way for all the painting tools.

OPACITY: Note the Painting mode and Opacity settings at the top of the Options palette. The default Painting mode is Normal and the default Opacity is 100%. Try out the different Painting modes and try painting with different opacities. You can change the opacity by typing in a number from 0–9 while using one of the brush tools

COOL BRUSH TIP: While you are painting, you can change the size of the brush by using the right and left bracket symbols, [and], on the keyboard. Pressing the right bracket moves you to the next bigger brush and pressing the left bracket takes you to the next smaller brush. If you set General Preference Painting Tools to Brush Size, you can change the brush size even as the brush sits over the area you want to paint. You'll see when you've reached the right size. Pressing Shift-] takes you to the last brush and Shift-[to the first brush.

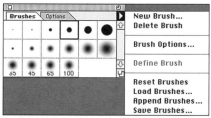

Brushes palette and its options.

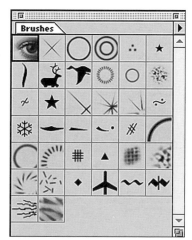

Assorted brushes from the Goodies folder that loads with Photoshop 5.

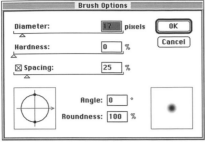

Double-clicking any brush takes you to its Brush Options dialog box.

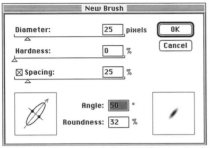

Custom brushes can be built using the New Brush option...

Lines drawn with the brush shape above and Spacing turned off.

(1 equals 10%, 2 equals 20%...9 equals 90%, and 0 equals 100%). If you type two numbers quickly, like 25, you can set the opacity to that double-digit percent. Also, please note that the tools do not all handle paint buildup the same way. The Pencil, Paintbrush, and Rubber Stamp tools paint only in strokes. That is, if you lay down a stroke of color or image at a certain opacity, holding down the mouse button and moving back over that stroke has no cumulative effect. You must release the mouse and paint a new stroke to build up the amount of paint. In contrast, the Smudge tool, Focus tools, and Toning tools add paint cumulatively. Holding down the mouse button and moving back and forth over a stroke increases the effect on each pass. Finally, the Airbrush and Blur tools produce a cumulative effect whether stationary or moving. Changes continue to be applied in the mouse location until you let go of the mouse button.

FADE: The Fade distance causes color painted with the tool to fade to transparent or the background color over the number of pixels you choose for the distance. If you leave the distance box empty—the normal setting—you get no fade-out.

...or by defining a rectangular selection as a brush shape.

STYLUS PRESSURE: You can vary the size, color, and opacity based on stylus pressure only if you have a graphics tablet instead of a mouse.

MODIFIER KEYS: If you hold down Shift when using any of the painting tools, you draw vertically or horizontally. Also, clicking once with the tool, letting go of the mouse button, and then Shift-clicking somewhere else, draws a straight line between these two points with the current brush.

BLEND MODES: You can now toggle through the different Blend modes as you paint by pressing Shift-+ to move forward or Shift-– to move backward through the various modes. In addition, see the chart on the next page for the specific keystrokes for each Blend mode. These keys can also be used to change the Blend modes for layers.

PENCIL/LINE TOOL

KEYBOARD SHORTCUT: Type the letter N. Type Shift-N to toggle between the tools.

When you use the Pencil tool, the edges of your drawing are jagged because there is no anti-aliasing here. Use the Pencil when you want to be sure to get a solid color even on the edge of the painted area.

BRUSHES: Note that when you switch from an anti-aliased paint tool, such as the Paintbrush, to the Pencil tool, the brushes in the Brushes palette switch to hard-edge brushes.

AUTO ERASE: The Auto Erase option replaces any pixels that are currently the foreground color with pixels of the background color. You usually want to leave this option off.

The Line tool makes great anti-aliased lines in whatever thickness you specify. To make a line, click where you want the line to start, drag, and then release where you want the line to end. You can also have arrows at the beginning or end of a line, and you can edit the width, length, and concavity of the arrows by clicking the Shape button.

Pencil options.

Line Tool options.

AIRBRUSH TOOL

KEYBOARD SHORTCUT: Type the letter J.

The Airbrush nib looks similar to the Paintbrush except that it continues to add density as you hold down the mouse button and go over the same area again and again. If you click the Airbrush down in one spot and continue to hold down the mouse button, paint continues to be applied until you reach 100% opacity. Instead of the Opacity setting, this tool has a Pressure setting that controls how

Airbrush options.

fast the density increases. Using the Airbrush is like painting with an airbrush or a spraypaint can. For even more of a real airbrush effect, use the Brushes options to set the spacing on your brush to 1 and then set the pressure to very, very low—about 5–10% or lower. You might also like the effect of turning the spacing off completely.

PAINTBRUSH TOOL

KEYBOARD SHORTCUT: Type the letter B.

The Paintbrush tool has anti-aliased edges that make the edge of where you paint blend more evenly with what you are painting over.

When painting with the Pencil or Paintbrush, the Opacity setting from the Brushes palette is not exceeded so long as you hold the mouse button down, even if you paint over the same area again and again.

Paintbrush options.

WET EDGES: If you turn this option on, more color is laid down on the edges of your brushstroke. It's sort of a watercolor effect.

ERASER TOOL

KEYBOARD SHORTCUT: Type the letter E.

The Eraser tool erases to the background color in the background layer and to transparency in any other layer. The default background color is white but can be any color. Erasing a layer to transparent allows you to see through the erased area to the layers below it. You can choose from four options for the type of eraser nib: Paintbrush, Airbrush, Pencil, and Block. The first three give you eraser nibs that act exactly like their painting tool counterparts in respect to style, so refer to the Paintbrush, Airbrush, and Pencil sections of this chapter, respectively. The Block option is most like the eraser from early versions of the program. It does not have anti-aliased edges and the size of the area you erase is determined not by brush size, but rather by the magnification of the image that you are working with. The higher the magnification, the smaller your erased area, until you reach the point that you are erasing individual pixels. If you hold down the Option key and click the Eraser icon, or if you type Shift-E, you cycle through the tool's Painting options. The Stylus options work only if you have a graphics tablet attached instead of a mouse.

Eraser options.

TO ACCESS SPECIFIC BLEND/PAINTING MODES

for	Macintosh	Windows
	Option-Shift	Alt-Shift

plus

Normal	N
Dissolve	I
Multiply	M
Screen	S
Overlay	O
Soft Light	F
Hard Light	H
Color Dodge	D
Color Burn	B
Darken	K
Lighten	G
Difference	E
Exclusion	X
Hue	U
Saturation	T
Color	C
Luminosity	Y
Threshold	L
Behind	Q

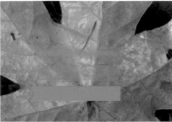

The four different erasers at 50% opacity.

ERASE TO HISTORY: You usually use the Eraser tool when you want to completely remove something in a small area. If you hold down the Option key when erasing or click the Erase to History option, you get the Magic Eraser, which erases to the current position of the History Brush. For more information on using the History Palette, see the chapter "History Palette, History Brush, and Snapshots."

RUBBER STAMP/PATTERN STAMP TOOL

KEYBOARD SHORTCUT: Type the letter S. Type Shift-S to toggle between the tools.

The Rubber Stamp has undergone some revisions in Photoshop 5. It is now two different tools: the Rubber Stamp and the Pattern Stamp. Both tools allow you to choose Aligned if you want to paint a continuous image or Pattern, even if you let go of the mouse or stylus. With the Rubber Stamp, you can clone from an image onto itself, from one layer of an image to another layer, or from one photo to another.

If you'd like to try some of the options that we show here, open the file Starry Night in the Tool Palette folder on the CD.

Aligned is the option you will use most often. You can use it to remove spots and scratches and also to copy part of an image from one place to another. To use it, pick a brush size from the Brushes palette, then hold down the Option key, and click at the location where you want to pick up the image (called the pickup location). Now, without holding down the Option key, click the place where you want to clone the new information (called the putdown location). As long as you hold down the mouse, information copies from the pickup location to the putdown location. Both of these move correspondingly when you move the mouse. When you release the mouse button and then move it and click down again, the relative distance between the pickup location and the putdown location remains the same, but both move the offset distance that you move the mouse. Therefore, you can clone part of the image, stop for lunch, and then come back and finish the job without worrying about misaligning your clone. This makes Aligned very good for removing spots. You can also clone from one image or one layer to another by Option-clicking in the pickup image or layer and then clicking down to clone in the putdown image or layer. See the chapter "Grand Canyon Tweaks," for more information on removing spots and scratches with the Aligned option. In the Starry Night picture here, we've first been asked to clone a group of stars. The Aligned option works well for this.

Rubber Stamp options.

For Rubber Stamp (aligned), Option-click at the pickup location...

...then click with no Option key at the location where you want to put down the clone. Notice the **+** that shows you the current pick-up location, and the **O** that shows the put-down location. We have our Cursors preference set to Brush Size.

You would use non-aligned (Aligned unchecked) to copy the same object into various places within the image. When you use this option, the pickup location remains the same when you move the mouse and click down in a new putdown location, which allows you to copy the same part of the image to multiple places within the image. When you want to change the pickup location, you need to Option-click again. Non-aligned would work better if you need to copy one star over and over.

PATTERN STAMP: Patterned cloning uses the current Photoshop pattern and copies it wherever you paint with the mouse. If the Align box is checked, different painting areas come up against each other; the patterns line up even if you have released the mouse button and started drawing more than once. This is the tool you want to use if you are painting wallpaper or some pattern that must match. To define a pattern, you select a rectangular area with the Rectangular Marquee and then choose Edit/Define Pattern. It remains the current pattern until you define a new one. In the example here, we used the file Fish Art, opened the Layers palette, and chose the Fish layer. We defined the pattern from a rectangle in the pink gill area, and then used the Pattern Stamp with Aligned on and our blend mode set to Normal at 100%. Notice that even if you use discontiguous strokes, the pattern aligns correctly.

Non-aligned is the same as Aligned except that the patterns do not necessarily match when different painting areas come up against each other. You would not want to use this option to paint wallpaper, but by changing the Painting modes you might find that you can build up some interesting textures. Here we've used the same pattern but stroked the Pattern Stamp over the same area several times, letting go of the mouse each time. The patterns do not align. While you're here playing, try lowering the opacity or using Multiply, Screen, Dissolve, or Difference as a Blend mode to lay texture over the flat color areas. Groovy.

THE HISTORY BRUSH

KEYBOARD SHORTCUT: Type the letter Y.

The most important addition to the Tool palette is the new History Brush. This brush works in conjunction with the History palette to give you multiple levels of Undo and multiple snapshots from which to paint. You have so many options now you can wander around painting different versions ad infinitum. My head hurts thinking about it. The quick explanation is: The position of the History Brush icon in the History palette determines the state of the file that you will paint from using the History Brush. The tool options are the same as the regular Paintbrush with the addition of the Impressionist, option which used to be part of the Rubber Stamp tool.

With the Aligned option on, if you let go of the mouse and move to a new location, the Rubber Stamp remembers the original location of your Option-click and maintains the relative distance.

With Aligned not on, if you let go of the mouse and move to a new location, the Rubber Stamp begins cloning again from the original location.

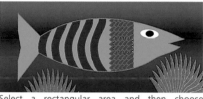

Select a rectangular area and then choose Edit/Define Pattern.

The Pattern Stamp (Aligned) clones the pattern in perfectly abutted regularity, even if you lift the mouse and begin a new clone.

Using non-aligned clones over an existing pattern if you lift the mouse and begin a new clone.

Here we used the Pattern Stamp with Align on in Multiply mode at about 30% opacity for some quick texture on the fish.

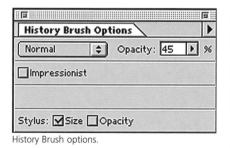

History Brush options.

The original Fish art.

The History Brush gives you far more flexibility than the multiple undos of any other program. Here, even though we moved objects and ran filters on them, built new layers and layer masks, and changed Blend modes, we were still able to use the History Brush to paint 45% of the original Green Fan layer onto a new layer for a 3-D effect.

THE EDITING TOOLS

Open the files CeramicFruit and Fish Art from the CD to follow the next part of this chapter.

SHARPEN/BLUR/SMUDGE TOOLS

KEYBOARD SHORTCUT: Type the letter R. Type Shift-R to cycle through the three tools.

Sharpen tool after several applications.

You can switch between the Blur, Sharpen, and Smudge tools by Option-clicking the tool, typing Shift-R, or using the pop-up. You use the Blur tool to help blend jagged edges between two images being composited, as well as to remove the jaggies from a diagonal line or just to soften selected parts of an image. You can use the Sharpen tool to locally sharpen an area without making a selection. Both tools work best when you try different levels of pressure (opacity) from the Options palette, and you should start out with a low pressure, as they can work quite quickly.

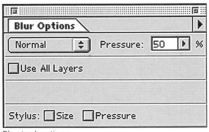

Sharpen tool options.

The Smudge tool turns your image into wet paint. You can click and drag to smear one color area into another. This blends the colors within the brush area, so the size of the blend depends on the size and softness of the brush you use. The pressure controls the amount of paint that mixes with each stroke and how far into the stroke the paint smears. At 100%, the color that you pick up is laid down the whole length of the stroke. If you hold the Option key down when you start a paint stroke or click the Fingerpaint mode, a dab of the foreground color mixes in with the rest of the colors being smudged.

Blur tool after several applications.

Blur tool options.

USE ALL LAYERS: The Use All Layers option reads all of the layers that have the Eye icon turned on to make whatever adjustments are specific to that tool. If you are Smudging colors, the Smudge tool looks at all colors in the current composite and

Smudge tool in action.

Orange foreground color mixed with the image with Fingerpaint mode.

Smudge tool options.

Chapter 7: The Tool Palette

smears them together. Ditto for Sharpen and Blur. But be aware that the Smudge, Sharpen, or Blur only occurs on the active layer, so make sure the layer that should show the change is currently active.

DODGE/BURN/SPONGE TOOLS

KEYBOARD SHORTCUT: Type the letter O. Type Shift-O to cycle through the three options.

You can switch the Dodge tool to the Burn or Sponge tool by using the pop-up option menu. If you Option-click the tool, it toggles between the Dodge, Burn, and Sponge tools. You use the Dodge tool when you want to make localized areas of your image lighter, and the Burn tool to make localized areas of your image darker. Both tools work best when you try different levels of exposure (opacity) from the Options palette. Start with a low value, about 30%.

When you use the Burn and Dodge tools, you need to specify the part of the image area you are working on. Set Highlights, Midtones, or Shadows depending on the part of the image you are dodging or burning.

We describe other techniques for dodging and burning, which we like better because they are more flexible and adjustable, in the chapters "Buckminster Fuller," "Grand Canyon Tweaks," "Blend Modes, Calculations, and Apply Image," and "Filters and Effects."

The Sponge tool allows you to saturate or desaturate the area you brush over. It is very useful for desaturating out-of-gamut colors (colors that you can see onscreen but are unprintable) to bring them back into gamut (printable colors).

TYPE/TYPE MASK/VERTICAL TYPE/ VERTICAL TYPE MASK TOOLS

KEYBOARD SHORTCUT: Type the letter T. Type Shift-T to cycle through the four Type tools.

When you use the Type tool, you enter text by clicking on the image in the location where you want to insert the text. (Text looks better if you have Adobe Type Manager installed and the Anti-Aliased option on, except for very small type.) Type is added to your image as a new layer with the type surrounded by transparency. The layer is named using the characters that you just typed in, which makes identifying the layer easy. The text comes in as the current foreground color at 100% opacity unless you choose a different color

Options for both the Dodge and Burn tools.

The original image.

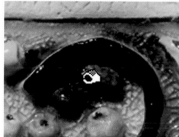

After dodging with the Dodge tool.

After burning with the Burn tool.

With the Sponge tool, you can saturate or desaturate the colors.

Several applications of the Saturate Sponge.

Several applications of the Desaturate Sponge.

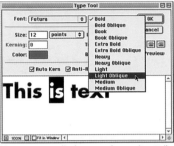

Type dialog box that appears after you click in your file with the Type tool.

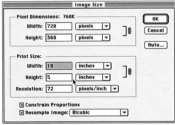

You can now edit the text, change its attributes, transform it, or add layer effects and still maintain the editability of the text.

A 760K file at 72 ppi is five inches high.

The same file at 300 ppi is 1.2 inches high.

while in the Type dialog box. You can access this new layer through the Layers palette, where you can modify the Opacity and the Paint mode. But the best news is that you can now edit the text in this layer. You can change the color, kern it, track it, baseline-shift it, and change the attributes character by character. If that's not enough, you can transform the layer or add layer effects and still be able to edit the text.

The Type Mask tool adds a selection of your type boundaries to the currently active layer. If a type layer is the active layer, you'll get a type mask but be unable to do anything further with that layer until you render it. For the highest resolution output and more control over type modifications, text often looks better if you add it using Illustrator, FreeHand, or your page layout program. We show you how to integrate type from Illustrator in "Bike Ride in the Sky."

FONT: Font is the name of the typeface that you will be using. Sometimes the name starts with a letter that categorizes the weight or cut of the font. Generally, you

This text has been skewed, rotated, and has layer effects applied to it, but you can still edit it.

look for the name of the typeface, such as Times or Garamond (we used Futura here) and then select the weight of the face that you wish to use, such as light, book, bold, or italic. If you are using Adobe Type Reunion, the weights of each face are grouped together. If you are not using Type Reunion, all the bold fonts appear in the menu together prefaced by the letter B. All the italic fonts are grouped together prefaced by the letter I, and so forth.

SIZE: The size that text appears depends not only on the size you choose in the Type Tool dialog box, but also on the resolution and dimensions of the image you set using the Image/Image Size command. If you set the resolution to 72 ppi, Photoshop thinks the image is large, in this case, five inches high; 12-point type would look quite small in this file. If you change the resolution to 300 ppi without changing the file size, however, Photoshop then thinks that the image is 1.2 inches high. Your 12-point type will look considerably larger. You can set your text in pixels also.

KERNING: Photoshop 5 allows you to kern letter pairs, that is, change the amount of space between any two characters. A positive number gives you more space between the letters; a negative number tightens the space. Place the cursor between two letters and turn off Auto Kern to type a value.

COLOR: You can now click the color square to change the color of the type at any time. You change the color of all the text when you click the color square, so if you want to do something fancy, once again, you probably want to do it with another program.

LEADING: Leading is the amount of vertical spacing between the baselines of the lines of text. A positive number gives you more space between the lines, and a negative number, less space. If you set type in all capitals, a negative number usually gives better spacing between the lines.

TRACKING: Tracking refers to the horizontal letter spacing of the text. Whereas kerning is the space between any two characters, tracking is the space between more than two characters. As in kerning, a positive number gives you more space between the letters, spreading them out, and a negative number draws the letters tighter together.

ALIGNMENT: The three icons above the Preview button change the alignment of your text from flush left to centered or flush right.

The Vertical Type tool and the Vertical Type Mask tool work exactly like their horizontal counterparts with the addition of the following option.

ROTATE: When you type vertical text, the characters are placed upright, one on top of the other. If you want the characters to lie on their sides, select the character or characters you want to rotate (you can do Command-A to select all of the letters), and click the Rotate button.

PAINT BUCKET TOOL

KEYBOARD SHORTCUT: Type the letter K.

The Paint Bucket tool does a similar thing as the Magic Wand in that it makes a selection when you click, but it also fills the selection with the foreground color after the selection is made, then deselects after the fill. We seldom use the Paint Bucket, preferring to make the selection first with other selection tools and then, once we have the right selection, use the Fill command from the Edit menu. The Fill command (Shift-Delete) also offers many more options than does the Paint Bucket. The Bucket is very useful and faster than Fill for colorizing black-and-white line drawings like cartoon drawings, animations, or solid color areas.

PAINTING MODES: We discuss the various Painting modes in a later chapter, "Blend Modes, Calculations, and Apply Image."

OPACITY: Changes the opacity of the fill.

PATTERN: To access the Pattern option, you must first define a pattern. Use the Rectangular Marquee with no feather and choose a selection that you'd like to turn into a pattern. Now choose Edit/Define Pattern. You can define only one pattern at a time, so if you like to have lots of neat patterns available, you need to save these rectangular selections as separate files or together in one file.

USE ALL LAYERS: If you are using several layers, you can choose which layers you want the Paint Bucket to search for the color tolerance range. If you click on Use All Layers and have the Eye icon on in more than one layer, Photoshop samples the data in every layer currently visible. The Paint Bucket fills only the currently active layer.

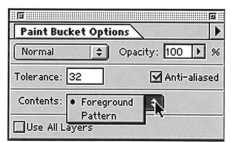

The Paint Bucket options.

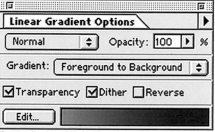

Define Pattern in the Edit menu.

GRADIENT TOOL

KEYBOARD SHORTCUT: Type the letter G. Type Shift-G to cycle through the different gradient styles.

The basic function of the Gradient tool is to make a gradual blend in the selected area from one color to another color. A blend is accomplished by clicking and dragging a line the length and angle you want the blend to happen. The Gradient tool is often used in a mask channel to blend two images together seamlessly by making a blend from black to white. Black represents one image and white the other. We use the Gradient tool for masking in Chapter 37: Bike Ride in the Sky and Chapter 33: The Band. If you'd like to experiment with the tool, open the files The Leaf, Fish Art, and GrColOrPur from the Tool palette folder on the CD. You can use Select/Load Selection to load the Leaf Mask as a selection.

The Gradient tool default settings.

We'll also do a few tricks with Layers, so you might want to open The Fish file again. Show the Layers palette (Window/Show Layers) and click the name of the appropriate layer. Turn on the Preserve Transparency option.

Photoshop five has five types of Gradient blends, Linear, Radial, Angle, Reflected, and Diamond. Radial creates a radial blend done as a circle. If Gradient

The TheLeaf file. Open this file if you want to play along with the Gradient tool. Now use Select/Load selection to load the Leaf Mask.

This file, called GrColOrPur, has an orange foreground and purple background. These are the colors we used to illustrate the Gradient tool. To use the same colors as you experiment, use the Eyedropper tool by itself to click the orange square and set your foreground color. Then hold down the Option key with the Eyedropper and click on the purple square to set your background color.

is set to Foreground to Background, the first click of the mouse is the circle's center using the foreground color, the line length that you drag is the circle's radius, and the mouse release location is at the outside edge of a blended circle using the background color. The Angle blend gives the effect of sweeping a radius around a circle. The line you draw is the "angle" of the radius in the foreground color (or first color of the blend) that then sweeps around the circle changing gradually to the background color (or moves through the colors of your selected blend). The Reflected gradient reflects two symmetrical linear gradients outward from your starting point, and the Diamond gradient uses the line you draw as one of the corners of the diamond shape that is created.

THE DEFAULT SETTINGS: When you set the Blend mode to Normal, the Type to Linear, and the Gradient to Foreground to Background, everything from the first click on the line to the edge of the selection is solid foreground color. Everything from the mouse release to the other end of the selection is solid background color. Along the line, there is a blend from foreground to background color, and at a place 50% along the length of the line, the two colors each at 50% opacity.

BLEND MODES AND OPACITY: You can set the Blend mode and Opacity of the gradient you are about to create using these settings in the Gradient Options palette. We discuss the various blend modes in the chapter, "Blend Modes, Calculations, and Apply Image." However, you might want to try some of the modes, like Color, Multiply, Difference, and Hard Light as you explore the Gradient tool.

THE DITHER OPTION: Leaving the Dither option on results in smoother blends with less banding. We recommend that you leave it on unless you want a banded and uneven gradient.

THE GRADIENT EDITOR: Notice the different gradients in the Gradient pop-up menu within Gradient Options. Each of these was created by Adobe using the Gradient Editor. To open the Gradient Editor, click the Edit button in the Gradient Options palette.

A blend across the selected area with the default setting...

...gives a blend from foreground to background with 50% of each color at the midway point.

A blend that begins or ends before the selection boundaries...

...will be 100% of the foreground color before the beginning of the blend and 100% of the background color after the blend line ends. When using the default settings, the midpoint, where color is 50% foreground and 50% background, will still be at the midway point.

Foreground to Background Color Only.

Foreground (Purple) to Transparent blend inside the mask of the leaf.

Transparent to Foreground (Purple) blend inside the mask of the leaf.

Linear blend from orange to purple, fins to mouth.

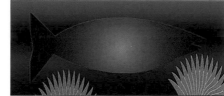

Radial blend center to top of fish.

Angle blend, center to nose of fish.

Reflected blend, center to top of fish.

Diamond blend, center to top of fish.

Here we made a copy of the fish layer and then used the reflected blend shown above on the top copy. We then set the Blend mode of the top layer to Hard Light at 100% opacity.

The Gradient Editor provides a list of the currently defined gradients. If you want to base your new gradient on an existing one, click the name of the existing gradient and then click the Duplicate button to make a copy of it. To create a new gradient from scratch, click the New button and you'll get the default name Gradient 1, which you can rename if you like. To modify an existing gradient, just select it and start making changes. To rename or remove a gradient, select it and then click Rename or Remove. You can also save and load gradient sets using the Load and Save buttons.

You can use the Adjust radio buttons to change either the color or transparency of a gradient. Here we see a gradient that has three colors: red to the left, purple in the middle, and green to the right. The bar below the Adjust choices, which is now colored, allows you to choose the colors of the gradient and where you want each color to appear along the gradient line that you draw. Each point below this color bar represents a different color. You can add a new point by clicking below the Color Bar and you can move this point by dragging from left to right. The Location box tells you the location of this color as a percentage of the length of the line you draw to create the gradient. You can set a point to a particular color by first clicking that point and then either clicking the F point below and to the left to get the foreground color, the B point to get the background color, or in the color box below and to the left to bring up the Color Picker and pick a new color. The color point you are currently working on will have its triangle top highlighted in black. You can click these points and drag them to any location along the length of the bar and the colors in the bar, and the transparency indicator below changes to show the effect of your movement. The little diamond points above the colored bar represent the halfway point between the color point below and to the left and the color point below and to the right of that diamond point. Click and drag it to have the Location window show you the location relative to the percentage of distance between these two points. The default location of the diamonds is always 50% of this distance, but you can move them left and right.

If you click the Transparency setting of the Adjust radio buttons, you can change the transparency of the gradient at each point along its length. You can turn off the

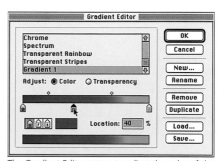

The Gradient Editor set up to adjust the color of the gradient. You access this by typing G to get to the Gradient tool, pressing Return to bring up the Gradient Tool Options palette, and then pressing the Edit button. Here the bottom transparency bar shows 100% opacity because we haven't edited the Transparency.

The Editing Tools

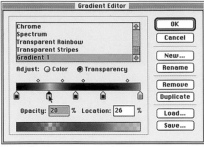

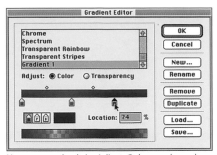

This is the Transparency mode where you move and change the the opacity of the points below the black-and-white bar to effect the opacity of the color preview at the bottom of the dialog. Here we have five different points, and the one that is currently selected has an opacity of 20% and a location of 26%. Transparency is shown as the same checkerboard pattern used by transparent layers.

Here we are back in Adjust Color mode and we have changed the rightmost color point to the color blue and moved it from Location 100% to Location 74%. Notice that the Opacity bar at the bottom now shows the Transparency that you set up in the previous dialog box.

transparency of any gradient by turning off the Transparency check box on the Gradient Options palette. Try turning off Transparency and then using the Foreground to Transparent option. You get just the solid foreground color. The bar that had color in it when you were adjusting the gradient colors now is black or white, representing the opacity of the transparency. (Black represents 100% opacity and white represents 0% opacity.) The length of the bar again represents the length of the line you draw when making the gradient. You can place Opacity points anywhere along the bottom of the bar by clicking below the bar. When you click a point, the top of it turns black, indicating that it is the point you are currently editing. The Location window shows you the location of this point relative to the total length of the line and the Opacity window shows you its opacity. You can see the effect of your changes in opacity by looking at the Opacity preview bar at the bottom of the dialog box. Just as when adjusting the gradient color, you can click above the Opacity bar to place diamonds that represent the midpoint between the Opacity point to their left and the Opacity point to their right. Bring the Gradient Editor up and play with it a bit and it will become obvious how

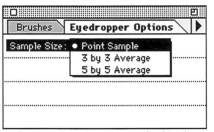

A gradient created with the Gradient 1 setting and Transparency turned off. There is no transparency here.

A gradient created with the Gradient 1 setting and Transparency turned on.

it works. I must admit that when I first saw this extension it was not intuitively obvious how it worked, but hopefully, this description will help you along your way.

EYEDROPPER/COLOR SAMPLER TOOL

Eyedropper options: Use Point Sample when choosing specific colors and 3 by 3 Average when color correcting.

This is the menu that comes up when you Control-click while using the Eyedropper tool.

KEYBOARD SHORTCUT: Type the letter I. Type Shift-I to toggle between the tools.

You use the Eyedropper tool to choose the foreground and background color within an image onscreen. You can click the Eyedropper tool to use it and then click the color that you want to make the foreground color, or Option-click to get the background color. You access the Eyedropper tool by holding down the Option key when using any of the painting tools and then clicking where you want to pick up a new foreground color.

New to Photoshop 5 is the Color Sampler tool. This tool allows you to place eyedropper-type samplers in up to four locations in your file. During manipulation of your image, you can watch how your changes are affecting the areas where you placed samplers. Samplers can be moved after they've been placed and can be hidden completely by using the Info palette pop-up. You can change the read-out values from RGB to CMYK, grayscale, HSB, Lab, Actual Color, or Total Ink percentages even in the middle of making adjustments to the file, by clicking the specific sampler pop-up triangle. You can delete a sampler from the screen by dragging it off the image. To see

The new Color Sampler tool is a pop-up on the Eyedropper tool, or type Shift-I to switch between the tools.

You can set up to four Color Samplers and change the read-out at any time. Here, we've changed Sampler #3 to give us the Total Ink percentage while in the middle of a Curves adjustment.

AUTOMATIC EYEDROPPER: The Eyedropper tool automatically shows up whenever you are in Levels, Curves, Color Balance, or any of the color correction tools and you move the cursor over the image. This allows you to see the color values of any location in the Info and Color palettes while you are correcting and changing those values. As a preference setting for this type of use with continuous tone images, you should double-click the Eyedropper and set the sample size to 3 by 3 Average rather than the default Point Sample setting.

how the Color Sampler tool can be used, read Chapter 26: Buckminster Fuller, Chapter 27: Color Matching Images, and Chapter 32: Versailles.

HAND TOOL

KEYBOARD SHORTCUT: Type the letter H.

Hand tool options.

Use the Hand tool to scroll the image. Scrolling doesn't change your document; rather, it allows you to look at a different part of it. You can access the Hand tool more efficiently by using the Spacebar on the keyboard along with a mouse click, which can be done any time. If you double-click the Hand tool in the Tool palette, the image resizes to the largest size that fits completely within the current screen and palette display.

ZOOM TOOL

KEYBOARD SHORTCUT: Type the letter Z.

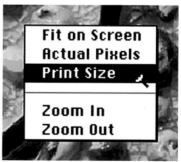

This is the menu that comes up when you Control-click while using the Zoom tool.

Use the Zoom tool to magnify the image and, with the Option key, to shrink the image. The location where you click is centered within the bigger or smaller image. Using this tool is like moving a photograph you are holding in your hand either closer to your face or farther away. The actual size of the photograph doesn't change, only how closely you are looking at it. It is best to access the Zoom tool using Command-Spacebar-click to zoom in closer, or Option-Spacebar-click to zoom out further. You can use these command keys any time, even when a dialog box, like Levels, is up. If you double-click the Zoom tool within the Tool palette, the image zooms in or out to the 100% size. At 100%, the image may be bigger than the screen, but you see every pixel of the part of the image you are viewing. Use this for detailed work. The Resize Windows to Fit option resizes your normal window to surround your zoomed size, if possible. I leave it off because I don't like my windows automatically resizing.

8 PICKING AND USING COLOR

A look at RGB, CMYK, HSB, and Lab color spaces,
what they are, when to use each, and how to access them
from Photoshop; the Photoshop Color Picker and the
Picker, Swatches, and Scratch palettes explained in detail.

There are different color spaces available in Photoshop that you can use for different purposes at different times. Instead of just working in one color space, like RGB or CMYK, it is a good idea to learn the advantages and disadvantages of the different color spaces. Photoshop has various tools for picking and saving colors. We summarize these color space issues in this chapter, mostly for how they relate to picking and choosing color. For more information on setting up and using the RGB, CMYK, and Lab color spaces in Photoshop 5, see Chapter 14: Color Spaces, Device Characterization, and Color Management.

THE RGB COLOR SPACE

For overall color correction and ease of work, using the Red, Green, Blue (RGB) color space offers many advantages. I recommend keeping your final master files in RGB format. Red, green, and blue are the additive colors of light that occur in nature. White light consists of wavelengths from the red, green, and blue spectrums. All scanners, even high-end drum scanners, actually have sensors that originally capture the data in RGB format. You can use RGB for final output to computers, multimedia and TV monitors, color transparency writers, digital video, Web sites, and some digital printers because these are all native RGB devices. RGB files are smaller than CMYK files because they have only three components of color instead of four.

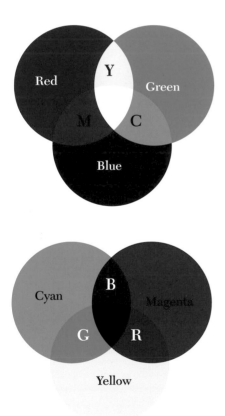

THE CMYK COLOR SPACE

Cyan, magenta, and yellow are the complementary colors to red, green, and blue. Red and cyan are opposites, so if you take away all the red from white light, cyan is what you have left. Cyan is formed by mixing green and blue light. Green and magenta, as well as blue and yellow, work similarly; that is, they are complementary colors. When you print on a printing press, the colors of ink used are cyan, magenta, and yellow. These are called subtractive colors because when you view something that is printed, you actually see the light that is reflected back. When white light, which contains all the colors, hits a surface painted cyan, you see cyan because the cyan paint subtracts the red from the white light, and only green and blue reflect back for you to see. To print red using CMY inks, you use magenta and yellow inks. Magenta subtracts the green light and yellow subtracts the blue light so what reflects back to your eyes is red light. The cyan, magenta, and yellow dyes that make up printing inks are not pure, so when you print all three of them at the same time, instead of reflecting no light and giving you black, you get a muddy gray color. Because of this problem, the printing trade adds black ink (the K in CMYK) to the four-color process so that dark areas are as dark as possible.

The Amount of Black

The amount of black ink used in the printing process and the way that it is used depends on the type of paper and press that you use. Newspaper presses typically use a lot of black ink and as little color ink as possible because black ink is cheaper. High-quality advertising color for magazines and other coated stock is printed with much more colored ink and less black. A skilled printer can create the same image in CMYK using a lot of black ink or very little black ink. You can use many different ways to combine the colored and black inks to get the final result.

Converting RGB to CMYK

Because of these different choices, converting from RGB to CMYK can be a complicated process. After an image is converted to CMYK, whether by a high-end scanner or by you in Photoshop, managing the relationship between the CMY colors and the black ink can be tricky. That's just one of the reasons you're better off doing your overall color corrections in RGB so that you are taking a correct RGB file and then converting it to CMYK. You then end up with a CMYK file that has the black in the right place in relationship with the final, or close to final, CMY colors. The main reason to use the CMYK color space is that your final output will be on a printing press or a digital printer that uses CMYK inks or dyes. We discuss color correction in both RGB and CMYK as we present the examples in this book. Because you want to customize the creation of your CMYK file to the type of printing you are doing and because colors can get lost when you convert to CMYK, you should keep your master file in RGB format, for the highest quality and versatility across all media.

The Hue, Saturation, and Lightness Color Space

Another color space used in Photoshop is Hue, Saturation, and Lightness. You can no longer use the Mode menu to convert an image to HSL mode like you could in some older versions of Photoshop, but the many color tools allow you to think about and massage color using this color space. Instead of dividing a color into components of red, green, and blue, or cyan, magenta, and yellow, HSL divides a color into its hue, its saturation, and its lightness. The hue is the actual color and can include all the colors of the rainbow. A particular red hue differs from a purple, yellow, orange, or even a different red hue. The saturation is the intensity of that particular hue. Highly saturated colors are quite intense and vivid, so much so that they almost look fluorescent. Colors of low saturation are dull and subtle. The lightness of a part of an

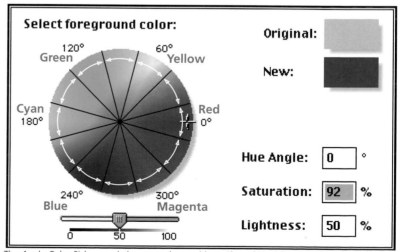

The Apple Color Picker can help you understand how Photoshop delineates Hue. I've broken the color wheel into 30° segments with black lines, and typed the names (in green) for the six true color segments. Photoshop considers Red hues to be the area from 345° to 15° with 0° being pure red. Cyan hues (red's compliment) range from 165° to 195° with 180° being true cyan. The in-between ranges (red/yellow, yellow/green, green/cyan, and so forth) are considered the fall off ranges when you adjust the hue in Photoshop.

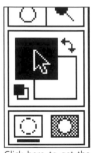

Click here to get the Color Picker and change the foreground color.

image determines how light or dark that part is in overall density. Lightness is the value in the image that gives it detail. Imagine taking a black-and-white image and then colorizing it. The black-and-white image originally had different tonal values of gray. The details show up based on the lightness or darkness of the black-and-white image. Removing the lightness value would be similar to taking this black-and-white detail part out of a color image. If you increase the lightness, the image starts to flatten and show less depth. If you increase the lightness all the way, the image loses all its detail and becomes white. If you decrease the lightness, the image may appear to have more depth, and if you decrease it all the way, the image becomes black. For working with the image using the Hue/Saturation/Lightness model, you use Image/Adjust/Hue/Saturation or Image/Adjust/Replace Color. The different color pickers also allow you to work in the HSL color model.

THE LAB COLOR SPACE

The Lab color space is a device-independent color space that has as its color gamut the colors that the human eye can see. The Lab color space is used internally by Photoshop to convert between RGB and CMYK and can be used for device-independent output to Level 2 PostScript devices. The Lab color space is quite useful for some production tasks. For example, sharpening only the Lightness channel sharpens the image without "popping" the colors. You can work in Photoshop using Lab color, and we have converted a Lab color example, Chapter 29: Bryce Stone Woman, for this version of *Photoshop Artistry*.

USING THE COLOR PICKER

The main tool for picking colors in Photoshop is the Photoshop Color Picker. You access the Color Picker by clicking on the foreground or background color swatch at the bottom of the Tool palette or by double-clicking the foreground or background color swatches on the

Current hue

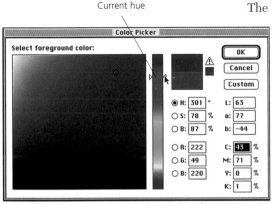

The Color Picker in Hue mode, which is the default. Sliding the color slider (shown with the arrow cursor above) up and down changes the hue in Hue mode. For a particular hue, purple here, click and drag the circle in the color box to the left to pick a particular color. As you move the cursor around in the color box with the mouse button down, left to right movement changes the saturation and up and down movement changes the brightness. You will see the values for saturation and brightness change in the number boxes to the right. You also see the corresponding RGB and CMYK values for each color. Hue is frozen by the color slider position.

Current saturation

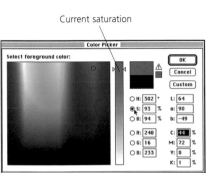

Put the Color Picker in Saturation mode by clicking on the S radio button. Now sliding the color slider up and down changes the saturation. Left to right movement of the cursor circle changes the hue and up and down movement changes the brightness.

Current brightness

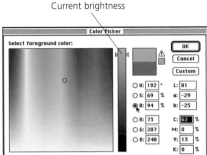

Put the Color Picker in Brightness mode by clicking on the B radio button. Now sliding the color slider up and down changes the brightness. Left to right movement of the cursor circle changes the hue and up and down movement changes the saturation. Brightness here is similar to Lightness, mentioned earlier in this chapter.

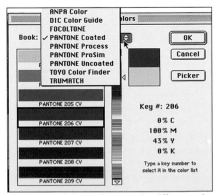

The Custom Colors picker with the different color systems that it makes available in the pop-up menu. Drag the slider or click on the up/down arrows to locate a color, click on a color to choose it, or type in the number associated with a particular color to choose that one. Choosing OK picks that color, and clicking on Picker returns you to the Color Picker where you can see and pick the RGB and CMYK equivalent to that color.

Red mode

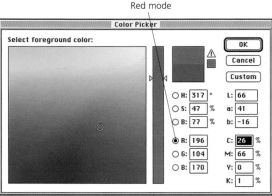

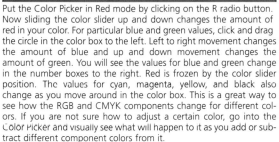

Put the Color Picker in Red mode by clicking on the R radio button. Now sliding the color slider up and down changes the amount of red in your color. For particular blue and green values, click and drag the circle in the color box to the left. Left to right movement changes the amount of blue and up and down movement changes the amount of green. You will see the values for blue and green change in the number boxes to the right. Red is frozen by the color slider position. The values for cyan, magenta, yellow, and black also change as you move around in the color box. This is a great way to see how the RGB and CMYK components change for different colors. If you are not sure how to adjust a certain color, go into the Color Picker and visually see what will happen to it as you add or subtract different component colors from it.

Out-of-gamut warning   New in-gamut color

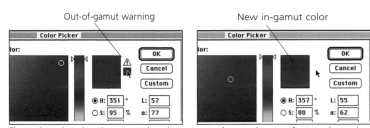

The exclamation sign shows you that the current color may be out-of-gamut (not printable in CMYK). Click on the sign to change the chosen color to the closest in-gamut color (shown at right). See the chapter, "Kansas—Final Tweaks" for a discussion of out-of-gamut colors.

Color palette. You can use this picker in Hue mode, Saturation mode, Brightness mode, or Red, Green, or Blue mode. See the diagrams here for an explanation of each mode. In addition, you can set a specific color by typing in its Lab, RGB, or CMYK values.

The Custom button brings up the Custom Picker for choosing PANTONE, Trumatch, and other standard colors. You can use these as separate color channels within Photoshop's Multichannel mode, choose one or more colors for Duotone mode, set spot color channels in CMYK or RGB mode, or the color automatically converts to RGB or CMYK for painting, depending on the active color space.

USING THE COLOR PALETTES

Besides the Color Picker that you access from the Tool palette, you can also access the Color palette and the Swatches palette from the Window menu. Normally these are grouped together on the desktop, but you can separate them by clicking on their name tabs and dragging each of them to some other specific location on the desktop. Because the big Color Picker is a modal dialog box that you cannot access on-the-fly when using the painting tools, the Color and Swatches palettes come in very handy for getting the colors you need quickly.

THE COLOR PALETTE

In the Color palette, you can move the RGB, CMYK, HSB, or other color sliders to create a color that you like. You pick this color for the foreground or background depending on which of the swatches is chosen in the Color palette. You change the display mode in the Color palette using its pop-up option menu. You can also pick colors from the color bar along the bottom of the palette. This color bar offers different display modes to choose from using the Color palette's options. The Color palette is also useful to have around while you're in Levels,

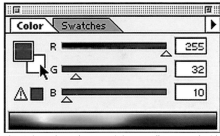

The Color palette shown as it is normally grouped with the Swatches palette. The foreground and background colors are shown to the left. You know that the foreground color is currently active because of the double line around it. If you move the sliders, you adjust the foreground color. The arrow cursor is over the background color. If you click on the background color, it becomes the active color and moving the sliders modifies it. If you double-click on either color square, you get the Color Picker. This palette also shows you the Gamut Warning icon.

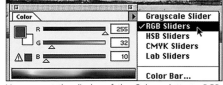

You can set the display of the Color palette to RGB, CMYK, HSB, Lab, or Grayscale.

The Color Bar choice brings up options for how to display the color bar at the bottom of the Color palette. You can choose the foreground color by clicking on a color in the color bar; Option-click for the background color.

65

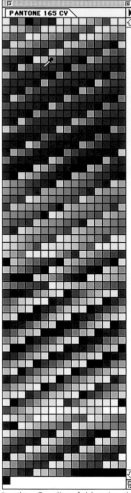

In the Goodies folder in the Photoshop folder, a Color Palettes folder contains swatch sets for PANTONE, Trumatch, and other standard color systems. Here we see all the PANTONE colors loaded into the Swatches palette. When the Eyedropper gets over a particular color, the Swatches tab changes to tell you which PAN-TONE you are about to choose. This may be a quicker way for you to find the custom color you want.

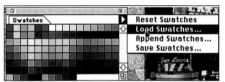

You can load and save different sets of swatches to files. If you have certain colors that you use for a particular client, you may want to save these in a file under that client's name. You can append swatches, which adds the swatches stored in a file to the ones you already have in the palette. Reset Swatches just goes back to the default set of swatches.

Curves, and the other color correction tools. It remembers the colors at the last location where you clicked the Eyedropper in an image, and it shows you how the color adjustments you are making are changing that location. See Chapter 27: Color Matching Images for more details.

The Swatches Palette

The Swatches palette allows you to save and then later access your favorite set of colors. To pick a color from the Swatches palette, check whether the foreground or background square is active. Clicking on the color swatch using the Eyedropper tool will give you a new color for that square. Option-clicking picks a new color for the other square. You automatically get the Eyedropper when the cursor moves over the swatches area. To save the current foreground color in the Swatches palette, Shift-click on the swatch you want to overwrite. If you want to add a new swatch without overwriting the ones there, Option-Shift-clicking on top of a swatch shifts it and all the other swatches one slot to the right, making room for the new swatch. Pressing the Command key gives you the scissors, and clicking over a swatch with them removes it. Using the pop-up options menu, you can load custom swatch sets into the Swatches palette, including sets for custom colors, like PANTONE, that are supplied in the Color Palettes folder that comes with Photoshop. Remember, however, if you paint with a custom color, it is converted to the current color model and does not separate as a custom color.

If you have a continuous tone 24-bit color image that has many colors that you might want to use for other projects, there is a quick way to load 256 of these colors into the Swatches palette. First, choose Image/Mode/Indexed Color to convert a copy of your image into Indexed Color mode. (Be sure to use a copy so you don't destroy your original image.) Using the 8 bits/pixel color depth,

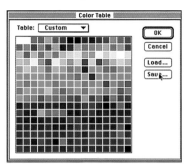

Converting a 24-bit color image to Indexed Color to create a color table for loading into the Swatches palette.

Saving your indexed color table using the Color Table editor. After saving this table, you choose Replace Swatches from the Swatches palette pop-up menu to make this the current set of colors in the Swatches palette.

Adaptive Palette, and Diffusion Dither settings in the Indexed Color dialog box gives you the 256 colors most common in the image. Click on OK in the Index Color dialog box; then choose Image/Mode/Color Table to see a table of the 256 colors you have created from the image. Click on the Save button in the Color Table to save these colors in a file. You can now use Replace Swatches in the Swatches palette to load all these colors. They are now easily available for painting projects in Photoshop. You can also use Load Swatches to add these colors to the swatches already present. This is more of a noteworthy technique for Web work where you might commonly add 3-bit (or whatever) palettes to one another, say for an animation. For more information on 8-bit color and creating images for the Web and multimedia, see the "Images for the Web and Multimedia" section of this book.

Chapter 8: Picking and Using Color

9 COLOR CORRECTION TOOLS

Overview of Photoshop's many color correction and gamma adjustment tools; which ones are most useful for what and why, and which ones are fairly useless for the professional.

Photoshop offers many tools for adjusting color and modifying image gamma or contrast. This chapter gives you a general overview about what the different tools do and when to use each tool. The color correction tools are in the Image/Adjust menu. Levels, Curves, Hue/Saturation, Replace Color, Selective Color, and Channel Mixer are the ones we use most. Auto Levels, Color Balance, Brightness/Contrast, Desaturate, and Variations are the ones we don't use much. In later hands-on chapters, we actually go through the details of each tool's features and how they're used in real-world examples. Invert, Equalize, Threshold, and Posterize are used more for effects and masking, which are covered in other parts of the book.

USING THE INFO/COLOR SAMPLER AND COLOR PALETTES

When you use any of the color correction tools, it is very helpful to have the Info and Color palettes visible onscreen too. Use Window/Show Info (F9 with ArtistKeys) and Window/Show Color (Shift-F9) to bring up these palettes. While working in any color correction tool, Photoshop automatically gives you the Eyedropper tool for measuring colors in the image. The Info palette shows you the RGB values and the CMYK values of the pixel or group of pixels you currently have the Eyedropper tool above. It shows you these values both before (left of slash) and after (right of slash) any changes you have made during the current iteration of the color correction tool you are now using. The Color palette has a subtle but important difference from the Info palette in that it displays the values of the last place where you clicked with the Eyedropper. This allows you to click on a picture tone or color area and see how the pixel values of that particular area will change as you make adjustments with the Color tool. The new Color Sampler tool, to the right of the Eyedropper in the Tool palette, allows you to click (Shift-click while in a color tool) up to four locations where you want to monitor the color of your image while working. These four color values show up in the bottom of the Info window. This is a great new Photoshop 5 feature because you can see how the color values at these four locations change throughout your color correction process. You don't have to

The color correction tools are in the Image/Adjust menu.

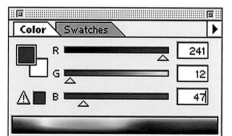

The Color palette remembers the values at the last location you clicked with the Eyedropper and then shows you how those values change when you make adjustments in a color correction tool.

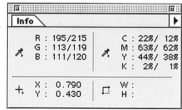

The Info palette with the before values to the left and the after values to the right of the slash.

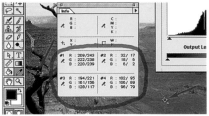

By Shift-clicking on the screen while in a color correction tool, you can place up to 4 Color Sampler points whose values will show up at the bottom of the Info window and will continue to update as you make color changes. This is a new 5.0 feature! These locations continue to update throughout your editing session, even as you switch tools and measure other locations with the regular Eyedropper.

measure them again; their values will constantly update as you work. Each open image can have up to four Color Samplers attached to it.

When adjusting a digital image, you want to make as few separate file modifications as are necessary to achieve the desired result. A file modification is when you click the OK button for any of the color correction tools and you are not in an Adjustment layer. Each file modification changes the original data, and too many changes can eventually degrade the quality of the data. Therefore, you don't want to constantly go from one color correction tool to the other frantically trying to get the effect you need. You want to use these tools intelligently, knowing what each one is good for and keeping the total number of uses down to the minimum required to do the final adjustments on a particular image. If you do your changes using Photoshop adjustment layers, the actual image pixels do not change until the image is flattened. Adjustment layers allow you to go back and change the color over and over again without suffering from this cumulative degrading effect on the digital values.

COMMON COLOR CORRECTION TECHNIQUES

All the color correction tools share a few things in common. When using Levels, Curves, Color Balance, and Brightness/Contrast on the entire image, you often want to have the Preview button turned off. When you have the Preview button turned off when working with these tools, Photoshop adjusts the color and brightness output of the video card controlling colors on the monitor, which gives you instant results onscreen when you make changes. This technique of adjusting the video card to preview color and contrast changes is called Video LUT Animation. The changes happen over the entire computer screen, not just in the active window. Also, when you have the Preview button off, you can click the title bar of this color tool's dialog box and hold the mouse button down to see the image as it looked before you make the adjustment. Click and release the mouse on the title bar and you instantly see a before and after view of your image. Video LUT Animation doesn't work with a few older Macs and with many PCs and compatibles. This Video LUT feature makes a difference when you are making subtle color adjustments, because when you stare at an image on the computer screen for more than a few seconds your eye tends to adjust to make the image look more correct. This quick before/after toggle stops your eye from having time to do this and you can better decide if you really like the color adjustments you have made. Video LUT Animation, with the Preview button off, gives a quick preview of your results no matter how big the file. It's usually fairly accurate and you should use it when possible when you make changes to the overall image in Levels, Curves, Color Balance, and Brightness/Contrast. After you make your changes, you might want to turn on the Preview button to force Photoshop to calculate all the changes and show you exactly how they will look, not just the approximation the Video LUT Animation gives you. When you use the Hue/Saturation, Replace Color, and Selective Color commands, the corrections are too complicated for Photoshop to simulate them simply by changing the video board, so you usually need to work with the Preview button turned on. Video LUT Animation also doesn't work with adjustment layers, so you need to use them with the Preview button on. If your video board does not support Video LUT Animation, just always work with the Preview button on. I have heard that the specs for Windows 98 include Video LUT Animation and also support for more than one monitor. (Windows 95 and NT allow only one monitor; the Mac allows up to six.) Time will tell how it works and if it is supported by third parties.

When working with a selected subarea, comparing one window to another, or adjusting an area in one layer to blend with nonadjusted items in other layers within Levels, Curves, Color Balance, or Brightness/Contrast, you usually work with the Preview button on so you can compare the changes you make to the selected area to the rest of the image. If the Preview button is on while working in a tool, clicking the title bar doesn't give you the quick before/after toggle. Also, you can *never* get this quick toggle during the Hue/Saturation, Replace Color, or Selective Color commands.

In any of the color correction tools, you can Option-Cancel (Reset) to stay in the tool but cancel any changes you have made in that tool so far. Many of these tools also let you load and save a collection of settings. This is useful when you have many very similar images in a production situation. You could carefully make your Levels setting for the first image and then use the Save button to save those settings in a file. If you have subsequent images in the group, you can use the Load button to automatically run the same settings. You can also use the Save and Load features to make Levels or Curves changes while looking at a layer with Video LUT Animation and then saving those changes and actually reloading them in an adjustment layer where you can't use Video LUT Animation.

LEVELS AND CURVES

The Levels and Curves tools have the broadest range of capabilities of any of the color correction tools. When you color correct an image from its original scan, you want to do so in a particular order. (We discuss that order in great detail in "Creating the Master Image," and you should read it for a better understanding of this overview.) The first step after you do a scan is to do overall color correction; that is, correct the complete image without any selections. Levels is the best tool to use because it gives you a Histogram of the data in the image. You can use the Histogram to judge the quality of the scan and to fix many scanning problems. You also can use Levels to precisely adjust the highlight and shadow values, the overall brightness and contrast, and the color balance, while viewing the results onscreen and in the Histogram. You make all these changes in one step and must choose OK only once for all these improvements. Levels is the color correction tool we use most often.

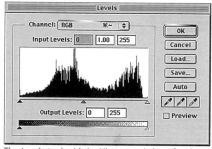

The Levels tool with its Histogram is best for doing the overall color correction right after bringing in a scan.

You can also use the Curves command to do your initial overall color adjustments of the entire image. Curves enables you to do all the same adjustments that Levels does. The Curves command has a different user interface than Levels, however. Instead of furnishing a Histogram, it provides the curve diagram shown here. The horizontal axis of the diagram represents the original image values with black and shadows on the left and white and highlights on the right. The vertical axis represents the modified image values with the shadows at the bottom and the highlights on the top. When the curve is a straight diagonal, as shown here, the image has not been changed. Moving the curve down in the middle darkens the image, and moving it upward lightens the image. The endpoints of the curve are used to change the highlight and shadow values. Using Curves, you can measure individual colors, see the range of values they represent on the curve, and then change only that color range. Curves' advantage is that it allows you to independently modify specific portions of the image's tonal range in different ways with more flexibility than Levels. The advantage of using Levels is being able to see the Histogram as you make changes.

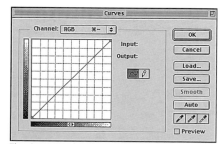

The Curves tool with a curve showing no adjustments to the image. The horizontal axis shows the original image values and the vertical axis shows these values as modified by the curve.

Levels and Curves are the most powerful color correction tools. See the chapters "Grand Canyon," "Kansas," and "Desert Al" for good discussions of using Levels and Curves in the ways for which they are best suited. Also read the chapter

"Digital Imaging and the Zone System" to understand how Levels Histograms and Curves relate to the original photograph.

THE HUE/SATURATION COMMAND

Hue/Saturation is often used to increase the saturation of all the colors by 10% to 20% after doing the overall color correction using Levels. This change is done with the Master button on. Using the Reds, Yellows, Greens, Cyans, Blues, or Magentas, you can change the hue, saturation, or lightness of objects in the image that have one of these standard colors as their primary color without actually making a detailed selection. In Photoshop 5, you can fine-tune these color selections further. You should use Hue/Saturation when you want to change the color, saturation, or lightness of a particular object or color range without changing its gamma or other characteristics. The first part of the process is to select the object(s) you want to change and use the Eyedropper with plus and minus to get a model of the representative color, which shows up in the Color Strip at the bottom of the Hue/Saturation window. This Color Strip shows changes to your representative color as you make them. Unlike Levels and Curves when Video LUT is on, with this tool you need to use the Preview button to see your changes within a file on a 24-bit color monitor.

The Hue slider looks at hues in a circular fashion, sort of like the Apple Color Picker or a rotary color wheel type Color Picker. The initial hue value, 0, is the degree value where you find your initial color. To change just the color, slide the Hue slider to the right (like rotating counter-clockwise on the Apple Color Picker). If your initial color was red, then red would be your 0. A Hue change of 90 degrees would make the color green. A Hue change of –90 degrees would make your color purple. A Hue change of 180 or –180 would yield the opposite of red, which is cyan. Sliding the Saturation slider to the right makes the selected items more saturated and sliding to the left makes them less saturated. This is like moving further from the center or closer to the center on the Apple Color Picker.

Moving the Lightness slider to the right takes away gray values and moving it to the left adds gray values (similar to the sliding bar on the right side of the Apple Color Picker). See Chapter 23: Grand Canyon, Chapter 24: The Car Ad, and Chapter 27: Color Matching Images for more information on the Hue/Saturation tool.

THE REPLACE COLOR COMMAND

The Replace Color command allows you to make a selection based on color and then actually change the color of the selected objects using sliders built into the command's dialog box. The selections are similar to selections made with the Magic Wand, but this tool gives you more control over them. The Magic Wand requires you to make a selection by using a certain tolerance setting and clicking a color, and then selects adjacent areas based on whether their colors fall within the tolerance value you set for it. If the selection is incorrect with the Magic Wand, you need to change the tolerance and then select again. This process takes a lot of time and iteration. The Replace Color command allows you to change the tolerance on-the-fly while viewing the actual objects or colors you are selecting.

The tolerance here is called Fuzziness. Increasing the Fuzziness, by moving the slider in the dialog box to the right, enlarges your selection, and decreasing it shrinks the selection. You see a preview of what is happening with the selection in a little mask window in the dialog box.

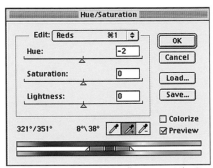

The Hue/Saturation tool. Usually you want the Preview button on when using Hue/Saturation. Notice the new color bars and sliders at the bottom of the dialog. These, along with the Eyedroppers allow Photoshop 5 to do a much better job picking a color range to modify with Hue/Saturation.

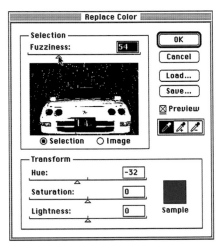

The Replace Color command has a selection capability based on object color and has some of the controls from Hue/Saturation built into it. Use it for quickly selecting and changing the color of objects. Use the sample swatch as a quick reference to see how your color will change; then use the Preview button to see the change happen within the file.

After you perfect the color selection, you then use the Hue, Saturation, and Lightness sliders in the Replace Color dialog box to change the color of the selected objects. You can see this color change in the image by clicking the Preview button, and that allows you to make further tweaks on the selection while actually seeing how they're affecting the color change. Replace Color selects and changes color on these objects from everywhere in the image selected using the selection tools before you entered Replace Color. To learn more about using Replace Color, see the Chapter 25: Yellow Flowers.

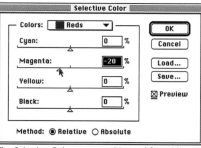

The Selective Color command is used for adding or subtracting the percentage of cyan, magenta, yellow, or black inks within the red, green, blue, cyan, magenta, yellow, black, neutral, or white colors in the selected area of a CMYK image. These percentages of change can be relative to the amount of an ink color that is already there or they can be absolute percentages.

THE SELECTIVE COLOR TOOL AND CMYK

The Selective Color tool works great when you are working with CMYK images. It is a good tool for making final tweaks to CMYK colors after converting from RGB to CMYK. With this tool, you adjust the amount of cyan, magenta, yellow, or black ink within the red, green, blue, cyan, magenta, yellow, black, neutral, or white colors in the selected area. It's also a great tool for fine control over fixing color areas that fade a bit when converted to CMYK. For more information about using this tool, see Chapter 25: Yellow Flowers, and Chapter 27: Color Matching Images.

THE CHANNEL MIXER

The new Photoshop 5 Channel Mixer allows you to take a percentage of the color from one channel and use it to create part of another channel. This technique can be used to improve CMYK separations and also the process of creating a black-and-white image from a color image. You could always do this type of thing in the past using Image/Calculations or by just pasting one channel on top of another and changing the opacity; the Channel Mixer just makes this process easier. See Chapter 28: Desert Al for an example of using Channel Mixer.

The new Photoshop 5 Channel Mixer allows you to take a percentage of the color from one channel and use it to create part of another channel. Here, we are taking 20% of the Cyan channel and 80% of the Magenta channel and using it to create a new Magenta channel.

COLOR BALANCE, BRIGHTNESS/CONTRAST, AND VARIATIONS

You will notice that we don't use Color Balance, Brightness/Contrast, and Variations tools much in this book. We consider them less precise than the other five color correction tools previously mentioned. We explain the advantages and disadvantages of using these three tools in this section. In general, they are more for color beginners and don't offer as much control as the Levels, Curves, Hue/Saturation, Replace Color, or Selective Color commands.

THE COLOR BALANCE TOOL

The Color Balance tool shows the the relationship between the additive colors (red, green, and blue) on the right and the subtractive colors (cyan, magenta, and yellow) on the left. You move three sliders, the Cyan/Red slider, the Magenta/Green slider, and the Yellow/Blue slider, either to the left to get the CMY colors or to the right to get their complementary RGB colors. If you don't understand the relationship between RGB and CMY, this tool makes it a little easier to see. When you use

The Color Balance tool. Color levels of 0 means that no adjustment has been made. Negative values mean adjustments in the CMY direction, and positive values are adjustments in the RGB direction. Preserve Luminosity is the only feature this tool has that can't be done with more precise control using Levels or Curves.

Color Balance, you need to adjust your shadows, midtones, and highlights each separately, which can take longer than using Levels or Curves.

In general, the Color Balance tool is much less powerful than Levels or Curves because you can't set exact highlight or shadow values, and you don't have much control over brightness and contrast. If you were to use Color Balance to do the overall correction of an image, you probably would have to go back and forth between it and Brightness/Contrast several times, and that would break the rule of clicking on OK as little as possible—and you still have less overall control than with Levels or Curves. Moreover, if you have a setting that you use all the time in Levels, Hue/Saturation, or Curves, you can save it in a file and load it later to use on a similar image, which is very useful when you want to save time and make a group of images have similar color adjustments—once again, the Color Balance tool doesn't have this option.

Overall, I would say that the Color Balance tool is more of a toy for beginning color correctors and not the tool I would recommend for imaging professionals. The one exception is that you can make adjustments in Color Balance with the Preserve Luminosity button on, which allows you, for example, to radically alter the color balance of a selected object toward red without the object becoming super bright like it would if you made such a radical adjustment in Levels or Curves. There are times when this is very useful.

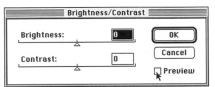

The Brightness/Contrast tool. Moving the sliders to the right increases the brightness or contrast, generating positive numbers in the respective boxes. Moving the sliders to the left decreases brightness or contrast and results in negative numbers.

THE BRIGHTNESS/CONTRAST TOOL

The Brightness/Contrast tool allows you to adjust the brightness and/or contrast of your image using Brightness and Contrast sliders. Usually we adjust the brightness and contrast using Levels or Curves because those tools allow you to also adjust the color balance and highlight/shadow values at the same time. Like the Color Balance tool, I would say that Brightness/Contrast is more of a toy, an entry-level tool. Most professionals use Levels and Curves. The only time you might use Brightness/Contrast is when you don't need to make any color adjustment and need only a subtle brightness or contrast adjustment. We demonstrate an example of its use in the "The Band" chapter: in it, we do a subtle adjustment to match the brightness and contrast of two grayscale channels.

THE VARIATIONS TOOL

The Variations tool is a neat idea, but it has several serious flaws. Variations is useful for the person who is new to color correction and may not know the difference between adding a little cyan and adding a little green to an image. When you use it, you see the current image surrounded by different color correction choices. The main problem with Variations is that you cannot zoom in on the current image or any of its new choices to see the details of what will happen when you make possible changes.

Variations works better on a 19" or 21" monitor, simply because the small images used

The Variations color correction tool shows you the original and current version of the image up in the top-left corner. As you change the current image, you can easily compare it here to the original. The big box in the bottom-left corner shows the current image in the middle surrounded by versions with more green, yellow, red, magenta, blue, or cyan added to it. You click one of these surrounding versions of the image if you like it better. It replaces the current image in the middle of this circle (also at the top), and then another round of new color iterations surround this new current image. On the right side, the current image is in the middle with a lighter one above and a darker one below. Again you can click one of these to make it the current image.

to illustrate the changes are a little bigger on a larger monitor. Still, when you make the changes and say OK to Variations, you are often surprised by how the changes that looked cool in small size inside the Variations dialog have adversely affected certain color areas. Like the Color Balance tool, you can't set precisely where the highlight and/or shadow values begin. You have to adjust highlight and shadow values separately using the radio buttons at the top right of the Variations dialog box. You can't set the highlights or shadows to known values like you can in Levels and Curves.

In Variations, you can also adjust the saturation by selecting the Saturation radio button. The saturation, highlight, and shadow settings show you out-of-gamut colors if you have the Show Clipping box checked. When shadows are going to print as pure black or highlights as pure white, these clipped areas show up as a bright complementary warning color. In Saturation mode, colors that are too saturated for the CMYK gamut show up the same way.

If you are not used to doing color corrections, Variations is a good way to prototype the corrections you want to make. Maybe you'll decide to add some yellow, darken the image, and increase the saturation a bit. After you make these decisions with the aid of Variations, you probably want to go back to Levels, Curves, or Hue/Saturation and make the corresponding changes there. Then you can also set

RGB to CMY Relationship

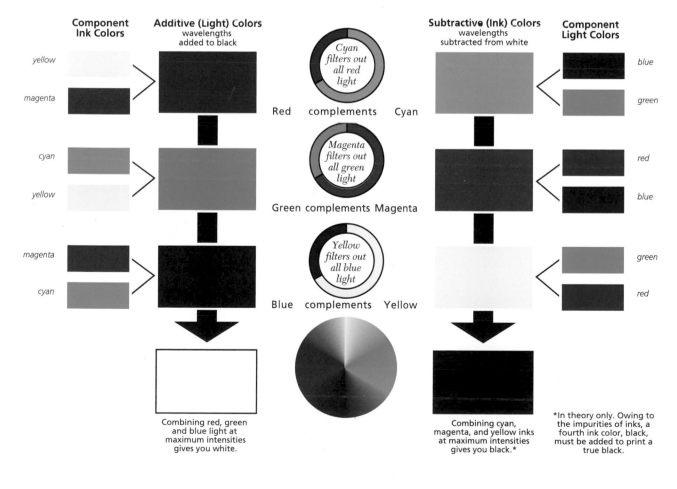

the highlights and shadows more exactly and see the details of the changes you are making as you make them. We do not use Variations in this book. For more details on Variations, see the Photoshop manual.

THE AUTO LEVELS AND DESATURATE COMMANDS

The Auto Levels command does an automatic color correction of your image. I would not recommend using it for quality color control, but it's okay for a quick color fix to an FPO proof. The Desaturate command completely desaturates your image, taking all the hue or color values out of it, leaving you with a black-and-white image in RGB or CMYK mode. Desaturate does not do exactly the same thing as Image/Mode/Grayscale; with Desaturate, the image appears flatter. To convert from color to grayscale, I would correct the color image first and then choose Image/Mode/Grayscale. If you need an RGB image, then convert this grayscale back to RGB. You get better contrast that way.

WHERE TO LEARN MORE

To learn more about the color correction tools mentioned in this overview, read the chapters "Creating the Master Image," "Digital Imaging and the Zone System," and "Setting System and Photoshop Preferences," and do the step-by-step examples in "Grand Canyon," "Kansas," and "Desert Al." The chapters "Yellow Flowers," "Color Matching Images," "The Band," "Versailles," and "Bryce Stone Woman," also have color correction techniques.

Chapter 9: Color Correction Tools

10 SELECTIONS, PATHS, MASKS, AND CHANNELS

Terms and concepts for working with
selections, paths, masks, and channels.

Before you can understand all the possibilities, we first need to explain several important concepts. You need to understand the concept of a selection and how to make a selection using the Photoshop tools. You need to understand what a mask channel is, how to turn a selection into a mask channel, and how to edit a mask channel using different tools to allow you to isolate the necessary parts of an image to achieve a particular effect. This includes understanding what a selection feather or a mask blur is and how these affect the edges of blended selections. We will discuss the concept of opacity, which also affects image blending. We also show you how to effectively use the Channels palette.

MAKING SELECTIONS

Let's start out by talking about the concept of a *selection*—an isolated part of an image that needs special attention. You may want to make this part of the image lighter or darker, or you may want to change its color altogether. You might also select something in an image that you wanted to copy and paste into a different image.

THE SELECTION TOOLS

There are various tools for making selections. The simplest ones are the Rectangular and Elliptical Marquees, which allow you to draw a box or an ellipse around something by clicking at one side of the area you want to isolate and then dragging to the other side. This will create a box or oval-shaped selection that is denoted by dotted lines around the edge. The next level of selection complexity is the Lasso tool, which allows you to draw a freehand shape around the selected objects. Using the Lasso in Photoshop, you can draw either freehand or straight line segments, or combinations of both. Another selection tool is the Magic Wand, which allows you to click a certain color in an image and automatically select adjoining areas based on that color. A totally different way to make selections is to use the Pen tool. The Pen tool creates selections, called paths, that are mathematical descriptions of points joined by straight and curved line segments. With the Pen tool, you can create the most exact paths along subtle curved surfaces. Ultimately though, paths are converted back to normal selections when you are ready to use them to modify your image. Photoshop 5 has added three new selection tools: the Magnetic Lasso, the Magnetic Pen tool, and the Freeform Pen tool.

There are ways to increase the size of a selection and also to select all objects of similar color or brightness within the image. In this chapter, we learn about the

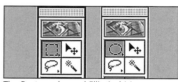

The Rectangular and Elliptical Marquees are the simplest selection tools. Click and drag in the Tool palette on the arrow in the bottom corner of the Rectangular Marquee, or type Shift-M, to change to the Elliptical marquee.

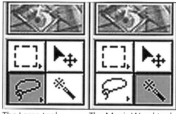

The Lasso tool.   The Magic Wand tool.

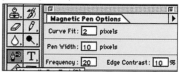

The new Magnetic Lasso (above) and Pen (below) tools automatically trace around the edge of an object depending on the way you set up their parameters.

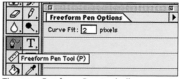

The new Freeform Pen tool allows you to make Pen selections in a similar way to using the Lasso tool.

concept of a selection and how selections fit in with the rest of Photoshop. To learn about using the regular Selection tools and the three new selection tools, go to Chapter 7: The Tool Palette, and Chapter 22: The Car, and for the Pen tool also look at Chapter 30: Bob Goes To… and Chapter 40: The Portable Computer Ad.

WORKING WITH AND INVERSING SELECTIONS

Here you see the Paris Dog Image, in which we have selected the dog using the Lasso tool. When the Dog is selected, anything we do (painting, changing color, and so on) can happen only within the boundaries of the selected area. That is one purpose of a selection, to isolate your work to a particular object or area within the image. If you compare working on an image in Photoshop to painting a mural on a wall, selecting just the dog would be equivalent to putting masking tape everywhere else on the wall, allowing us to paint only on top of the dog. If we choose Select/Inverse, then everything except the dog becomes the selection. Now we have selected the background and not the dog. So, any time you have a selection of an object, you also have, via Select/Inverse, a selection of everything except the object. Returning to the wall analogy, using Select/Inverse would be like removing the masking tape from the background and putting tape over the area of the dog.

CHANGING A SELECTION

Changing a selection is a lot easier than moving masking tape. You can add to any selection made using any of the Marquees, Lasso, or Magic Wand selection tools by using any of these tools with the Shift key down when you create the new selection. You can subtract from a selection by pressing down the Option key when you define the area you want to subtract using these same tools.

SETTING THE FEATHER VALUE

Using most of the selection tools in their default mode is similar to placing masking tape along the edge of the selection, in that there is a defined sharp edge to the selection. Such a selection is said to have a feather value of 0. The selection feather is something that determines how quickly the transition goes from being in the selection to not being in the selection. With 0 feather, the transition is instantaneous. You can change the feather of a selection using the Select/Feather command. If you change the feather of the selection to 20, the transition from being fully selected to being fully unselected would happen over the distance of 40 pixels (actually, at least 20 pixels on either side of the zero feather selection line). If you used this type of feathered masking tape to paint the selection of the dog green, the feather would cause the two colors to fade together slowly over the distance of 40 pixels.

PIXELS AND CHANNELS

A pixel is the basic unit of information within a digital image. Continuous tone digital images (scanned photographs of real objects) are a two-dimensional array of pixels. If the image were 2,000 pixels wide by 1,600 pixels high and we were printing it at 200

Here is the Paris Dog where we have used the Lasso to select just the dog.

The above selection after choosing Select/Inverse.

Dog selection with no feather filled with green.

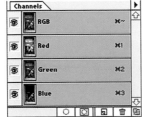

Dog selection with a 20-pixel feather filled with Green.

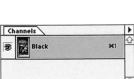

The Channels palette for a grayscale image with the single black channel, Channel #1, which is the image.

The Channels palette for an RGB image. Each of the red, green and blue channels is a grayscale image. You only see color when you view the RGB channel by choosing Command-~ or clicking the name RGB.

pixels per inch, then the image would print at 10 inches wide by 8 inches high (2000/200 = 10, 1600/200 = 8).

If we are working with a black-and-white image, each one of these pixels contains one byte of information, which allows it to have 256 possible gray values. A black-and-white image has one channel in which each pixel is one byte in size. A channel is just a term referring to a two-dimensional array of bytes. If we are working with a RGB color image, it has three channels (one for each of red, green, and blue). A CMYK image has four channels. You can see these channels by choosing Window/Show Channels. In an RGB file, Channel #1 is red, Channel #2 is green, and Channel #3 is blue. There is also an imaginary Channel #~, which allows you to see the red, green, and blue channels at the same time. (This is how you see color.) The RGB channel, Channel #~, is an imaginary channel because it doesn't take up any additional space beyond that which the red, green, and blue channels take up.

SAVING SELECTIONS AS MASK CHANNELS

When you make a selection, you are making what is called a *mask*—the selection masks out the part of the image that you don't select. You can save a selection to a mask channel, which allows you to use it again later or to do further selection editing on the mask with the painting tools. This is especially useful for a complicated selection that you don't want to have to remake later. To do this, choose Select/Save Selection or just click the Save Selection icon at the bottom of the Channels palette. The new mask channel you would create by doing the Save Selection would be named #2 if you were working in a grayscale image and #4 if you were working in an RGB image. When you are working with a grayscale image, Photoshop assumes Channel #1 is the image and Channels #2 and higher are mask channels. In RGB, Photoshop assumes Channels #1, #2, and #3 are red, green, and blue, and that Channels #4 and higher are mask channels. You can rename a mask channel by double-clicking the channel, entering the name you want, and then clicking OK. If you Option-click on the Save Selection icon, the Channel Options dialog box opens as you make the mask channel and you can type in the new name right there.

HOW MASK CHANNELS WORK

A *mask channel* is just another channel like the others we've described. When you save a selection to a mask channel, the parts of the image that you selected show up as white in the mask channel, and the nonselected parts (the masked parts) show up as black. When you have a blend between two partial selections, it shows up as gray in the mask channel. Feathered selection areas also show up as gray. A mask channel has 256 possible gray values, just like any other grayscale image.

Load Selection from Channel or Path.

Save Selection to Channel.

New Channel, Layer, Action or Path.

Throw away Channel, Layer, Path or Action .

LEARN THESE SHORTCUT ICONS AND WHEN TO USE THEM!

Image with dog selected.

Saving this selection using the Save Selection icon.

The mask that gets saved for this selection.

The Channels palette after doing the Save selection and renaming Channel #4 DogMask.

Load Selection the quick way; dragging the mask channel to the Load Selection icon at the bottom of the Channels palette. You can also hold the Command key down and click the Mask channel you want to load.

Load Selection from the menu bar.

EDITING MASK CHANNELS

You can actually edit a mask channel just like you would edit any grayscale image. Sometimes you may want to make a selection using one of the selection tools, save it to a mask channel, and then edit the selection within the mask channel. When you edit a selection, you usually use the selection tools. When you edit a selection saved as a mask channel, you use pixel editing tools, like the Pencil, Paintbrush, and Gradient tools, from the Tool palette. White in a mask means totally selected and black means totally unselected. If you edit a white area to be gray, you make it less selected, or, partially selected. You can edit a black area and make part of it white; doing that adds the white part to the selected area. You may save a selection in a mask channel so you can edit it there, or you may just save it so you can use it again later.

We do many things with mask channels in this book. Sometimes we use the terms selection, mask, and mask channel interchangeably since they all refer to an isolated part of the image. To do something to the image with a mask that is saved in a mask channel, you must first load it as a selection. Choose Select/Load Selection from the menu bar or click the mask channel you want to load and drag it to the Load Selection icon at the bottom left of the Channels palette. You also can load a selection by Command-clicking on the channel you want to load. When a selection is loaded, you can see the marching ants.

Sometimes people get confused about the need to have both selections and mask channels. Remember, a selection actually masks out the nonselected areas of the currently active channel(s) and layer. After you create a selection or do a Load Selection, you can change the active channel(s) or layer within a document and the selection remains. It just always affects what you do to the active channel(s) or layer. A mask channel is just a selection saved for later. Unless the mask channel is currently loaded, it doesn't affect any other channel(s) or layers or anything that you do to them with the painting tools or filters. You can have up to 21 mask channels in an RGB Photoshop document plus the Red, Green, and Blue channels, for a total of 24 channels. You can load any of these mask channels as a selection at any time.

Here are the options you have when you do a Load Selection. The Add, Subtract, and Intersect options only show up if you have an existing selection at the time of the load.

COMBINING SELECTIONS

When you load a selection, you can combine that new selection with any existing selection present before the load. Command-clicking on a mask channel loads it as a new selection and throws out any existing selection. Command-Shift-clicking on a mask channel adds this new selection to any existing selection. Command-Option-clicking a mask channel subtracts this from an existing selection and Command-Option-Shift-clicking on a mask channel intersects the new selection with the existing selection, giving you the parts that the two selections have in common. If you don't want to remember all these command options, they show up in the Load Selection dialog box, which you can access by choosing Select/Load Selection.

DELETING, MOVING, AND COPYING CHANNELS

You can remove a mask channel by clicking that channel and then choosing Delete Channel from the Channels palette's pop-up menu, or by clicking the channel and dragging it to the Trash icon at the bottom right of the Channels palette. If you delete the Red, Green, or Blue channel this way, Photoshop 5 will assume that you want to produce spot color plates of the other 2 channels and will give you cyan, magenta, or yellow channels,

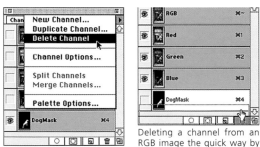

Deleting a mask channel from an RGB image using the Channels palette's pop-up window.

Deleting a channel from an RGB image the quick way by dragging to the Trash icon at the bottom right of the Channels palette.

To copy a channel, drag it to the New Channel icon at the bottom of the Channels palette.

The copied channel appears at the bottom with its name being Alpha1, Alpha2, etc. If you use Duplicate Channel from the Channels palette menu, the new channel will be the same name with "copy" at the end.

To move a channel, click it and then drag it until the line is dark between the channels where you want to put it.

The moved channel appears in its new location.

depending on which of the RGB channels you trashed. If you look at Image/Mode, you'll see that you are now in a Multichannel file.

You can copy any channel, including the Red, Green, and Blue channels, by clicking on the channel and dragging it to the New Channel icon at the bottom of the Channels palette. You also can make a copy of a channel by choosing Duplicate Channel from the Channel palette's pop-up menu.

You can move a channel from one location to another by clicking the channel you want to move and then dragging it until the line becomes dark between the two channels where you want to put this channel. Let go of the mouse at that point and you have moved the channel. You cannot, however, change the location of the original Red, Green, and Blue channels.

USING THE CHANNELS PALETTE EYE ICONS

After you save a selection in a mask channel, you can then work with it in a different way than by just seeing the marching ants lines around the edge of the selection. Notice that the Channels palette has two columns. The left-most column is the thin one that has the Eye icons in it. This column signifies the channels that you are currently seeing—the ones with the Eye icons on. The right-most column is the one that has the name of the channel. Clicking in the right-most column for a particular channel highlights that channel, which signifies that you are working on it. That makes it the Active channel. Clicking in the right-most column for Channel #~ (the RGB composite channel), highlights the Red, Green, and Blue channels because Channel #~ represents all three of them. If you also have a mask channel defined, like the picture here with the dog mask, then there are different things you can do to work with that mask channel in relation to the other channels.

The Eye icons for the Red, Green, and Blue channels normally are turned on, and those channels are highlighted when you are working with an RGB image. The normal state is displayed in this first picture to the right.

Normal state for working in RGB, Channel #~, with Red, Green, and Blue Eye icons on and the DogMask off.

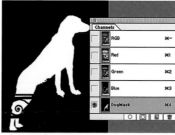

When working on a mask channel directly in black-and-white, you normally have its Eye icon on with its channel grayed. All the other channels have their Eye icons off and they are not grayed.

79

If you click the right-most column of the DogMask channel, that channel becomes the active one. It shows up in black-and-white and if you do any editing with the painting tools, you do so in black-and-white in the DogMask channel. The Eye icons for the RGB channels turn off now. The second picture to the left shows this state.

To change the overlay color, double-click on the mask channel to bring up its Channel Options, click here on the color swatch, and change its color.

If you want to edit the mask channel while also seeing the RGB image, do the following. After you make the mask the active channel by clicking in its right-most column, you can then click the Eye icon column of Channel #~, which turns on the Eye icons for RGB. You will see RGB, but these channels are not active. They are not highlighted, which means that you are seeing them but are still working on the high-lighted DogMask channel. The parts of the mask that are black will show up with an overlay color, usually red. If you paint in black with the Paintbrush tool, you add to this black part of the mask. The paint shows up in the red overlay color. If you paint with white, you add to the selection and subtract from the red overlay color. If you want to change the overlay color, double-click the mask channel to bring up its Channel Options, click on the color swatch, and change its color in the Color Picker. Be sure to leave its opacity at lower than 100% so you can see the picture through the overlay.

If you want to, you can also view the DogMask while working on the RGB image. Click the right-most column of Channel #~, which activates the RGB channels so that when you paint with the Paint-brush, you modify the RGB image. Now if you click the Eye icon column of the DogMask channel, you see this channel as an overlay while working in RGB.

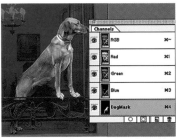

You can also work on a mask while looking at the RGB image too. To get into this state, first click in the second column of the Dog-Mask channel to activate the mask and then click in the first column of Channel #~ to turn on the RGB Eye icons without activat-ing the RGB channels. Here you will be edit-ing the DogMask channel.

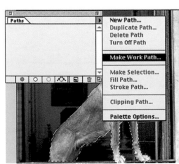

If you want to work on the RGB channels while seeing the mask, first click the right column of Channel #~ to activate RGB, then click in the Eye icon column of the DogMask channel. Here you will be editing the RGB channels.

CONVERTING BETWEEN PATHS AND SELECTIONS

Use the Make Work Path and Make Selection commands in the Paths palette to convert between Selections and Paths or vice versa. To use a Path, you will usually convert it into a selection and then maybe into a Mask channel or a Layer Mask.

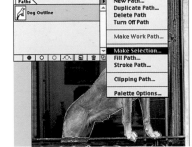

Use Make Work Path from the Paths palette to make a Path from a Selection.

Use Make Selection from the Paths palette to turn a Path into a Selection.

Chapter 10: Selections, Paths, Masks, and Channels

11 LAYERS, LAYER MASKS, AND ADJUSTMENT LAYERS

Terms and concepts for working with layers, adjustment layers, and layer masks, and using them for prototyping and effects variations.

Think of each layer in a RGB Photoshop document as a separate RGB file. Each layer has its own separate Red, Green, and Blue channels. As you look at the layers in the Layers palette, imagine that the one at the bottom of the palette is a photographic print laying on the bottom of a pile of prints on your desk and that each layer above that in the Layers palette is another photographic print laying on top of that bottom one in the order you see them in the palette. You have a pile of photographic prints on your desk. Now imagine that you can look at the top of this pile of photographs and see through them, seeing all of them at the same time, all the way through to the bottom of the pile. It's even better than that because you can control how much of each photo you see, as a percentage of the whole, and you can control what parts of each photo you see. You can run a variety of effects, called Blend modes, on each photo in the pile, so the possible combinations of how you see them all together numbers in the thousands. You can change the order of the photos in the pile and also move them and distort them in relationship to each other. All these things and more is what Photoshop layers allow you to do.

"Night Cab Ride in Manhattan"—an image with many layers. Here we see all the layers. This image, called LayersIntro, is included in the Layers&LayerMasks folder on the CD; open it and play while reading this section.

LAYERS AND CHANNELS

Layers are similar to channels in the ways you move them around, copy them, and delete them. To work with layers, you use the Layers palette, which you activate from Window/Show Layers or by using F10 with ArtistKeys. If you use layers and channels at the same time, which you usually do, you will learn about them faster if you separate the palettes so you can see them in different places onscreen at the same time. Just click the Layers or Channels name tab at the top of that palette and drag it to a new position onscreen. You can then hide or bring up the Channels palette with Window/Show Channels or by pressing Shift-F10 with ArtistKeys.

Each layer is like a separate Photoshop file that you can superimpose on top of other Photoshop layers in the same document. Take a look at the NightCabRide image at the beginning of this chapter; we created it using six layers. Photoshop 5

Making a copy of the Dog layer by dragging it to the New Layer icon. You could also choose Duplicate Layer from the Layer Palette menu to accomplish the same result.

After the Dog Layer has been copied and named Dog Pointillize.

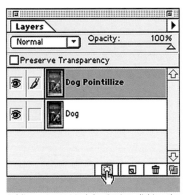

Adding a Layer Mask by Option-clicking the Layer Mask icon. Clicking the Layer Mask icon removes everything but the selection from this layer. Option-clicking removes the selected area. If there is no selection, clicking on the Layer Mask icon selects the entire layer and Option-clicking hides the entire layer.

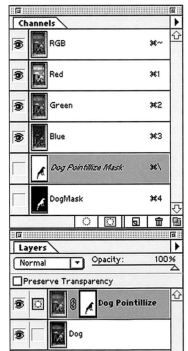

After a Layer Mask is added, it shows up as a thumbnail to the right of the Layer thumbnail in the Layers palette. It also shows up in the Channels palette below the Blue channel. Because the eye icons are on for RGB in the Channels palette but the Layer Mask is active, we can now edit the mask but we will see the changes in RGB.

allows you to have up to 100 layers. Each layer has its own set of Red, Green, and Blue channels. When working with layers, you can view one layer at a time, several layers at a time, or all the layers at once.

A SIMPLE EXAMPLE

Consider the Paris Dog image we were working with in the last chapter. You should open a copy of this from the Layers&LayerMasks folder on your CD. Make sure your Channels and Layers palettes are visible, using Shift-F10 and F10 (if you have ArtistKeys loaded), or by going to Window/Show Channels and Show Layers. You start out with a simple image that has a single layer, called Dog. You can make a copy of this Layer by clicking the Dog layer in the Layers palette and dragging it to the New Layer icon at the bottom of the Layers palette. Holding down the Option key while doing this opens the Duplicate Layer dialog box, where you can give this new layer a name. We will call it Dog Pointillize, because we're going to run the Pointillize filter on it. Notice that the Layers palette now has a second layer above with the name we gave it. New layers come in above the current active layer and they then become the active layer.

Now choose Filter/Pixelate/Pointillize and run the Pointillize filter on this new layer with a value of 5. Because this layer is on top of the Dog layer, you can no longer see the Dog layer. The Dog Pointillize layer has its own set of RGB channels, so now the document is twice as big as it was when we started.

MAKING A LAYER MASK

Do a Load Selection from the DogMask channel in the Channels palette by Command-clicking that channel. Now we have a selection of the dog. Option-click on the Add Layer Mask icon at the bottom left of the Layers palette to add a layer mask to this layer. Notice that the layer mask thumbnail now appears to the right of the Dog Pointillize Layer thumbnail and it is black where the dog is. Also, notice that it shows up in the Channels palette and is called Dog Pointillize Mask. Now the Dog Pointillize layer is removed in the area of the Dog, where the selection was, and you see the original dog in the layer below. If you press Command-I at this point, to invert the Dog Pointillize mask, you can see the original background with the dog now pointillized.

When you first add a layer mask, it comes up in the mode in which you can edit the mask but see RGB. In this mode, the masks thumbnail has a black line around it in the Layers palette and shows up as highlighted (active) in the Channels palette. Option-clicking this layer mask thumbnail in the Layers palette at this point switches you to the mode in which you can edit and see the mask. The Eye icon is now on for the mask and off for RGB in the Channels palette. Option-clicking again returns you to the original mode where you can edit the mask and see RGB. Try this on the ParisDog sample image.

Chapter 11: Layers, Layer Masks, and Adjustment Layers

To edit the layer itself and also see the layer, click the Layer thumbnail in the Layers palette. For each layer in the Layers palette, the Layer thumbnail is the one to the left and the Layer Mask thumbnail is the one to the right. To the left of the Layer thumbnail, in Photoshop, you see an icon that looks like a mask when you are editing the Layer Mask and like a paintbrush when you are editing the Layer itself. The item you are editing also has a black highlight line around it.

When editing the layer, you see the Paint-brush icon to the right of the Eye icon and the Layer thumbnail has the dark highlight.

ADDING AN ADJUSTMENT LAYER

Now click back on the Layer thumbnail for the Dog Pointillize layer (that is, the thumbnail on the left, not the Layer Mask thumbnail on the right). You should now see the Paintbrush icon between it and the Eye icon. Command-click the New Layer icon at the bottom middle of the Layers palette to bring up the New Adjustment Layer dialog box. Enter the name Darken Curve then set the Type to Curves to choose a Curves adjustment layer. Click OK and click in the center of the curve line and drag to pull the curve down and to the right to darken the entire composite. (This works because this new adjustment layer is on top of all the others.) Choose OK. An adjustment layer can be of Type Levels, Curves, Brightness/Contrast, Color Balance, Hue/Saturation, Selective Color, Channel Mixer, Invert, Threshold, or Pos-terize. Although an adjustment layer acts like any other layer, it does not make you pay the price of adding another set of RGB channels for the new layer. The color cor-rection adjustment you make in the adjustment layer applies to all the layers below that adjustment layer. You can turn this correction on and off simply by turning the Eye icon on or off for that particular adjustment layer. If you double-click the name of the adjustment layer, you can actually change the adjustment—in this case, the curve settings—as many times as you want without degrading the color in the file. If you had a selection when you created this new adjustment layer, its layer mask would only darken the selected area. Adjustment layers have only a Layer Mask thumbnail; they don't have a Layer thumbnail because there is actually no RGB data associated with adjustment layers. Notice that you are currently not allowed to click on any of the RGB Channels in the Channels palette because they don't exist for an Adjust-ment layer. Click on this Darken Curve Adjustment layer in the Layers palette and drag it down between the Dog Pointillize layer and the Dog layer until you see a black line form between these two layers. Release the mouse button at that point. This moves the adjustment layer down so that now it darkens only the Dog layer and not the Dog Pointillize layer.

When editing the layer mask, you see the Mask icon to the right of the Eye icon and the Layer Mask thumbnail has the dark highlight.

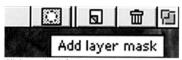

Click on the left-most icon to add a Layer Mask showing only the selected area. Option-click to show the inverted selection.

Click the middle icon to add a Layer. Com-mand-click this icon to add an Adjustment layer.

The New Adjustment Layer dialog box allows you to choose the type of adjustment layer and also give this new layer a name.

You now see *Darken Curve Mask* in the Channels palette below the Blue chan-nel because now the Darken Curves layer is active. Click back on the Dog Pointillize layer to make it active and notice that the Dog Pointillize mask is now below the Blue channel in the Channels palette. Finally, click back on the Dog layer and notice that all the layer masks have been removed from the Channels palette. Only the layer mask, if there is one, for the active layer shows up in the Channels palette. The Dog Mask channel is not associated with any layer, so it continues to be in the Channels palette all the time.

MORE ABOUT LAYERS USING NIGHTCABRIDE

Let's take a look at the NightCabRide image with its several different layers to see how this works. Open the LayersIntro file in the Introduction to Layers folder, and use that file to try out the different options that we discuss here. In the Layers palette for Layers Intro, you see that this image has six layers. Currently, we are

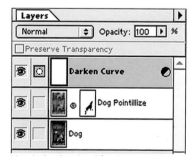

Here is the thumbnail for the Layer Mask of the Darken Curve Adjustment Layer. An Adjustment Layer will always have a Layer Mask, although it is often totally white, showing that the adjustment is happening to the entire image area. Adjustment layers only have a Layer Mask thumbnail; they don't have a Layer thumbnail because there is actually no RGB data associated with adjustment layers.

83

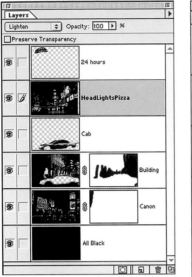

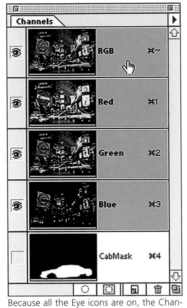

The Layers palette with the HeadLightsPizza layer active and all the Eye icons on. Here we are viewing the largest thumbnails. Choose Palette Options from the Layers palette menu to set the size of your thumbnails.

Because all the Eye icons are on, the Channels palette shows you a view of the Red, Green, and Blue Channel thumbnails of all layers as a composite image.

Option-click on the HeadLights-Pizza layer's Eye icon and all the other layers are no longer visible.

With only the HeadLightsPizza Eye icon on in the Layers palette, you see just that layer's Red, Green, and Blue Channel thumbnails in the Channels palette.

LayersIntro with just the HeadLightsPizza layer visible.

looking at all of them because the Eye icons, in the left column of the Layers palette, are all on.

Imagine that all the layers are in a pile with the bottom layer, here called All Black, at the bottom of the pile. As you add layers on top of this, like Canon, Building, and Cab in this example, they are blended with the layers below them. The active layer, the one that is highlighted, HeadlightsPizza, is the layer that is modified by changing the settings for Opacity and Blend mode at the top of the Layers palette. You click in the right column of the Layers palette to make a layer active. The active layer will also be changed by anything you do with any other Photoshop tools, like the Paintbrush, Levels, or Curves. If you do something to the active layer while all the other layers' Eye icons are on, you can see the changes as they are combined with the other layers, but the other layers themselves do not change.

The Channels palette shows you the Channel thumbnails and Eye icon state for the layer you are working on. What you see in the Channels palette depends on the layer you have activated and which Eye icons are on in that layer and other layers. If you just want to work on that one layer and see only that layer, you can click the Eye icons of the other layers to turn them off. Another, quicker, way to turn them all off is to Option-click the Eye icon in the Layers palette of the layer you want to work on. Doing that also changes the RGB display of the Channel thumbnails in the Channels palette so that you see just the Red, Green, and Blue channel info of the one layer. To turn all the other layers back on again, just Option-click again the same layer's Eye icon in the Layers palette. Also, then, the RGB channel thumbnail display in the Channels palette once again shows a composite of all the visible layers.

THE BACKGROUND LAYER

If you open any single layer image into Photoshop, like a TIFF file for example, and look at the Layers palette, you will notice that the image's layer is called Background. It is called Background in italics because the Background layer differs from a normal layer. The Background layer, when it has that name, must be the bottom layer and cannot have any transparent areas. If you make a selection in the Background layer and clear or delete that selection, the selected area fills with the background color (usually white). If you delete a selection in any other layer, that area fills with transparency (the checkerboard pattern). Transparency is a hole where you can look through a layer and see other layers below it. You cannot move other layers below the Background layer or move the Background layer above other layers. To convert a layer from a Background layer into a normal layer, just double-click it and give it a new name. It becomes a normal layer and you can move it above other layers, as well as create transparent areas in it. The Background layer determines the initial canvas size for your layered document. You want to make sure the canvas is large enough to encompass the parts you want to see in all your layers. Therefore, you may

Chapter 11: Layers, Layer Masks, and Adjustment Layers

want to put your largest picture element, often your main background, down as your first layer. If you add additional layers that are larger in horizontal or vertical pixel dimensions than your Background layer, you can see only as much of the image as fits on the Background layer onscreen. However, you can still move these other layers by using the Move tool to expose parts left hanging outside the canvas area. In Photoshop, these parts that hang off the edge are permanently cropped only when you use the Cropping tool or the Image/Crop command. To expose these parts of the image, you can always increase the canvas size using Image/Canvas Size.

When you turn off the other Eye icons and look at the Cab layer alone, the transparent area appears as a checkerboard.

WORKING WITH ADDITIONAL LAYERS

When you add additional layers that are smaller than the *Background* layer, or if you copy a small item and do an Edit/Paste with it, the extra area around these smaller items shows up as transparent (a checkerboard pattern). When we look at just the Cab layer in this NightCabRide image, we see that it's entirely transparent aside from the cab itself. Through those transparent parts, when all the Eye icons are on, we will see the lights and buildings from the other three layers below the cab.

DRAG AND DROP, MOVING, AND LINKING

You create additional layers in Photoshop by copying something from another image and then choosing Edit/Paste. You can name these layers by double-clicking them in the Layers palette. Using the Move tool, you can also click a layer in the main document window, or the Layers palette in image A, and drag and drop it on top of image B's main document window to create a new layer in image B. In Photoshop, you can also drag and drop a whole set of layers if they're linked together. Having one layer in a perspective set active, you can link other layers to it by clicking on the Link column (the one to the right of the Eye icon) of the other layers you want to link to it. Layers that are linked can all be Moved and Transformed (scaled, rotated, and so on) together. This is a great feature of Photoshop especially for Web and multimedia designers.

Moving the cab and building with the Move tool.

You can move layers from side to side or up and down using the Move tool. Just click to activate the layer you want to move in the Layers palette, then select the Move tool from the Tool palette (V or the Command key), click and drag on the layer in the main document window, and drag it to its new location. If you have all the Eye icons on, you can see its relationship to the other layers change.

The moved cab and building.

You can influence layers using the Opacity and Blend modes. The Cab layer is partially transparent because its opacity is set to 85%. The reason that it looks like you are seeing headlights through the cab, however, is that the Blend mode on the Head-LightsPizza layer is set to Lighten.

The Layers palette setup for moving the cab and building that are linked together. Notice that the cab opacity is set to 85%.

MORE ABOUT LAYER MASKS

If you want part of a layer to be temporarily removed, or made invisible, you can add a layer mask to any layer. The parts of the layer mask that are black are transparent in that layer, which allows you to instantly prototype a layer and its composite with the other layers without seeing the masked-out part. If you later decide you want to restore that part of the image, just remove the layer mask by Shift-clicking its thumbnail to turn it off. When you activate a layer that has a layer mask, that mask is also added to the channels in the Channels palette. It only appears in the Channels palette while you have that layer activated. If you want to edit the layer mask while still looking at the layer, just click the layer mask's

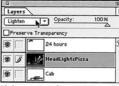

Lighten mode causes the headlights, and not their black background, to show through the cab. Try Normal mode instead of Lighten mode here to see the difference.

The Building layer without its layer mask. Only the hole where the car will sit is transparent.

The Building layer mask.

The Building layer with its layer mask removing the newly transparent areas from the final composite.

thumbnail within the Layers palette. When you paint with black in the main document window, you add the black to the layer mask and remove those areas from view in the layer associated with the layer mask.

In Photoshop, you can create a layer mask by choosing Layer/Add Layer Mask/Reveal Selection or by clicking the New Layer Mask icon that is leftmost at the bottom of the Layers palette. If you have a selection at the time of that click, the selected area will become the only thing that is white in the mask and therefore the only visible part of that layer. If you choose Layer/Add Layer Mask/Hide Selection or Option-click the New Layer Mask icon, everything except the selected area will now be visible and the selected area will be made black in the layer mask.

If you want to edit the layer mask while looking at the mask itself, Option-click the layer mask's thumbnail within the Layers palette. The main document window will now just display the black-and-white mask and your Layers palette will have all the Eye icons dimmed out. The Channels palette now shows this layer mask channel as active with its Eye icon on. When you want to return to editing the layer itself, click the layer's thumbnail within the Layers palette.

MOVING, REMOVING, AND COPYING LAYERS

You can remove a layer by clicking it, choosing Delete Layer from the Layer palette's pop-up menu, or clicking the layer and dragging it to the Trash icon at the bottom right of the Layers palette.

You can make a copy of any layer by clicking the layer and dragging it to the New Layer icon, the middle icon at the bottom of the Layers palette. You can also make a copy of the active layer by choosing Duplicate Layer from the Layers palette's pop-up menu. The copied layer will have the same name but with "copy" appended to its end.

You can move a layer from one location to another in the Layers palette by clicking the layer you want to move and then dragging it until the line becomes dark between the two layers where you want to put this layer. Let go of the mouse at that point, and the layer is moved. When you move a layer, it changes the composite relationship of that layer with the layers around it. Notice how the headlights no longer show through the cab after you move the HeadlightsPizza layer from above the cab to below the cab.

To edit the layer mask while still looking at the layer, just click the layer mask's thumbnail. You will see the Layer Mask thumbnail to the right of the Layer thumbnail. The Channels palette will display the mask as above, active, with its Eye icon off. The Eye icons are on for RGB, so you see those channels, yet you edit the mask because it is active.

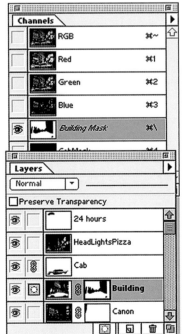

To edit the layer mask and see just the mask in the Document window, Option-click the Layer mask's thumbnail. You will see the Layer mask thumbnail to the right of the Layer thumbnail. The Channels palette will display the mask highlighted with the Eye icon on as above. The Eye icons are off for the RGB channels because you don't want to see them. Now Option-clicking the layer mask's thumbnail will toggle between just seeing the layer mask and then seeing the RGB channels but you will always be editing the mask until you click the Layer thumbnail again or click on RGB in the Channels palette.

Chapter 11: Layers, Layer Masks, and Adjustment Layers

GROUPING, LINKING AND ALIGNING LAYERS

A layer can be Grouped with the Layer or Layers below it. The bottom layer in a group determines the transparency for the entire group. This means that if the bottom layer in the group has a layer mask that removes its center portion, that same center area will be removed from all the layers in the group. To group a layer with the one below it, choose Layer/Group With Previous (Command-G). You can always ungroup a layer later by choosing Layer/Ungroup (Command-Shift-G). You can also group or ungroup a layer with the one below it by Option-clicking the line between the two layers. It is obvious when layers are in a group because the bottom layer in the group has its name underlined because this layer determines the transparency for the group. The other layers above it in the group are all indented to the right with dotted lines between them.

By clicking in the middle column of a layer in the Layers palette, that layer can be linked with the currently Active layer. When you click in this middle column, the link icon will show up letting you know this layer is linked to the currently active layer. More than one layer can be linked together and when you activate a layer, all the layers that are linked to it will have this link icon in their middle column. If you move or scale any of the layers that are linked together, they will all move or scale together proportionately. If you drag and drop any layer that has others linked to it, those other layers will also be copied to the other document. This allows you to link together a group of layers that represent a button, for example, and then drag that button, with all its layers, to any other document. You could use this feature to make up a Photoshop library file of the buttons you use most often. When you need a particular button, just drag and drop one of its layers and they all come along for the ride. This is a very powerful feature especially for Web and multimedia people who use the same elements over and over again.

If you have a bunch of layers linked together and one of them is the active layer, you can use the new Photoshop 5 Layer/Align Linked to align the rest of the linked layers with the active layer in six possible ways: Top, Vertical Center, Bottom, Left, Horizontal Center, Right. Remember, the results of the Align Linked command will depend on the layer that is currently active. There is also a new Layer/Distribute Linked choice which will distribute the linked layers evenly in the same six ways. If you currently have a selection on the screen, you can use the new Layer/Align to Selection to align the currently active layer and any that are linked to it to the selection in the same six possible ways. For examples of how to use these alignment features, see Chapter 40:

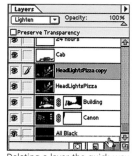

Deleting a layer the quick way by using the Trash icon at the bottom of the Layers palette. If the Layer is active, you can just click the Trash icon. If you don't want the delete warning message to come up, just Option-click.

To copy a layer, drag it to the New Layer icon at the bottom of the Layers palette. Just clicking this icon creates a new blank layer with a generic name, or an Option-click allows you to name it while creating it.

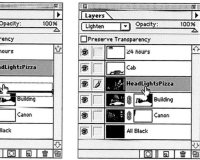

To move a layer, click on it and drag it until the line is dark between the layers where you want to put it.

The moved layer appears in its new location now below the cab.

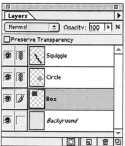

Here are three linked layers. Doing a Layer/Align Linked/Left will align the left edge of the nontransparent parts of the other two layers with the left edge of the Box layer because Box is the active layer.

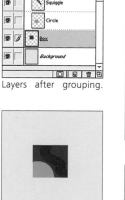

Layers before grouping.

Layers after grouping.

Image before grouping

Image after grouping

Before Align Left.

After Align Left.

Double-click a layer to get the Layer Options for that layer. Layer Options allows you to name a layer and change its opacity and blend mode. It also allows you to set the range of pixel values that come from This Layer as well as the range of pixel values that come from the cumulative effect of the current composite of all the layers underlying this layer. The This Layer and Underlying options are very powerful, as you will see later in this book.

The Portable Ad, Chapter 41: Creating Shadows and Edge Effects, and Chapter 35: South Africa In Focus.

THE LAYER OPTIONS DIALOG BOX

If you double-click a layer, you bring up the Layer Options dialog box, which enables you to name a layer, group it with other layers, or composite it using only a partial range of its 0–255 pixel values. This partial compositing feature is very powerful! Chapter 38: Posterize, Bitmaps, and Patterns, Chapter 36: Blend Modes, Calculations, and Apply Image, and Chapter 35: South Africa in Focus explain Layer Options in great detail.

FLOATING SELECTIONS

When you have made any type of selection and it is highlighted on the screen with the dotted lines moving around it (those marching ants), you can now choose Command-option and then click and drag to float that selection. A floating selection is another copy of the pixels of the active layer in that selected area floating on top of the original layer below. A floating selection is sort of like a temporary layer although in Photoshop 5 it doesn't show up in the Layers palette. To change the opacity and blend mode of a floating selection in Photoshop 5, you now need to use the Filter/Fade command. Before Photoshop had layers, it always had floating selections and they were more powerful. In older versions of Photoshop, all the things we do with layers today had to be done one at a time using a floating selection. You can only have one floating selection at a time and when you deselect it, by clicking outside it or choosing Select/None or by running a filter or any command on it, it becomes embedded in the layer it is floating above. At that point, you can no longer move it. A layer, on the other hand, is like a permanent floating selection and you can have many layers. Layers don't go away like floating selections do. In Photoshop 5, you can no longer turn a floating selection into a full-fledged layer by double-clicking it in the Layers palette. If you really want a layer from a selection though, just choose Command-J (Layer/New/Layer Via Copy) to create a new layer with a copy of the current selection. Floating selections had most of their power removed in Photoshop 5. (It might be simpler if Adobe removed them completely.) If you used floating selections a lot before, you should learn to do things with layers now! In Photoshop 5, if you do a Paste on top of an individual channel in the Channels palette, you get a Floating Selection that also doesn't show up in the Layers palette and you must use Filter/Fade to change its mode or opacity.

CONTROL KEY (RIGHT MOUSE BUTTON) CONTEXT-SENSITIVE MENUS

If you Control-click while working in the Move tool, you will get some very useful context-sensitive menus. On Windows systems, you use the right mouse button instead of doing Control-click. When you are using the Move tool, or with Control-Command-click if not in the Move tool (Control Right mouse for Win), you get a context-sensitive menu showing all the layers with Eye icons on that have pixels at the current mouse location. You can then drag through this menu to activate the layer you want to work on. If you are in a selection tool or a painting tool, you will get a different context-sensitive menu. These context-sensitive menus are great power user tools!

Chapter 11: Layers, Layer Masks, and Adjustment Layers

12 HISTORY PALETTE, HISTORY BRUSH, AND SNAPSHOTS

Using the History palette, History Brush, and the new Photoshop 5 Snapshot features to give you added power with Photoshop 5.

You can bring up this History Options dialog from the History palette menu and use it to set the Maximum History States to up to 100 levels of Undo. You can also turn on Allow Non-Linear History, which will then no longer automatically throw away future history when you go back into the past and change the sequence of events by entering a new command.

The simple explanation for the History palette is that it allows Photoshop 5 to have up to 100 levels of Undo. Actually though, the History palette allows a lot more flexibility than that. between the History palette, the History Brush, and the way they work with the new Snapshot design, you initially wonder if this is yet another flavor of Layers. There are some important distinctions between using History with snapshots versus layers and as we will explain, they can be used in different and also similar ways, but the reasons for using one versus the other are quite distinctly different.

THE SIMPLE CASE OF USING HISTORY

Every time you do a Photoshop 5 command that changes your image, that command gets saved in the History palette. It may be creating a new Layer, painting a stroke in your file or even using the Levels command. In the History palette, you see a

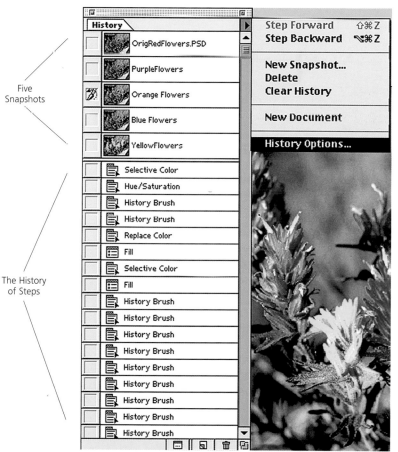

Here we see the History palette with five snapshots at the top and then a long list of commands in the lower section. In this photo all the original flowers were red. I used Selective Color, Hue/Saturation, and Replace color to make versions of this image with all Purple, Orange, Blue, and Yellow flowers. As I did this, I made a snapshot of each set of colored flowers. I then kept changing the source of the History Brush, currently set to the Orange Flowers snapshot, as I painted with the History Brush to recolor any flower with any of the five colors. If you wanted to be able to change the colors again after saving the file, you would use Adjustment layers to get a similar effect with lasting flexibility. All this history information goes away when you close or quit!

The Photoshop 5 Edit/Fill command, which now has the Use History option. This allows you to Fill a selection, or your entire Layer, from any previous History or Snapshot state.

Create a new Snapshot from the current history state.

Create a new Document reflecting the image at the current history state.

list of all the commands you have done in order from the oldest on top to the newest on the bottom. As it has always been, Command-Z toggles between Undo and Redo of the last command you did. Command-Option-Z now marches back up the history chain undoing command after command. Command-Shift-Z goes back and redoes those same commands in the same order they were originally done.

At any time you can create a Snapshot that will remember the state of your image at that particular point. In Photoshop 5, you can have multiple Snapshots and they are all saved at the top of the History palette. Photoshop is by default set up to automatically take a Snapshot of your image when you first enter the program. This Snapshot is used to implement the Revert to Saved type commands. The Erase, Paint, and Fill from Saved and Snapshot options in the Photoshop 4 Eraser, Rubber Stamp tool, and Fill commands have all been replaced in Photoshop 5 by Erase, Paint, or Fill from History. This is now much more flexible! To paint from History, you need to use the History Brush. This is a new painting tool that paints from your image as it existed at a particular state within the History palette. Clicking in the left-most column of the History palette next to any Snapshot or History State sets the History Brush to paint on your current image with the image as it looked at that previous point in history. See the Case Study with flowers on page 92 for an example of how this is used. You are not just painting with what that particular step did; you are painting with the cumulative effect of everything you did up to and including that state. This is cool stuff because it makes certain things, like painting with any of the tools that use brushes, much more undoable, repeatable, and totally flexible.

MAKING SNAPSHOTS AND DOCUMENT COPIES ALONG THE WAY

When you use the History palette's New Snapshot menu or the middle icon at the bottom of the History palette to create a Snapshot, this saves not only the current appearance of your image on the screen but also its selection state and the state of the Layers palette and the rest of the file. This is a lot more than the old Take Snapshot command. You can take a Snapshot at any time whenever you want to make sure you can get back to this point within your document. If you crop your image after taking a Snapshot, you may not be able to paint from this snapshot onto the current state of the document because that state will now have a different Canvas Size. Just like in the older versions of Photoshop, you could not Rubber Stamp from Saved if the saved file had a different crop size. Also, remember that snapshots do not survive after a crash, so you should still save the file often enough to protect from any system failure. If you are in the middle of a project using Snapshots and you have to close the file, you can make documents of the Snapshots you want to save and then drag the opening snapshots from those documents back into the window of your original document when you reopen it. The snapshots will return to the History palette, and you can continue to paint from those snapshots as long as the image size of the snapshot and the current state of the file are the same. Or you could make new layers and use Edit/Fill/From Snapshot for each snapshot that you want to save.

You can click in the left-most icon at the bottom of the History palette to create a new document showing the image at the current History state. This is like choosing Image/Duplicate, except you don't get the Merged Layers Only choice and the new document will automatically be given the name of the command you just finished doing in the current History palette. This new document will now have its own empty History palette and its own empty set of Snapshots and History states, which you will develop as you start to work on it. All the Layers are copied into the new document. This allows you to branch off in several directions from a particular state in the history of your image and then explore all the options, each in its own document, until you are happy with the outcome. After working in a new document, you can always go back to the document it came from and all its history will still be intact. This is somewhat subtle but very powerful, especially for creative people who like to try a lot of options.

PAINTING FROM THE FUTURE

To choose where the History Brush paints from, you click in the leftmost column next to a particular History or Snapshot state. The History Brush will then paint on your current layer from that particular past state of your file. If you click in the left column of the History palette to set the History Brush on a certain state, and then click in the right column of the History palette to return the working image to a previous state that happened before your History Brush state, your image returns to that previous state. If you start entering more commands, they will enter after the current History state, that previous state, and all states between the current History state and your History Brush state will be removed. The state of your History Brush stays there, sort of in the future, as long as that is the location where your History Brush will be painting from. This allows you to, in a way, paint from the future.

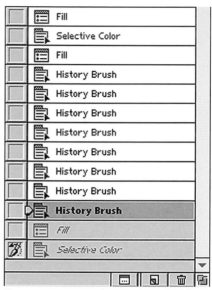

Here we see a case where we have the History Brush set on the command called Selective Color, which is in front of the current state we are working on in the History palette. This allows you to paint from the future!

LINEAR VERSUS NON-LINEAR HISTORY

You can turn on the Allow Non-Linear History option by choosing History Options from the History palette. When you do this, the History system does not throw away future History states. Say you enter 10 commands so you have a History palette with 10 things in it. Normally, if you click the fifth thing to return your image to that previous state, states 6–10 disappear as soon as you do another command. That new command appears at position 6 and states 6–10 are removed. When you turn on Allow Non-Linear History, then states 6–10 stay in the History palette, without actually appearing in your image and that new command appears at position 11. Your actual image, however, appears as it would if you had done states 1–5 and then state 11. Still, if you clicked back onto state 8, for example, the effects of states 9–11 go away and you would be back where you would have been if you never returned to state 5 and then did the new state 11. Non-Linear History makes finding a state in the History palette a bit more confusing, but it always leaves you the option of returning to one of those previously removed states.

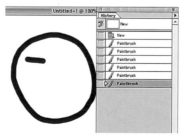

1. Here we have used five strokes of the Paintbrush to paint a face. Let's say we like the head but don't like the eyes, nose and mouth. We can click back on the first Paintbrush command, which drew the head, and the other strokes will be turned off.

2. With Linear History, when we make that first paint stroke to draw the new eye, the old paint strokes for the eyes, nose, and mouth go away.

3. With Allow Non-Linear History turned on, the first stroke to draw a new eye skips the old strokes for the eyes, nose, and mouth and starts in a position beyond those. This gives you the option to return to the old face by clicking the stroke just above the currently highlighted one. It also gives you the option to use the History Brush to paint any of those old face parts onto a new face where you might want just one part from the old face.

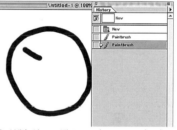

4. Here, using Non-Linear History, I have painted a second set of eyes and a second nose; then I used the History Brush to paint the old mouth back in from the previous History state. That old mouth state would not have been there if I had not had Allow Non-Linear History turned on.

91

A History Case Study with Flowers

I opened a photograph of some red flowers taken in the high sierras at Yosemite. I wanted to have this same picture with multiple flower colors. (I wouldn't actually do this to one of my "true nature" photos.) Without making any selections, I used either Replace Color, Selective Color, or Hue/Saturation to change the color of all the flowers to first Purple, then Orange, then Blue, and finally Yellow. After each new color, I used the middle icon at the bottom of the History palette to create a Snapshot of all the flowers at each of these four new colors. I then clicked in the leftmost column of the Original Red Flowers Snapshot to set the History Brush there and followed that by a Fill from History to return my current state to the original red flowers. I then used one of the color change commands to change this red into yet another color. After I had the five colors I wanted, I then refilled back to all red. Next, I set the History Brush onto one of the other colors by clicking in the left-most column of its Snapshot. At that point, I used the History Brush to paint over some of the red flowers with flowers of new colors. I just had to reset the History Brush source on a different color Snapshot when I wanted to change colors. With this setup, I could paint over each flower as many times as I wanted and could even go back to the original red flowers at any time. The only problem is that when I close the file or quit Photoshop, my neat Snapshot/History setup goes away. To see how to change the color of objects, check out Chapters 22: The Car Ad, 25: Yellow Flowers, and 27: Color Matching Images. To see how to set this type of situation up with Layers so you can make changes to the flower colors even after saving the file, check out Chapter 29: Bryce Stone Woman, Chapter 32: Versailles, and the other Layer color correction examples.

Here you can see the five different color Snapshots at the top of the History palette. I'm currently painting with the History Brush from the Blue Flowers Snapshot to change this flower from Red to Blue.

The original photo with the actual red flowers.

The photo after modifying the flowers using the History palette and its Snapshots along with the History Brush.

HISTORY ALL GOES AWAY WHEN YOU CLOSE OR QUIT

If you are doing anything where you want several options created in a way that you can later reopen and change them, you should use Layers, Layer Masks, and Adjustment Layers to give yourself that ability. By turning layers on and off, modifying Layer masks and switching the settings in Adjustment Layers, you can make almost anything changeable in a variety of ways. You can also now do this in a sometimes simpler way with the History palette. The trouble with the History palette is that it gets cleared every time you close the file and reopen it. Also, if you made a change in the History palette, like a Curves setting, for example, you cannot go back to that History state and double-click it to see what the actual change was, like you could with an Adjustment Layer; you can only click that state and your image returns to where it was at that state. You can also paint with the History Brush on your current state from the image in that previous state. This History Brush feature adds a lot of power to History, Snapshots, and Photoshop.

CREATING A MASTER

COLOR SPACES AND COLOR MANAGEMENT

CALIBRATION

OVERALL COLOR CORRECTION

THE ZONE SYSTEM FOR DIGITAL IMAGES

MASTER IMAGE WORKFLOW

SCANNING, RESOLUTION, HISTOGRAMS, AND PHOTO CD

DIGITAL IMAGE

This 4x5 was taken in Yosemite using Fuji Velvia film, scanned with a Tango drum scanner, and corrected in Lab color using Photoshop 5.

13 DIGITAL IMAGING AND THE ZONE SYSTEM

Digital imaging as it relates to traditional
photography and the Zone System, and
how to create a high-quality original photograph.

Images in nature that you see with your eyes have the greatest beauty because they usually are illuminated by very wonderful light and have depth and texture that we can only simulate on a print or computer screen. The range of light, from the darkest black shadow to the brightest sparkling highlight, reflected from reality to our eyes is far greater than we can reproduce in any printed or screen image. Our eyes can adjust as we gaze into a shadow or squint to see a bright detail. When you look at a scene in nature, it has the best quality and the most detail. The T.V. set, which we watch so much, has the least amount of detail and sharpness. Go out and see the real world!

TRANSITIONS TO THE DIGITAL WORLD

There are many reasons to copy a scene from nature, a pretty face, or a product and reproduce the image so it can be carried around and seen again. How to do this, and get the best quality, is an important subject of this book. I give thanks to Ansel Adams, perhaps the most well-known nature photographer, and his great series of books, *The Camera, The Negative,* and *The Print,* for my introduction to an understanding of artistic photography. These titles by New York Graphic Society Books are must-reads for anyone who wants to understand how to take the best quality photographs. *Ansel Adams: An Autobiography* is also a wonderful book. Many of Adams' discussions are about black-and-white photography, but the concepts still apply to color and even digital imaging. The depth and joy of his philosophies are something all people who deal with images should have a feeling for.

Although he died in 1984, before digital imaging became easily available and popular, Ansel Adams was ahead of his time and says in his book *The Negative:*

> *"I eagerly await new concepts and processes. I believe that the electronic image will be the next major advance. Such systems will have their own inherent and inescapable structural characteristics, and the artist and functional practitioner will again strive to comprehend and control them."*

This chapter should help you to understand the nature of an original image and how to control and improve it in the digital world.

ACHIEVING YOUR VISUALIZATION

The Zone System, developed by Ansel Adams in 1940, gives photographers a way to measure an image in nature and then capture it on film so it can be reproduced with the photographer's intentions in mind. Adams uses the term "visualization" to explain a technique where photographers imagine what they want a photo to look like as a print before taking the photo. Once this image, the visualization, is in the photographer's mind, the photographer uses the Zone System to get the correct data on the film so that visualization can be achieved in the darkroom. Getting the right data on the film or into a digital camera is very important in the process of creating a digital image too. We use the Zone System to explain what the right data is, and then we discuss how to get that data onto film or into a digital camera. If you get the right data into a digital camera, you can transfer it directly into your computer. When you capture the image on film, you need to scan it correctly to make sure all the information gets into your computer.

CAPTURING THE DYNAMIC RANGE

When you look at an image in nature or in a photography studio, you can use a photographic light meter to measure the range of brightness in the image. On a very sunny day, out in the bright sun, you may have a very large range of brightness between the brightest and darkest parts of your image area. We will call this range, from the brightest to the darkest part of an image, the *dynamic range* of that image. Each photographic film, and each digital camera, has its own dynamic range of values from brightest to darkest that the particular film or camera can capture, called its *exposure latitude*. Many photographic films and digital cameras cannot capture the full dynamic range of brightness present in the original scene, especially on a bright contrasty day. I'm sure you have all taken photographs where the prints don't show any details in the shadows or where a bright spot on a person's forehead is totally washed out. The objective of the Zone System is to measure, using a light meter, the brightness range in the original scene and then adjust your camera so the parts of that brightness range that you want to capture actually get onto the film or into the digital camera.

DIVIDING AN IMAGE INTO ZONES

The Zone System divides an image into 11 zones from the brightest to the darkest. Ansel Adams uses Roman numerals to denote the zones from 0 to X. These zones in the printed image reference how light or dark each area will be. Zone 0 is pure black where there is no detail showing whatsoever. In a photograph, a Zone 0 area would be solid black; in a halftone you would see no white dots in the solid black ink. Zone I is still a very dark black, but it is not pure black and has no real measurable detail. If you look at a Zone I halftone with the naked eye, it still looks black without detail, but if you were to use a loupe or other magnifier, you would see very small white dots in a sea of black ink.

On the other end of the scale, Zone X is solid white, so in a print this would be the color of the paper; in a halftone there would be no dots in a Zone X area. You would use Zone X to represent a specular highlight like the reflection of the sun on a chrome bumper. Zone IX is a very bright white without detail, but again you can see some very small halftone dots if you use a loupe. The range of image brightness areas that will have obvious detail in the printed image include Zone II through Zone VIII. Zone VIII will be very bright detail and Zone II will be very dark detail. In the middle of this area of print detail is Zone V. In a black-and-white print, Zone V would print as middle gray, halfway between pure black and pure white. In a color print, a Zone V area would print as normal color and brightness for that area if you were looking at it in normal lighting conditions with your eyes adjusted to it. When you set the exposure setting on your camera, areas in the image that have a brightness equal to that exposure setting are getting a Zone V exposure. We will explain this further in this chapter.

GETTING A GOOD EXPOSURE

Let's talk for a moment about how you take a picture with a camera. We will use black-and-white negative and color positive transparency as examples in this discussion. Normally, when you take a transparency picture with a camera, you measure the range of brightness in the original scene and set the exposure on your camera so as to reproduce the range of brightness on the film to look the same way it did in the original scene. When you use an automatic exposure camera, the camera does this for you. When you use a manual camera with a hand-held light meter, you need to do it manually. Even though many of you probably have automatic cameras as I do, let's describe the manual camera process so we all understand what needs to happen to take a good picture. The automatic cameras of today have computerized light meters that do all this for you, although you sometimes still need to do it manually to get exactly what you want. This discussion also applies to getting a good exposure with a digital camera.

MEASURING THE BRIGHTNESS

To get a good exposure, you need to measure the brightness range of different subjects within the photograph. Let's say you were taking a photograph of a Spanish home in Costa Rica. You want to set the exposure somewhere in the middle of the brightness range that occurs naturally in the setting. That middle position, wherever you set it, then becomes Zone V. A hand-held spot light meter allows you to point at any very small area in a scene and measure the amount of light reflected from that area. The light meter measures the brightness of light, the *luminance*, reflected from the metered part of the image. Unless you plan to use filters or different film to modify the light's color, this is all you really need to measure regardless of whether you are taking a black-and-white or color photo.

In the Spanish home picture, the brightest areas are the little bit of sky at the top and the reflection of the sun in the right side of the window frame at the bottom. The darkest areas are the shadows in the bottom right corner. Measuring these with a light meter that allows spot readings might produce readings like exposure value 17 for the bright section of sky at the top and exposure value 7 for the dark shadow at the bottom. Each change in the exposure value settings on a professional light meter is equal to a difference of two in the amount of light measured.

In the building picture, if we have exposure value readings from 7 in the darkest area to 17 in the brightest area, there is a difference of 1,024 times the brightness from the darkest amount of light to the brightest amount of light. This is because each jump in the exposure value represents twice as much light. Here's

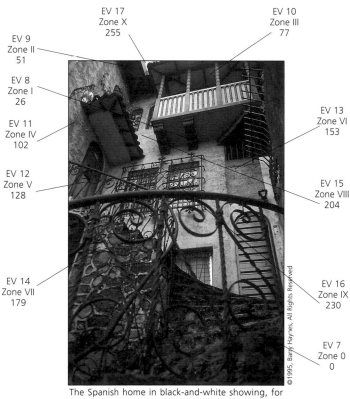

EV 17
Zone X
255

EV 10
Zone III
77

EV 9
Zone II
51

EV 8
Zone I
26

EV 13
Zone VI
153

EV 11
Zone IV
102

EV 12
Zone V
128

EV 15
Zone VIII
204

EV 14
Zone VII
179

EV 16
Zone IX
230

EV 7
Zone 0
0

The Spanish home in black-and-white showing, for each zone, the exposure value (EV) read by an exposure meter, the corresponding zones, and lastly the 0 to 255 digital value based on placing Zone V at exposure value 12 on the door.

how we get 1,024 times as much light: exposure value 7 = 1 (the lowest amount of light), EV 8 = 2 (twice as much light), EV9 = 4, EV10 = 8, EV11 = 16, EV12 = 32, EV 13 = 64, EV14 = 128, EV15 = 256, EV16 = 512, EV17 (the brightest reading) = 1024. This is 1024 times as much light from the darkest area to the brightest.

PLACING THE ZONE V EXPOSURE

After measuring the range of exposure values within a scene that you want to photograph, you usually set the camera's exposure to a value in the middle of that range. The value that you set your exposure to causes the areas that have that exposure value within the scene to show up as a middle gray value on the film and print in black-and-white or as a normal middle detail exposure in color. Where you set your exposure on the camera is called "where you are placing your Zone V exposure." Here we are placing our Zone V exposure at exposure value 12, the reading we got from the door. Usually you set your exposure to the area within the image that you want to look best or most normal. If a person were standing on the steps in this photo, you might set the exposure to a reading that you would take off the person's face.

When you decide where to set the exposure, you affect what happens to each of the zones within the image area, not just Zone V. If the Spanish home image were a transparency, it would reflect an exposure where you set Zone V based on the reading taken from the middle of the door. If the film is then processed correctly, the middle of the door in the transparency would look correct, as though you were looking straight at it with your eyes adjusted to it. When you set the exposure to the middle of the door, the areas that are lighter or darker around it, the zones above and below Zone V, become correspondingly lighter or darker on the film. The bright window, at exposure value 16, will then be placed at Zone IX and will show up as very bright and with almost no detail on the film. This is because it is four zones above, or 16 times brighter than, where we set our exposure (at exposure value 12).

If you were to set the exposure on the camera to exposure value 16, the exposure value for the bright window, you would do to the camera and film what happens to your eye when you

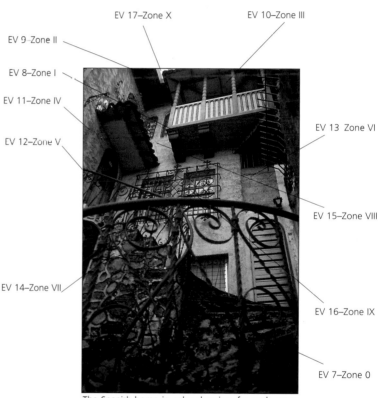

The Spanish home in color showing, for each zone, the exposure value read by an exposure meter and the corresponding zone based on placing Zone V at exposure value 12 on the door. For the color image, the RGB digital values vary for each color channel depending on the color of the area.

move up very close to the bright part of a contrasty scene. The iris on your eye closes and you start to see a lot of detail in that bright area. It is no longer a white area with no detail, because the focus of your field of vision moves up and your eyes adjust to encompass just that area. If you set the exposure on your camera to exposure value 16, that bright window area in the picture would show up as a middle gray for black-and-white or a normal color in a transparency. By changing this exposure, you would then be placing Zone V at exposure value 16. Now the door would be at Zone I, 16 times darker, and everything darker than the door would be in Zone 0, totally black.

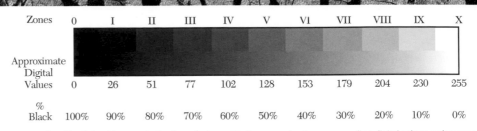

Zones	0	I	II	III	IV	V	VI	VII	VIII	IX	X
Approximate Digital Values	0	26	51	77	102	128	153	179	204	230	255
% Black	100%	90%	80%	70%	60%	50%	40%	30%	20%	10%	0%

A stepwedge file of the 11 zones in the Zone System with the approximate corresponding digital values and percentages of black ink. The digital values shown here fall somewhere in the center of each zone. Where the actual zone values and digital values appear for each image depends on the type of output you choose. You have more latitude where the Zone I detail begins and Zone IX details end when you print at a higher resolution and line screen. If you are printing to newsprint, all of Zone I may print as 100% black and all of Zone IX as 100% white.

This would give you details in the highlights, but you would lose the details in the darker parts of the scene. By measuring the scene and noticing that the bottom of the stairs has exposure value 7 and the sky has exposure value 17, then setting the exposure on your camera in the middle at exposure value 12, you place Zone V there and thereby obtain the full range of these values on the film.

UTILIZING YOUR EXPOSURE LATITUDE

Different films and different digital cameras have different exposure latitudes. The *exposure latitude* of a film is the number of different exposure values it can record at once. The Zone System covers a range of 11 exposure values, a brightness going from 1 to 1,024 times as bright. Most films cannot capture detail in so broad a range of lighting situations. This range of light would be found in a contrasty scene on a sunny day with the sun shining directly on it. Some films can capture detail over a range of seven exposure values and some over a larger range. In Adams' description of his zones, detail is captured only from Zone II through Zone VIII, or over a seven-zone range. Things in Zones 0, I, IX, and X are pretty much void of detail and either black or white. Some films have a lesser exposure latitude and others a greater one. Some digital cameras, like the Dicomed digital backs, have a larger dynamic range than most film. If you know the exposure latitude of your film or digital camera when taking a picture, you can determine which parts of the picture will have detail and which will be black or white by measuring the range of your image area and setting your exposure, your Zone V area, so the other zones, or brightness ranges, fall where you want them.

We could have gotten more details in the highlights in this picture by placing Zone V, our exposure setting, at exposure value 13 or 14 instead of 12, but then the shadow areas at exposure values 8 or 9, the areas underneath the roof and balcony overhangs, would have shown up as totally black. Some pictures will not be very contrasty, and you will know, by taking light measurements, that the exposure latitude of your film, or digital camera, can handle the total number of zones in the image. All you need to make sure of then is that you set the exposure in the middle of that range so all the areas of different exposure values fall within the latitude of the film or digital camera and you thus capture their detail.

If you want to know more about the Zone System and how to take the best photographs, you should read Ansel Adams' book The Negative. *It contains very useful information. It also shows you some very good techniques for extending or shortening the exposure latitude of your film by under- or over-developing. Another great book on the Zone System is* The New Zone System Manual *by White, Zakia, and Lorenz from Morgan Press, Inc.*

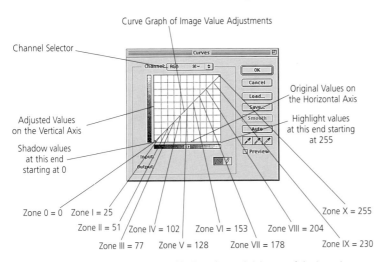

Using the Curves tool, if you want to modify the colors or brightness of the items in a certain zone or zone range of the image, this diagram points out the part of the curve you would modify to change those zones. Using the Eyedropper tool with Curves, you can measure any part of the image and the location of its values will show up on the curve as a small circle. This makes it very easy to adjust any range of values or colors using Curves.

The measurements and diagrams in this chapter don't accurately measure any particular film or camera. They simply illustrate how the process works.

THE ADVANTAGES OF A DIGITAL IMAGE

Once you have captured all the information you need on the film, you want to move it into your computer by doing the best possible scan. If you have a digital camera, you don't need to scan; you can digitally transfer the image from the camera to the computer. Your objective is to make sure that your image retains all the zone detail you captured for you to play with. For more information on scanning and bringing images into the computer from Photo CD, see "Scanning, Resolution, Histograms, and Photo CD."

When you look at the histogram of a digital image using the Levels or Curves commands in Photoshop, you see all those values, all those zones, and you can move them around and adjust them with much more precision than you would have in the darkroom.

If you are not familiar with Levels and Curves, read "The Grand Canyon," "Kansas," "Grand Canyon Tweaks," "Kansas Tweaks,"and "Creating the Master Image," later in this book.

Looking at a scan of the Spanish home image in Levels, we can actually see how many values in the image fall within each zone. Notice that in this image many values fall in Zones I, II, and III. That's because this image has a lot of dark areas in it. There are not many values in Zones IX and X because this image does not have many very bright areas. To move the values that are in Zone V toward Zone IV, making the image brighter, or toward Zone VI, making the image darker, you can use the Brightness/Contrast slider in Levels. To move the values in Zones I and II over to Zone 0, making the shadows darker, you can use the Input Shadow slider. In later chapters, we show you how to use these techniques with the Levels command to give you more control over the different brightness and color zones in your images. We will also show you how to use Curves to do pretty much anything you want with your image data.

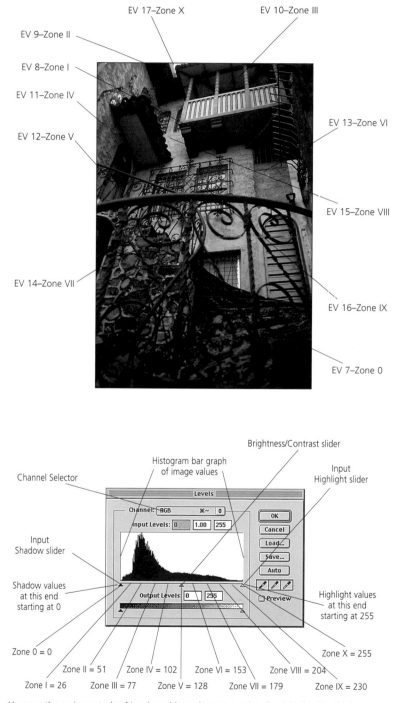

Here are the main controls of Levels and how the zones pointed out in the Spanish home image above show up in the histogram of that image. The approximate digital value, in the 0 to 255 range, is also shown for each zone.

COLOR SPACES, DEVICE CHARACTERIZATION, AND COLOR MANAGEMENT

An overview of how we see color, how color is measured, and how to decide what color space, gamma, and bit-depth you should use with Photoshop.

WHAT IS COLOR & HOW WE SEE IT

It's night and we can barely see; then the sun slowly comes up, and things begin to become recognizable. The light from the sun is allowing us to see more and more things. In that early morning light, things seem very warm and yellow. Then as the sun gets higher in the sky, that warm yellow appearance goes away and we get a whiter light. That white, midday light is actually made up of many wavelengths of light. Light is actually waves of excited electronic particles and those waves come in different wavelengths. When those light waves hit a surface, each different type of surface absorbs some of the wavelengths of light, and other wavelengths are reflected back toward us if we are looking at that surface. Now instead of the white light that comes from the sun, we are only seeing part of that light reflected back from a surface. The part or wavelengths that are reflected back to us determine the color of that surface.

Our eyes have sensors called rods and cones. The rods sense brightness or light intensity, but it is the cones that actually detect color, and there are three different types of cones each sensitive to a different wavelength of light. One type of cone is more sensitive to Red light, one is more sensitive to Green, and the third is more sensitive to Blue.

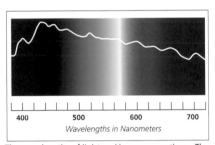

The wavelengths of light and how you see them. The white line is an approximation of daylight wavelengths.

AN IMAGE ON PAPER

When we look at an image printed on paper, the color we see depends on the color of the incoming light that is illuminating that paper; that incoming light supplies all or most of the wavelengths of light that we could possibly see although there might be several different types of light illuminating the paper that increases the possibilities. The color and surface texture of the paper itself will subtract some of the wavelengths from that incoming lightsource and give the paper a certain color. The inks or other types of color that are painted on that paper will subtract further wavelengths from that original light and reflect back different colors that are the remaining nonsubtracted wavelengths. The angle that you view the paper might also influence how much light is reflected back.

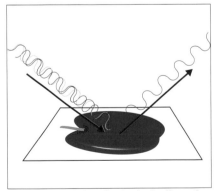

Seeing color by light reflecting back off a surface while the other colors are absorbed.

AN IMAGE ON A COMPUTER MONITOR

Color on a computer monitor comes from particle energizers, a type of light source, behind the monitor's glass that hits the coating on the inside of the monitor glass and produces different colors and light intensities depending on the numerical values that are driving the different colored light particle energizers. There is also light hitting the monitor from the outside due to other light sources within the room, and this light will have some effect on the color and brightness that you see from the internal monitor particle energizer. The way you see color on a computer monitor is quite different from the way you see color on a printed piece of paper. It is difficult to exactly match the brightness, color, and contrast characteristics of these two mediums.

SLIDE ON A LIGHT TABLE

When you see color by looking at a slide on a light table, the color you see here depends on the color of the lightsource behind the slide, the colors in the emulsion of the slide material, and also on the amount and intensity of the other light sources in the room.

COLOR GAMUTS

There is a very large range to colors, wavelengths of light, that the human eye can see. There are also wavelengths of light that our eyes can't see. A particular range of colors is called a color gamut. The color gamut of the human eye is described in a color space called Lab color. A color space is a description of range of colors to be used for a particular purpose. In the 1930s, an organization called the CIE (Commission Internationale de l'Eclairage) did a bunch of scientific measurements with human observers to develop a description of the colors the human eye could see. Without filling in all the details here, this description has evolved into two very useful tools we will use in this book for measuring and quantifying color. (Note: to learn a lot more about the CIE and color history and theory, I'd recommend "The Reproduction of Color" by Dr. R.W.G. Hunt, Fifth Edition, 1995 by Fountain Press. Also the Color and Measurement Primer that comes in the manual for the Colortron spectrophotometer which has a great history and explanation of color theory and measurement.) One of these tools is the Lab color space, that Photoshop supports, that consists of a color gamut of this range of colors that the human eye can. The second tool is the CIE xy chromaticity diagram that shows these colors on an xy graph again representing the colors the human eye can see. This CIE xy chromaticity diagram is useful for plotting other color gamuts and comparing one against the other. When you are working on a project using the Lab color space, you won't be throwing out colors that the eye can see and you won't be working with any colors that the eye cannot see. Using the Lab color space, you can potentially be working with all the colors the eye can see; however, the eye can actually see more colors than many of the color capture and display mediums we work with can reproduce.

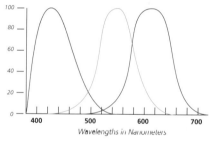

Wavelengths of light the eye can see.

MEASURING COLOR

To measure color, we need to be able to measure wavelengths of light. A device called a spectrophotometer does this, and we will be talking about how the spectrophotometer, along with some new software, is now being used to improve our use and accuracy of digital color. We want to be able to measure the colors that a particular film can record, that a particular scanner can scan, that a particular monitor can display, and that a particular printer can print. To do this people have developed test target systems, like the IT8 color target from the CIE, to measure color. In its purest form, this IT8 target consists of a group of many color swatches, light wavelength descriptions, covering a large range of colors that the human eye can see, as well as various films could capture, scanners could scan, monitors could display, and printers

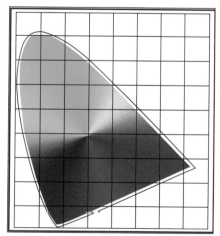

A CIE Chromaticity diagram showing the Lab color space.

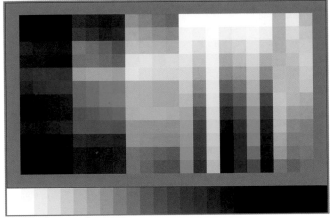
An IT8 color measuring target.

could print. I use the word could here because you need to know that each color device, each film, scanner, monitor, or printer, has its own color gamut. The color gamut of a device is the range of colors that particular device can detect, reproduce, or display. With a spectrophotometer, one can use the IT8 target to measure the color gamut of any particular device.

MEASURING THE GAMUT OF A FILM

To measure the gamut of a film, you photograph a scientifically printed version of the IT8 target when that target is illuminated by a known light source. You then process that film exactly and use the spectrophotometer to measure each swatch in the target as it is reproduced on that film. Different film manufacturers will sell you film swatches with IT8 targets already correctly exposed on them for you to scan and measure. The film needs to be illuminated by a known light source while taking the measurements. Those measurements are then entered into a profile-making software program, which generates an ICC color profile of that film. The software program knows the empirical values each swatch is supposed to have and did have on the scientifically produced original that was photographed. Based on the differences between the original values of each swatch and the values actually recorded on the film, the ICC profile is generated that characterizes that particular film. A characterization is a description of the differences from the original empirical values, which ends up also telling you the color gamut or range of colors that film can represent. The ICC stands for International Color Consortium, which is basically a group of companies and international groups that have agreed on a standard for specifying color. The ICC profile standard is that standard, and an ICC profile is a description of color that is in a standard format that can be recognized by many different color software applications including Adobe Photoshop 5, Apple ColorSync, QuarkXpress 4.0, and Adobe Pagemaker 6.5.

CHARACTERIZING A SCANNER

To measure the color gamut, or characterize, a scanner, you need a scientifically produced IT8 target on film, which you can get from the film manufacturer, or on a printed medium that can be scanned with the scanner. The resulting digital values that the scanner gets are entered into the profile-making software that will make an ICC profile describing that particular scanner.

CHARACTERIZING A MONITOR

To characterize a monitor, a scientifically created digital file of the IT8 target is measured with a spectrophotometer while being displayed on the screen in a room lit with controlled lighting conditions. Then those measurements are entered into the profile making software to generate the ICC profile of that monitor.

CHARACTERIZING A DIGITAL PRINTER

To characterize a particular digital printer or printing press, the scientifically produced digital version of the IT8 target, or some other target, is printed on that printer or press using the standard process for outputting to that device. Then the results are measured with the spectrophotometer, and the profile generating software creates the ICC profile from those results.

Chapter 14: Color Spaces, Device Characterization, and Color Management

Now we know what ICC profiles are and how they are made. By the way, there are various targets that the industry uses to create ICC profiles; the Kodak IT8 is just an example, and there are various companies that create ICC profile making software. In this industry, a commonly used set of profile-making software is PrintOpen for profiling printers, ViewOpen for profiling monitors, and ScanOpen for profiling scanners. These are all available from Linotype-Hell. When you are using this process to characterize, or describe, the color gamut, or range of colors, that a particular device can record, scan, display, or print, the accuracy of this characterization is based on the accuracy of the way the test was performed and measured. When you make a profile or get a profile made, make sure it is done properly, or the profile you get might actually do you a disservice.

Bill Atkinson's Grayscale Target that is used in the first step of characterizing a printer. This file is available in the Calibration folder on the CD.

AN EXACT PROCESS FOR CHARACTERIZING A DIGITAL PRINTER

As Bill Atkinson points out, "The photographic process introduces all kinds of nasty nonlinearities and color crossovers that can only be accurately modeled by an empirically measured lookup table." Bill's process for characterizing his Fujix and LightJet 5000 output is the following:

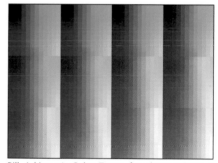

Bill Atkinson's Color Target for characterizing a printer. This file is available in the Calibration folder on the CD.

"This is exactly what I do quite successfully to get an excellent color and tonality match between all my devices, so that my small Fujix test prints look very close to my larger EverColor Luminage* fine prints. The profiles that I create are not based on a computational model of how the light and colorants combine and interact, but instead on a black-box approach that simply interpolates between entries in a large array of empirical measurements.

I use a Gretag Spectrolino spectrophotometer on a SpectroScan X-Y table to make automated color measurements, and ColorSavvy's SMPKit profile building software to create an accurate ICC profile from the CIE-Lab color measurements.

First I print out a series of grayscale patches to the Fujix or LightJet printer, and then use the Spectrolino to measure the resulting densities on the developed photograph. This data is used to create a Photoshop curve that empirically linearizes the device response to grayscale. The curve doesn't look at all like a gamma curve or a dot-gain curve. It has lots of bumps and quirks that reflect the actual measured response of a complex interaction.

Then I prepare an RGB target which is initially 12 by 12 by 12 equal steps in RGB. The linearization curve is applied to the target to spread out the RGB numbers such that they more evenly and efficiently span and sample the device-specific RGB colorspace. Next this pre-compensated RGB data is sent to the printer, exposed by lasers, and the photograph developed.

The resulting 1,728 patches of photographic color are measured on the SpectroScan, getting accurate CIE-Lab values for each patch. The whole target is remeasured with a spatial offset a total of five times to get more accurate readings by averaging the measurements in Excel. At three seconds per automated reading, it still takes seven and a half hours to gather the data. Then I use ColorSavvy's SMPKit software to build an accurate ICC printer profile from the averaged CIE-Lab color measurements and the actual RGB input data that was sent to the printer after linearization.

These "black-box" RGB profiles work very well, since the printer's response is very repeatable, and is recalibrated back to the same set-points each time I load a new roll of photographic emulsion or receiver paper. In the case of the EverColor LightJet, EverColor purchases 200 rolls of 50 inch wide Fujicolor Crystal Archive paper at a time, and every time they switch paper emulsions, they prepare a new profile and email it to all their customers. They also use a Gretag SpectroScan and ColorSavvy SMPKit, and use the same procedure to build their profiles as I do."

You should check out Bill's images at ***www.natureimages.com*** and if you ever get to see some of his wonderful prints, you'll discover what calibration is all about. His Fujix prints are as close as possible to identical in color to his LightJet ones and even to the original transparencies when printed straight from the scans. By the way, at natureimages.com, there are also a lot of useful action scripts for sharpening images, resampling for different size prints, and so on, as well as all the latest discoveries from Bill Atkinson Photography. You should check out his site which is also one of the better photography sites I have seen. Some of Bill's Actions scripts are also included in the Actions folder on the *Photoshop 5 Artistry* CD.

CHOOSING YOUR COLOR WORKING SPACE

When you are working in Photoshop 5, you have the option of choosing various different color spaces as your working color space. Color spaces available with Photoshop 5 use either the RGB, Lab, or CMYK color model. Each color space also encompasses a particular color gamut. So when working in Photoshop 5, you need to decide which color model, RGB, CMYK, or Lab, makes the most sense for your type of work, and then within that model, what color gamut you need for the type of work you are doing.

Let's first discuss the color gamut issue. For any particular body of work that involves human viewing, you will probably not need to work with colors outside the gamut of Lab because the gamut of Lab is the set of colors the human eye can see. If you are outputting your work on color film, digital printers, computer monitors, or printing presses, you also need to consider the color gamut of those devices. It turns out that the color gamut of a CMYK printing press is much smaller than the color gamut of the human eye, the Lab color space. If you are only outputting to CMYK presses but you are working within the Lab color space, you may be constantly disappointed because many of the colors you would see on the screen could not actually

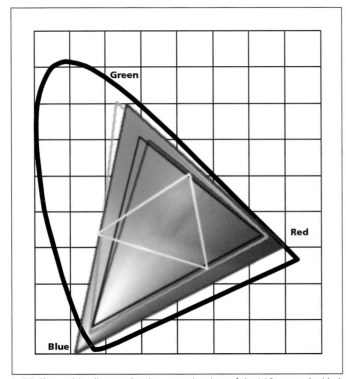

A CIE Chromaticity diagram showing approximations of the LAB space, the black outline which includes all the colors within that black outline, Joe Holmes Ekta Space PS5 with the Red Outline, Adobe RGB (SMPTE-240M) in Green, ColorMatch RGB in Blue, sRGB in purple and the CMYK SWOP print space in yellow. The actual color gradients you see here probably doesn't accurately display the actual colors in the space but it gives you an idea of the trade offs. You have to choose one of these spaces, or something similar to work in. The biggest space shown here, other than the Lab space, is a custom space defined by Joe Holmes to encompass the gamut of Ecktachrome film. He works in this space, mostly using Live Picture, to create his beautiful art prints on the LightJet 5000.

be reproduced on a printing press. The color gamut of computer monitors, color film recorders and some of the new digital color printers is much larger than that of a CMYK press. So if you are also outputting to devices other than a press, you would not want to limit your gamut to colors only available on a press, especially if your goal is to produce art prints for gallery use or exciting colorful images for the Web and multimedia. The ideal circumstance would be to work in a color space that encompasses the entire color gamut of all the input scanners or digital cameras, display

Chapter 14: Color Spaces, Device Characterization, and Color Management

monitors, and output color film recorders, photographic and ink-based printers, digital printers, and CMYK or 6 color presses that you would be outputting to now and in the reasonable future. I got the term "reasonable future" from my friend Bill Atkinson, and it seems like a good term because foreseeable future could include a time when we all wear special glasses, like Geordi La Forge on Star Trek, that increase the gamut of what the human eye can see. That would complicate things too much. We could measure the gamut of each of those devices and plot those gamuts on a CIE chromaticity diagram. If we then created a color space that encompassed the gamut of all those devices, then we would be set!

Now lets discuss the Color Model issue. What we have available in Photoshop is Lab, RGB, and CMYK. In the Image/Mode menu, there are also Index color, Duotone, and Grayscale, but I would put them in the category of special case models that we only work with under certain circumstances.

THE LAB WORKING SPACE

The Lab model has the advantage that its color gamut encompasses all the colors that the human eye can see. This is a very wide gamut and would certainly encompass the devices we would be working with in the reasonable future. Bill Atkinson and Charlie Cramer, two photographer friends of mine whose work I really admire, do actually work in the Lab color space using Photoshop 5 and also Lino-Color. Bill's images can see be seen at www.natureimages.com and both their prints can be seen at the Ansel Adams gallery in Yosemite. Charlie's prints are also at the Photographer's gallery in Palo Alto and the Weston gallery in Carmel among others. Anyhow, check out Chapter 29: Bryce Stone Woman that was redone using a new Lab color scan, an awesome Bill Atkinson scan, in the Lab space for this version of *Photoshop Artistry*.

I'm also considering using the Lab color space for my art prints but the potential problems with the Lab space are that it encompasses a larger gamut than most of the output devices I will be using that are color film via a film recorder, LightJet 5000 digital prints, prints on other digital printers and display on color monitors. The other potential problem with Lab is that the tools for working in Lab within Photoshop might not be as easy to work with than if I were working in RGB. In the Lab space, there are three channels: Lightness, a, and b. Another great thing about Lab is that the Lightness channel allows you to adjust the brightness and contrast of the image as well as sharpen the image without modifying the color of the image. Using Levels to look at a histogram of the Lightness channel of a Lab image is similar to looking at a histogram of RGB, all three channels at the same time, in an RGB image. The color values in Lab are stored in the a and b channels. The a channel controls the red/green range of color, and the b channel controls the yellow/blue range. Most of us are used to working with color using Red, Green, and Blue along with their complements of Cyan, Magenta, and Yellow. Using a and b takes a little getting used to, and it works pretty well in Photoshop if you start out with a scan that is very close to what you want. When you have to make major color shifts with the a and b channels in Photoshop, this can be more difficult.

Bill and Charlie have been using LinoColor, which has color controls that are more flexible in Lab, to get their colors close, then using Photoshop for all the final color tweaks, masking, spotting, sharpening, and final image production. The other thing about the a and b channels in Lab images is that if you look at their histograms you will see that the values are usually all within the center part of the histogram. The blank parts at the left and right side of the a and b histograms represent colors that are in the very wide gamut Lab space but were not captured by the film or scan-

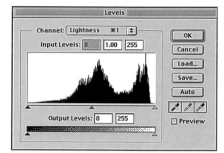

The Lightness channel in a Lab color image looks similar to an RGB histogram, but check out the a and b channels below where very small adjustments can make major changes.

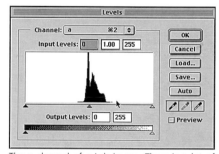

The a channel of a Lab image. There is a lot of unused space here that could be use for a more detailed spec of this color if this were a reduced gamut Lab space like Lab LH.

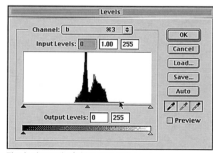

The b channel of this same Lab image.

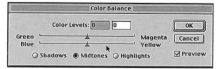

The Color Balance tool gives you different controls when working in Lab color, and you may find that you use it more in this color mode.

107

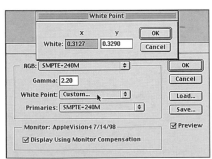

You can use the RGB pop-up in RGB Setup to set you default RGB workspace; here it is set to Color-Match RGB.

In the initial Photoshop 5.0 release, the Adobe RGB color space was called SMPTE-240M. Adobe renamed it to Adobe RGB, actually Adobe RGB 1998, in version 5.02 of Photoshop which was a free bug fix version coming out after version 5.0. If you see the name SMPTE-240M in this book, just know that it is exactly the same color space as Adobe RGB and vice versa.

Here we have set the workspace to SMPTE-240M (Adobe RGB).

When you pick a workspace, that also sets up the default Gamma, White Point, and CIE xy primaries describing that workspace. You can then go in and modify these by hand. For Gamma, just type in a new value, and you will quickly see a change in the appearance on the screen. If you choose Custom under White Point, you can enter your own values there too. There are also some typical standard white points you can choose from.

ner and therefore don't get represented in most Lab images. To represent a digital image in 24 bits of digital space in Lab, we have 256 possible lightness values, 256 possible a values, and 256 possible b values. The concern about Lab is that for most images the a and b channels are using much less than the 256 possible range of values. The possible color range for the a and b channels is so wide that the actual range used is often covering a span of only 140 to 160 values or fewer within the center of their histograms. This brings up the concern of posterization of color values within Lab images. To address this problem, LinoColor has actually defined a smaller Lab space called Lab LH that encompasses a smaller a and b gamut that is more in line with actual digital output devices but Photoshop 5 doesn't support this space.

THE RGB WORKING SPACE

When using the RGB color space in Photoshop 5, you choose different versions of the RGB color space. Older versions of Photoshop assumed the gamut of your RGB space was the gamut of your monitor as described by the old Monitor Setup dialog. This caused colors outside of that space to be clipped even though those colors might have been printable on higher gamut output devices like color film recorders or the LightJet 5000 digital printer. With Photoshop 5, you use the RGB Setup dialog to specify the gamut and other characteristics of your RGB space. You can choose an RGB color space that has a wider gamut than your monitor and, if you have Display using Monitor Compensation on, Photoshop will adjust the display of your space to preview most accurately on your monitor, but Photoshop 5 will not clip the colors that are outside of the monitors gamut from your RGB file. That way you will see those colors when you print the image. Using the RGB pop-up dialog, you can choose from the default RGB spaces Adobe has provided. You can also enter your own Gamma value, use the Custom setting under White Point to set a Custom white point using CIE xy values, and use the Custom setting under Primaries to enter your own CIE primaries in xy space. Unless you have the tools available to measure the gamut of your input and output devices and create your own RGB workspace, you should probably pick one of the spaces provided by Adobe or something that seems to be moving toward becoming some sort of an industry standard.

WHICH RGB SPACE TO USE?

Of the spaces provided by Adobe, only four of them have much interest to people dealing with professional images. I will describe those here, and you can look in the Photoshop 5 manual for information about the other spaces if you want it. The four most useful spaces are Adobe RGB, ColorMatchRGB, AppleRGB, and sRGB.

ADOBE RGB (SMPTE-240M)

The widest gamut of these spaces, Adobe RGB, is a proposed standard for HDTV production. But more importantly, its gamut includes essentially the entire CMYK gamut and more because it also better encompasses the gamut of things like color RGB film recorders, the LightJet 5000 digital printer, and other more advanced color output devices. If you set your RGB workspace to Adobe RGB, you will be least likely to be throwing out values that you'll be able to see in today's digital output devices, and yet the gamut is not so large that you'll be wasting a lot of your color space and thus having posterization problems. With Adobe RGB though, you will be able to see more colors on a good monitor than you'll be able to print in CMYK on a press. The technical description for Adobe RGB is: white point = 6500, gamma = 2.2, red x = .6400 y = .3300, green x = .2100 y = .7100 and blue x = .1500 y = .0600.

ColorMatch RGB

The ColorMatch RGB space has a smaller gamut than Adobe RGB but a bigger gamut than sRGB and AppleRGB. This space is based on the Radius PressView monitor that is an industry standard for quality color work. There are several advantages to the ColorMatch RGB space, especially for people who are doing print work. One is that people who have been working with a PressView monitor can open their old untagged files into this space without any conversions. The other advantage is that it has a fairly large gamut, at least for CMYK print work, and it is a well-known space within the color industry. If you have been working in older Photoshops with a quality monitor calibrated to gamma 1.8 and 5000° Kelvin color temperature, this color space will give you a very similar working situation within Photoshop 5. The technical description for ColorMatch RGB is: white point = 5000, gamma = 1.8, red x = .6300 y = .3400, green x = .2950 y = .6050, and blue x = .1550 y = .0770.

sRGB

The sRGB RGB color space is the current default for Photoshop 5. This space is good for people who are primarily working on Web images and want to see what they are going to look like on a typical PC monitor. The problem with sRGB is that it is the smallest gamut space of the four, and working in this space will mean that you are potentially throwing out certain colors, even for CMYK print work, and you are certainly throwing out colors if you are planning to output to a color film recorder or LightJet 5000 type digital printer. If you are working in a larger gamut space, like Adobe RGB or Lab, and you want to create an image for the Web, you could save your file from the Adobe RGB space, temporarily set your space to sRGB, and then reopen and convert your file into that sRGB space. This will allow you to do your main work in Adobe RGB or Lab space and keep more colors; then use sRGB to preview the work as it will look on the average PC Web user's monitor. At this point, you can resave the file under a different name, or in JPEG format for your Web consumers, and it will be in sRGB space that is optimized for that market. If you just want to stay in Adobe RGB or Lab space all the time, you can actually just output files for Web consumption by using the ColorSync 2.5 export filter and transform from your wider gamut space into sRGB. If you are a service bureau, you will probably find that you get a lot of files from the sRGB space just because it is the Photoshop 5 default and many people who don't take the time to learn about color won't bother to change this. The technical description for sRGB is: white point = 6500, gamma = 2.2, red x = .6400 y = .3300, green x = .3000 y = .6000, and blue x = .1500 y = .0600.

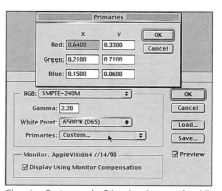

Choosing Custom under Primaries gives you the ability to change these settings that describe the range of colors within your space. You should probably not change any of these Gamma, White Point, or Primary settings from the defaults unless you have the equipment and know-how to correctly measure your changes and know why you want to make them. For example, let's say that you measured a particular new film or digital camera that you are using and determined from its ICC profile that the Adobe RGB (SMPTE-240M) primaries did not contain a small portion of the film's color range. You could then change the Red, Green, or Blue xy values of Adobe RGB to extend the range of the space adding those colors.

AppleRGB

The AppleRGB space is based on the old standard Apple 13" Trinitron color monitor. There are probably a lot of files out there in this space because Illustrator and older Photoshops have been using it as their default RGB space. Its gamut is not that much better than sRGB, so we really are not suggesting you use this as a current RGB working space. You will probably find it useful to use this as a Source Profile when opening old Photoshop files that were not from Radius PressView monitors, especially files from people who never changed their Photoshop Monitor Setup from the default settings. You'd be surprised how many people never change this. The technical description for AppleRGB is: white point = 6500, gamma = 1.8, red x = .6250 y = .3400, green x = .2800 y = .5950, and blue x = .1550 y = .0700.

Choosing Your Color Working Space

CMYK as a Master Workspace

The CMYK print gamut is smaller overall than the gamut of any of the RGB monitor gamuts above, but there are a few colors CMYK can print that sRGB and Apple RGB don't include. These days, it is not that common for people to have images that are only used in CMYK print. Even if you are using an image for just CMYK print, it is likely that you may have to print that image several times, and at several sizes and on different types of paper. For these situations, it is better if you have your master image in RGB or LAB, then when you size, you can get more exact sharpening and you can also more accurately generate new separations for different papers and presses. But most of us will be using that same image in print, on the Web, and for output to several digital printers. Because the RGB and Lab spaces are both bigger in color gamut than CMYK, it makes more sense these days to leave our master image in RGB or Lab format. If you do still decide to create your master images in CMYK, remember that some of the filters don't work on CMYK either. In any case, while viewing your CMYK images on the screen, even if the separations were done elsewhere, Photoshop compensates for the appearance of the image on the screen based on the CMYK settings parameters you have set up. If you open an image that was separated to be used in a 20% dot gain situation and display it with the Photoshop CMYK Settings set up for 30% gain, the image will appear too dark on the screen. When you reset the Photoshop settings to 20%, the same image appears correct again. You need to be careful when opening Photoshop images that your prefs are set up correctly.

Hardware Monitor Gamma and Color Space Gamma

Another thing you need to consider when working in Photoshop is the hardware gamma your monitor is set at and whether you work in an RGB workspace that is 1.8 or 2.2 gamma. If you are using your monitor to work with images that are for CMYK print output, you may be better off if your monitor hardware gamma is set to 1.8, which has also been the typical gamma of Mac systems. If you are doing primarily output to the Web, you may want to set your monitor hardware gamma to 2.2, which is the typical gamma of PC systems. Now the gamma of your RGB workspace is a different story. A workspace that has a gamma of 2.2 does a more even job of displaying the values in a histogram and allows you to see more separation in the shadows. Your shadow detail will less likely be posterized. Many people in the print world are used to working with PressView monitors and the ColorMatch RGB workspace with their gamma set at 1.8. In general, more people who work in print have been working with a workspace having a gamma of 1.8, and people who use the Web or work on the Web are more likely use a workspace with a gamma of 2.2. If you open a file that has been color adjusted in a gamma 1.8 space into a gamma 2.2 space without converting, the file would seem darker and more contrasty. Similarly, if you initially corrected the file in a gamma 2.2 space and then opened it into a 1.8 space without converting, the file would seem too flat and light. Whatever space you adjust your files in, you will get used to and make the appropriate choices as to your color adjustments. It's just when you open or print that file into a different gamma environment without compensation, you will notice a problem. Try a gamma 1.8 workspace like ColorMatch RGB and then compare it, with the same images open on the screen, by changing the RGB Setup to a gamma 2.2 workspace, like Adobe RGB, without conversion. Then see which gamma range space is going to work for you. You can also open the Stepwedgefile (from the Calibration folder on the CD) and screen grab it, Command-Shift-3 on the Mac, while your RGB Setup is set to ColorMatch. Then while the same unmodified file is still open, change RGB Setup to Adobe RGB and

Using Apple monitor calibration software to set the hardware Gamma on my AppleVision 750 monitor, now called the ColorSync 17, to 1.8. I use a white point of D50 when I'm working on CMYK print jobs, like this book, and currently also when working on my LightJet prints. The viewing light you are using to display LightJet prints, or whatever prints you are workin on, can make a difference as to where you set your monitor color temperature. You will want the whites on your monitor to match the whiteness of your printer paper when viewing that paper under your chosen viewing light. Check our Web site at www.maxart.com for my lastest discoveries in the best ways to calibrate your monitor and set things up for different types of printing situations. I'm currently evaluating some new calibration products I received at the September 99 Seybold and will post my findings on our site.

Chapter 14: Color Spaces, Device Characterization, and Color Management

do anther screen grab. Now bring those two grab files up on the screen at the same time, crop them to just the grayscales, and compare the results. The grab done in the 2.2 workspace should be perceptually more even.

USING 48-BIT COLOR

Another thing to consider, especially when working on the highest-quality art prints, is if it would make sense to work in 48-bit color instead of 24-bit color. Photoshop 5 supports most of the important color corrections tools, the Eyedropper and the Rubber Stamp in 48-bit color mode. To convert an image to 48-bit color, just choose Image/Mode 16 Bits/Channel. If you get a scan from a really good scanner, the scanner will be actually scanning the file getting 48-bit RGB information. When you adjust the curves and other controls in scanner software, what you are really doing is deciding how to convert from the 48 bits of information that the scanner gets down to the 24 bits of information that is in a standard RGB file. You are throwing away information that you got from the scanner, and sometimes you end up throwing away the wrong information or you want some of it back for a different rendition of the image. At this point, you may need to rescan your original if it was a 24-bit scan. Some scanners actually allow you to save all 48 bits of information exactly as it comes from the sensors on the scanner, a raw scanner. This way, assuming you have a great scan from a great scanner, you might never need to scan the original again because you can always reprocess that 48-bit scan data down to 24 bits in a different way to pull out a different area of detail. You can actually run Levels, Curves, Color Balance, Brightness/Contrast, Hue/Saturation, and Channel Mixer on 48-bit files in Photoshop 5. This would allow you to do one raw scan and then save that and actually be able to make the most of your scanner decisions later or over again without actually rescanning. Of course, a real issue here is that a 4x5 film scanned at 5,000dpi (what you need to get all the info out of the film) in 24 bit is 1.43Gb; that scan in 48-bit would be 2.86 Gb! For 35mm it is not that bad, about 100Mb in 24-bit and 200Mb in 48-bit.

PREVIEWING COLOR

When you are working on a CMYK file in Photoshop or when working on an RGB file with View/Preview/CMYK on, Photoshop gives you a fairly accurate preview of how that CMYK file will look when printed on a press. Photoshop does this using the CMYK Setup information you have given it. Photoshop builds a table for RGB to CMYK, which it uses to make the actual color separations, and then it also builds a table for CMYK to RGB that it uses to display CMYK files on the screen because a computer screen uses RGB technology to get its colors. Part of the CMYK to RGB process includes not displaying colors that you can't actually print. When you are working in RGB or Lab, you can see a preview of what your image would look like if you were going to print it on a CMYK press by using View/Preview/CMYK. But what if you were going to print your image on an RGB device like the LightJet 5000 digital printer or the Fujix printer and you wanted to get a preview of how that would look? There is actually a way to do this in Photoshop 5 by tweaking the CMYK preview logic in Photoshop. When you do this, it breaks CMYK preview until you put it back by returning to CMYK Setup's Built-In or ICC settings.

Remember now that the proper way to make a LightJet 5000 or Fujix print from Photoshop 5 is to edit the file in either Lab or your chosen RGB workspace, like Adobe RGB; then choose File/Export/Tiff with ColorSync Profile to create a Tiff file

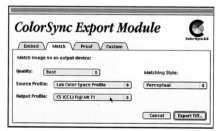

Using Apple ColorSync 2.5 to export a Lab format image to make a print on the LightJet 5000 at Ever-Color Fine Art. You want the Quality set to Best, the Input Profile set to Lab, or your RGB workspace if you are working in RGB, the Output Profile set to the current profile for the LightJet, or Fujix, and for photographic images, the Matching Style set to Perceptual. Make sure you are using ColorSync 2.5, it's more accurate than the older versions.

that is actually tagged with the profile of the output device. You have, of course, saved your master file in either Lab or your RGB workspace because this export is just to print the file on this version of paper with this printer. When you later want to print the image on another printer or another batch of paper, you do another ColorSync Export using the profile for that printer or paper batch. We are doing this with the ColorSync Export instead of using Photoshop's Profile-to-Profile feature because we want the saved file to be tagged with the profile of the printer, not Lab or your RGB workspace. If you saved the file as Tiff directly from Photoshop 5, it would either save no tag, if tagging were turned off, or it would tag the file with your current monitor space, which would no longer be correct after the transform.

So now, here's the cool recipe Mark Hamburg, Photoshop's chief engineer from Adobe, came up with so you can soft-proof from your normal workspace to see what the file will look like when printed on your RGB printer.

1. Find the Calibration Sources files: Lab Colors and CMYK Colors in the Goodies/Calibration folder. Open these without color conversion. Make sure your Profile Setup is set to Ask When Opening.
2. Add an alpha channel to the Lab Colors file and fill that channel with white.
3. Using Image/Mode/Profile-to-Profile, convert the Lab Colors file from Lab to the profile for the RGB device you are interested in proofing. Use the intent that you would use for doing mode conversions, Perceptual for this type of situation.
4. Save the result in Raw format as "<Profile Name> to CMYK" with the file type in the Raw dialog set to 8BST.
5. Close the file.
6. Use Image/Mode/Multichannel to convert the CMYK Colors file to Multichannel and then use Image/Mode/RGB to convert it to RGB Color, which will relabel the channels.
7. Discard the fourth (Black) channel. A more complicated version of this procedure would create phony black behavior. The steps given here just result in black ink that has no effect.
8. Use Image/Mode/Profile-to-Profile to convert from the profile for the RGB device to Lab. You probably want to use Relative Colorimetric conversion here to match Photoshop's standard proofing behavior.
9. Save the result in Raw format as "<Profile Name> from CMYK" with the file type in the Raw dialog set to 8BST.
10. Close the file.
11. Choose File/Color Settings/CMYK Setup and click on the Tables mode at the top to the CMYK Setup dialog.
12. Load the files saved in steps 4 and 9. They should end up in the appropriate portions of the dialog.
13. Choose save to create an ICC profile representing the result of combining these two tables. You can later reload this profile, or one from a different batch of paper or a different RGB device, to get back to a soft proof of this device any time you want. The CMY portion of CMYK now works just like the RGB for the target device. The K portion has no effect. You can now use CMYK Preview (Command-Y) to proof the appearance of the file on the RGB device. Gamut Warning (Command-Shift-Y) will also now work to show you the areas of your image that are out of gamut for this printer. Remember, to be exact, you would have to rebuild this proofing setup whenever you get a new profile for your RGB device, like in the case of a new batch of paper for the LightJet. This is a great and powerful hidden feature of Photoshop 5!

15 CALIBRATION

Here you learn how to use the tools that come with Photoshop (and the images on the Photoshop 5 Artistry *CD) to calibrate your monitor and output devices.*

To fully understand this chapter, you should also read Chapter 5: Setting System and Photoshop Preferences, Chapter 14: Color Spaces, Device Characterization, and Color Management, and Chapter 18: Steps to Create a Master Image. Let me also mention that unless otherwise stated, you should assume that the files on the Photoshop 5 Artistry CD were created in a ColorMatch RGB environment and they should be tagged with ColorMatch RGB.

COLOR MANAGEMENT SYSTEMS AND HOW THEY FIT INTO THE PHOTOSHOP 5 ENVIRONMENT

Color management systems, like ColorSync, take an image that you have corrected on your computer screen and remap that image based on the color gamut of the particular output device it is being printed on. The color gamut of an output device is the set of colors and brightness ranges that the output device can print. Each different output device, such as a digital printer, CMYK proofing system, transparency writer, and so on, has its own specific gamut. If you take the same digital file and print it, unmodified, on a number of different output devices, each print will look different—from each other, and also probably different from the image on your screen. The purpose of a color management system is to adjust for these differences so the same image will look as close as possible on different computer monitors and will print as closely as possible on different types of output devices.

The monitor calibration technique we used to use with older versions of Photoshop showed you how to calibrate your monitor to make it look as much as possible like the output of one particular output device, but then you had to do this calibration routine separately for each output device. A color management system measures the difference between different types of output devices and creates a device profile for each device. Photoshop and ColorSync use ICC profiles to characterize devices. When you send an image to a particular device, the color management system changes the image, on-the-fly, using that image's device profile to try to make it print in a standard way on that device. If you print the same picture on many devices, the color management system does its best to make all those pictures look as close as possible to each other. I say "does its best" because you cannot always get the same colors on one device that you can on another. Each device has its own color gamut.

Apple's ColorSync color management system is a generic one that allows many other third-party companies to contribute device profiles for their specific products. The problem with Color Management Systems in the past has been that they haven't incorporated a good way to deal with the subtle differences between each instance of a particular device. I have, for example, an Epson Stylist Photo inkjet printer. I love the photographic quality prints it gives me. But if I took the digital file that produced a print on my Epson printer and printed the same file, unmodified, on someone else's Epson printer, you would see subtle differences between the two prints. The other printer might have a different batch number on its inks, it might be slightly out of alignment, the temperature and humidity at the other printer's location might be different, and for whatever reason, there may be other subtle differences. Color management systems have not dealt well with these matters in the past, but they are now doing a better job.

To solve these problems, the systems need to be able to measure the output from your particular device and create a custom ICC device profile for it at any particular time. Some newer products emerging on the scene are starting to help users take these measurements and create much better color profiles. Color management systems can also characterize different types of scanners and film input types, different types of monitors, and other factors that affect color production along the way to final output. Given the great many variations in what can happen to the colors, it's no wonder color calibration and correction often prove so difficult.

Color management systems can help you deal with the differences in the gamut and characteristics of different types of input and output devices, and they are improving all the time. Some color management system marketing implies that these systems can automatically scan, correct, and output images so that they print like originals. And although color management systems can be adjusted to give you a higher degree of calibration and control between devices, doing this correctly still requires a lot of careful measurement and control of every part of your color production system. See the "An Exact Process for Characterizing a Digital Printer" section in Chapter 14: Color Spaces, Device Characterization, and Color Management for an example of how to accurately do this characterization process.

CALIBRATING YOUR OUTPUT DEVICE

Many issues arise in attempting to get quality output to a digital printer, film recorder, or imagesetter. First among them are calibration issues. You must calibrate the output device and keep it calibrated. When your output device is not calibrated and consistent, any calibration and correction you do on your computer is less useful. Next, you need to send some known, good test output to your output device and compare that output print to the image that made the print on your monitor. You characterize and adjust your monitor so the image on your monitor looks like your print when you view both under your standard lighting conditions.

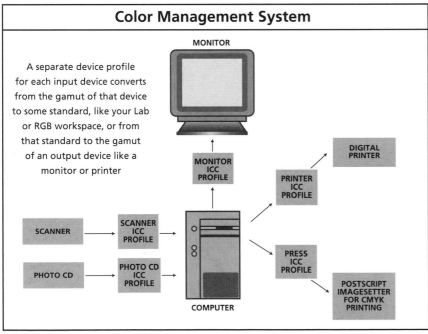

Color Management System

A separate device profile for each input device converts from the gamut of that device to some standard, like your Lab or RGB workspace, or from that standard to the gamut of an output device like a monitor or printer

MONITOR

MONITOR ICC PROFILE

SCANNER → SCANNER ICC PROFILE →

PHOTO CD → PHOTO CD ICC PROFILE →

COMPUTER

PRINTER ICC PROFILE → DIGITAL PRINTER

PRESS ICC PROFILE → POSTSCRIPT IMAGESETTER FOR CMYK PRINTING

The standard file format your files are stored in, on your computer, should be either Lab or your default RGB workspace. The ICC profiles will then translate files into that space, from a scan or digital camera, and out of that space, to display on a monitor or print on a printer of some kind.

When you scan an image or have it scanned or put onto Photo CD, you need to be sure to get the best scan and,

with Photoshop 5, it would be very helpful to have an ICC profile of your scanner. If you are not doing the scanning yourself, you need to know how to check the scans that others have done to make sure that the maximum amount of information is available. And, you need to understand how to make the most of the information that you have. We cover the scanning part of the process in Chapter 16: Scanning, Resolution, Histograms, and Photo CD.

Trying to calibrate your monitor or perfect your process of making color corrections doesn't do any good unless the output device you are sending to (imagesetter, color printer, film recorder, or whatever) has been calibrated. A good way to test calibration is to send a group of neutral colors to your output device. I have created this file, called the StepWedgeFile, for use as a test file for calibrating your output device. The StepWedgeFile consists of wedges of neutral gray that have a known value. Two issues are involved in calibrating your output device. The first issue is whether the device will print the correct density. If you send a 50% density value (numerically, 128) to the device, it should measure and look like 50% when it prints. All densities should print as they are expected. The second issue is getting colors to print correctly. If you get the output device to print, using all its colors, these neutral gray values correctly, it's a good sign that it will also print colors correctly. You want the densities on the gray wedges to be correct, and you also want each wedge to continue to look gray.

To calibrate an imagesetter, send a grayscale version of the StepWedgeFile to the imagesetter and output it as one piece of film. Use a densitometer to measure the densities of the swatches on the film. They should match (plus or minus 1%) the densities that you sent from the file. Make sure the imagesetter is calibrated for density before you start worrying about color.

PRINT KNOWN CMYK COLOR OUTPUT TO MAKE A TEST PRINT

When you know that your output device has been calibrated for density, you should also check it for color. For CMYK output, you need a CMYK file that you know contains good color separation values and images. For RGB output, you need a known quality RGB original. On the following pages, we present examples of the types of files you should create or use for your tests.

A file that is in our Calibration folder, called KnownOutputTest, contains known CMYK values at the top in the neutral grays and also various colors that you can use to test how known CMYK colors print on your output device. We created these swatches in a CMYK file by selecting the area of each swatch and then going into the Photoshop Color Picker and typing in the CMYK values that make up that swatch's color. If you are doing this yourself, use Edit/Fill to fill the selection with the color you just created. The KnownOutputTest file also contains photographs that were separated using known color separation techniques. We have a version of the Ole No Moiré image from Adobe; the Bryce Canyon and Santa Cruz images are mine; the flying books is an Apple magazine cover shot by Marc Simon with effects by me; and the fourth image is by one of my students, Will Croff. All these images and these separations have been previously printed on a press with very good results.

You can make a test image of your own by creating grayscale bars and color bars like the ones shown in KnownOutputTest and then include several images that you know are good separations of work typical of the type of image you normally

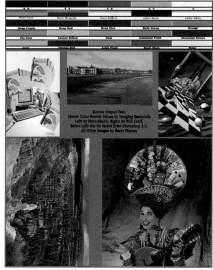

Here is our KnownOutputTest CMYK file. This file uses known CMYK values and separations. You can use it to make a test proof and to calibrate your monitor to that proof. You can also make your own Known Output test image.

separate. You can also include the Ole No Moiré image, which you can get from the Calibration folder within the Other Goodies folder on the Photoshop 5 installation CD. Check out the Read Me file within that same calibration folder for more information on how to calibrate with this file. After you output and proof your KnownOutputTest (or the one on the Photoshop 5 CD or the one in the Calibration folder on this book's CD) in the way you would normally work, you open the file that you used to create the proof and calibrate your monitor so the image onscreen matches the proof as closely as possible. We will show you how to do that shortly. For calibrating an RGB output device, use similar images that you know have worked well when output to that type of device.

CHECKING PHOTOSHOP SEPARATIONS OR RGB OUTPUT ON YOUR CMYK OR RGB OUTPUT DEVICE

If you are doing CMYK output, to see if your Photoshop color separation preference settings are working well, we will create a Photoshop separation test. This RGB file can also be used to test output to your RGB printer or other RGB output device. Before doing any tests, be sure to read Chapter 5: Setting System and Photoshop Preferences, and set up your Photoshop RGB Setup and CMYK Setup preferences correctly. If you already have Photoshop separation preferences that work well for you in Photoshop 5, you might want to continue to use those. To make your own test image, create an 8.5x11 canvas in RGB mode, fill it with a neutral gray background, and save it as Photoshop Separation Test. Now convert the grayscale Step-WedgeFile, in the Calibration folder on the CD, to RGB and paste it into the Photoshop Separation Test file.

Next, find some RGB images that are typical of your normal work. Copy these images and paste them into your test file. (We have created a Photoshop Separation Test file from some of the images in this book. It is called RGBOutputTest and is included in the Calibration folder on the *Photoshop 5 Artistry* CD and also printed in this chapter.) Save the final RGB version of your RGB test file. Use your Photoshop Separation Test, or ours, to output to your RGB printer or device or, if converting to CMYK, to output all four of the cyan, magenta, yellow, and black pieces of film in the same way you do your normal production. If you normally use the Photoshop Mode menu to convert from RGB to CMYK, do just that on the Photoshop Separation Test. If you use someone else's separation tables, do it that way. If you normally save your files as EPS/DCS from Photoshop and then put the file into Quark, do the same thing in your test. Save your final CMYK version of the file under a different name than the RGB version.

Print the Photoshop Separation Test to your RGB output device or for CMYK to film or plates on your normal imagesetter or platemaker and make one of your normal proofs. The densities should look correct in the stepwedge on the test print and they should also look gray. If the stepwedge densities are not right, or if they have a cyan, magenta, or some combination of color casts, it's a sign that either the RGB output device, imagesetter, platemaker, or proofer isn't calibrated or something's not right about the way you created this output. You should not have altered or color corrected the stepwedge file using your monitor, so it should be gray. If it doesn't look gray or the densities are not correct, you will have to calibrate your printer, or for CMYK adjust your separations to solve this problem. If the stepwedge looks good and this test prints with the correct densities and no color casts, you know you're set to calibrate the rest of your system.

The Calibration test files on the Photoshop 5 Artistry CD were created using the ColorMatch RGB workspace. If you open them into a different RGB workspace,

Here is our RGBOutputTest RGB file. This file uses known corrected RGB images from this book. You can use it to make a test print on an RGB device or convert it to CMYK to test out your Photoshop CMYK Setup settings.

like Adobe RGB, they will look different than they did using the ColorMatch RGB workspace, but you should not convert them into your other monitor workspace before making any output tests. Actually, these calibration files were saved with the Embed Profiles check boxes in the File/Color Settings/Profile Setup dialog turned off. Because I explicitly turned off Embed Profiles, Photoshop embeds a profile called None, and when you open one of these files into a different space, you won't be asked if you want to convert the file and the file will not be converted. This is what you want for a test file like this. A behavior that may seem strange however, is that when you have RGBOutputTest or StepWedgeFile open in any RGB space, the RGB readings in the Info palette will be correct, that is, the same readings I got, because the file was not converted. The CMYK readings for these two files, however, will depend on your current RGB Setup and CMYK Setup settings. When you have the KnownOutputTest file open, a CMYK file, in any CMYK Setup space, the CMYK readings you get in the Info palette will be correct, the same as mine, but the RGB readings you get will depend on your RGB Setup and CMYK Setup settings.

If you have an ICC profile for your output device, like the Lightjet 5000 for example, you may get a better looking print from these test images if you choose File/Export/Tiff With ColorSync Profile to export this print using the profile of your printer. If you do this, you will want to choose ColorMatchRGB as your Source profile, your printer's ICC profile as the Destination, set the Quality to Best, and set the Matching Style to Perceptual. This will create a TIFF file that you should then print on your printer. If you don't have a ColorMatch RGB setting within your ColorSync profiles, you can create one by using the Save button within the RGB Setup dialog while the RGB setting is set to ColorMatch RGB.

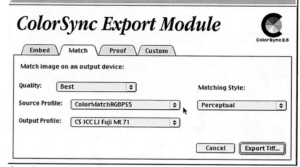

If you have an ICC profile to characterize your output file, you might get a better test by using the ColorSync Export module to transform into that space first. You would do a transform like this if you were normally outputting via an ICC profile. If you are printing directly from Photoshop, your Print dialog might also have the logic built in to do an ICC profile transform on-the-fly while printing.

CALIBRATING YOUR MONITOR

Now you are going to take your Known Output Test and your Photoshop Separation Test and use these files along with their proofs to calibrate your monitor. Consistent lighting in your office for color correcting images is a must. If you have an office with a large window right next to your screen, achieving consistent lighting onscreen is just about impossible. Ideally, you should have a color correct, 5000° Kelvin viewing box next to your monitor where you can place your proofs for consistent viewing. 5000° Kelvin is the standard viewing condition for viewing proofs in a CMYK printing environment, but if you or working in some other medium, like LightJet prints for gallery display, you will want to view your prints under a different light source. I use halogen flood lights to view my gallery prints because that is the most common gallery lighting source, and they have a color temperature around 2700 or so depending on the type of flood light you buy. You want a room where the lighting on your monitor is always the same. You can then adjust the monitor so the color and contrast of the image onscreen looks as close as possible to the proof.

Now that we are using Photoshop 5, we need to create an ICC profile for our monitor. If you have a monitor with a calibrator that can calibrate itself and generate an ICC profile, that is what you want to do. If you just have a normal monitor with no built-in software or hardware for calibration, you can use the Adobe Gamma utility that comes with Photoshop 5 to calibrate your monitor to a known color temperature and gamma and then create an ICC profile for that monitor. In either case, you will have to calibrate your monitor to some color temperature and gamma value. If

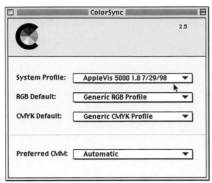

No matter how you calibrate your monitor, you need to set your ColorSync system profile to the ICC profile of your monitor after it's calibrated.

you are mostly working on CMYK print projects, I would recommend that you calibrate your monitor to gamma 1.8 and color temperature 5000. Gamma 1.8 works the best for most print work. If you are printing to a digital printer, the color temperature of your monitor should try to match the white on your print paper. CMYK match print paper is typically sort of yellowish in color, that is why we suggest 5000° K, but some digital printers actually have a more blueish paper so you might want to calibrate to 6500°K in that case. If you are mostly working on images for the Web, you might want to set your gamma to 2.2. After you have calibrated your monitor, either with hardware or Adobe Gamma, make sure you go into ColorSync, or the Windows equivalent, and set the System Profile to the ICC profile you have created with the calibration.

USING A BUILT-IN CALIBRATOR

I have an AppleVision 750 17" monitor, currently called a ColorSync 17 that has a built-in calibrator system that doesn't even require a suction cup. For the price, I'm pretty happy with what this monitor can do, and it is certainly more easy to use than some other calibration monitor systems I have played with. To the side here, I show the settings I use with this monitor when I am working on CMYK print projects, like this book. These settings get me very close to calibrated, and then I use the technique described at the end of the chapter for tweaking the CMYK preview. The combination of these things gets me very happily calibrated.

I also have a Radius PressView 21 SR 21" monitor that is supposed to be the industry standard for calibrated print monitors. When this monitor is working and you have a good one, it is a great monitor. I have lots of friends that do high-end color work who would use no other monitor. I have been very happy with mine too. I must say though that it took me three of these to get one that had consistent color across the entire screen, and then after using the monitor for two years, it broke and cost me over $600 to repair. I have also talked with other people who have had problems getting one of these monitors set up correctly, yet all of us really like them when all is working properly. I'd also like to thank Radius for all the help and support they have given me with the PressView. You may find, and I have heard this too, that the 17" pressview is more consistent and reliable. At any rate, if you want a monitor that you can calibrate, using hardware, to a particular color temperature and gamma, I'd recommend the Radius Pressview or the Apple ColorSync monitors. You do usually get better more consistent results with a hardware calibrator than by using the Adobe Gamma utility we are going to describe next. If you do get a hardware calibrator system, make sure you follow the directions that come with that system.

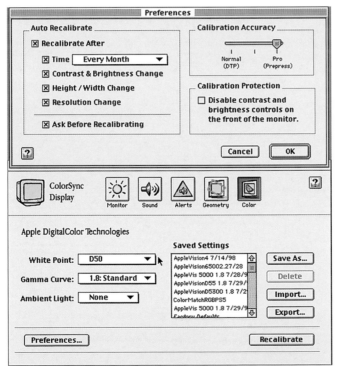

Here are the settings I use with my Apple ColorSync 17 built-in hardware calibration system. For working with this book, I'm using a color temp of 5000 and gamma of 1.8. I have the preferences, at the top, set to use the maximum Pro accuracy and to recalibrate any time something with my monitor changes. If other people were playing around with my system, I'd probably also turn on the check box to disable the brightness and contrast controls on the front of my monitor. The Recalibrate button runs a bunch of tests to measure the monitor hardware and then sets it to 5000 and 1.8. I then Export an ICC profile to load as my ColorSync System Profile. That automatically passes the information on to Photoshop.

Using the Adobe Gamma Utility

First, make sure the background on your monitor is neutral gray. On the Mac, go to Control Panels on the Apple menu and locate the Desktop Pattern Desk Accessory. Click the arrows on either end of the slider until you find a neutral gray, then click the Set Desktop Pattern button to invoke the change. In Windows 95 and NT, click the Start button, select Settings, Control Panel. Now click the Display icon then click the Background tab and select None in the Pattern and Wallpaper drop-down menus. Select the Appearance tab and click the Color button. Now choose one of the neutral grays from the pop-up swatches or click the Other button to open the Color dialog box. This dialog box gives you more color swatch selections and also allows you to choose a gray value from the Color Picker or to enter a value, like 128, for RGB in the Red, Green, and Blue settings. If you use the Color dialog box, you will have to press OK to apply the change from this dialog box, in either case, press OK from the Appearance tab to apply the changes.

To describe the use of this Adobe Gamma utility, we will show you screen grabs of the 10 steps that you have to go through, and under each grab, we'll have a caption that explains that step.

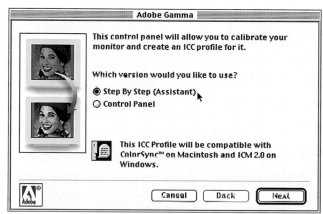

Step1: When you open Adobe Gamma, you can either choose the Step By Step Assistant, which give you more help along the way, or the Adobe Gamma Control Panel, which comes without much explanation. We will use the Assistant version here. You might want to try the Control Panel after more experience.

Step2: Here you press the Load button to choose an initial ICC profile to describe your monitor. For example, if you had a Radius PressView monitor, you could probably start out using the ColorMatch RGB profile. For this monitor, I initially use the Apple 17" D50 profile.

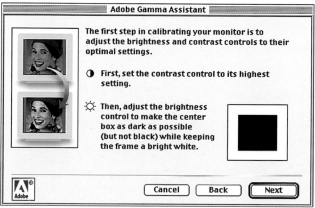

Step3: This screen of the Adobe Gamma Assistant helps you to correctly set the Brightness and Contrast controls on you monitor. When they are correct, you should barely be able to see the smaller box in the center of the black area, and you should also have bright whites.

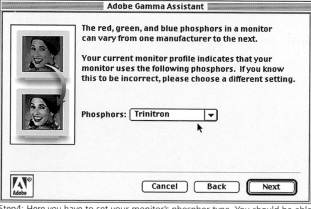

Step4: Here you have to set your monitor's phosphor type. You should be able to get that information from the documentation that comes with your monitor. If you use a correct starting monitor profile, that information might also be included there.

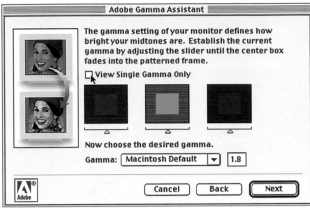

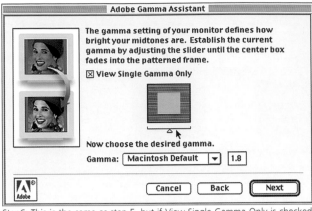

Step5: In this step, you choose a desired monitor gamma. For print work, or for print and Web work, I would suggest setting this at 1.8. If you are doing exclusively Web work, set it to 2.2. To get the color to match correctly, sit back and squint while moving the slider until the box in the middle is least visible.

Step6: This is the same as step 5, but if View Single Gamma Only is checked, you make the gray box in the middle disappear within the surrounding box. I'd try both methods to see which works best for you. When it is correct, the boxes in the middle should be least visible in both gray and color modes.

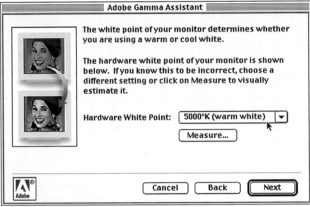

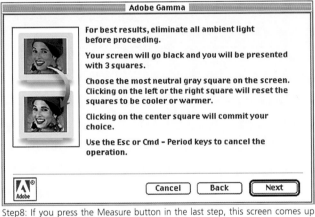

Step7: Here you are choosing the hardware white point of your monitor. Many monitors these days have a settable white point, and if yours does, you should set it before running Adobe Gamma; then choose that setting here. For CMYK print work, you will probably want to use 5000 Kelvin.

Step8: If you press the Measure button in the last step, this screen comes up giving you directions on how to measure your monitor's default hardware white point. If you don't have a monitor with a settable white point, read these directions, then click Next in this dialog to get the next step below.

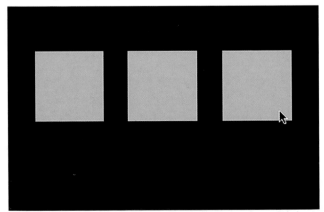

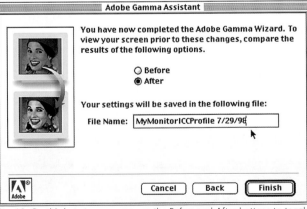

Step9: To help you judge which square is actually a neutral gray, it helps to have a Macbeth Colorchecker chart or a Kodak grayscale chart placed in your 5000° Kelvin viewing box. You can then adjust the squares here until you get a gray that matches the neutral gray on one of those charts.

Step10: On this last step, you can use the Before and After buttons to toggle between the way your monitor was set up before and how it will be set up after this session with Adobe Gamma. If you are happy with your Adobe Gamma session, save your changes into a newly named ICC profile of your monitor. When you leave Adobe Gamma, on the Mac make sure your Color-Sync System Profile is correctly set to this new monitor ICC profile on WIndows make sure ICM is set correctly for this profile.

GETTING EXACT CMYK SOFT PROOFS

After using Adobe Gamma, or a hardware calibration technique to calibrate your monitor, if you find that your CMYK files on the screen (or your RGB soft proofs) still don't look like your proofs—hopefully they are close at this point—there is a trick you can use to adjust the CMYK preview logic in Photoshop to have your CMYK files match your proofs more closely. Here are the steps to do this:

1. With your CMYK digital file (or RGB soft proof) on the screen, bring up Hue/Saturation or Selective Color Adjustment layers and adjust your onscreen image until it matches your proof as closely as possible. Do this all within your standard controlled lighting environment. If your neutrals are off, the Neutrals choice under the Colors pop-up does a good job of adjusting neutrals. When your onscreen image matches as closely as possible, go into each Adjustment layer in order and use the Save button to save the changes made in that layer.
2. Open the CMYK Colors file (or the <Profile Name> from CMYK file) inside the Goodies/Calibration folder in the Adobe Photoshop 5 folder and make each of those changes to that file in the same order as your Adjustment layers were. So, for example, if your first change was a Selective Color adjustment, you would choose Image/Adjust/Selective Color and then use the Load button to load that change; then choose OK. You would then go ahead and make the next change, and so on to this file until all the changes were made.
3. Convert the CMYK Colors file to RGB using Image/Mode/RGB; then convert it to Lab using Image/Mode/Lab.
4. Choose File/Save As to save the file with a different name, like MatchPrint-ProofTweaks or something, in RAW format with the File Type set to 8BST.
5. Go into CMYK Setup and then set the CMYK Model to Tables. Now click the Load button and choose the file you just saved, in my case MatchPrint-ProofTweaks. Notice that this only changes the From CMYK Table part and not the To CMYK Table part. The From CMYK Table part controls how CMYK files are converted to RGB for display on the screen. You just modified how Photoshop does screen display for CMYK files so your display shows them more accurately. Items within () above imply that you can also use this technique here to fine tune the Previewing Color technique described on pages 111 and 112.

This process allows you to keep your monitor calibrated to a standard setting, like gamma 1.8 and color temperature 5000 or gamma 2.2 and color temperature 6500, and yet have a very accurate way to tweak your soft proofs of CMYK images. If you switch to a different soft proofing system, or actually use a press proof, you just need to create a new custom table for that proofing system. Make sure you leave your original CMYK Setup file untouched and start out with this every time you go back to a new proofing system. When you change your CMYK Setup back to Built-in, Photoshop will automatically alter the From CMYK tables to the defaults based on your Ink Options settings. Doing this for CMYK soft proofing is very similar to the process called Previewing Color described at the end of Chapter 14 for soft proofing RGB output devices. Both these techniques are the most useful I've found for exactly calibrating your monitor to a particular output device. Thanks a lot to Jim Rich, author of *Photoshop in Black and White*, and Bruce Ashley for all their help in explaining and testing out this method. They have both been using this technique for some time to get more accurate CMYK monitor calibration. This technique actually works quite well with Photoshop 4 ,too; the steps are just a little different there!

No matter how you calibrate your monitor, you need to set your ColorSync system profile to the ICC profile generated by the calibration of your monitor. Photoshop on the Mac gets its information about your monitor from the ColorSync System Profile.

121

16 SCANNING, RESOLUTION, HISTOGRAMS, AND PHOTO CD

Here you learn how to make a good scan at the right resolution and file size, how to use histograms to evaluate and improve scans, and how to make the best use of Photo CD scans.

WHAT ARE BYTES, BITS, AND DPI?

To learn how to make a good scan, you need to understand resolution and the issues involved in determining what size to make the scan. Because we're going to be talking about size in bytes, let's take a minute to talk about bytes, bits, and dpi. A *byte* (8 bits) is the most common unit of measurement of computer memory. All computer functionality is based on switches that can be turned on and off. A single switch is called a *bit*. When a bit is off, it has a value of 0. When a bit is on, it has a value of 1. With a single bit, you can count from 0 to 1. With two bits lined up next to each other, you can count from 0 to 3 because now there are four possibilities (00=0, 01=1, 10=2, and 11=3). Add a third bit, and you can count from 0 to 7 (000=0, 001=1, 010=2, 011=3, 100=4, 101=5, 110=6, and 111=7). When there are 8 bits, or a byte, you can count from 0 to 255, which is 256 possible values.

A grayscale digital image has one byte of information for each value scanned from the film. A value of 0 is the darkest possible value, black, and a value of 255 is the brightest possible value, white. Values in between are different levels of gray, the lower numbers being darker and the higher numbers being lighter. You can think of these values like you would think of individual pieces of grain within a piece of film: the more values you have per inch, the smaller the grain in the digital file. Also, the more of these values that you have per inch, the higher the resolution (alias dpi [dots per inch] or samples per inch) in your file. An RGB color digital image has three bytes of information (24 bits, one byte for each channel of red, green, or blue) for each value scanned from the film. And CMYK files have four bytes per pixel.

If you have an enlarger in the traditional darkroom, you can make a 20x24 print from a 35mm original. Its quality will not be as good as a 20x24 print on the same paper from a 4x5 original of the same type of film, because the 4x5 has more film area with which to define the image. If you were printing on different types of paper, the paper's grain would affect the look of the final print. It's the amount of grain in the original film that makes the difference when you project that film on the same paper to make a traditional darkroom print.

When you make a print on a printing press, the line screen of the halftone is analogous to the grain in the photographic paper. When you make a print on a digital printer, the dpi (dots per inch) of the printer is analogous to the grain in the photographic paper. The dpi of a digital printer is the number of individual sensors, or ink jets, or laser spots, that the particular printer can put down per inch. Each digital printer has its own maximum possible dpi, based on its own specific physical limitations. The relationship between the dpi of a scan and the line screen or dpi of a digital printer is analogous to the relationship between the grain size of film in the enlarger and the grain size of the paper you are printing on in a traditional darkroom. A scan of 100 dpi will print on a digital printer that can output at 300 dpi, but it won't look as good as a 300 dpi scan for the same printer. Similarly, a print on photographic paper from ASA 1600 (large grain) film won't look as good as a print on the same paper from ASA 25 (small grain) film.

How Big Should I Make a Scan?

When you are having an image scanned, you should know the intended purpose of the scan well ahead of time. When you have more than one purpose and image size, scan the image at the maximum size you would use it.

The formula for calculating the optimal byte size for a scan of a 6x7 image to be printed at 300 dpi is (6x300 dpi) x (7x300 dpi) x 3. This file would be 11,340,000 bytes in size. (The final factor represents the number of bytes for each pixel in the image; 3 is the number for an RGB color image.) For a CMYK scan, the factor is 4 instead of 3 because there are 4 bytes for each pixel in a CMYK image. If you do a black-and-white scan, you can remove this factor because they require only one byte per pixel. When scanning for publication, you generally should scan an extra ¼ inch for each dimension to give the stripper (electronic or manual) a little extra space for fine adjustment. Here's the general formula for the required byte size of final publication scans:

Scan Size = ((height of image + ¼") x (2 x line screen dpi)) x ((width of image + ¼") x (2 x line screen dpi)) x 3 (for RGB)

If you scan a file for output to a digital printer, such as the Epson Stylist Photo or the LightJet 5000, you need to do the scan at the same dpi as the resolution of the printer you plan to use. For output to the LightJet 5000, which has a resolution of 120 pixels per centimeter (304.8 dpi), the formula and byte size would be (6x304.8 dpi) x (7x304.8 dpi) x 3 = 11,705,783 bytes. Most dye sublimation digital printers (Fargo, Tektronics, Mitsubishi, GCC, et al.), and also the IRIS ink jet printer, have a printed dpi of 300. The Epson Stylist Photo and the Epson 600, 8000, and 3000 have printed dpis of from 720 to 1440. The way the Epson uses dots, however, is different from digital printers like the dye subs and the LightJet 5000. I have found that for these type of Epson printers, you get good results if you use a file of about 360 dpi. You should find out the resolution of the printer your service bureau is using and do your scans accordingly.

If you scan a file for output to a film recorder, such as the Kodak LVT (Light Valve Technology), or Cymbolic Sciences' Light Jet 2000, remember that they require a very high dpi. If you want the output to have the same quality as original film, the dpi can be around 2000 or more. Outputting a 4x5 RGB transparency at 2,000 dpi requires a file size of (4x2000) x (5x2000) x 3, or 240,000,000 bytes. For

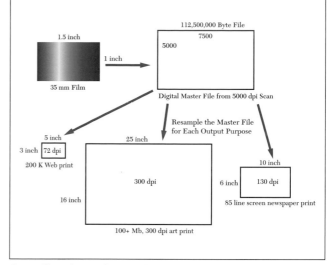

If you will use the scan for more than one purpose, make the original scan for the size of the biggest file you will need. Do your overall color correction, image enhancement, and spotting on this biggest master file. You can then resample that corrected file down to whatever resolution and file size you need. Above you see some sample uses. When scanning most files on a high end drum scanner, you will find that you will not get anymore detail information from the film by scanning it at more than 5000 dpi. If you scan at a higher dpi than this, you probably will not get any better data than just resampling up the 5000 dpi file. A file of this dpi can certainly be resampled down with Image Size or the Cropping tool to 72 dpi for the Web, 300 dpi for a digital art print, 170 dpi for a newspaper print, or anything else you need.

If the image is to be published as a halftone on a printing press and you want the best quality, you need to scan it at a dpi (dots per inch or scan samples per inch) of twice the line screen of the publication. For example, if you are printing a six-inch by seven-inch photograph in a 150-line screen publication, you should scan it at 300 dpi for the number of inches you're printing it at.

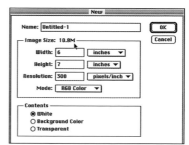

Use File/New to calculate the size of the scan you will need.

film recorders, the dpi of the file needs to match the maximum dpi of the film recorder for optimal quality.

If you have trouble remembering formulas and don't want to bother with a calculator, there is an easy way to calculate the file size you will need: by using the New command in Photoshop. Choose File/New, and then enter the width and height dimensions in inches for the largest size you expect to print the image you are scanning. Based on the current discussion, set the resolution in pixels/inch to match what you will need for your line screen or printer resolution. Now set the mode to Grayscale, RGB, or CMYK, according to the type of scan. The image size that shows up at the top of the dialog box is the size in megabytes that you should make your scan. Now you can cancel from this dialog box; Photoshop has done the calculation for you.

The formulas for file size that we present here are the ones you would use to obtain the best quality. Making even larger scans than these is unlikely to improve the quality but definitely increases the time necessary to work with and output the files. Making smaller scans than these most likely reduces your quality but also decreases the time necessary to work with and output the files.

If you scan small files, usually measured in pixel dimensions, for Web sites or multimedia applications, you often can get better results if you scan a simple factor larger in each dimension. I recently did some Web images where the final spec for the GIF file size was 180 by 144 pixels. I scanned the files at 720 by 576 and did all my color corrections and masking at this larger, more detailed size. One of the final steps before creating the GIF files was to scale the corrected and sharpened files to 25% of the larger size. This 25% scale factor is a simple ratio that allows for very accurate scaling. See "Creating Small Transparent GIF Composites" for the details of this process.

If you need some digital files to prototype a project, you don't need to start with the large scans we describe here. I find that RGB scans of about one megabyte usually provide plenty of screen detail for any prototyping I do. If you JPEG-compress these scans, you should be able to get 10 or so on a 1.4Mb disk and hundreds on a ZIP. When you decide on the final dimensions for the images in your project or printed piece, you can do a final scan for the intended output device at those final dimensions. When you get a big final scan, archive the original digital file as it was scanned and use copies of it to do color corrections, color separations, and crops, so that you can go back to the original if you make a mistake and need to start over. Happy scanning!

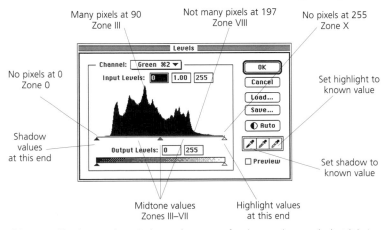

A histogram, like the one above, is the graph you get of an image when you look at it in Levels. For more information on levels and histograms, turn to "The Grand Canyon," where we furnish a detailed introduction to levels. Also refer to "Digital Imaging and the Zone System" to see how histograms relate to traditional photography and light.

EVALUATING HISTOGRAMS TO MAKE THE BEST SCAN FROM ANY SCANNER

Now that you know how big to make the scan, you need to know how to make a good scan and also how to do a good job of bringing an image into Photoshop from Photo CD. The key to these techniques is learning how to use the histogram in Levels to evaluate scans. This section presents a few histograms and talks about what they reveal about the images they are describing. By the way, some of the Levels histogram screen grabs from this chapter and others are from earlier versions of Photoshop. We usually only update screen grabs if the features in the tool or the tool's

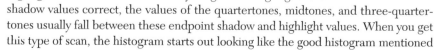

layout have changed. This has not changed in Levels; Photoshop 5 just uses the new platinum appearance.

A *histogram* is a bar graph of the samples of each possible setting in the 0 to 255 range in the entire image. The diagram on the previous page shows you some of the useful information that a histogram can provide. When you have normal subject material, the best possible circumstance is to have an original image, transparency, or negative that has a good exposure of the subject matter and shows a full range of values from very dark to very bright and some detail in all areas. The previous chapter, "Digital Imaging and the Zone System," tells you how to create a high-quality exposure with a camera. If you have a high-quality image that contains values in all zones and has been scanned correctly, you see a histogram like the one shown to the left.

When you scan a normal full brightness range image, you should aim to get a scan that has a full range of the values present in the original. For most common commercial uses of photography, you want a histogram that has similar traits as the one shown here.

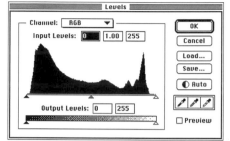

A histogram that has a full range of values. The shape of the histogram in the middle is different for each image.

SCANNING SHADOWS AND HIGHLIGHTS

When you scan an image, there are several areas in which you need to be careful what values you obtain. There can be places within the scanned image that are totally black. These should occur only if the original has areas that are totally black (*black shadows*, Zone 0). Then there are the regular shadows, which are the darkest places in the image that still show texture or detail when printed (Zones I and II). On the other end of the spectrum are specular highlights, which are areas in the original that are totally white, such as the reflection of the sun in the chrome bumper of a car (Zone X). Next, there are regular highlights, the brightest areas of the image where you still want to see some texture or detail (Zones VIII and IX).

To some extent, we can call everything between the regular highlights and the regular shadow areas *midtones*. At the dark end of the midtones, are the *three-quarter-tones* (shadow areas where you can see a fair amount of detail) and at the bright end of the midtones, the *quartertones* (highlight areas where you should also be able to see a fair amount of detail).

ADJUSTING THE SCANNER TO GET THE RIGHT VALUES

When you do a scan, the values that you want to obtain for the shadows and the highlights depend on the type of output device you are directing the final image toward. If you are not sure of the output device or if you might be using different output devices, the highlights (Zone IX) should have a value in the range of 245–250 and the shadows (Zone I) should have a value in the range of 5–10. With an original image that has a full range of colors in each of the red, green, and blue channels, you need to adjust the scanner to get these types of highlight and shadow values. If you get the highlight and shadow values correct, the values of the quartertones, midtones, and three-quartertones usually fall between these endpoint shadow and highlight values. When you get this type of scan, the histogram starts out looking like the good histogram mentioned

You may not want the shadow values to go right down to 0 and you may not want the highlight values to go right up to 255, depending on the range of values in the original image and on the intended output device.

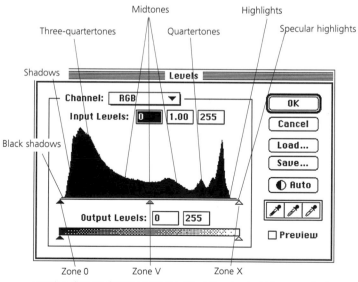

Here is a diagram showing what the different parts of a histogram refer to.

Histograms of different scanning problems and how to fix them.

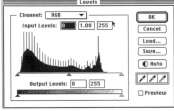

Highlights not bright enough, increase overall exposure on scanner.

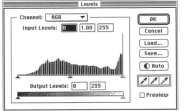

Highlights too bright, decrease overall exposure on scanner.

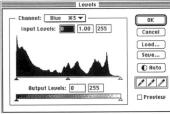

Blacks too dark in the Blue channel, lost shadow detail. Make sure original has detail in the shadows, and if it does, then change black setting in the scan for less black or for lighter shadows.

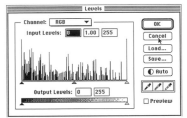

Original is posterized, or this is a bad, gappy scan.

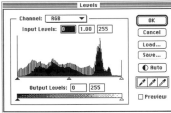

This type of look may indicate one channel was scanned badly. See the Red channel in the histogram to the right.

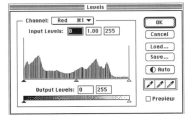

The Red channel from the histogram to the left. Need to lower exposure on red and also lighten black setting.

If the scanner allows you to make separate adjustments for each of the Red, Green, and Blue channels, look at the histogram from each channel and adjust the Red, Green, and Blue scanner settings separately to get the best histogram in each color.

earlier. With this complete scan, you can always adjust the image in Photoshop to get different highlight, midtone, and shadow values, as well as different contrast, and you will know that you started with all the information from the scanner. I usually do my scans with the normal default scanner settings. Some scanners allow you to add a curve that adjusts the image as you scan it. I generally don't use a preset curve in the scanner because I'd rather do the adjustment myself in Photoshop. When you have a scanner that scans more than 8 bits of info per color, for example 12, using a pre-set curve may help the scanner to decide which of the 12-bit range is used to reduce down to 8 bits per color. See if you get better results by applying the curve in the scanner versus doing it in Photoshop.

SCANNING STEP BY STEP

Whenever I scan in Photoshop, using any scanner, I always use the same simple technique. First I set up the default brightness, contrast, and color balance controls on the scanner. I remove any pre-set curves that would change the contrast of the scan from the scanner setting. I make sure that I set the scanner for the correct type of film. I then do a prescan, which shows me the image in the scanner's preview window. I crop the image to scan the area I want to scan. In the Nikon Scan dialog box at the top of the next page, the prescan and crop are shown on the right. Next, I set the scanner to do about a 1Mb scan. I usually don't tell desktop scanners to sharpen the image, because I don't know how good their sharpening software is. If I get a good focused raw scan from the scanner, I know Photoshop sharpening can do a great job. The next step is to do the 1Mb scan at the default settings. I would only buy a scanner that had a Photoshop plug-in allowing it to scan directly into Photoshop. This saves a lot of time over scanning into another package, saving the file, and then having to reopen it in Photoshop.

Next, I evaluate the 1Mb scan for correctness by first cropping any extra information from around the edges of the scan and then using Levels in Photoshop to look at the image. You want to crop any black or white borders before you look at the histogram because they distort the accuracy of the histogram. At the end of this chapter, I show you some sample histograms and explain their problems and how to correct them by adjusting the scanner.

Keep on doing 1Mb scans and adjusting scanner settings until you get the best histogram you can. Once you get the levels to look correct on the small 1Mb scan, use the same scanner settings for exposure and color balance, and increase the size of the scan to give you the final number of megabytes that you will need. It is always best to get a good-looking histogram from the scanner before you make corrections to the histogram in Photoshop. If you aren't personally doing the scan, you at least now know how to evaluate the scans you get. When you cannot improve the scan using the scanner itself (you didn't do the scan, you don't have the scanner, or you already did the best that the scanner can do), the next step is to get the histogram correct using Photoshop's color correction utilities. I cover this process after the next section.

GETTING THE RIGHT HISTOGRAM

Time and again I am asked in classes, "What is a good histogram?" Let me ask a question in response. If you have three different photographers take a picture of a basket of apples, which would be the "good" photograph: the one that is dark, moody, and mysterious; the one that is light, delicate, and ethereal; or the one that is an accurate representation of a basket of apples in the sunshine? In actuality, any or all of the three may be excellent photographs. Judging a histogram is similar, in that many different histograms could be the "right" histogram for a given photograph, depending on the artist's interpretation of the subject.

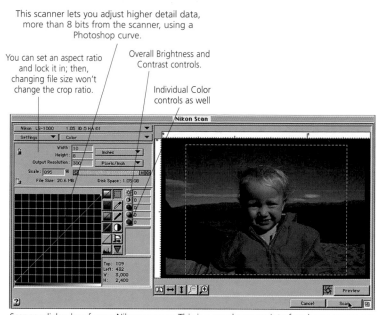

This scanner lets you adjust higher detail data, more than 8 bits from the scanner, using a Photoshop curve.

You can set an aspect ratio and lock it in; then, changing file size won't change the crop ratio.

Overall Brightness and Contrast controls.

Individual Color controls as well

Scanner dialog box from a Nikon scanner. This is a good scanner interface because you can create the cropping box in the prescan window to the right, and set its dimensions and its dpi independent of each other. Nikon scanners also have good controls for brightness in each of the Red, Green, and Blue channels, as well as good controls for overall brightness and shadow settings.

COMPARING THE HISTOGRAM TO THE ORIGINAL

The histogram cannot be viewed separately from the original slide or photo. A good histogram of the original is one that accurately reflects the amount of information in the original. A good histogram of the final output accurately represents the artist's visualization. Never does the adage, "garbage in, garbage out" apply more fully than in digital imaging. If you have an original with no highlight detail, there is absolutely zero possibility that even a high-end scanner can give you something to work with. A good scan of a good original, however, gives you a full range of information that can be manipulated digitally, just as you would manipulate information traditionally in the darkroom.

If you start with a very low contrast original, your histogram will have a shortened value scale; that is, the representation of the pixel values will not stretch across all the values from 0 to 255. In general, as you color correct this scan, you force the values of the pixels in the scan to spread out along the luminosity axis all the way from deep shadows (between about 3 and 10) to bright highlights (around 245)—notice that we say "in general." If the effect that you wish to achieve is a very low contrast image, say, a photo that appears ghosted back, you may need to do very little adjustment to the histogram. It all depends on what you are visualizing for the final output. Just as you use the Zone System to set where the values of the actual subject matter

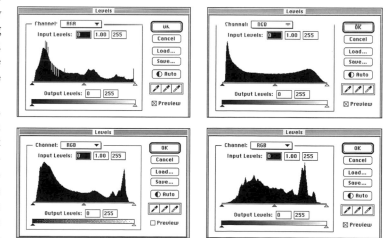

These could all be good normal histograms. Generally, the important characteristic in a good histogram of a typical photograph is to have values that go all the way from one end of the histogram to the other. This histogram would represent an image that has values from black, Zone 0, all the way to white, Zone X. The way the graph actually looks in between these two endpoint areas varies with the particular image. **For some images, such as soft fog on a mountain lake after sunset, or a subtle snow scene, there may not be bright highlights or dark shadows, and then you wouldn't have values that go all the way from one end of the histogram to the other. That is OK for that type of image.**

will fall on the film, in digital imaging you choose (by manipulating the histogram) where the values of the scan will fall in the final output. Therefore, you must view the histogram in the context of the original input and the desired output. You must ask yourself, "What is actually there?" and "What do I want the audience to see?"

SCANNING UP TO 16 BITS PER COLOR PER PIXEL

Many scanners these days scan a lot more than 8 bits of information per color per pixel. The scanner gets this information out of the film and then the scanner software uses a curve or other scanner settings to reduce this down to 8 bits per pixel when it gives it to you in Photoshop. If you later decide you are not happy with the 8 bits of information you got, you will have to rescan the image to get a different set of values. For example, the scanner may actually pull more shadow range information from the film but, due to the fact that 8-bit files are limited to a total of 256 tones per color, the software throws out a lot of this shadow info when it reduces the file to 8 bits. Since Photoshop 5 has much better support for actually working with files that have more than 8 bits per color, it would be much better to have the option of getting all the information the scanner gets from the film before the scanner software reduces it down to 8 bits. That way you could save this info on disk and modify it many different ways without having to rescan the image. Photoshop 5 allows you to work with up to 16 bits of information per channel using many of its tools including Levels, Curves, Hue/Saturation, Brightness/Contrast, Color Balance, Equalize, Invert, and Channel Mixer. You can also Crop, Rubber Stamp, Image Size, and Rotate Arbitrary, as well as use the History Brush with 16-bit channel files. Some scanners allow for the saving of files with more than 8 bits per color channel, but many, even some very expensive ones, don't. This is now an important feature to check for when buying a scanner to use for doing high end color work.

MODIFYING WITH LEVELS AND CURVES

Once you get a good scan with a good histogram, you can modify it with Levels and Curves to get your visualization of that image for your final print. If you move the Levels Input Highlight slider to the left, you move your Zone VIII and IX values toward Zone X, brightening the highlights. If you move the Output Highlight slider to the left, you move your Zone X, IX, and VIII values toward Zone IX, VIII, and VII, respectively, dulling the highlights. Similarly, you can use the Shadow sliders to move the zone values around in the shadow parts of the histogram. If you move the Input Brightness/Contrast slider to the right, you move Zone V values toward Zone IV or III, making the midtones darker and more contrasty. If you move the slider to the left, you move Zone V values toward Zone VI or VII, making the image lighter and brighter.

The Curves tool allows you to make even finer adjustments to values in specific zones. Read "Grand Canyon," "Kansas," and "Desert Al" chapters to try out these techniques and see how digital imaging gives you more power to realize your vision. As Ansel Adams says in his book *The Negative,* "Much of the creativity in photography lies in the infinite range of choices open to the photographer between attempting a nearly literal representation

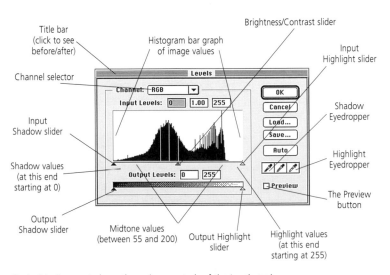

Study this diagram to learn the various controls of the Levels tool.

of the subject and freely interpreting it in highly subjective 'departures from reality.'" Many people think of Adams' prints as straight photos from nature. Actually, Adams did a lot of adjusting with his view camera and in the darkroom to create the visualization of the image that would bring forth his feelings and impressions from the original scene. I believe he would enjoy digital imaging.

WORKING WITH PHOTO CD IMAGES

Photoshop 5 now has some pretty good built-in support for Kodak Photo CD. First let's talk a little about Photo CD. When you get an image scanned onto Photo CD, there are two possible formats: Regular and Pro Photo CD. Regular Photo CDs have five scans of different sizes of each image. The five pixel dimensions are 192x128, 384x256, 768x512, 1536x1024, and 3072x2048 pixels. For about $1 to $2 a photograph, you get all five sizes of scans of each photograph. The largest of these is an 18Mb file, which is useful for a 10"x6.8" separation at 300 dpi (that is, for a 150 line screen separation). With these 18Mb files, I have actually made some very high-quality 11x17 prints by using a ProofPositive dye sublimation printer (no longer available), resampling up the images, and sharpening them. I have also made great prints from Photo CD scans on my Epson Stylist Photo printer.

Kodak also offers Pro Photo CD scans. These scans have the same five resolutions as above, plus a sixth resolution that is 4096x6144, or up to 72Mb in size—big enough for 11x17 by 300 dpi without resampling up the scans. I have made high quality 16x20 LightJet 5000 prints from 4x5 Pro Photo CD scans. The Pro scans cost about $15 to $20 each and they seem to be very good as long as you give them a proper original exposure. I have been getting my Photo CD and Pro Photo CD scans done at Palmer Photographic and have been quite happy with the results. Palmer takes jobs from Federal Express and gives you 48-hour turnaround. To try them out, copy the free coupon at the end of the book.

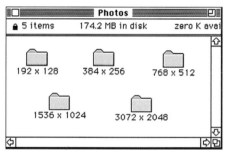

Here are the five pixel dimensions of regular Photo CD scans.

If you have a difficult negative—one that is improperly exposed, too dark or too light—and you want to get the absolute most out of the scan, you may do better with a high-end drum scan. On the other hand, if the original is a good exposure with a full range of data, and you make sure that you tell the people doing the Photo CD scans the type of film you are sending them, you should be able to get very usable scans. As with any scan, however, the operator of the scanner and the quality control of the service bureau doing the scans is going to affect the results. If you are not happy with the results at your service bureau, try a different Photo CD scanning location.

The Photo CD scan puts your image onto a CD. A regular CD, be it an audio CD, multimedia CD, or whatever, can hold up to 650Mb of digital information. The Photo CD scans are compressed so that even if a file is 18Mb when you open it, it takes up only 4Mb to 6Mb of storage on the disc. That means you can get about 100 to 120 regular Photo CD scans on a single CD. The Pro format takes much more disk space; you can only get about 30 of them on a single CD.

BRINGING PHOTO CD INTO PHOTOSHOP

There are various options for bringing a Photo CD image into Photoshop and in the past I had liked the Kodak Acquire module version 2.3 because it gave me the best histograms of my scans and more absolute control over how the scan was opened. Now, the Photoshop 5 built in Photo CD support available from the Open dialog allows me to open Photo CD images in an ICC profile compatible way.

For great Photo CD scans, call Palmer Photographic in California at 800-735-1950. We usually ship to them using Federal Express.

Poor Scans and Their Problem Histograms
(Different types of problems require different scanner adjustments)

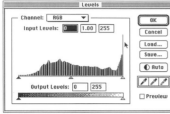

No highlight detail. Rescan with a lower exposure setting.

The image is too bright, obscuring the detail in the clouds and other highlights.

This scan has quite different ranges for each of the Red, Green, and Blue channels. Best to rescan and adjust each channel separately.

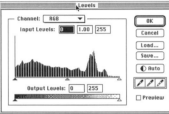

No shadow detail. Rescan and change the shadow setting on the scanner.

No matter what we do in Photoshop, we won't be able to bring out shadow detail because it was lost in the scan.

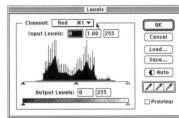

The Red channel for the scan above. Rescan with more exposure on red, and a different black value.

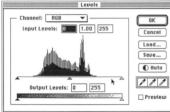

Not a broad enough range on the scan. We could correct this in Photoshop by bringing in the highlight and shadow sliders, but then we would end up with a gappy scan like below. We are better off rescanning with more exposure and a different shadow setting.

The highlights and shadows are way too dull.

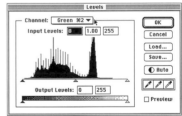

The Green channel for the scan above. Rescan with larger exposure for green; black is okay here.

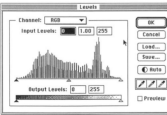

The histogram of the image above after fixing it in Photoshop; it now has a bunch of gaps in it that represent lost tonal values. You will get more detail in the printed result by rescanning.

The corrected image with the gappy histogram still prints better than the uncorrected histogram.

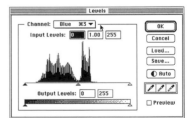

The Blue channel for the scan above. Rescan with a much larger exposure and possible black adjustments.

Corrected Photographs and Their Good Histograms
(Values in the middle of a histogram look different for each photo)

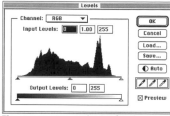

The correct scan and print for the sample image on the previous page. Lots of ¾ tones on the dark parts of the beach. The large number of ¼ tones are probably in the sky and the waves.

Santa Cruz sunset from the boardwalk.

Young Lakes.

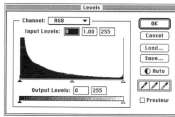

Lots of very dark areas and very bright areas, even totally black and white, are OK in this photo.

The Paris Cafe.

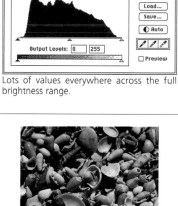

Lots of values everywhere across the full brightness range.

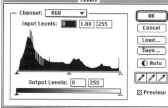

This histogram has lots of dark shadows in the trees and the fence. The spike at the far right is the white buildings.

The Burnley church.

Shells in Costa Rica.

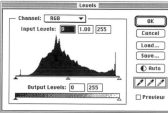

Notice the small spike for the dark shadow areas that are small but so important in the photograph.

Man on the beach at sunset.

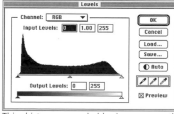

This histogram probably is so smooth because all the objects have a similar range of colors and subtle tones.

Edit Image...

OK
Cancel

[748K]

Video RGB
Photo CD YCC
Grayscale
GAMMA 1.4 5000
GAMMA 1.8 5000
GAMMA 2.2 5000
GAMMA 1.4 6500
GAMMA 1.8 6500
GAMMA 2.2 6500
GAMMA 1.4 9300
GAMMA 1.8 9300
GAMMA 2.2 9300

Resolution: Base   (512x768)
Metric: GAMMA 1.4 5000°K

Edit Functions:
Saturation: 0
Cyan/Red: 0
Magenta/Green: 0
Yellow/Blue: 0
Dark/Light: 0

The older Kodak Acquire module, version 2.3, allows you to choose the gamma and color temperature with which to open the file. Although this is from before ColorSync, I still like the histograms it produces. I usually use Gamma 1.4 and color temp of 5000°K which tends to give the most histogram information in Levels. If you are not happy with the results from the built-in Photo CD support, you may still want to try out this Plug-In if you can find one.

Kodak ICC Photo CD

Photo CD
Image: IMG0010.PCD;1
Image   1536 by 1024
File Size: 4.5 MB

Source
KODAK Photo CD 4050 K-14 V3.4

Destination
Lab Color Space Profile

OK
Cancel
Image Info
Source
Destination

Here are the controls for the built-in Photo CD Open command that you access from File/Open. It allows you to specify an ICC profile for the source device and the destination device. The source device specification is an ICC profile that you should get from your Photo CD provider. The name they seem to use for it is a film term, which will describe what the Photo CD scanner will do with a particular type of film. There is usually one Film term for Kodachrome and another for E6. The Destination profile should be set to your standard RGB or Lab workspace. You can always save an RGB workspace profile by just using the Save button in RGB setup. When you have an accurate Source and Destination profile, this appears to give pretty good results but the results will not be very good if you use the wrong Source or Destination profile. Talk to your Photo CD supplier for more detailed information about how to use this. If you make your Destination profile your current RGB or Lab workspace, then you should choose Don't Convert when the Missing Profile dialog comes up right after the above Photo CD dialog is finished. This Open logic will have done the conversion for you.

Depending on how you open the image, you should be able to get a better Photoshop histogram of it. When I first started to use Photo CD with the built-in support of an older version of Photoshop, I thought that the quality was not very good. The main problem seemed to be loss of highlight detail in bright clouds and other areas. I tend to take very contrasty photographs and require that the scan maintain the full range of contrast. I later learned how to use the Kodak Photo CD Acquire module to get a full range of data from the same CDs that had earlier given me problems.

OPENING PHOTO CD

To Open a Photo-CD file from the File/Open dialog, choose File/Open then use the Open dialog to navigate to the numbered files within the Photo_CD/Images folder on the Photo CD disk. You will have to use the little picture directory that comes with a Photo CD to decide which image to open because the images just have numbered names on the CD. Double-clicking one of the numbered images brings up the Kodak ICC Photo CD dialog to the left. Use the Source button to set the Source profile to the ICC profile you receive from your Photo CD scanner operator that describes the "Film Term" used to scan your type of original. Set the Destination profile to your RGB or Lab workspace, for example, SMPTE-240M. When you set these, they should remain the same until you change them. Choose which of the 5 (or 6 with Pro) images sizes you want and then click OK to bring up the image into Photoshop. When the dialog is finished, you will get the Missing Profile dialog, and you should choose Don't Convert if you chose your RGB or Lab workspace as the Destination in the Photo CD dialog.

To us Kodak version 2.3 Acquire module, which you used to be able to get from Kodak but 2.3 is actually an older version which I like better, you have to put it in the Plug-Ins folder within the Photoshop 5 folder and then access it from File/Import. When you first enter the Acquire module, you choose the particular scan that you want from the image glossary that comes with the CD. It shows you a tiny picture of each image along with the number that represents that image on the CD. Because a CD is a write-once device, the images are always stored by a number and you can't write a name on the CD.

After you select an image in Acquire 2.3, you get a little preview picture of it. If you click the Edit Image button, you get a more detailed dialog box. The Edit Image dialog box lets you see a bigger version of the image that you can crop more easily. If you crop the image before you open it, opening becomes a much faster process because Photoshop then reads less data from the Photo CD. You can also choose the size (one of either 5 or 6 sizes) of the scan you want to open. However, the best aspect of the Kodak Acquire module is that it allows you to choose the gamma and color temperature that you want to use when opening the image. I seem to get the best results in 2.3 with gamma 1.4 and color temperature 5000°K.

The Edit Image dialog box allows you to sharpen the image as well as to adjust Saturation, Cyan/Red, Magenta/Green, Yellow/Blue, and Dark/Light balances as you open the image. I usually leave these controls alone and just try to get the best histogram by changing the gamma and color temperature settings. You can do the other adjustments more accurately in Photoshop after you get the best raw information from the Photo CD.

Chapter 16: Scanning, Resolution, Histograms, and Photo CD

17 TRANSFORMATION OF IMAGES, LAYERS, PATHS, AND SELECTIONS

Using all the Photoshop 5 transformation features to scale, resize, and distort your images.

You want to initially scan your image at a size that will be big enough to encompass all the needs you will ever have for that image. You then color correct and spot that image to create your Master version. You then archive that Master file and when you want to use it for a particular purpose, you first resample a copy of it using Image Size, or the Cropping tool with Fixed Target Size, set to the dimensions and resolution you will need. Then you may want to convert it to CMYK or GIF or some other format for final output. This information about scanning and resampling your file is covered in the previous "Scanning, Resolution, Histograms, and PhotoCD" chapter.

This Transformation chapter talks about how you can use the Edit/Free Transform command as well as the Edit/Transform/Scale, Rotate, Skew, Distort, and Perspective commands to distort a version of a file, layer, selection, or path. The Transform and Free Transform tools in Photoshop 5 have been improved and generalized to work in a consistent way no matter what it is that you are transforming. We will start out with a more simple case and then move into more complicated transforms. Let me first mention, however, that whenever you are doing a transform, the Info window will show you your progress with the current change in angle, position, or dimensions. At any time while in the middle of the transform, you can choose Edit/Transform/Numeric to see the Numeric Transform dialog, which will show you what you have done to the item so far and allow you to modify them numerically. All the Transform commands along with Free Transform are interrelated, and you can go from one to the other while in the middle of a transform.

Let's take a look at each one of these Transform options by themselves and then we'll see how they can be combined using Free Transform and the Edit Transform menu. Take the case of the Square Button we see on the next page.

The Info window (F9) shows you on-the-fly progress during your transform even when the mouse is down and you are dragging a point. Use this for real-time feedback about your transformations.

At any time during a transformation, you can go into Numeric Transform to see what changes you have done so far. You can then edit those changes here. Not all the possible transformations show up in this dialog, however.

Here we see the Transform menu with all its individual options. You can choose any item from this menu to transform the image in one way at a time. While you are in the middle of a Free Transform, you can still choose any single option from this menu, which allows you to combine single transformation elements, working on them one at a time, before you have to accept any changes. This way, instead of typing in a Scale value, pressing OK, typing in a Rotate value, pressing OK, and typing in a Skew value and pressing OK, you are able to begin the Free Transform, choose each option separately, set its value, and press OK only once to make all the changes you entered. This gives you more control than simply dragging handles in a Free Transform.

TRANSFORMING A SQUARE BUTTON

To begin, open the Square Button file in the Transformation folder of the Photoshop 5 Artistry CD. Type an F to put the image in Full Screen mode then type Command-Option-0 to zoom to 100%. Bring up the Info palette (F9) so you can see numerically what you are doing as you move the cursor during each transform. Make sure Square is the Active layer in the Layers palette and then choose Edit/Transform/Scale. Click the top-right handle and drag it up and to the right. Pressing down the Shift key while dragging the corner forces the scale to be proportional. Scale it to 125% in the Info palette with the Shift key down. Now release the mouse, choose Edit/Transform/Rotate, and use the same top-right handle to rotate the image -14% by dragging up and to the left after clicking the handle. Now choose Edit/Transform/Skew and drag the top-middle handle to the left until the skew angle is 9.6 degrees. Finally choose Edit/Transform/Perspective and then click the top-right handle again and drag it down until you see the dimension of the right edge decreasing from both the top and bottom at the same time. If you now choose Edit/Transform/Numeric, you will see the cumulative results of the four transforms you have made so far. The Rotate and Skew angles have changed due to the effects of the Perspective command you did at the end.

Choose OK from Numeric Transform and go ahead and try Edit/Transform/Distort. This allows you to click any corner handle and independently drag that corner in any direction while leaving the other corners alone. You can also click one of the handles in-between two corners and this allows you to distort that entire side of the image as a unit. Play around with Distort for a while, and remember that if you don't like what you do, you can always exit and cancel the entire transform by choosing the Escape key. If you do this though, the image returns to the original rectangular button. While you are entering the individual Transform commands, Photoshop keeps track of all of them while showing you a quick preview. When you hit Escape, they all go away and when you press Return or Enter, they are all executed in the final hi-resolution manner. This final hi-res transform may take a little longer, especially on a large file. I went ahead and used the Distort transformation to make the button appear as though the bottom of it was closer to me and the top was farther away. To do this in Edit/Transform Distort, bring the top-right and bottom-left edges toward the center and move the top left edge a bit until it looks right to you. Now go ahead and choose Return or Enter to finish the transformation and you will notice that it has a lot more detail.

If you choose File/Revert to revert your image to the square button again, I'll show you how to do this transformation all in one step. This time choose Edit/Free Transform (Command-T), which will allow you to do all the different transformations at the same time. To do the Scale to 125%, just click in the top-right handle and drag up and to the right with the Shift key down until you see 125% in the Info palette. Make sure you release the mouse button before the Shift key to keep things proportional. Now move the cursor a little above and to the right of the top-right handle and you should see a cursor curving to the left and down. When you see this cursor, it is telling you that if you click and drag at this point, you can rotate your object. While seeing the curved cursor, click and drag up and to the left until the angle in the Info palette is -14 degrees. To do the

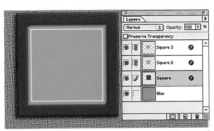

Here we see a button that has been made up of three layers. Each of these layers has had Layer Effects applied to give it shadows, beveled edges, and so on. Because the Layers Square, Square 2, and Square 3 are all linked together, with the middle linking column in the Layers palette, any transformation done to any one of them happens to all three of them. Because each layer is an object surrounded by transparency, we do not need to make a selection before transforming the entire object. The transparency itself is assumed to be the selection.

Here we see the Info palette after scaling to 125%, rotating by -14°, and skewing by 9.6°.

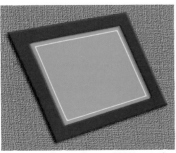

The image after scaling to 125%, rotating by -14°, skewing by 9.6°, and then applying perspective.

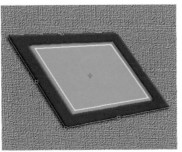

The above image after using Edit/Transform/Distort to make the bottom seem closer and the top farther away.

Skew, Command-click in the top middle handle and drag to the left while keeping the mouse down until the angle is 9.6. Don't move the mouse up or down while dragging to the left or you will also be changing the vertical scaling, and it may be hard to get the angle exactly at 9.6 without the scale changing too. When you get the angle to 9.6, you can release the Command key and you are then just adjusting the vertical scaling. Since Free Transform does many things at once, it is sometimes hard to keep a particular component of your transform exact and you may have trouble getting back to exactly 125% scaling. The way to fix this is to now release the mouse, then go into Edit/Transform/Numeric, put the exact 125% value back in and then click OK on the Numeric Transform box. You are still in Free Transform, so let's do some more transformations before we finish. To do the Perspective, hold down Command-Option-Shift and then click and drag the top-right handle down and to the right. Finally you do distort by just holding down the Command key while you click and drag in any corner handle and then move it to where you want it. You can now press Return or Enter to finish the Free Transform.

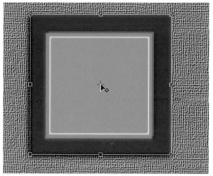

This is the default location for the rotation point, in the center of the object's area. We have placed the cursor on top of it and you can see the little black circle at the bottom-right of the cursor. This is telling you that you can now click the rotation point and drag it to its new location.

CHANGING THE CENTER POINT OF A ROTATE

A new, very useful feature that was added for Photoshop 5 is the capability to change the center of rotate during a transform. Go ahead and open the original SquareButton file again from the hard disk. Now choose Edit/Free Transform (Command-T) and in the center of the button you will notice a small crosshair with a circle in the middle of it. Let's call this the rotation point. When you put the cursor on top of it, the cursor gets a small circle at its lower right, as in the diagram to the left. At this point, you can click and drag this rotation point anywhere on the screen. Now when you release the mouse, this moved location becomes the new center for rotation. After releasing the mouse, move the cursor to just outside one of the corner handles of the button until you see the curved rotate icon. Click and drag at that point to rotate the button and you will see that it is rotating around the center point wherever you placed it. You can even place it outside of the button's area. It is very powerful to be able to rotate around any center. This was one feature that Live Picture had that Photoshop didn't and it does allow you do make certain useful transformations. I'm glad Photoshop 5 has added this feature. You can, of course, move the center point over and over again and then rerotate around that new center point. If you want to get the rotation point back to the center of the object, just drag it to the vicinity of the center and it will jump to and lock on the center when it gets close enough.

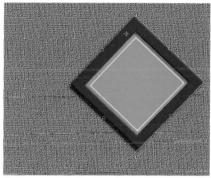

Here we are rotating the above button around a center point that was moved to the upper-right corner of the button. Now that we have rotated the button, the center point appears just to the left of the top of the button. You can see the curved rotation icon at the bottom below the center of the button.

TRANSFORMING THE CONTENTS OF A SELECTION VERSUS TRANSFORMING THE SELECTION ITSELF

Click the Square 3 layer in the Layers palette to activate that layer. Now Command-click the thumbnail for that layer to load that layer's transparency as a selection. Actually, the things that are not transparent are loaded as the selection. This layer has the Inner Glow effect on it to create the highlight around the green area in the center of the button. Let's say we want this area to be smaller in the center of the button. Now choose Edit/Free Transform (Command-T), then Option-Shift-click the top-right handle, and keep the mouse button down while you drag that handle toward the center to make this center square smaller. Remember that the Shift key forces the Scale to be proportional. The Option key makes the transformation happen symmetrically around the center of the area to be transformed. Press Return

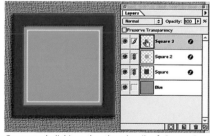

Command-clicking the thumbnail of Square3 to load its non-transparent area as a selection.

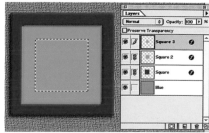

Square 3 after making it smaller with Option-Shift-click and drag using Free Transform of the layer.

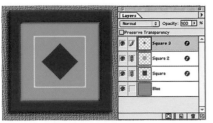

The final button after using Select/Transform Selection to create the center diamond area and then filling it with red.

after you have made the square smaller, as shown to the left. We just did a Free Transform of the contents of a selection. When you have a selection, if you choose Edit/Free Transformation and then do a transformation, you transform the contents of the selection within that layer, not the selection itself. To transform the selection and not its contents, you need to use the new Photoshop 5 feature Select/Transform Selection. Your selection should still be there, but if it is not, just Command-click the Square 3 layer again to reload it. Choose Window/Show Info (F9) to bring up the Info palette. This time, choose Select/Transform Selection, which puts you in a Free Transform mode where you are working on the Selection itself. Now hold down Option-Shift while you drag the top right corner handle and scale the selection inward until it is at 50% in the Info palette. Move the cursor just outside the top-right handle to get the rotate cursor and then rotate the selection up and to the left until you get 45 degrees in the Info palette. If you can't get the exact values you want in the Info palette, choose Edit/Transform Numeric and tweak the values there, then

press OK on the Numeric dialog, and finally press Return or Enter to finish your transform. This time you have transformed the selection itself and not the contents of the selection. Again, the only difference is that to transform the selection itself, you start the process with Select/Transform Selection instead of Edit/Free Transform or Edit/Transform. Now press I to get to the Eyedropper tool and click on the red color on the outside of the button to load it as the foreground color. Choose Edit/Fill (Shift-Delete) to fill that selected area using the Foreground Color. Your image should now look like the one to the right.

TRANSFORM OF A PATH

Click Square 2 in the Layers palette to make it the active layer. Command-click the Square 2 thumbnail to load a selection of the non-transparent area of this layer. Now choose Window Show Path (Shift-F11) to bring up the Paths palette. Choose Make Work Path from the Paths palette to turn this selection into a Path and choose OK when asked if you want the Tolerance set to 2.0. You now have a Path of the area around the edge of this layer. Now choose Edit/Free Transform Path. Notice that the names have changed because a Path is now active and also notice that you could have also chosen Edit/Transform Path along with all the nor-

Here we notice that when a Path is active the Edit/Transform choices change to Edit/Free Transform Path or Edit/Transform Path. You now have all the same transformation options with your path.

mal Transform options. Choose the Arrow tool by clicking and dragging the arrow in the bottom-right of the Pen tool area in the Tool palette. Now click in the top-right point of the path and drag it down and to the left until that point is just below the top-right highlight on Square 3. Now click the bottom-left point and drag it up and to the right until it is just below the bottom-left highlight on Square 3. Now choose Fill Path from the Paths palette's menu to fill this area with the red Foreground Color. You should now have the image to the left.

The final Double Diamond Button after filling the Path with Red.

Moving the Path points with the Arrow tool.

Chapter 17: Transformation of Images, Layers, Paths, and Selections

LINKED LAYERS TRANSFORM AND MOVE AS A GROUP

The three layers in this example are all linked together, which you can see by noticing that the link icon, the middle icon in the Layers palette, is on for the other two layers whenever a particular layer is active. Had we not loaded a selection to do the transformations on Square 3, all three layers would have transformed in the same way. Why don't you try this to see for yourself. Click back on the Square 3 Layer and without loading a Selection, just choose Edit/Free Transform. Now start to Scale the image and you will notice that all three layers, the entire button, scale together. If you use the Move tool to move any of these layers, they will also all move together because they are linked. This is a very useful feature when you create an object that is made up of more than one layer and yet you want to move it or scale it as a whole. You can also drag and drop this linked object to another document and all the layers will be copied to the other document having the same names as they have in your current document. This allows you to create component or library documents that contain your standard objects, like buttons, for example. When you need one of these objects, you just open that library document and drag and drop that component into your current working document. To get around this linking so you can move or transform a layer that has other layers linked to it, you need to first click in the linking column of any other layers where the link icon shows up. This unlinks those layers from the one you want to change. If there are a lot of other layers linked to this one, it may be faster to just activate one of the other layers and then click the linking column of the layer you want to modify. This single act unlinks it from all the rest of the group. In either case, you can now transform or move the current layer. If you want to relink the layers after the change, just reclick in the linking column of the layer(s) you unlinked before and the link icon should show up again. You can also click and drag through a bunch of layer's linking columns to do a group linking in one step.

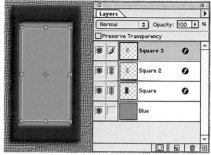

Here we are using Free Transform to scale only Square 3 and yet the other 2 layers are scaling too because they are linked to Square 3.

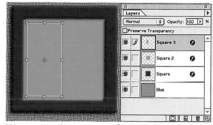

Here we see the same transform as above, but only the Square 3 layer is changing because we unlinked the other two layers.

EDIT/TRANSFORM ROTATE AND FLIP VERSUS IMAGE/ROTATE AND FLIP CANVAS

Edit/Transform Rotate or Edit Transform Flip of a Layer only rotates or flips the currently active layer and any other layers that are linked to it. Image/Rotate Canvas/Rotate or Flip rotates or flips the entire document, including all layers whether they are linked or not.

OTHER USEFUL EXAMPLES OF TRANSFORMS IN THIS BOOK

Check out the Chapter 30: Bob Goes to..., Chapter 22: The Portable Computer Ad, Chapter 44: Creating Small GIF Composites, and Chapter 35: South Africa In Focus for real-world examples of using Free Transform in production situations.

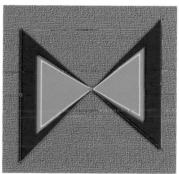

With Free Transform, you can hold the Command key down while dragging the corners across each other to create the bowtie twist look.

Square Button Reentry Vehicle #1. Free Transform of the button and a stretched ghost image.

Square Button Reentry Vehicle #2. The image to the left using Color Dodge between the ghost image and the button layers.

18 STEPS TO CREATE A MASTER IMAGE

Choosing your master color space, the color correction process, archiving the master and then targeting resampled versions for different uses, sharpening, soft-proofing, device-specific tweaking, and saving final output files.

CHOOSING YOUR MASTER COLOR SPACE

When working on an RGB file using older versions of Photoshop, Photoshop assumed the gamut of your RGB space was the same as the gamut of your monitor, which was specified using Monitor Setup. Photoshop 5 allows you to choose an RGB or Lab workspace that is not limited by the gamut of a particular monitor or device. You need to decide which RGB workspace, or the Lab space, you are going to use as your default color working space. To help you in making this decision, you should read Chapter 14: Color Spaces, Device Characterization, and Color Management. This chapter is an overview of the workflow we suggest you use to create master images within your default color workspace and then color correct those images, archive the master and finally output copies of it to several different device-specific color spaces like CMYK, the Lightjet 5000 color laser printer, a film recorder, and also to the Web.

COLOR CORRECTING YOUR SCAN OR PHOTO CD

When you get the best possible histogram from the scanner or the Photo CD, you usually need to do some color correction work. The first step in color correction is to work some more on the histograms until you get them as close to perfect as you can given the data available. Before you start the color correction process, make sure that your Photoshop preferences are set up correctly for all the color spaces you will be working in for this project, that is, if your master color space is RGB but you will print a version of this image in CMYK on a web press, you need to be sure your prefs are set up correctly for your master RGB workspace and your CMYK for that press and paper. The parts of the preferences that affect color correction and the appearance of images onscreen are as follows:

- RGB Setup
- CMYK Setup
- Grayscale Setup
- Profile Setup
- Setting the Eyedropper
- The Highlight and Shadow settings in Levels and Curves

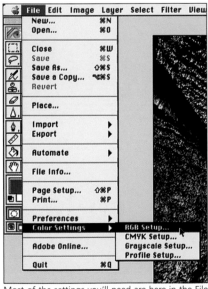
Most of the settings you'll need are here in the File menu under Color Settings.

Using Chapter 5: Setting System and Photoshop Preferences at the beginning of this book as a guide, make sure your preferences are set up as recommended. You should do color correction in a specific order. The next few pages offer an overview of the order and steps you should use in making color corrections and in creating a Master image and your device-specific images. "The Grand Canyon" chapter, which is next, goes into much greater detail.

THE STEPS FOR COLOR CORRECTING

The first step in color correcting is to bring up the Info palette and the Color palette by choosing Window/Show Info (F9) and Window/Show Color (Shift-F9), respectively. The Info palette shows you the RGB and CMYK values of the current location of the Eyedropper tool while in Curves, Levels, Hue/Saturation, or any color correction tool. It also shows you how your color correction is modifying these values by displaying before values on the left and after values on the right. When you move the cursor into the Levels or Curves dialog boxes, the values in the regular Info palette go away but you can use a Color Sampler, with the new Color Sampler tool to the right of the Eyedropper, to keep track of values at specific locations you choose or use the Color palette to keep track of values at the last location you clicked with the Eyedropper. When you click down in a particular location, the values in that location show up in the Color palette. These values change only when you click in a new location or use Levels, Curves, or Hue/Saturation to make a color adjustment that affects the location where you last clicked. The Color Sampler values, up to four per image, show up at the bottom of the Info palette. It is useful to always have the Info palette showing and sometimes also the Color palette when you are making color corrections.

Before you start any color correcting, make a copy of the original scan and color correct the copy so that you can return to that original if you make any mistakes while color correcting. You also wan to make sure your original scan is scanned for the biggest possible usage for that image. For example, I make 16x25 prints of my 35mm transparencies. For this type of print, I scan at 5,000dpi, which also gets all the possible info from the film and gives me about a 100Mb file. I can resample the file down for smaller prints, this book, and for my Web site. The basic order for color correction when starting with an RGB scan is as follows:

1. Go into Levels.
2. Set the Highlight.
3. Set the Shadow.
4. Adjust the overall brightness and contrast of the image.

You do the first three steps in RGB mode using either Levels or Curves, although Levels is better because you see a histogram when you use it.

5. Go into the Red, Green, or Blue channel and remove color casts, being especially careful that neutral colors are neutral and don't have a cast.
6. Save your Levels or Curves settings in a Levels or Curves Adjustment layer so you can change them Later without image degradation if needed.
7. Go into a Hue/Saturation Adjustment layer and increase or decrease overall saturation. Make adjustments to the hue, saturation, and lightness of specific color areas.
8. Make color changes to isolated image areas using Selections followed by Levels, Curves, and Hue/Saturation Adjustment layers.
9. Remove Spots and Scratches from your Image.

At this point, you have a color-corrected Master RGB or Lab image. You will archive this Master Image and then resample a copy of it down, or sometimes up if

Before values   After values

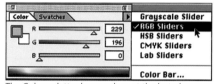

Here we see an Info palette with the standard RGB and CMYK readouts as well as two of the possible 4 Color Sampler readouts. The Info palette shows you the original values, upon entering the tool, on the left of the slash. On the right, after the slash, it displays the values resulting from the tool's adjustments since you entered it this time.

The Color palette shows values at the last place you clicked. You can see how the values at that location change when you make an adjustment using one of the color correction tools.

needed, for each different usage of that image. After the copy image is resampled to the final size, then you will do a final Sharpening and Spotting. You can print resampled copies of this image directly to RGB printers or output to an RGB film recorder to make transparencies. You can use the RGB file for Web and multimedia projects and as the final file if you use a third-party method to convert your images to CMYK on-the-fly from Photoshop or Quark. You can also convert an image to CMYK using Photoshop for separations.

10. Resample each copy of the image to final size and do final Sharpening, and after the sharpen, Spotting.

11. Convert to CMYK using the Mode menu, if you need CMYK. This will set up the CMYK Preview for you to soft proof in CMYK on your screen. If you are going to output your Lab or RGB file to a Lightjet 5000 or other RGB printer that you have an accurate ICC profile for, you can set up your prefs to use the View/Preview CMYK and View/Gamut Warning to give you a soft proof of what your master image will look like on that device. See the Previewing Color section of Chapter 14: Color Spaces, Device Characterization, and Color Management to learn how to do this very useful thing.

12. Make minor color adjustments to specific color areas using Hue/Saturation, Curves, and Selective Color with or without selections.

13. If you are outputting to an ICC profiled RGB space, you would now use the ColorSync Export filter to convert from your Master Lab or RGB workspace into the ICC space for that output device and save a TIFF file tagged with that ICC profile for your specific device and paper combination.

Now I'm going to take you through these steps in more detail.

SETTING HIGHLIGHT

Go to Image/Adjust/Levels (Command-L). You work in Channel zero, the composite channel, to set the highlight and shadow. The *highlight* is the brightest point in the image where you still want to have texture. Everything brighter than the highlight prints totally white, with no dots. The RGB values here should read somewhere in the range of 240 to 250 depending on your device. Remember that after you set the highlight, everything brighter than the highlight location will print totally white. Setting the highlight also removes color casts from the whole highlight part of your image. You need to set the highlight at a place you want to be white in the end, as well as at a location you want to print as a neutral value. You want to pick a spot where the detail or texture is just fading but is not completely gone. This usually falls at the brighter end of Zone IX in the Zone System. Using the highlight Eyedropper, click down at the location where you want to set the highlight, and at the same time, watch how the Info palette shows the values (before and after in RGB and CMYK). When you click, the after values should change to the default preference white point values. Because not all images have a good white point, you can also set the highlight by going into each color channel and moving its highlight slider separately.

SETTING SHADOW

Now pick the point where you want to set the shadow. The RGB values here should read about 5 to 10. It should be at a location you want to print with a neutral shadow value. This location would be at the darker end of Zone I in the Zone System. Everything darker than this point prints as totally black after you set the shadow. If you want a lot of totally black places in your image, set the shadow at a location

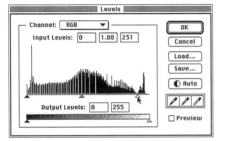

It is often hard to distinguish what point is the brightest on the computer screen. You can find the highlight by holding down the Option key while moving the RGB Highlight slider to the left. The first area to turn white on the screen is where you want to look for the highlight. Make sure you move the slider back to 255 when you see where the highlight is. This method only works if your computer supports Video LUT Animation.

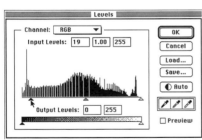

It is often hard to distinguish what point is the darkest on the computer screen. You can find the shadow by holding down the Option key while moving the RGB Shadow slider to the right. The first area to turn black on the screen is where you want to look for the shadow. Make sure you move the slider back to 0 when you see where the shadow is. Again, the Option key technique only works with Video LUT Animation, so to use it, you need a Mac or Windows 98 with a PC video card that supports Video LUT.

that isn't very dark, say 15, 15, 15. Everything darker than that location goes black. If you want a lot of shadow detail in your image, set the shadow at a location that is as close as possible to 0, 0, 0 in RGB. These initial RGB highlight and shadow values vary somewhat from image to image. The purpose of setting the white and black is to normalize these values to neutral grays and also to set the endpoints of detail in the reproduction. Some images do not have a good point at which to set the highlight and shadow with the Eyedroppers. See the Chapter 20: Kansas and Chapter 29: Bryce Stone Woman for examples of how to deal with this situation.

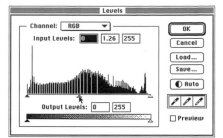

Adjust the overall brightness and contrast by moving the middle slider using Channel RGB.

ADJUSTING THE OVERALL BRIGHTNESS AND CONTRAST

Use the RGB Channel of Levels again for this step. Move the middle slider to the right to make the image darker and more contrasty. Move it to the left to make the image brighter and less contrasty. Move it around until the image has the level of brightness and contrast you want. In a Lab Image you would do all the work we've covered so far in the Lightness channel.

ADJUSTING THE OVERALL COLOR CAST

If the overall image seems too green, go to the Green channel in Levels and move the middle slider to the right. This will add magenta to the image and remove the green cast. If the image is too blue, go to the Blue channel and move the middle slider to the right to add yellow to the image. You just need to remember that the Red channel controls red and its complement, cyan; the Green channel, green and magenta; and the Blue channel, blue and yellow. The middle sliders of each channel are going to mostly affect the midtones as well as the quartertones and three-quartertones. The Highlight and Shadow sliders should have been adjusted correctly when you set the highlight and shadow at the beginning.

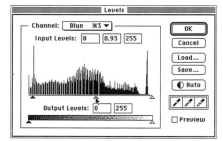

Now deal with color casts by adjusting the middle slider in the color channel that effects the color cast.

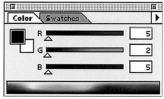

Here we can see the unbalanced values in the Color palette. The green value is less than red or blue.

Sometimes you can get a color cast in the highlight or the shadow if the point at which you set the highlight was not a neutral location. Some images do not have neutral locations. In such cases, click the normal Eyedropper at a highlight or shadow location while in Levels and look at the values for that location in a Color Sampler or the Color palette. The values in the Color palette change only when you click down with the mouse. The Color palette remembers the last place you clicked. If the numbers are not neutral (for coated stock, the highlights should be around 244, 244, 244 and the shadows should be around 5, 5, 5), use the Highlight or Shadow sliders for the color channel(s) that are out of adjustment to correct the numbers in the Color palette or Color Sampler. Afterward, you may have to go back to readjust the midtone sliders to slightly adjust the midtone color cast again.

You should modify all these corrections in the Levels dialog box as one step. You don't want to say OK until you complete all these steps. If you say OK too many times in the color adjustment dialog boxes, you degrade the image. You don't want to go into Levels or Curves repeatedly. Do it all in one step if possible. After you finish the overall color correction in Levels, and only then, choose OK in the Levels dialog box. To have the ability to modify your changes over and over again, do them with Adjustment layers instead of regular layers. For hands-on examples using these techniques, see Chapter 19: Grand Canyon, Chapter 20: Kansas, and Chapter 28: Desert Al. If you find that doing a color shift by moving the middle slider of a color channel in Levels affects the brightness and contrast too much, use Color Balance with Preserve Luminosity turned on. This will change the color without changing the brightness or contrast. If you were working in Lab color, you would make these cast changes using the a and b channels of a Lab image.

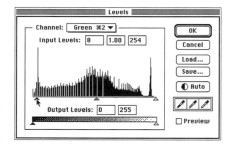

Make the change using the Shadow slider from the Green channel while looking at the values in the Color palette.

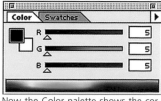

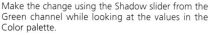

Now the Color palette shows the correction implemented to neutralize the shadow value in green.

Color Correcting Your Scan or Photo CD

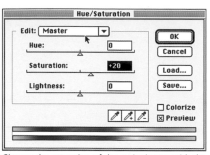

Change the saturation of the entire image with the Master menu chosen.

Change the hue, saturation, and lightness of just the red colors in the image with the Red menu chosen. With Photoshop 5, you can also use the Eyedroppers to refine the definition of Red.

MAKING OVERALL AND SELECTED CHANGES TO HUE, SATURATION, AND LIGHTNESS

You often want to increase the overall saturation using the Hue/Saturation tool, especially if you had to brighten the image in Curves or Levels. To increase the overall saturation, move the Saturation slider to the right with Master selected. You can also selectively correct color if a certain color range in the image is off. For example, if the reds in the image were too orange, you could make them redder by first selecting the Red pop-up and then moving the Hue slider toward the left. This operation would add magenta to only the red areas of the image. This method differs from adding magenta using Levels or Curves because the latter method usually adds magenta to everything in the image.

When the Red menu button is selected, only the items in the image that are red have their color changed. If these items were unsaturated, you could add saturation to just the red items by moving the Saturation slider with Red selected. Similarly, you could add or subtract lightness in the reds. If your image contains different tones of red and you only want to adjust some of them, you can use the Eyedroppers in the Hue/Saturation dialog to fine-tune the range of reds you want to adjust. For even more control, you could also select those areas *before* you make the red adjustment. The Color Range, Replace Color, and Selective Color tools are also good choices for tweaking colors.

MAKING COLOR CHANGES TO ISOLATED AREAS USING SELECTIONS, LAYER MASKS, AND ADJUSTMENT LAYERS ALONG WITH LEVELS, CURVES, AND HUE/SATURATION

The color corrections I have discussed so far have been global color corrections to an entire image. If a particular area is the wrong color or too light or too dark, you may now want to make a selection of that area using Photoshop's selection tools, and then you may want to adjust the colors in that area using Levels, Curves, or Hue/Saturation. You can also use a layer mask to integrate that area from another layer or Adjustment layer where the color has been changed.

Go through Chapter 23: Grand Canyon Tweaks, Chapter 24: Kansas Tweaks, Chapter 29: Bryce Stone Woman, and Chapter 28: Desert Al, for a complete description and some hands-on practice in using these techniques to change isolated areas.

SPOTTING THE IMAGE

You will want to clean up your master image by removing spots, scratches, and other blemishes with either the Rubber Stamp tool or the Dust and Scratches filter. You can either do this to the copy of the original scan image that is at the bottom of your Layers palette under all your Adjustment layers or you can Merge all your changes into a new "Merged" layer at the top of all your existing layers and then spot that. If you spot the original scan at the bottom of the Layers palette, then you won't need to respot if you later change any of your Adjustment layers. This does make permanent changes to this layer, however, although you could spot a copy right above the bottom layer. If you spot a "Merged" layer on top of all the others, as we did in Chapter 28: Desert Al, then you will have to respot this if you make any changes to the Adjustment layers underneath. Still, you save time by spotting the master image because you only do that once; then the spots that have to be made after you sharpen each resampled version later will be a lot fewer.

SAVING YOUR MASTER IMAGE

After Spotting, your master image is ready to be saved and archived. You can now use this image for any future projects or prints to RGB printers, film recorders, CMYK print jobs or for Web or multimedia use. For any of these uses, you will make a copy of the master, rename it, then resample it to the size needed, and convert it to the format needed for this particular purpose.

MAKING RESAMPLED COPIES FOR EACH USAGE

With your master image opened, you can choose File/Save a Copy to save a Flattened version without extra channels on the disk. This can then be opened, resampled, and saved for a particular project. You can also choose Image/Duplicate and turn on Merged Layers Only to make a nonlayered copy of the master that is already open and on your screen. After you have one of these copies up on the

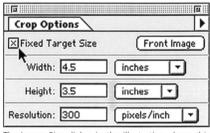

Make sure the image Width, Height, and Resolution are set correctly for your layout dimensions and line screen when printing on a press. You don't want Quark or Pagemaker to resample your image. For best results, place it into other apps at 100%. For Web images, change the Inches pop-up to pixels before typing in your pixel dimensions.

You can use Image/Duplicate Image to make on screen copies of your Master image, one for each usage. Choose Merged Layers Only to compress all the layers in the master into just one layer in the duplicate.

screen, you need to choose Image/Image Size or use the Crop tool with Fixed Target Size on to resample the image to the size and resolution you need for this project. See Chapter 16: Scanning, Resolution, Histograms, and Photo CD or Chapter 23: Grand Canyon Tweaks to learn the details of this resampling process. Just remember that you will get better results when you take a big image and sample it down than if you take a small image and sample it up. If you had already scanned your original at 5,000dpi from film or if your original is the highest resolution from your digital camera, then sampling up is certainly a viable choice. When you scan film at more than 5,000dpi, it is unlikely you will get any more real information.

The Image Size dialog in the illustration above this does not allow you to crop and resample your image at the same time. To do that, you want to use the Cropping tool with the Fixed Target Size option shown here.

SHARPENING THE IMAGE

As a final step, on each resampled version of your image, you will want to use the Unsharp Mask filter or one of the other sharpening filters to sharpen the image. You will have to run some tests to determine the type and amount of sharpening that works best for your different categories of images. It is sometimes useful to run tests on a section of the image and do side-by-side comparisons. Select a section of the image that represents the entire image using the Rectangular Selection tool, and then make a copy of it. Next, choose File/New and create a new file. Because you just made a copy, the new file will be the size of the copied section. Choose OK in the New dialog box and then do an Edit/Paste followed by Select/None. To compare different parameters of the Unsharp Mask filter, you can repeat this or now use Image/Duplicate, until you have several files that you can place next to each other onscreen.

Let me explain the three parameters of this filter.

AMOUNT: Controls the overall amount of sharpening. When you compare sharpening effects, zoom the image to at least 100% so you can see all the detail. Compare different copies of the same image area using different settings for Amount.

RADIUS: Photoshop sharpens an image by looking for edges in the photograph and enhancing those edges by darkening one side of the edge and lightening the other side. *Edges* are sharp color or contrast changes in an image. The Radius setting in the Unsharp Mask filter controls the width of pixels along an edge that are modified when you sharpen the image. Again, try running the filter with different settings, as well as comparing two copies of the same image side to side.

THRESHOLD: When you set the Threshold to 0, everything in the image becomes a candidate edge for getting sharpened. If you set the Threshold to 10, Photoshop finds and sharpens an edge only if there is a difference of at least 10 points (in the range from 0 to 255) in the pixel values along that edge. The larger value you give to the Threshold setting, the more contrasty an edge must be before it is sharpened and the more you are just sharpening the edges. When you find the correct Unsharp Mask values, use them to sharpen the entire file. See Chapter 24: Kansas Tweaks for a detailed hands-on example of using Unsharp Mask.

CONVERTING FROM YOUR RGB OR LAB WORKSPACE TO FINAL OUTPUT

If this is a CMYK usage, make sure that your CMYK preferences are set up correctly for this printer, then go to the Image/Mode menu and choose CMYK Color to convert the image from RGB or Lab to CMYK. If you don't correct the RGB or Lab file before converting to CMYK, Photoshop would create the Black channel on your CMYK file incorrectly. Unless your scans are done directly into CMYK, you should do overall correction on your master RGB or Lab file before converting to CMYK. Scans made by high-end scanners in CMYK should already have had overall color correction done for you by the trained scanner operator.

If you are working on an image for output to an RGB printer, like the Lightjet 5000 or the Epson Stylist Photo, you can leave the resampled and sharpened image in your RGB or Lab workspace and still get a soft proof on the screen of how the image will look when printed to that output device. To do this, you use the method called Previewing Color, described at the end of Chapter 14: Color Spaces, Device Characterization and Color Management. To see the soft proof, this technique uses the View/Preview CMYK menu option after you change the CMYK color separation tables to actually preview to the ICC profile of your RGB device. This is a very useful feature, check it out!

MAKING FINAL SUBTLE COLOR ADJUSTMENTS

When you are comparing the image on your screen to a proof made from CMYK film or to a print from a particular RGB printer, you want to compare the CMYK version, or the Lab or RGB version with Soft Proofing set up, of the image on the screen to the proof. There are colors that will show up on an RGB monitor, and in your RGB workspace, that may not be able to be printed with printing inks on a press or RGB printer. When Photoshop displays a CMYK image on the screen or with Soft Proofing set up, it adjusts the colors to try to give you an accurate representation of how the colors will actually print on a press or on your printer. It changes this adjustment based on the settings in RGB Setup for your workspace and CMYK Setup for your printer. When working in CMYK, you need to be sure that the preferences values used to convert from RGB to CMYK are the same values that you are using for displaying the CMYK image. When working on a file for an RGB printer or film recorder, you need to be sure soft proofing is set up with an ICC profile from that printer.

Because the CMYK or Soft Proof image onscreen more closely matches the image on a press or your printer than the Master RGB image, you may need to do final subtle color corrections in CMYK mode or after setting up your Soft Proof. For some images, the CMYK or Soft Proof version will look the same on the screen as the Master RGB version, depending on the colors in the image and the gamut of your device. Certain colors, for example, bright saturated red or deep blue, may get duller or change when you convert to CMYK. Also, the shadow or highlight areas may require a slight modification to be sure the correct balance is achieved in the

Here we are converting a file from Lab color space, where the color corrections were done, to CMYK where the output will happen.

Chapter 18: Steps to Create a Master Image

neutral areas. To add contrast to CMYK images, you may want to run a curve or increase the black midtone values. You can make these final color adjustments using Curves, Levels, Hue/Saturation, Replace Color, or Selective Color.

Just to make sure you understand what is happening here, when you are using the Soft Proofing technique to soft proof your Lab or RGB workspace image to your output device, after changing the separation tables to simulate your device's ICC profile, when you turn on View/Preview CMYK, you see the RGB or Lab image in the simulated color space of your device. When you turn View/Preview CMYK off, you see your image in your standard Lab or RGB workspace. This works similarly to Preview CMYK when you are working in Lab or RBG, and you actually want to get a CMYK preview of that Lab or RGB file, except in that case the CMYK separation settings would actually be set up for CMYK instead of your RGB device's ICC profile.

If this version of the image is destined for the Web, you might want to temporarily change your RGB workspace to sRGB, using File/Color Settings/RGB Setup, and then use Image/Mode/Profile to Profile to convert this image from your default RGB or Lab workspace to sRGB. Now you should see an accurate example of how this image will display on the average PC monitor. Do the final save of this Web image while in sRGB space, so the tag is correct; then return your RGB Settings to your normal RGB workspace.

Saving the Device Specific Image

For output to a press, especially if printing directly from Photoshop, you might need to go into Page Setup in the File menu to adjust some of the settings. You should talk to the print shop or service bureau doing the output and ask them if you need to set Negative and Emulsion Down. Also, ask the service bureau how to set the Halftone Screens. Often, they will want you to not set either value in Photoshop because they will set them using Quark, the imagesetter or platemaker. You really should coordinate with the printer or service bureau concerning who's going to set what. Also ask the service bureau whether they want you to save the images as Photoshop EPS, use one of the DCS options or use CMYK TIFF, or use some other format because this varies according to the type of output device that particular bureau uses.

If you save the image in EPS/DCS format for input into Quark, you will most likely use the settings in the dialog box here. You should check the Include Halftone Screen box only if you set up the screen angles and frequencies using the Screens dialog box (which you access from the Page Setup dialog box). If the screens are going to be set in Quark, leave the Include Halftone Screen check box unchecked. Good luck with your color. If you have any questions or comments about these techniques, please email us at www.maxart.com or reach us via our contact information at the end of the book.

If you are outputting to an RGB printer, like the Lightjet 5000, make sure the correct ICC profile is embedded in the file. When I send Lightjet prints to Evercolor Fine Art, the final step is to use File/Export ColorSync Tiff to convert the file from my RGB or Lab workspace to an RGB Tiff tagged with and using the ICC profile of the Lightjet with their current paper batch. Evercolor emails me the latest ICC profile whenever it changes paper batches on its printer. To tag a file with a profile other than the current RGB workspace or none, you need to save through the Color Sync export filter as we just mentioned here.

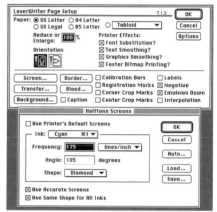

Settings for EPS to Quark. Check Include Halftone Screens only if you set the screens in Photoshop. To get an EPS/DCS format, you now need to choose either the Photoshop DCS 1.0 or Photoshop DCS 2.0 option.

The Page Setup dialog box and its Halftone Screens dialog box. Check with your service bureau for how to set the screens and other settings here. They might want you to leave these unset in Photoshop if they're planning to set them in Quark.

Here is the dialog from the ColorSync RGB Tiff Export filter. It is currently set up to convert a file from the Lab workspace to the current ICC profile of the Lightjet 5000 at Evercolor fine art.

19 HANDS-ON SESSION: Grand Canyon

Introduction to Levels, using Levels and Hue/Saturation for overall color correction, introduction to Curves, and using Curves to change specific color ranges.

In Chapter 5: Setting System and Photoshop Preferences, we showed you how to set the default highlight (C=5, M=3, Y=3, K=0, or R=244, G=244, B=244) and shadow (C=95, M=85, Y=83, K=95, or R=2, G=2, B=2) values for printing on a sheet-fed press to coated stock. This Grand Canyon chapter is done using those settings and also with the RGB Setup set to ColorMatch RGB and the CMYK Setup set as in Chapter 5. If you didn't already do so, go through Chapter 5 before doing this exercise. Before you proceed, also read Chapter 15: Calibration, Chapter 16: Scanning, Resolution, Histograms, and Photo CD, and Chapter 18: Steps to Create a Master Image. These chapters give you an overview of the entire reproduction process, show you how to calibrate your monitor, and give you a further understanding of histograms within the Levels tool. You should calibrate your monitor before proceeding with this chapter.

INTRODUCTION TO LEVELS

Before you start actually color correcting the GrandCanyon image, let's take a tour of the Levels tool and explain its different parts and functions. Levels contains two sets of controls, Input and Output, which can make the image lighter or darker as well as change its contrast. The Input controls on top include the histogram, the Input Levels numbers, and three sliders. The Input Shadow slider darkens shadows, the Input Highlight slider lightens highlights, and the Brightness/Contrast slider, in the middle, controls brightness and contrast. The output controls on the bottom of this dialog box contain the Output Levels numbers, the Output Shadow slider for making shadows lighter, and the Output Highlight slider for making highlights darker or duller. The names "Input" and "Output" are chosen by comparing what happens with

The initial uncorrected GrandCanyon image. Notice the green tint in the clouds and the overall flatness.

the Levels Highlight and Shadow sliders to what happens when you move the endpoints of a straight curve in Curves either along the horizontal (Input) axis or along the vertical (Output) axis of Curves. This might seem a bit obscure at this point, but maybe it will make more sense to you after you read this whole chapter; then look again at the Curve diagrams and their captions at Step 23.

STEP 1: From the Grand Canyon folder on the CD, open the GrandCanyonPCDRaw file in Photoshop. If your RGB Setup is not set to ColorMatch RGB, you will get the Profile Mismatch dialog. You should Convert the file into your RGB workspace and then realize that the exact numbers you get when doing this exercise will be slightly different than ours. Use the Marquee and then use Image/Crop to select; then crop any white or black borders that you're not going to print. Use File/Save As GrandCanyon PS in Photoshop format on your hard disk; it is always good to save things in Photoshop format while you are working on them, because that also saves all your channels and layers.

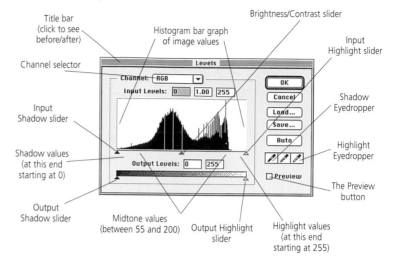

Study this diagram to learn the various controls of the Levels tool.

STEP 2: Bring up the Info palette from the Window menu. If you have loaded ArtistKeys, the predefined set of function keys explained in Chapter 5, just press F9 to bring up the Info palette. Be sure to set up the Info palette's Options to show you both RGB and CMYK values. You will also be using the Color palette (Shift-F9).

STEP 3: Choose Image/Adjust/Levels and move the Levels dialog box out of the way as much as possible. You want to see as much of the image as you can while color correcting it. Use the levels diagram on this page as you review or learn the basic functions covered in steps 4 through 9. Make sure the Preview button is turned off on a Mac; for Windows you probably want the Preview button on.

STEP 4: Move the Input Highlight slider to the left, and observe as you do so that the highlight areas in the clouds get brighter and that the Input Levels number on the right decreases from 255. Move the slider until the number reads about 200. Let go of the slider and move the cursor over an area of the image where the clouds have turned completely white. When you use any of the color correction tools, you automatically get the Eyedropper tool when you move the cursor over an area of the image. The Info palette shows you two sets of values for this white area. The values to the left of the slash are the original values at the Eyedropper location when you first entered Levels, and the values to the right of the slash show you what your levels changes have done to the digital values at the Eyedropper location. You can now see that moving the Input Highlight slider to the left makes the highlights brighter but also causes you to lose detail in the highlights if you move it too far. The original RGB numerical values that were in the range of 210 to 220 have now all changed to 255, which is pure white and prints with no color or detail—and you don't want that.

STEP 5: Move the Input Shadow slider to the right until the Input Levels number on the left goes from 0 to about 50 and the shadow areas of the image darken. Move the Eyedropper over a dark area and measure the changes in the Info palette. The RGB

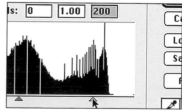

STEP 2: The Info palette with before values on the left of the slash and after values on the right.

STEP 2: The Color palette. Hold the mouse button down and measure an image color area to change the values in this window.

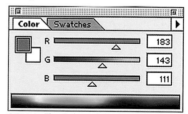

STEP 4: Move the Input Highlight slider to the left so the right Input Level reads about 200.

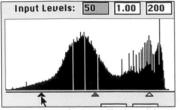

STEP 5: Move the Input Shadow slider to the right so the left Input Level reads about 50.

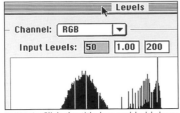

STEP 6: Click the title bar and hold down the mouse to see before; let go to see after.

STEP 7: Use the Eyedropper tool to click on the red rocks. (In Levels, you are automatically in the Eyedropper.) If you Shift-click, that will create a Color Sampler.

STEP 7: A Color Sampler shows up at the bottom of the Info palette. If will always show you the before and after values at that location.

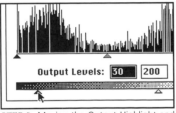

STEP 8: Moving the Output Highlight and Shadow sliders and looking at the Output Levels numbers.

values originally in the range of 0 to 40 have all moved to 0 now; they have become totally black.

STEP 6: Move the cursor to the title bar at the top of the Levels dialog box. When you click on the title bar and hold the mouse button down, the image returns to the way it looked before you changed anything in Levels. When you release the mouse button, the image returns to the changed state with no highlight and shadow details. This quick preview feature is very useful for toggling quickly between before and after versions of an image to see if you really like the changes you have made. But it works only when the Levels Preview button is turned off. If the title bar toggle isn't working for you (mostly Windows users), your video card may not support Video LUT Animation and, if so, you will need to work with the Preview button on all the time and then turn the Preview button off to see the before state. See Video LUT Animation in Chapter 5 for more information. Now, hold down on the Option key and click the Cancel/Reset button. The Cancel button changes to Reset, and clicking it restores the levels to their starting values when you entered Levels this time. All your changes are removed but you don't leave Levels. Calculating the Levels histogram can take a long time when you're working on large files, and this Reset feature saves time when you want to start over. Notice that the values in the Info palette

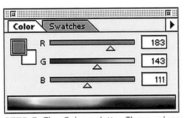

STEP 7: The Color palette. These values change as you move the Input Brightness/Contrast slider.

disappear when you move the cursor back into the Levels dialog box. Using the Color palette lets you remember values at the last place you clicked and see how a change in Levels modifies those values.

STEP 7: Use the Eyedropper tool to click a midtone value in the GrandCanyon image; the orange/red rocks in the foreground will work. When you press down on the mouse button, the values in the Color palette change. If you Shift-click the red Rocks, this creates a Color Sampler area at the bottom of the Info palette that will always show you the values at that location. Now move the cursor back into Levels; notice that these values in the Color palette and Color Sampler don't go away, even when you're in the dialog box. Press down on the Input Brightness/Contrast slider and move it to the left; the image gets brighter and less contrasty and the numbers in the Color palette and Color Sampler get larger. Move the slider to the right, and the image gets darker and more contrasty, and the numbers in the Color palette and Color Sampler get smaller. Also, observe that the middle number (the *gamma*) in the Input Levels numbers boxes is changing. When you move the slider to the left, the gamma goes above 1.0, and when you move it to the right, the gamma goes below 1.0. If the Input Levels numbers read 0, 1.0, 255, you know you haven't changed the Input Levels. When you click another area of the image, the Color palette's values will change to show you the reading at that new location. The Color Sampler you created before will not move however. If you Shift-click in a new location, a new Color Sampler, up to four per image, will be created at that location. To move an existing Color Sampler, you need to Shift-click and drag the old sampler location to a new location.

STEP 8: Move the Output Highlight slider to the left until the Output Levels number on the right reaches 200. Then measure the brightest cloud values; notice that values originally in the 200 to 220 range have all dropped below 200. You changed the

Output Levels number from 255 to 200, and the difference of 55, or close to it, has been subtracted from all these highlight values, darkening and dulling your highlights.

STEP 9: Move the Output Shadow slider to the right and notice how doing that makes the shadows lighter and duller. If you measure the changes with the Eyedropper and Info palette, you will notice that moving this slider increases the shadow's numerical values (which makes the shadows lighter).

SETTING THE HIGHLIGHT AND SHADOW VALUES

STEP 10: Steps 4 through 9 show you the basic functions of the different parts of the Levels tool. It is important to use those functions in the right order and to take careful measurements of your progress using the Info palette, Color Samplers, and Color palette. We will start out working with the Highlight and Shadow Eyedroppers to set the highlights and shadows on this image—a very important step in this process. All reproduction or printing processes, including sheet-fed presses, web presses, newspaper presses, digital printers, and film recorders, have certain endpoints to their reproduction process defined by the highlights and shadows. Many newspaper presses can't show detail for shadow values that are more than 85% to 90% black, and some newspapers are even worse. Sheet-fed presses, on the other hand, can sometimes show detail in areas with more than 95% black. In a digital file, these percentages are represented by numerical values ranging from 0 (100% black) to 255 (white, or 0% black).

When you color correct an image, you don't want that image to contain areas that the output medium you are using can't reproduce. Setting the highlight and shadow values correctly for your output device ensures that this won't happen. You also want the white parts of your image to print as white (not with a color cast of yellow, cyan, or magenta) and the black parts of your image to print as black (not dark gray with a green cast). You can ensure this by setting your highlights and shadows correctly. When you set the highlight, you are setting the brightest point in the image that is a neutral color, white, and that still has a dot pattern (doesn't print as pure white paper). The highlight would be the brightest part of Zone IX in the Zone System. Any point brighter than the highlight will print as totally empty paper with no dots. When you set the shadow, you are setting the darkest point in the image that is a neutral color, black, and that still has a dot pattern. The shadow would be the darkest part of Zone I in the Zone System. Any point darker than the shadow will print as totally black ink with no white holes to give detail.

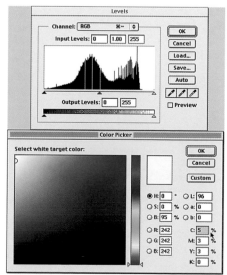

STEP 11: Photoshop allows you to decide where you want it to set the highlight. The highlight should be the brightest neutral point that still has detail. Double-click the Highlight Eyedropper button and make sure that the CMYK values in the Color Picker are 5, 3, 3, 0 and the RGB values 242, 242, 242. If you are using a different RGB workspace, you may have slightly different RGB values here. These are the neutral values you would want your highlight to have for a sheet-fed press on coated paper, and they also work for most other purposes. Due to the impurities in printing inks, you get a neutral color by having more cyan than magenta or yellow. Because this is a highlight, there is no black. Click the OK button if you need to change any of the values.

STEP 11: Make sure the highlight values are 5,3,3,0.

149

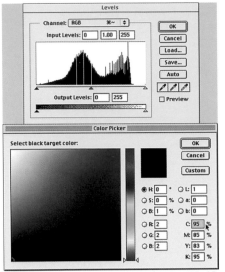

STEP 12: Make sure the shadow values are 95, 85, 83, 95.

Info

R : 205/242   C : 20/ 5%
G : 221/242   M : 4/ 3%
B : 220/242   Y : 11/ 3%
             K : 0/ 0%
X : 485   W :
Y : 180   H :

STEP 13: The before and after values for the highlight. Notice how the green color cast was removed and the default neutral 5, 3, 3, 0 values were inserted.

Info

R : 9/ 2   C : 72/ 75%
G : 7/ 2   M : 65/ 65%
B : 3/ 2   Y : 67/ 64%
             K : 91/ 97%
X : 1299   W :
Y : 938   H :

STEP 14: The before and after values for the shadow. Notice that the shadow CMYK values to the right are not the same as the 95, 85, 83, 95 default values you entered, but you should get exactly 2, 2, 2, or very close to it, in RGB.

STEP 12: Now double-click the Shadow Eyedropper and make sure the shadow values are 95, 85, 83, 95 in CMYK and 2, 2, 2 in RGB. If both these shadow values are not correct, simply fixing the CMYK values should change the RGB values to 2, 2, 2. If not, you need to return to Chapter 5: Setting System and Photoshop Preferences, and check the preferences for Monitor setup, Printing Inks setup, and Separation setup. Click the OK button if you need to change any of the values.

SETTING THE HIGHLIGHT

STEP 13: Next, you use the Highlight Eyedropper to click on a highlight, which should be the brightest area of the clouds. You want the highlight to be a neutral white area—the last possible place where you can see a little texture. The RGB values in the Info palette should be in the 240 to 255 range and the CMYK values in the 0 to 10 range. If you have specular highlights (the sun reflected off a chrome bumper, for example), these will not have detail and should have values of 255. You're looking for something just a hair less intense than that. Move the Levels dialog box out of the way so you can see the entire clouds area. To find the correct area for setting the highlight, hold down the Option key and move the Input Highlight slider to the left. The whole image area first turns black and then, as you move the slider to the left, white areas appear. Because this image has no specular highlights, the first white area that appears in the clouds is the point at which you should set the highlight. Remember where that location is in the window. Now move the Input Highlight slider back to 255 because you were only using it to locate the brightest point. Click the Highlight Eyedropper in the Levels dialog box. Now move this Eyedropper up to that bright place in the clouds, and move it around in the area while looking at the RGB values in the Info palette for the highest set of numbers. When you find those numbers (I chose 205, 221, 220), click once and release the mouse button; don't move the mouse after you click. The numbers to the right of the slash in the Info palette should now display 242, 242, 242 for RGB and 5, 3, 3, 0 for CMYK at that exact spot where you clicked. Now go to the Levels title bar and click it. When the mouse button is down, you see the original image. When the mouse button is up, you see the image after the highlight change. Notice that this process of setting the highlight has removed the subtle green cast in the entire clouds area. The clouds should appear whiter when you are not clicked down on the title bar. (If your computer doesn't support Video LUT Animation, as with most PCs, you will have to find the highlight point by measuring the areas that seem the brightest on your screen and setting the highlight where the largest numbers are. Then turn the Preview button on and off to see how the image looks before and after the change.) Setting the highlight actually moves the highlight sliders in each of the Red, Green, and Blue channels, which in turn moves the histogram in RGB all the way to the right. Press Command-Z once to undo and then Command-Z again to redo this change while watching the RGB histogram and the white color or the sky. See the differences?

SETTING THE SHADOW

STEP 14: Now we are going to use the Shadow Eyedropper to click a shadow, which should be the darkest neutral area where you still want a little detail. The RGB values in the Info palette should be in the 1 to 10 range. The CMYK values in the Info palette will be in the 60% to 100% range. Move the Levels dialog box to the top so you can see the entire bottom half of the image. To find the correct area for setting the shadow, hold the Option key down while moving the Input Shadow slider to the right. The whole image area first turns white, and then as you move the slider to the right, black areas appear. The first black area to appear, in the rocks to the lower right or in the tree, is the place where you should set the shadow. If you set the shadow at a location that has a value of about 1, 1, 1, you are setting up your image in such a way that almost no areas will be totally black when it prints. If you set your shadow at a location whose value is around 10, 10, 10, you are saying that you want everything darker than that totally black—and you will get lots of totally black areas. Now move the Input Shadow slider back to 0 because you were only using it to locate the darkest point. Click the Shadow Eyedropper in the Levels dialog box. Now move this Eyedropper up to that darkest place, and then move it around in the area while watching the RGB values in the Info palette. You might want to zoom in to that particular area before you pick the darkest spot. Try clicking at a spot around 10, 10, 10 to see how dark this makes your shadows. I clicked at a spot around 9, 7, 3, one of the darkest spots under the rock, where I set the shadows for this image. When you find the right spot, click once and release the mouse button; don't move the mouse after the click. The right numbers for RGB in the Info palette should now display 2, 2, 2 (or very close to it) for that exact spot where you clicked. Now go up to the Levels title bar and click it. When the mouse button is down, you see the original image and when it's up, you see the image after the highlight and shadow changes. If you don't have Video LUT Animation, you will have to find the shadow point by measuring the areas that appear darkest and then clicking the one with the lowest numbers, and you'll do the title bar compare by turning Preview on and off.

SETTING OVERALL BRIGHTNESS AND CONTRAST

STEP 15: As you look at this image, notice that it's sort of flat. Move the Input Brightness/Contrast slider to the right until the middle Input Levels number reads about .90. Notice the increased depth and contrast. If you think back to our discussion of the Zone System, you can equate the initial location of the Brightness/Contrast slider with Zone V, the middle gray values. Moving the slider to the right moves Zone V up toward Zone VI or VII, depending on how far you move it. What was a Zone VI value now becomes a Zone V value; darker, and with more depth. This effect is similar to the one you would get by setting the original camera exposure at Zone VI or greater, except moving the Brightness/Contrast slider by a zone or two wouldn't change Zones I and IX as much. If you move the slider to the left, the image would look even flatter. Leave this slider at about .90, and a few steps from now I will show you how to saturate your colors to add contrast and drama without sacrificing shadow detail.

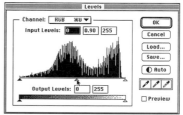

STEP 15: Move the Input Brightness/Contrast slider to the right to add depth and contrast to the image.

CORRECTING FOR COLOR CASTS

STEP 16: All adjustments so far have been done with the Levels Channel selector set to RGB (Channel ~). You can now use the Channel selector in Red (Channel 1), Green (Channel 2), and Blue (Channel 3) modes to control the color balance of the image and to correct for color casts. You can switch between channels by clicking the pop-up menu and dragging up or down, or by using the key combinations Command-~ through Command-3. The Red channel controls red and its complement, cyan; the Green channel controls green and its complement, magenta; and the Blue channel controls blue and its complement, yellow. Try to commit this set of complementary colors to memory. To learn more about the complementary colors, refer to the RGB/CMYK table at the end of Chapter 9: Color Correction Tools. This image has a slightly blue color balance, which makes it seem a little cold. Use the Channel

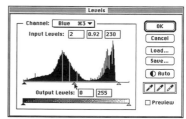

STEP 16: Move the Blue Input Brightness/Contrast slider to the right to add yellow to the image.

Correcting for Color Casts

selector or Command-3 to move to the Blue channel. Move the Input Brightness/Contrast slider far to the right until the middle Input Levels number reads about .5 and notice how yellow the image is. Now move the same slider far to the left to about 1.5 and notice how blue the image is. You can use this middle slider to control the color balance of the midtones. Move it back to the right until it reads about .92 and notice the difference in the color of the green grass and bushes in the foreground as well as the overall warmer tone of the image compared to when the slider was at the initial value of 1.0. You have added yellow to remove the blue cast in this image.

STEP 17: Press Command-2 to switch to the Green channel. As you move the middle slider to the left, you add green, and as you move it to the right, you add magenta. I moved it slightly to the right, to .92, which adds a little magenta to the whole image. If you press Command-1, you can use the middle slider to move between red and cyan. Again, I moved it slightly to the right, to .97, and added just a little cyan by removing just a little red. You may make these adjustments slightly differently depending on your preferences for color and depending on your monitor. So long as you have calibrated your monitor to your output device, you should be able to obtain results that you like. If you made major cast changes to any particular channel, go back to RGB (Command-~) now and double-check your Brightness/Contrast adjustments. Before leaving Levels, click the title bar to see how the image looked before you made any of the changes, and release the mouse to see the new improved image (Preview off/on for Windows). You should see the improvements on your monitor. When the Preview button is off, you can use Video LUT Animation on the video board to instantly simulate the changes you will see based on your levels adjustments. We have been doing these changes in Levels assuming the Preview button is off.

Many PC systems and compatibles, and a few Macs, don't support Video LUT Animation in their video boards. Video LUT Animation also does not work when you use a Levels Adjustment layer. If you don't have Video LUT Animation, just work with the Preview button on to see the changes as you make them, or turn it off to see the original image. You can't use the title bar as a before/after toggle without Video LUT Animation.

STEP 17: The GrandCanyon image after the Levels corrections.

Also, on *all* machines, you may want to turn the Preview button on before leaving Levels and Curves just to check on the screen to be sure that the calculated changes, with the Preview button on, actually match the Video LUT Animation simulated changes. You also want to have the Preview button on if you are viewing a composite of several layers while making changes to only one of them. Click the OK button to complete all the changes you have made in Levels. You'll notice that in layer chapters we have you use the Save button at this point followed by Cancel so you can move your Levels changes to an Adjustment layer. We skip that here to simplify things. At this point, you should File/Save in case you want to revert to this version of the image later. Go back into Levels and notice that the histogram, especially the Red channel, now has gaps in it because you stretched out the original set of tonal values. These gaps now represent missing tonal values in the 0–255 of possible values. Step 18 will fill in those tonal ranges again.

Chapter 19: Grand Canyon

ENHANCING COLOR WITH HUE/SATURATION

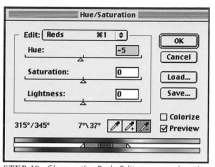

STEP 18: Type I to get the Eyedropper; then Shift-click to add Color Samplers to the brightest highlight area in the clouds and to the darkest shadow area in the rocks. You should still have your Color Sampler in the red rock areas. If the samplers don't show up in the Info palette, choose Show Color Samplers from the Info palette's Options menu. In Step 15, when you moved the Brightness/Contrast slider to the right to increase contrast, you might have had the urge to go even further for a more dramatic effect. Going too far to the right would remove too much shadow detail, however. You can add contrast and drama without losing shadow detail by choosing Image/Adjust Hue/Saturation and moving the Saturation slider to the right to about +17%. The screen may take a few seconds to update, but you will notice all your colors become more saturated, which builds more contrast into the image. When you saturate all the colors, only the midtones change; the highlights and shadows remain the same. You can verify this by looking at the values in your Color Samplers. The Red Rocks Sampler will have changed, but the highlight and shadow area samplers should be pretty much the same. When using the Hue/Saturation tool, you want to have the Preview button on, because Photoshop can't calculate these more complex changes using the monitor on-the-fly the way it can in Levels and Curves.

STEP 19: Choose the Reds Edit menu and notice how the red rocks change as you move the slider between -5 and +5. I moved the Hue slider to -5 to add Magenta to the Reds and then dragged the Eyedropper Minus tool over the lighter areas of the tree so it would not turn a redder color.

STEP 19: Besides using the Hue/Saturation tool to saturate and desaturate all the colors, which you do with the Master Edit choice selected, you can also use it to change particular color areas in the entire photo. Click the Edit pop-up menu and choose Reds; then move the Hue slider a little to the left, to about –5, to add magenta to the red areas of the image. Notice all the red rocks become a richer, darker red color. Now move this slider in the other direction to +5. This takes away magenta and adds yellow to the red parts of the image. Now the rocks appear more of a brown color. When you use channel 2 or 3 to add magenta or yellow in Levels, you add magenta or yellow to everything in the image. When you use the Red Edit choice in Hue/Saturation, you change only things in the image that are already red. With a new Photoshop 5 feature, if you find that the Red adjustment you made changed too wide a range of red values, you can use the Eyedropper Minus tool, at the bottom of the Hue/Saturation dialog, to click and drag on a range of red values in the image that you don't want to change. If you want to change a broader range of reds, use the Eyedropper+ tool; then click and drag over areas you want added to the definition of Reds for the change. Notice that the gray bars between the two rainbow sliders at the bottom of the Hue/Saturation dialog move and change when you use the Eyedroppers to change the range of Reds that will be edited. They are showing you the range of Reds that are being effected.

STEP 21: The GrandCanyon image after the Levels and Hue/Saturation corrections.

STEP 20: Choose Edit: Blues and now you can change the hue of blue objects toward cyan (to the left) or magenta (to the right). Move the Hue slider between –10 and +10 and observe how the colors in the sky change. You might combine this change with the adding or subtracting of saturation from the blue colors in this image. Remember that changing the blue values not only changes blues in the sky but also any other blues in the image. Keep an eye on the entire image as you make these adjustments. I moved the blues +7, toward magenta and the cyans +8 toward blue to try to make the sky more blue. I also saturated both cyans by 5% and blues by 7%. I also use the Eyedropper Minus and Plus keys to try to lessen any casts in the white clouds. Turn the Preview button off and on to see the image before any of these changes and then after all the changes. Click the OK button after you finish the Hue/Saturation changes. We will soon learn how to completely isolate a portion of the image using selections and layer masks for very fine color control of that area. Go back into Levels and notice that the gaps in the channels are now filled in by the added saturation.

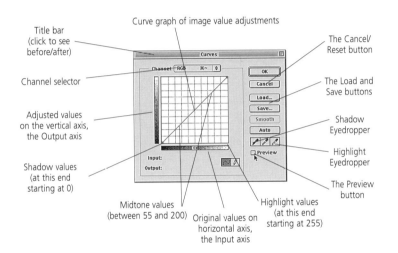

Study this diagram of the Photoshop 5 Curves dialog to learn the controls of the Curves tool.

STEP 21: Save this color corrected version of the GrandCanyon image in Photoshop format so that you can use it in future steps.

INTRODUCTION TO CURVES

This section shows you how to adjust specific color ranges using Curves. Before you start making further adjustments to the GrandCanyon image, take a moment to examine the Curves tool and its different parts and functions.

Curves is a graph of input and output values with the input values at the bottom of the graph on the horizontal axis and the output values to the left side of the graph on the vertical axis. When you use Curves, the input values are the original unadjusted values before you invoked Curves. The output values are the adjusted values and depend on the shape of the curve graph.

In Levels, the histogram is a picture of the actual data that makes up the particular image. In Curves, you see a graph of how this curve would modify any image, but you don't actually see the data that is part of the image. That is why I recommend using Levels first after you do a scan because you can see how the scan worked. Many of the controls in Curves are the same as those in Levels. Both tools provide an OK button, which you press when you

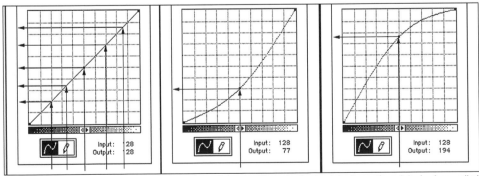

To understand the curve graphs, look at these three diagrams. Along the horizontal axis are the original values, called Input, with 0 (black) on the left side and 255 (white) on the right side. On the vertical axis of the curve, to the left side, are the modified values, called Output, with 0 (black) on the bottom and 255 (white) at the top. Imagine that the original values are light rays that travel straight up from the bottom of the diagram. When they hit the curve graph, they make an immediate left and exit the diagram on the left side. When the curve is the straight default curve, the values go out the same as they come in, as you can see by the left-most curve above. When the curve is dragged downward, like the middle curve, a value that comes in at 128 hits the curve sooner so it will go out at 77. Because lower values represent darker numbers, pulling the curve down makes the image darker. When the curve is dragged upward, as in the right curve, the input value of 128 doesn't hit the curve until it gets to 194, and that is the brighter output value.

Chapter 19: Grand Canyon

want the changes to become permanent, and a Cancel button, which you press when you want to leave the tool without any changes taking effect. If you hold the Option key down and then press Reset, you stay in the tool, all changes are undone, and the curve goes back to the default straight curve. Both Levels and Curves also have Load and Save buttons that you can use to load or save settings to the disk.

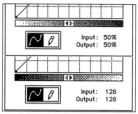

By clicking on the arrows in the middle, you can give the horizontal axis shadows on the left or the right. Leave shadows on the left for working with this book.

If you particularly like a curve that corrected one image, you can click Save to save it, go into Curves while working on another image, and click Load to run it on the other image. Curves, also like Levels, has Highlight and Shadow Eyedropper tools to set the highlight and shadow the same way you do in Levels. In fact, Curves uses the same preference values for the highlight and shadow numbers as you set in Levels. These preferences are systemwide. The curve graph is just a picture of what happens to all the values from 0 to 255. To move the curve, you click it and drag it to a new position. When you let go, Photoshop leaves a point along the curve graph, a point that causes the entire curve to move. To get rid of a point, you click it and drag it outside of the Curves window. When you do this, the curve bounces back to where it would be without that point. Let's experiment a bit now with Curves before you make final adjustments to the GrandCanyon image.

STEP 22: Using the same image you saved at the end of step 21, choose Image/Adjust/Curves (Command-M) and look at the Curves dialog box. If the curves graph area is divided into only four sections, both horizontally and vertically (the default), you can get a more precise grid. Move the cursor to the middle area of the Curves graph, and Option-click in this center area. Now the Curves graph will have 10 sections in each

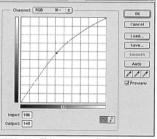

STEP 23: This curve makes the image lighter and brighter. To do this in Levels, move the Input Brightness/ Contrast slider to the left.

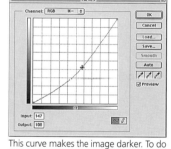

This curve makes the image darker. To do this in Levels, move the Input Brightness/Contrast slider to the right.

This S-curve makes the midtones more contrasty and the shadows and highlights less contrasty. You can't do exactly the same thing in Levels.

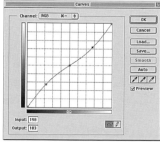

STEP 23: This backward S-curve makes the midtones flatter and increases contrast in the highlights and shadows. You can't do this exactly in Levels.

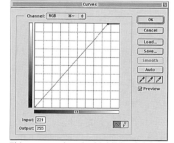

This curve makes the highlights brighter. This is similar to when you move the Input Highlight slider in Levels to the left.

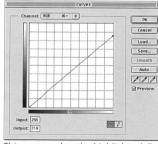

This curve makes the highlights duller. This is similar to when you move the Output Highlight slider in Levels to the left.

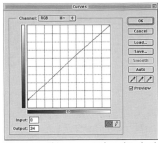

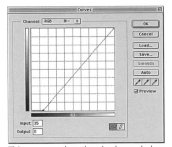

STEP 23: This curve makes the shadows brighter, like moving the Output Shadow slider in Levels to the right.

This curve makes the shadows darker, like moving the Input Shadow slider in Levels to the right.

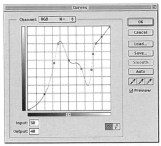

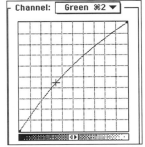

Try this curve to see a prehistoric Grand Canyon! You can't do this kind of adjustment in Levels.

STEP 24: This type of curve adds green to the entire image.

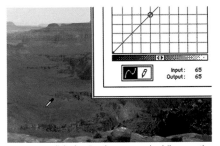

STEP 24: Click the Eyedropper tool while over the green field and hold it down while moving around to measure the range of greens in the field. The circle appears to show you where these values are on the curve graph. Command-Shift-click in the middle of that range to automatically place a point on each of your Red, Green and Blue Curves.

STEP 25: If you click in the little grow box at the top-right of the Curves dialog, the dialog toggles between the normal Curve dialog and a larger, more accurate display, allowing you to enter more points and see more detail.

direction. To get a bigger Curve window where you can enter more points with greater precision, click in the box at the top-right area of the title bar, the middle right box in Windows. Clicking in this area again will go back to the smaller curve diagram. Make sure that the Preview button is off; leave it on if you don't have Video LUT Animation.

STEP 23: Now click down in the middle of the curve and move the mouse up and down, left and right, and notice how the curve shape changes, and notice the corresponding changes to the image. Try out all the curves in the diagram above and on the previous page. Option-Cancel between each one to reset the curve to straight. Make sure you understand why each curve changes the image the way it does. Remember that each input value has to turn instantly to the left and become an output value as soon as it meets the curve. Trace some values for each of these examples, and I think you will understand how the curve graphs work. You need to understand these curve graphs because they come up all over the place in Photoshop (in Curves, Duotones, CMYK Setup, and Transfer functions), as well as in many books and other applications dealing with color.

CHANGING COLOR RANGES WITH CURVES

STEP 24: Cancel all the different things you tried with Curves and go back to the image you ended up with at the end of step 21. Choose File/Revert if you somehow destroyed the image while playing with Curves. Now you're going to use what I call the LockDownCurve to do fine adjustments to the greens in the valley of the Grand Canyon. Enter Curves (Command-M) and move the Curves dialog box so that it isn't covering the green field in the middle of the GrandCanyon image. Because we want to change the greens in the field, select the Green channel from the Channel selector. If you move the cursor out over the field, it changes to the Eyedropper tool; you are automatically in the Eyedropper whenever you use a color correction tool. If you click the Eyedropper and hold the mouse button down as you move it around over the green field, a circle appears on the curve showing you where the values you are measuring occur along the curve. Observe where the range of those values occur within the curve, and when you reach a point in the middle of that range, Command-Shift-click at that point. This new Photoshop 5 Command-Shift-click feature places a solid black point in each of the Red, Green, and Blue curves where the color occurred in that curve at the spot you clicked. (Command-clicking the image now places a point on the RGB curve that you would use to adjust Brightness and Contrast in that area.) Click the Green curve at that placed point and move it diagonally, either up and to the left for more green, or down and to the right for more magenta. You want to brighten these greens in the field. Notice, however, that the rest of the curve also moves, causing you effectively to add green, or magenta, to the entire image. What you want to do is add green to just the greens that have the same green color range as this field.

STEP 25: Option-Cancel to restore the curve to the default. You will now create what I call a *lock-down curve*. Click at each intersection of the vertical and horizontal lines in the green curve to leave a point that locks the curve at its present location. Make sure that the Input and Output numbers are equal before you click. Now you have a lock-down curve in the Green channel. Remeasure the green field, by holding the mouse button down as you move around it, to see where the measurements fall between the points on the lock-down curve. Clicking in the box at the top-right area of the title bar to get a bigger curve at this point might help. Command-Shift-click the image in a position that is in the middle of the greens range in the curve for this green field. Move the points on either side of this range so that only this range is open and so that there are lock-down points at either end. Now move the placed point in the middle of the range either by using the mouse, by typing values into the Input and Output boxes, or by using the up and down arrow keys to nudge the number up or down. Move the curve up and left for more green, or down and right for more magenta. I added green to this Green curve and a little yellow to the Blue curve too. Notice that the only greens that changed were the ones in this valley and in other parts of the image that had the same range of greens. To save time when doing lock-down curves, we have a precurve, called LockDownCurve, that has locked points on all four channels. You can use the Load button to load this from the Preferences folder on the CD.

STEP 26: Save this image as GrandCanyonPart1. You will work on it again in Chapter 23: Grand Canyon Tweaks, where you lighten the dark tree and rock areas, remove the scratch, and spot the image to turn it into a Master RGB image.

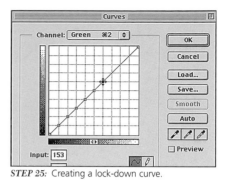

STEP 25: Creating a lock-down curve.

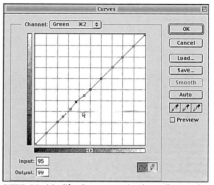

STEP 25: Modify the greens in the valley's color range.

STEP 26: The GrandCanyon image after using Curves to pop the greens in the valley.

Changing Color Ranges with Curves

*Overall color correction using Adjustment Layers
on a problem scan without good white or black points.*

The initial Kansas Photo CD scan.

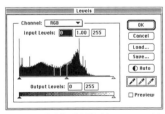

STEP 2: Original RGB histogram with lack of highlight values.

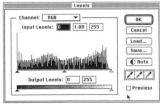

STEP 2: Final RGB histogram data is spread from 0 to 255.

In this example, you will do overall color correction but use some different techniques than in the Grand Canyon session because the histogram of this scan looks different. For the purposes of this example, we assume that you have done the Grand Canyon example.

SETTING HIGHLIGHTS WITH CHANNELS

STEP 1: Open the file KansasRawPhotoCD. This is a 4Mb Photo CD scan of a Kodachrome shot I took while driving through Kansas during a summer vacation when I was in college. Use the Crop tool or Marquee to crop the copyright notice from the bottom. Choose File/Save As and save this file as Kansas-Levels. Put the image in Full Screen mode by clicking the middle icon at the bottom of the Tool palette. Bring up the Info palette (F9 with ArtistKeys) and the Color palette (Shift-F9 with ArtistKeys), and then choose Image/Adjust/Levels (Command-L) to enter Levels.

STEP 2: Look at the original RGB histogram pictured here and notice that the values don't go all the way to the right, highlight, side, which is why the picture looks dull. Press Command-1, then Command-2, and then Command-3 to look at the Red, Green, and Blue channels, respectively. I always do this when I first look at a scan to see if it has any potential problems. In this image, all the channels have dull highlights but each of them has highlight detail that ends at a different point on the histogram. Press Command-~ to go back to RGB, and then hold down the Option key while dragging the Input Highlight slider to the left. (Remember, the Option key technique only works if you have Video LUT Animation and the Preview button is off.) You would normally set the highlight at the first area to turn white. In this photo, there is no good, neutral place to set a highlight, which should be pure white after that setting. The "white" buildings aren't really that white, and the brightest area is actually in the blue clouds somewhere. That's a sign that the Eyedropper may not be the best way to set the highlights in this image. Type Command-1 again and move the Red Input Highlight slider to the left until it reaches the first real histogram data, at about 213. Do the same things for the Green (189) and Blue (171) channels, and then press Command-~ to return to RGB. Notice how much brighter the image looks now and also how much more complete the RGB histogram looks. We have set our highlight for this image.

STEP 3: Notice that the shadow values in the Blue channel suddenly drop off a cliff on the left side, unlike those in the Red and Green channels, which taper off like they should; this is a sign that the scanner did not get all the shadow detail in the Blue channel or that there was no more detail in the film. Because this is a Photo CD scan, we have to live with it or buy our own scanner. When this happens to you, look at the original transparency and see if there was actually detail in this area. If there was, you might be able to get better results by rescanning with a high-end drum scanner. However, in the real world, we often have to correct problem images and scans, so hold the Option key down (only if you have Video LUT Animation) and move the Input Shadow slider to the right to test for a shadow point. There are some good shadow locations on the right side of the wheat in the front and also within the big green tree by the house. Click the Shadow Eyedropper and measure these shadows until you find the darkest neutral spot (I found a few at 5, 5, 5) and click on that spot with the Shadow Eyedropper. The new value for that spot , on the right side of slash in the RGB numbers in the Info palette, should be around 2, 2, 2 and your black shadows should look neutral. If they don't, click a new neutral darkest spot until your shadows look and measure neutral. Now you have set your shadow.

BRIGHTNESS, CONTRAST, AND COLOR CAST

STEP 4: Move the Input Brightness/Contrast slider in RGB until the overall brightness of the image looks correct. I moved it to the left to bring out a little more shadow detail in the foreground wheat and in the dark trees around the house. You can't bring out more detail in an area that is totally black, so don't go too far on this shadow detail thing.

STEP 5: Because we moved the highlight sliders differently on each of the color channels, we need to go into each channel and correct for color casts, which is easiest to do if you try to fix the most annoying cast first, and then fine-tune the other colors and other casts that appear along the way. The wheat in the foreground seems to have a greenish cast. I often have a hard time with these greenish casts because they're sometimes both green and cyan. This one looks greener, so go to the Green channel (Command-2) and move the middle slider to the right to add magenta; that should improve the situation and make the wheat look more golden. Move the slider until the wheat looks *too* magenta, move it back until you start to see the green again, and then add just a little magenta. If the image still has a greenish tinge, it might be that there is a cyan problem too, so move to the Red channel (Command-1) and add

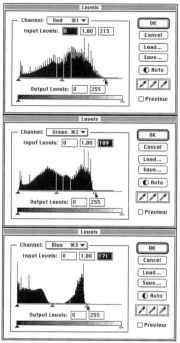

STEP 2: Move the Input Highlight sliders of the Red, Green, and Blue histograms to the left until they touch the beginning of the data. This moves all the data to the left of that point all the way to the right, spreading out the values in each histogram.

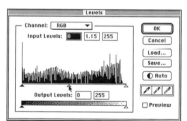

STEP 4: After setting highlight and shadow, set overall brightness and contrast. Move middle slider to left in RGB.

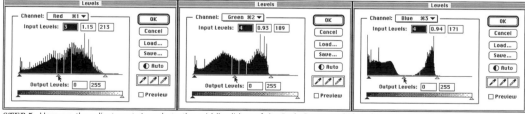

STEP 5: Here are the adjustments I made to the middle sliders of the Red, Green, and Blue channels to adjust for color casts in this image. Because the wheat is the major component here, getting that to look good was the main goal. Other parts of the image can be fine-tuned later.

STEP 5: Kansas, after all the Levels adjustments.

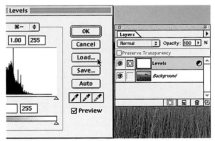

STEP 5: Creating a Type Levels Adjustment Layer. Press OK after setting the type to Levels.

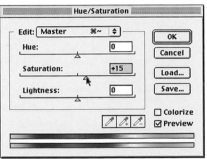

STEP 5: After you enter Levels as an Adjustment layer, press Load to load your settings from before when you were working in Levels on a real layer and were able to use Video LUT Animation. Notice that Video LUT doesn't work here in an Adjustment layer.

Hue/Saturation

Edit: Master

Hue: 0

Saturation: +15

Lightness: 0

☐ Colorize
☑ Preview

STEP 6: In Edit Master, saturate all the colors by 15.

a little red by moving the middle slider to the left. Finally, add a little yellow by moving the middle slider in the Blue channel a little to the right. At this point, before leaving Levels, you might want to click the Preview button just to make sure that the Video LUT simulation of your corrections matches the calculated changes that you set when you click Preview. They usually match really well on my system. Of course, if you don't have Video LUT Animation, work with the Preview button on anyhow. When you're happy, you could click OK to make your Levels changes permanent but, to have more flexibility in tweaking these changes later while keeping the most quality, it would be better at this point to press the Save button in Levels to save your Levels settings, call them KansasLevels, and then press the Cancel button to cancel from Levels on the actual *Background* layer. Now choose New Adjustment layer from the Layer palette menu and set the type in the Adjustment layer dialog to Levels. Now choose OK to this dialog, and you will find yourself back in Levels, but this will be a Levels Adjustment layer. Press the Load button to load the Levels settings you just saved then choose OK. Now you have your Levels changes in a Levels Adjustment Layer, and you can turn these changes on an off using the Eye icon for that Layer which is above the Background layer in the Layers palette. Choose File/Save to save your changes so far. Now you have done the initial Levels adjustment on this difficult image.

SATURATING COLORS

STEP 6: Having completed the initial overall histogram correction with Levels, you're ready to use the Hue/Saturation tool to saturate and enhance the colors that are most important to this image. Choose New Adjustment Layer from the Layers palette and set the Type to Hue/Saturation, then press OK. Make sure that the Preview button is on when you reach the Hue/Saturation dialog. When you use Levels or Curves on the whole image, you want to initially work with the Preview button off on a real layer, because when you do, Photoshop gives you an instant preview using Video LUT Animation, a technique that instantly changes the internal adjustments on the monitor. The calculations performed on your image in Hue/Saturation are too complicated to preview with Video LUT Animation, though, so you need the Preview button on. For flexibility later, you might as well create a Hue/Saturation Adjustment Layer, as we just did here, instead of just doing Image/Adjust/Hue/Saturation. Video LUT Animation doesn't work in Adjustment layers. When you first enter Hue/Saturation, the Edit Master menu is selected. Any master changes you make apply to all the colors at the same time. Move the Saturation slider to the right to about 15, making all colors more vivid.

Chapter 20: Kansas

STEP 7: Because the wheat is mostly composed of yellow, this is an important color to tweak. Choose the Yellow Edit menu to restrict the changes you make to apply only to the yellow parts of the image. Move the Saturation slider to the right by 15 and move the Hue slider a little to the left toward red; –1 makes the yellows a little warmer and more intense. The changes you make might be a little different depending on your personal taste and exactly how you have adjusted your version of this image so far.

STEP 8: Chose the Red Edit menu and move the red Hue toward the left by –3, add magenta, and saturate reds also by 5. Chose the Cyan Edit menu and move the cyan Hue toward the right, blue, by 5, and saturate them by 10. The cyan changes mostly affect the sky. When you choose OK to this Hue/Saturation dialog, your changes are archived in a Hue/Saturation Adjustment layer that you tweak as many times as you like, without damaging the original image, even after saving the file. We will learn a lot more about the advantages of Adjustment layers later in this book—it's just important that you get used to using them as soon as you can.

STEP 9: In color correcting this image, we have made all the corrections we can make without creating selections. Save this image as KansasAfterLevelsandHS so you can return to it to do some final color tweaks using selections along with Curves and Hue/Saturation later in Chapter 24: Kansas Tweaks.

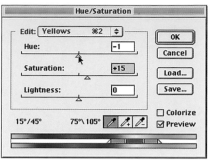

STEP 7: In Yellow, saturate the yellow colors by 15, and move yellows slightly toward red.

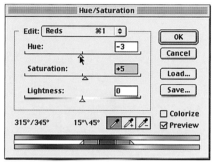

STEP 8: Red Hue/Saturation changes.

STEP 9: The final Layers palette.

STEP 9: Kansas, after Levels and Hue/Saturation adjustments using Adjustment layers.

Saturating Colors

HANDS-ON SESSION: Burnley Graveyard

*How to work with duotones, how and
why to adjust duotone curves, and how to
save and calibrate your duotone output.*

STEP 1: The BurnleyGraveyard image printed as black and white using only black ink.

Duotones are used when printing black-and-white photos on a press to get more tonal range. Black-and-white (B&W) digital images can have up to 256 tones in digital format, but you can't get those 256 tones on a printing press with just the single black ink. If you use two or more inks to print B&W images, part of the tonal range can be printed by the first ink and part of it by the second ink. Many of Ansel Adams' well-known B&W posters are actually duotones. Besides giving you a larger tonal range, duotones allow you to add rich and subtle color to your B&W images.

Typically, you use black ink for the dark shadows and a second color, maybe a brown or gray, for the midtones. You can add a third and even a fourth color to enhance the highlights or some other part of the tonal range. Many books are printed with two colors, black for the text and a second color, such as red or blue, for text section titles, underline, and other special colored areas. If this type of book has photographs, you can often make them more interesting by using duotones instead of just B&W.

CREATING A DUOTONE

STEP 1: This photo was originally a color photo but I felt a B&W or duotone printing of it would better convey the feelings I have about this stark graveyard where my grandfather and uncle are actually buried. Before using Image/Mode/Grayscale to convert the image to B&W, I did the overall color correction with Levels to get the best version of the RGB image I had scanned. It is usually best to do overall color correction before converting an image from RGB to either B&W or CMYK. After converting to B&W, I edited the contrast of the sky and the foreground separately to bring out the drama of the scene. I also fixed a section of the sky which was blown out due to the high dynamic range of the original photo. Open and crop the Burnley-Graveyard image from the Burnley Graveyard folder on the CD. Choose Image/Mode/Duotone to start working with the Duotone Options. Start out with the Type set to Monotone and the curve for Ink 1 straight. If the curve is not already straight, click on the Curve box, the leftmost one, for Ink 1, and bring up the curve. Click and drag any extra points in the middle of the curve to outside the dialog box to remove them. The horizontal axis of the curve diagrams in Duotone Options has the

STEP 1: Change type to Monotone mode and start with a straight curve.

highlights on the left and the shadows on the right, the opposite of the default for Levels and Curves. The numbers in the boxes represent a percentage of black. Box 0, for the brightest highlight, should read 0, and box 100, for the darkest shadow, should read 100. All the other boxes should be blank when you have a straight curve. Click on OK in the Duotone Curve dialog box. The Ink box for Ink 1 should be black and Black should be its name. Change the Type to Duotone to activate Ink 2 with a straight curve. To pick the color of Ink 2, click in the Color box, the rightmost one, for Ink 2, to bring up the Custom Colors picker, and then select a PANTONE, Focoltone, Toyo, Trumatch, or other color from one of the Custom Color Systems. Look in Chapter 8: Picking and Using Color, if you need help using the Custom Colors picker. If you were going to print your duotone on a two-color book job or a job with a spot color, you would probably use one of these color systems. We selected PANTONE Warm Gray 10 CV for Ink 2. You now have a black ink and a medium gray ink, both with straight curves. Make sure the Preview button is on in the Duotone Options dialog box to give you a preview of what it should look like with the current inks and curves. Printing two inks, both with straight curves, is like printing the image in black and then printing the exact same image again with the second ink color. When printing with halftone screens, the second ink will be printed with a different screen angle to add some additional tonality over just using one ink. Printing the two inks using the same curve will cause the image to have too much density and thus seem very dark. This is not taking advantage of the real possibilities for duotone improvements.

STEP 1: The BurnleyGraveyard image created in Duotone mode as a duotone with black and PANTONE Warm Gray10 CV inks, both having straight curves, and later converted to CMYK for this final output.

ADJUSTING YOUR DUOTONE CURVES

STEP 2: Click on the Curve box, the leftmost box, for Ink 1. You want to adjust the black ink to make it prevalent in the shadows but less prevalent in the midtones and highlights. To do this, click on a point in the middle of the curve and drag that point downward to remove black from the midtones and highlights. Now click on the shadow end of the curve, to the middle right, and drag it up to add a little more black to this area of the image. See the illustration of the black curve here. Click on the OK button for black and then click on the Curve button for Ink 2, middle gray, so you can work on its curve. Because we want the dark areas of the image to be represented mostly by black, we need to remove the gray from the shadows. Click at the top right of the curve and drag it down to about 55. Now you need to put the gray back into the highlights and midtones, so click a couple of points in the middle of the curve to pull it up so it looks like the curve here. New for Photoshop 5 is the Preview option. When it's on, you should be able to see these changes as you make them. You have now made the basic adjustments for your duotone curves. Now change each curve just a little bit, one curve at a time. Tweak these curves until you are happy with your duotone; then choose OK to Duotone Options and save the image as BurnleyGraveyardDuo.

CREATING A TRITONE

STEP 3: To further enhance this image, you can add a third ink for the highlight areas just to alter them in subtle ways. Before doing so, however, take time to make a copy of the two-ink version of the image so you can compare them onscreen. Choose

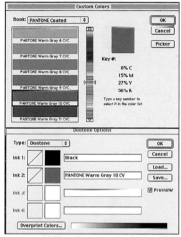

STEP 1: Picking the second color by clicking on the rightmost color square for Ink 2.

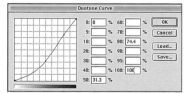

STEP 2: The black curve emphasizing the shadows.

STEP 2: The midtone curve for Ink 2, lowering this color in the shadow areas.

STEP 2: The BurnleyGraveyard image created in Duotone mode as a duotone with black for the shadows and PANTONE Warm Gray 10 CV for the midtones and highlights, after adjusting the curves for those two colors, and then converting to CMYK.

Image/Duplicate and name this copy BurnleyGraveyardTri. Choose Image/Mode/Duotone, and select Tritone from the Type menu in Duotone Options so that a choice for Ink 3 will be added. Click on the Ink Color box and choose a lighter gray for the highlights. (For Ink 3 we chose PANTONE 422 CV.) Adjust the curve for this highlight color so that it has ink only in the brightest part of the image. Here is the curve we chose for the third ink. Notice how we moved the 0 position of the curve up to 6.3 instead of leaving it at 0. This strategy actually adds some density to the brightest parts of the image; that is, in the clouds and where the sun reflects off the gravestones, two areas that previously were pure white. Here, we are using a third ink to subtly fine-tune the main image created by the first two main inks.

STEP 4: You may want to measure some values on the screen using the Eyedropper. When working with duotones, you want to set the top-left area in the Info palette to Actual Color so that it will give you measurements of the ink density percentage of each color. If you measure one of those highlight areas in the clouds, you can see that there is no density there from Inks 1 and 2, but that Ink 3 has 6% density in that area. If you measure a shadow area, the maximum density there will be from Ink 1, black. There will be some density from Ink 2 and there will be no density from Ink 3, because its curve specifies no ink in the shadow areas.

STEP 5: You have added a third color specifically for the highlights; therefore, you may want to go back to Ink 2 and remove some of the midtone ink from the highlight areas. Click on the Curve box for Ink 2, and lower its curve in the highlight areas by clicking a point there and dragging it downward. Here is the final curve we used for Ink 2 in the tritone. Our final tritone image appears on the next page.

STEP 6: Go back and try some different colors and different curves for this duotone or tritone. Try some blues, greens, purples, magentas, yellows—lots of wild things. Experiment with some radical inverted curves to discover the great range of effects you can achieve with the Duotone options.

STEP 3: Final tritone values with details of the highlight curve. Notice how this curve actually starts above 0 on the Y axis. This adds density in the very brightest areas.

CALIBRATING AND OUTPUTTING YOUR DUOTONES

If you are not having any particular calibration problems, especially if you are converting Duotones to CMYK for final output, we recommend that you leave your calibration and preferences set up the same as those for CMYK output in Chapter 5: Setting System and Photoshop Preferences. However, you may find that you need to calibrate your monitor differently for duotone output than for CMYK output. If duotones on your monitor aren't matching the final output, redo the monitor calibration steps for duotones, and make a duotone proof to create separate preference settings for working with duotones.

When you output your duotones, you have several choices to make. If you actually print with PANTONE or some other custom spot color, you need to save the file as a duotone in Photoshop EPS format. You can set your screen angles for the duotone in Photoshop using the File/Page Setup/Screen button, or you can set your

STEP 4: The Info palette measuring a highlight in Tritone mode.

STEP 4: Set the Info palette to Actual Color for duotones.

STEP 5: The midtone curve for the tritone with a small dip in the highlight area and a bigger dip in the shadows.

164

Chapter 21: Burnley Graveyard

screen angles in Quark Xpress or PageMaker if you are placing your duotone into one of those page layout applications. Talk to your service bureau about how and where to set your screens and what screen angles and frequencies to use; they may be different depending on the type of imagesetter your service bureau uses. Make sure the Short PANTONE Names option is chosen in File/Preferences/General. This option makes the PANTONE names chosen in Photoshop more compatible with those specified in Quark, Illustrator, and other layout and graphic applications. Make sure the name of each color is exactly the same (including upper- and lower-case letters) in your page layout application; otherwise, your duotone may be output as CMYK. To save from Photoshop as a duotone, leave the Mode menu set to Duotone, choose File/Save As, and then set the Format to Photoshop EPS. In the EPS dialog box, set the Preview to Macintosh (8 bits/pixel) and the Encoding to Binary, and click on the Include Halftone Screen check box only if you have set your screens and frequencies using Page Setup in Photoshop. On Windows systems you may want to set the Encoding to ASCII depending on the page layout application you will be placing the duotone into. Check with the manual for that application.

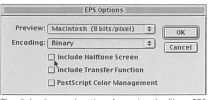

The dialog box and settings for saving the file as EPS Duotone.

If you want to convert the duotone to CMYK to output it with process colors, use the Image/Mode menu to convert the image to CMYK color. You will probably still save the file as an EPS, but there will be an additional option for DCS, which you should set to "On" (72 pixel/inch color) to get the 5 file format with a color preview. For more information on the options for saving CMYK files, see Chapter 18: Steps to Create a Master Image.

You can also convert your duotones to RGB format if you want to composite them with other images for Web or multimedia use, or for output to a film recorder or some other RGB device. To do the conversion to RGB, just select Image/Mode/RGB.

When you work on a duotone or tritone, the Channels palette just displays a single channel, your original black-and-white image. When you print the tritone, this same black-and-white channel prints three times, and each time the separate curve for the particular tritone color is used to modify it before it goes to the printer. If you

Converting a file from Duotone to CMYK format for output to process colors.

want to see each of these three-color tritone channels as they will look after the curves are applied, switch the Image/Mode menu to Multichannel. The Channels palette will now show you three channels: Channel 1 for black, Channel 2 for PANTONE 10, and Channel 3 for PANTONE 422. You can then click on each channel in the Channels palette to see how that channel will look on film. If you wanted to edit each of these channels separately, you could do so now, but after doing that, you could not convert them back to Duotone mode. They would have to be output as three separate black-and-white files. If you were just looking at the three channels and not editing them, you would choose Edit/Undo to undo the mode change and put things back into Duotone mode.

The final BurnleyGraveyard image created in Duotone mode as a tritone with black shadows, PANTONE Warm Gray 10 CV midtones, and PANTONE 422 CV highlights, then converted to CMYK for final output.

Calibrating and Outputting Your Duotones

IMPROVING COLOR AND MOOD

MAKE DETAILED SELECTIONS AND LAYER MASKS

SHARPENING AND SPOTTING

RETOUCHING AND COLOR CORRECTING
USING ADJUSTMENT LAYERS

COLOR MATCH IMAGES

USING BLACK AND WHITE AND LAB COLOR

WITH SELECTIONS, LAYERS, ADJUSTMENT LAYERS, AND LAYER MASKS,

This Kodachrome was taken using a Canon F-1 with a 28mm FD lens. It has always been one of my favorite images.

22 HANDS-ON SESSION: The Car Ad

*Using the Magic Wand, the Lasso tool, Quick Mask mode,
the new Magnetic Lasso tool, and new Hue/Saturation
capabilities to select the red car and change its color.*

STEP 1: The original perspective Acura ad with the red Acura.

STEP 1: The Magic Wand tool with its tolerance set to 75 and Anti-aliased on.

STEP 1: This is about as much of the selection as you should try to get with the Magic Wand. Now use the Lasso tool.

Suppose the image for an ad has been created and the clients love it. They are ready to run the ad, when the art director and the boss enter insisting on a purple car. You try to explain to them that red really looks better because the background is mostly purple, but they insist on a purple car. You don't want to have to go out and reshoot the car—that never happens in the digital world—so you just select the car and change its color.

Making selections is one of the most basic Photoshop tasks but also one of the most important. Often the difference between work that looks polished and work that looks hack is dependent upon how well you make your selections. Here we'll show you a couple of different ways to achieve the same result. With practice, you'll find which tools you're most comfortable with and which give you the type of accuracy and flexibility you need.

SELECTING THE CAR

STEP 1: Open the RedAcura.psd file from The Car folder. Double-click the Magic Wand tool, set its tolerance to 75, and make sure Anti-aliased is on. The larger the tolerance, the more adjacent colors the Magic Wand selects. Having the Anti-aliased feature on makes edges of the selection blend easier with their surroundings. Click on the bright red color just to the right of the Acura emblem above the bumper to select most of the bumper area. Now Shift-click the reddest part of the hood, in the middle. Holding the Shift key down while making a selection adds that selection to what you have already selected. Change the tolerance to about 45 and then continue to Shift-click unselected red areas with the tolerance set to 45. If adding any new area makes the selection lines go outside the area of the car, choose Edit/Undo (Command-Z) to undo that last part of the selection. Your previous selections should still be there. After you select most of the red areas of the car without going beyond its boundaries, your selection should look like the one pictured here. If you lose your selection at any time, you can reselect using Select/Reselect or Command-Shift-D.

STEP 2: Double-click the Lasso tool, make sure its feather is set to zero, and make sure that Anti-aliased is also on for the Lasso. Again, hold down the Shift key first and then circle areas that you didn't select with the Wand. While adding to the selection with the Lasso tool, you should zoom in closely to the area you are working on. Make sure that the Shift key is down or you might accidentally move the selection instead of adding to it. When you hold down the Shift key, the cursor appears as either a crosshair or the Lasso, depending on how your preferences are set up. In either case, you will see a little plus to the bottom-right of the cursor to tell you that you are adding. When the Shift key is not down, the cursor looks like a white pointing arrow with a selection box. Clicking and dragging at this point will move the selection. If you do this by accident, immediately choose Edit/Undo (Command-Z), or if you notice that you moved the selection a few steps ago, use the History palette to back up to a state where the selection had not been moved. Use Shift with the Lasso tool to circle all the areas not selected. When adding to the selection, first put the cursor on top of an area already selected, hold the Shift key down, and then press and hold down the mouse button while circling the areas you want to add. If you accidentally select something along a border that you don't want to select, move the cursor into an area nearby that isn't selected, hold the Option key down, press the mouse button down, and use the Lasso to circle the part of that border area you want to deselect. When you hold down the Option key, you see a minus to the right of the cursor signifying a subtract from the selection. When doing selections along a border with the Lasso tool, you have to trace the edge pixel by pixel. The Lasso tool has no intelligence to detect where color or brightness changes, so this is a hand-eye coordination exercise. Be sure to select everything that is part of the red car, even the reds that have a purple tone or are almost black. If they're part of the painted car, you should select them. Just like an auto body shop that is putting masking tape on the chrome and other areas for a paint job, you need to make sure that all areas to be painted are selected and all areas not to be painted are not selected. Pretend that the unselected areas have masking tape on them.

After you have started a Lasso selection, addition, or subtraction, the mouse button is down and you are drawing with the button down. At this point, if you hold the Option key down, you can release the mouse button and draw straight line segments between mouse clicks. If you want to draw in freehand again, hold the mouse button down again while drawing. In any case, the Option key or the mouse button needs to remain down until you are done with this selection change because when you release the Option key and the mouse button at the same time, the two end points of the selection will join. The hand-eye-mouse coordination in this maneuver can be tricky! Let's go through the most difficult case, when you are subtracting from the existing selection. First press the Option key and hold until you click down on the mouse button. Starting with the Option key tells Photoshop you want to subtract. Next, you click the mouse button and hold it down while drawing in freehand. Now you can release the Option key as long as you keep the mouse button down. If you want to draw straight line segments, press down the Option key again after its initial release. Now each time you mouse click, you are defining a corner point, and straight lines will be drawn between clicks. To draw in freehand again, press and hold down the mouse button while drawing. When you have looped around what you wanted to subtract, release the Option key and the mouse button, and the end points of this

STEP 2: The Lasso tool and its options.

STEP 2: No Shift key down, so white arrow cursor moved selection. Choose Edit/Undo (Command-Z) immediately if this happens.

STEP 3: Click on the Save Selection icon to save your selection.

selection will be joined. Remember, this works for both adding to (Shift key starts) and subtracting from (Option key starts) a selection.

SAVING AND LOADING YOUR SELECTIONS

STEP 3: After you work on this for a while, you might get nervous fearing you could lose all your hard work with a random mouse click. Remember, if you click without holding down the Shift key, you make a new selection and will lose and the selection you have worked on so hard. If this happens by accident, choose Command-Z to Undo. Another way to protect against this happening is to save your selection into a mask channel. To do this, bring up the Channels palette, Window/Show Channels (Shift-F10 with ArtistKeys), and click the Save Selection icon (second from the left) at the bottom of the palette. A new channel is created; it's white in the selection and black (or masked) everywhere else. If you want to save your selection a second time after you work on it some more, choose Select/Save Selection, and then choose Channel #5 and the Replace Channel option. This new selection overwrites the old saved selection. To retrieve your selection from the mask channel, choose Select/Load Selection of a New Selection and set the Channel pop-up to #5. A shortcut for doing Load Selection is to hold the Command key down and click Channel #5 in the Channels palette. That selects the white parts in the channel. The mask channel CarColor is a completed selection that you can use to check the accuracy of your selection. Leave this mask channel on the palette until the end, and then compare your finished selection to it for an idea of what you need to improve, if anything. If you have questions about how channels or the Channels palette works, see Chapter 10: Selections, Paths, Masks, and Channels.

STEP 3: To load your selection again, click on the channel and drag it to the Load Selection icon at the bottom-left area or just Command-Click on the channel.

CHOOSING A NEW COLOR

STEP 4: When you think you have finished the selection process, choose Command-H with your selection loaded and active to hide the selection edges. This operation removes the marching ants and lets you see the edges of your selection as you change the color of the car. If your selection is not correct, problems usually show up along the selection edges. Now choose Image/Adjust/Hue/Saturation (Command-U) to bring up the Hue/Saturation dialog box. While you are in a color correction tool, the Eyedropper is automatically selected from the Tool palette. Click down with the Eyedropper on the red area of the car just above the Acura emblem. The Foreground color swatch in the Tool palette or the Swatches palette will show this red. To use the swatch as a preview, you need to first set it to your starting color, as we just did. Move the Hue slider, the top one, to the left until the number reads –70. Notice that the swatch changes from red to purple, indicating that making the change would make your reds purple. If the Preview button is selected, the car will also change to purple after a brief delay. When you are working on a large file, this delay can be long, so you might want to move the Hue slider back and forth with the Preview button off, and use your swatch to get the new color in the ballpark of what it should be. The swatch will change instantly. When the swatch seems correct, click the Preview button to see your selection change color. If the Preview button isn't on yet, turn it on now.

STEP 4: The sample swatch in the Tool palette changes to purple when you move the Hue to –70. With the Preview button on, the selected area will change also.

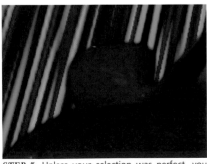

STEP 5: Unless your selection was perfect, you might have a red border around the edge and you might notice other areas that are still red after you turn the car to purple. Zoom in using Command-Spacebar-click to see selection edges closely.

WORKING WITH QUICK MASK SELECTION MODE

STEP 5: In the Hue/Saturation dialog box with the Preview button on, use the Spacebar to scroll around the edge of your selection, making sure all the red areas of the car have changed to purple. You might notice a red edge around the car and in other areas, such as on the Acura emblem, which indicates that your selection isn't perfect. If you find some red, press the Cancel button in the Hue/Saturation dialog box to return the car to red. Now you're going to use Quick Mask mode along with the Paintbrush tool to clean up your selection. In the Tool palette, double-click the Quick Mask mode icon toward the bottom right of the palette to bring up your Quick Mask options. Click the color swatch, and set it to a bright green. The default color for this swatch is red, which won't work here because we have a red car. The default for Quick Mask mode is that the masked area, the nonselected area, is covered by a colored semitransparent layer. This is like seeing a rubylith in traditional masking. The selected area is not covered. When you're in Quick Mask mode, you use the painting tools to add or subtract from your

STEP 5: The Quick Mask mode selector is toward the bottom-right area of the Tool palette. Here we see the color swatch in the Quick Mask Options dialog box. Note: As a shortcut, you can also use (Q) to toggle back and forth between the regular and Quick Mask modes.

STEP 5: In the default Quick Mask mode, the Quick Mask icon has gray on the outside, a white circle on the inside, and a semitransparent green mask that overlays the nonselected areas. Painting with black here subtracts from the selection.

STEP 5: In the Selected Areas Quick Mask mode, the circle in the Quick Mask icon has gray on the inside. The green mask area overlays the selected areas. Painting with black here adds to the selection.

selection by painting with a brush. This gives you finer pixel-for-pixel control than you can get with the selection tools.

Type a D to set the default black and white colors. When the masked areas are overlayed, which is the default, painting subtracts from the selection and adds to the masked area. The default Quick Mask icon is gray on the outside. If you Option-click the Quick Mask icon, it changes so the gray is on the inside and the selected areas are overlayed with green. When you paint in this mode, painting adds to the selection. Put yourself into this mode by Option-clicking the Quick Mask icon until the circle in the middle of it is gray and the outside is white. Now the green overlay will be wherever your selection was.

STEP 6: Using the Paintbrush tool, in Normal mode, with 100% opacity in the Paintbrush options, choose a 5-pixel brush, third from top left, in the Brushes palette (F12 with ArtistKeys). If you see a red border around the edge of your selection, paint this border area with the brush. You may need to pick a larger or smaller brush. You can use the left and right bracket keys to change your brush size without moving the cursor to the Brushes palette while painting. You can also double-click any brush to change its size and attributes. If you are not sure how to pick brush sizes and options, see Chapter 7: The Tool Palette.

Paint any red areas that still show up so they are overlayed in green. If you accidentally paint beyond the edge of

STEP 6: Notice that the Channels palette will get an extra channel called Quick Mask when you are working in Quick Mask mode. This goes away when you return to Normal Selection mode.

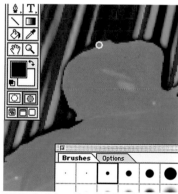

STEP 6: Using the Paintbrush tool to remove the red border from around the edge of the red car selection by adding to the selection.

STEP 6: What the edge should look like with a perfected selection, before switching back to Normal Selection mode.

the red area, you can Option-click the Quick Mask icon and invert the overlay; then you're subtracting from the selection instead of adding to it. A faster way to erase mistakes is to type an X, which exchanges the foreground and background colors and allows you to paint with white. While you're in Quick Mask mode with selected areas overlayed, painting with black adds to the selection and painting with white subtracts from the selection.

When you have perfected your selection, the selection overlay should look like the diagram here. You shouldn't have a red border protruding around the overlay edge.

Be sure to check the Acura emblem and the red roof of the car. For an area where the red color fades into another color at the edge, you can use less than 100% Opacity on the Brush to blend the selection of the red into the other edge colors.

Working in Quick Mask mode can be confusing if you Load Selections or work with the selection tools at the same time. For now, use the Paintbrush and other painting tools to edit in Quick Mask mode.

STEP 7: What the Quick Mask icon should look like (gray on the outside with a white circle inside) after switching back to Normal Selection mode.

RETURNING TO NORMAL SELECTION

STEP 7: At this point, Option-click the Quick Mask icon so that the masked areas are overlayed and the icon appears gray on the outside and white on the inside. Then click the Regular Selection icon to get the marching ants back around your selection. If you leave the icon gray on the inside and white on the outside, when you save a selection after that your masks will be inverted. The selected part will be black instead of white. This may confuse you. Believe me, it has confused many of my students! Now use Select/Save Selection to update your selection in the Channels palette.

STEP 9: The final purple Acura.

FEATHERING THE SELECTION

STEP 8: Choose Select/Feather and put a 1-pixel feather on the selection border before going into Hue/Saturation. This may blend away very fine reddish hues along some edges of the car.

MAKING THE CAR PURPLE

STEP 9: Now choose Command-H to hide the edges of your selection, go back to Image/Adjust/Hue/Saturation (Command-U), and move the Hue slider back to –70. Your purple car should now look great and have no red edges. If it does, choose OK from the Hue/Saturation tool. If it still isn't perfect, choose Cancel in Hue/Saturation (or choose Edit/Undo if you already said OK), and go back to Quick Mask mode for more fine-tuning with the Paintbrush tool. When you're done, choose File/Save As to save your final purple car under a different name.

After your save, reopen the original TheCar.psd file and get ready to do this example again using the new Photoshop 5 Magnetic Lasso tool and new Hue/Saturation capabilities.

MAKING THE INITIAL SELECTION

STEP 1: We are going to use the Lasso tool again, but this time we'll use the Magnetic Lasso option. Type Shift-L until you see the icon for the Magnetic Lasso, then press the Return or Enter key to bring up the Options palette if it's not already open. Set your Feather value at 0, but turn Anti-aliased on. Start with 10 as the Lasso width. This gives you a brush size large enough to cover the edge between the car and background but not so large that you include a lot of the background streaks. The Frequency is how often the Lasso will put down anchor points to anchor the selection marquee. We're going to use 40. For Edge Contrast, type in 20%.

STEP 2: Let's begin at the lower-left corner of the car. Click to start the Lasso selection; then draw around the edge of the car being careful to keep the cursor on the edge and hold the mouse button down. If you have your cursor preference set to Brush Size, keep the middle of the circle over the car's edge. If you see that the selection is being drawn into the car's body or into the background, you can move the mouse back over the previous selection, retracing your steps until you get back to the last anchor point that was laid down. If you've placed the last anchor point in a poor position, you can delete that anchor point by pressing the Delete key. Continue to retrace your path, pressing the Delete key until you get back to a place where you like the path you've drawn. Then continue forward again, clicking once to add an anchor point where you feel one is needed. (Photoshop will continue to add automatic anchor points, but it's nice to put some down where the curve changes directions sharply, such as around the mirrors, or where the background and the color of the car are too closely matched for Photoshop to place accurate anchor points.) If at any time you become hopelessly entangled in lasso lines, you can press the Escape key to quit drawing and start again. When you reach the windshield area or the bottom of the car, you might

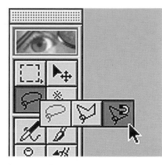

STEP 1: The Magnetic Lasso icon.

STEP 2: The Magnetic Lasso places anchor points as you move along the edge. Click once to place an anchor point manually. Hold down the Option key and click to draw with the Polygonal Lasso as we did here around the windshield.

STEP 2: The selection marquee from the Magnetic Lasso. Don't worry about the areas where the path is incorrect. We'll fix those later.

STEP 3: Use the Magnetic Lasso with the Option key to subtract from your selection just as you would with the regular Lasso.

STEP 4: Command-clicking on the New layer icon while your selection is active will give you an Adjustment layer with a Layer mask.

find it useful to switch to the Polygonal Lasso tool. You can access the tool while in the Magnetic Lasso by holding down the Option key and clicking from point to point letting up on the mouse between points. (The Lasso will draw the line but not place anchor points.) To switch back to the Freehand Lasso, press the Option key and continue drawing while keeping the mouse button down.

Finish the selection by drawing all the way back to your starting point. You'll see the Magnetic Lasso icon again, with a little circle at the bottom-right, which means that when you click, the selection will be closed. The selection will also close if you double-click at any time or press the Enter key.

STEP 3: To subtract areas from the selection, use the same Magnetic Lasso tool and settings but hold down the Option key before you start to draw. For the headlights, I brought the Lasso Width down to 7 and the Contrast down to 10%. Use this technique to take out the four round headlights, the license plate, and one of the yellow turn signal lights. Leave the other signal light and the Acura emblem in the selection for now.

ADDING AN ADJUSTMENT LAYER

STEP 4: When we did this example before, we built a channel, loaded it as a selection, and then used Hue/Saturation to change the color of the car directly on the *Background* layer. We're still going to change the color of the car, but this time we'll do it via an adjustment layer. This will keep all the pixel information of our original intact and give us more flexibility to change the hue again and again without risking degradation of our file. Because you've already worked in Quick Mask mode, you'll quickly grasp editing the Adjustment layer mask. But, if you have trouble or find it confusing, read Chapter 29: Bryce Stone Woman or Chapter 32: Versailles.

Create the Adjustment layer while your selection is still active by Command-clicking on the New Layer icon at the bottom of the Layers palette. You'll see that you now have a new layer above the background layer, which consists of a mask thumbnail and an icon denoting an adjustment. Immediately when you click, you'll also get a dialog box that allows you to choose the type of adjustment you want, in this case set Type to a Hue/Saturation Adjustment layer. Chose OK to the New Adjustment Layer dialog and you'll get the Hue/Saturation tool. As you did before, change the Master hue setting to –70 and chose OK again.

STEP 5: Now go back to the car and take a look at edges to see how good your mask is. You'll probably see areas that you want to include in your Adjustment Layer mask and others that you want to exclude. Remember the turn signal that we didn't knock out of the original selection? Let's work on that first because it's easy to see the change there.

The Hue/Saturation layer should still be the active layer in the Layers palette. Choose the Paintbrush (B) and a medium size brush (10–13 pixels). Type D and then X to make Black your foreground color. When you begin to paint, you'll be painting on the Layer mask for the Adjustment layer. Painting with black will mask out (remove the color change) from any of those areas that you've just changed with the Hue/Saturation Adjustment layer. As you paint the turn signal, you'll see the original color from the Background layer return. If you want to see how your painting is affecting the Adjustment Layer mask, Option-click the Adjustment Layer thumbnail.

STEP 5: After you've changed the hue, it's pretty easy to paint out the areas that shouldn't be adjusted by painting directly on the Adjustment Layer mask with black.

Option-click again to continue to paint with black any areas that should remain the original color. Switch to white by typing X while in the mask to paint any areas that should be purple. When you used Quick Mask mode, you were doing essentially the same thing, only this time, you're editing the Adjustment Layer mask and therefore your changes are saved automatically. Plus, you don't have to remember to get out of Quick Mask mode to go back to selection mode.

STEP 6: After you've worked on your edges, you're probably itching to get to the Acura emblem to finish your job. But wait! We're going to go a little further with the Hue/Saturation tool and let Photoshop do some of the really hard work for us. Double-click the name of the Hue/Saturation layer to bring up the Hue/Sat dialog box again. Hold down the Option key to get the Reset button and reset the colors to their original hues. Now use the Edit pop-up to switch to the Reds. This way, you'll be editing only the red pixels in the selection. Change the Hue slider to -70 to once again have a purple car.

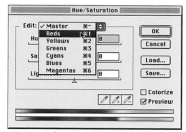

STEP 6: After resetting the Master to 0, use the pop-up to select only the Reds in your selection.

STEP 7: Check the area around the Acura emblem to see if there are any errant red pixels hanging out there. More than likely, there will be. Photoshop didn't consider these pixels "red" enough to change them during your last Hue/Saturation adjustment. Double-click the Hue/Saturation Adjustment layer to bring up the dialog box once more. Now click the +Eyedropper because we're going to add those red pixels to the range of reds that we are editing. Click one or more of the red pixels. Notice how the colors quickly come into line with the other purples around them. Check other areas of the car, especially the highlight areas, for pixels that still appear red to you and include those pixels in your red range. If you look at the range indicator (the darker gray rectangle between the two color bars) in the Hue/Sat dialog box, you'll see that the range is now larger because you've added those shades.

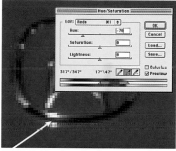

STEP 7: Use the +Eyedropper to click on the red pixels that still appear near the Acura emblem to add those colors to the red range being modified.

The beauty of using the Adjustment Layer method is that you can now go back and change the color of the car again and again without risking any degradation to the pixels in the file. Fast, clean, flexible…who could ask for more?

STEP 7: Notice that the range of colors you are editing (denoted by central, dark gray slider) is now larger than the original range.

STEP 7: With Quick Mask mode, paintbrushes, and Hue/Saturation set to Master, you might find it difficult to clean up around the emblem to get rid of all the red pixels.

STEP 7: Selecting the red colors with the Hue/Saturation adjustment layer tool, you can continue to add to or subtract from the range of colors you are editing to fine tune your changes.

HANDS-ON SESSION: Grand Canyon Tweaks

*Using selections and Adjustment layers to change
shadow areas, using the Rubber Stamp tool to
remove spots and scratches to create your
Master Image, and making a print and Web version.*

STEP 1: Tree shadow selection with anti-aliased on.

STEP 1: Tree shadow selection with anti-aliased off.

USING SELECTIONS AND ADJUSTMENT LAYERS TO BURN AND DODGE

STEP 1: Open the final color corrected version of the GrandCanyon image that you create in the earlier Grand Canyon. Put the image in Full Screen mode by typing an F. If the tree trunk, the big rock on the lower-right side, the bushes on the lower-left side, or some other parts of the image are too dark or too light, you might want to change them like you would in a darkroom by holding something over the enlarger light source in the trouble area or by adding extra light to that area while making the print. In traditional darkroom terms, this is called *dodging* or *burning*. I often burn and dodge using selections and Adjustment layers instead of the Dodge and Burn tools because they give me greater flexibility with different types of effects that I can always undo.

Bring up the Layers palette (F10); then double-click the *Background* layer and rename it Orig Image to change it from a *Background* layer into a normal layer. Type W and then Return, and type 8. Then press Return again to set the Magic Wands' tolerance to 8, which makes it select a smaller range of colors. Make sure the Anti-aliased option is turned on. When Anti-aliased is on, the edge of the selection is given something like a very slight feather to blend changes you might make to that selected area with the background. If you don't have Anti-aliased on, the edge of the selection is very abrupt; you get no blend between the edge and the surrounding area. Now click down in the dark part of the tree trunk with the Magic Wand. It will select the tree trunk and it may select more than that. If you don't like what it selects, press Command-Z for Undo to return to your last selection state and try again. You may want to select other dark parts of the tree trunk by holding down the Shift key while clicking those parts. If you don't like a selection, you can also choose Select/None to remove that selection and then change the tolerance on the Magic Wand, and try again.

STEP 2: The tree shadow areas I selected, Command-clicking the New Layer icon to get a new Adjustment layer.

STEP 2: When you are happy with your selection, choose New Adjustment Layer from the Layers palette menu or Command-click the New Layer icon at the bottom middle of the Layers palette. You want to add a new Curves Adjustment layer (be sure to choose Curves from the Type menu). Name this Layer Wand Selection. The new layer will automatically be set up with its mask isolating the selected area. Click the Load button in Curves to load the LockDownCurve from the folder of this example.

Use the Eyedropper to measure the range of values in the tree trunk, remembering to click and drag on the trunk if you want the circle to show up in the Curve diagram. Command-click the image at a point that is in the middle of this range, and this will place a point there in the RGB curve, which is the one you want to use for changing brightness and contrast. The placed point will be in the shadow parts of the curve, so click there and drag up and to the left to make the tree trunk lighter or down and to the right to make the trunk darker. You might have to move or toss some of the existing points from the Lockdown curve at the shadow end. Notice how the edges of the selection blend with both other parts of the trunk and the background. The Preview button needs to be on for you to see this. When you have a selection or are working in an Adjustment layer, you always need the Preview button on to see your changes; you don't want to use Video LUT animation in this case. If you do too much lightening or darkening, the edges start to distort. When you're happy with your changes (I darkened the darker parts of the tree) click the OK button.

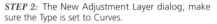

STEP 2: The New Adjustment Layer dialog, make sure the Type is set to Curves.

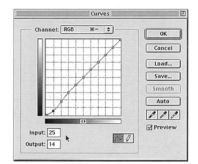

STEP 2: The Wand Curve adjustments we made to darken the tree trunk.

STEP 3: The great thing about using an Adjustment layer is that you can always go back to this Curve later and change it. The pixels in the Orig Image layer below are not permanently changed until you flatten the image or merge the Adjustment layer with the one below. Now you can now see this change before and then after by turning the Eye icon on and off for this layer. You can make a second Adjustment layer using a different selection technique or just a different selected area or different Curve adjustment and then choose between the two by turning the Eye icon of either one, or both on or off. You don't have to decide which of your different Adjustment layers you want until you save a flattened version of the image. Only the Adjustment layers whose Eye icons are one become part of a final flattened image. I usually save my layered version, without flattening, in Photoshop format in case I want to change one of the layers later. To make a flattened version, I turn on the layers I want and then choose File/Save A Copy, enabling the Flatten option and then save as a TIFF or EPS file under a different name. Go ahead and make some other Adjustment layers by making a selection of some other area you want to change and then choosing New Adjustment Layer from the Layers palette menu and adjusting that selected area.

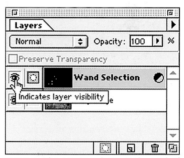

STEP 2: The Layers palette at the end of Step 2 with the Wand Selection Adjustment layer turned on. To view the Original Image without the Wand Selection, click to turn off the Wand Selection's Eye icon. Notice the Yellow Tool Tip that tells you what the Eye icon does. You can turn off the Tool Tips by unchecking the Show Tool Tips check box in File/Preferences General.

SPOTTING THE MASTER IMAGE

STEP 4: After using selections on specific items and color areas to do any necessary brightness/contrast and color fine-tuning, you need to spot the image. Make sure your general preferences for tools are set up as recommended in Chapter 5: Setting System and Photoshop Preferences. Specifically, be sure to set Painting Tools to Brush Size and Other Tools to Precise. Click the right-most column of the Orig Image layer in the Layers palette to activate it. The active layer, the one with the gray highlight, is the one that any changes will affect. Type Command-Option-0 to zoom your image in to 100%. Move the cursor to the sky in the upper-right corner of the image, and do a Command-Spacebar-click to zoom in to that area; you will notice many dust spots. You should be zoomed in to 200%. In Full Screen mode, you can see the zoom ratio for your window in the Window menu. You can also see it in the bottom-left area of the Navigator palette. You now want to remove any spots and scratches from your master image so that later when you sharpen any individual versions of this image, the sharpening won't add many, if any, new dust spots to those versions.

STEP 4: You can see the zoom ratio, 100%, in the Window menu.

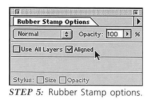

STEP 5: Rubber Stamp options.

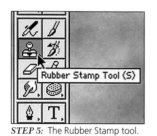

STEP 5: The Rubber Stamp tool.

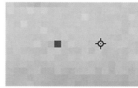

STEP 6: The Brushes palette and your brush.

Another technique for removing dust is to use the Dust and Scratches filter. Select part of the sky with the Lasso, feather set to about 4, and then do Filter/Noise/Dust & Scratches. This technique seems to do a good job on clouds and soft areas, but it often blurs areas that are sharp, so you don't want to run it on the entire image. You should test it on a particular selection by comparing the image with and without the Preview button on in the filter to make sure it doesn't blur the image too much. You can also try different radius and threshold values in the filter. A Radius of 2 and a Threshold of 20 works well in this exercise.

STEP 5: Double-click the Rubber Stamp tool and set the options as shown here. Make sure that you are in Clone (aligned), Opacity is set to 100%, and Blend mode is set to Normal. You can most easily get these default options by choosing Reset Tool from the Options palette menu.

STEP 6: Now choose Window/Show Brushes (F12 in ArtistKeys) and choose the third brush from the top left, a 5-pixel brush. Refer to Chapter 7: The Tool Palette if you need help understanding and setting the Brushes options.

STEP 7: You're going to use the Rubber Stamp tool to remove the spots in the sky and the scratch in the canyon. Move the cursor near a spot you need to cover. You should be about 1/4 inch from the spot and over a color and texture that you want to use to fill that spot. Hold down the Option key and click the mouse. This tells the Rubber Stamp tool where to pick up image detail to use in removing the spot. (When the Option key is down, the cursor turns into a crosshair with a circle in the middle.) Now, move the cursor to the spot you want to retouch and click the spot without holding down the Option key. Without the Option key down, the cursor should appear as a clear white circle the size of the brush you're using. Image detail copies over the spot from where you Option-clicked. If it's a big spot, you might have to move the cursor a little with the mouse button down to completely erase the spot. When you hold the mouse button down, you will notice a circle where the cursor is and an x where the Rubber Stamp tool is picking up the pixels to copy. As you move the cursor with the mouse button down, the x and the cursor move together; Aligned is on, showing you where the tool is copying from and to. When the Aligned option is turned on, the copy from and copy to location keep their relative positions as you move the mouse and click different locations.

STEP 7: A spot to the left with the Option key down and cursor on the right. Option-click next to the spot to show Photoshop where to pick up color and detail.

STEP 7: Click the spot without the Option key down. The cursor should look like this before you click, and the spot should be removed when you click using the pixels from where you Option-clicked before.

STEP 7: The circle and the crosshair that you see while cloning with the mouse button down. Photoshop picks up detail from the crosshair and places it down at the cursor circle.

STEP 8: Use the technique described in step 7 to remove all the other spots in the sky on this image. Don't forget that you can scroll by pressing down the Spacebar and clicking and dragging with the Hand tool. If you are trying to make sure that you remove all the spots in the image, you can go back into Normal Screen mode and start out in one corner, like the top-right corner here. After spotting that top rightmost area, click in the gray area of the horizontal scrollbar to scroll the image one full screen at a time. Move across the image, screen by screen, removing the spots in each of these areas. When you get to the other side of the image, you can scroll down one full screen by clicking in the gray area of the vertical scrollbar. Now work your way back across to the other side. If you go through spotting your image in tiles in this manner, you are less likely to miss a spot.

Chapter 23: Grand Canyon Tweaks

REMOVING SCRATCHES

STEP 9: If you look in the rocky area to the right, just below the horizon, you can see a one-pixel wide white scratch, which we created to simulate the types of scratches you get when the film processor has dirt on it and puts a streak right across your favorite picture. You're going to remove that scratch, and you can use the same technique to easily remove film processor scratches. Before you remove this scratch, use Option-Spacebar-click to zoom out until the image is below 25% zoom ratio. In Full Screen mode, you can see the zoom ratio by clicking the Window menu and looking at the name of this window (it will have a check mark next to it). Notice that at this small size, less than every fourth pixel in the image is displayed and the scratch is not visible. This is why when you spot or remove blemishes, you should always zoom in to at least 100%. Use Command-Spacebar-click or the Navigator palette to zoom back to 200%.

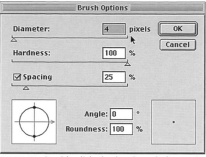

STEP 10: Double-click the brush and change its Diameter to 4 pixels.

STEP 10: Put the cursor above the scratch and check to make sure the brush is just a little bit bigger than the scratch. I double-clicked the third from the left brush in the Brushes palette and changed its Diameter to four pixels. Now move the cursor to about 1/8-inch below the left end of the scratch line. Hold down the Option key and click the mouse to tell Photoshop to pick up image detail here. Now move the cursor directly upward and click on the left end of the scratch (no Option key this time) with the cursor centered vertically on the scratch. A piece of the image is cloned here from below the scratch where you Option-clicked. Release the mouse button, move the mouse to the right end of the scratch, and then Shift-click the right end of the scratch. The scratch should fill in with image data from right below it, as though you had cloned from below by holding down the mouse and drawing on top of the scratch from left to right. You may have to practice this trick several times to get it correct. Also, you might have to Rubber Stamp out certain patterns that might repeat from copying the information from below the scratch into the scratch. This is usually only required in a few small areas however. Choose File/Save As and save the image as GrandCanyonMaster.

STEP 10: First, Option-click below the left end of scratch.

STEP 10: Second, click the left end of the scratch, centered on the scratch, directly above where you Option-clicked before.

STEP 10: Third, Shift-click the right end of the scratch, centered on the scratch. The scratch should disappear!

ARCHIVING YOUR MASTER AND THEN MAKING CUSTOM VERSIONS

STEP 11: Now you have completed color correcting and spotting this image. This is your master version that you want to archive along with all its layers. There are not many layers in this example but there will be more in future examples. Here we wanted to make sure you got the idea what the workflow was like for creating this, your master image, and then making several different versions of that image for different production situations. You want to leave your master image intact in your RGB or Lab workspace and as the largest file you might need. For other smaller versions of the image, that is, a brochure or book version or something for your Web site, you will flatten and resample down a copy of this master and then sharpen it and do a final spotting at the final size for this use. The file will then be converted to CMYK, for print situations, saved as JPEG or GIF for the Web, or exported through a ColorSync ICC profile that characterizes your output device and saved as an RGB TIFF. For this example, we will create one version to print on a press and a second version for your Web site.

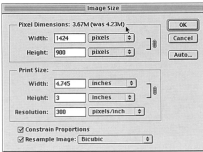

STEP 12: The Image Size dialog with Resample Image off, which allows us to see how big of an image we can get at the resolution we want without resampling. If the Width and Height shown here are bigger than what we need, we know that we will be resampling down and not up, which is what we want.

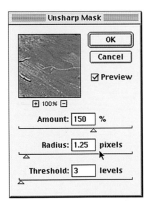

STEP 12: The Image Size dialog with Resample Image turned on again after we have typed in the Height we wanted. This shows us that we will have some extra Width. To get an exact crop and resample in one quick-and-easy step, use the Fixed Target Size feature of the Cropping tool as we do in step 15.

STEP 13: Here are the Unsharp Mask settings we are using for the CMYK version of the image.

MAKING A CMYK PRINT VERSION

STEP 12: Choose Image/Duplicate (F5) to make an onscreen copy of your master image. Turn on the Merged Layers Only option in the Duplicate dialog and name this image CMYK 300dpi 3x4.5. Choosing Merged Layers Only will blend all the layers in this copy into one Photoshop layer. Now go to the Layers palette and choose Flatten Image from the Layers palette menu. Notice that this turns your one layer into a *Background* layer. To save your file as a TIFF and in many other formats, you need to have a *Background* layer that doesn't have all the properties of a normal Photoshop layer and is compatible with more file formats. Press F for Full Screen Mode and then Command-0 to fill the screen with this copy. Go into Image/Image Size (F7) and turn off the Resample Image option at the bottom of the dialog. This allows you to play around with numbers to see what you will get without resampling your image. If you don't need to resample, that is better, and when you do resample, you want to resample down and make a larger image smaller, rather than resample up. Set the resolution to 300dpi, which is the resolution you would use to print this on a 150-line screen press, your typical glossy magazine. With the resolution set to 300dpi and Resample Image off, you can see that this image has enough information to print 5.093 inches wide and 3.22 inches high. You need to go 4.5 inches wide and 3 inches high so, because these numbers are smaller, you now know you can do this and resample down instead of up. Turn Resample Image back on and set the height to 3 inches; notice that the width now says 4.745. Your numbers may be slightly different depending on how you did your initial crop. The point here is that the Image Size dialog is showing you that with the height set to 3 inches, you have a little more width than you need. If you look at Pixel Dimensions, at the top of the dialog, it is also showing you that the image is going to be made a little smaller than it was if we choose OK at this point. Choose OK to Resample the image. Because the image is a little wider than we need, the person placing it into the CMYK publication layout will have to choose how to crop the extra image off the sides. In the Web version, we'll show you how to make it exactly the size you want.

STEP 13: Now we need to sharpen the image because it is at its final size. You will get better sharpening results if you don't sharpen the image till it reaches its final resample size. Choose View/Actual Pixels (Command-Option-0) to zoom the image to 100% and then do Filter/Sharpen/Unsharp Mask (F4). The details of the Unsharp Mask filter are explained in the next Kansas Tweaks chapter, but what you need to know here is that you will use different settings in this filter depending on the size of the image and also on the particular image. Also, you are usually best judging the results of a sharpen or a blur while looking at the image at 100%. For this image, I have decided to use the 150, 1.25 and 3 setting. You can play with the setting and see what they do to the image as long as the Preview button is on. Again, we will go into the details of what each setting does in the next chapter. Check and Respot your image after the final sharpening; there should be little additional work!

STEP 14: Now make sure your CMYK Setup settings are correct based on the decisions you made after reading Chapter 5: Setting System and Photoshop Preferences; then choose Image/Mode/CMYK to convert this image to CMYK mode. Depending on your monitor calibration and your other preferences setup, you might notice a certain color and/or contrast shift after converting to CMYK. You can use Command-Z to toggle back and forth between RGB and CMYK to help you decide if you need to make adjustments after converting to CMYK. You can actually do this and make the adjustments in RGB mode by turning on View/Preview/CMYK to see what your

RGB file will look like when converted to CMYK. Because I don't usually adjust my RGB master files based on how they will look in CMYK, my normal workflow is to go ahead and do the conversion to CMYK and then fix any problems in that particular CMYK version at that time. This is my preference because the main focus of my images is my larger art prints that are destined for RGB output devices, like the Lightjet 5000. Now choose File/Save to save this CMYK version in TIFF format.

MAKING A WEB VERSION

STEP 15: Use the Window menu to go back to your GrandCanyonMaster image; then choose Image/Duplicate again with Merged Layers Only on naming this GrandCanWeb250x175. Choose Flatten Image again from the Layers palette menu and then F for Full Screen Mode and View/Fit On Screen (Command-0) to fill the screen with this image. Type C to switch to the Crop tool, and press Return to bring up its options. Turn on Fixed Target Size and set the Width and Height to Pixels. Type in 250 for the Width, 175 for the Height, and 72 for the Resolution. Now start in the gray area above and to the left of the image and drag a cropping box to the bottom of the image. Because Fixed Target Size is on, the Crop tool will force the box to the aspect ratio you have chosen. You can now click and drag the center of the box left and right to decide what gets cropped off the edges. Press Return and the image will be cropped to exactly the size and resolution you entered. Because we know we are making a smaller image here, this is OK but realize that the Crop tool would just as easily make a bigger image if you typed in different values. But then your quality might not be as good as you want. Now choose Command-Option-0 for 100% and then press F4 for Unsharp Mask and use the 300, .5, and 0 settings. Larger amounts and smaller Radius values seem to work better for the small Web images. Now choose File/Save As and save this file in JPEG format with the Quality set at High (6) and Baseline Optimized On. These JPEG settings are explained in great detail in the last section of the book: Images for the Web and Multimedia.

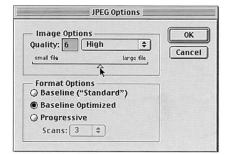

STEP 15: Here we use the Fixed Target Size settings for the Web version of our image. Fixed Target Size allows you to crop to the exact size and resolution in one step, but you need to first make sure you have enough data to be resampling down and not up because the Cropping tool will go ahead and do it regardless.

STEP 15: The JPEG options to use to get high-quality and good compression.

STEP 15: Here is the JPEG version of this image we made in step 15 but printed at 300 dpi.

STEP 14: Here is the CMYK version of this image we made in Step 14.

24 HANDS-ON SESSION: Kansas Tweaks

*Using selections and Adjustment layers with Curves,
Hue/Saturation, and Unsharp Mask to finish color correcting
a problem scan; learning about Preview CMYK and fixing
out-of-gamut colors with Gamut Warning and Color Range.*

In this session, you use Curves and Hue/Saturation to add color adjustments to specified areas of the overall color correct image of Kansas. This session also demonstrates using the highly important Unsharp Mask filter, the Gamut Warning, and CMYK Preview.

IMPROVING SELECTED COLOR AREAS

STEP 1: Open your corrected file from the earlier "Kansas" session, or use our version, called KansasAfterLevels&HS. Double-click the Magic Wand tool and make sure that the Tolerance is set to 32 and that Anti-aliased is on; these are the defaults. You are going to select parts of this image and improve their color balance and/or density. Start out with the green strip of grass that separates the field from the sky, and the two big trees next to the house. This whole area seems a bit magenta to me, and the trees seem too dark. Click the grass and then Shift-click to add to the selection until you have selected all the grass and the two big trees. Be sure to click only in the green areas; stay away from the almost black parts of the trees. You can also use Select/Grow to increase the selection adjacent to areas you have already selected. If you accidentally select something that you shouldn't, choose Edit/Undo (Command-Z) and try again. You can also use the Lasso tool with the Shift key to add to the selection or with the Option key to subtract from the selection. After you select the entire area, choose Select/Feather and enter 1 to create a one-pixel feather. This feather will blend the color changes you will make along the edge of the selection.

STEP 2: Choose New Adjustment Layer from the Layers Palette menu and set the Type of Curves and the name to Change Green Curve. Press the Load button to

STEP 1: Create the selection of the grass and trees with the Magic Wand.

Load the LockDownCurve from the Kansas Tweaks folder. Select the Green channel in the Curves dialog, and then click down on the image with the Eyedropper and hold in the area where the green grass seems a bit magenta. Look at the circle on the curve and move the cursor around a bit in the green area while holding down the mouse until you can see where an average magenta/green area is. At that point, Command-Shift-click on the image and Photoshop will place a point on the curve representing the place you clicked. Move that point in the curve diagram up and to the left to add green to that part of the curve. Now measure the magenta in the darker parts of the big trees next to the house and add green to that part of the curve, too. Switch to the RGB curve (Command-~) and measure the

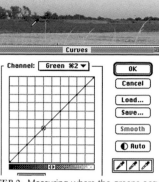

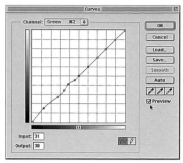

STEP 2: My final adjusted Green curve

STEP 2: Measuring where the greens occur in the green grass. Command-Shift-click to add a point to the Red, Green and Blue curves and Command-click to add a point at the corresponding location in the RGB curve.

brightness of the dark trees. Don't measure the totally black places; they're too dark to have any detail worth saving. Measure the medium to darker parts of the trees and see how the circle moves around on the curve as you move the cursor around over these parts of the trees. Command-click on the image to place a point on the RGB curve representing that place in the image. Move that point up and to the left to make the trees lighter. Notice that making the trees lighter also makes the darker bushes in the selection lighter. Turn on the Preview button so you can see the changes you have made in the selection and how they blend with the unselected, unchanged areas. If the borders are not seamless, either you made a poor selection or your changes are too radical. If you have problems with the way the border looks, first back off on the amount of change you made, and if that doesn't work, cancel the Curves command and go back to edit your selection.

STEP 3: Use the Magic Wand again to select the red parts of the red barn, which is most of it except for the roof. For this job, you may get better results if you set the Tolerance to about 8 and then use the Shift key with the Magic Wand to keep adding to the selection. You can also use Shift or Option with the Lasso to add or delete from the selection. Again, choose a Select/Feather of one pixel to soften the edge of the selection. Choose New Adjustment Layer or Command-click the New Layer icon at the middle of the Layers palette to add a new Adjustment Layer of Type Hue/Saturation. Set the Edit menu to Red so you change only the things that are red in this selection. Move the Hue toward the left, magenta, by −10, and increase the saturation by +10 points to make the red more vivid. Make sure that the Preview button is on so that you can see your changes.

STEP 4: Notice that each time you create a New Adjustment layer, your Layers palette grows toward the top. Also notice that these last two Adjustment layers have mostly black Thumbnails to their left in the Layers palette. If you Option-click one of these Thumbnails, you will notice that you see a mask and that mask is black everywhere except the area that was selected before you created the Adjustment layer. When you create an Adjustment layer when having a selection, Photoshop assumes the selection is the part you want to adjust and creates a mask that is white only in that area. Only the white parts of the masks are actually changed in color or contrast by the Adjustment layer. The two Adjustment layers we created in the initial Kansas chapter, which are the two right above the *Background* layer, have totally

STEP 4: We now have four Adjustment layers but notice how the top two have layer masks that are not all white. The white areas in these masks correspond to the selections we had made prior to creating the Adjustment layer.

STEP 4: Close up of the layer mask for the Barn Adjustment layer

Improving Selected Color Areas

STEP 5: The Kansas image after specific color corrections using Selections and Adjustment layers.

white Thumbnails because those layers adjust the entire image. These Thumbnails are called the Layer Masks for these Adjustment layers.

STEP 5: The white buildings in this image aren't very clean either. The building closest to the red barn is too dark and has a bluish cast. The other white buildings have various degrees of yellow tinge to them. Using similar techniques to what you used on the grass and barn, first select the dark building and then use a Curves Adjustment layer to brighten it up. Then select all the yellow buildings and use either a Curves or Hue/Saturation Adjustment layer to clean them up. Save the image as KansasMasterLayers. You could have made these changes by using Image/Adjust/Curves or Image/Adjust/Hue/Saturation but then you would have to change the actual pixels of the original *Background* layer or a copy of it. If those changes later turned out to be a problem after printing a proof, you would not have a record of your mask and exactly what you did or find them as easy to further modify as you will with these Adjustment layers. To further modify an Adjustment layer, double-click the name of the Adjustment layer, and your old modifications will come up allowing you to change them again and again without slowly destroying the integrity of the original image. One thing you should do to the *Background* layer, however, is use the Rubber Stamp tool to remove all the spots and scratches. Click the *Background* layer to activate it and then use the rubber stamp techniques you learned in the last chapter to spot this image, especially the sky.

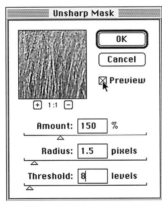

STEP 6: The Unsharp Mask filter dialog box with its three settings.

THE UNSHARP MASK FILTER

STEP 6: When I want to make a final output file the exact same size as my master file, so I don't need to resample before sharpening, I often create a sharpen layer on the top of the Layers palette that encompasses the effects of all the other layers and is then sharpened. Do this now by clicking back on your top-most Adjustment layer. Now choose New Layer from the Layers palette naming this layer Merged. Now hold down the Option key, and keep it down while Photoshop is thinking; then choose Merge Visible from the Layers palette. This will merge the effect of all the layers into this merged layer, but it will also leave the rest of the layers intact. If you end up with only this one Merged layer when you are done, you let up on the Option key too early, so Command-Z and try again. Now use Filter/Sharpen/Unsharp Mask to sharpen your image for final output. The Unsharp Mask filter has three different settings (Amount, Radius, and Threshold) that affect different parts of the sharpening process. You will have to run some tests to determine what value to use in each of these settings. It is often useful to compare tests on a small section of the image. Photoshop does have a Preview button in the Unsharp Mask filter that allows you to see the filter of a selected area of the image, but it still doesn't allow you to compare one group of settings to another.

Select a section of the image that can represent the entire image, and whose sharpness is most important, and make a copy of it using Edit/Copy. (See the images on the next page to see what I selected from this photograph.) Now choose File/New (Command-N) to create a new file. Because you just made a copy, the new file will

Another technique for sharpening very saturated files is using Mode/Lab Color to convert the file to Lab Color mode and then sharpening the L channel. This method prevents your saturated colors from popping as much during the sharpening. You can then convert back to RGB unless your master workspace is Lab; then no conversions are necessary to do this step.

be the size of the copied section. Say OK to the New dialog box and then do Edit/Paste (Command-V). Repeat this action several times, until you have five or six small files that you can place next to each other on the screen for comparison. Now run different tests on each file to see what the three parameters of Unsharp Mask each do.

AMOUNT: This setting controls the overall amount of sharpening. When you compare sharpening effects, you want to zoom in to the image, to at least 100% to see all the detail. Compare different copies of the same image area using different settings for Amount. You sharpen an image by looking for edges in the photograph and enhancing those edges by making one side of them darker and the other side of them lighter. Edges are sharp color or contrast changes in an image.

RADIUS: This setting controls the width of pixels along an edge that you modify when you sharpen the image. Again, try running the filter with different settings and comparing several copies of the same image side by side.

THRESHOLD: When you set Threshold to 0, everything in the image becomes a candidate for being an edge and getting sharpened. If you set the Threshold to, say 10, then an edge will only be found and sharpened if there is a difference of at least 10 points (in the range from 0 to 255) in the pixel values along that edge. The larger value you give to the Threshold setting, the more contrasty an edge needs to be before it is sharpened and the more you are doing just Sharpen Edges.

When you find the correct Unsharp Mask values, use those to sharpen the entire file. If the original image is very grainy, I might increase Threshold, which lessens the sharpening of the grain. If the image is very fine grained, I might decrease Threshold, which allows me to sharpen the file a bit more without getting more than the normal grain appearance in the final image. You have to be careful not to over-sharpen. If your final output is a halftone, you can get away with more sharpening than you can for a transparency film recorder or even a digital print output, because the screen angles and dots in a halftone tend to lessen some sharpening artifacts. All artifacts show up if you output to a color transparency film recorder, however. We usually use the Unsharp Mask filter instead of the other Photoshop sharpening filters because Unsharp Mask provides much finer control over the many different types of images.

Image with no sharpening. We need some!

Unsharp Mask 150, 1.5, 0. Too much grain!

Unsharp Mask 450, 1.5, 0. Too much sharpening and grain!

Unsharp Mask 150, 4.5, 0. Too large a Radius for a real look.

Unsharp Mask 150, 1.5, 8. I used to use this a lot but now I experiment more on each image.

Unsharp Mask 300, .5, 4. Compare this to the ones on either side.

Unsharp Mask 500, .5, 8. Let's see how this prints.

RESPOTTING WITH THE RUBBER STAMP

STEP 7: After you sharpen any image, you should zoom in to at least 100% and then go through each section of the file, checking for spots that appeared after sharpening. Sharpening tends to enhance spots that may not have been obvious before, which is why you should double-check the spotting of your Master file after any final sharpening. The procedure is the same as the spotting work demonstrated in Chapter 23: Grand Canyon Tweaks. Do another File/Save (Command-S) to save your final spotted file with your Sharpened and Spotted Merged layer on top. Now choose Image/Duplicate to create a copy of your layered image and choose Merged Layers Only so only one layer exists in this copy. Choose Flatten Image from the Layers palette to prepare this version of your image for final output.

OUT-OF-GAMUT COLORS

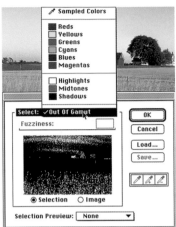

STEP 8: In Color Range, selecting out-of-gamut colors.

STEP 8: You can see many vivid colors on the computer screen in RGB or Lab that won't print in CMYK on a press. If you are working in RGB to send your final output to a film recorder and color transparency film, you can get more colors on film than you can on a press. If your final output is some Web or multimedia presentation, you can also get the colors there. You need to realize that each different type of computer monitor or digital color printer, or even press and paper combination, might have a different color gamut. The *gamut* of your output device is the range of colors it can actually print. For more information about these issues, see Chapter 14: Color Spaces, Device Characterization, and Color Management. If you are going to print this file on a press in CMYK or if you are using the RGB output device soft-proofing technique described at the end of Chapter 14, you might want to check your out-of-gamut colors and see if you need to correct them. Refer to Chapter 5: Setting System and Photoshop Preferences and make sure that your CMYK preferences are set up correctly before you use any of the CMYK Preview or Gamut Warning commands. Choose Select/Color Range, and then choose Out-of-Gamut from the Select pop-up in the dialog box. Click OK to see a selection of all the colors that you can see in RGB but which won't print exactly the same in CMYK or on your RGB device. Choose View/Hide Edges (Command-H) to hide the edges of this selection.

STEP 9: Some out-of-gamut colors, like red, often look quite different and usually muted when printed in CMYK. In many other colors, you might not notice the difference. Choose View/Preview CMYK (Command-Y) for an estimate of what the image will look like when printed in CMYK while you are still working in RGB or Lab. If you made the red barn really bright, you will notice it fades a bit. How many other changes did you see in the image? The sky might look a bit duller. Now choose View/Gamut Warning (Command-Shift-Y), and all these out-of-gamut colors will change to gray or whatever color you have set in Preferences as the gamut warning indicator. Remember that you have a selection, which you made using Color Range, of all the colors that are actually out-of-gamut. With Gamut Warning on, you can use this selection in conjunction with the Hue/Saturation command to fix much of the gamut problem. Colors often are out-of-gamut because they're too saturated. Choose Command-U for Hue/Saturation and move the Saturation slider to the left. Notice that the Gamut Warning areas get smaller the more you desaturate the selected out-of-gamut area. You might want to desaturate your out-of-gamut colors in several stages, or use the Sponge tool from the Tool palette, so you don't further desaturate colors that have already come back into gamut. To desaturate in stages, move the Saturation slider to the left, to, say, –10. Choose OK and then choose Select/None. Now go back to Color Range (see step 8), and choose the new smaller set of out-of-gamut colors. Reduce the saturation on these also by –10. Continue this iterative process until you have no more out-of-gamut colors, or until the out-of-gamut areas are so small they won't show.

STEP 10: Gamut Warning is a very useful tool for seeing colors that are going to be difficult to reproduce in CMYK or on your RGB output device. However, if you always desaturate all your colors so that no Gamut Warning areas show up, you may end up with duller colors on press or your device than you would have gotten if you were a little less strict about desaturating all your RGB colors. I compared two conversions to CMYK of this image. The first had been pre-adjusted, via steps 8 and 9, to remove out-of-gamut colors, and the second was of the same image without the out-of-gamut adjustments. The pre-adjusted image didn't change much at all when converted to CMYK, which is good. The image that I hadn't pre-adjusted for out-of-gamut colors did change and got a little duller, as with the red barn, but overall was a bit brighter and more vivid in CMYK than the pre-adjusted image was. So if you work in RGB and use bright colors, even out-of-gamut ones, you might get brighter color results by going ahead and converting these to CMYK. You know that some bright colors may get a bit duller, but you can deal with those dull or changed colors when you are in CMYK mode, instead of dulling them ahead of time by desaturating based on Gamut Warning and possibly desaturating them too much. Do some tests to see what works best for you! When printing on an RGB device, like the LightJet 5000, you might find you lose a few less details in your extreme saturated areas if you bring things into gamut with the device a bit before sending a file to the printer. Again, you should experiment and see.

CONVERTING TO CMYK

STEP 11: Now you have your final color corrected version of the RGB image for this particular job. If your final output device is an RGB device, such as a film recorder or a video screen, your work is done. If you use a color management system or printer software that automatically converts your file from RGB to CMYK as you output it, you also are done. If your final output device is CMYK and you are going to do the conversion from RGB to CMYK in Photoshop, you need to make sure all the preferences are set up correctly for CMYK conversion and for this particular printing project. Choose Mode/CMYK to convert the image to CMYK. When in CMYK, Photoshop automatically adjusts the image display on the monitor to try to simulate your actual CMYK printed output. Consequently, some of the brighter colors may get duller or change slightly. You might want to do additional small color tweaks now that you are in CMYK, using the same tools you used in RGB. You can also use the Selective Color tool and other tools to tweak CMYK colors, as explained at the end of Chapters 25: Yellow Flowers and 27: Color Matching Cars. For this particular image, we created a curve called CMYK Tweak Curve to adjust the image after it was converted from RGB into CMYK to make the CMYK image look more like the RGB image. When you are happy with your CMYK image, save it as Kansas-FinalCMYK.

STEP 11: The final RGB version of Kansas after all color corrections and using the Unsharp Mask filter.

25 HANDS-ON SESSION: Yellow Flowers

*Using Color Range and Replace Color
to change the colors of flowers and to
enhance those colors; using Selective Color
to improve the CMYK version.*

Original version of the flowers picture. We will select the flowers and change their color.

The Color Range tool lets you make selections based on these different color choices. When you use the Sampled Colors choice, you click on the colors you want to select within the image.

In this session, you use the Color Range and Replace Color tools to select the flowers and change their color from yellow to orange. You then use the Selective Color command to enhance the color of the orange flowers. This image is tagged with Color-MatchRGB and was created in a ColorMatchRGB workspace. Using a different workspace to do this example might yield slightly different measured values.

ABOUT COLOR RANGE AND REPLACE COLOR

The first thing you do in this example is select all the flowers. There are two similar tools for making selections based on color in Photoshop 5. Select/Color Range allows you to specify a color using the Eyedropper tool and then shows you a mask of all the areas in the current selection that contain that color. You can add to or subtract from that mask using + or – Eyedroppers, so that when you leave Color Range, you have a selection that contains the final colors you specified. Another command that is similar to Color Range is Image/Adjust/Replace Color. It lets you make selections similarly and also change the colors of the selections at the same time, using controls that are like those in the Hue/Saturation command but not quite as powerful. You can load and save color selection sets between these two tools, so you need to understand the subtle but important differences between them.

The Color Range tool always returns a selection, which you can then use as you would any other selection to modify the selected areas using other Photoshop tools. Because Color Range lets you make selections, it furnishes some very useful features for seeing exactly what you have selected. When you choose the Sampled Colors option from the Select pop-up menu in Color Range, you select colors by clicking on them with the Eyedropper (you do the same in Replace Color). You can add to the colors that you select by using the regular Eyedropper and Shift-clicking, and you can subtract from the selected colors by Option-clicking. Also, the + and – Eyedroppers always add to or always subtract respectively from the selected areas. You see what colors are selected by looking at a black-and-white mask window in the dialog box. Here, white shows you the selected areas. To see the selected items in the most detail, choose the Quick Mask option in the Selection Preview pop-up, and you will get a Quick Mask overlay on top of the unselected areas in the Actual Image window. If you choose the correct color for your Quick Mask (notice the purple in the diagram here), you can see when your selection is complete. You choose the color for your Quick Mask by double-clicking on the Quick Mask icon at the bottom of the Tool palette. (You need to do this before you enter Color Range.) See Chapter 22: The Car Ad for a discussion of Quick Mask mode. You can also choose no preview in the image area, or a Grayscale, Black Matte, or White Matte preview. These can also be very useful in different types of situations. Try them all and see what works best for you. By the way, the other options in the Select pop-up allow you to select all the reds, yellows, greens, cyans, blues, magentas, highlights, midtones, shadows, or out-of-gamut colors in the part of the image that you selected before you entered Color Range. The out-of-gamut colors option can be very useful (see Chapter 24: Kansas Tweaks). Although Replace Color doesn't give you these other Select options, you can get them by using the Save button in Color Range to save selections made with these options, and you can use the Load button in Replace Color to load these selections.

The Replace Color tool also allows you to select colors with the Eyedropper in the same way as Color Range, but it has no Quick Mask Preview mode and no Select options. Replace Color doesn't provide as many options for selecting the colors or for seeing the selection as Color Range does, but after you make a selection in either one, you can click on the Save button to save the description of the selected colors. This feature allows you to select similar colors in other images or make the same color selection in the current image from Color Range or from Replace Color by going into either tool and using the Load button to load that color selection description. When you have the selection you want, the Replace Color tool allows you to change the color of the selected items by using the Hue, Saturation, and Lightness sliders at its bottom. The Preview box here shows you the color changes happening in the image on the screen. For changing color, Replace Color is even better than a selection preview because you see whether the selection is correct as you actually change the colors you want. So, when you use Color Range, you are selecting a range of colors in an image and ending up with a selection. When you use Replace Color, you select a range of colors and replace those colors simultaneously. Now, let's try this out!

USING COLOR RANGE TO SELECT THE FLOWERS

STEP 1: Open the FlowersYellow image in the YellowFlowers Example folder. Put Photoshop into Full Screen mode by pressing F or by clicking on the middle icon at the bottom of the Tools palette. Double-click on the Quick Mask icon, click on the colored square, and then set the color to medium blue or purple. Find a color that has no yellow in it so that any flower parts not selected show up easily. Make sure the Opacity is set to 50%. Say OK to these dialog boxes and click back on the regular Selection icon to the left of the Quick Mask icon. Now press the Tab key to remove all the tool windows from the screen. Choose Select/Color Range. Set the Fuzziness to 40. The Fuzziness, which works the same in Replace Color and Color Range, is

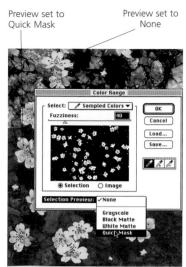

Preview set to Quick Mask
Preview set to None

In the top part of this illustration, the Selection Preview is None and you see the image. At the bottom of the illustration you see the purple Quick Mask preview, which is very useful.

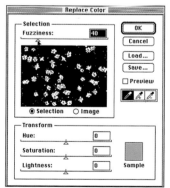

The Quick Mask icon
Click here to change the Quick Mask color

Click on the Quick Mask icon to get the Quick Mask Options dialog box; and then click on the color square and select a new color with the Color Picker.

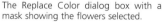

The Replace Color dialog box with a mask showing the flowers selected.

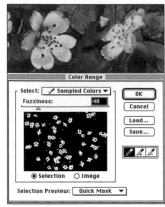

STEP 2: Part of the flower on the right is covered by purple. Shift-click on it to add it to the selection.

like the Tolerance on the Magic Wand; the higher the Fuzziness, the more similar colors are selected. Unlike using the Magic Wand, you can move the Fuzziness after you make a selection to change the range of selected colors. Set Select to Sampled Colors and set Selection Preview to None, for now. Use the Eyedropper to click on the yellow flowers and you will notice that wherever you see a flower, you should get some white showing up in the mask window. Hold the Shift key down and click on different areas of the flowers, adding more to the mask. If white areas or spots show up in the mask window where there are not any flowers, press Command-Z to undo that last Eyedropper click. When you think you have selected all the flowers—and no areas that are not flowers—set the Selection Preview to Quick Mask.

STEP 2: In Quick Mask, you will notice a see-through purple layer covering everything not selected by the mask. That's the Quick Mask preview. If you notice that parts of the flowers are covered by purple, Shift-click on them to add them to the selected areas. If you select a really bright part of the flower or a really dark part of the flower, you may also notice the purple overlay coming off other areas of the image that are not flowers. If so, you have selected too much, and should press Command-Z.

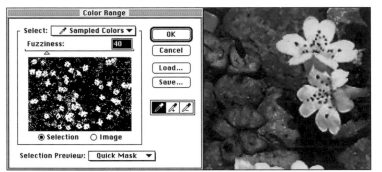

STEP 2: Here we have selected too much. You can see the mask coming off things that are not flowers, like the green leaves to the left of the flowers. Use Command-Z on the minus Eyedropper to fix this.

STEP 3: When the purple mask doesn't cover any flowers but still covers everything not a flower, you have done what you can do with Color Range to select the flowers. You might want to try the Grayscale, Black Matte, or White Matte Selection Preview modes to see if there are any errors that show up there. If so just use the plus or minus Eyedroppers to fix them. Click on the Save button and save this set of colors as ColorRangeToRC. Click on OK now and you end up with a selection of the flowers. If you wanted to work on these selected items with one of the other color correction tools, such as Hue/Saturation or a filter, you could have used this procedure to get a selection of the flowers. We had you do the first part of this exercise in Color Range so that you could see the differences between it and Replace Color. You could have done the whole session in either Color Range or Replace Color. Just so you know, you can click inside the preview window itself with the Eyedropper tools to add and subtract in Color Range. This may not be accurate enough for this difficult selection, but it can be faster in simpler selections.

USING REPLACE COLOR TO SELECT AND CHANGE THE COLOR

STEP 4: You are now going to use Replace Color for the rest of the exercise. Choose Select/None (Command-D) because you're actually going to improve on this selection using Replace Color. Double-click on the Eyedropper tool and set the Sample Size to Point Sample. Choose Image/Adjust/Replace Color, and click on the Load button. Select the ColorRangeToRC file you just saved from Color Range. This will give you the same selection you just had, but this time you only see the black-and-white mask in the dialog box. Choose the middle Eyedropper Plus tool; then click on a yellow flower at a place that is a middle yellow color. This color should be a shade of yellow that best represents the flowers as a whole. Notice that the sample box at the bottom-right of the Replace Color dialog now has the yellow color you clicked

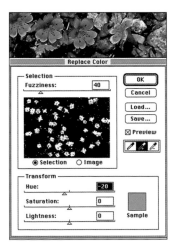

STEP 4: The Replace Color dialog box previewing yellow to orange.

on in it. Getting the color into the sample box is why you clicked here with Eyedropper Plus. This tool adds a color to the color selection range instead of starting a new selection range. Now go down to the Hue slider and move it to the left to –20. The yellow sample is now orange. When you click on the Preview button, all the selected yellow flowers will turn orange. This is the one type of selection preview that you can't do in Color Range, and it is very useful. If most of the flowers look orange but have a little bright yellow around their tips, you have 'em right about where you want 'em. If all the flowers are orange without a trace of yellow, you should look around the rest of the image and make sure you didn't change the color of anything else that had some yellow in it but wasn't totally yellow, such as the green leaves on the ground.

The flowers, after changing them to orange.

STEP 5: Now you need to change the yellow in the tips of the flowers to orange. Since the Eyedropper is set to Point Sample, this will allow you to select minute color differences that are only one pixel in size. Zoom in (Command-Spacebar-click) on any flowers that still have too much yellow around the tips of their petals. Carefully click on those yellow tip colors and add them to the color set. As you do this *with Preview on*, the tips of other flowers also turn orange. You can also increase the Fuzziness; you will notice that more little dots show up as selected in the mask. This may also improve the blending of any remaining yellow in the flower tips. Some of the brighter tips may actually just be highlights, so you don't need to change every last one. They just need to look natural as orange flowers. Some of the flower petals were originally burned and dried on the yellow flowers, so don't try to get them to turn orange also. If you do, you will make the Color Set too large and change colors where you shouldn't.

Click the Save Button in Replace Color and save the final Color Set as YellowFlowerSet. Later in Step 9, you will use YellowFlowerSet to learn about a more advanced way to do this that gives you more control over your flower color details. For now though, click on the OK button in Replace Color when you are happy with your flowers. It may be faster to change the dried tips using the Rubber Stamp tool, cloning color from another flower or another part of the same flower. You still will want to do this in the Clone (aligned) setting using either the Normal or Color blend mode.

STEP 7: After measuring the orange flowers, we notice in the Color palette that this orange color is made up of 97% yellow and 52% magenta. We then choose yellow as the color to change with the Colors pop-up.

STEP 6: Use File/Save As to save the file as FlowersOrange, and then open the original Flowers file and compare the two images. The flower colors and tones should look as natural in orange as they did in yellow. Bring back the Tool palette by pressing Tab, and then double-click on the Eyedropper tool to set the Sample Size back to 3x3 average.

USING SELECTIVE COLOR

STEP 7: When you are happy with the RGB version of this image and have saved it (in Step 6), you should convert it to CMYK using Mode/CMYK. You may notice a slight dulling of the flowers when the image converts to CMYK, although this particular orange color converts to CMYK quite well. When in CMYK, it is best to use the Selective Color command to make further subtle tweaks on colors. This command changes a particular color based on the respective amounts of cyan, magenta, yellow, and black that comprise it. Bring up the Color palette using the Window menu (Shift-F9 with ArtistKeys). Use its Options menu to change it to CMYK Display mode. Now choose Image/Adjust/Selective Color to bring up the Selective Color tool. With this tool, you have to select the main color that you would like to change using the Colors pop-up menu at the top. The choices are Red, Yellow,

STEP 8: The orange flowers after adding 20% magenta. Notice that the Magenta value actually changes from 52% to 61%.

STEP 8: The orange flowers after removing 25% magenta with Selective Color. If you click on a sample color after entering Selective Color, the Color palette shows you the actual new CMYK percentages as you make adjustments in Selective Color.

Green, Cyan, Blue, Magenta, White, Neutral, and Black. If you want to change the orange flowers, you'll probably notice that orange is not one of these colors. Use the Eyedropper and click on an orange flower in a shade of orange typical of the orange color of all the flowers. Notice in the Color palette that this bright orange consists mainly of yellow and magenta. Because yellow is the main component of this orange color (it's 97% yellow, in fact), you should now choose Yellow from the Colors pop-up. Next, you change the percentages of the other colors that make up your yellows.

STEP 8: Notice that the orange color already is very close to completely saturated in yellow but that the magenta component is only 52% saturated. On the left side of the Color palette, you see a swatch of the color where you last clicked. The Magenta bar in the Color palette shows that if you add magenta to this color, the flowers will look a deeper orange, and eventually reddish, in color. If you take away magenta, the flowers will become more yellowish. Move the Magenta slider in Selective Color (not in the Color palette) to the right, to +20%. In our example, the Method radio button at the bottom of the dialog box is set to Absolute, which should mean that you're adding 20% magenta ink to the 52% magenta already in the yellows, resulting in 72%. If you were to set Method to Relative, you would add 20% of the 52% of magenta already there, which should bring it up to about 62%. In reality, Absolute mode brings the 52% magenta up to 61%, and Relative mode brings it up to 57%. If you are trying to add a specific percentage, you should measure the results you actually get using the Color palette rather than assume the percentages in the Selective Color dialog box will be exact. Now subtract 25% magenta from these orange flowers to get the lighter, more yellowish orange you see in our third Selective Color illustration. These operations are examples of how you use the Selective Color tool to make subtle tweaks in specific color ranges. When you set Colors to Neutral, Selective Color is also very good at removing color casts in the neutral areas. Photoshop is good at identifying which colors should be composed of equal quantities of cyan, magenta, and yellow.

A MORE FLEXIBLE WAY TO SET THIS UP

For a more advanced way to set this up, try this. Choose Select/Color Range, use the Load button to load the YellowFlowerSet that you saved in Step 5, and click on OK. You now have a selection of the parts of this image that you want to change. Now choose New Adjustment layer from the Layers palette menu and set the Type pop-up to Hue/Saturation, make the name Orange Flowers, and then click on OK. This adds a Hue/Saturation Adjustment layer above the existing still yellow *Background* layer. Now you are in the Hue/Saturation dialog box, so set the Hue to –20. Your flowers will now change to orange and only the flowers will change because your selection will have been automatically put into the layer mask of this Hue/Saturation adjustment layer. When an Adjustment Layer is active, you are automatically working on this layer mask. With the Adjustment layer active, you can now use Gaussian Blur and the painting tools to fine-tune the Adjustment layer's built-in layer mask, and you can double-click on the name of the Adjustment layer (Orange Flowers) at any time to change the color of the flowers. I found that a Gaussian Blur of 1 on this Adjustment layer's mask improved the color change blend. Do Filter/Blur/Gaussian Blur (Shift-F4) and set the Amount to 1. This solution allows for an infinite number of changes without degrading the image. See the Yellow/Orange Layers file in the Extra Info folder for this chapter and try this out for yourself!

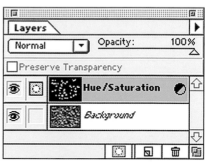

A MORE FLEXIBLE WAY: The Layers palette for this more flexible way to change the color of the flowers and leave your options much more open.

The flowers with the burned petals have to be fixed with the Rubber Stamp tool.

The orange flowers after the color correction choices have been made with Selective Color.

Making a fine black-and-white print the digital way: increasing contrast, brightening the white areas using electronic ferricyanide, and burning in the edges to emphasize the middle. Colorizing a B&W image.

(Original Concept by Bruce Ashley)

The original Fuller scan.

You start out with a scan of an original black-and-white negative of Buckminster Fuller, and in order to make it a fine print, you need to darken it and increase its contrast. You also want to brighten the white shirt and the candles a bit, and finally, add a little twinkle to Fuller's eyes, sharpen the center, and burn in the edges of the print.

BRIGHTENING THE IMAGE

STEP 1: Open the Fuller file from the Buckminster Fuller folder on the *Photoshop 5 Artistry* CD, crop out the bottom copyright notice and use File/Save As to save it as FullerFixed. Bring up the Info palette with Window/Show Info, (F9 with ArtistKeys). You'll also need to bring up the History palette, which we'll be using in conjunction with the History brush a bit later.

Use the Color Sampler tool (type I or Shift-I) to set three samples that we'll be checking as we make our Levels and Curves adjustments. Set sampler #1 on the collar to the left of the tie (look for values around 215), set sampler #2 on the cuff of Fuller's shirt, and set sampler #3 on the dark edge of the highboy in the background. Notice that each step you take is chronicled in the History palette.

STEP 1: Set your color samplers to measure the whites of the shirt and the blacks of the furniture in the background.

STEP 2: Choose Image/Adjust/Levels (Command-L). Move the Cursor around in the bright area of Mr. Fuller's collar, noting that the RGB values that show up in the Info palette are not very bright whites. If we move the Input Highlight slider to the left, this would brighten the collar, but it would also blow out any remaining detail in the wall by the bright lamp. Instead, we are going to make a bright version of this image and then use that to selectively lighten (Electronic Ferricyanide) the shirt, candles, and eyes. Adjust the Input Brightness/Contrast slider in Levels to the left to brighten the collar until the values in the collar that were 215 read about 235. The Info palette values to the left of the slash are the original values, and the values to the right of the slash show the adjustments you made using this iteration of Levels. Now look at the Color Sampler numbers below the main part of the Info palette. You'll see that Photoshop is giving you ink percentages before and after this levels adjustment. Using the color samplers in this fashion, you can take your level adjustment to the ink percentages that the press you're using can handle. In this case, we're assuming that the press can hold about a 7-8% dot. If you feel more comfortable using RGB values to make your Levels changes, you can click the pop-up beside any of the color sampler icons in the Info palette to view values in Grayscale, RGB, CMYK, HSB, or Lab color space, or view the total ink percentage. When you are happy with your adjustment, exit Levels by clicking on the OK button to make the change.

STEP 3: Make sure the History palette is open and click on the New Snapshot icon to make a Snapshot version of the file. Now click on the step prior to the Levels adjustment in the History palette. You'll see your file revert to the state it was in before the adjustment. If you use Undo Levels immediately after you've taken the snapshot, you'll achieve the same result. Just know that with the History palette, you could move back several steps even after you've taken the snapshot.

STEP 4: Choose New Adjustment Layer from the Layers Palette menu or Command-click on the New Layer icon to add a Levels adjustment layer. Make sure that the Type is set to Levels. Now move the Brightness/Contrast slider of Levels to the right to adjust this image for greater contrast. Make sure that large sections of the blackest blacks don't fall below 2 or 3 in the Info palette. It's okay to have a few small sections that go to 0, but you don't want them to be very large, because they will show up as pure black in the printout. Exit Levels using OK. The overall effect of giving the picture more contrast is pleasing, but the whites of Fuller's shirt are now muddy. Next, you adjust the whites using the

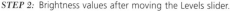

STEP 2: Brightness values after moving the Levels slider.

STEP 2: If you prefer to work in a different color space when using the color samplers, choose it by using the pop-up next to the appropriate sampler in the Info palette.

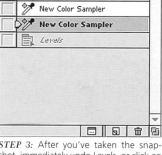

STEP 3: Click the Make Snapshot icon after you've done the Levels adjustment.

STEP 3: After you've taken the snapshot, immediately undo Levels, or click on the step previous to the Levels adjustment as we've done here.

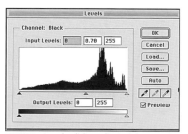

STEP 3: Levels slider adjusted for greater contrast.

following "Electronic Ferricyanide" technique. We did not adjust the highlight and shadow values within Levels in this image because they were correctly set by the original scan.

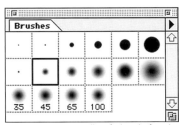

STEP 5: This is how the History and Layers palettes should look before you begin to lighten the collar and cuff with the History Brush.

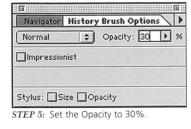

STEP 5: Set the Opacity to 30%.

STEP 5: Option-drag the Background layer to the New Layer icon at the bottom of the Layers palette. Call this new layer Working Image. You will make any actual changes on this layer, leaving the background image untouched. In the History palette, click the space to the left of Snapshot 1 to make that the state of the file from which you want to paint. Next, type Y to get the History brush and press Return or Enter to bring up the Options palette. In History Brush Options, set the Opacity to 30% (you can do this by typing 30 if the current Opacity is highlighted, 3 if it is not highlighted).

STEP 6: Choose Window/Show Brushes (F12 with ArtistKeys) and select a medium brush with a soft edge. You can use the left and right bracket keys to go to the next smaller or larger brush.

STEP 6: Use a small soft brush for the candles.

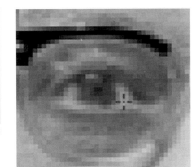

STEP 6: Zoom in to make the eyes brighter.

STEP 7: You are now painting from the Snapshot taken after your first Levels Adjustment. Lighten the collar and cuff by painting on them with the History Brush. Each time you paint over a section, it lightens it using 30% of the lighter version in Snapshot 1. If you want to remove the shadows on the white shirt next to his tie, several strokes there should turn them white. Look at the color sampler percentages in the Info palette to see how much you are lightening the whites. Remember, however, that there is a Levels Adjustment layer affecting the white that you are painting. Unless you add a layer mask to the Adjustment layer, you will not bring the white all the way up to the 7-8% setting that you got when you made your lighter snapshot. If, at any time, you want to hide the color samplers, you can do that from the Info palette menu.

Next, choose a very small brush, and click on the twinkles in Fuller's eyes to lighten them. Experiment with different size brushes; zoom in and out as you work. Command-Spacebar-click on the candles to zoom in to them, and continue to use the History Brush to paint from Snapshot 1 to lighten them. Use the left and right bracket keys to pick a brush the width of a candle. Click on one end of a candle and then Shift-click on the other end to draw a straight line the length of the candle. You may need to lower the opacity as you work on the candles to get more subtle shades of white. You may want to save your file now using File/Save (Command-S).

SHARPENING THE CENTER AND BURNING THE EDGES

STEP 8: Option-click on the Elliptical Marquee tool in the Tool palette or type Shift-M until you have selected the oval-shaped icon. Select from the center by positioning the cursor on the tip of Fuller's nose, holding down the Option key before you click, and then clicking and dragging to isolate the oval area you want to sharpen and inversely burn in. If you've made the size and shape oval that you like, but it's not in exactly the position you want, click inside the selection border and drag to move the selection. You can also hold down the Spacebar while in the middle of selecting to move the selection. Choose Select/Feather (Command-Option-D) to set the feather to about 35 pixels, which creates a soft slow transition between the sharpened and nonsharpened areas and also between the burned and nonburned areas.

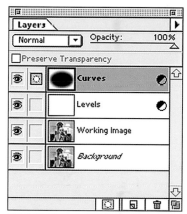

STEP 8: Make the oval selection on Fuller look something like this.

STEP 9: Go to Filter/Sharpen/Sharpen to emphasize the center of the portrait by making it a little sharper. Then use Select/Inverse to invert the selection, and select the outside of the image for burning. Click on the Levels layer so that the next layer you add will be above Levels.

STEP 10: Command-click on the New Layer icon, this time setting the Type to Curves to add a Curves adjustment layer. Make sure that the Preview check box is on so that you can see how the changed area on the outside will blend with the unchanged area in the middle. Now adjust the Brightness/Contrast (move the center of the curve down) to darken the outside of the image. Move the curve up and down until you like the amount of darkness. Click on OK when you are happy. Notice that the feathered selection of the outside part of the image has been automatically saved as a layer mask in the Curves adjustment layer. The black part of this layer mask stops the Curves adjustment from happening in that center area.

The advantage to this approach is that you now have a layered document where major steps in the process of refining this image can be looked at separately, and even changed or undone. If you turn off the Eye icon for the Curves layer, you remove the burn-in. If you want to change the amount of burn, just double-click on the word Curves and you can still change the Curve. You can turn the Levels adjustment layer on and off by using its Eye icon, and later you can change it too. If you click on the Working Image layer's Eye icon, you can see the original unsharpened, unwhitened image underneath in the *Background* layer. Try some of these things to quickly review your progress and changes on this image.

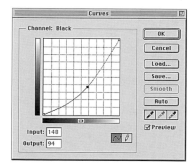

STEP 10: The Layers palette at the start of Step 10.

STEP 10: Move the curve downward to darken the edges. Make sure the Curves dialog box is out of the way so you can see most of Fuller.

REMOVING THE BANDAGE

STEP 11: Option-drag the Working Image layer to the New Layer icon to make a backup copy and name it Working Image BU. Click and drag this backup copy to below the Working Image layer, and then click on the Working Image layer to activate it. Next, double-click on the Rubber Stamp tool and set its Option to Aligned. Use the Rubber Stamp tool with different size brushes and with the Blend mode Normal and Opacity set to 100% to remove the bandage on Fuller's glasses. To make the retouching realistic, the patterns of light and dark on the forehead must match the rest of the picture. You need to make sure the wrinkles on his forehead, for example, continue into the areas where the bandage was. Copy skin at 100% opacity from different areas next to the bandage on top of the bandage. You'll have to copy lots of small sections to make the effect work. Don't copy the same piece of skin over

197

STEP 13: Final adjustments were made to burn in edges. We also used the Rubber Stamp tool to remove the bandage and fix his ear.

and over again or you'll get a sort of patterned look. For the wrinkles, place the cursor so you Option-click on the center of a wrinkle; then click to clone where you want the center of the wrinkle to continue on top of the bandage.

STEP 12: Adjust skin shading, by changing the Opacity to 50% and cloning lighter or darker skin areas over what you have already done to make sure that the subtle shading on the head looks right. In this step, you can choose areas farther away from the bandage to get the shading you need. After cloning out the bandage, and adjusting the lightness, you may need to use the Blur tool at a low opacity, perhaps 10%, to blend your changes together.

STEP 13: As a final step after blurring a bit, I used the Lasso tool to select the area that was cloned and blurred, feathered the selection by 3, and then used Filter/Noise/Add Noise to add about 3–5 of Gaussian Noise on top of the selected area. This will make the noise there match the rest of the image. You can always start over again on the bandage removal by using another copy of Working Image BU. When you are happy with the removal of the bandage, you can throw away Working Image BU.

COLORIZING MR. FULLER

STEP 14: Make sure your layers are in the final state you want for this image; then choose Image/Duplicate (F5) to make a duplicate copy of the image in Photoshop. Check the Merged Layers Only check box so the copy just has a single layer showing you the layers that currently have their Eye icons on. Choose Image/Mode/RGB to convert this image to RGB, which you need to do if you want to colorize it. Double-click on the Paintbrush tool and set its Blend mode to Color. This will change the hue and saturation when you paint but not the luminosity. The *luminosity* is the gray values that give the image detail and brightness.

STEP 15: Use the Color Picker or the Color palette to choose a nice bright red for his tie, and then paint that color over the tie. At 100% opacity you'll notice a few problems. One, it's very difficult to get an accurate edge no matter what size brush you use, and two, the color is pretty garish. Undo what you've painted and try again at about 30% to 40% opacity. While painting, you can change the opacity simply by typing a number, such as 35, to get 35% opacity. This helps make the edges a little less abrupt and the color is more subdued. If, however, you paint over the same section again and again, you'll be adding color until you are back at 100% opacity. You can use this to your advantage as you add subtle shading, but it can also be frustrating.

STEP 16: Now use the Lasso tool to select Fuller's vest. Make sure that the Lasso feather is set to zero. Pick a color, and then choose Edit/Fill (Shift-Delete) to fill this area with the color you choose, making sure the mode is set to Color and the opacity is in the 30% to 50% range. You can use this technique to colorize most of the objects in the scene. Remember to try different feather values on the selection and different opacities of a color if needed. This is certainly quick and pretty effective, but there's little flexibility—when it's done, it's done.

STEP 17: If you want to easily change the color of an object that has been selected with a rough Lasso selection, Command-click on the New Layer icon to add a Hue/Saturation adjustment layer. Click on the Colorize option in Hue/Saturation; then move the sliders to get the color you want with your selected item. The Lasso selection was automatically converted to a layer mask for this layer, so you can now fine-tune the edges of the selection by painting with black where you want to remove the color and painting with white where you want to add the color. You can now go back into the Hue/Saturation adjustment layer to later change the color.

STEP 18: Another cool trick, for example, to add some wallpaper to the background, is to run a filter—try Pixelate—on the whole image. Then click Take Snapshot followed by Edit/Undo of the filter, at which point the filter effect should be in the Snapshot, enabling you to paint it in where you want it using the History Brush set to that Snapshot. Go ahead and paint in the wallpaper. To get a more even opacity on the wallpaper, you can also select an area and then choose Fill in From Snapshot mode to fill that area with your pattern from a filter effect stored in the Snapshot. You could also run a different filter on another layer that is a copy of the image and use a layer mask to have that filter effect appear wherever the layer mask is white. There are always at least three different ways to do anything in Photoshop. Have fun as you create your color version of Mr. Fuller!

STEP 18: Here is my colorized version of Mr. Fuller. Have fun creating yours, and try colorizing in as many ways as you can. That's how you find what works best for you!

Measure and adjust the color of objects so differently colored items can be changed to match, and do subtle color tweaks after CMYK conversion to deal with faded CMYK hues.

The long shot is a red car, and you need to end up with two matching red CMYK images.

The close-up shot is a green car; you need to change its color to match the red car to the left.

Imagine that you want to create an advertisement using two photos of the Acura Integra. One of the photos is of a red Integra and the other of a green one. You need to convert the green car photo so that its color matches that of the red one. You also need to convert both cars to CMYK and do some final color matching there. The files in this example were saved using the Color-MatchRGB settings and the example was done with ColorMatchRGB as the RGB workspace. Your numbers should come out very similar if you use this RGB workspace for this example but you might get somewhat different numerical values if you choose to convert these original images to another RGB workspace.

STEP 1: Here is the color match spot in the red car.

STEP 1: Here is the color match spot in the green car.

CHOOSING THE COLOR MATCH SPOTS

STEP 1: Open the RedAcuraCM and GreenDetail files from the Color Matching Cars folder. Find a spot on the red car where the color appears to be an average intermediate color that could represent the color you want for the whole car. Both of these photos have highlight and shadow areas that you are going to want to match also. I've found that if you can locate a good midtone area in both images and get those midtone areas to match, the rest of the image will also match pretty well. I used the area on the front of the car to the right of the chrome Acura emblem just above the word "Acura," embossed in the red bumper. Because this spot exists—and the lighting on it is similar—in both photos, you can use this location on both cars to get the colors to match. We call this location the *color match spot*. Bring up the Info palette (F9) and set the top-left viewing area to HSB mode. Type an I to choose the Eyedropper tool; then Shift-I to switch to the Color Sampler Eyedropper. This tool is new for Photoshop 5 and allows you to place a measurement location within an image and then see how the values at that location change when you make color adjustments. You can place up to four Color Sampler locations in each image that you have open. If you now press Return, this will bring up the Color Sampler Options palette and you should make sure the Sample Size is set to 3 by 3 average. Put the Eyedropper over the color match spot and click to take a measurement. Hold the mouse button down and measure around a bit to make sure the spot you are using as this first measurement is an average measurement for this area. I used just above the E in Ingetra. When you release the mouse, the Color Sampler added to the bottom of the Info palette will remember values for that location. Change the current display of those values to HSB and write down the HSB values within the Red image. I got 358° for the hue, 89 for the saturation, and 81 for the lightness but slightly different values will work also. We will now match these in the green image.

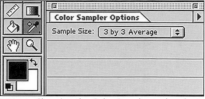

STEP 1: Choosing the Color Sampler tool and setting the Sample Size to 3 by 3 Average.

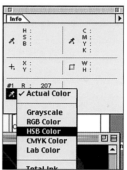

STEP 1: Setting your Color Sampler readings to HSB.

STEP 2: Switch to the green car and find the same location right above the embossed E. Click here to create a Color Sampler reading in this image too. Change the Color Sampler display of this spot in the Info palette to HSB. If you ever have trouble seeing the Color Sampler part of the Info Palette, which is at the bottom, you can always choose Hide Color Samplers followed by Show Color Samplers from the Info Palette's Options and this will bring all your Color Sampler values back into view. Choose Image/Adjust/Hue/Saturation (Command-U) to bring up the Hue/Saturation color adjustment tool. Move the Hue slider so that the Hue value in your color match spot for the green image matches the one you wrote down for the red image. You need to have the windows open on the screen so you can see both cars at the same time, and you might want to zoom in for now so that you see this part of both cars at the same time. Now move the Saturation and Lightness sliders back and forth until you get saturation and lightness values in the Color Sample that match the numbers you

STEP 2: Adjusting hue, saturation, and lightness to get the green Color Match spot to match the values in the red car.

wrote down for the color match spot on the red car. The Color Sampler continues to show you how the Color Match Spot where you set it in the green car has changed based on the Hue/Saturation slider movements. Try to get all three numbers to match exactly but don't worry if one of them is off by one point in either direction. The Saturation and Lightness settings influence each other as you move them. As you change one, the other also changes, so you must tweak both of them for a while until you get as close as possible to what you had in the red car. When you are happy with the adjustments, click on the OK button in Hue/Saturation. You could have also made a Hue/Saturation Adjustment layer if you wanted to easily go back and modify these settings again later.

STEP 3: Now click and drag the little Eyedropper pop-up menus in the Info Palette to convert the Color Sampler displays for both images to RGB mode. Write down the Red, Green, and Blue values from the Color Match spot in the original red car. My values were 207 for Red, 23 for Green, and 29 for Blue. Switch to the green car, now converted to red, and choose Image/Adjust/Levels (Command-L). Go into the

Choosing the Color Match Spots

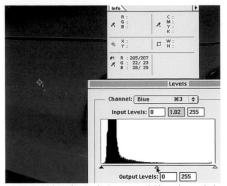

STEP 3: Using the Red, Green, and Blue channels in Levels to match the green car's RGB values to the red car's values.

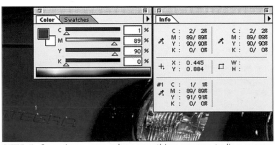

STEP 5: When you put the Eyedropper tool exactly over the Color Match spot, the circle and crosshair will disappear and you will just see the number 1 that denotes Color Sampler number 1's position. At this point, you can click and get all the values to match exactly between the different palettes.

STEP 5: Sometimes, even when everything appears to line up correctly, the values will not match exactly between the different palettes or even between two readouts from the same palette. Just get things as close as possible.

Red channel (Command-1) and move the Input Brightness/Contrast slider, the middle slider, until the Red value in the Color Sampler matches the Red value you wrote down for the original red car. Switch to the Green channel and do the same thing until the Green value matches on both. Finally, do the same thing for the Blue channel. Now the two cars should match fairly well.

CONVERTING TO CMYK MODE

STEP 4: Now bring up the Color palette (Shift-F9), which is useful here because it shows you, with its colored sliders, how to adjust colors to get more of what you want. In older versions of Photoshop, I always used the Color palette for all my matching color situations. Now the Color Sampler in Photoshop 5 gives you the advantage of remembering the location of the sample point and also having up to four sample points for each image. It is good to know the trade offs between using the Color Sampler and the Color palette and here we'll learn them. Using its Palette Options menu, convert the Color palette to CMYK mode. Also convert all your Color Sampler readouts to CMYK. Type Shift-I to switch the Tool palette to the regular Eyedropper tool. This is the tool you will use for getting measurements into the Color palette.

STEP 5: Make sure your File/Color Settings/CMYK Setup settings are set correctly and then use Image/Mode/CMYK Color to convert both cars to CMYK mode. Based on your CMYK preference settings, the colors onscreen should now be as close as possible to your printed colors. You might notice the intense red of these cars fade somewhat as you convert to CMYK. Now we'll use the Selective Color tool to do final subtle tweaks of your red color in CMYK mode. Selective Color is a great tool for doing subtle adjustments to particular color areas in CMYK. Switch to the original red car, the long shot, and make sure you can see both the Info palette and the Color palette. Now go into Image/Adjust/Selective Color (Shift-F6). Make sure that Colors is set to Reds, because you're going to be adjusting the red colors in the car. Set the Method to Absolute, so that you can make the color adjustments more quickly. Move the cursor until it is exactly on top of the Color Match spot; at that point the circle and crosshair will disappear. At this exact point, click to take another measurement at the color match spot on the car and notice that when you click, the values come up in the Color palette. Values only change in the Color palette when you click or take a reading with the mouse button down. The values in the top-left area of the Info palette change whenever you move the mouse, and the values in your Color Match spot in the Info palette will only change when you change the color of that Color Match spot. These values should now match the values in the Color Match spot within the Info palette although, as we show you the illustration, the match might not be completely exact.

STEP 6: Notice that the color consists mostly of magenta and yellow. The colors of the sliders on the Color palette show you how the color at the color match spot will change if you add or subtract more cyan,

Chapter 27: Color Matching Images

magenta, yellow, or black ink. If the cyan value is greater than 0, subtract cyan using the Selective Color slider, until the cyan value reads 0 in the Color palette. You should also now see the 0 value in your Info palette Color Sampler reading. This maneuver adds red to the car color. Add magenta with Selective Color until the magenta value in the Color palette is about 99 to make the car a deeper, richer color. Adjust the yellow until the yellow value in the Color palette reads about 94. To get a slightly darker, richer color, add some black until the black value in the Color palette reads about 4. The colors in the Color Palette's sliders will give you hints on what to do to improve the CMYK color of the spot you are reading in your image. You don't have to use the exact same numbers that we have; just adjust the cyan, magenta, yellow, and black percentages on the color match spot until you like the car's shade of red. Write down these final adjusted CMYK values from the Color palette.

STEP 7: Switch to the image that was originally green and then again enter the Selective Color tool. Press down on the mouse button while taking a measurement of the color match spot in this image. The values in the Color palette should now match those in the Color Match spot for this image in the Info palette. Now adjust the cyan, magenta, yellow, and black inks, using the sliders in Selective Color, until the percentages match the final adjusted percentages you just wrote down from the other image. We used Cyan = 0, Magenta = 99, Yellow = 94, and Black = 4, but your values can be different. You just want the two red colors to match and both look the way you like them. This method is a good way to match the colors of objects that start out differently but have to end up the same.

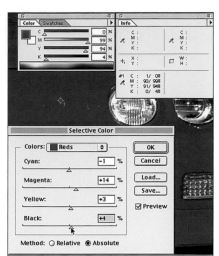

STEP 6: Here are the final Selective Color adjustments we made to get the 0, 99, 94, 4 values for the car that was originally red.

The final green car after converting to red and CMYK adjustments.

The final long shot of the original red car after conversion and adjustment in CMYK.

28 HANDS-ON SESSION: Desert Al

*Color correcting this difficult exposure and scan and
using color channel swapping, Adjustment layers,
and intralayer blending to produce a print with natural,
consistent, and pleasing tones overall.*

The original uncorrected image.

One of my favorite pictures has always been this photo of my best buddy Al, taken on a desert trip we made together back around 1980. I always wanted to make a print of it, so when I got my Epson Stylist Photo printer, I had it and many other favorite pictures put onto PhotoCD. When I brought in the photo, it was obviously oversaturated in the shadow area of the face. Because this is not a major area of the image, the first step to correct it is to do overall color correction to get the rest of the image to look right. This file was saved using ColorMatch RGB tags so if you want your values and histograms to look exactly the same, set your RGB colorspace to ColorMatch RGB. If you use a different color space, that will be okay but the image may look somewhat different on the screen, and you will have to make slightly different corrections.

OVERALL COLOR CORRECTION

STEP 1: Open the OrigAl file from the Color Correcting Al folder on the CD. Crop any areas from around the edge of the image that are not going to be in the print. In this case, my copyright notice is the only thing you need to crop. Double-click on the Background Layer and Name it Original Al. Use F9 to bring up the Info palette and Shift-F9 to bring up the Color palette. Now go into Levels and use the steps outlined in Chapter 19: The Grand Canyon and Chapter 20: Kansas to set the Highlight, Shadow, overall Brightness/Contrast, and finally the color cast. Here are the Levels settings I ended up with for Al. To set the highlight, I used the Highlight Eyedropper in Levels and set it to the white area on the tip of Al's right shoulder (on the left side of the image). For the shadow, I used the Shadow Eyedropper and set it to the shadow on the black tuft of hair below Al's ear and behind his neck. I then adjusted the overall brightness and contrast as well as the color balance. When you are done with your basic color corrections, to give yourself the option of changing them later without image degradation, use the Save button in the Levels dialog box to save your Levels changes as AlBasicLevels; then Cancel from Levels. Command-click on the New Layer icon in the Layers palette to create a Levels Adjustment layer. Now, use the Load button to load AlBasicLevels and choose OK. This enables you to later change the levels without remodifying the file's pixel values. Doing the initial settings using Levels in the

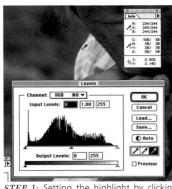

STEP 1: Setting the highlight by clicking with the Highlight Eyedropper on the whitest area of Al's shirt.

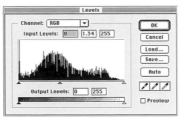

STEP 1: The overall corrected RGB histogram.

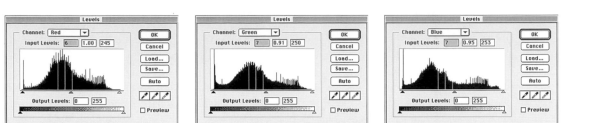

STEP 1: The overall red adjustments. STEP 1: The overall green adjustments. STEP 1: The overall blue adjustments.

actual layer enables you to use Video LUT Animation to find the white and black points. Use File/Save As to save this as AlLevels. If your computer doesn't have Video LUT Animation, just start out directly in the Levels Adjustment layer.

STEP 2: Command-click on the New Layer icon to add a Hue/Saturation Adjustment layer above the Levels Adjustment layer. Here are the settings I made in Hue/Saturation. The goal was to saturate all the colors, as I normally would do, but then to not add more saturation to the reds in the face. To get the set of reds that I want to desaturate, I first used the new Photoshop 5 Hue/Saturation Eyedropper and dragged it over the really saturated areas of his face because these are the ones that need desaturation. I then used the Eyedropper minus to subtract out the normal red flesh tones by dragging over them and then the Eyedropper plus to add any too saturated colors back in. As you are doing this, notice that the range of reds that are selected changes based on the width of the gray slider bars between the two rainbow color bars. Try my settings and feel free to modify them and make your own to improve the image.

FIXING THE OVERSATURATED AREAS WITH CHANNEL MIXER

STEP 3: Click back on the Original Al layer so you can then use the Channels palette to look at the Red, then the Green, and then the Blue channels of the image to see if one of them has a noticeable pattern within the oversaturated area. The Levels and Hue/Saturation layers have no Red, Green, and Blue channels because they are Adjustment layers. You can see that the Green channel is very dark, magenta, in all the saturated areas. Click back on the Hue/Saturation layer to activate it; then option-click on the New Layer icon to add a new layer above it (call it Color Merged). Hold down Option and leave it down while choosing Merge Visible from the Layers palette

STEP 3: Al's RGB before using the Red channel to fix the saturated areas.

STEP 3: The Red channel we will use to fix the Green and Blue channels.

STEP 3: The unfixed Green channel is dark in all the saturated areas.

STEP 3: The Color Merged Fixed layer after fixing the Green and Blue channels.

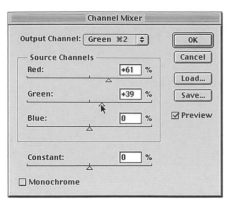

STEP 3: Here we see the Channel Mixer settings for the Green channel.

menu and while the calculations are happening. This maneuver merges the effects of the Levels and Hue-Saturation Adjustment layers into the new Color Merged layer. You can now look at its channels and see which colors are causing the saturation problem. Option-drag the Color Merged layer to the New Layer icon and call this copy Color Merged Fixed. Drag this layer to just below the Color Merged layer and Option-click on the Color Merged Fixed Eye icon to just work on and see that layer. Command-click on the New Layer icon to create a new Adjustment layer; then set the type to Channel Mixer and choose Group with Previous Layer. Channel Mixer is a new feature in Photoshop 5 that makes this kind of operation much easier and more flexible. We are going to use the Red channel to fix the oversaturation problems in the Green and Blue channels. Make sure the Preview button is on in the Channel Mixer dialog; then set the Output Channel to Red and leave the Source Channels set to 100% Red. Now set the Output Channel to Green; then change the Source Channels to about 61% Red and 39% Green. This will change the Green channel to actually be made up of 61% of the Red channel and you will notice more detail returning to the saturated areas of Al's face. Now set the Output Channel to Blue; then set the Source Channels to about 47% Red and 53% Blue. You can change these percentages as many times as you like, and as you do, you will notice small changes in color balance and the amount of detail in the saturated areas of Al's face. To fix the Green and Blue channels, you want to use the least amount of the Red channel that both repairs the dark areas and keeps a compatible color balance that will be somewhat fainter. Compare my Color Merged layer (with the layer mask off) to my Color Merged Fixed layer to see the relative color balance and lightness I used. My final version of this example is in the Extra Info Files folder of Color Correcting Al on the CD.

BLENDING THE TWO LAYERS

STEP 4: Turn on the Eye icon for the Color Merged layer and click on it to make it the active layer. Now click on the left-most Layer Mask icon to add a layer mask to the Color Merged layer. Use the Air Brush at 5% Pressure with soft brushes to paint black in the Color Merged layer mask. Doing so lets you slowly remove dark and oversaturated parts of the Color Merged layer to reveal the lighter fixed version of the Color Merged Fixed layer underneath. You want to have the Eye icons on for both Layers while doing this. Don't worry if the color balance of Color Merged Fixed isn't exactly right; just work on getting the saturation down in the damaged areas. If you are having trouble making this work, see the Extra Info Files folder to check out my layer mask for the Color Merged layer. When you are happy with the basic detail that you have added with the layer mask, click on the Channel Mixer layer to activate it. Then Command-click on the New Layer icon to add a grouped Levels adjustment layer above it. Now you can change the color balance and contrast of the Color Merged Fixed layer while watching how these changes affect the Color Merged layer's appearance. You should find that you can get Al's face to look much better. Now activate Color Merged and click back on its layer mask. Use black or white with the Airbrush to make further changes to the mask and fine-tune the face composite. Add a new layer above the Color Merged layer. Make sure that the Eye icons are on for Color Merged Fixed, the Channel Mixer and Levels Adjustment layers above it, Color Merged, and the new layer. Then choose Merge Visible with the Option key down to merge the four lower layers into this new layer. Name it Final Retouch and make it the active layer.

STEP 4: Al before retouch and sharpening.

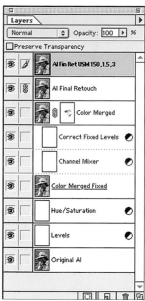

Step 8: The final Layers palette for this example. Check out my version in the Extra Info Files folder on the *Photoshop 5 Artistry* CD.

CLEANING UP SOME BLEMISHES

STEP 5: Now use the Lasso tool to select the white part of Al's left eye. Use Select/Feather to put a one-pixel feather on this selection. Go into Hue/Saturation (Command-U) and try to brighten the white of Al's eye and to make it more white. I added +10 to the lightness in Master mode, and then I moved the Hue to +8 in Reds mode, all of which made the eye stand out a little better and removed some of its red tint.

STEP 6: Now use the Rubber Stamp tool with different size soft brushes and opacities to remove any blemishes and to tone out areas that are too magenta. If you set the opacity to 30–50% and then clone from an area next to the one you want to fix, it's easy to even out color areas that aren't quite right without losing the original detail in that area. You can also clone with the Blend mode set to Color to change the color of something without losing its original detail. Remember that you can change the opacity by typing a number on the numeric keypad between 0 and 9. Zero is for 100%, 9 for 90%, 8 for 80%, . . . 1 for 10%, or even 25 for 25%. You can also use the bracket keys, [and], to move to the next smaller or the next larger brush. Make sure that you use File/Preferences/Display & Cursors to set the preferences for Painting Cursors to Brush Size so that if the cursor is over your image, you can see the brush size relative to your image and zoom factor as you change the brush size with the bracket keys. Be careful not to blur the facial detail with too much cloning.

STEP 7: Option-drag the Final Retouch layer to the New Layer icon and name the copy USM. Go into Filter/Sharpen/Unsharp Mask (F4) and use the techniques demonstrated in Chapter 24: Kansas Tweaks to find the right sharpening settings for Al. I used 150%, 1.5, and 3. You may want to rename this USM layer with the sharpen settings you used. This will help if you need to change them later. After doing the sharpen, you may want to do another quick sweep at 100% to check for spots that the sharpen adds. I do my sharpen in a layer that is a copy of Final Retouch to give me the option of later trying a different sharpen amount!

STEP 8: Save the file as your final RGB version of Al, and call it AlFinalRGB or something like that. Use Flatten and Image/Mode/CMYK to convert Al to CMYK mode if necessary. You want to save the flattened version under a different name to preserve the layered RGB version for later use and changes.

STEP 8: The final version of Al, after retouching and sharpening.

207

29 HANDS-ON SESSION: Bryce Stone Woman

Color correcting an image in Lab color using most of the techniques in this book.

The final Bryce Stone Woman image after correcting it in Lab color. You can see the "before" version of this image on the last page of this chapter.

This is one of my favorite photos of Bryce Canyon. The light rock formation in the front center, if you use your imagination a bit, could be a naked woman with long bushy hair sitting on the rock and admiring the view. Because the rocks are predominately red, it is hard to make the rocks look their best without making the green trees and shrubs look too dark and magenta. The solution is to use a layer mask to combine several versions of the image, one that optimizes the red parts and another that optimizes the green parts. For those of you that have earlier versions of *Photoshop Artistry*, you have seen this image before but we completely redid it for this version of the book starting with a different scan, which was a Lab file, and then learning how to color correct an image that was in Lab Color mode. You should read chapter 14: Color Spaces, Device Characterization, and Color Management to learn more about Lab color before doing this example. Also, this will not be a normal step-by-step example; because this is my first example in Lab color, I decided to share the experience of creating the image with you instead of worrying about writing down every step. Therefore, to better understand this example, you should first do the examples in Chapters 25: Yellow Flowers, 28: Desert Al, 31: Bob and the Kestrel and 32: Versailles. They use similar techniques but include all the details. Also, I'm new to Lab color so I'm not even sure there is a good reason for everything I did here, so just sit back and enjoy the show!

When I first got the new scan for this image from Bill Atkinson and his Tango drum scanner last year, I converted it to RGB from the Lab format he had given it to me in and made a very nice LightJet 5000 print of it. The color correction techniques that I had used to make that print were similar to those for this image in *Photoshop 4 Artistry* although a little more elaborate. When I started working on this example, I took my master RGB image from that print and thought I would start over with the original Lab scan to see if I could duplicate what I had done in RGB, using Lab this time. Following is the process I went through to arrive at the Layers palette, shown here, for the final Lab image printed on the previous page. You should open my final Lab image, called BryceLab.psd, from the folder for this chapter on the CD. You can then look at the layers setup on your screen and turn each layer on one at a time as we go through the purpose of each layer.

TRYING TO DUPLICATE WHAT I DO IN RGB

STEP 1: When I reopened the Lab scan, I realized that it was still uncropped and I had cropped the RGB version I was trying to duplicate. I had not resampled the RGB image though, just done a crop, but I would need to line the two up. To do this, I went into Image Size on the RGB version and noted the actual number of pixels in each dimension. This would be the crop size I would use on the Lab version too, so I set the Fixed Size style on the Marquee to that size.

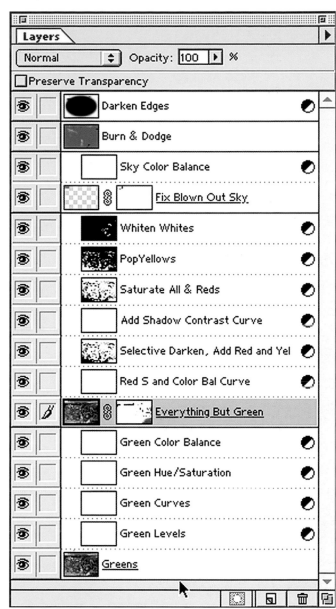

Here is the final Layers palette for this example. We are going to go through the steps I went through in creating this image and all its layers.

Next, I copied a single layer version of my RGB image and pasted it on top of my Lab version, and of course, it was a bit smaller. I inverted this temporary RGB layer and set its Opacity to 50% because a positive and negative image on top of each other at 50% Opacity gives you 50% gray if they are perfectly lined up. I then used the arrow keys while in the Move tool to nudge the inverted layer until it lined up with the Lab image I had to crop underneath. At that point, I turned the Eye icon off for the the layer underneath and then clicked with the Marquee, which was already set for the correct size, and lined the marquee up with the edges of the already cropped RGB image on top. Now my Marquee selection lines were lined up exactly, so I chose Image/Crop to do the crop and then threw away the temporary layer on top. Actually, before I did this line up and crop I had already resampled each of these

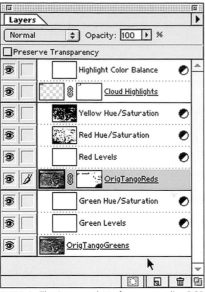

STEP 2: The Layers palette from my earlier RGB rendition of Bryce. I reused the Layer mask separating the Red and Green elements as well as the Yellow Hue/Saturation mask and the Red Hue/Saturation mask, although the way I used them was sometimes different in Lab color.

STEP 2: The Layer mask that separates the Green and non-Green layers in my Lab image. The white areas of the mask are where you will see the non-green areas from the upper of the two layers, and the black and gray parts of the mask are where you will see all or some of the image from the Green layer.

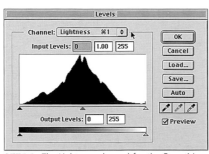

STEP 2: The Lightness channel for the Everything-ButGreen layer. This histogram looks very similar to a corrected RGB histogram. The Lightness channel contains the brightness and contrast information for a Lab image.

images by 50% to make them more manageable than the original 100Mb scans. Because I resampled both by the same percent, I was still able to line them up.

STEP 2: You might be wondering why I wanted to crop this Lab image so it lined up exactly with the RGB image I had made before. The reason is that there were some complex masks I had created for the RGB version of this image, and I was hoping to reuse them in doing the Lab version. Here is the Layers palette for my previous RGB version of this image, and I did reuse the masks as you will see.

My traditional basic setup for an RGB image is to first use Levels to correct the histogram; then use Hue/Saturation to saturate the colors and finally use Curves to tweak problem areas. What I did in the RGB version, as you can see to the right here, is create one real Layer, OrigTangoGreens, for the Green elements in the photograph and a second real layer, OrigTangoReds, on top of that, for the Red elements. The Layer mask to the right of the OrigTangoReds layer controls which parts of the image come from each of these two main layers. You'll notice several Grouped Adjustment layers above the OrigTangoGreens layer that set its Levels and Hue/Saturation settings. Then above the OrigTangoReds layer is the grouped Adjustment layer for the Reds histogram, and then two different Hue/Saturation Adjustment layers above that. For this image I used one Hue/Saturation layer to adjust the reddish tones and a separate one for the yellows, each with its own layer mask. Trying to do it all with one Adjustment layer caused too much crossover between the Red and Yellow areas especially where they mixed a lot. The layer mask that separates which part of the image comes from OrigTangoReds and which part from OrigTangoGreens was created using Image/Adjust/Threshold in a similar way that we created the Bike Mask in Chapter 31: Bob and the Kestrel. To create the Red and Yellow Hue/Saturation masks, which are close to inverses of each other, I went into Select Color Range to create a selection of either the Red or Yellow areas and then used Select/Save Selection to save that selection in the Channels palette where I edited it and then later used Load Selection to load it before creating my Red Hue/Saturation layer. For more details on this mask creation technique, see Chapter 25: Yellow Flowers in this book or the previous version of the Bryce example in *Photoshop 4 Artistry*.

When I started working on the Lab version, I went ahead and created one Layer for the Greens and a second layer for the Reds. You can see in the Lab Layers palette that these two layers, called Greens and Everything But Green (RED), and the Layer mask separating them, remained. Now I tried to use Levels to do the initial overall color correction on the Red and Green layers. You can see these two layers, called Selective Darken, Add Red and Yellow, and the other, Green Levels. I discovered that in Lab mode, the Lightness channel is great to work with for setting the highlight and shadow values because there are not color balance problems mixed in with setting the brightness and contrast values in the Lightness channel. The difficulty for me came when I went to the a and b channels within Levels and tried to adjust the color balance. Try this out for yourself using the BryceLab you have opened. Turn off all the Eye icons above the Everything But Green layer and activate that layer, then create a new Levels Adjustment layer above it. You'll notice when you go into Levels that you are in the Lightness channel. This is a pretty normal histogram and you do the obvious thing of moving the endpoints in to where the data starts. Then use the middle slider to adjust the brightness and contrast. This is great to be able to adjust this separately from the color balance. Also, if you just sharpen the Lightness channel of a Lab image, you avoid the color shifts you always get when sharpening all the channels of an RGB image. There is no need to

Chapter 29: Bryce Stone Woman

sharpen the a and b channels within a Lab image because they only contain color information and no brightness and contrast information as all the channels have in an RGB or CMYK image.

STEP 3: Now choose the a channel. Moving the middle slider to the left makes the image more red, and moving it to the right makes the image more green. Try it and notice that moving this more than a small amount dramatically affects the color of the image. That is because all the color information in this Lab image is squashed into that small area of the histogram spanning only about 51 in the a channel and 91 in the b channel of this image. The Lab color space is so large, all the colors that the human eye can see, that the rest of the histogram is reserved for other colors that are not in this image. Moving the Input Highlight slider of the a channel to the left makes the highlights more red and the Input Shadow slider to the right makes the shadows more green. Moving the Output Highlight slider of the a channel to the left makes the highlights more green, and moving the Output Shadow slider right makes the shadows more red.

Now try out the b channel where moving the middle slider to the left makes the image more yellow and moving it to the right makes it more blue. Try out the Input and Output shadow and highlight sliders to see what they do too. Now hold down the Option key and choose Reset to put everything back where it started. Start out with the Lightness channel, and adjust the brightness and contrast of the red and yellow parts of the image, actually everything but the greens. Then switch to the a and b channels and try to get the red and yellow colors the way you want them. You realize that the controls are quite different than when working in RGB or CMYK.

STEP 4: I duplicated the layer structure I had used in my RGB image. Of course, the adjustments I made, especially in Levels, were quite different, and I was able to get a Lab image that looked somewhat similar, but it didn't seem to have the same amount of contrast and separation of colors. The Layers I had created so far were Green Levels and Green Hue/Saturation to adjust the Greens and Selective Darken, Add Red and Yellow (my Red Levels layer), as well as Saturate All & Reds and Pop Yellows for the Everything but Green layer. Things looked a bit flat and muddy, and I could not get this image to look as good as the RGB one. Then I thought maybe Curves would work better, instead of Levels, as the initial adjustment for a Lab image, so I created the Layers Red S and Color Balance Curve for the non-Greens and Greens Curve for the greens. As you can see, the S curve I

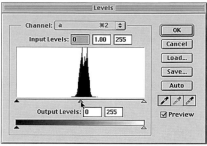

STEP 3: The a channel for the EverythingButGreen layer.

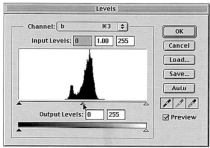

STEP 3: The b channel for the EverythingButGreen layer.

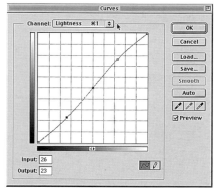

STEP 4: The Red Lightness S curve I used to add some contrast to everything but the greens.

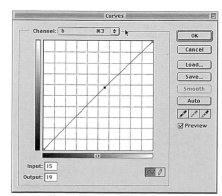

STEP 4: The Red b Curve adds some yellow to the color balance.

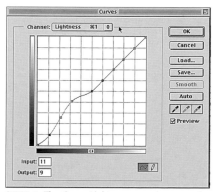

STEP 4: The Green Lightness curve increases the slope of the curve, and thus the contrast, where most of the green values lie in the image.

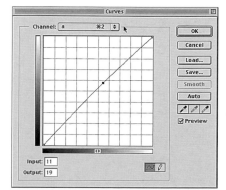

STEP 4: The Red a Curve adds some red to the color balance. You want to be very subtle with your Lab a and b curve movements.

Trying to Duplicate What I do in RGB

used for the Lightness channel of the non-Greens helped increase the contrast and in the a channel I moved the curve up and to the left to add red and I did the same thing in the b channel to add yellow. The Green Curves, as you can see, was mostly a move in the Lightness channel to lighten and brighten the greens by increasing the slope of the curve where most of the green values were sitting, to the bottom-left half of the curve. I initially turned off the Eye icons for my Levels adjustments and replaced them with these Curves adjustments leaving the Hue/Saturation layers as they were. At some point though, I accidentally turned on all the layers, by Option-clicking the Eye icon of a Layer, and noticed that the image looked even better with both the Levels and Curves layers on at the same time. I tweaked each layer a little further and was getting happier with this image, except the shadow areas in the Reds and Yellows looked a little flat, and the color balance on the greens was not what I wanted.

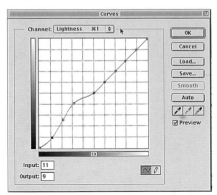

STEP 5: The Lightness adjustment in the Green Curves Layer helps the shadow areas in the Green parts of the image.

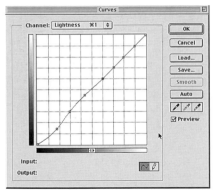

STEP 5: The Add Shadow Contrast Curve helps the shadow areas in the non-Green layers of the image.

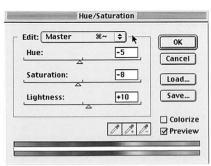

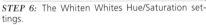

STEP 6: The Whiten Whites Hue/Saturation settings.

STEP 5: To solve this problem, I added the Add Shadow Contrast Curve to the group of Red, non-Green, layers. This curve does a similar thing as the Green Curves above by increasing the slope of the part of the Lightness curve that corresponds to the tonal range of the image we wanted to modify. I added a Color

STEP 5: The Green Color Balance Adjustment layer. We also changed the Highlight and Shadows settings. You can check those out on your screen with my final image open.

Balance Adjustment layer at the top of the Greens layers to just pop the Greens, especially the green highlights, a bit. Remember, I didn't modify the pixels in the Greens or EverythingButGreen layers, so you can always throw my Adjustment layers away, or turn their Eye icons off, and try out your own adjustments making your own Adjustment layers.

FINE TUNING THE IMAGE

STEP 6: By editing the PopYellows layer mask, I created a mask for the Whiten Whites Hue/Saturation Adjustment layer whose job is to take the pinkish cast out of rocks that I wanted to be white in the final image. The effect was mostly created by lowering the Saturation and increasing the Lightness on the Edit Master part of this Hue/Saturation dialog. The Hue shift here takes a little yellow out of the whites.

STEP 7: If you turn off the top four Layers of my final Lab image, you'll notice that the sky in the top-left corner is badly blown out. There wasn't a whole lot of detail in the original image or scan here anyway, so I created the Fix Blown Out Sky and Sky Color Balance layers specifically to patch that blown-out corner. Fix Blown Out Sky is just part of the sky to the right copied and edited to make it appear as though it were raining in that top left corner also. The color of this new sky area wasn't quite right so we added a Grouped Color Balance Adjustment layer just to tweak that part of the image. Remember that a Grouped Adjustment layer is indented from the first real layer below it. It only affects the pixels in that real layer below it and the Grouped layer also gets its transparency from that real layer below. To created a Grouped Adjustment layer, you need to turn on the Group With Previous Layer check box in the New Adjustment Layer dialog or Option-click the line between that already created Adjustment layer and the real layer below it.

Chapter 29: Bryce Stone Woman

STEP 8: The Burn and Dodge layer is a normal layer, not an Adjustment layer, filled with 50% Gray using Edit/Fill, with its Blend mode set to Soft Light. Soft Light mode ignores 50% Gray but will darken the cumulative effect of all the layers underneath in areas that are darker than 50% Gray and lighten those layers in areas that are lighter than 50% Gray. This allows you to burn and dodge the image using the Airbrush along with large, soft brushes having a low opacity. Before you start this type of work, you type D to set the default colors of Black and White. Then you can use X, for eXchange, to toggle between painting on this Gray layer with either Black or White.

STEP 9: As a final step, we created a mask and Adjustment layer curve to very slightly darken the outer parts of the image. We then edited this by hand with the Airbrush to re-lighten some of those darkened areas.

We know that this has been a whirlwind tour of color correcting and editing using Lab images. Based on the great results my friends Bill Atkinson, Charlie Cramer, and Bruce Hodge are getting, I believe I will be using Lab color a lot more in the future and will keep you posted on my progress with it at my Web site, www.maxart.com. After this book is printed, I plan on spending a lot more time shooting nature images and making fine art prints. Please keep me up to date with your discoveries and questions doing the same at barry@maxart.com. Enjoy!

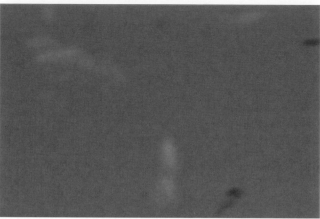

STEP 8: The Burn and Dodge layer. Areas that are darker than 50% gray will be darkened in the underlying layers, and areas that are lighter will be lightened.

STEP 9: The mask for the Darken Edges Curves Adjustment layer. This was a very subtle darkening of the Lightness channel curve.

The original Bryce Image before we made any color corrections.

COMPOSITING MULTIPLE IMAGES

LEARN THE PEN TOOL

CREATE THRESHOLD AND GRADIENT KNOCKOUTS

REPLACE HEADS AND COLOR MATCH FACES

COMPOSITE TWO SCANS
TO INCREASE DYNAMIC RANGE

CREATE COMPLEX COMPOSITES

WITH LAYERS,
ADJUSTMENT LAYERS,
AND LAYER MASKS

Taken with a Canon-F1 and 28mm FD lens using Kodachrome in Venice, Italy.

30 HANDS-ON SESSION: Bob Goes to...

Using the Pen tool for smooth curves and
Levels for hair to create a knock-out of Bob, and
then using layers to send Bob traveling!

In this session, we explore various techniques for creating a knock-out of Bob. First we will use the Pen tool to trace the outline of Bob and remove his background. We will show you how you can use Threshold and Levels to automatically Knock out difficult hair and shapes that are hard for the Pen tool. After you separate Bob from his background, you'll use layers, layer masks, and Free Transform to send him to different locations.

You will find the selection and basic compositing techniques we show you here useful in many places. Because Bob has subtle, curved edges and a somewhat soft distinction between him and the background, you can get a more exact selection if you use the Pen tool rather than the Lasso or Magic Wand. Before you do this example, you should be sure to read Chapter 3: Navigating in Photoshop and set up your Actions palette using ArtistKeys. Also, read Chapter 10: Selections, Paths, Masks, and Channels as well as Chapter 11: Layers, Layer Masks, and Adjustment Layers.

SETTING THINGS UP

STEP 1: Open the BigBob file in the Bob Goes To folder. Click the middle icon at the bottom of the Tool palette (F) to put yourself in Full Screen mode and use Command-0 to zoom BigBob so it fills the screen. Bring up the Channels palette (Shift-F10 with ArtistKeys) and then the Layers palette (F10). You can get these from the Window menu but using the function keys is faster. When you have loaded the ArtistKeys Actions, the function keys F9 through F12 and their Shift alternatives take care of most of the palettes. Put your Channels and Layers palettes along the side of the screen but make sure that you can see all of both of them at the same time. Notice that the Layers palette just has one layer, called *Background*. Double-click the word *Background* and type in the name Bob, to change it from a *Background* layer into a normal layer. Now open the Vegas file from the same folder. Choose Select/All (Command-A) to select all of Vegas and then Edit/Copy to copy it. Then choose Window/BigBob to switch to the Bob file, and finally, choose Edit/Paste to paste Vegas as a new layer on top of the Bob layer. Notice that this new layer (called Layer 1) has been created in the Layers palette. Notice also that Layer 1 is black and white because you pasted on top of a black-and-white document. All the layers in a document have to be in the same color mode. Do Command-Z to undo the Paste; then choose Image/Mode/RGB to convert Bob to RGB. Red, Green, and Blue channels appear in the Channels palette, each a copy of the old Black channel. Now do Edit/Paste again and the Vegas image will be in color. Double-click its layer,

STEP 1: The BigBob image as it appears when you first open it.

name it Vegas, and then choose OK. Imagine that Bob was a print laying on your desk and then you dropped the Vegas print on top of it. Think of each layer as a separate image; after all, it is—each layer has its own set of RGB channels. Review Chapter 11 during this exercise if you need to refresh your understanding of layers.

STEP 2: You're going to want Bob standing in front of a background, so you want Bob to be the top layer. Click the Vegas layer and drag it downward until you see a black line below the Bob layer. At this point, release the mouse to change the order of the layers. Bob is now on top and will completely hide Vegas for now. Press Command-Shift-S, for Save-As, and save the file as Bob Goes To. You can now close the Vegas image because you have created a layer for it in Bob Goes To. Choose Window/Show Paths (Shift-F11) to bring up the Paths palette. Click the Pen tool in the Tool palette (P) and press Return to bring up the Pen tool's Options. Turn on the Rubber band option by clicking in it so you see an X in the box. Setting this option causes the Pen to show you how a line or curve will draw between two points.

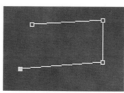

STEP 3: Clicking to enter corner points on a path.

CREATING A PATH FROM SCRATCH

STEP 3: If you already know how to use Paths, you can skip steps 3 and 4. You can now use the Pen tool to learn how to create a new path. The Pen tool allows you to make selections, called *paths,* by clicking to create points between either straight or curved lines. If you click a point and immediately release the mouse, you create a corner point. If you click a point and drag before releasing the mouse, that point becomes a curve point. When you create or move a curve point, you get two lines coming out of the curve point; I call these *handlebars.* The handlebars control the shape of the curve. Try this out now! It's sort of like tracing—but more fun!

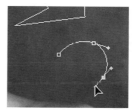

STEP 3: Clicking and dragging to enter curve points on a path. The handlebars should be tangent to the curve shape you are trying to draw.

Click anywhere on top of the Bob Image with the Pen tool and immediately release to create a corner point. Click four or five corner points to create a box. When you put the last corner point on top of the first, a little circle appears next to the arrow, indicating that you are closing the path. When you see the circle, click on top of the initial point again to close the path. If you're going to turn your path into a selection (as you are going to do here), you usually want the path to be closed. After closing the first box path, move the cursor down below that box, and in a new area, click and drag to create a curve point. Where you click is the location of the point, and dragging out the handlebar beyond the point affects the shape of the line segment between that point and the previous point as well as between that point and the next point. Draw an oval shape by clicking and dragging four curve points. Close the path by clicking again on the original point. You now have a box path made up of corner points and an oval path made up of curve points. If you look at the Paths palette, you can see them both in a new path called Work Path. Work Path is a temporary place where you can create a path without naming it. Actually, each of these two disjointed paths is a subpath of Work Path. Double-click Work Path and rename it Play Path. After you name a path, any changes you make to it automatically save as part of that path.

STEP 3: To close the curve, click the first point a second time when you see the small circle next to the Pen icon.

STEP 4: Now select the Arrow tool in the Tool palette by typing an A. See the diagram on this page; it gives the names of each tool. You can also scroll through the different Pen editing tools by continuing to type Shift-P until you get to the tool you want;

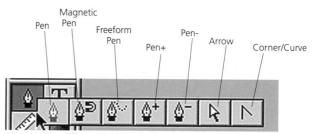

STEP 4: The different tools available from the pop-out menu for Pen in the Tool palette. NOTE: Adobe calls the Corner/Curve tool the Convert Point tool. The Pen tool, Magnetic Pen, and Freeform Pen tools are for entering points initially. The Arrow tool allows you to edit points that have been entered. The Pen+ and Pen– tools are for adding and deleting points, and the Corner/Curve tool is for changing points between corners and curves and for decoupling the handlebars.

Creating a Path from Scratch

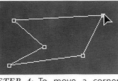

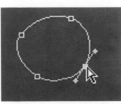

STEP 4: To move a corner point or a curve point, click it and drag.

STEP 4: To adjust the shape of the curve, first click the point whose handlebars affect the part of the curve you want to change. Second, click the end of the handlebar and make it longer or shorter or change its angle. This changes the shape of the curve.

STEP 4: Moving a curve point to make the oval longer.

STEP 4: Changing the shape of a curve segment by dragging one end of a handlebar.

although, Shift-P now only toggles through the Pen, Magnetic Pen, and the Free Form Pen. Now use the Arrow tool to edit the path. First click the box shape you made with the corner points. When you click the box shape, its points become highlighted. To move one of these points, just click it, drag, and then let go in the new location. This change saves automatically in your Play Path. Click the oval subpath now and its points become highlighted. If you want to move one of these curve points to elongate the oval, just click and drag it like you would a corner point. To adjust the shape of the curve, first click the point on one end of the curve segment that you want to change. This brings up the handlebars for that point. Now click the end of the handlebar next to the segment you want to change, and make it longer or shorter, or change its angle to change the shape of the curve.

You can also add points with the Pen+ tool and delete points with the Pen– tool. To add a point, just click along the line segment where there currently isn't a point using the Pen+ tool. You used to be able to access the Pen+ tool from the Arrow tool by holding the Command and Option keys down while over a location that doesn't already have a point and then clicking to add a point. Now in Photoshop 5 if you do this, or just hold down the Option key and click, and then you drag a little after the click, you get the Arrow plus tool that makes a copy of the entire path. To just add or subtract a point, you now need to be in either the Pen+ or Pen– tool. If you are in the Pen– tool, the Option key will temporarily give you the Pen+ tool and vice versa. When you add a point with the Pen+ tool, it is a curve point. You can then change the shape of the curve by adjusting that point's handlebars with the Arrow tool.

If you want to change a curve point to a corner point, or vice versa, click it with the Corner/Curve tool (Adobe calls it the Convert Point tool). To change a corner to a curve, you click and drag the corner point to define the length and angle of your handlebars. You also can use the Corner/Curve tool to decouple a curve point's handlebars. Clicking either handlebar and moving slightly with this tool allows you to then use the Arrow tool to drag each end of the handlebar to change its curve segment shape without changing the one on the opposite side of the handlebar's point. To recouple the handlebars together again, use another click of the Corner/Curve tool. You can also access the Corner/Curve tool from the Arrow tool by holding down the Command and Option keys and putting the cursor over an existing point. Using the Pen tool in Photoshop is a lot like using the Pen tool in Illustrator, more so Photoshop 5 as some of Photoshop's command keys were changed for Illustrator compatibility. If you are not familiar with the Pen tool or if you want to know all the little details, read the "About Paths" section in the Selecting chapter (Chapter 7) of the Adobe Photoshop 5.0 manual. We show you how to use paths as you work on projects in this book. Click on the Play Path you just created and drag it to the trash at the bottom-right area of the Paths palette.

MAKING A PATH AROUND BOB

STEP 5: Make sure you are currently using the Pen tool. (Type Shift-P until you get it, or click and drag on the Pen area in the Tool palette and then choose the Pen icon from the pop-out menu.) Press Command-Spacebar-click to zoom into the bottom-left of where Bob sits against his background. Click the Pen tool to make the first point in the lower-left corner of Bob's body along the edge between Bob and the gray background. Now move the cursor up the curved shape of his arm and click and drag out a curve point for the second point. Release the mouse when the line segment between the first point and the second point matches the edge of Bob against the background. You want the handlebars on curve points to always be tangent to the curved edge of Bob at the point's location. Now click and drag the Pen tool to create curve points around the edge of Bob and his background. Stay zoomed in close and use the spacebar to scroll when needed. If you make a mistake, you can Command-Z to remove the last point you entered. If you hold down the Command key while entering a path, you get the Arrow tool and you can go back and click any other point you have entered so far and move it. Releasing the Command key puts you back in the Pen tool so you can enter more points. You can use the Tab key to get all the current palettes out of your way. Don't worry about making it perfect as you enter it because you can use the Arrow tool later to adjust the selection you're making here now.

STEP 6: Move your way up the left side of the Bob layer entering curve points all the way until you get to the hair. It is hard to do a good job of selecting hair using the Pen tool, so just rough out the basic shape of the hair as you go through that part of the selection. Selecting hair like this properly is one of the most common things people have trouble doing. We show you how to do this later in the session. When you get to the top-left corner of the edge of Bob's hair with the background, click there to make a corner point and then click again on the top-right edge of Bob's hair with the background to make another corner point. Now trace down the right side of Bob, making mostly curve points by clicking and dragging each once until you click to make another corner at the bottom-right edge. To make a curve point, you click and continue to hold down the mouse button while you drag out the handlebars. You don't click, release the mouse, and then click again and drag! Now go back to the bottom-left edge and click back on the original point when you see the small circle next to the Pen tool. This completes the path around Bob, and you should now double-click the Work Path name in the Paths palette and call it Bob Outline.

STEP 7: Use the Pen's pop-out in the Tool palette, or just type an A, to switch from the Pen tool to the Arrow tool. Click once on the outline of your path to bring the points back. If you were doing this for a comp, the path you have made so far probably would be fine. However, if you were going to use it for an ad or magazine cover, you would want to make the path as accurate as possible. For the most accuracy, zoom in close; now go back and scroll around the edge as you use the arrow key to move points and handlebars when the curve edge is off. You will want the edge of the curve to be just a hair inside the edge of Bob's surface because you don't usually want to have any pixels from Bob's old background showing on top of the new background. Remember, now in Photoshop 5 you use the Command and Option keys to get the Corner/Curve tool. To add or delete points, you need to switch to either the Pen + or Pen– tool. When in one of those tools, you can get the other by holding down the Option key while over a segment, to get Pen +, or while over a point, to

STEP 5: Start by clicking a corner point where Bob's arm meets the background. Now click and drag curve points as you follow Bob's shape upward and around.

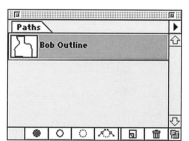

STEP 6: The Photoshop 5 Paths palette. The icons on the bottom, from left to right, fill a path with the current foreground color, stroke a path with current painting tool and brush, do a Load Selection from a path, turn a selection into a path, create a new or copied path, and throw a path into the trash. To use them, you click on the path you want and drag to the appropriate icon, then release when the icon highlights. Dragging to the New Path icon copies the path. To create a path from an existing selection, click the fourth icon from the left. Option-dragging or clicking any icon brings up any option dialog box that the icon has.

get Pen—. If you are not in one of these positions, you might get the Arrow tool or the Arrow Plus tool. As you edit the path, it automatically updates to Bob Outline in the Paths palette.

TURNING PATHS BACK TO SELECTIONS AND MASKS

STEP 8: Click in the empty space below your last path to dehighlight a path.

STEP 8: When you are happy with the shape of your Bob Outline path, choose Make Selection from the Paths palette pop-up menu. Make it a New Selection with the feather set to 0 and Anti-aliased on. When you choose OK, you will see the selection as well as your path still highlighted. To dehighlight your path, click in the empty area below the name Bob Outline in the Paths palette. The faster way to turn a path into a selection is to click the path name in the Paths palette and then drag to the Load Selection icon, which is third from the left at the bottom of this palette. Your path turns into a selection using the options last set in the Make Selection dialog box, and it also becomes dehighlighted.

STEP 9: Make sure the Bob layer is active; then click the Add Layer Mask icon at the bottom-left area of the Layers palette to create a layer mask for the Bob layer with the selected parts of Bob showing but the background now removed. Remember that the black areas of a layer mask remove those parts of that mask's layer. When you clicked the Add Layer Mask icon, your selection turned into the layer mask with only the selected parts then visible. You can also choose Layer/Add Layer Mask/Reveal Selection if you are not used to using the icons.

STEP 10: Click the Vegas layer to make it the active, highlighted, layer. Use Command-0 to make sure that you're zoomed in so you can see the entire image in the screen. Now choose Edit/Free Transform (Command-T) to get the Free Transform command. Click in the center of the Vegas layer and drag it so its top-left corner aligns with the top-left of the document canvas. Next, hold down the Shift key while dragging the bottom-right handle down and to the right, to scale the Vegas image. The Shift key makes the scale proportional. You can drag beyond the edge of the document canvas into the gray area to scale the image bigger than the canvas. Release the mouse button when you are happy with the scale. Press Enter (or Return) to finish the Transform or press the Escape key to cancel the Transform. Now that you have sent Bob on a trip to Las Vegas, let's try another location, too.

STEP 11: Use File/Open to open the Packard file in the "Posterize, Bitmaps, and Patterns" folder on the CD. Move the Packard window so you can see part of the Bob Goes To window below it. Type V to make sure that you are in the Move tool, and then click in the image area of the Packard image and drag until your cursor sits on top of the Bob Goes To image. The cursor should change to a hand at this point, and if you then release the mouse, you will drop a new Packard layer on top of the Vegas layer in the Bob Goes To file. Bob is now in Miami, where there are many photo shoots along the beach. Double-click Layer 1 and rename it Packard,

STEP 10: Using Free Transform to scale the Vegas image.

and then use Command-T (Free Transform) again to move and scale the Packard image so it is stretched across the screen. Press Enter or Return to end the Free Transform session. Now you can see Bob in either Vegas or Miami by turning on the Eye icon for the layer you want to see as his background.

CLEANING UP BOB'S LAYER MASK

STEP 12: Click the Bob layer and use the Move tool (V or hold down Command) to move Bob until his hair on both sides is over the clear blue sky of the Miami scene. It should be pretty obvious that your Pen tool selection of his hair is not too natural. Bring up the Channels and Layers palettes and separate them so you can see both at the same time. Click the left-most rectangular thumbnail in the Bob layer to activate the layer. This thumbnail, I call it the Layer thumbnail, should now have a black highlight around it in the Layers palette. It is easier to see this if your highlight color is set to gray or something nonblack. The Channels palette should show RGB as active with the RGB Eye icons on for channels ~ through 3. Type a B to go to the Paintbrush tool, and then type D to get the default colors. And finally, press the 0 number key to set the Brush Opacity to 100%. Try painting on Bob's face and you will see black paint on

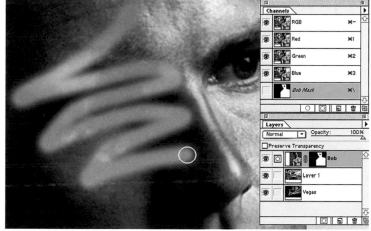

STEP 12: Painting Black in the layer mask removes that part of the layer. Here is what your Channels and Layers palettes should look like if you want to paint in the mask but view the RGB composite image.

top of his image. Whatever you do now permanently affects Bob's layer. Use Command-Z to undo this painting or Command-Option if you have to undo more than one step. Now click the Layer Mask thumbnail, which is the right-most thumbnail in the Bob layer, and notice that it now highlights in black. The Channels palette now has a channel called Bob Mask activated, even though the Eye icons are on for the inactive Red, Green, and Blue channels. Type D again, followed by X, and then paint with black on top of Bob's face. You're now painting black into Bob's layer mask, and you will notice the Packard layer through the area you paint with black because black in a Layer Mask removes that area of the layer. Use Command-Z again to remove your changes. Here you are changing the mask but seeing the changes happen to the composite of the RGB layers. The Channels palette shows that you are seeing RGB but working on the layer mask. If you now Option-click the Layer Mask icon, you will see the mask and will still be working on the mask. Again, look at what is active and which Eye icons are on in the Channels palette. Option-click the Layer Mask icon again to return to seeing RGB but working on the mask. You need to really be aware of whether you are working on the layer mask or the layer, as well as how the Layers and Channels palettes show you the current state.

STEP 13: Bring up the Brushes palette, F12, and choose a midsized soft brush. Type a 5 to set the opacity to 50% and then paint with black where Bob's hair blends with the background to create a more subtle blend than you did with the Pen tool. Painting with black fades out and eventually removes parts of the hair and painting with white brings it back. Remember that you can use the left and right bracket keys to change brush size as you work. You sometimes want to paint with white at 100% along the hair edge to bring back all the hair and even some of the background. Then use X to Xchange the colors, and use black at 50% with different size brushes to slowly blend away the background and keep the hairs you need to make the composite look natural. After getting the hair correct, scroll around the entire edge of Bob and use a hard-edge black brush at 100% to remove any light ghosts along the edge. Now do a File/Save.

USING LEVELS FOR BETTER, FASTER HAIR KNOCK-OUTS

STEP 14: Doing a knock-out of hair using the above by-hand method is one of the most difficult tasks and how to do it with less work and more accuracy is one of the most asked questions. You can use Threshold or Levels to create a mask that will sometimes do the knock-out for you. Here, we look at an alternative method to doing the hair knock-out and maybe even the entire knockout of Bob. Click and drag the Bob Mask channel in the Channels palette to the New Channel icon and make a copy of this channel called MaskByHand. Now click back on the Layer thumbnail for the Bob layer to reactivate the Red, Green, and Blue channels. Hold down the Shift key, and then click the Bob Layer Mask thumbnail in the Layers palette to turn off this layer mask until you Shift-click again. Click and Option-drag the Red channel to the New Channel icon and call it Levels. Choose Image/Adjust/Levels to make some changes to this temporary mask channel. Move the Input Shadow slider, the top-left one, toward the right until it reads about 50. Move the Input Highlight slider, the top-right one, toward the left until it reads about 74. Next, move the Brightness/Contrast slider, the one between the other two, until it reads about .76. You will see a pretty good mask of the hair. You want the background white and the head and hair black with some grayish hair where they blend together. Now choose OK on Levels. You will use this mask only to replace the hair area of the existing Bob layer mask. Using Levels and moving the Highlight and Shadow sliders close together to create a mask of hair allows you to have some brightness variation from the pure black-and-white mask that you get when you use Threshold as you do in the next example, "Bob and the Kestrel." This variation can help blend the hair into the new background. I got the idea for this Levels technique from watching a demo Deke McClelland gave at the Photoshop conference in Orlando. In his technique, he used the High Pass filter first to isolate the edges and then followed that by Levels or Threshold.

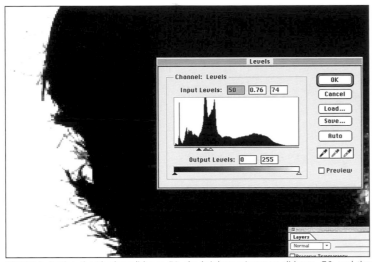

STEP 14: Setting the Shadow slider to 50, the brightness/contrast slider to .76, and the highlight slider to 74 creates a pretty good mask of the hair in my version of Bob.

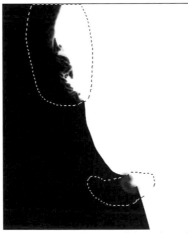

STEP 15: Here is the part of the Bob mask you should select before doing the Paste Into. As shown here, you might also want to get the tuft of hair below Bob's ear.

STEP 15: First notice that the head in the existing Bob layer mask is white where the head in our new Levels mask is black. To fix this, choose Image/Adjust/Invert (Command-I) to invert our new mask. Now choose Select/All, and then choose Edit/Copy to copy the entire mask. Choose Select/None (Command-D) and then click on the Bob mask in the

Chapter 30: Bob Goes To...

Channels palette to activate it. Turn on the Eye icon for the Bob mask and turn off the Eye icons for RGB, Red, Green, and Blue. Now you are just working on and seeing the Bob layer mask. Type L to get to the Lasso tool, and then select from the area of hair above Bob's ear to the top of his head. Now, choose Edit/Paste Into, which will use the new Levels mask to replace the Bob mask just in that selected area. To see the before and after results, click the Eye icons to turn the RGB, Red, Green, and Blue channels back on. Just click the Eye icons, not the right part of the channel. Now click the Eye icon for the Bob mask channel to turn it off. You are now seeing the composite with the new modified mask. Command-Z to see it again with the old mask, and then use Command-Z to toggle back and forth to decide which mask is better. Choose Select/None if you like the new mask better; otherwise, Command-Z one more time to remove your floating selection and revert to the old mask. If you choose the new Levels version, you can now further improve it by doing more hand editing on it or by applying a very slight Gaussian Blur, about .5 pixels, in this new Levels area.

USING THE FINAL BOB MASK WITH FREE TRANSFORM TO SEND BOB TO DIFFERENT LOCATIONS

STEP 16: Now that you have a final mask of Bob, you can bring up different potential background layers and send Bob to many places. You can make a different Bob layer for each background by clicking and then dragging the Bob layer to the New Layer icon at the bottom of the Layers palette. Give each Bob layer an appropriate name, like Bob Vegas for the Vegas scene, Bob Miami for the Packard scene, and so on. Now use the Move tool to move this version of Bob to the appropriate place in this scene. If you need to scale or transform a scene or the Bob for a scene, activate the layer you want to scale by clicking it in the Layers palette and then typing Command-T to bring up the Free Transform command. This will add handles to the corners and middles of a box that is drawn around the Layers contents. You can scale the layer by clicking and dragging one of the handles to make the image bigger or smaller. To scale proportionately, hold down the Shift key while scaling. To rotate the layer, move the cursor a little outside one of the corner handles; you should see the curved rotate icon. Click and drag at this point to rotate. You can move the layer while transforming it by clicking in the middle and dragging to the location you want to go to. Use the Command key while clicking and dragging a handle to distort the image, the Option key to scale evenly around a center point, and Command-Option-Shift to scale the image with perspective. The Escape key

STEP 16: Here we used the final Versailles image from the "Versailles" example, along with Free Transform, to move and scale Bob until his eye lined up correctly with the sun. To create the composite effect, the Blend mode on his layer was set to Overlay, and we modified his layer mask to remove him from where the palace of Versailles buildings start.

STEP 16: In this version of Bob's travels, we used the Fill command in Color mode with 15% of the red from the Mint sign to colorize Bob, and then we moved him into place and made some minor adjustments to his layer mask using the Paintbrush so that his hair would blend best with the dark background.

223

allows you to cancel Free Transform. To accept your transform, press Return or Enter. You may find that you need to do minor fine-tuning on Bob's layer mask to properly blend each different background. For more information on Free Transform, see chapter 17: Transformation of Images, Layers, Paths, and Selections.

STEP 16: Here we used Layer/Transform/Flip Horizontal on Bob's layer to make him face the other way, and then Free Transform (Command-T) to rotate, scale, move, and skew Bob. Finally, we tinted him with a Grouped Hue/Saturation Adjustment layer having the Colorize check box on.

SAVING CLIPPING PATHS FOR QUARK OR ILLUSTRATOR

When you finish editing the Bob Outline path at the end of step 7, you could easily have used it to knock-out Bob as a clipping path in Quark or Illustrator. Importing with a clipping path into Quark or Illustrator would allow you to place Bob as an object with a transparent background. This way you could wrap text around him or you could place him on top of a background created in Quark or Illustrator.

To save a path in this way, choose Clipping Path from the Paths Palette menu. Choose the path you want for your clipping path from the Path pop-up menu. In this case, you would choose Bob Outline. We recommend leaving the flatness value blank, which will use the printer's default setting. The flatness controls the accuracy of curved line segments created with PostScript. For more information on flatness, see the Photoshop manual and/or ask your service bureau for a recommended flatness setting for the type of output you are doing. To use the Clipping Path, save this file in Photoshop EPS format and when you open it into Quark, Illustrator, or other layout packages that support clipping paths, the background will be transparent in that application. Clipping path knock-outs don't allow for the subtle blending we have been doing here in Bob's hair using layer masks. Clipping path knock-outs cannot have a varied feather on their edges.

31 HANDS-ON SESSION: Bob and the Kestrel

Using Threshold with hard- and soft-edged masks and Paste Into to combine images.

(Original concept by Bruce Ashley)

This is a technique that would be difficult and tedious to do in the darkroom. Here, using digital imaging, it's easy. In this session, you create a complicated mask of the bicycle using Threshold and editing in a mask channel. You then add a gradient to the mask and use it to seamlessly place Bob behind the bicycle.

PREPARING THE KESTREL IMAGE

STEP 1: Use File/Open to open the OrigKestrel file in the Bob & Kestrel folder. Choose File/Save As (Command-Shift-S) and save it in Photoshop format to your hard drive with the name Bob&Kestrel. Open the OrigBob file from the same folder.

STEP 2: Crop the white and black borders from both of these files. Type C for crop, and then draw a box around the images to exclude the borders. You can click and drag the handles on the edges of the box to change it after you draw it. Hold down the Command key to stop the automatic lock-to-edges feature in the Photoshop 5 Cropping tool. Press Enter or Return to do the crop. Zoom in to 100% using Command-Option-0. Use Filter/Sharpen/Sharpen Edges followed by Filter/Sharpen/Sharpen to sharpen both images. You can use an action in the ArtistKeys Actions palette (F11) called SharpEdgesShp to run both these filters in the correct order by clicking on SharpEdgesShp or using the Play icon to play it. Whenever you sharpen something, you should be zoomed in to at least 100% so you can see all the details. We normally use Unsharp Mask for sharpening, as in Chapter 24: Kansas Tweaks, but SharpEdgesShp is a quick technique that works well with these small images, and also for comps.

STEP 3: Type the letter D, for the default colors. Use the Window menu to bring the Bob&Kestrel file to the top and then click in the middle icon at the bottom of the Tool palette to put it into Full Screen mode. Use Image/Canvas Size (Command-F8) to make the image window the same width but 750 pixels high. Put the image in the lower center of the canvas by clicking on the middle square at the bottom. It will turn gray to indicate where the original image will be in the new canvas. This will cause all the new whitespace to be added to the top of the image.

The original Bob.

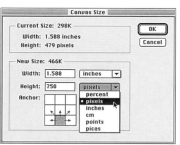

The original Kestrel.

STEP 3: Set up the canvas size with the height of 750 pixels and the gray box at the bottom center to make room at the top of the file.

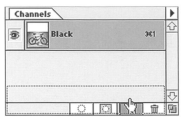

STEP 4: Option-drag to the New Channel icon and make a copy of the Black channel to create a mask. Name it Bike Mask.

STEP 5: The Black/White box forces colors to white for the foreground and black for the background when you work on a mask channel.

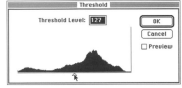

STEP 5: With the Preview button off, move the Threshold slider until you have the best mask for the bike. About 127 worked for us.

STEP 6: Selection to be deleted (turned to white).

STEP 7: The mask with the bicycle filled in.

MASKING OUT THE BIKE

STEP 4: Go to Window/Show Channels (Shift-F10) and Option-drag Channel #1, the Black channel, to the Channel Copy icon. Option-dragging brings up the Duplicate Channel dialog box, allowing you to enter a name. Name it Bike Mask by typing in the name and choosing OK. You will use this new channel to create a mask to separate the bicycle from Bob. Wherever Bob is to be in the final composite, the mask needs to be white (and it should be black where the bike will be). Check out the final image at the end of this chapter to see what we are trying to create here. Now imagine the mask you would need to create this composite.

STEP 5: Using Image/Adjust/Threshold (Shift-F7), adjust the slider with the Preview button off (leave Preview on if you don't have Video LUT Animation—most PCs don't) until you have created a good dropout of the bike frame. You don't want to etch too much from the edges around the bike frame and the seat. If gaps start to show on the frame edge, you have taken too much away. Don't worry about getting the tires completely; you can fix them later. Click on OK to finish your Threshold selection. Now type a D to make the foreground white and the background black, and then type an X to make the foreground black and the background white. Each time you type an X, the foreground and background colors will exchange.

STEP 6: Using the Lasso tool with Feather set to zero, draw freehand selections around the areas of black that remain in the background on the mask and then use the Delete key (Backspace on Windows) to set them to white. (You need to do this only above the center of the wheels.) Type Command-D to remove the selection.

STEP 7: Choose the Pencil tool (N) and press Return to bring up its options. Choose Reset Tool from the Pencil Options palette's menu. Go to Window/Show Brushes (F12) and pick the third brush from the top left. This should be a 5-pixel brush with the hardness set to 100%. Use the Pencil tool to add black to areas of the bike not yet filled in. You want the entire interior of the bike frame to be black so that when you combine the bike and Bob, Bob doesn't show through those areas. You only need to do this to areas above the height of the center of the wheel. Don't paint out beyond the edge of the original bicycle boundary. Without leaving the Pencil tool, you can switch between black, to fill in the bicycle, and white to erase around the tires, by typing an X to exchange colors. You can speed up this painting process by using the shortcut of clicking on one end of a line and Shift-clicking on the other end to draw a black line with the Pencil tool. After you finish this step, you will have done a lot of work editing this mask, so do a Save (Command-S) to update your file on the disk in case you make a mistake in the following steps.

CREATING A GRADIENT MASK

STEP 8: Make a copy of the Bike Mask by Option-dragging the mask to the New Channel icon at the bottom of the Channels palette. Name this Gradient Mask.

STEP 9: Type G for the Gradient tool, and then press Return to make sure its options are set as shown here. Notice that you are creating a Linear Gradient with the Blend mode set to Darken. The Linear Gradient tool is the left-most choice in the new

Photoshop 5 Gradient pop-out from the Gradient area of the Tool palette. You are going to use the Gradient tool to add a gradual blend from Bob at the top of the image to the bicycle at the bottom of the image. We are doing this in a copy of the Bike Mask so that if we make a mistake, we still have the original Bike Mask to try again. Of course with Photoshop 5, we could always use the History palette to save the day if we make a mistake. That is, so long as we are saving enough History States. You use the Gradient tool by clicking in the place where you want 100% of the foreground color and dragging to where you want 100% of the background color. Everything between these two points will be a blend of the two colors. Everything outside these two points will be 100% foreground or 100% background. The Darken option will make the gradient change the Bike Mask only when the gradient makes the image darker than it was before. This will not modify the existing black parts of the mask.

STEP 9: Use the default Foreground to Background Linear Gradient tool options but set the Blend mode to Darken.

STEP 10: Click on the Black/White icon at the bottom of the Tool palette, or type D, to set the foreground color to white and and the background color to black. With the Shift key down, click and then drag the Gradient tool from just above the seat downward to ⅓ down the wheel from the top of the back wheel. Release the mouse button before releasing the Shift key to be sure the Shift key is applied. The Shift key forces the gradient line to be vertical. You should now have the final mask shown here. When you do a Load Selection on this mask, the white area at the top will be fully selected with the black areas fully not selected. The gray blend becomes less and less selected the darker it gets.

STEP 11: Click on Channel #1, the Black channel, in the Channels palette. Now you should see the original Kestrel image. Load the Gradient Mask as a selection using Select/Load Selection or by Command-clicking on the Gradient Mask in the Channels palette. The bottom of the gradient selection (the marching ants line) shows up at the 50% gray point. All of the gradient is actually selected to some extent, although it is selected less and less as it gets darker and is only selected to a very small amount as it turns to almost all black.

PUTTING BOB IN THE PICTURE

STEP 12: Use the Window menu to switch to the OrigBob image. Choose Select/Select All (Command-A), followed by Edit/Copy to place Bob on the Clipboard.

STEP 13: Use Window again to return to the Bob&Kestrel window. Now do Edit/Paste Into, not just Paste, to paste Bob into the selection loaded from the Gradient Mask. Bob is now in a new layer called Layer 1. You will notice that there is also a layer mask on this layer that looks the same as your Gradient Mask. Where this layer mask is black, the Bob layer is made transparent, and

STEP 10: To create the gradient, Shift-drag the gradient tool from starting just above the seat and ending ⅓ down the wheel.

STEP 10: Your final gradient mask should look like this.

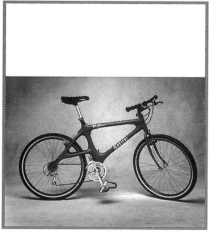

STEP 11: The appearance of the selection after doing a Load Selection.

STEP 15: Here is the final appearance for the Layers and Channels palettes of this example. Notice (see the Hand icon) that the layer and layer mask are not linked in layers created by Paste Into. This means that when you move either, the other will not move with it, as is the case when you normally create a layer mask. Also notice that the Layer 1 mask shows up in the Channels palette when Layer 1 is the active layer.

you can see the Kestrel in the layer below. Turn off the Eye icon on the Kestrel layer, the bottom layer, to see how parts of Bob are now transparent. Turn this Eye icon back on to see the Kestrel again.

STEP 14: Make sure that Layer 1 is still active (highlighted in the Layers palette), and then choose the Move tool from the Tool palette (type V or hold the Command key down). Click and drag to adjust the position of Bob. Make sure no gray transition line is visible at the bottom of Bob as he blends into the bicycle. You need to drag him down until the bottom of his image reaches the place where the Gradient Mask turns completely black. You can check that location in the mask channel by switching back to it using Command-3 or by clicking on the channel you want in the Channels palette. Do Command-1 to go back to the Black channel before moving Bob again. While in the Move tool, you can use the arrow keys to move 1 pixel at a time and Shift-arrow to move 10.

STEP 15: When Bob is in the correct location so that the transition between him and the Kestrel is completely transparent, then Crop (C) any extra white from the top of the image. Save this as Bob&Kestrel in Photoshop format. Saving in Photoshop format with both layers will later allow you to reopen the file and move Bob again.

The completed Bob&Kestrel image after cropping.

Chapter 31: Bob and the Kestrel

32 HANDS-ON SESSION: Versailles

Using two scans to get the full range of detail in a high-contrast image; using layers, Adjustment layers, and layer masks to color correct an image by combining the two scans, and how to apply filters selectively using layers.

This technique shows you how to get more detail in a contrasty image by doing two scans, one for the highlights and another for the shadows, and then combining the two images using Layers. Multiple layers of the same image will be lined up with each other exactly. When shooting an image, if the camera is on a tripod, you can bracket your exposures and also use the compositing technique in this chapter on two scans from two bracketed shots of the same image. This actually works very well as a way to extend what you can get on just one piece of film.

SCANNING THE IMAGE IN LAYERS

STEP 1: Open the Sky file in the Versailles folder. This file was originally opened using the Kodak Photo CD Acquire module with a gamma of 1.4 and color temperature 5000, which gave the most detail in the sky but made the foreground look too dark. We will call this version of the image Sky.

STEP 2: Open the Buildings file. This file was originally opened using the Kodak Photo CD Acquire module using gamma 2.2 and color temperature 5000, which gave the most detail in the buildings and foreground but made the sky too light. We will call this image Buildings. If you were going to use this technique with two different scans of the same piece of film or of two different scans of two bracketed exposures, you would need to make sure that both scans were pixel-for-pixel aligned. To do this, scan a single piece of film at the same time and size without moving the original inside the scanner, or use the Move tool with the arrow keys to line up the scans of two bracketed exposures while each is in a separate layer.

STEP 3: Make the Buildings image active, choose Select/Select All, and then choose Edit/Copy. Now switch to the Sky image and do an Edit/Paste. Double-click this new layer and name it Buildings; then rename the sky layer, currently called *Background*, to Sky. We now have a two-layered document, with the Sky layer as the bottom layer and the Buildings layer as the top one. You also could have used the Move tool to drag the Buildings and then drop that image on the Sky file as a new layer. That's actually faster because it doesn't use the copy buffer, but in Photoshop 4 and 5, you need to remember to hold down the Shift key if you want drag-and-drop layers to be centered in their new location. You can now close the original Buildings image because it is now a layer in Sky. Use the Crop tool to crop the black borders from around both images. Because you first made the

STEP 1: The original Photo CD Acquire using gamma 1.4 to get the most detail in the sky.

STEP 2: The original Photo CD Acquire using gamma 2.2 to get the most detail in buildings and foreground.

STEP 3: You now have both images inside a two-layered document with the Buildings layer on top and the Sky layer on the bottom.

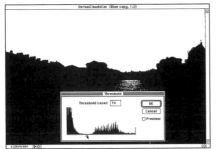

STEP 4: Use Threshold of around 74 to make a mask of the building/sky at the edges of the image.

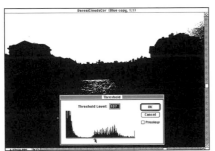

STEP 4: Use Threshold around 107 to make a mask of the building/sky at the middle of the image.

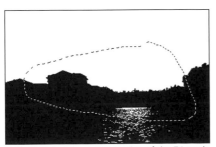

STEP 5: Select the center portion of the 74 mask, where the 107 mask gives better detail, using the Lasso tool with a feather value of 0.

Buildings image a layer on top of Sky, both images will be properly aligned and cropped exactly the same. Do File/Save As, save the two-layered file in Photoshop format, and call it Versailles Layers.

MASKING THE SKY FROM THE BUILDINGS

STEP 4: You now need to make a mask that separates the sky from the rest of the image. Look at the different color channels by clicking in the right-most column in each of the Red, Green, and Blue channels in the Channels palette. Find the channel that has the most contrast between the tops of the buildings and the sky. In this case, it's the Blue channel from the Sky layer. The channels that show up in the Channels palette change depending on which layer is active and which layers are visible. Make sure that the Sky layer is active and the Buildings layer has its Eye icon turned off, as shown here in step 4. Then choose the Blue channel in the Channels palette. Make two copies of this Blue channel using Duplicate Channel from the pop-up menu in the Channels palette, or by dragging the Blue channel to the New Channel icon at the bottom of the palette. Name the first copy Edges and the second copy Center. Now use Image/Adjust/Threshold (Shift-F7 with ArtistKeys) to make two masks using these copies of the Blue channel. You want these masks to separate the sky and the buildings. Zoom in to different areas along the edge of this boundary and notice how different values of Threshold do a better or worse job of accurately defining this boundary. You can click the title bar of Threshold (make sure the Preview button is off) to toggle between the mask you're making and the original Blue channel. This makes it easier to accurately see the boundary. If your computer doesn't have Video LUT Animation (most PDs), work with the Preview button on and turn it off when you need to see the original version.

I used a Threshold value of 74 in the Edges copy of the Blue channel to get the most detail between the buildings and the sky at the edges of the image. In the Center copy, I used the value of 107 to get the best detail between the buildings and the sky in the lighter middle portion. If you need more information on creating Threshold masks, see Chapter 31: Bob and the Kestrel.

STEP 5: Type D for the default colors. You will now combine these two masks to make your final Threshold mask. Choose Select/Select All and then Edit/Copy the Center mask. Choose Select/None, and then using the Lasso tool with a feather value of 0, first click the Edges mask in the Channels palette and then select the center portion, where the Center mask gave better detail. Do an Edit/Paste Into to replace this portion of the Edges mask with that from the Center mask. Choose Select/None, Command-D, and then rename this combined mask HardEdge. Now use the Lasso tool followed by Delete (Backspace on Windows) to fill in any of the white reflections in the brick area with black. The only thing you want selected in

STEP 4: Drag and drop the Blue channel from the Sky layer to the New Channel icon to make channels for your sky mask.

Chapter 32: Versailles

the end here is the sky area. You can now throw out the Center Threshold mask by dragging it to the Trash icon in the Channels palette.

MAKING A LAYER MASK

STEP 6: Click on RGB in the Channels palette to go back to viewing color. Now click in the right-most column of the Buildings layer in the Layers palette to activate that layer as well as to turn its Eye icon back on. Command-click the HardEdge mask in the Channels palette to load it as a selection. The sky should now be selected. Now Option-click the Add Layer Mask icon, which is left-most at the bottom of the Layers palette, to create a layer mask in the Buildings layer that removes this selected area from view in the Buildings layer. You should now see the sky from the Sky layer and the buildings from the Buildings layer. Try turning the different layers off and on using the Eye icons, so you can gain an understanding of the control you have over viewing the different parts of the image.

STEP 6: The Layers palette after adding the layer mask in step 6. Notice that this mask is inverted from the one you made in step 5.

OVERALL COLOR CORRECTION

STEP 7: Do a Command-Shift-S to save the image under a different name, and call it VersaillesColorCor. This will allow you to go back to the previous version if you make a mistake in doing the color corrections. Click the Building Layer thumbnail, the left-most picture icon in the Buildings layer, and then do the overall color correction steps on the Buildings layer. Remember that you're concerned only with making the buildings look best from this layer because the Sky will come from the Sky layer. You are going to do these corrections using Adjustment layers. Command-click on the New Layer icon in the Layers palette, and then set the Type to Levels and choose the Group with Previous Layer option to group this layer with the Buildings layer. Doing this creates a Levels adjustment layer that will change only the color of the Buildings layer. Using an Adjustment layer will allow you to change these color settings again later.

With Levels: set highlight, set shadow, set overall brightness/contrast, and then correct color cast. Now Command-click on the New Layer icon again to create a Hue/Saturation Adjustment layer that is also grouped with the previous layer. In this Hue/Saturation layer, set overall saturation and adjust specific colors. See Chapter 19: Grand Canyon and Chapter 20: Kansas if you need a review of overall color correction. Now click the Sky layer and do overall color correction on it by first adding a Grouped Levels Adjustment layer and then a Grouped Hue/Saturation Adjustment layer. When using these Levels Adjustment layers, work with the Preview button on, so you can see the relationship between the colors you adjust in the Sky layer and the ones you adjust in the Buildings layer. When you do this, focus on getting the part of each layer you will use in the final composite to look the best. The great thing about doing this with Adjustment layers is that you can always go back and change the color adjustments later without further degrading the original images. You can also turn off the Eye icons for any of the Adjustment layers and see what the images looked like before the color adjustments.

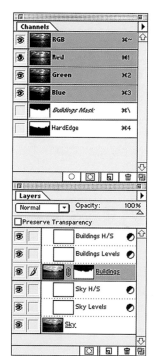

STEP 7: The Layers and Channels palettes after adding the Adjustment layers to color correct the Buildings and the Sky layers.

IMPROVING THE FOREGROUND

STEP 8: Now we will use an Adjustment layer with a layer mask to improve certain areas in the foreground image. You may notice that the buildings and the brick courtyard on the left and right sides of the image have a green tinge to them, and that they are also a little dark. Use the Lasso tool with a 0-pixel feather to select these areas

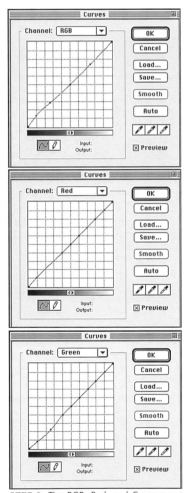

STEP 8: The selection, before the Gaussian Blur of 25, used to fix the dark and green area in the Buildings layer.

STEP 8: The RGB, Red, and Green curve changes to fix the dark and green areas in the Buildings layer. Yours may be different.

that are too dark and too green. Don't worry about the selection going up into the sky; the sky will eventually come from the Sky layer and we are currently working on things in the Buildings layer. Click the Save Selection icon in the Channels palette to save this new selection, and then name it Green Fix. Click Green Fix in the Channels palette and choose Select/None. You will want the edge of this selection that is in the courtyard and on the buildings to have a large feather so that the color and darkness changes will blend over a larger area. Use Filter/Blur/Gaussian Blur, Shift-F4, to give this about a 25-pixel blur. Doing a Gaussian Blur of a channel, instead of just choosing Select/Feather, allows you to see the distance over which the blend will happen and change the blur amount (similar to Feather amount) as needed. Now click this channel and drag it to the Load Selection icon, which is left-most at the bottom of the Channels palette. Click the top layer, which should be the Hue/Saturation layer for the Buildings. Now Command-click the New Layer icon in the Layer palette to create an Adjustment layer of type Curves. The selection you loaded will automatically save into the layer mask of this Adjustment layer so that only the selected parts of the Buildings layer will be modified. Measure with the Eyedropper to find the areas you want to adjust. Pressing down with the Eyedropper tool while in Curves will show you where that dropper location occurs in the Curve to make the adjustment for the darkness of the area as well as the green color balance.

You can use these great, new Photoshop 5 features to help you in this situation. When you find the location in the curve you want to adjust, Command-clicking the screen where the Eyedropper is, at that location, will place a point on the corresponding location on the RGB curve. This is great for adjusting the brightness and contrast of that location. If you Command-Shift-click the screen at the Eyedropper location, Photoshop 5 will place points on each of the Red, Green, and Blue curves where that clicked location is on each of those curves. It may be a different location on each curve. This is a great, new feature that you can take great advantage of in this type of subtle color correction situation! Now go into each of the Red, Green and Blue curves and tweak the color at the point Photoshop placed there. You may have to place other points on either side of that point to lock down other parts of the curve. Also new for Photoshop 5 is the ability to place up to four Color Sampler points in the image and track how the color is changing at each of these points when you make a Curve, or other, color adjustment. To do this, just Shift-click on the screen to place a new Color Sampler point. The Color Sampler readout values show up at the bottom of the Info Palette. If you want to move an existing Color Sampler point, Shift-click it and drag to a new location.

I used the curves pictured here to fix this part of the image. You may want to use one Curve Adjustment layer to lighten the dark areas and a second one to adjust the color balance. Click OK in Curves when you are happy with your changes. Now you should zoom out so you can see the entire image and then toggle between having and not having this change by turning the Eye icon for this Curves layer on and off. If you made a good correction, you should see a significant improvement in the selected area of the image. If you are not happy, double-click the Curve layer and change the curve. You can also use the Paintbrush to paint white or black in the layer mask for each Adjustment layer to modify which areas are actually changed by this curve adjustment. Do a Command-S to save the file and these new layers.

TWEAKING THE LAYER MASK

STEP 9: Now that you have your final color corrections done, you will notice some jagginess or tell-tale brightness variation along the edge between the sky and the buildings. Wherever the layer mask is black, you are seeing the sky from the underlying layer. Wherever the layer mask is white, you are viewing the Buildings layer. You may notice that the edge between the buildings and the sky is sort of jagged. That's because you made this mask using Threshold. Click the Buildings layer mask thumbnail in the Layers palette so that the Channels palette Buildings Mask is active, highlighted, but the Eye icons are on for RGB, Red, Green, and Blue. Now go into Filter/Blur/Gaussian Blur to blur your mask by about .5 to .7 pixels. This will make the edge blend better. Type D to set the default colors, and then you can use the Paintbrush, B, to paint with white in the layer mask to see more from the Buildings layer. You can also type X to exchange the colors. Then you can paint with black to see more from the darker Sky layer. Use a small brush and fine-tune the mask along the edge to get even better blending between the two images. Remember that you can change the opacity of the Paintbrush by typing a number like 5 for 50% or 0 for 100%. Often a partial opacity mask adjustment is just what you need. You can use the left and right bracket keys to move to the next brush on the left or right in the Brushes palette. To draw straight line segments, click one end of the line and then Shift-click the other end. When you are finished here, do a Command-S to save the file.

MERGING THE LAYERS AND SMOOTHING THE BORDER

STEP 10: Click on the top layer in the Layers palette to activate it and then Option-click the New Layer icon to create a new layer and name it Merged. Hold down the Option key while choosing Merge Visible from the Layers palette menu. This will merge all the visible layers into this new top layer. You can now use the Gaussian Blur filter to reduce any remaining edge jagginess. Command-click the Buildings layer mask to load a selection from it. Choose Select/Modify/Border and set the border to 4 pixels. This will make a selection of 4 pixels wide on either side of the border between the buildings and the sky, and also around the sides and bottom of the image. Now use the Lasso tool (L) with the Option key down to circle the sides and bottom of this selection and remove them, leaving only the selection along the border between the sky and buildings. Choose Select/Feather to feather this selection by 1 pixel. Now do Select/Hide Edges (Command-H) to hide this selection, and then do a Filter/Blur/Gaussian Blur (Shift-F4) of .5 to blur the edge in the selected area. This should remove any remaining jagginess or color differences along the edge of the two images. Scroll along the edge at 100% to see if this improves your image. If it does, choose OK, if it doesn't, choose cancel. Option-click the Save Selection icon in the Channels palette to save this selection, and name it Border. You may want to use it again later.

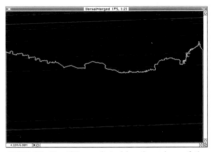

STEP 10: Use this mask to blur the edges of the border you have merged together.

SHARPENING AND SPOTTING

STEP 11: Now do Filter/Sharpen/Unsharp Mask (F4) of 150, 1.5, 4 to finalize this image. If the edge along the border becomes jaggy again, undo the sharpen and do a Load Selection of the channel you called Border. Choose Select/Inverse to select everything except for the border. Now redo the Unsharp Mask, and the border will be excluded from the sharpen. You might not want to sharpen the edge along the border because it could emphasize any imperfections generated from the merging of the two images. The Gaussian Blur and Unsharp Mask have to be done after the Merge Layers for their effects to be properly seen along the edge of the selection.

STEP 12: The Versailles image after removing the green tinge, lightening the edges, and using the Rubber Stamp tool to remove any spots or blemishes. This version of the image was also sharpened using the Unsharp Mask filter with the 150, 1.5, 4 settings.

STEP 12: Zoom into the image at 100% or closer. Use the Rubber Stamp tool with a small brush to clone out any dust spots. You always have to recheck this after final sharpening because sharpening can enhance dust spots that previously were not visible. Do Command-S to save this image along with all its layers and channels.

USING LAYERS TO APPLY FILTERS

By scanning, combining, color correcting, and sharpening, we've created a great straight photograph that we could use as our final image. If you would like to create a photo with a more surrealistic look, the following steps give you some ideas of how to use layers to enhance an image by applying filters with different opacities and Blend modes.

STEP 13: Start with the final Versailles image from step 12 of this chapter. Click on the Merged layer at the top and Option-drag it to the New Layer icon at the bottom of the Layers palette. Call this layer NoiseSky. Choose Filter/Noise/Add Noise to create Gaussian noise with an amount of 25. This will add a grainy appearance to the image. Command-click the Buildings layer mask in the Layers palette to load the mask as a selection; then Option-click the new Layer Mask icon to add a layer mask to the NoiseSky layer. The Option-click inverts the mask to remove the buildings, instead of the sky, from this layer. Now you see only the noise in the sky.

STEP 14: Option-drag the Merged layer to the New Layer icon in the Layers palette and call this layer UM500,10,0. We are going to apply the Unsharp Mask filter to this layer and use it as a special effect. Click this new layer and drag it to the top of the Layers palette. Then release when you see the black line above the NoiseSky layer.

STEP 15: Choose Filter/Sharpen/Unsharp Mask (F4) and set the parameters to 500 for the Amount, 10 for the Radius, and 0 for the Threshold. Click OK to run the filter on this layer. This gives the photo a dramatic effect, but we may not want this effect to be completely applied.

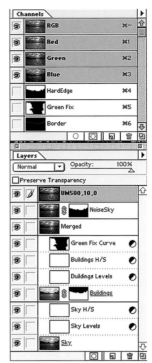

STEP 15: The Layers and Channels palettes at the end of step 15. My final image uses this order of layers but has the opacity of the UM500,10,0 layer set to 25% and the Opacity of the NoiseSky layer set to 75% with its Blend mode set to Overlay.

STEP 16: Change the mode on the NoiseSky layer to Overlay and set the Opacity to 75%.

STEP 16: Now you have two copies of the final Merged layer with filters applied to them. You can now combine the Merged layer and these new filter layers to produce a variety of effects. What we want to do now is apply the mask/filter layers at different opacities and use different Blend modes until we get the effect we want. The noise filter was a little bit too grainy, so I changed the NoiseSky Blend mode to Overlay and its Opacity to 75%. Because I had applied this layer using a mask of only the sky area, these changes affect only the sky. To see these changes, you need to turn off the Eye icon on the UM500,10,0 layer.

STEP 17: The Unsharp Mask filter of 500,10,0 produced a dramatic effect, but what I wanted to do was use this effect to slightly dramatize the image but still leave it in a more natural state. To do this, I activated the UM500,10,0 layer by clicking it and then set its Opacity to 25%.

STEP 18: You can also turn on or off a particular layer completely by turning on or off its Eye icon. This allows you to see what the image looks like with or without that layer applied. You can Option-click the Eye icon of a layer to look at just that one layer. Try turning off or on particular layers to see how it affects your final image. Try changing the opacity of different layers and also changing the composite modes.

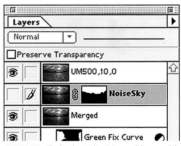

STEP 18: To look at the Merged layer with just the Unsharp Mask layer applied at 25% on top, turn off the Eye icon for the NoiseSky layer.

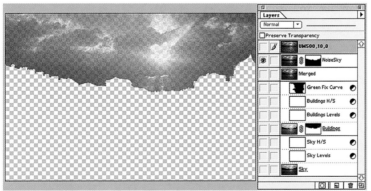

STEP 18: To look at the NoiseSky layer only, Option-click its Eye icon. The bottom part of this layer is removed by its layer mask, and the sky is partially transparent because the Opacity is set to 75%. Option-click its Eye icon again to turn all the other layers back on.

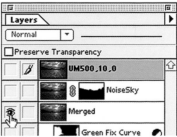

STEP 18: To look at the Merged layer only, Option-click the Eye icon for that layer.

Using Layers to Apply Filters

STEP 19: To move USM500 to between NoiseSky and Merged, click USM500 and drag it downward. When you see the line between the other two layers turn black, let go.

STEP 19: Besides changing the opacity and composite mode of your layers, you can also change the order of the layers. By applying the filters in different orders, you can change the appearance of the final effect. To change the order of a layer, just click the layer that you want to move and drag it up or down to its new location. When the line between two layers becomes black, then you can release the mouse to drop your layer between these two. Try all these things out to see which variation you like best.

The final version of this image, along with the filter effects, was produced by using three layers. The original Merged layer was the image from step 12 of this example after we removed the green tinge and ran Unsharp Mask for basic sharpening. We then made a layer to add 75% of the Noise filter to the sky using the Overlay Blend mode. The third and final layer adds 25% of the Unsharp Mask 500, 10, 0 to the entire image area. This makes the image more dramatic without taking away all the image detail that 100% of Unsharp Mask would have removed.

3 HANDS-ON SESSION: The Band

Create a composite of the band, Only Human, from nonmatching original files using channels, layers, and graduated masks; color correct and adjust these images to match as closely as possible.

When you are compositing photographs, you need to either color correct each of them separately before you composite them, or you can combine them first and then color correct the final image as one. The Layers feature in Photoshop 5 will allow us to combine the images first and still color correct each of them separately after compositing them. This will allow us to do the color corrections while we are looking at how the images are combining. To do this example, you will be using the Tool palette, the Channels and Layers palettes, the Info palette, and sometimes the Color palette. Refer to the chapter on navigating to learn the most efficient ways to use these palettes. Refer to Chapter 5: Setting System and Photoshop Preferences to see how to set up the ArtistKeys Actions to open and close the various palettes. You will also be using the Levels and Curves tools, and should have already gone through Chapter 19: The Grand Canyon, which explains their basic functionality. These images were saved using the ColorMatch RGB settings so working on them in that RGB color-space will give you the same histograms and numerical results as this example.

SETTING THINGS UP

STEP 1: Open the three files—Johnny, Chris, and Beth—from the folder The Band. Place them in order with Johnny on the left, Chris in the middle, and Beth on the right. This is the order in which we will composite the photos together.

STEP 2: Click on Chris to make him the active window, and double-click on the Background Layer and rename it to Chris. By renaming Chris' background layer, we converted it into a normal layer. Adding Canvas to a normal layer will make the extra canvas transparent versus the canvas of the background color we would have gotten if we had left it as a background layer. Transparent canvas won't effect the Histograms of Chris when color correcting, but canvas of the background color would. Now go to Image/Canvas Size (Command-F8) to change the width of Chris to be three times the original width. We will be placing Johnny at Chris' left and Beth at Chris' right, so keep the gray area in the middle of the grid, which will add the extra whitespace evenly to either side of Chris. Just triple the value in the width field and click on OK. Now save this version of Chris in Photoshop format and call it TheBand.

STEP 3: Using the Move tool to drag and drop Johnny on top of Chris.

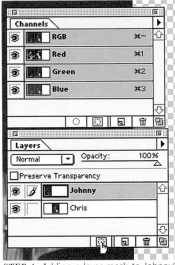

STEP 4: Adding a layer mask to Johnny's layer.

STEP 5: What Johnny and Chris look like after the gradient is created and before Johnny is moved over.

BLENDING JOHNNY INTO CHRIS

STEP 3: Use the Move tool to drag and drop Johnny on top of Chris. Just click on the center of Johnny's image and drag the cursor over the top of Chris' image; then release the mouse button. This adds Johnny as a new layer on top of Chris. You could close the Johnny file now, if you are short on memory.

STEP 4: Double-click on the new layer in the Layers palette and call it Johnny. Use the Move tool (choose V, or press the Command key) to move Johnny over to the left of Chris. Click on the Add Layer Mask icon at the bottom left of the Layers palette to add a layer mask to Johnny's layer. Click on the Black/White Default Colors icon, or type D to force the foreground color to white and the background color to black. D gives us white in the foreground (which means select this image) and black in the background (don't select this image) when working on a Mask channel. When working on an image layer, D gives us a black foreground and a white background.

STEP 5: Double-click on the Linear Gradient tool (G) and choose Reset Tool from the Gradient Tool Options menu. This will reset all the default options in the Gradient tool. Use the tool while holding down the Shift key to create a blend from white to black starting just to the right of Johnny's face and dragging right to the right edge of the Johnny layer. The Shift key will constrain the blend to horizontal. You should let go of the tool when you reach the right edge of Johnny. Don't go beyond this right edge or this image will not fade completely out and you'll see a faint line. In the layer mask, you have defined the area where Johnny and Chris will blend together. Where the layer mask is black, Johnny's image is completely gone and where it is white, Johnny's image is completely there.

STEP 6: Use the Move tool (V or Command) and slowly drag Johnny to the right until the transparent area between Johnny and Chris disappears completely. If you find that you are having trouble making subtle movements with the mouse, you can use the arrow keys to move your selection one pixel at a time (Shift-arrow moves your selection 10 pixels at a time). We'll color correct Johnny after we add Beth to the image.

STEP 5: Creating the gradient that will blend Johnny into Chris.

STEP 6: What Johnny and Chris look like after Johnny is moved over.

BLENDING BETH INTO CHRIS

STEP 7: Switch to the image of Beth and use the Move tool to drag and drop Beth on top of Chris. Move her completely to the right of Chris. Double-click on the new layer and call it Beth. Add a layer mask to her layer by using the left-most icon at the bottom of the Layers palette. Use the Gradient tool (G) and click to the left of her face; drag to the left edge (not beyond) with the Shift key down to blend out this part of her image. Use the Move tool (V or hold Command key down) to move her to the left until she blends in nicely with Chris. You can always change how Beth or Johnny blend with Chris by just using the Gradient tool again in their layer masks and then moving their layers as needed.

REMOVING PICTURE ELEMENTS

STEP 8: Press Command-0 to zoom out and see the entire Chris canvas. Type C to get the Crop tool and then click and drag a rectangle around the edge of the three band members. Click and drag in the handles (the little squares around the edge) to fine-tune the cropping box, making sure all the white or transparent borders are removed. Hold down the Command key while dragging the Cropping box handles to turn off the new Photoshop 5 default "snap-to-grid" along the edge of the image area. Now press Return (or Enter) to do the crop. You now have the three images blended together and cropped in their final size. Press Command-S at this point to save the file on top of the existing version of TheBand. Now you can revert to this version of the image if you are not happy with the following changes.

STEP 9: At this point, we have a problem with Beth's image, because the amplifier covers up Chris' arm and his cymbal. Click on the right column of Beth's layer in the

STEP 10: The amplifier before it is removed by the layer mask.

STEP 10: The amplifier after it has been removed by the layer mask.

Layers palette to activate (highlight) Beth's layer. This allows you to work on Beth's layer without changing Johnny or Chris. If you click on the Eye icon of Beth's layer, it will turn off and you will see that Chris' layer is black underneath the area where the amplifier is added beside Beth. If we could just remove the area of Beth's image where the amplifier is and see Chris' image in its place, that would solve our problem. To do this, we will use the existing layer mask. Click on the Eye icon of Beth again to make her layer visible. Her layer should also be the active layer, the one that is highlighted. Click on the layer mask thumbnail to the right of Beth's layer thumbnail. Arrange things on your monitor so you can see the entire Layers palette and the entire Channels palette at the same time. Depending on the state of the Layers palette, it is important that you understand which channel(s) are actually being edited versus the channels that are only being viewed. Only the highlighted channels can be changed. You will notice that the Eye icons are on for Red, Green, and Blue, but the layer mask is active (highlighted). Painting now will affect the mask.

STEP 10: With Beth's layer mask activated, edits will change only the mask, which will add or subtract things to the appearance of Beth's layer without actually changing her layer. Because the Eye icons are selected on all the layers and all the channels, you will see everything while this is happening. Only the activated (highlighted) channel is actually changed.

STEP 10: Anything that is black in the layer mask will make the corresponding part of Beth's layer not show. This is how the gradient removed her left side. Use the Paintbrush tool with 100% opacity and a large brush to paint over the amplifier with black as the foreground color. As you paint, the painted parts of Beth's layer will disappear and Chris' layer will show through from below. Paint over the amplifier and also over Chris' shirt and arm in the area where Beth's black background overlaps Chris. Now type a 5 to set the brush to 50% opacity. Then switch to a soft edge brush, and use this to blend in the two backgrounds above where the amplifier used to be. As you move further away from the amplifier, you may want to use only 30% opacity; to do this, type a 3. Blend the two images around the edges of the area you removed.

STEP 11: If a transparent area starts to appear as you paint, you have reached the edge of the Chris layer's data. You will have to click on the Chris layer and clone (with the Rubber Stamp tool) some of the background area beyond the edge so it can replace Beth's background in the layer above. Now Option-click on the Beth's layer mask thumbnail and you can view the mask without the layers. Notice how the black and gray areas in the mask cause the two layers to blend.

STEP 11: Option-click on the layer mask to see it by itself.

COLOR CORRECTING THE IMAGE

STEP 12: Notice the coloration on Johnny is much redder than that of Chris or Beth. He was standing under a red light when photographed. Because he is so different, we should correct him to make him look closer to the others before proceeding with overall color correction. All these photos were taken without flash, using ASA 1600 film, which is why they are so dark and grainy. Click on the right column of Johnny's layer, making it active (highlighted) and allowing us to edit this layer while still seeing the others. Click in the right column in the Channels palette of each of the channels: Red (Command-1), Green (Command-2), and Blue (Command-3). You will notice that the Red channel of Johnny has lots of detail but the Green and Blue channels have very little detail, especially when compared to those channels of Beth and Chris. This is why Johnny looks so red and so flat. Because Johnny doesn't have detail in the Green and Blue channels, we will first have to add some detail there to be able to color correct him in the normal way using Levels or Curves.

STEP 13: We are going to modify the individual channels of Johnny to make them look more like the channels of Chris and Beth. This will make his color in RGB a lot closer, and will add detail to the Green and Blue channels so we can color correct him further using the color correction tools. Click on the Johnny layer to make sure it is the active layer. Choose Red (Command-1) from the Channels palette. Use the Image/Adjust/Brightness/Contrast slider and move the contrast to the left to about –7 and the brightness to the right to about +12 to make the Red channel of Johnny have similar brightness and contrast to the Red channels of Chris and Beth. You want the Preview button in Brightness/Contrast on so you can see the changes to Johnny without any screen changes happening to Chris and Beth. Click on OK in the

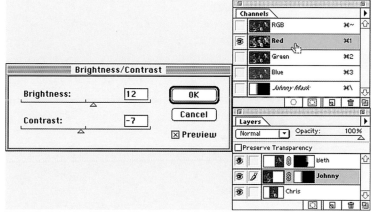

STEP 13: Adjusting Brightness/Contrast on Johnny's Red channel. Make sure your Layers and Channels palettes look like this.

Brightness/Contrast tool. Type a D to get the default colors. Choose RGB (Command-~) from the Channels palette to select the Red, Green, and Blue channels of Johnny. Choose Select/All, Command-A, from the Select menu, followed by Edit/Stroke, and stroke the border with a 100% opacity, normal stroke of 4 pixels on the center of the selection. This will draw a black 4-pixel border around the entire image in Johnny's layer. Now choose the Red channel of Johnny again (Command-1) and do a Select/All followed by Edit/Copy to make a copy of the Red channel of Johnny. The black border needed to be drawn to remove transparency from the right two-thirds of the channel, so when we paste this channel on top of the Green channel, it goes down in exactly the same place. If we had not done this, the Copy would have only copied the left one-third of Johnny's Red channel (the nontransparent part) and then the paste on the Green channel, in the next step, would not line up correctly.

STEP 14: Switch the Channels palette to the Green channel (Command-2). Paste Johnny's Red channel on top of Johnny's Green channel. Use Filter/Fade to change the opacity of Johnny's pasted Red channel to somewhere around 52%. Change the opacity until Johnny's Green channel looks like and blends well with Chris' and Beth's. Look at the tone and brightness of Johnny's face and also make sure the backgrounds look similar as they blend together.

STEP 15: Switch to the Blue channel (Command-3); your change to the Green channel has now been made permanent. Now paste Johnny's Red channel (still in the Copy Buffer) on top of the Blue channel and use Filter/Fade to adjust the opacity to

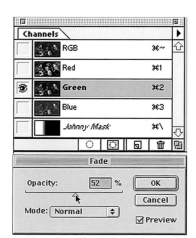

STEP 14: Use Filter/Fade to change the opacity of Johnny's Red channel (on top of the Green channel) to about 52% or until Johnny looks similar to Beth and Chris in the Green channel.

make Johnny's blue look like the Blue channel of Chris and Beth. Set it to somewhere around 18%. If you click on the Eye icon of the RGB channel, this will turn on the ability to see full color but the Blue channel will still be the only one highlighted. You can now change the opacity of Red on top of Blue while seeing how this changes the color of RGB. This process is similar to using the new Photoshop 5 Channel Mixer feature. The advantage of doing it this way is that you can see how each channel blends as a single channel in grayscale or turn on the Eye icons for RGB and see the effect on color. The Channel Mixer (used to fix a similar problem in Color Correcting Al) gives you a nice color preview but doesn't allow the black and white preview of each channel. The advantage of using the Channel Mixer is that it can be done as an Adjustment layer, which gives you the ability to more easily make changes later.

STEP 16: Using the Channels palette again, switch back to the RGB channel (Command-~). This will make the Blue channel change permanent. Now Johnny should look much closer to Chris and Beth than when we started. Johnny is never going to look as good colorwise as Chris and Beth because we are making most of his color from the Red channel. Don't try to be a perfectionist here; just get them close and understand the process for future corrections on your own projects. Now use the Crop tool (C) to crop the 4-pixel black border from around the image. Make a selection just inside this border and press Return to crop. Don't forget to use the Command key to stop the Crop tool from locking on the edges of the image. Now that there is color information in each of Johnny's channels, you can use the other color correction tools to make him seem even closer in color to Chris and Beth.

TheBand after Step 16 and before final overall color correction.

STEP 17: You now want to do overall color correction for the entire image. It is best here to correct each image layer separately while looking at the merged image to make sure the corrections match. This approach gives you more control and demonstrates an advantage of leaving the image in layers until the last possible minute. Do a File/Save As to save this version as TheBand.2.

OVERALL COLOR CORRECTION

STEP 18: Now we will do the standard overall color corrections to each of the three layers, matching them as we go. You will adjust the overall contrast and color balance of each of the layers using Levels, with the techniques discussed in Chapter 19: The Grand Canyon. Click on the Chris layer (right column) to make it the active layer. Choose Command-L for Levels and look at the histogram of Chris. Because Chris is in the middle, let's first set the white and black points. Use the techniques described in Chapter 19: The Grand Canyon to decide where to set the white and black points. I used the Option key with Video-LUT animation to set the white to the brightest place on his shirt using the Highlight Eyedropper, and I set the black by moving the Input Shadow slider on each of the Red, Green, and Blue channels to the right until it reached the Histogram data for each color. I decided not to use the Shadow Eyedropper to set the black because the blacks in this image are not very consistent. By moving the Shadow Eyedroppers over to where the data starts in each color, you get

Chapter 33: The Band

a definite dark value. You then need to look at and measure the black values on the screen and adjust them so each of Chris, Beth, and Johnny have a visually matching black. I actually moved each of Chris' black values over 5 more points to the right. After the overall white and black are set, adjust the Input Brightness/Contrast slider in RGB mode, and then go back to the individual channels to correct for color casts. Review Chapters 19 and 20 if you have any questions on overall color correction.

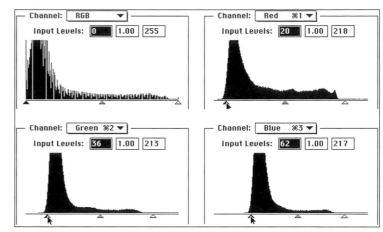

STEP 18: My final Levels color correction settings for Chris. Yours may be different.

STEP 19: Click on the Save button to save the Levels changes you want to make to Chris; call it ChrisFinalLevels. Now Cancel from Levels and Command-click on the New Layer icon, or choose New Adjustment Layer from the Layers Palette menu, to add a Levels adjustment layer to Chris' layer. Name it Chris Levels and set the type menu to Levels. Click the Group with Previous Layer option so that the adjustments you make here will affect only Chris' layer. Using adjustment layers here will allow us to go back and change the Levels adjustment on any of the three images as many times as needed without damaging the data of the image because the changes are not actually made until the image is flattened. Choose OK in New Adjustment Layer; then click on the Load button to load the changes we just saved at the end of working on the Chris layer in Levels. Now click on OK in Levels. We made the changes in Levels first because Adjustment layers don't allow you to use Video LUT Animation to instantly see before and after while evaluating subtle color changes to a layer. For more info on Video LUT Animation, see Chapter 19.

STEP 20: Now click on Beth's layer to color correct it. Command-click on the New Layer icon and add an Adjustment layer of Type Levels that is grouped to the Beth layer and called BethLevels. Because we want to see the changes to Beth in relation to Chris, we will have to work with the Preview button on in Levels this time because we went directly into an Adjustment layer. I set the white point with the Highlight Eyedropper in RGB on Beth's forehead, but not at the absolute brightest spot there. You don't want her whole forehead washed out, but a little bright spot there looks good. Remember, you set the white point at the last place where you want to see detail, and everything brighter than that will be pure white with no dots or detail. If you set it on the absolute brightest spot, there will be no specular highlight and that is not really what you want either. I set the black on Beth in the same way I did on Chris by moving the Input Shadow sliders for each color channel to the right until the data starts. I then adjusted the color balance on Beth to match Chris—his face, lighting, and background. Click on OK to finalize the Levels changes. Beth may be further improved by using Hue/Saturation to clean up the yellows in her hair. Some of the yellow hair looked green to me, but adding magenta in Levels messed up the rest of the image. I did this by Command-clicking again on the New Layer

STEP 20: My final Levels color correction settings for Beth. Yours may be different.

STEP 20: Final Hue/Saturation/Lightness changes for the yellows in Beth.

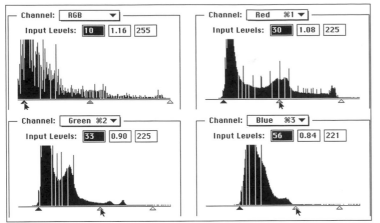

STEP 21: My final Levels color correction settings for Johnny, called JohnnyFinalLevels, in the Extra Info Files for this chapter on the CD. Notice how little data there is in the Blue channel here. Your settings for Johnny will probably be different because each of us have already adjusted Johnny in a slightly different way.

icon to add a new Hue/Saturation adjustment layer Grouped to the Previous Layer(s) so only Beth was changed. Now just make the changes to Beth's Hue and Saturation in Yellow and click on OK.

STEP 21: Now we need to adjust Johnny to make him look like Chris and Beth. As usual, Johnny will be the hardest image to adjust. Again, you want to switch the active layer you are working on to Johnny by clicking in the right-most column in the Johnny layer. Now, again Command-click on the New Layer icon in the Layers palette to add a Levels Adjustment layer Grouped with the Johnny layer. The only white point on Johnny is the reflection in his guitar, and this is pretty much a specular highlight. It is most important to make sure that the lighting on Johnny's face matches Chris and Beth as much as possible. To set the highlight, I moved the Input Highlight sliders for each of the Red, Green, and Blue channels over to the left until they were at about 225. This made Johnny's face look the best. I set the shadows on Johnny again by moving the Input Shadow sliders over to the right to where the data started and then a little bit more, moving each slider by the same increments. Then it's back to RGB to adjust the Brightness/Contrast slider in the middle and at the same time moving the Input Shadow slider (RGB) to the right to darken the shadows a bit more in all colors. Go back and forth between these two sliders so the shadows and the brightness/contrast looks like the best match with Chris and Beth. Remember to leave the Preview button on. Now go back into the individual color channels and make any color cast adjustments and then press the OK button to finalize your Levels changes to Johnny.

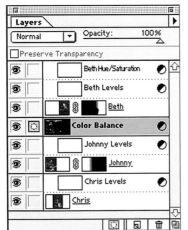

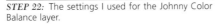

STEP 22: The settings I used for the Johnny Color Balance layer.

STEP 22: With this layer and adjustment layer setup, we can go back and change the color of each of the band members as many times as we like. Since the changes are happening in an adjustment layer, the actual data in the digital file will not have permanent changes to it until we create a flattened version of the image.

STEP 22: Johnny's face is sort of flat compared to Beth and Chris, and his background doesn't match either. To fix this, click on the Johnny Levels layer and then Command-click on the New Layer icon to add a new Color Balance Adjustment layer above Johnny Levels and Grouped to Johnny Levels. Turn on Preserve Luminosity in Color Balance and then add lots of red and magenta in the midtones to make a stronger version of the highlight color you will add to Johnny's face. Click on OK in Color Balance. Now choose Edit/Fill (Shift-Delete, Shift-Back Space on Windows) and fill the layer mask of this Adjustment layer with black to remove this color change everywhere. Type a D to get the default colors of White for the foreground and Black for the background. Now airbrush with white at 5% Opacity with the Airbrush tool using a soft brush to add red highlights to Johnny's face. Wherever you paint with white in the mask, the Color Balance change will be applied. Just slowly add the reddish highlights to Johnny's face to better match that of Chris and Beth. In the end, I noticed a few greenish areas in the upper-middle background of Chris, and also on his shirt, so I Option-clicked on the line between the Johnny Levels layer and this new Color Balance layer to ungroup this from Johnny Levels. I was then able to paint with

Chapter 33: The Band

white in the mask above Chris to remove these greenish tones also. To use this layer to alter anything in the Beth layers, I would have had to drag it above the Beth layers as well. If you are having problems matching the background areas or the faces, use the new Photoshop 5 Color Sampler to add sampling Eyedroppers to the hard to match areas of each image. You can then create a grouped Curves Adjustment layer with a Lockdown Curve over a layer to change and match the value read in a different layer. See Chapter 27: Color Matching Images and Chapter 32: Versailles for examples of this type of situation.

STEP 22: The final mask used for the Color Balance layer.

MAKING FINAL ADJUSTMENTS

STEP 23: Now you have completed the compositing and color correction steps. Use File/Save As to save a version of this image and call it TheBandFinalLayers. You can use this version to show your clients the image, and you can also use the Move tool to move Johnny and Beth up and down and in closer to Chris if you want variations. If you want to move Beth and Johnny out farther away from Chris, drag Chris' layer to the New Layer icon at the bottom of the Layers palette. This will make a copy of

STEP 25: The final completed version of TheBand.

Chris' layer right above the current one. Select the bottom version of Chris and fill it with Chris' background color. Now, if you move Johnny or Beth outward, instead of the transparent halo you got before, you just get more of Chris' background and it looks pretty natural.

STEP 24: Before sharpening and spotting this image, you need to choose Flatten Image from the Layers palette pop-up menu. This will merge everything back into a single document that you can save as a TIFF, EPS, or in some other format. Save it under a different name if you want to still be able to play with your layered version. Now that you have just one layer, use Filter/Sharpen/Unsharp Mask to sharpen the image and then use the Rubber Stamp tool to remove any scratches or spots or imperfections in the image. There is a hairline scratch from the top to the bottom of the image just to the right of Johnny's face. Beth has a black hole in the corner of her lip and there are various dust spots and lines. These all need to be removed. For further information on sharpening and spotting, see Chapters 23 and 24.

STEP 25: Save the final version of the file. You can compare your different versions of this image to the ones of the same name that I created. They are in the Extra Info Files folder.

HANDS-ON SESSION: The McNamaras

Using Adjustment layers and layer masks to color correct and composite the McNamaras' family portrait, where we need to move six smiling faces into the final image to create one where everyone is smiling.

I was an only child, so while growing up it was always more fun to go over to the McNamaras and play with their six kids. Now, as adults, we still get together a lot and I have had the joy of taking two of their five-year family portraits. Taking a family portrait of this many people, and especially this many kids along with their parents, is not the easiest task. I also wanted to use my 4x5 camera so there would be the maximum amount of detail in the image. All the kids are wiggling around, so it's hard to get them to smile at the camera, and then the parents often look down and give directions to their children at just that moment when all the children are actually looking at the camera. I knew this would be difficult to do with the 4x5, so I also brought along my trusty Canon F1 and shot two rolls of 35. With the 35mm stuff, I actually did get one picture where everyone was smiling and looking at the camera. That was the shot we used for the McNamara family. Still, though, I wanted to make a 4x5 version, because it would have so much more detail. Scans, with the Leaf 45 scanner, were made of enough of the 4x5 images that I had at least one smiling face of each person. Here we are going to composite all of them together to create the family portrait where everyone is smiling!

The images in this chapter were created using the ColorMatchRGB workspace. If you are using a different RGB space, things may look a little different on your system.

STEP 1: Make sure that the version of Photoshop you are going to use for this example is already running. Bring up the new Photoshop 5 History palette (Command-F8) and use the History Options menu to make sure you are saving about 40 steps of history. This will help you undo any mistakes made when retouching to blend the new images in. If you have not used the History palette before, read Chapter 12: History Palette, History Brush, and Snapshots because you will find the History palette very useful here. From the Finder or File Manager, open the McNamaras

The original McNamaras image before color correction or the addition of the smiling faces.

folder and do Select All on all the files that end in JPG. The files for this example were JPEG-compressed. Choose File/Open from the Finder and all of them will open into Photoshop at once. If this doesn't work on your system, just open each of the files using the File/Open command in Photoshop. Choose the file McNamaras-Orig from the Photoshop Window menu and put it in Full Screen mode by clicking on the middle icon at the bottom of the Tool palette or by typing F. Type C to bring up the Cropping tool and crop out any black or white borders around the image. Choose File/Save As and save it as McNamarasPortrait.

STEP 2: Choose Image/Adjust/Levels to start the overall correction for the main McNamaras image. We are going to do this in Levels, on the layer versus an Adjustment layer, so we can use Video LUT Animation in the initial correction. Then we will save the Levels settings, cancel from Levels, and load those settings into a Levels Adjustment layer. Go through the basic levels adjustment, which you learned about in Chapter19: The Grand Canyon. You may want to review that chapter if you are not sure what to do here. I used the Highlight and Shadow Eyedroppers to set the highlight on one of the white chairs and the shadow in the darkest leaves along the top of the photo. You can load my levels settings, called LevelsOne, from the Extra Info Files folder on the CD if you want to check them out. When you are happy with the Overall Levels settings, click on the Save button in Levels and save these settings in a file called MyLevelsOne. Then hit the Cancel button to exit Levels. Now Command-click on the New Layer icon to create an Adjustment layer of Type Levels, and call it McLevels. Make sure you turn on the Group with Previous Layer option; then click on the Load button to load the MyLevelsOne setting you just saved. Now choose OK. We did this using an Adjustment layer so that we would have the option of changing it later after we get all the faces composited in. Now create another adjustment layer of type Hue Saturation, also Grouped with the Previous layer, and call it McHueSat. Do the Overall Saturation adjustments for the McNamaras family like we did in Chapter 19: The Grand Canyon. My adjustments are called HueSatMc, in case you would like to use the Load button in the Hue/Saturation dialog box to check them out. The contrast and saturation on this scan is just a bit off. In fact, some of the face scans look better and you'll need to bring the McNamaras image up to their level. In the end they just all need to match and also make a pleasing color portrait. Choose OK in the Hue/Saturation dialog box when you are happy with the added saturation and tonal changes.

STEP 3: The Layers palette after moving all the smiling faces into the work file.

ADDING THE SMILING FACES

STEP 3: Type M to switch to the Move tool; and then use the Window menu to switch one at a time to each of the smiling face images and drag and drop it with the Move tool on top of the same person's face in your McNamarasPortrait image underneath. If you put the cursor on the nose in the smiling version, and then drag to the same person's nose in the McNamaras layer and release the mouse button at that point, you will have a good start on lining up the two heads. Go ahead and drag and drop each smiling person into their own layer, giving that layer the name for that person. The names of the smiling people's files are the actual names of that particular person. After dragging each person into their own layer, you can File/Close (Command-W) the file for that person. When you have moved all six people into their approximate position, go ahead and press Command-S to save the McNamaras-Portrait with all their layers. Your Layers palette should now look like this one here.

Chapter 34: The McNamaras

STEP 4: Some of the smiling layers will overlap each other, but don't worry about that now, because we are going to work on each one of them separately to integrate it into the image in a custom way. Turn off the Eye icons for all the smiling face layers except for Jackey. You still want the Eye icons on for the McNamaras layer and its Adjustment layers. Click on the Jackey layer to make it active, and then type a 5 to set its opacity to 50%. You can now see 50% of the Jackey layer and 50% of the original image of Jackey underneath. Use the Move tool (V) to move the Jackey layer around a bit until you figure out which 50% comes from this layer. The face in the Jackey layer is a bit bigger than the original face underneath. Use the Move tool to line up the

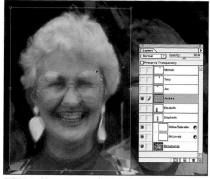

STEP 4: Here you see the two Jackeys before they are lined up. Pick an absolute position in the center of the image area, like her glasses' corner here, put the cursor on that position, and then drag the cursor to the same position in the other layer to move the Jackey layer and line them up. You can use the arrow keys to scroll by one pixel and fine-tune the positioning. After you adjust the position, you may have to rescale a bit, readjust a bit, and so on, until you get it right.

STEP 4: Here is how the two Jackeys look after they are lined up.

glasses and lips on each layer as best you can. Now choose Layer/Free Transform (Command-T) and use the Free Transform command to scale this Jackey layer exactly and move it into the exact position above the original head below. Remember to hold down the Shift key while clicking and dragging in one of the corner handles to make your scaling be proportional. To move the layer while in Free Transform, just click and drag in the middle of the box that defines the current image or use the arrow keys for fine adjustment. Press Return to end the Free Transform.

STEP 5: Type L to bring up the Lasso tool, and then press Return to bring up its Options palette. Now type a 2, and then press Return again to set the feather at 2. Now make a selection around the inside of Jackey's face. This is the part of her face we are going to use from the Jackey layer. Now click on the Layer Mask icon (the left-most one at the bottom of the Layers palette). You may notice a color difference between the skin and hair on the Jackey layer and the skin and hair in the original image. To fix this, add a Levels or Curves Adjustment layer above the Jackey layer and grouped with the Jackey layer. I added Curves and Hue/Saturation Adjustment layers above the Jackey layer and used them to match the color and contrast of Jackey's face and hair. I also added a Curves Adjustment layer above the McNamaras layer, and I used it with an S curve to add a little contrast to the McNamaras layer to better match Jackey. We may have to modify all of these as we add other smiling faces to the composite. After you get the colors to match fairly well, type a B to switch to the Paintbrush tool and then click on the Layer Mask for the Jackey layer. Type a 0 (zero) to get 100% opacity; then use a soft brush to paint in the layer mask to blend the two faces together even more. Paint with black to include more of the original Jackey face and with white to include more of the face from the Jackey layer. Sometimes you might want to paint with 50% opacity to blend the two images together. I also used the Rubber Stamp tool to clone away a little of Jackey's hair at the top of her head in the McNamaras layer.

STEP 6: The original Jackey actually had a pretty good smile, but I like the one from the Jackey layer better. You can now choose the one you like best by just turning the Eye icon on and off for the Jackey layer. The original image of Joe was definitely not

STEP 5: Make a Lasso selection (feather 2) of the inner area of Jackey's face; then click on the Layer Mask icon to create a layer mask only showing that part of the Jackey layer.

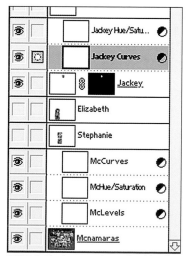

STEP 5: The Layers palette after blending Jackey's better smile into her previous head.

Adding the Smiling Faces

STEP 7: Before Joe, Jackey, Tony, and Michele's heads are replaced by smiling versions.

STEP 7: After the smiling heads are installed.

STEP 8: The initial Lasso selection for the Elizabeth layer with Opacity at 50%.

smiling very much. Turn on the Eye icon for the Joe layer and you'll see that the new Joe definitely has a better smile. Now go through the sequence of adjustments you did for Jackey in steps 4 and 5, but this time do them for Joe and the Joe layer. You'll find that the area of each person's face that you have to change is different. Pull up the McNamarasLayers file from the Extra Info Folder in the McNamaras example on the CD. This is my version of the final image. You can look at each of my layer masks and my Adjustment layers to see what I did. Press Command-S to save your McNamarasPortrait file.

STEP 7: Let's do Tony next, and because he's actually standing behind Jackey, click on the Tony layer in the Layers palette and drag it down underneath the Jackie layer. Now do steps 4 and 5 for the Tony layer. Don't worry about any overlap between Tony and Jackey; that will go away when you create the layer mask for the Tony layer. To get Tony's head to look right in the composite, I ended up adding first a Levels, then a Hue-Saturation, and finally, a Curves Adjustment layer above Tony and grouped with Tony's layer. To the right of Tony is Michele, so turn on the Eye icon for her layer and do her after Tony. To get Michele to look right, I had to include part of her neck as well as her head. You have to Rubber Stamp the collar and neck a bit on the right side. Turn the Eye icon on and off for Michele as well as Shift-clicking on her layer mask in my final version of the McNamaras to see what I did to make her look correct. If you make a mistake while rubber stamping, use the History palette to go back to an earlier version or you can also paint from an earlier version using the History Brush. See the Using History and Snapshots chapter for more info on how to do this. For the color correction on her, I just used a Levels Adjustment layer. In a similar way as you did Tony and Michele, now you should turn on the Eye icon for the Stephanie layer and blend in the slightly better expression for Stephanie. Do steps 4 and 5 for her. I just had to add a Levels Adjustment layer to get her facial color to match the original. Now might be a good time to save the file (Command-S).

ADDING THE SMILING ELIZABETH

STEP 8: The last person who needs a better smile is Elizabeth. Because her feet were in sort of a strange position in the original and she was sitting in the front, I decided to replace her entire body. The best way I found to line up the two images of Elizabeth was to make the chair she is sitting in line up between the two shots. Because there is quite a bit of movement between the two images of her, my initial Lasso selection included more than just the new Elizabeth. It also included the old Elizabeth. We will need to get rid of all of her from the original photo, so we might as well start by seeing how the locations where she was in the original photo look if used from the new photo in those areas. After making your Lasso selection, click on the Layer Mask icon to add a layer mask that includes only the selected area; then set the opacity on the Elizabeth layer back to 100%. Now you need to use the Paintbrush tool in the

Chapter 34: The McNamaras

layer mask, painting in either black, to remove the Elizabeth layer, or in white, to add parts of the Elizabeth layer. Do this until you get the two layers to merge the best that you can.

STEP 9: You will find there are some fringe areas that won't work from either the Elizabeth layer or the original McNamara layer. You will have to use the Rubber Stamp tool (S) to clone some of what you need in those areas. Before you do this though, go ahead and add a Grouped Levels Adjustment layer and get the color of the Elizabeth layer to match the original photo. A good place to compare is the white chair that Stephanie is sitting on behind and to the right of Elizabeth. Part of the armrest for this chair will come from the original image and part of it will come from the Elizabeth layer. Get those whites to match and you will have the color pretty close. I also added a Hue/Saturation Adjustment layer above Levels and Grouped with Elizabeth to saturate her colors a bit. Now that the colors match pretty well, use the Rubber Stamp tool to clone the areas that won't work from either layer. For me, this was the top-right edge of the lower-left corner of Stephanie's dress, which came from the Elizabeth layer, and little sections of the pants on the boy to the left of Elizabeth. Remember, the Rubber Stamp tool lets you clone from one layer onto another. Just have the first layer active when you Option-click to define where you are cloning from, and then activate the layer you are cloning to before you begin to paint in the clone. To get the part of Stephanie's dress that I used from the Elizabeth layer to match, I lassoed that part of the dress, then added a Curves Adjustment layer (again, Grouped with the Elizabeth layer), and used it to match the two dresses. Because I had the dress area selected when I Command-clicked on the New Layer icon to create the Adjustment layer, this automatically created a layer mask that allowed the Curves adjustments only in that dress area. As you Rubber Stamp and paint in the layer masks to get Elizabeth to look correct, it is easy to get confused and forget which layer or layer mask you are using or which tool you are using. It is even hard for me

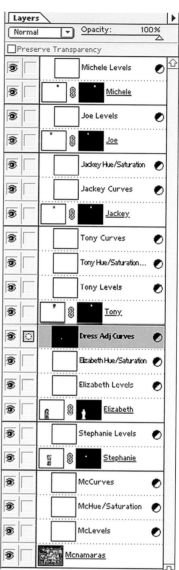

STEP 10: The final Layers palette after working on the new image of Elizabeth. This file is in the Extra Info Files folder for the McNamaras chapter on the CD.

The final McNamaras' image after color correction and the addition of all the smiling faces. This was sharpened with Unsharp Mask at 150 percent, Radius of 1.5, and Threshold of 3.

Adding the Smiling Elizabeth

sometimes when I'm doing something like this. Slow down and concentrate; think twice and make sure you are using the right tool in the correct state. Sometimes it helps you get your bearings to turn off the Eye icon of a layer or Shift-click a layer mask thumbnail to see the image without a layer or a mask. You will be switching between the McNamaras and Elizabeth layers as you rubber stamp and you'll also switch between rubber stamping on a layer and using the Paintbrush to edit a mask. Remember that you can always use the History palette or the History Brush to restore any layer, or just part of a layer, to a previous state.

STEP 10: You now have all your smiling faces added and you have color corrected and masked them to match as best you can. Now it is time to look at the image as a whole and further tweak the color or contrast of any head that doesn't seem quite right. A particular person might seem slightly off color or have a different brightness or contrast than the rest. You might also decide to adjust the contrast or color balance of the entire McNamara layer. Because you did all your color adjustments using adjustment layers, you can double-click on the name of any of them and change the Adjustment as many times as you like without degrading the original pixels in any of the layers. The final color changes to the pixels will not be made until you flatten the image; even better, use File/Save A Copy to create a flattened version. When I zoomed out and looked at the image, I ended up changing the Joe and Jackey heads a little to make them fit in better with the rest of the faces. I used Joe's Levels Adjustment layer to make his face a little darker and warmer, and I used Jackey's Curves Adjustment layer to make her face a little warmer. My final version, called McNamarasLayers, is on the CD in the Extra Info Folder for this chapter. If you're having a problem with anything, pull up my version and see how I did it. Press Command-S to save your file when you finish it. Before printing this, I did Image/Duplicate to create a merged version, and then Unsharp Mask to sharpen it—and of course I converted it to CMYK.

35 HANDS-ON SESSION: South Africa In Focus

Building a flexible multilayered file to create various composite screens for multimedia use; Layer masks, Adjustment layers, Clipping groups, Text effects, Filters, and Actions help you get the job done.

When you work in multimedia you have to build many files to accomplish even the shortest project. How you set up your Photoshop files can make an enormous difference in how quickly you accomplish your tasks and how quickly you can adjust to the demands of a different application or end product. This chapter is a mere introduction to some of the issues that will crop up if you decide to use your Photoshop skills to do work for CD-ROMS, kiosks, or video.

BUILD THE BACKGROUND SCREEN

STEP 1: We'll be working on a project that is going to be used several different ways. There's going to be a video of the opening segment as well as an informative CD for educational use. Because we're unsure of exactly who's going to be doing the work with the files after we've done our Photoshop work, we want to build a file that has great flexibility to go out to other programs. Use File/New to open a new file, 648 pixels by 486 pixels in RGB mode at 72 pixels per inch. Although, 640x480 is the most common file size in multimedia, 648x486 works for most uses, and it's the preferred size for analog video transfers. You're working with low resolution files because video, television (but not DTV), and computer monitors are low-resolution media. Bring up the Color palette (Shift-F9), the Info palette (F9), and the Layers palette (F10) to assist you. Make sure your Info readout is in pixels by using the X and Y coordinates pop-up on the Info palette. Move the sliders on the Color palette to R-224, G-139, B-0 to set the foreground color. Now, option-Delete to fill the entire screen with this foreground color. Save your file as In Focus.psd.

The final composite we'll build during this session!

In the coming of DTV (Digital Television), HDTV is a component. However, all DTV signals will not include HDTV. Some will be SDTV (Standard Definition Television). How all this shakes down remains to be seen. For now, be prepared to need several different sizes for your graphics.

STEP 2: Now we'll add a bit of texture to the screen. Choose Filter/Texture/Texturizer and use Sandstone as the texture. Chose 100 percent as the scaling, and Top as the Light Direction, but use a Relief of only 2. Remember, there's going to be a lot happening on this screen; you want a little texture but you don't want the texture to

STEP 2: The Texturizer filter has built-in textures, additional textures in the Goodies folder that loaded with Photoshop 5, or you can create your own.

compete with information or images that are truly important. Double-click the Background layer and rename it Sandstone texture.

By the way, if you haven't played with the Texturizer filter, now might be a good time to take a few moments to do so. You'll see when you choose your texture that you can load additional textures that came with Photoshop (look inside the Goodies folder in your Photoshop folder and also inside the folder, Other Goodies/Textures for Lighting Effects), textures that you've purchased from third-party sources, or that you've scanned in or created from scratch. To create your own texture, use File/New to open a grayscale image the same size as your file filled with white. If your texture is smaller than your file, you might see tiling or repeating of the same pattern over and over again. You sometimes see this with the small textures that came with Photoshop. Now use Filter/Noise/Add Noise of about 50 Gaussian on your texture. Now use Filter/Brush Strokes and any of the Brush Stroke filters. Just play. When you have something you think looks interesting (hint: white and black areas remain flat when you Texturize), save the file with a meaningful name (like inktexture.psd) in Photoshop format. Go back to your In Focus.psd file and make a new layer by clicking the New Layer icon at the bottom of the Layers palette, and Option-delete once again to fill this layer with the same background color that we used before. Go to Filter/Texture/Texturizer again; only this time choose Load Texture as your option and search for the grayscale file that you just created. You'll still get options of how much scaling and how deep you want to make your texture. Experiment a bit and then say "OK" and take a look at what you've created. It's such fun that you can lose whole days creating textures and checking them out. If you've created a background that you like better than the one we made using the Texturizer and Sandstone, name it My Texture, keep it with the file on its own layer, and see how it works with the composite.

SET ZERO ORIGIN AND GUIDES TO ESTABLISH SAFE AREAS

One of the issues you have to deal with in multimedia is the overscanning (cropping) that happens when your pictures are displayed on a television screen. If you have text or images that are highly important (and which ones aren't?), you need to make sure that they appear in an area of the screen that will be readable. To make sure of accurate placement, we're going to build guides for both the *image safe* (the area that will display artwork accurately) and the *title safe* (the area that will display text legibly). Normal image safe on a 640x480 file that is the most common size used for this type of work is 33 pixels from each side of the frame and 25 pixels from the top and bottom. Title safe for the same size file is 65 pixels from each side and 49 pixels from top and bottom. As you can see, your live area diminishes a great deal when you start to put text onscreen.

About now you may be remembering that the file that we're working on is not 640x480 but rather 648x486. That's because the video editor who will be working with some of the files later has requested this size and we've built the file to accommodate her. However, we still need to set our safe areas for 640x480 because some of the files will be used in this format. So we're going to set a different zero origin for the file to help us correctly position our guides.

STEP 3: Show the ruler by typing Command-R if it is not currently onscreen. In the top-left corner of the window where the horizontal and vertical rulers meet, there is a small square that has two perpendicular dotted lines. This is the zero origin positioner. Right now, the zero point is at the top-most and left-most pixel of the image—that's normal. But you can set the zero point anywhere to help you measure and

When you work in multimedia (or do any complex artwork for that matter), it's a good idea to work with a notepad to write down what you're doing. Date the page and name the job you're working on. That way if you need to re-create a certain effect for another job, you have a record of how it was done. Also, save the layered version of your Photoshop file for reference.

position items accurately. To do this, click and drag on the two perpendicular lines and when you let go, notice the rulers. The zero origin has moved to the place where you let go. If you move the mouse around the image, you see that the pixel readout on the Info palette is negative when the mouse is above or to the left of the new zero point. Reset the zero origin by double-clicking on the intersection of the two rulers. We need to set the zero origin at exactly 3 pixels from the top of the image and 4 pixels from the side of the image to position safe guides accurately for our 640x480

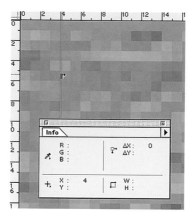

STEP 3: Shift-drag guidelines to four pixels from the left and three pixels from the top of your screen.

size files. To make this easier, zoom in on the top-left corner of the file; you need to be at 1,200 to 1,600% size. (Remember you can type in the percentage you want in the view box on the bottom-left area of the screen.) Hold down the Shift key as you drag a guide from the horizontal ruler three pixels. Holding down Shift constrains the guides so they snap to the edge of a pixel and not somewhere in-between, which can be very important when you're aligning objects for programming in multimedia or image maps for the Web. Now, look at the Info palette; the Y axis should read 3. Then repeat the process with the vertical ruler, Shift-dragging a ruler across four pixels until the X axis readout is 4. Make sure that Snap To Guides is turned on (View/Snap to Guides or Command-Shift-;) and once again, drag your zero origin out to the intersection of your guides.

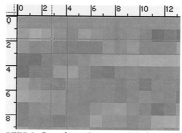

STEP 3: Drag from the zero origin box and make sure Snap To Guides is turned on.

STEP 4: Still zoomed in, click the vertical ruler and drag a guideline out 33 pixels from your new zero position, making sure to hold down the Shift key as you drag. This is the guide for action safe. Shift-drag another guide from the vertical ruler 65 pixels in from the side. This will be the title safe. Click the horizontal ruler and Shift-drag a guide down 25 pixels from the top of the image for the action safe, and Shift-drag another guide 49 pixels from the top for title safe. You might need to use the Hand tool (Spacebar-drag) to reposition the file so you can place your guides, but zooming in assures that you can read the rulers accurately.

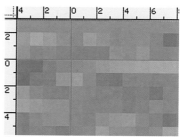

STEP 3: The new zero origin.

STEP 5: Now that you have the first set of guides placed, we'll use a shortcut to position the second set and avoid having to do the math (but feel free if you're so inclined). Command-Option-Spacebar-click (zoom out) until you can see the four large rectangles, created by the guides you just placed, in the corner of your file. Select the Rectangular Marquee (M or Shift-M) and draw a rectangle from the edge of your file to the lower-right corner of the first large rectangle. Next, hold down the Shift key and draw a second marquee that encompasses the forth rectangle. You should have two rectangular selection marquees that look like the illustration here. Type Command-Option-0 (zero) to fit the image in the window and, still using the Marquee tool, drag the selections down toward the lower-right corner.

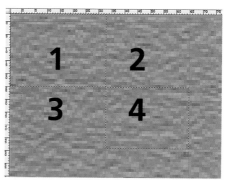

STEP 5: When you Shift-select the areas, they should look like this.

STEP 6: First choose Select/Transform Selection, and then choose Edit/Transform/Rotate 180° to rotate the selection 180°. After you've rotated the selection, press Return to accept the transformation. Still using the Marquee

Set Zero Origin and Guides to Establish Safe Areas

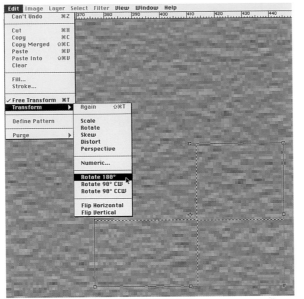

STEP 6: Photoshop 5 allows you to transform a selection as well as a layer. In this case, we're rotating the selection marquee itself using first, Transform Selection, then Edit/Transform/Rotate 180°.

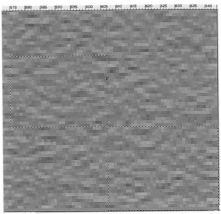

STEP 7: Shift-drag the new guidelines for the right and bottom edges of your file.

tool, move the selection to the bottom-right corner of your file. Zoom in to the area and use the arrow keys to move the selection one pixel at a time until it's in place exactly at the edge of the file.

STEP 7: Shift-drag guidelines from both the vertical and horizontal rulers. As long as Snap to Guides is still on, you'll feel the guides snap to the marquee edges. When your guides are in place, you can double-click the intersection of the ruler bars in the upper-left corner of the window to reset your zero origin.

If you're wondering if there's an easier way to establish the safe areas, of course there is. You could simply take half of the extra width (8 pixels/2=4 pixels) and height (6 pixels/2=3 pixels) of the larger file and add it to the number of pixels needed for safe. That is, image safe would now be 37 pixels from each side and 28 pixels from the top and bottom. Title safe would be 69 and 52, respectively. But, if we had done it the easy way, you wouldn't know how to set a new zero origin, would you?

STEP 8: Choose Edit/Transform/Scale to scale Africa by eye.

BRING IN AFRICA

STEP 8: Zoom out until you can see the entire screen and deselect (Command-D) the rectangles you were using to place your guides. Open the file Africa.psd. Use the Move tool and drag the Africa layer into your file to create a new layer. Remember, if you hold down the Shift key as you drag, you automatically place the file in the middle of the screen, which is what we want to do here. The artwork will be larger than the background screen, so use Edit/Transform/Scale to scale it to fit. Remember to hold down the Shift key as you scale to scale the image proportionately. You want the continent to "bleed" a bit, and I've placed it just a bit left of center, as there is more imagery on the right side of the final design than on the left. You can drag a guideline to the center of the file (324 pixels) to help you decide where you want to place Africa, but don't get too picky until you've put all the pieces together. If your guides are turned on (type Command-; if they're not), you can see how much of Africa is hanging over the image safe area.

Turn off View/Snap to Guides; then choose Edit/Free Transform (Command-T). Hold down both Option and Shift as you click and drag the top-right corner handle down and to the left until Africa is the correct size. If you immediately choose Edit/Transform/Numeric at this point, the Scale number will show you how much you have already scaled the artwork. To scale the art further, or to scale to a whole number, turn on the Constrain Proportions check box and type in the number that you want. Choose OK on the Numeric dialog and then press Return or Enter to accept the entire transformation.

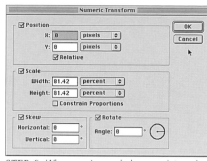

STEP 8: When you've scaled your picture but before you press Return, you can go immediately into Transform/Numeric to type in an exact amount for the scale or to see how much you've already scaled the art.

STEP 8: Place Africa a bit to the left of center of the background. The shadow is a Layer Effect.

ADD THE LAYER EFFECT.

STEP 9: We'll use one of Photoshop 5's new Layer Effects, the Drop Shadow effect, for this layer. Because shadows sometimes need to be separated from the primary object, it's not always possible to use this Layer Effect for materials that go into other programs, but in this case, we'll be fine.

It's easy to add these quick effects, and, best of all, they remain completely interactive with the layer. You move the layer, the shadow goes with it; add or adjust the layer mask, the shadow changes. And if you don't like the color or angle or depth of the shadow at any time, it's a no-brainer to go in and fix it.

To add the shadow to Africa, go to Layer/Effects/Drop Shadow and click the color square to bring up the Color Picker. Use a rich red-brown—I've used R:180, G:83, B:24—and keep the rest of the default settings. You don't want a lot of shadow here because it might look too busy with all the other things going on. But remember, if you want to change it later, you can.

BLOCK IN OTHER MAJOR ELEMENTS

STEP 10: Next, we're going to block in the three photos. I like to put placeholders down before I actually bring in the photos to have an idea of how much space I have to work with. So, click the color square on the Tool palette or show the Color palette to choose a light brown. Color doesn't really matter, we're eventually going to throw these layers in the trash; we just want to get a feeling for how things will lay out. Type M or Shift-M to get the Rectangular Marquee tool. Draw a marquee about one-third of the width and one-third of the height of the file. That's about 210 pixels by 150 pixels; there's not an exact size that we need. You can use the W and H measures in the bottom-right of the Info palette to see the size. Option-click the New Layer icon at

STEP 9: Drop Shadow is just one of the many Layer Effects you can now add with Photoshop 5.

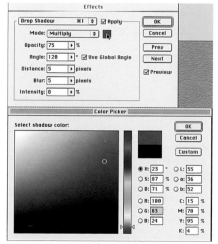

STEP 9: Use the default settings for the Drop Shadow effect, but use R:180, G:83, B:24 for the shadow color.

Block In Other Major Elements

STEP 10: Your photo boxes should be placed something like this.

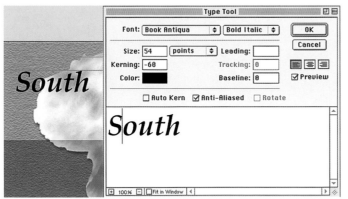

STEP 11: With the Preview box checked, the new Text tools allow you to preview the type as you place it as well as change the kerning, tracking, leading, baseline shift, and alignment. You can even change the style or color of individual letters.

STEP 11: To kern a letter pair, click between the letters and turn off the Auto Kern check box. You can then type in a kern amount or use shortcut keys to tighten or loosen the kerning.

the bottom of the Layers palette to create a new layer called Animal Block, and then Option-delete to fill the selection rectangle on that new layer with the light brown color you chose. Change the Blend mode of the layer to Multiply. This gives you the basic shape you'll be working with. Choose Select/Deselect (Command-D) and then Option-drag that layer to the New Layer icon at the bottom of the Layers palette twice to create two copies of the layer. Call one Art Block and the other People Block. Use the Move tool (V) to position each layer where you'll want your photos to appear. Animals will appear in the top-right section, People in the bottom-right, and Art in the left-middle of the frame. Make sure your guidelines are showing (Command-;) so you can position the three photo blocks within the image safe for the most part.

STEP 11: Next, let's type in the South Africa text. We're going to put each word on a separate layer, so we can move them independently of each other. Type T to get the Text tool and make sure it's set to the regular, horizontal Text tool. Type D to get the default colors; then click in the upper-left are of the file to get the Type dialog box, and type in the word "South." I've used Book Antiqua Bold Italic at 54 points; you'll have to improvise depending on what typefaces you have installed in your system. After you type in a word, you have to highlight any letters that you want to edit, whether you're changing the actual letter itself or its size, leading, kerning, baseline shift, or color.

I found that the spacing between the letters was good except between the S and the O. To kern a letter pair, place the cursor between the two letters you want to tighten or loosen and click off the Auto Kern button. When you turn off Auto Kern, you can type a value in the Kerning box or use shortcut keys to move the letters (See "Taking Advantage of Photoshop 5" at the beginning of this book for a table). I used –60 to tighten the space between the letters. The Type dialog box gives you an onscreen preview of any changes you make, a welcome addition to version 5. When you like the way the text looks, click OK to accept the text. Notice the layer in the Layers palette now is named "South" and has a T on the far-right side to let you know that this is a text layer and is still interactive. You can now double-click on the layer's name to change the type, but certain operations, like filters, can not be done to this layer until it is rendered.

STEP 12: Option-drag the South layer to the New Layer icon at the bottom of the palette and name this new layer, Africa. Double-click on this layer name to bring up the Text dialog box. Double-click or click and drag on the word South to highlight it and type in the word Africa. Turn Auto Kern back on, click OK, and then use the Move tool on this layer to shift Africa below and to the right of South.

Chapter 35: South Africa In Focus

STEP 13: Go to File/Place and place the Focus.ai logo. This is an Adobe Illustrator file that we'll place, resize, and rasterize in Photoshop. When the logo comes in, it comes in at the size it was created in Illustrator. Photoshop gives you the opportunity to resize the logo before you rasterize it, avoiding any loss of clarity that might occur if you rasterize first and then resize. Keep your eye on the Info palette as you resize by Shift-dragging on a corner handle, and bring the logo down to about 70% of its original size. Then press Enter to accept the change and rasterize. Use the Move tool to move the artwork down and to the left a bit.

BRING IN THE PHOTOS

STEP 14: It's time to start bringing in the photographs and setting up the text for the three main areas of our production, currently called "Animals," "Art," and "People." Open the files Giraffe.psd, Ayanda.psd, and Masks.psd. If you go to Image/Image Size on any of these files, you'll notice that they are all considerably bigger than we need, but we won't worry about changing the resolution or image size in the original photos; we'll do all of our resizing in the In Focus file. Start with the Giraffe.psd file and use the Rectangular Marquee tool to select primarily the giraffe's head and neck with some of the foliage in the background. Take a bit more than you think you'll actually use. Command-C to copy the area; then switch to your In Focus file and Command-V to paste the giraffe as a new layer. Your selection probably fills most of the screen because the Giraffe.psd file was at a much higher resolution than the 72dpi we're using. Double-click on this layer and name it Giraffe.

STEP 13: When you bring in vector artwork, you get a bounding box and a preview of how the art will look when rasterized. The arrow in the corner means you are ready to resize the art.

STEP 13: Place the Adobe Illustrator logo, Focus.ai.

STEP 15: In the Layers palette, move the Giraffe layer just above the Animals block layer. Option-click the line between the two to make a clipping group, that is, to clip the Giraffe layer to the shape of the the Animals block layer. Because you already set the Blend mode of the Animals block layer to Multiply, the Giraffe layer will assume the same Blend mode. To scale the Giraffe, choose Edit/Free Transform (Command-T) and hold down the Shift key while dragging the corners of the transform box inward. Click and

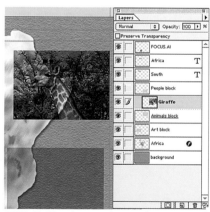

STEP 15: Your Layers palette and your artwork should look something like this after Step 15.

drag in the middle of the box to move the image. When you're happy with the size and position, press Return or Enter to accept the transform.

STEP 16: Repeat the same basic process for Masks.psd and Ayanda.psd. Copy an area from the original file and paste it into the In Focus file as a new layer. Rename the layer and move it to above its corresponding block layer; then make a clipping group by Option-clicking the line between the layers. Use Edit/Free Transform to resize the artwork while holding down the Shift key to about 150% of the size of the block that "clips" it. You want some extra because later we'll feather the mask to give the artwork softer edges. Wait for a few seconds after you make your transformation to

Build the Text and Text Effects

STEP 16: Your file and Layers palette should look something like this after Step 16. The dotted lines between layers signify Clipping groups.

get a preview of how the art will look before you press Return to accept the transformation. When you are happy with the size of each image, click the linking column (the middle column) of each image to link it with its Block layer. Now you can use the Move tool to move each two-layer group together.

BUILD THE TEXT AND TEXT EFFECTS

STEP 17: Now that the major elements are in place, we'll type in the text to finish up our original comp, and then we'll go back and finesse some of the elements after we get approval of the initial concept. Make the Giraffe layer the active layer; then type I to get the Eyedropper tool and sample the light blue color on the Africa map to make that the foreground color. Type T to get the Text tool and click near the bottom of the Giraffe to place type there. When the Text dialog box comes up, you'll notice that the foreground color is the color that the type will appear. You'll get an onscreen preview, so if you don't like the color you selected, you can change it on-the-fly or at any time later. I typed "animals" and used Arial Black at 40 points with tracking of 50 to give a little air between the letters. If you don't have the same type-

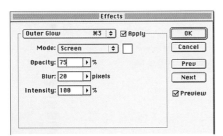

STEP 18: The Outer Glow settings for the three titles: Animals, Art, and People.

face, you can experiment with the type you have installed in your system and see the screen update as you change faces. Just remember that you need to highlight the text to change the typeface, or any other attribute, after you've typed it in. When you're happy with the text, click OK. Your layer will now automatically be named "animals."

STEP 18: Let's go ahead and add the text effect to this text before we type in the other words. Choose Layer/Effects/Outer Glow and use the default color, Mode, and Opacity, but change Blur to 20 pixels and the Intensity to 100%. Click OK or press Return or Enter to accept this.

STEP 19: We'll use two different methods to set the other two titles. Each way works just fine; it's up to you when you work which method to use. For art, use the method to set the type that we just used, that is, make the Masks layer active, use the Text tool (the settings that you last used will still be there), and simply type in the word "art" and click OK. Now, click on the animals text layer and go to Layer/Effects/Copy Effects. After the effect has been copied, you can click the art text layer and do

STEP 19: You can copy any effect that you've already applied to one layer to any other layer in your file.

Layer/Effects/Paste Effects to get the same glow, color, and everything, that you used on the animals text layer.

STEP 20: The other way to do this is to click the animals or art text layers and Option-drag that layer to the New Layer icon at the bottom of the palette to make a copy of the layer. Double-click the layer name to get the type dialog box, highlight the old text and type in the new word, people, and click OK. Use the Move tool (V) to move the text over the picture of Ayanda and, in the Layers palette, move that layer above the Ayanda layer. You can make a copy of the layer and change the text if you just drag the layer to the New Layer icon instead of Option-dragging, but the name of the layer will not represent the text. In this case, double-click the layer thumbnail to get the Layer Options dialog box and type in the new name.

STEP 19: "art" after the effect has been pasted.

STEP 21: At this point in the process, the client has decided to change the area currently titled "animals" to "nature." In Photoshop 4, you would have to build a completely new layer and make sure you had written down all the attributes of the text so you could match it. In Photoshop 5, you merely double-click the layer name, highlight all of the text, and type in the new text. Not only is the text changed, but the Layer effect is added to the new text and the name of the layer changes.

STEP 21: To change a word, simply double-click on the layer name and highlight the letters, word, or words that you want to change…

…type in the new material and say OK. You can even highlight one letter to change its characteristics.

STEP 21: The basic elements are in place and the concept has been approved. Now it's time to get creative.

Build the Text and Text Effects

STEP 22: With the art block selection active, click on the Save Selection as Channel icon and you'll get Alpha1.

STEP 22: After you have the new channel, deselect the area (Command-D) and you're ready to do the Numeric Transformation and filtering.

FINESSE THE CLIPPING MASKS OR LAYER MASKS

STEP 22: After the original concept has been approved, you can start to add the touches that make your production stand out. First we're going to add a feathered edge to our masks for the three photographs. Depending on how you're sending out your files, you could work with the Clipping group mask (the bottom layer of the Clipping group). For our example, we are going to make black and white alpha channels that are employed as layer masks in Photoshop but will be used as alpha channels in Adobe Premiere through which video clips will be played. Let's start with the "art" area. Command-click on the art block layer to load that shape as a selection. Show the Channels palette (Windows/Show Channels or Shift-F10). While the selection is active, click the Save Selection as Channel icon on the bottom of the palette and then deselect the area (Command-D).

STEP 23: Make sure Alpha 1 is the active channel by clicking on its name. You should see only the black and white alpha channel at this point. When we feather the mask for the the artwork, it's going to need to be about 10% bigger, so go to Edit/Transform/Numeric and type in 110% for both the width and height scaling. Choose OK.

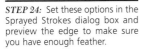

STEP 24: Go to Filter/Blur/Gaussian Blur (Shift-F4) and blur the entire channel by about 10 pixels. Next, go to Filter/Brush Strokes/Sprayed Strokes and set the Stroke Length and Spray Radius both to 15 with the Stroke Direction as Right Diagonal. Preview your results in the window and make sure that you have enough feather.

STEP 24: Set these options in the Sprayed Strokes dialog box and preview the edge to make sure you have enough feather.

STEP 25: When you're happy with the results, choose OK. We're now going to make a layer mask from this channel. Command-click on the Alpha 1 channel to load it as a selection; then switch over to the Layers palette. Click on the "masks" layer to make it the active layer and click on the Add layer mask icon at the bottom-left area of the Layers palette to add your selection as a layer mask.

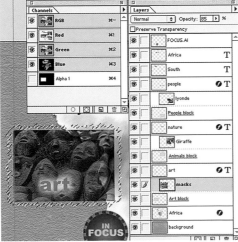

STEP 25: With the selection loaded and "masks" layer active, you're ready to make a layer mask by clicking the leftmost icon at the bottom of the Layers palette.

STEP 26: You now have a layer mask but the artwork is still being clipped by the Art block layer below it. Option-click on the dotted line between the two layers to release the Clipping group. Click the Eye icon on the Art block layer to turn that layer off. The Masks layer is now controlled by its layer mask. Set its Blend mode to Multiply and the Opacity to about 85%. If you find that you have hard edges, or you don't like the placement of your artwork, click the linking icon between the Layer thumbnail and the Layer mask thumbnail. You can then move the layer and the mask separately from one another. If you still have a hard edge on part of your artwork, you may find that your artwork is simply not large enough to fill the entire mask area. In this case, you'll need to go back to the original Masks.psd file and make a new selection, bring it in, and resize it. At any rate, make sure you relink the layer to its layer mask before continuing.

STEP 27: Repeat steps 22–26 for each of the other two photo layer groups. Command-click the Clipping group block layer to select its shape, make a new channel of the selection, enlarge it 10%, blur it, and filter it with the Sprayed Strokes filter (steps 22–24). Then follow steps 25 and 26 to attach those channels as layer masks.

MAKE THE MASKS LAYER MORE INTERESTING

STEP 28: To add a bit more visual interest to the Masks layer, click on the Masks layer, and then Command-click the New Layer icon to add an Adjustment layer. Turn on the Group With Previous Layer button to make the adjustment to only the Masks layer, and choose a Hue/Saturation Adjustment layer; then choose OK. Click the Colorize button and the Preview button and make sure you move the dialog box out of the way to see your changes. I used 335 as my Hue adjustment, but you can try other colors and see what you like best.

STEP 29: At this point, you really want to show the History palette (F8) because you'll be creating many different effects, and you'll want to take snapshots of several of them and then click between snapshots to see which effects you like. With the History Brush, you can selectively paint in areas from the snapshots that you've taken using different Blend modes and opacities.

STEP 30: There is another possibility for making the Masks layer more exciting. Turn off the Hue/Saturation Adjustment layer, click on the Masks layer, then Option-click on the New Layer icon and turn on the Group With Previous Layer option. This creates a Clipping group based on the layer mask. Name this layer, Gradient, and change the Blend mode to Color.

STEP 30: Make sure you turn on Group With Previous Layer to have the Adjustment Layer affect only the Masks layer.

STEP 30: Click the Load button to load the SA In Focus gradient from the Photoshop 5 Artistry CD. Feel free to edit the gradient.

STEP 30: Check the Reverse option to begin with yellow and end with purple.

Type G for the Gradient tool and choose a gradient style by typing Shift-G until you get the style you want to use. You will be dragging a gradient line across the area of the Mask image. I first tried the Angled gradient that gives interesting color shifts, but I often got a hard line where the angle started. Even when I edited the gradient, the color shifts were often too hard-edged. I got the best results using either the Reflected gradient or the Diamond gradient. As for color, you can try any of the colored gradients that automatically load with Photoshop, but I built a custom gradient that you can load. Click the Edit button on the Gradient Options palette and then click the Load button on the Gradient Editor. The file you want to load is Artwork Gradient and the gradient is called SAIF.grd. Click OK on the Gradient Editor; then experiment with making gradients of different lengths and different directions on the Gradient layer. Each time you achieve an effect that you really like, click the New Snapshot icon at the bottom-middle area of the History palette. If you like, you can

It's useful to know that while in the Move tool, to quickly access any layer in the Layers palette, you can Control-click on the screen and get a menu of al layers having pixels at that location. Just choose the layer you want from the pop-up. If you are not currently in the Move tool, Command-Control-click does the same thing. For Windows, you use the right mouse button instead of the Control key when in the Move tool and Control-right mouse when not.

double-click the Snapshot name and rename each snapshot with a name such as Blue-Orange Diamond.

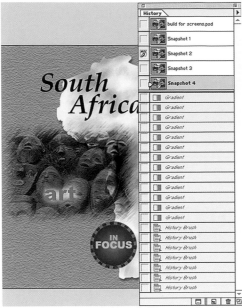

STEP 37: Here, we've tried lots of different gradient blends and made snapshots of four that looked good. We've then used the History Brush several times to selectively take portions of the snapshots that we liked to achieve the final result. Note that in this illustration, Snapshot 4 is the active snapshot, the one that you are viewing, but if you paint, the History Brush is set to Snapshot 2.

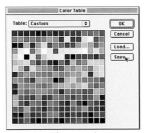

STEP 33: After you change your file to Indexed Color, you can go to Image/Mode/Color Table and save the Color palette to load in Photoshop or other applications.

STEP 31: When you have three or four snapshots, click each one to view it and decide what you like best in it. Type Y to get the History Brush and make sure the active layer is Gradient. Use an opacity of about 30% to begin with. Click the left column in the History palette of the snapshot that you'd like to paint from and begin to paint on the Gradient layer. Remember that you can use different Blend modes if you like. To paint from another snapshot, click in the left column of that Snapshot to place the History Brush icon there and continue painting. Once again, if you achieve an effect you like, take a snapshot of it and name it. With so many variations, you can get confused, so take your time and make sure you know what is happening. And remember, the mark of the true artist is knowing when to quit. When you finish painting the Gradient layer, turn off its Eye icon in the Layers palette and turn on the Hue/Saturation Adjustment layer. Decide which you like better for your final version of the file and leave on the Eye icon for that layer.

READY THE TYPE FOR ANIMATION

STEP 32: We have used Photoshop to create this image and get approval for the final layout. Now all of the pieces are in place. It's time to make the adjustments necessary to send parts of the final file out to other programs for multimedia. In the case of the type for Nature, People, and Art, we need to separate the text from the effect. Click the Art layer and go to Layer/Effects/Create Layer. You now have two distinct layers, Art and Art's Outer Glow. Repeat the process for the Nature layer and the People layer. If the files are sent to Macromedia Director for animation, you'll send the type for all three of these layers as tiny PICT files that can be animated rapidly, or you might set the type in Director. The glows will be treated differently. Because Director does a rather poor job with soft anti-aliased edges, we'll be animating the glows against the background file and sending these out separately. There are several extensions for Director that can help you when you need to achieve some special effect that Director doesn't normally handle. You might want to take a look at Photocaster and Alphamania.

ACTIONS HELP YOU ANIMATE THE GLOW

STEP 33: We're going to animate the glows for the text against the background screen and that means there's going to be lots of files that we have to crop, convert to indexed color, and save as PICT files. Actions can help you automate much of the work. Let's build the action using the Art's Outer Glow layer. One of the first things we'll need is a Color palette to work with. Our Director file will be limited to 256 colors, and we'll need a custom palette that will load with the animation to give us the best possible color accuracy on many different platforms. First, make sure all the layers that will appear in your final screen have their Eye icons turned on. So choose which textured background and which effect for the Masks layer you want in your final image. Choose Image/Duplicate (F5) and turn on Merged Layers Only. Using the duplicate file, go to Image/Mode/Indexed Color, say OK to Flatten, and choose

Adaptive as the palette type, Color Depth of 8 bits/pixel, diffusion Dither, and Best color matching. This will create a color table of 256 colors that occur most often in this file. Next, go to Image/Mode/Color Table and click the Save button to save this color palette, so it can be loaded for the Director movie or any other files that we create for this production. I've saved my color table and it's on the Photoshop 5 Artistry CD for you. It's called, SAIFclut.aco and it's in the Extra Info Files subdirectory for this example. Switch back to the In Focus file with all the layers.

STEP 34: We'll save a version of the file with the opacity of each glow at 0% and then 45%. Then save a version with the glow at 10% increments until we reach 95% opacity. In Director, we'll load these files in order, making the glow appear to "burn in" or get brighter. Turn off the Eye icons for Nature, Nature's Outer Glow, People, People's Outer Glow, Art, and Art's Outer Glow. This leaves the main title, the In Focus logo, the Continent, and the three photos in place as the background for the Director production. However, to accurately position the files in Director, we'd like a file size of 640x480 pixels. So turn your guides back on if they are currently off (Command-;) and choose the Rectangular Marquee tool. Begin your selection at the intersection of the guides at the top-left corner of the file, the ones that are four pixels from the left edge and three pixels from the top. Watch the Info palette and draw a selection that is exactly 640 pixels by 480 pixels. Switch to the Channels palette, Option-click the Save Selection icon to make a new channel, and name this channel 640Crop. This is the channel we'll load each time we want to crop the file to 640x480 and save it. Switch back to the RGB channel.

STEP 35: The first file that we'll need to save is this generic background without the three text areas or their glows. Save your file so you can revert to this state if necessary. We won't record the action now, but simply go through the steps (or most of them) that will be contained in the action. First, Command-click on 640Crop to load it as a selection. Second, choose Image/Crop to crop the file. Third, go to Image/Mode/Indexed Color and use the Custom Palette option to load your saved color table from step 34 as the custom palette. Fourth, do a Save A Copy (Command-Option-S) and save the file in a new folder called PICS as SAIF001.pct. (When you choose PICT File format, Photoshop will automatically append the extension if you've chosen Always for Append File Extension in the Saving Files preferences setup.) Fifth, go back to the load selection state in the History palette to put the file back the way it was before you did the crop.

STEP 36: Now it's time to build the action to animate the glows of the three words. For safety's sake, do a Save As and save this file as SAIF Actions Test to build the action and test it out. If anything blows up, you'll still have your original file intact. Make sure that Art's Outer Glow is the active layer. Bring up the Actions palette (F11) and turn off Button Mode. Look at the illustration on this

More and more multimedia productions are being created in thousands of colors, instead of the 256 we use here. This is because end users have larger, faster machines with better video cards and more RAM for processing. But you must always create with your intended audience in mind, and often that still means 256 colors.

In reality, creating a Color palette for a multimedia production can be a much more complicated process. Here, we're dealing with only one portion of a production. You might need to find a Color palette that works with multiple background screens that are very different one from the other. See Chapter 43: GIFs, JPEGs, and Color Palettes for more information on creating custom Color palettes in Photoshop and check out other programs such as DeBablizer, Director, and Adobe's new ImageReady if you have to create many complex Color palettes.

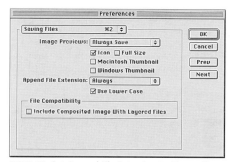

STEP 35: Set Append File Extension to Always if you want Photoshop to always give you the appropriate extension for the type of file you are saving.

STEP 36: Click the New Set icon on the bottom of the Actions palette to create a new set of actions specific to the work on this production. You may be able to use these actions again, or modify them to use for different multimedia productions.

265

STEP 36: When you click the New Action icon, you can name the action, decide which set to put it in, and give it a function key and/or color.

File size, naming conventions, and exact pixel dimensions and locations are all vitally important elements of a well-produced multimedia presentation. If you're building your own presentation, make sure you keep a log with all the vital information. And, if you know a good database program, here's where you want to use it.

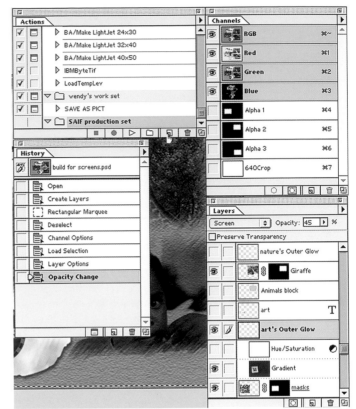

STEP 36: This should be the palette state when you get ready to create your new action by clicking the Record button on the Actions palette.

page to see how your palettes should look before you start to record your action. Click the New Set icon on the bottom of the Actions palette to create a set called SAIF Production Set. Any actions that you record to help you produce files for the job will go in this set. Then, next time you work on a job with similar needs, it's possible that you can use the same actions or modify these actions to complete your work. When you start using actions, you'll wonder how you ever worked without them. Now, with the SAIF production set highlighted, click the New Action icon and name the action, Crop&Save. If you want to set a function key or color, you can do so now. Click Record when you're ready to record your steps, and don't be nervous. Remember, you can go back and edit an action that doesn't work properly or delete it and start again. And, because you're working on a copy of the file (you did make a copy of the file, didn't you?), you don't have to worry about ruining a day or two of work.

STEP 37: Here are the steps you take during the recording of the action. Double-click the Opacity area of the Layers palette (Art's Outer Glow must be the active layer) and type in 45. Command-click the 640Crop channel to load it. Go to Image/Crop and crop the image. Go to Image/Mode/Indexed color and load the SAIF.clut Color palette. Go to File/Save a Copy (or Command-Option-S) and save this as a PICT file in the PICs folder that you created. Give the file the name SAIF002.pct. In the History palette, click back on the Load Selection state. Then click the Stop button on the Actions palette to stop recording. And you're done. Well, almost.

Chapter 35: South Africa In Focus

STEP 38: In the Actions palette, click the triangle to the left of Crop&Save to open the action and look at the steps. You can click the triangle on any step to view the specific information about that step, too. Right now, we want to put a breakpoint in the action at two places to allow the user to input specific information. Click in the second column of the Set current layer step and the Save step. This will cause the action to stop at those points to allow you to input specific information, in this case the opacity of the layer and the filename.

STEP 39: Play the action by clicking the Play button on the bottom of the palette. When the action stops at the Layer options dialog, type in the new opacity for the file you want to create. When the action stops at the Save dialog box, type in the name of the new file. These files will be handed over to the person doing your multimedia programming to animate in another application such as Macromedia Director. If you have trouble setting up the action, you can load SAIFProductionSet.act from the *Photoshop 5 Artistry* CD. Also, don't forget to refer to Chapter 4: Automating with Actions.

STEP 38: Click the triangle beside Crop&Save to open the action and view the individual steps.

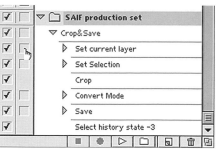

STEP 38: Click the second column (the breakpoint column) to set a breakpoint at the Set current layer step and also the Save step. This allows the user to input specific information at those stages.

HINTS FOR PREPARING GRAPHICS FOR AN ONLINE VIDEO EDIT

72ppi (pixels per inch) is the preferred resolution for videotape.

All of your images should be created at a 4:3 aspect ratio.

For nonbroadcast, 640x480 pixels is okay. However, as more people upgrade their computer systems, more multimedia productions are being built at higher resolutions, such as 800x600 and using thousands of colors rather than 256.

For transfer to D1digital tape, images need to be 720x486.

For Broadcast spec, images must be 648x486 pixels (analog transfers), 720x486 pixels for digital transfers.

All your files should be the same resolution. It's a bad idea to give post-production facilities files of different resolutions (that is, 500x400, 640x480, and 32x200 pixels).

Most post-production facilities prefer that your graphics be either in the PICT format or QuickTime format. For PC graphics, facilities can usually handle TARGA, FLI, or FLC formats. If you are transferring an animation composed of numerous individual images, such as PICT or TARGA files, those files ideally should be numbered (that is, 001, 002, 003, 004, and so on). For PCs you will probably need files numbered with an extension after (that is, 001.tga, 002.tgs, 003.tga) Don't give the post facility a folder of images that all have different names such as Chip1, Chip1a, Fire1, Fire2, Dog, Today1. Just use numbers (not letters) if you have Mac files.

If you are importing Photoshop files into Adobe Premiere, you'll either have to flatten the image or import one layer at a time. If you import a single layer, Premiere will recognize the layer's transparency as an alpha channel. However, Premiere does not recognize layer masks or layer effects so you need to apply layer masks and create layers from any effects before importing.

You can import a layered file into Adobe After Effects, and After Effects will see all the layers, layer masks, layer transparency, and Blend modes. After Effects recognizes Adjustment layers and precomposes them. The program does not currently recognize layer effects, so you need to create a separate layer using Layer/Effects/Create Layer.

Hints courtesy Nancy White, Lizmar Productions

CALCULATIONS, PATTERNS,

USE THE NEW TYPE TOOL AND LAYER EFFECTS

COMPOSITE WITH TRANSFORMATION
AND BLEND MODES

USE PHOTOSHOP AND ILLUSTRATOR TOGETHER

USE FILTERS, TEXTURES, PATTERNS, AND BITMAPS

MANY WAYS TO CREATE SHADOWS

USING CALCULATIONS AND APPLY IMAGE

FILTERS, AND EFFECTS

Taken on location in Bandon, Oregon with a Canon EOS 10-S/28-105 Canon Zoom. Fuji Velvia film was used and the Image was scanned with a Lino/Hell Tango scanner. Corrections and final output from Photoshop.

BLEND MODES, CALCULATIONS, AND APPLY IMAGE

How each of the Blend modes work; the subtleties of using modes in Calculations, Apply Image, Layers, Fill and the painting tools; when and how to use Calculations versus Apply Image versus Layers.

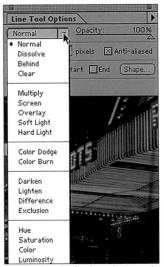

The Blend modes for the painting tools.

The Blend modes for the Fill command.

The Blend modes are used to determine how two groups of image information combine. The two groups of image information could be of various types within Photoshop. The first type could be a photographic image and the second a solid color that is painted or filled on top of the first image. You could do this using one of the painting tools or the Fill command. If you created a layer that was a solid color, you could also combine this layer with a photographic image on a second layer by using a Blend mode in the Layers palette. In the Layers palette, you can determine which Blend mode to use to combine two photographic images in the same layered Photoshop document. You can use the Apply Image command with different Blend modes to combine two-color photographic images that are in separate documents and have the exact same pixel dimensions. Finally, you can use the Calculations command with Blend modes to combine two images of the same size when you want a black-and-white mask channel as a result. The Blend modes appear in the painting tools, the Fill tool, the Layers palette, the Apply Image command, the Calculations command, and the Stroke command. Not all of the Blend mode options are offered in each of these areas. As we

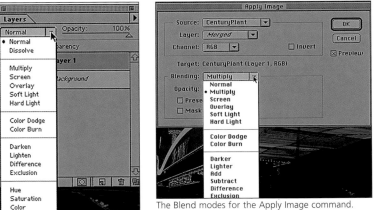

The Blend modes for Layers.

The Blend modes for the Apply Image command.

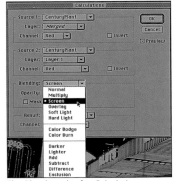

The Blend modes for Calculations.

explain each Blend mode, you'll see why some of them make more sense in one or another area. All of these options also offer you a way to use a mask as you combine the two groups of image information. The mask will affect the parts of the two groups that are combined.

THE TOOLS FOR BLENDING

First, we discuss the different tools and methods for blending and when it makes the most sense to use each of them. Later, we discuss each of the Blend modes and its unique applications within each of the different blending tools. You can find many of the images we use in this chapter in the Blend Modes Cals & Apl Im folder on the CD. Although this is not entirely a step-by-step hands-on session, we encourage you to play and explore these techniques with the images. By playing on your own, you learn new things, and you can have a lot of fun, too.

THE FILL COMMAND

The Edit/Fill command (Shift-Delete) is used to fill a selection, or the entire layer if there is no selection, with something like the foreground or background color, or from the pattern or History Brush location. The Blend mode and Opacity in the Fill tool just determine how this filling image will combine with what was there before. Normal, at 100% opacity, completely covers what was there before with the new color or image. I mention Image because you can change the "Use" pop-up to fill from the current History Brush setting or from the current pattern. An opacity of 50% will give half what was there before and half the new filled image or color. We usually use Fill to completely cover a selection or the entire image with a solid color or a tint. We also use Fill a lot to revert the selected area to a Snapshot or other location in the History palette. When you use Fill, you need to pick a Source, Opacity, and Blend mode before you do the operation, and then you have to undo it if you want to change it. If you need to prototype the opacity or mode of your Fill, use the layer techniques we show you in the book because it is quicker to make variations in the Layers palette. We used Fill to get the highlight effects in the pop-up dialog box on the previous page. Because we wanted them all to look the same, we just used the Rectangular Marquee to select the Blend Mode pop-up menu, used Select/Inverse to invert that selection, and then used Fill with 40% black in Normal mode to get the effect.

THE PAINTING TOOLS

You use a painting tool when you want to apply an effect by hand and softly blend it in and out, like you would do with an airbrush or paintbrush. These tools in Photoshop have a lot more power, however, due to the magic of digital imaging and the blending modes. Go through "The Tool Palette" to learn about the subtleties of each painting tool. With the Blend Mode options in the painting tools, you don't just lay down paint, or even a previous version of the image. Instead, you can control how this paint or image combines with what is already there. Add the Photoshop 5 History palette and the ability to use the History Brush to paint from any step in the last 100 steps, and you have super power and flexibility. This History Brush also allows you to use the Blend modes. See Chapter 12: History Palette, History Brush, and Snapshots for more information.

COMBINING IMAGES USING LAYERS

Layers and adjustment layers are the most powerful ways to combine two or more images while keeping the most options open for further variations and many

Here's how we created the highlighted pop-ups on the previous page with Fill. We selected the pop-up with the Marquee tool and then used Select\Inverse followed by the above Fill command.

The Night Cab Ride image produced using many layers.

versions of your composite. Sometimes we use layers even when we are dealing with a pattern or solid color. The reason is that with layers, you can always go back and change something, move something, change the opacity or Blend mode without having to totally redo your image. Unlike the contents of the History palette, which go away when you close the file, layers stay around as long as you want. You can try an effect and be able to turn it on and off at will. Layers gives you the most sophisticated control of the Blend modes as well as many other abilities at the same time. If you don't understand layers, and if you haven't read Chapter 11: Layers, Layer Masks, and Adjustment Layers, you should read it now before you continue. When you use layers, your files may get much bigger because many layers add at least the original size of the file in that layer to your document size. Adjustment layers allow you to do color changes with a new layer without adding all the extra file size. Layered documents have to be saved in Photoshop format to maintain the flexible layer information. Still, layers are WAY COOL!

COMBINING IMAGES, LAYERS, AND CHANNELS USING APPLY IMAGE

The basic function of Apply Image is to copy one image, layer, or channel, called the Source image, and use it to replace another image, layer, or channel, the Target image, of exactly the same pixel resolution. To combine two items with Apply Image, they must be exactly the same width and height in pixels. The two images are combined using a blending mode and opacity that are chosen from the Apply Image dialog box. You can optionally choose a mask, which will combine the images only where the mask is white. Apply Image is useful when copying a channel or layer from one place to another, especially when you want to put it on top of an existing channel or layer and combine the two with a Blend mode.

Before you enter Apply Image, you should choose the Target image, layer, or channel. This will be modified when you leave Apply Image by choosing OK, so you may want to first make a copy of that target item.

The Las Vegas Night image.

The Century Plant image.

The Vegas Lights mask.

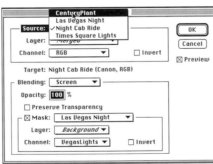

Here we see most of the possible options of Apply Image. Before we entered Image/Apply Image, we made Night Cab Ride the active document in Photoshop. Canon was the active layer within that document. This active item is always selected as the Target of Apply Image, so you will be changing that document, channel, or layer. The Source pop-up window shows you only documents that are the same pixel size and dimensions as the target document. Here, we chose the Century Plant as the Source. The Blending pop-up is where you choose the Blend mode. There is an optional mask, selected here, which causes the blending to happen only within the areas of the mask that are white. If the Preview button is on, you see the results of the Apply Image in the Target window. This lets you try different options and see what they do.

The results of the Apply Image settings shown in the previous illustration. The Century Plant image is brought into the Night Cab Ride composite where the Las Vegas Night mask was white. In that area, it is blended with the Canon layer using the Screen Blending mode.

Chapter 36: Blend Modes, Calculations, and Apply Image

If the Preview button is on, you can see the results of the operation in the target window. In choosing the source, you can pick any open document, layer, or channel, as long as it's the same exact pixel dimensions as the target. Like the source, the mask can be any open document, layer, or channel that is the same pixel dimensions as the target. The Preserve Transparency option will stop the Apply Image command from changing any transparent areas within a layer. Both the source and the mask have an Invert check box that you can check to turn that selection to its negative.

In this chapter, we use three images that we have cropped to be exactly the same pixel size. They are the Las Vegas Night image, the Century Plant image, and a modified Night Cab Ride image. The Las Vegas Night image has a mask, called VegasLights, that is white where the neon lights are. There are no particular masks in the Century Plant image. Here are some other examples of using Apply Image, using the same three images, so you can get an idea what the com-

Here we see a more simple application of Apply Image. The source, target, and resulting images are shown here. The Screen Blend mode is analogous to taking transparencies of the two images and projecting them onto the same screen from two different slide projectors. The light areas of the images are emphasized. Setting the opacity to 85% made the Las Vegas Lights a little less bright in the composite image below.

The Times Square Canon image.

The Las Vegas Night image.

The composited image.

mand does. If you want to get a result that is more than one channel deep, you need to use Apply Image instead of Calculations. The effects you can create with Apply Image can also be achieved by using layers, by first copying the different components into a layer document. Layers give you more flexibility because the different layers don't have to start out being the exact same size and you can move them around side-to-side as well as above-and-below in relationship to each other. Effects within layers can also be done and undone in multiple combinations using the Eye icons.

You should use Apply Image mostly in cases where you already know the spatial relationship between the objects being combined, and you have to do the operation quickly for some production purpose. Motion picture and multimedia work (where you are compositing many frames of two sequences together that have been preshot in registration, to be lined up exactly) is a good example of how you would use Apply Image. This process could be automated over hundreds of frames by using actions or by using some other application automation software.

COMBINING CHANNELS USING CALCULATIONS

The main purpose of the Calculations command is to use the Blend modes to combine images, layers, or channels and end up with a single black-and-white channel as the result. When you need a color result, use Apply Image; when you need a channel result, use Calculations. Calculations provides for two source files, Source 1 and Source 2, and a Result file. When you enter Calculations, all three of these files are set to the active window within Photoshop. You can use the pop-up menus to change any of these files to any other open file that has the same pixel dimensions. The source files are the two that will be combined using the Blend mode that you choose. The Layer pop-up on each of these files is available for layered documents and allows you to choose the merged layer, which is the composite of all layers that

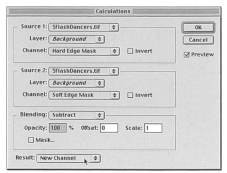

Here are the Calculations settings to produce the mask of the glow without the sign. When doing a Subtract, the item that you want to subtract should be in Source 1. The item you are subtracting from should be in Source 2. In this case, the result was a New channel. Depending on the choice we make for the Result, it could be a new Channel in the existing file, a new file itself, or a selection in the existing file.

The Flashdancers sign where we want to make a mask of just the glow without the sign so we can have separate control over each.

We have a hard-edge mask of just the sign. We put this into Source 1.

We have a soft-edge mask of the glow, including the area of the sign. We put this into Source 2.

Here is the resulting glow mask where we subtracted the hard-edge mask from the soft-edge mask.

To move the sign to another background, we used the hard-edge mask to copy the text into one layer and the glow mask to copy the glow into another layer. We then had separate color, blending and blur control over each item in the sign that allowed us to get the result we wanted on the new background.

With the Channel pop-up, you can select any channel including Transparency and layer masks.

currently have their Eye icons on or any other layer in the document.

The Channel pop-up allows you to choose any channel in the chosen file or layer. To access a layer mask channel, you need to first choose the layer that owns that layer mask. You can also choose the Transparency channel, which is a mask of any transparent areas in the chosen layer. This interface allows you to blend any two documents, layers, or channels that are open by using the blending modes, and to then put the result into a new channel, document or selection. These open items must have the same pixel dimensions as the active window. The blending interface also allows an optional mask, which will force the blending to happen only in the areas that are white in the mask. Both source items and the mask have an Invert check box to optionally invert any of them before doing the composite. You will learn more about Apply Image and Calculations as you go through each of the Blend modes next.

UNDERSTANDING EACH BLEND MODE

Let's start out with the Blend modes listed in the Edit/Fill command, which would have the same effect as the Blend modes used by the painting tools if you were painting with the same color, pattern, or image that you were filling with. When you use the Fill command, you fill a selected area. You can fill with the foreground or background colors as well as from the History palette or from a pattern. All these options are available to paint from by using different flavors of the painting tools. When you paint, you select your "fill area" as you paint instead of from a selection. In either case, the modes work the same. Some of these modes also apply to layers and to the Calculations and Apply Image commands.

274

NORMAL

When painting or filling in Normal mode, you are filling the selected or painted area with the foreground or background color, the History palette, or a pattern. Normal mode for a top layer in the Layers palette means that the top layer will be opaque at 100% opacity. You will not see any of the layers below through this layer. You use Normal mode in Calculations or Apply Image to copy the source layer or channel to the target, or destination layer, or channel without any blending. This totally replaces the target, or destination, with the source.

DISSOLVE

Depending on the opacity of the dissolve, this mode appears to take the opacity as a percentage of the pixels from the blend color and place them on top of the base color. The base color is the color or image that was there before the dissolve. The blend color is the color or image that is being dissolved on top of the base color or image. Try this with two layers, setting the mode between them to Dissolve. If you set the opacity to 100%, you get all of the top layer and don't see the bottom layer. The same thing happens if you use a fill of 100% or paint at 100% in Dissolve mode. When you set the opacity to 50% and look at the pixels up close, you will see that there are about 50% pixels from the top layer and 50% from the bottom. If you set the opacity to 10%, only 10% of the pixels are from the top layer or color.

With Dissolve, the pixels seem to be entirely from one image or the other; there doesn't seem to be any blended pixels. If you want to achieve this type of look between two images but have more control over the pattern used to create the dissolve, create a layer mask on the top layer filled with solid white. Now, go into the Add Noise filter and add Gaussian noise to the layer mask. Where the noise is black, the bottom layer will show through and you will get an effect similar to Dissolve. This way you can use Levels or Curves or even a filter to change the pattern in the layer mask and thus change how the two images are combined. The more noise you add, the more you will see of the bottom layer. Also, in this case, some of the pixels can actually be blends between the layers, especially if you use Gaussian Blur to blur your layer mask too. Dissolve is not an option with Apply Image or Calculations, but you can get a similar effect here by using a Gaussian noise mask as you combine images, layers, and channels.

BEHIND

This Blend mode is used to paint into the transparent part of a layer. It is available only from Fill and the painting tools and only if the layer has a transparent area. It is not available if the Preserve Transparency check box is checked for that layer. Behind allows you to paint a shadow or color behind an object (like a circle) in the layer, using a painting tool or the Fill command. The actual image in the layer won't be affected because Behind only paints into the transparent area. Painting in Behind mode is like painting on the back of the acetate. Here we see a shadow that was added to a circle using the Paintbrush tool in Behind mode with a large soft brush.

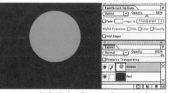

The green circle is in the top layer with red in the bottom layer. Now both layer's Eye icons are on.

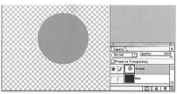

Here is just the circle with the Red layer turned off. The transparent area shows up as a checkered pattern.

We have painted black into this transparent area using Behind mode with a large soft brush.

Here we see the shadow without the background color. When painting in Behind mode, we didn't have to worry about painting on top of the green. It is automatically masked out because it is not transparent.

CLEAR

The Clear mode is available only when in a layered document from the Fill command, the Paint Bucket tool, and the Line tool. It will fill the selected area, the line in the case of the Line tool, with transparency. This is the little checkerboard pattern that means you can see the layers below through the transparent areas. Clear is also available as a menu item from the Edit menu, although Edit/Clear behaves a little differently depending on whether you are in a normal layer or a *Background* layer. When in a normal layer, Edit/Clear fills the selected area with transparency. When in a *Background* layer, Edit/Clear fills the selected area with the background color.

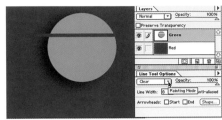

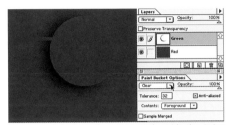

Here we used the Line tool to create the red line going across the circle by drawing the line in Clear mode.

This brings up an interesting thing about Photoshop and how it deals with layers and the special layer called the *Background* layer. When you open a TIFF file or some other file that doesn't contain layers into Photoshop and then go into the Layers palette, you will notice that these files contain a single layer called *Background*. This isn't really a layer in the true sense of the word, because it can't have any transparent areas. If you make a selection in a Background layer of an image and then choose Edit/Clear, the selected area will be filled with the background color. You will notice that Clear does not show up as an available option for a Background layer within Fill or the Line and Paint Bucket tools. If you double-click on this special Background layer within the Layers palette and rename it something else, it will turn into a normal layer. Now, Edit/Clear will fill a selection with transparency, and Clear is available in the Line and Paint Bucket tools. Until you rename the *Background* layer and make it a real layer, you can't interchange its order in the Layers palette with other layers.

Here we clicked on the green circle with the Paint Bucket in Clear mode leaving only the shadow with this nice effect.

MULTIPLY

Multiply is a very useful Blend mode that is available within all the Blend mode pop-ups. When you multiply two images together, it is analogous to what you would see if both the images were transparencies and you sandwiched them together and placed them on a light table or projected them onto a screen. Anything that was black in either image would be black in the resulting composite image. Anything that was white or clear in either image would let you see through it to what was in the other image in that area. When you multiply two images together, the 0–255 values of the corresponding pixels in each image are actually multiplied together using the following formula:

A Multiply of the Century Plant and Las Vegas Night images, from the third page of this chapter, emphasizes the darker areas of each image.

(Source 1) x (Source 2) / 255 = destination

Just like doing a multiply in mathematics, the order of the Source 1 and Source 2 images doesn't matter. Dividing by 255 at the end forces all the values to be in the 0–255 range. You can see that when either Source value is 0, black, you are going to get 0 as the result. When either Source value is 255, white, you are going to get the other Source value as the result, because 255/255 = 1, so you end up multiplying the other Source value by 1.

SCREEN

Screen is sort of the opposite of Multiply, in that when you do a Screen between two images, anything that is white in either of the images will be white in the resulting image. Anything that is black in either image will show the other image in that black area. Screen, like Multiply, is also available in all the different Blend mode pop-

The original Glow mask we want to drop a gradient into.

Doing a Load Selection on the glow, left, and dropping the gradient into the selected area, produces the halo around the glow at the right side.

Unwanted halo effect

Create the gradient in a separate mask channel and use Calculations to Multiply for the effect at right.

A Calculations Multiply of the Gradient and Glow mask channels drops the gradient into the glow area without a halo.

A powerful use for Multiply is to seamlessly add a gradient to an existing selection. Let's say we wanted to use the Glow mask to create a glow that was bright at the left side and fading toward the right. To do this, we would want to drop a gradient into this mask. If you do a Load Selection on the mask and then create the gradient within that selection, you will get a light halo around the edge of the gradient toward the right side. This is caused by the loaded selection. To avoid getting this halo, just create the gradient in a separate channel and then multiply the two channels together, giving you a better fade.

ups. When you Screen two images together, it is analogous to what you would see if both the images were projected from two different slide projectors onto the same screen. Here is the formula for Screen:

255 - ((255 - Source 1) x (255 - Source 2) / 255) = destination

You can simulate the Screen command using the Multiply command if you first invert both of the Source images and then multiply them together, and finally, invert the result of that multiply. That is exactly what this formula for Screen does: (255 - Source1) does an Invert of Source 1. With the Screen formula then: the Invert of Source 1 is multiplied by the Invert of Source 2 and then is divided by 255. That part of the formula does the multiply of the two inverted images. Finally, subtracting that result from 255 at the end does the Invert of the result of that multiply, giving you a Screen. The important thing to remember between Screen and Multiply is that a Screen of two images will emphasize the lighter areas and a Multiply will emphasize the darker areas.

A screen of the Century Plant and Las Vegas Night images emphasizes the lighter areas of each image.

Soft Light

In Soft Light mode, the original image is blended with the blend color, pattern, or image by making the original image either lighter or darker depending on the blend image. If the blend image is lighter than 50% gray, the original image is lightened in a subtle way. Even where the blend image is pure white, the resulting image will just be lighter than before, not pure white. If the blend image is darker than 50% gray, the original image is darkened in a subtle way. Even where the blend image is pure black, the resulting image will just be darker than before, not pure black. The tonal values and details of the original are fairly preserved, just subtly modified by the blend image. If you add a 50% gray layer above an original image and set the Blend mode to Soft Light, you can then use a soft brush and paint or airbrush with white or black to dodge or burn the image by lightening or darkening this gray layer. Use less than 100% opacity on your brush to get more subtle effects. This is better than using the dodging or burning tool because it's infinitely adjustable because you're not actually changing the original image. You can easily get a 50% gray layer by clicking the New Layer icon in the Layers palette, choosing Edit/Fill, and filling at 100% with Use: 50% Gray and Mode: Normal.

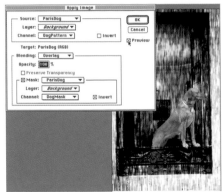

Apply Image was originally used to prototype the Paris Dog examples. The mask used to isolate the dog is seen here but we Invert it to actually get the effect in the background.

The original ParisDog image.

The original Dog pattern.

The Dog mask before inverting.

To actually produce the five final images, I set up a two-layer document and then used File/Save A Copy to save each flattened version after changing only the mode between each save. That was just a faster production choice.

The examples shown here use Apply Image and layers to combine my ParisDog image with a pattern that I created in Photoshop and a mask that stops the dog itself from being affected by the pattern. I ini-tially tried this out using Apply Image. The original ParisDog image, the grayscale DogPat-tern, and the DogMask were all in the same file. Before entering Apply Image, I selected the RGB background layer of ParisDog; this made that the target. For the source, I selected the DogPattern, which applies the pattern on top of the ParisDog. I set the mode to Overlay to create the effect and then decided that I didn't want the pattern on the dog. Choosing the Mask option allowed me to pick the Dog mask, and the Invert check box was turned on because the mask was actually white in the dog area. Turning on Invert made the mask white in the background and the white area of the

Chapter 36: Blend Modes, Calculations, and Apply Image

mask is where the DogPattern image is applied. With the Preview button on, I tried all the different Blend modes and could see that I wanted to use this as an example. At this point, I was going to have to produce five versions of this image, one for each Blend mode. When you use Apply Image, it actually changes the Target image, so to do five versions with Apply Image, I would have had to make five copies of the ParisDog, one for each Blend mode.

A more efficient way to do this, after prototyping the effect with Apply Image, was then to create the five versions from a layered document. The

bottom layer was the ParisDog image. I added a layer above this for the DogPattern, and to that layer I added a layer mask for the inverted Dog-Mask channel. Now to produce the five different versions, all I had to do was change the Blend mode in the Layers palette, once for each version, and then choose File/Save A Copy for each version to make a flattened TIFF copy with all channels and layers removed. For more information on using layer masks, see Chapter 40: The Portable Computer Ad or Chapter 31: Bob and the Kestrel.

Again, Photoshop layers are a great prototyping and production tool! When I took this photo on a residential alley in Paris, the dog was in this pose as I walked by. I pointed and focused my camera, and then the dog went back inside just as I was about to shoot. I stood there for a bit with the camera ready, and, sure enough, the dog returned and posed for me. It has always been one of my favorite shots.

Overlay: This is contrasty but it still preserves some of the tone and detail from the original.

Multiply: Notice how dark the shadows are compared to Overlay.

Screen: Notice how bright the highlights are compared to Overlay.

Soft Light: This preserves the most tone and detail from the original.

Hard Light: The highlight and shadow values and the lightness values come pretty much directly from the pattern.

Understanding Each Blend Mode

HARD LIGHT

In Hard Light mode, the original image is blended with the blend color, pattern, or image by making the original image either lighter or darker depending on the blend image. If the blend image is lighter than 50% gray, the original image is lightened and this lightening is a contrasty effect. If the blend image is pure white, the resulting image will be pure white. If the blend image is darker than 50% gray, the original image is darkened and this darkening is a contrasty effect. If the blend image is pure black, the resulting image will be pure black. In Hard Light mode, the resulting image seems to take its lightness value from the blend color, pattern, or image. Because the tonal values of the original are not very preserved, the adjustment is a radical one. If you add a 50% gray layer above an original image and set the Blend mode to Hard Light, you can then use a soft brush and paint with white or black to dodge or burn the image by lightening or darkening this gray layer. This will be a radical, contrasty dodge and burn. Use less than 100% opacity on your brush or you will get pure white or black. Remember that this effect is infinitely adjustable because you are not actually changing the original image. See the "Soft Light" section for how to get a 50% gray layer above the image.

OVERLAY

Overlay does a combination of Multiply and Screen modes. The dark areas of an original image are multiplied and the light areas are screened. The highlights and shadows are somewhat preserved, because dark areas of the image will not be as dark as if you were doing a Multiply and light areas will not be as bright as if you were doing a Screen. The tonal values and details of the original are preserved to some extent, but this is a more contrasty transition than Soft Light, just not as radical as Hard Light.

DARKEN AND LIGHTEN

The Darken and Lighten Blend modes are easy to understand. In the Darken mode, each of the corresponding pixels from the original image and the blend color, pattern, or image are compared, and the darker of the two is chosen for the result. In the case of Lighten, the lighter of the two pixels is chosen for the result. Within Apply Image and Calculations, these modes are called Lighter and Darker. These Blend modes are most useful in combining masks to create new masks. An example of this, shown here, would be the situation in which you have pasted two objects into a composite scene and for each object you have a mask. When you Paste in Photoshop, you always have a mask of the object, which is the transparency of the object's layer. You have a mask of each separate object, and now you need one mask that contains both objects at the same time.

Using Calculations to set the Blend mode to Lighter between the two masks will create the mask of both the objects. You can then use the inverse of

The shoes and the glasses have each been placed here separately.

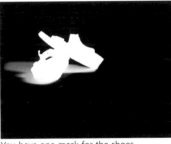

You have one mask for the shoes.

Another mask for the glasses.

These Calculations settings using Lighter will create the new mask below to the left.

This mask of both shoes and glasses was created with Calculations using Lighter.

To create this background mask with a single calculation, invert both the source masks and use Darker instead of Lighter.

Chapter 36: Blend Modes, Calculations, and Apply Image

this mask to give you a mask of the background. To do this in one step, select the Invert check boxes on both the Source channels in Calculations. Because both Source masks have now been inverted, you would have to use Darker to combine the two masks and get the final inverted mask with the white background.

Difference and Exclusion

Difference is one of the most useful blending modes. Difference compares two images and gives you a mask that is black where each of the two images are exactly the same and is nonblack and closer to white the more the images are different from each other. Here is the formula for Difference:

| *Source 1 - Source 2* | = *Destination*

Difference is similar to Subtract but the results are never inverted; they are always positive because the two vertical bars stand for absolute value and therefore make the result positive. With a little photographic planning, you can use Difference to automatically separate an image from its background. Pick a background that is quite different in color and brightness from the objects to be shot. First, place the objects, adjust your lighting, and shoot them. Without moving the tripod or changing the lighting, shoot the background without the objects. If these two photographs are scanned in register, doing a Difference between them can often automatically give you a mask of just the objects. The two objects in the example here were shot on a tripod using a Kodak DCS electronic camera. When using an electronic camera, scanning the images in register is no problem because they are sent directly from the camera to the computer. In this case, we had the computer in the studio, so we could try Difference between the two images and then adjust the lighting and exposure to make sure we'd get the best knock-out. Actually, to create the final mask of the objects in this case, we used Calculations first to do a Difference between the Red channels of the two images; then we used Calculations again to Screen the results of the Difference with itself. Screening an image (or mask) with itself brings out the brighter parts of the image. We then brought this Screened mask into Levels and increased its brightness and contrast slightly again to darken the blacks and brighten the whites. Finally we did some quick editing of the masks of the actual objects. Still, this process was faster using Difference and Screen than if we had done the knock-out by hand. Using Difference to do knock-outs works even better for objects that have no shadows or where the shadow is not needed in the knock-out.

A digital camera hooked up to a computer is starting to become a reality for more and more photographers today, especially those who do a lot of repetitive catalog work. Also, consider the motion picture industry or multimedia applications where artists

The objects as originally shot with the Kodak DCS system.

The background shot with the same lighting and camera position.

Difference between the Red channels of the background and the object shots. Try each channel and see which does the best job.

These Calculations settings using Difference will create the mask to the left.

Above mask after some quick edits and a brightness adjustment with Levels. Sometimes using Calculations to Screen a mask with itself will bring out the bright values even more. After that, Levels can by used to redarken the shadows, adjust the shadow midtones, and further brighten the highlights that represent the objects you are knocking out.

New background placed behind the objects using an inverted version of the mask to the left.

The Positive Version of the Image.

The Negative Version of the Image.

Exclusion of the top Black to White Layer with the Positive image in the Layer below.

Layer setup for Exclusion above.

Layer setup for Difference below.

Difference of the Top Black blending to White layer with the Positive image in the layer below.

or technicians might have to knock out hundreds or even thousands of frames to composite two sequences together. With Difference and a little computer-controlled camera work, this situation could also be automated. Say you're shooting some guys on horses riding across a field that you will later want to superimpose on another scene. Have a computer remember all the frame-by-frame motion of the camera while shooting the scene. Now immediately, while the lighting hasn't changed, use the computer to move the camera back to the original position at the beginning of the scene. With computer control, reshoot all those frames without the horses to just get the backgrounds. Now using Difference and an Actions Batch, to automate hundreds of frames, you can quickly create a knockout of all those frames.

Exclusion is similar to Difference but not as intense. An Exclusion with black will do nothing to the image, as will a Difference with black. An Exclusion with white will invert the image completely, as will a Difference with white. An Exclusion with 50% gray leaves you with 50% gray, whereas a Difference with 50% gray still changes the image to make it appear partially negative. A Difference from black blending toward white is a slow transition from a positive image to a negative image with no gray section in the middle. In an Exclusion from black blending toward white, the portion from black to 50% gray is actually a transition from the positive image toward 50% gray. From 50% gray, the image turns more negative as we proceed toward white where the image is totally negative.

ADD AND SUBTRACT

Add and Subtract are available only in Apply Image and Calculations. Add takes the corresponding pixels of the original and the blend image and adds them together using the following formula:

Add = (Source 2 + Source 1) / Scale) + Offset = Destination

Subtract takes the corresponding pixels of the original and the blend image and subtracts them using this formula:

Subtract = (Source 2 - Source 1) / Scale) + Offset = Destination

Scale and Offset are additional parameters that you use with these blending modes in Apply Image or Calculations. The normal values for Scale and Offset for both Add and Subtract are 1 and 0. The order of the Source 1 and Source 2 parameters doesn't matter with Add, but it definitely does with Subtract. The Source 1 parameter is always subtracted from the Source 2 parameter, and the result has to be in the 0–255 range. When Source 1 is white, 255, which represents a selection, the result of the Subtract will always be black. The effect of the Subtract is then to remove the selected areas of the Source 1 mask from the selected areas of the Source 2 mask. This is a very useful function. Of the two, Subtract is the Blend mode I use more often, and I usually do Subtracts between masks. See the example of Subtract with Calculations earlier in this chapter.

When doing either an Add or a Subtract, the Offset value will make the resulting mask lighter if the offset is positive, and darker if the offset is negative. The offset is a number, in the 0..255 range, that will be added to the result of each corresponding pixel's calculations. If we do an Add of two images and set the scale to 2, we are getting an average of the two. This would give us the same

Chapter 36: Blend Modes, Calculations, and Apply Image

result having one image in a layer on top of the other with the top image having a Normal Blend mode and 50% opacity. With the Add command, you have the additional control of using the Offset parameter to make the resulting image either lighter or darker.

Hue, Saturation, Color, and Luminosity

These blending modes will affect the original image by using either the hue, saturation, color, or luminosity of the blend color, pattern, or image as the hue, saturation, color, or luminosity of the original image. In these examples, combining the two sides of the desert (the original desert Century Plant and Las Vegas), you can see how the Century Plant scene is modified by the hue, saturation, color, and luminosity of the Las Vegas Night scene. The Las Vegas scene has very intense hues that are also very saturated, so it is easy to see what happens with these two images. To get these different effects, we placed the Las Vegas scene as a layer on top of the Century Plant layer and just changed the layer Blend mode of the Las Vegas layer. In Hue mode, you see the hues from the Las Vegas scene, but the saturation and the intensity of those hues, and all the details, come from the Century Plant scene. In Saturation mode, the highly saturated values from the bright neon lights intensify the more subtle hues and details from the Century Plant scene. Color mode combines the hue and saturation from Las Vegas with the details, or luminosity, of Century Plant. When you put the Las Vegas scene in Luminosity mode, then you are seeing all the details from that Las Vegas scene but the more subtle hue and saturation values from the Century Plant. In the Las Vegas scene, there are large black areas. These have no hue or saturation values, which is why they show up as gray when in Hue, Saturation, or Color modes.

The Las Vegas Night image.

The Century Plant image.

A more interesting way to combine these two images is to double-click on the Las Vegas layer to bring up the Layer Options. Moving the left, Shadow, slider to the right in the This Layer part of Layer Options, removes the black part of the Las Vegas scene from the composite. In the final example of this image, we have used the Move tool to move the Las Vegas layer up a little bit. Now Las Vegas is at the end of the trail in the desert. We then double-clicked on the Las Vegas layer to bring up its Layer Options. We are in Luminosity mode, but the colors of the Century Plant image show through in the black areas of Las Vegas because we have moved the Shadow sliders of This Layer over to the right.

First, we moved the Shadow slider to the right to 10. That removed all the digital values from 0 to 10 from the composite, allowing the Century Plant to show through. This produces jaggy edges on the transition between Las Vegas and the Century Plant backgrounds. By holding down the

The Las Vegas Hue with the Century Plant saturation and luminosity.

The Las Vegas Color (hue and saturation), with the Century Plant luminosity.

The Las Vegas Saturation with the Century Plant hue and luminosity.

The Las Vegas Luminosity with the Century Plant hue and saturation.

Understanding Each Blend Mode

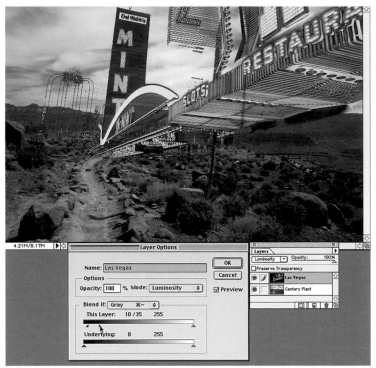

Here we see the results of using Layer Options in Luminosity mode to completely remove the black values in the 0–10 range and to blend out the black values in the 11–35 range from the composite of Las Vegas and the Century Plant. We double-clicked on the Las Vegas layer to get the Layer Options dialog box.

Option key and sliding the right-most part of the Shadow slider further to the right, the Shadow slider has now split. We moved the right-most part of this slider to 35. The meaning of this is that the black values in Las Vegas from 0 to 10 are completely removed, and the values from 11 to 35 are blended out making a softer edge between these two images. The Luminosity values in Las Vegas from 36 to 255 are still retained within this composite. For more information on this powerful Layer Options dialog box, see Chapter 11: Layers, Layer Masks, and Adjustment Layers, and Chapter 38: Posterize, Bitmaps, and Patterns.

COLOR DODGE AND COLOR BURN

Color Dodge brightens the original image as the blending color goes further toward white. A Color Dodge with black does nothing; then as the blending color gets lighter, the original image picks up brightness and color more and more from the blending color. Color Burn is similar but opposite. A Color Burn with white does nothing; then as the blending color gets darker, the original image picks up darkness and color more and more from the blending color.

Have fun with all the Photoshop Blend modes!

The Positive version of the image.

The Black to White layer by itself.

The Spectrum layer by itself.

Color Burn of the Top Black blending to White Layer with the Positive image in the layer below.

Color Dodge of the Top Black blending to White Layer with the Positive image in the layer below.

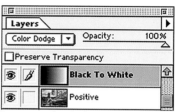

Layer setup for Black to White Color Burn and Dodge above.

Layer setup for Spectrum Color Burn and Dodge below.

Color Burn of the Top Spectrum Layer with the Positive image in the layer below.

Color Dodge of the Top Spectrum Layer with the Positive image in the layer below.

Understanding Each Blend Mode

HANDS-ON SESSION: Bike Ride in the Sky!

*Combining two color images using two gradient masks
and Multiply to create a high-flying bicyclist; using
Blend modes versus Illustrator text treatments to create
cool text effects; the new Photoshop 5 editable text;
bevel, shadow, and shading effects.*

The original bicycle.

Some interesting clouds!

I was playing in Photoshop one day and created one of my favorite images using two gradients to blend a cyclist into the clouds. Multiplying this image with its negative made it even more interesting. Here we use this image to play with some text effects.

COMBINING THE IMAGES WITH GRADATIONS

STEP 1: Open the Clouds and BikeRider files in the Bike Ride in the Sky folder and crop the copyright notices from the bottom of both. Click on the BikeRider file to make it active. Choose Window/Show Channels (Shift-F10) and Window/Show Layers (F10) if the Channels and Layers palettes are not currently visible. Click on the New Channel icon to the left of the Trash icon at the bottom of the Channels palette to create a new channel.

STEP 2: Linear Gradient Tool Options.

STEP 2: New channel with gradient blend.

STEP 2: Double-click on the Gradient Blend tool (or type G and then Return) and set the options as shown in the illustration for this step. Type D to make sure the foreground color is white and the background color is black. Click at the top of the channel and hold down the Shift key as you drag downward to blend from white at the top edge of the channel to black at the bottom. The Shift key forces the line you draw to stay vertical. Make sure you start your blend exactly at the top edge of the file and finish exactly at the bottom; otherwise, the top won't be pure white and the bottom pure black. If you use Full Screen mode or increase the window size to slightly larger than the file itself, finding the edges will be easier.

STEP 3: Drag the channel to the Load Selection icon at the bottom left of the Channels palette, or just Command-click on Channel #4 to load this selection. Now click on the RGB channel (Command-~) and choose Edit/Copy to copy the RGB channels of this file.

Now go to the Clouds file and choose Edit/Paste. Notice that the bike rider fades out toward the bottom because we did the Copy with the gradient selection loaded. We want a more dramatic fade-out with the wheels disappearing into the clouds, so choose Command-Z to get rid of the bike rider for the moment.

STEP 4: In the Clouds file, make a new channel and do a Gradient blend in this channel, just as you did in Step 2 with the bike rider. Command-click on this channel to load it as a selection. Click on RGB in the Channels palette to view the Clouds again.

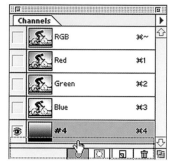

STEP 3: Command-click the channel or drag to the Load Selection icon to load the selection.

STEP 5: You still have the bike rider in the copy buffer from the earlier copy, but instead of just pasting the file this time, choose Edit/Paste Into. The already faded bike rider is being pasted into a selection of the Clouds file that also causes fading toward the bottom. Because of this, fewer and fewer of the pixels in the lower portion of the Clouds file are affected by the Paste Into command. By doing the Load Selection on the bike rider before copying him, you are applying a mask that fades the bike rider toward the bottom. Doing the Paste Into applies a second mask to the image and fades it further at the bottom. When you copy with a selection loaded and then Paste Into another selection, you are using two masks to affect the resulting composite. If you turn off the Eye icon for the *Background* layer, you will see the bike rider as faded by both masks. Now hold down the Shift key and click on the Layer 1 layer mask to turn it off. This is the bike rider you copied from the other file. The Layer 1 layer mask was created because you did a Paste Into. This is the mask you had loaded as a selection just before you did the Paste Into. Shift-click on the layer mask again to turn it back on; then turn the *Background* layer's Eye icon back on.

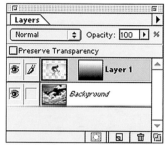

STEP 6: After doing the Paste Into, notice that the layer mask is not linked to the layer as it would be if we created a layer mask in the normal way.

STEP 6: Click on the leftmost Layer 1 Layer thumbnail to activate the layer and then use the Move tool (V or Command key down) to move the bike rider into a position that you like. Now use the Crop tool (C) to crop the composite to your liking, and then choose Flatten Image from the Layers palette menu to combine everything back to a single channel. Save this file in Photoshop format using the name NewBiker.

STEP 6: Move the bike rider and then crop the image; save as NewBiker.

USING MULTIPLY FOR A MORE INTERESTING EFFECT

STEP 7: Click on the *Background* layer and Option-drag it to the New Layer icon at the bottom of the Layers palette; name the new layer Inverse. The Inverse layer is now active (highlighted). Go to Image/Adjust/Invert (Command-I) to make a negative of the image. Change the Blend mode of the Inverse layer from Normal to Multiply. This does a Multiply of the pixels in this layer with the corresponding ones in the underlying layers. I have noticed that a Multiply of an image with its negative can often create interesting effects. We will be using Levels to look at this multiply composite and make it more interesting, but first we must merge these two layers or we will be running Levels on the Inverse layer alone. Choose Merge Down (Command-E) from the Layers palette menu. Now we can work on the composite as a single layer.

STEP 8: Go to Image/Adjust/Levels in the RGB channel and move the sliders to create more vivid color and contrast. Move the Input Highlight slider, the top right slider, to the left until you reach the beginning of the histogram information; then adjust the Brightness/Contrast slider to the right until you have an effect that you like. You may want to move the Input Shadow slider, the top-left slider, a bit to the right also to darken the blacks. Click on OK in Levels.

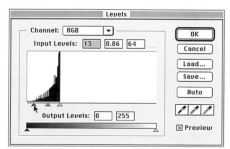

STEP 8: Adjusting levels makes this picture more interesting.

STEP 9: Type L to switch to the Lasso tool, and then press Return to bring up its Options palette. Now you can type a 5; then press Return again to preset the Lasso feather to 5 pixels. Lasso a portion of the clouds near one of what remains of the men that were originally holding up the bicycle. Now do Command-Option-click and drag to drag a copy of this selected area over on top of the man to cover what remains of him. Command-Option-dragging a selection creates a floating selection, a copy of the selected area, which you can move around by clicking and dragging inside its boundaries. Use Command-H to hide the edges of your copy; this makes it easier to see how it blends. When you are happy with its location, Choose Select/Deselect (Command-D) to make it a permanent part of the current layer. If you press the Delete key when working on a copy like this, it will go away. In older versions of Photoshop, these floating copies used to be called Floating Selections and they showed up as a temporary layer in the Layers palette. Now, in Photoshop 5, they no longer show up there; they have no name, and to change their Opacity or Blend mode, you use the Filter/Fade command. You may have to take portions of several clouds to make the image look smooth. You can use the Rubber Stamp tool to clone portions of the clouds, the Smudge tool to soften the effect, or the Blur tool to smooth transitions at this point also. When you have removed all traces of the men, press Command-S to resave this file as NewBiker.

TEXT EFFECT ONE

This first type of text technique was originally learned from Kai Krause's helpful tips on channel operations that have been posted on America Online for the last few years. Check out the keyword Photoshop on America Online for all of Kai's interesting techniques and lots of useful Photoshop info from all over. The steps we are using here are somewhat different from Kai's channel operations, and they are made easier to understand by doing them using layers. This is a more traditional Photoshop text and glow effect created using channels. Although this manual process is more work than the new built-in effects, I'm sure some of you will find creative uses for variations on this theme that can't be done with the new auto shadows and glows. We will show you some of the new Photoshop 5 text, shading and bevel effects later in this chapter.

STEP 1: Use File/New to make a new Mode Grayscale document called Text that is 600 pixels wide by 150 pixels high with a Resolution of 72dpi. Set the Contents to White, and then click on OK. Click on the default colors box or type D to make sure the foreground color is black. Type T to get the Type tool and then click down in the Text window to bring up the Type Tool dialog box and type "Bike Ride in the Sky!" in Times Bold 60 pt., or a similar heavy bold font, with Anti-aliased and Auto Kern on. Choose OK in the Type Tool dialog. Then use the Move tool to position the type in the center of the white background, and then choose Merge Down from the Layers palette menu. Double-click on the *Background* layer and name it Plain Text. Make a copy of this layer by Option-dragging it to the New Layer icon at the bottom of the Layers palette and name it Blur & Offset.

STEP 1: Rename the *Background* layer Plain Text.

STEP 2: Make the Blend mode for the Blur & Offset layer Darken. This chooses the darker parts of the two layers. Do a Filter/Blur/Gaussian Blur (Shift-F4) of 5 pixels and then a Filter/Other/Offset of 6 pixels to the right and 4 pixels down. Make sure Repeat Edge Pixels is chosen in the Offset filter. If you wanted black text with a gray drop shadow, you could stop now. We'll go further.

STEP 3: Option-drag the Blur & Offset layer to the New Layer icon and name the copy Multiply. Set its Blend mode to Normal for now. Choose Image/Adjust/Equalize to spread the blur even further in this Multiply layer. Then Gaussian blur this layer by 5 pixels to soften this spread, and finally, choose Image/Adjust/Invert (Command-I). We invert this blur at the end because we will eventually want to colorize it as a glow, and for that purpose we need a light gray blur area. We also want the area surrounding the glow to be black so we can later remove it. Now, set the Blend mode for this layer to Multiply. Remember that Multiply will emphasize the dark areas of either image.

STEP 4: Make a copy of this Multiply layer by again Option-dragging it to the New Layer icon. Name this one Difference. This actually copies step 3, part 2 (see illustration). Now change the Blend mode in this latest layer to Difference. Choose File/Save to save this layered version and then use Image/Duplicate (F5) with Merged Layers Only on to create a single layer version of this image called SkyText.

STEP 5: Now you are working on the single layer Sky Text file. Go to Image/Mode/RGB to change the mode to RGB. You need to do this to add color to the text. Now choose Image/Adjust/Hue/Saturation (Command-U). Click on both the Colorize and the Preview boxes and drag the Hue slider to the right until you get a nice purple, or some other color you like better. You may also want to increase the Saturation and lower the Lightness values to get a deeper, darker color. Choose OK when you are happy with the color. Now use the Move tool (V) to drag and drop a copy of this layer onto your New-Biker image. Use the Move tool to move the text to a location you like. Double-click on this new layer and name it SkyText. You will now be in the Layer Options dialog box. Drag the left-most This Layer slider to the right slightly until most of the black background is removed. Hold down the Option key and drag just the right side of that slider triangle further to the right until you get a shadow effect that you like. For more information on Layer options,

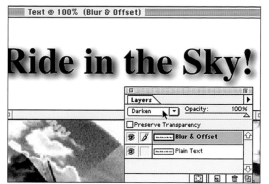

STEP 2: The Blur & Offset layer set to Darken mode.

STEP 3: Part 1, Equalize the Multiply layer .

STEP 3: Part 2, After the Equalize, Gaussian Blur 5 pixels and Invert with the mode set to Normal.

STEP 3: Part 3, After changing its mode to Multiply. That multiplies this layer with the step 2 results in the lower layers.

STEP 4: The result of a difference between step 3, part 2 and step 3, part 3. When you do a Difference, areas that are the same become black and areas that are far apart become white to gray depending on how far apart their corresponding pixels are.

STEP 5: Final text after Hue/Saturation.

Text Effect One

STEP 5: Move the Hue slider to colorize text.

STEP 5: Blend out black on the text layer gradually with Layer Options.

The final Text One effect.

see Chapter 11: Layers, Layer Masks, and Adjustments Layers, and Chapter 38: Posterize, Bitmaps, Textures, and Patterns. File/Save again as NewBiker.

TEXT EFFECT TWO: PHOTOSHOP AND ILLUSTRATOR

Now we will be switching between Photoshop and Illustrator. We will be using both programs for several reasons: first, we want to set our type on a path; second, we want our type to print at a very high resolution to avoid looking jagged; third, Illustrator will allow us to easily kern and resize our type; fourth, we'd like the ability to make further corrections to the underlying Photoshop file without disturbing the text. So fasten your seatbelts!

STEP 1: In the NewBiker image, double-click on the *Background* layer and rename it to Biker; then rename the Layer 1 layer to Text Effect One. We are going to add some text above the bike rider's back, and it would be nice to have some more space between the top of the bike rider and the top of the file. Click on the Biker layer; then choose Image/Canvas Size (Command-F8) and set the height to 1.4 inches. Click in the bottom center to put the gray Anchor there. This will force the new canvas to all come in at the top of the image. Choose OK on Canvas Size; then use the Marquee to make a selection the entire width of the image from just above the biker's head to where the transparent area of the new canvas starts. Choose Edit/New/Layer Via Copy (Command-J) to create a new layer using this selected area. Now use Layer/Transform/Scale and click in the top middle handle. Then drag to the top of the window to scale this part of the clouds to fill the transparent area. Press Return to end the Scale, and then choose Layer/Merge Down (Command-E) to merge this back into the Biker layer. Press Command-S to Save.

STEP 2: Open the Paths palette by going to Window/Show Paths (Shift-F11). Click on the Pen tool (P) in the Tool palette. If you haven't used the Pen tool before, it might take several tries to get used to the feel of the tool, but keep at it. If you need to, go back to Chapter 30: Bob Goes To... or Chapter 7: The Tool Palette and review the Pen tool sections. The Pen tool is a very powerful feature of Photoshop and when you get used to using it, you'll wonder how you ever worked without it. Press Return and make sure the Rubber Band option is on in the Pen Options. You are now going

STEP 2: The first click and drag.

STEP 2: The second click and drag.

to build a path on which you will set type. You want the path to curve over the back of the bicyclist, so click the Pen tool underneath the bicycle seat to set the first point on the path and drag a handle from this point at about a 45° angle toward the upper-left corner of the file. Then, let go of the mouse button and click and drag a point somewhere near the biker's shoulder or above his head. Drag this point almost directly horizontal and to the right. You'll see the actual path grow and curve as you manipulate this handle. Now, click on the Pen icon in the Tool palette and drag to switch to the Arrow tool (A). Use the Arrow tool to modify the curve until you get a curve that matches the biker's back and is offset from his shape several pixels. Double-click on Path in the Paths palette and rename this path Text Path. Click in the whitespace below Text Path in the Paths palette to deselect that path.

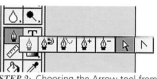

STEP 2: Choosing the Arrow tool from the Pen tool options in the Tool palette.

STEP 3: Choose Select/All to get the outline of your entire file and click on the SelectionToPath icon at the bottom of the Paths palette to make a new working path with this selection. Double-click on this new Work Path and name it Border. An alternative method is to Select/All and then make a path using the Make Work Path option in the Paths palette menu with the tolerance set to 2.0.

STEP 4: After you have named this second path, you should do File/Save to save this NewBiker image again. Now, choose File/Export/Paths to Illustrator, choose All Paths from the Write pop-up item, and click on Save to save a new file called New-Biker.ai. This will give you the default name, which is the name of the current file with the extension .ai. If you have enough memory to run Illustrator at the same time you have Photoshop open, start Illustrator now. If not, you'll have to quit Photoshop to work in Illustrator and return to Photoshop to do your effects later. If you have no experience using Illustrator, try not to get frustrated with this part of the exercise. Illustrator, like Photoshop, is a large and wonderful program with lots of power and opportunities to make mistakes.

STEP 3: Converting the Select/All into a path.

STEP 5: From Illustrator, first close the file Illustrator automatically creates called Untitled art 1; then open the file you just exported, NewBiker.ai. When the file opens, you will probably see only four sets of crop marks and the outline of the page size that you have set in your document layout option. Don't worry about how things look for now. Just go to View/Artwork and you should see a rectangle the size of your

Text Effect Two: Photoshop and Illustrator

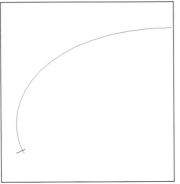

STEP 6: Click on the path with the Type tool.

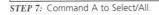

STEP 7: Command A to Select/All.

STEP 7: The Character dialog box in Illustrator. Your type sizes may be different depending on the font and resolution of your file.

STEP 7: Text kerned and resized.

Photoshop file and the path that you drew for the type.

STEP 6: Use the Magnify tool, Command-Spacebar-click as in Photoshop to zoom in on the path for the type. Click on the Type tool in the Illustrator Tool palette and you will notice that the horizontal baseline under the tool becomes wavy as you put the Type tool on top of the Text Path. This is the Path Type tool. Click down on the path near the bottom-left point and you get a flashing insertion point. Type "Bike Ride in the Sky!"

STEP 7: Then, with the Type tool still selected, press Command-A (Select All), and then Command-T to bring up the Character dialog box. Change the type face to Times Bold at a point size where all the type fits and looks good (or go wild, choose Futura or some nice fat face). If you know how to use Illustrator, kern and resize the type to your heart's content. When you are happy with the type, use File/Save As to save the file with the same name in Illustrator 6.0 or 7.0 format or the most modern Illustrator format you have. Just overwrite the existing file when it asks you about that.

STEP 8: Back in Photoshop, reopen NewBiker if you had to leave Photoshop to bring up Illustrator. Zoom out so you can see the entire image on your screen. Click on the Text Effect One layer to make it the active layer. Now go to File/Place and choose the Illustrator file NewBiker.ai. You will get a bounding rectangle with an X over it to show the size of the EPS file. In this case, it should be exactly the same size as the Photoshop file because of the Border path we created. Use Return to rasterize this text, and that will create a new layer called NewBiker.ai. Rename it to Illustrator Text.

STEP 9: This Illustrator Text layer is back in Photoshop, so you can use Photoshop to create a shadow from it. If you are printing this file with an imagesetter, the actual text should be output from Illustrator to get the smoothest edges. If this is a multi-media or Web project and the final image will be low-res screen pixels anyhow, then you might as well produce your text from this file in Photoshop. If you are going to produce the final text from Photoshop, you can use the new Photoshop 5 shadow, shading, and bevel effects on this text you imported from Illustrator. These are described in the next section of this chapter. In any case, you needed Illustrator to wrap the text around the path. If we are going to print the text from Illustrator, we will still want to create the shadow in Photoshop, so this is a case where the new built-in shadows won't work and we have to make the shadow manually. Option-drag this Illustrator Text layer to the New Layer icon and call the new layer Shadow. Choose Edit/Fill (Shift-Delete) and fill this with black, making sure the fill options 100%, Normal, and Preserve Transparency are on. Now drag this Shadow layer below the Illustrator Text layer, and then use the Move tool to offset the shadow depending on the direction of your desired light source. Finally, do Gaussian Blur of about 2 to complete the shadow effect. You can also change the Opacity of the shadow from the Layers palette. Now click back on the Illustrator Text layer and change its color by picking the color you want and then using Edit/Fill again to fill this text with the new color. This allows you to see the effect with the colored text and shadow in Photoshop. If you were creating the entire image in Photoshop, you could use File/Save A Copy to save a flattened version with the layers you want for that usage. If you are printing the text from Illustrator, we need to go back there to complete the project.

STEP 10: Your goal now is to create an image you can import into Illustrator with the shadow for the text created in Photoshop. Turn off the Eye icons in the Illustrator Text and Text Effect One layers because we don't want them in the final Illustrator file. The actual text will be created and output from Illustrator because it can then be output at Imagesetter resolution. Choose File/Save A Copy named NewBiker.eps in Photoshop EPS format with Flatten Image, Exclude Alpha Channels, and Exclude Non-Image Data on. In the EPS dialog box, make a Mac 8-bit preview (TIFF for Windows) and save in Binary. Close Photoshop if you must to reopen Illustrator.

STEP 11: Go back to Illustrator 7.0 and choose File/Place to place NewBiker.eps. After placing NewBiker.eps, if you are still in Artwork mode, you will see a bounding rectangle with an X across it. Use the Selection tool, the top-left tool in Illustrator's Tool palette, and the arrow keys to position this rectangle exactly above the existing rectangle. For accuracy, you may want to zoom in considerably using Command-Spacebar-click. When the file is in position, send it behind the type by using Object/Arrange/Send to Back. Then, use View/Preview to switch to Preview mode. You can use the Selection tool to click on the type baseline and change the color with the Illustrator Color palette at this point. Just click on the color you want. Use Window/Show Color to bring up this palette. Just use File/Save to resave this final file as NewBiker.ai. This can now be printed to an imagesetter from Illustrator to get much finer edges on your text with PostScript text output. If you do further revisions to the Photoshop file, or have other versions of the file that you would like to try, you can click on the Photoshop image in Illustrator and choose File/Place. Illustrator will ask you if you want to replace

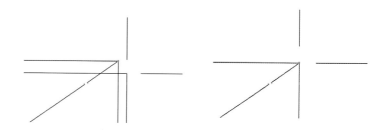

STEP 10: Layer palette setup and image as we save it in EPS format to be placed in Illustrator.

STEP 11: Your file may initially place out of alignment, like this.

STEP 11: Use the Selection tool and arrow keys to line up the file.

STEP 11: The final Text Effect Two as printed from an Illustrator EPS file placed in Quark.

Text Effect Two: Photoshop and Illustrator

the artwork that you have selected. If you say Replace to this prompt, your new artwork will pop into place automatically.

To see this Illustrator text with the new Photoshop 5 effects applied to it, open the NewBiker.psd file from the Extra Info Files folder of this chapter. To copy the effects from the bigger text version, I used Layer/Effects/Copy Effects while having the Bike Ride in the Sky layer active. Then I made a copy of the Illustrator Text layer and then used Layer/Effects/Paste Effects to add those shadow and bevel effects to that layer. I then when into each effect and edited the Global Angle and Blur amounts to work better with the smaller Illustrator text. Read the next section to find out about these exciting new Photoshop effects.

PHOTOSHOP 5 EDITABLE TEXT

Photoshop 5 has greatly expanded text capabilities although it does not have the capability to wrap text around a curve as we did in Illustrator. There are now the four options for text shown to the left that you get from the Tool palette. The two options that look like selections create a selection of the text area when you leave the Type Tool dialog. With these options you can still do individual kerning between letters, and you can also have different letters and words from different fonts, but you need to do all of this before leaving the Type Tool dialog. You would then have to fill the selection with a color or pattern or use the selection to create a mask allowing you to create text from an existing image layer. The more powerful new Type features are the Horizontal and Vertical Type options that actually create one of the new Photoshop 5 Type layers. When you click down on your image to create some type, you enter the redesigned Photoshop 5 Type tool. You type the text you want to create into the window at the bottom of the dialog box. You can then select any character, word, or group of words and change its font, face, size, and so on. You can have more than one font, face, size, and so on, just like you would be able to do in a word processor. When you click on the space between two characters, you can specify the kerning between those two characters. If the Preview checkbox is checked, you see a preview of all your text changes on the screen as you are making them. This is much more powerful than older versions of Photoshop. You can click in the Color box to bring up the Color Picker and specify the color of the text and you can also edit the Size, Leading, Tracking, and Baseline information just like a real word processor. The best thing about the new Text tool is that when you choose OK from this dialog, the text layer you create is editable even after you save the file and return to Photoshop on another day. To edit the text, just double-click on the name of this text layer in the Layers palette and the Type Tool dialog comes up again allowing you to change the text and all its attributes.

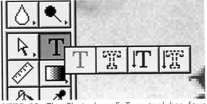

STEP 12: The Photoshop 5 Type tool has four options. From left to right, they are: regular horizontal editable text, horizontal text as a selection, vertical editable text, and vertical text as a selection. When you choose either text as a selection option, you end up with a selection of the text area when you leave the dialog. This cannot be further kerned or edited without re-creating it again from the dialog.

STEP 12: Here are the features of the greatly improved Photoshop 5 Type tool. Notice that we can set the font and face, kerning, size, color, and many more features of each character and word. We can then go back in here later and change them as many times as we want so long as we keep the type in a separate layer and don't choose the Layer/Type/Render Layer command.

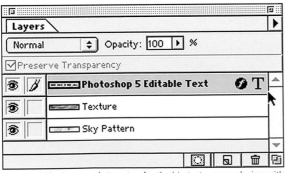

STEP 12: The Layers palette setup for the big text we are playing with here. The far-out thing is that we can double-click on the name of this text layer and then go back and edit the text itself, change the kerning, change the font or face of individual characters or words, change the size, and so on, and all the shadow and bevel features come along for the ride with no extra work!

STEP 12: Click on the Type tool (T) in Photoshop; then press the mouse button down at the top left of the screen in the NewBiker image. This will bring up the Type tool. Type the words Bike Ride in the Sky into the white box at the bottom of the tool. Click and drag to select all this text and pick a font, face, and size that you like. Notice that if you have the Preview button on, you will see the changes you

294

are making as you edit the text. Try clicking between two characters and changing the kerning between those two characters. It's great how you get instant preview on the screen. Click in the Color box and change the color of the text. Save your changes to this file but leave this file open so we can play with it more later. Open the file Photoshop5BigText from the folder for this chapter. Now we'll play with the new Photoshop 5 Shadow and Bevel and Emboss effects. It is a little easier to see and appreciate those effects when working with bigger versions of the type.

PHOTOSHOP 5 SHADOW, BEVEL, SHADING, AND EMBOSS EFFECTS

STEP 13: Switch back to the NewBiker image, and while working on the top Bike Ride in the Sky layer, choose Layer/Effects/Drop Shadow. Turn on the Apply button to add a drop shadow to your latest Bike Ride in the Sky text. Try out the different options with the Preview button on, and you will see the text changing while you play with the options. Choose OK to the Effects dialog and then use the Window palette to switch to the Photoshop5BigText image. I have already turned on a combination of effects here that we can look at and play with. As you see in the illustration to the left, each effect we are currently using has a check mark next to it in the menu bar. While in the Effects dialog, we can switch between the different effects by using the pop-up menu at the top of the dialog or using command keys for the different effects. With the Photoshop 5 Editable Text layer active, go to Layer/Effects/Bevel and Emboss first. The main effect we are using here is the Bevel and Emboss. Turn on and off the Apply button to see what this effect is doing. Here we are using the Global Angle so this effect can be in sync with the Shadow effect we are also using. You can see the parameters of both of these effects pictured here. I picked the Highlight color to make it appear that the highlight was a reflection relating to the yellowish paper in the background. The shadow color is a dark red that is also in sync with, but not as dark as, the color I used in the Shadow effect below. When you are using these new Photoshop 5

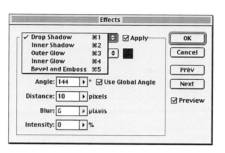

STEP 13: While in the Effects dialog, you can switch between effects by using command keys or this pop-up menu at the top of the dialog.

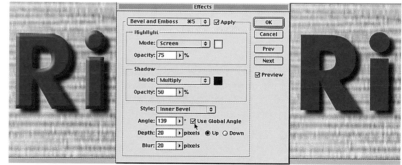

STEP 13: The Layer Effects menu for the text layer showing check marks next to the effects I'm using to create this beveled shadow text. Notice that you can use Copy Effects to copy a group of effects and then paste them into another layer. You need to do the Paste Effects command from this menu, not Command-V, to actually paste the effects into another layer. You can also change the Global Angle from here or choose to hide all the effects.

STEP 13: The features for Bevel and Emboss with those features turned on to the left and off to the right. The highlight color was chosen to almost appear as a reflection off the yellowish background. The Shadow colors between here and the Drop Shadow feature below were chosen to work well together. When you click on one of these colors, the Color Picker comes up, and you actually see the color changes preview on the screen while you are making them. This allows for very exacting control!

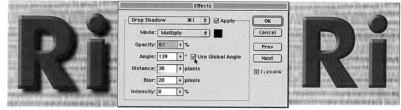

STEP 13: The features for Drop shadow with the shadow turned on to the left and off to the right. Notice that Use Global Angle is turned on here and in the Bevel and Emboss example so the shadows in the two features are in sync.

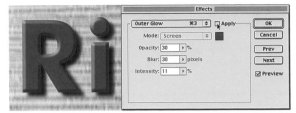

STEP 13: The features for Outer Glow. Here Outer Glow is off, and it makes the shadow a little darker than it would be with the glow on. The Outer Glow is on in the above illustration of the Drop Shadow on. Outer Glow makes the shadow appear like it is lighted a little from the glowing text above it.

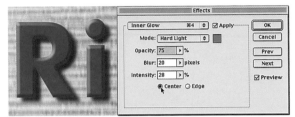

STEP 13: The features for Inner Glow. Inner Glow is making the inner nonbeveled part of the text brighter and more saturated than it would be with the feature off. The best way to see the difference here is to open the Photoshop5BigText file in the Extra Info Files folder and look at the difference on the screen with this feature on and then off.

effects, you will find that you switch back and forth between the 5 effect choices modifying each a little at a time until you get the combined effect you want. These effects can be added to any object that is surrounded by transparency within a layer. The nice thing about using these effects with the new Photoshop 5 editable text is that if you later go in and change the font, kerning, size or some other aspect of the text, the effects stay with you and just get applied to the new version of the text. Notice that in the Bevel and Emboss dialog (Command-5) that I am using the Inner Bevel style here. There are also Outer Bevel, Emboss and Pillow Emboss styles that you should try out to see what they do. For the Bevel and Emboss settings, I changed the Depth and Blur amount until they looked right with this size text. These would be different depending on the size and shape of text you are using. You also want to change the Opacity of the Highlight and Shadow to meet your needs. For the Drop shadow effect, you need to set the Opacity of the shadow, the Distance of the shadow from the object, the amount of Blur the shadow has and the Intensity of the shadow. Play with each of these to see what they do.

The other options we used in creating this text effect were Outer Glow and Inner Glow. Turn the Apply button on and off for Outer Glow and you will notice that Outer Glow adds a reddish tinge to the shadow and also lightens it as it gets nearer to the text, which is what would happen if the text were actually glowing. With this option, the Blur will change how the effect changes the appearance of the shadow, and the Opacity and Intensity also effect the appearance. Play with these settings so you can see what they do. The Inner Glow makes the solid interior parts of the text brighter and more saturated. Again, turn the Apply button on and off to see the difference on your computer screen. Play with the Opacity, Blur and Intensity options as well as with the Center and Edge choices. Try changing the color of each of these effects options to see how that shows up in the final composite effect. These new layer effects make it a lot easier to create quality text effects as well as effects on other objects. They are especially convenient when used along with the new Photoshop 5 Type tool!

The Layer/Type/Render Layer command turns your type and effects into pixels, as Photoshop 4 did, right away. After you render your text, it is no longer editable, so you usually don't use this command until you have to. When you use Save a Copy to save the image in a flattened form, like TIFF, the text and effects get rendered at that time, which allows you to leave the nonrendered, still editable text in the layered version of your document.

STEP 10: Photoshop 5 makes nice text, bevel and shadow effects!!!

Chapter 37: Bike Ride in the Sky!

STEP 13: Here we see the new Photoshop 5 text effect that we were able to get much more easily than the two previous manual effects—and I think it looks a lot better. Too bad we can't wrap this around a path too. Maybe that will be a feature for version 6.

STEP 13: Although we can't actually create the wrap around effect in Photoshop, we can apply the new Shadow, Bevel, and lighting effects to the text after we have imported it from Illustrator. This is fine if the file is being printed or output to the Web directly from Photoshop. If we want to print the text from Illustrator, however, we will have to use Layer/Effects/Create Layers to separate the effects into layers other than the text layer, and then turn off the Eye icon for the text layer. The text will be output from Illustrator. This might or might not work depending on the combination of effects chosen.

HANDS-ON SESSION: Posterize, Bitmaps, Textures, and Patterns

Create interesting texture effects using Posterize, bitmaps, and patterns along with layers and Blend modes.

STEP 1: The original photo of the Packard.

There are many ways to create and integrate patterning into Photoshop images. Here we use bitmaps, filters, and various Layer options to add texture effects to images.

STEP 1: Type the letter D to get the default colors. Open the Packard image in the Posterize Bitmaps & Patterns folder and bring up the Layers palette (F10 with ArtistKeys). Double-click on the *Background* layer and rename it Packard. Choose File/Save As and save this as PackardLayers. Choose Image/Duplicate (F5) and name the duplicate copy PackardStreaks. Use Image/Mode/Grayscale to change the mode on the duplicate copy to Grayscale and say OK to Discard Color Information. Choose Flatten if asked about flattening the image. You will use PackardStreaks later. Do another Image/Duplicate, naming this one Packard/Mezzo. Choose Select All (Command-A), then Edit/Copy, and finally File/New (Command-N) to get a grayscale file the same size as the other Packard files. Before clicking on the OK button in the New dialog box, name the file MezzoTint and make sure that the White radio button is selected to fill this copy with white. Choose Filter/Noise/Add Noise and add 100 of Gaussian noise. This is sort of a mezzotint pattern. Press Command-A again to select all of the grayscale pattern. Now choose Edit/Define Pattern to make this the pattern Photoshop is now using. You should now have four windows on your screen. The original color Packard, now called PackardLayers, and the grayscale PackardStreaks, PackardMezzo, and the MezzoTint pattern.

DIFFUSION DITHER BITMAPS AND MEZZOTINT PATTERNS

STEP 2: Return to the PackardMezzo window and choose Select/None (Command-D). Now choose Image/Mode/Bitmap and you will get a dialog box with a lot of options. Choose Diffusion Dither and say OK. Also say OK to the Flatten Image question if asked. The image will be zoomed to 100% because diffusion dithers don't look right unless the image is seen at 100% or closer. A diffusion dither bitmap is an image made up of only black and white dots; there are no grays. The Bitmap mode contains

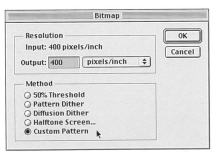

STEP 2: Here are the options when you choose Mode/Bitmap.

one bit of information for each pixel; it is either on or off, black or white. These images are very compact, which is useful for the Web and multimedia. A regular grayscale image contains 8 bits per pixel, so each pixel can have 256 different gray values. Diffusion dithers are very universal because you can display them on any computer monitor and print them on any printer that can print black dots. Now choose Command-Z to undo the diffusion dither, choose Mode/Bitmap again, and this time pick the Custom Pattern option. This will make a bitmap that uses the MezzoTint pattern you created and saved as the default pattern. Choose Select All, go to Edit/Copy, and then use the Window menu to switch to your color PackardLayers image and do an Edit/Paste. Name this layer MezzoPattern.

STEP 3: With the MezzoPattern layer active and both Eye icons on, change the opacity to 40%. Now you can see the original Packard layer with MezzoPattern on top of it. The colors on the Packard will be muted because you are in Normal mode. Change the Blend mode in the Layers palette to Multiply to make the black dots more black and drop out the white parts of the pattern. It will also bring out better color saturation in the nonblack areas, and you will see better colors from the original Packard. Choose File/Save to update your file.

A Subtle Posterize Effect

STEP 4: Click on the Packard layer to make it the active layer, and then Option-drag it to the New Layer icon at the bottom of the Layers palette. Name it Posterize and choose OK. Option-click on its Eye icon to turn off the other layers for now. Choose Image/Adjust/Posterize and set the Levels to 6. This reduces each color channel in the Posterize layer to only six levels of gray and gives this layer a posterized look. Now click on the Eye icon in the Packard layer to make that layer visible but leave the Posterize layer active (highlighted). Move the Opacity slider to 40%, which will show 60% of the original Packard layer from below. This will give you a subtle posterize effect while still maintaining most of the original image from below. To quickly see the image with and without this effect, click the Eye icon to turn the Posterize layer on and off. Now turn on the Eye icon of the MezzoPattern layer to see all three layers together.

Streaked Patterns

STEP 5: Now we will create another pattern and add some more layers to give you other options with this image. When we add the next layer, we want it to be added above the MezzoPattern layer, so click on the MezzoPattern layer to make it the active layer. Switch windows back to the MezzoTint file and zoom out so you can see the whole file onscreen. Use the Rectangular Marquee tool (M) to make a long, skinny selection on the left edge of the file the full height of the file. This rectangle should be about ¼ inch wide. Now use Edit/Transform/Scale and grab the middle-right handle and drag it across the screen to the right side of the window. This stretches out the dots within this ¼-inch selection and gives you a streaking pattern. Press Enter or Return to finish the scale process. Command-Option-0 to zoom to 100%. Now choose Filter/Stylize/Emboss and emboss this pattern by 4 pixels, 150% at 135 degrees. Notice how the pattern changes depending on the Angle of rotation and the other Emboss parameters. Choose OK from Emboss. Choose Select/All (Command-A) and then Edit/Define Pattern to make this the current Photoshop pattern. Choose File/Save As and name this pattern MezzoStreaks. Use the Window menu to switch

STEP 3: The Layers window should now look like this.

STEP 3: A section of the image with the 40% mezzotint pattern applied using Multiply mode.

STEP 4: After Option-clicking on the Posterize Eye icon, the other layers are not visible.

STEP 4: Seeing Posterize and Packard at the same time with Posterize being active at 40%.

STEP 5: The long, skinny selection on the left edge.

to PackardStreaks that you made in step 1. Use Image/Mode/Bitmap to convert this to another bitmap again using the Custom Pattern option. You will now get a streaked version of the Packard. Use File/Save As to save this as PackardStreaks.

STEP 6: Choose Select/All and then Edit/Copy in the PackardStreaks document; then switch to PackardLayers and do an Edit/Paste. This will make a new layer in the PackardLayers document above the MezzoPattern layer. Double-click on this new layer and name it StreakPattern. When you double-click on a layer, the Layer Options dialog box opens. After typing in the new name, move this dialog box out of the way so you can see the PackardLayers document as well as this dialog box. From the Layer Options dialog box, we can change the Opacity and Composite modes. There are two sets of slider bars that are very cool—This Layer, which allows you to remove some of the pixels in the 0–255 range from the active layer, and Underlying, which allows you to specify the pixels from the underlying layers that will definitely be in the composite. Move the right-most highlight slider on This Layer until it says 247. This means that all the pixels from 248 through 255, the white pixels, will be removed from this layer in the composite. Now you see black streaks added to the composite image as the colors and pattern from below show through the white areas. Now change the opacity to 50%, and the black steaks turn to gray. Click on the OK button, and then do a Save (Command-S).

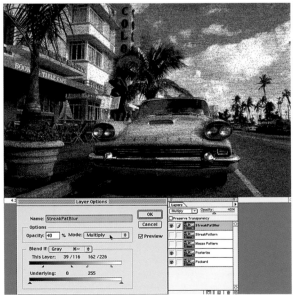

STEP 6: Using the This Layer slider to remove the whites from the pattern.

BLURRING BITMAPS TO ADD GRAY VALUES

STEP 7: Click on the StreakPattern layer and Option-drag it to the New Layer icon at the bottom-left part of the Layers palette. Name this new layer, which should be above the StreakPattern layer, StreakPatBlur. Set its opacity back to 100% and use Layer Options to move the right-most This Layer slider back to 255. Click OK. Turn off the Eye icons on the StreakPattern and MezzoPattern layers and then click on the StreakPatBlur layer to make it active. Choose Command-L to look at this Layer in Levels and you will notice that, because this is a Bitmap, only pure white and pure black values exist. Cancel from Levels. Use Filter/Blur/Gaussian Blur (Shift-F4) of 1 pixel to blur this new layer. Look at it in Levels again and you will notice that the Gaussian Blur added many intermittent gray values. Now double-click on StreakPatBlur to bring up the Layer Options dialog box again.

STEP 8: Now we can use the This Layer slider bar to do a lot of different types of effects. Zoom in to 100% (Command-Option-0) so you can see in detail what is happening. Move the left Shadow slider on This Layer to the right until it reads about 39. This removes the dark shadow values from 0 to 38. Now move the right-most highlight slider to the left until it reads about 226. This removes the bright highlight values from 227 to 255. Notice that this modified pattern contains jaggy edges where the whites and blacks have been removed. While holding down the Option key, click on the right side of the left shadow slider and slide it to the right, which will split the slider in two. Drag the right side of the left slider until it reaches 116. Option-click on the left half of the right-most slider and drag it until it reads 162. The numbers on the This Layer slider should now read, from left to right: 39, 116, 162, and 226. This means the shadow values from 0 to 38 are completely removed. The values

STEP 8: The StreakPatBlur layer with its Layer Options and the state of the Layers palette.

from 39 to 116 are blended out slowly, which removes the jaggy edges. The values from 117 to 161 are completely opaque. The values from 162 to 226 are blended out, and the values from 227 to 255 are completely removed. Try changing the Blend mode between Normal, Multiply, Screen, Lighten, Darken, and Difference until you get the one you like best. You can also readjust the Opacity for each different Blend mode you try. Click on the OK button in the Layer Options dialog box when you are happy with this layer's effect. Do Command-S to save this version of the document.

STEP 9: You can obtain another interesting effect by doing the following. Have the Packard Layer at 100% Normal, Posterize at 50% Normal, and turn off the Eye icons for MezzoPattern and StreakPattern. Now set StreakPatBlur to 40% and Multiply with the Layer Options, as in the step 8 illustration. Option-click on the New Layer icon and name the new layer Emboss. Make sure the new layer is above StreakPat-Blur. With the Emboss layer active, choose Option-Merge Visible from the Layers Palette menu to move all that you can now see into this Emboss layer. Make sure you leave the Option key down while Photoshop is doing the calculations. Now choose Filter/Stylize/Emboss and use the same settings you did in step 5. Choose OK on the Emboss Filter; then change the Blend mode of the Emboss layer to SoftLight. If you now turn off the StreakPatBlur layer, you will notice that the pattern is embossed into the original colors without changing those colors much at all. The Emboss layer has a lot of neutral gray in it and the SoftLight Blend mode ignores neutral gray. Try the Overlay and Hardlight modes that also ignore neutral gray. You can change the opacity on the Emboss layer to lessen any of these effects. See Chapter 36: Blend Modes, Calculations, and Apply Image to understand how these Blend modes actually work.

Here is the Layers palette setup for the image below.

TIME TO PLAY WITH LAYERS AND OPTIONS

STEP 10: Now you have several layers and effects that you can adjust until you get the final image you want. Remember that you can turn off any layer by clicking on its Eye icon. Play with Opacity, Mode, This Layer slider, and Underlying slider in the Layer Options dialog box for each layer until you get the final combined effect you like. Remember, the Underlying slider bar in the Layer Options dialog box forces pixels of lower layers into the composite. In the StreakPatBlur layer, if you move the right-most Underlying slider to the left until it gets to 128, then all the values in the final composite from 128 to 255 will come from the lower layers, not from the StreakPatBlur layer. Play with these features until you understand them. When you are happy with a particular effect, you can use File/Save A Copy to save a flattened version of the file using only the layers that are currently visible. This way, you can save many variations of this multilayered document.

My favorite layer combination has the Packard Layer at 100% Normal, the Posterize layer at 50% Normal, the MezzoPattern, StreakPattern, and StreakPatBlur layers off, and the StreakPatBlur Emboss layer at 100% SoftLIght.

HANDS-ON SESSION: Filters and Effects

*A tour of some of the more versatile Photoshop filters
as well as many useful layer and blending techniques
for getting the most out of all the filters.*

The best way to learn the simple filters is to just play with each of them. Try out all of the filters and all their features and compare different settings on the same image. Understand the range of possible things you can do with each filter. This is something that is fun and easy for you to do yourself and there are lots of other Photoshop books, including the Photoshop manual, that have charts of each filter and what it looks like during one particular iteration. Photoshop comes with a set of over 75 filters, and with them and the rest of Photoshop you can do millions of different effects. There are hundreds of other third-party filters on the market, and some of them are really unique, but a lot of them just give you a slightly easier way to do something that could already be done with the standard Photoshop filters by combining them with the other features of Photoshop.

In the rest of *Photoshop 5 Artistry*, we show you how to use the workhorse retouching filters in a lot of real world examples. Here in this chapter, we are going to concentrate on how to use layers and masks to combine filters in interesting ways. We are also going to talk about some of the more complicated filters and how to understand and make the best use of them. You need to play with all the filters and options because the possibilities for effects and combinations are in the millions; using the techniques we show you here, you can discover your own entirely new effects.

GETTING BOB READY

STEP 1: Open the file BobVegas from the Filters and Effects chapter.

STEP 1: Bring up your new Photoshop 5 History palette (F8), use History Options from the palette menu to set the Maximum History States to 100, and also choose Allow Non-Linear History. This will allow you to have the most flexibility when working with these images. Any time you want to look at a previous incantation of the image, you can always go back to it by clicking on that previous state in the History palette. If you decide you want to keep it around, use the History palette menu to take a Snapshot of that state, or for a really permanent copy, use File/Save a Copy. You can then continue to add new changes from that point, or you can click back on the most recent state in the History palette to continue from there. You can also use the History Brush to paint on the current state in the image from a previous state or Snapshot by clicking to the left of that previous state in the left-most History Brush Source column in the History palette. Check out Chapter 12: History Palette, History Brush, and Snapshots for an overview of this great new set of features. When you are playing with effects and are not sure exactly what the outcome will be, the History palette can be a big help.

Open the file BobVegas from the Filters and Effects folder. Use the Cropping tool (C) to crop out the white stripe and copyright notice at the bottom. Click on the Bob layer in the Layers palette to make it the active layer. Click on Bob's layer mask, called Bob Mask, in the Channels palette and drag it to the Copy icon at the bottom of the Channels palette. Name this copy Bob Orig Mask. We can use this Bob Orig Mask in different ways to run different effects on either Bob, the background, or some combination. Click on RGB in the channels palette to return to RGB color viewing.

STEP 2: Adding a red glow.

STEP 2: Use the Eyedropper (I) to select a bright red, green, or yellow from the Las Vegas background as the foreground color. Click on the left-most Bob layer thumbnail, not the layer mask; then choose Edit/Fill (Shift-Delete) and fill the entire Bob layer, in Color mode, with 20% to 30% of this color. This should give him an interesting glow.

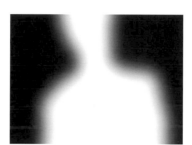

STEP 3: Click on the Bob Orig Mask in the Channels palette and make another copy of it, and call it Bob Blur Mask. Choose Filter/Blur/ Gaussian Blur (Shift-F4) and put a 25-pixel blur on this mask channel.

STEP 3: The Bob Blur Mask channel.

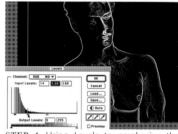

STEP 4: Using Levels to emphasize the main edges of the Find Edges filter.

STEP 4: Make a copy of Bob's layer by dragging it to the New Layer icon at the bottom of the Layers palette. Name the copy Bob Edges. Shift-click on the Bob Edges layer mask icon to turn it off for now. Click on the Bob Edges layer thumbnail; then run Filter/Stylize/Find Edges on this layer, and then press Command-I to invert it. Now go into Levels and manipulate the results of this filter to emphasize the main edges. First, move the Input Highlight (top right) and Brightness/Contrast (middle) sliders to the left to brighten the main edges and bring out more edges. Now move the Input Shadow (top left) slider to the right to darken the shadows and drop out the unneeded edges. Play with this for a while and then choose OK when the edges look right to you. Now Shift-click on the Bob Edges layer mask again to turn it back on, and you will see the Vegas scene again. Turn off the Eye icon for the Bob layer for now and see the Bob Edges version on top of the Las Vegas.

STEP 5: Bob Edges blended with Vegas.

STEP 5: To blend Bob Edges and Vegas together a bit, click on the Bob Edges layer mask thumbnail and then choose Image/Apply Image. Set the Source channel to the Bob Blur Mask channel, which will blend Bob Edges with the Las Vegas scene and make the top layer slightly transparent around the edges. You can always use Apply Image to copy any mask into a layer mask to change the appearance of the edges. Because we saved the Bob Orig Mask and Bob Blur Mask channels at the beginning, we can modify any other layer mask and still know we have these original versions to go back to later if we choose.

STEP 6: Bob Edges in Difference mode, with Bob partying in Las Vegas.

STEP 6: Now change the Blend mode on the Bob Edges layer to Difference, and see Las Vegas through the middle of Bob. Turn on the Eye icon for the Bob layer and notice that Bob is no longer see-through because this mask still has the original hard edges. Now his skin looks sort of hard baked. Do a File/Save As here, and then try out some of the other Blend modes for both the Bob and Bob Edges layers. Do File/Revert to continue with the exercise.

STEP 6: Your layers and channels should look like this after Step 6.

Getting Bob Ready

STEP 7: The new background with the Motion Blur effect.

STEP 8: 20% Radial Blur, Spin Draft mode on Bob's left eye, then inverted.

STEP 8: With other layers on, set the mode to Hard Light and set the Bob layer to 50%.

STEP 9: What the Layers palette should look like after Step 9.

MOTION BLUR

STEP 7: Option-click on the Vegas Eye icon to turn off the Eye icons for all the other layers. Option-drag the Vegas layer to the New Layer icon at the bottom of the Layers palette and name the copy Vegas Motion Blur. Use Filter/Noise/Add Noise to add 35 of Gaussian noise. Adding noise before a Motion Blur enhances the motion effect. Now use Filter/Blur/Motion Blur of 40 at 27° to blur the Las Vegas street in the direction of motion down the block. Change the Blend mode on this layer to Luminosity and you will get an interesting effect between the blurred Las Vegas and the original Las Vegas. Again, press Command-S to save; then play with the other Blend modes on the Vegas Motion Blur layer. Multiply makes this look like a dangerous street to walk on, Screen turns it into party time, Overlay is sort of halfway between these two, and Difference and Exclusion creates a strange trip. Each Blend mode here gives the street a different mood. That's the great thing about combining filters with layers; there are thousands of different effects, and you have to play with it to get the one that's right this time. Go back to the Luminosity Blend Mode when you are done playing. Besides using the Layers palette, another way to go back to Luminosity mode would be to click on the top-most line in the current group of Blending Change lines in the History palette. If Allow Non-Linear History were not on, the History palette would forget all the other Blend modes you tried above when you do the next step. With Allow Non-Linear History on as you have it, the next step will skip all the other Blending Change lines and be added to the History palette below them. That allows you to click back on them if you want to.

RADIAL BLUR

STEP 8: Make a copy of the Bob layer and call it Bob Radial Blur. Drag it to be the top-most layer; then Option-click on its Eye icon to turn off the other layers for now. Shift-click on its layer mask to turn it off, too. Use Filter/Blur/Radial Blur and click and drag in the Blur Center box to set the center of the blur to Bob's left-most eye. This may take you a couple of times to get right. For each iteration, first do Command-Z, then Command-Option-F to bring up the same Radial Blur filter, allowing you to change its options. Use Spin of 20 in Draft mode. The other quality modes will take longer, but don't forget that they are there when you need the absolute best quality radial blur. Use Command-I to invert this image to complete the first part of this step. Now Option-click on the Eye icon of this layer to turn the other layers back on. Set the Blend mode of this layer to Hard Light; then set the opacity of the Bob layer to 50%, and you get the second effect of this step. Try some more effects yourself by playing with all the layers.

STEP 9: Choose Command-S to save your creation so far. Turn off the Eye icons of the top two layers and set the opacity of the Bob layer back to 70%. Option-click on the New Layer icon and name the new layer Merged Layer. Drag it up to the top of all the other layers. While choosing Merge Visible from the Layers Palette menu, hold down the Option key until the merge finishes its calculations. This will stick a merged copy of the currently visible layers into this new top layer without actually merging the other layers into one. Whenever you get a certain look that you want to save, you can always do Option-Merge Visible to create this look in a single layer.

Chapter 39: Filters and Effects

THE WAVE FILTER

STEP 10: Now choose Filter/Distort/Wave and look at the many options in this dialog box. The first step in understanding what the Wave filter can do for you is to simplify the options. Set the Number of Generators to 1, the Type to Sine, both Wavelengths to 30, and both Amplitudes to 50. For now, set the Scale to 100% in the Vertical dimension and 0% in the Horizontal dimension. The wavelength is the distance from the top of one wave to the top of the next. The amplitude is the distance from the top of a wave to the bottom. Getting one simple sine wave across the screen makes it easier to see what this filter actually does. Choose OK to accept the filter parameters to see this in more detail. Now press Command-Option-Z to undo this but leave it in the History palette. Now press Command-Option-F to run the filter again, but

change the options. Now change the Type to Triangle waves , press OK, and you can see that these waves look like the stitch of a zig-zag sewing machine. Again press Command-Option-Z, then Command-Option-F, and choose the Square wave Type this time. This one is my favorite. It makes the image look like it went through a shredder and then was put back together again with the width of the shreds set by the wavelength and the separation of the two sets of shreds set by the amplitude. Now you will notice that the History palette has three Wave entries at the bottom, and as you click on each of them you see the image after each of the Wave options you tried so far. You can go back to any of them by clicking it or you can go back to the Stamp Visible step to try yet another option on the same starting image. This makes it a lot easier in Photoshop 5 to try things out and go back to them later.

Play around with these Wave parameters some more but keep it simple until you understand what each one does. They can be combined in interesting ways to create all sorts of wave shapes.

Undo your final set of play changes to the Merged layer, or use the History palette to go back to the state before running filters on this layer. Now go back into the Wave filter and set the shape to Square. Set the number of generators to 1, all wavelength and amplitude values to 50, and then set 100% Vertical and 50% Horizontal. Repeat Edge Pixels should also be turned on. This is a cool effect just by itself, but now try the different Blend modes and also different opacities to get lots of other neat effects. The one I liked best is shown here with all the layer's Eye icons turned back on, the Blend mode set to Overlay, and Opacity set to 100%.

Now you should experiment with the Bob and Vegas images on your own. Create a new Bob layer by copying one of the existing Bob layers. Try out each of the filters with each of its parameters on a

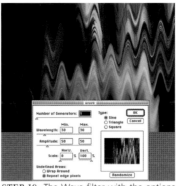

STEP 10: The Wave filter with the options simplified. The wavelength of a sine wave goes from one high point to the next. The amplitude is from the top to the bottom of a wave. It is a bit easier to see what the wave looks like because we are just doing it in the vertical direction.

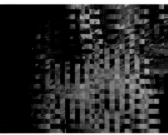

STEP 10: The new Merged layer after Square wave with the Blend mode set to Normal.

STEP 10: Changing the Blend mode to Overlay and turning on the other layers brings in an interesting effect.

History

Open
Crop
Duplicate Channel
Fill
Duplicate Channel
Gaussian Blur
Duplicate Layer
Find Edges
Invert
Levels
Apply Image
Blending Change
Duplicate Layer
Add Noise
Motion Blur
Blending Change
Blending Change
Blending Change
Blending Change
Blending Change
Duplicate Layer
Layer Order
Radial Blur
Invert
Blending Change
Opacity Change
Opacity Change
New Layer
Layer Order
Stamp Visible
Wave
Wave
Wave

STEP 10: Here is the History palette so far after running the Wave filter three times. We could now click back on any of these Wave steps to see it again or to remain in that step. We could also click on the Stamp Visible step to go back to just before we ran any of the Wave filter incantations.

STEP 11: The original Paris Dog image.

STEP 11: The Dog Edges layer after Find Edges, Invert, and Levels.

separate layer; then combine them using the Blend modes and opacities of these layers. You can turn any layer on or off by using its Eye icon. You can move any layer to the left or right, or up or down, by using the Move tool. Do this to have two or three Bobs standing next to each other. Play and be creative. I am amazed at all the different types of effects the thousands of students who have worked with these two images over the years have come up with!

LINE DRAWING

STEP 11: Now let's open a different image and try some other types of filters and effects. Open the file called ParisDog from the Filters and Effects folder. Notice that it already contains a mask of the dog and a pattern that we created in Photoshop. See Chapter 38: Posterize, Bitmaps, and Patterns for some ideas about how to create patterns like this in Photoshop. First, we will show you how to turn this image into a line drawing. Double-click on the *Background* layer and rename it Orig Dog. Make a copy of this layer by dragging it to the New Layer icon in the Layers palette. Name the copy Dog Edges. Use Filter/Stylize/Find Edges on the Dog Edges layer to find the edges of this image and use Image/Map/Invert (Command-I) to invert those edges. Use Command-L for Levels and move the Input Highlight and Brightness/ Contrast sliders to the left and the Input Shadow slider to the right to emphasize the main edges. You can also use the Load button to load the LevelsIsolateEdges preset levels settings from the Extra Info folder. Click on the OK button in Levels.

STEP 12: The Dog Edges B&W layer by itself after being Inverted.

STEP 12: Dog Edges B&W combined using Lighten with the Orig Image channel.

STEP 12: Choose Duplicate Layer from the Layers palette pop-up with a New destination to make a copy of this layer in a separate file. Use Image/Mode/Grayscale to turn the copy into black and white. You need to do this in a separate file or else all the layers will be turned into black and white. You will now have white lines against a black background. Use the Move tool (V) to click on this grayscale file; then Shift-drag it and drop it back on the Paris Dog file. You need the Shift key down in Photoshop to center the new layer when you drag and drop. Now you should have a new black-and-white layer on the top, so name it Dog Edges B&W. You should now have Orig Dog as the bottom layer, then Dog Edges, and finally, Dog Edges B&W on top. Turn off the Eye icon for Dog Edges and set the mode for Dog Edges B&W to Darken. Darken mode will give you a black background with colored lines where the white edges were. To get an even better effect, use Command-I to invert Dog Edges B&W, and then change the mode to Lighten. This will give you a white background with colored lines. I like this effect a little better. If you look at this layer by itself, you will see that it is just a black-and-white line drawing.

STEP 13: Now make another copy of the Dog Edges B&W layer, call it Dog Edges B&W Fat, and make sure that it is now the top layer. Turn the Eye icon off for Dog Edges B&W. You should now have the Eye icons on for Dog Edges B&W Fat (the active layer) and for Orig Dog. Run Filter/Other/Minimum of 1 on Dog Edges B&W Fat. This will make the edges here a minimum of 1 pixel wide and will give a chalk-drawing type effect. Try 2-4 pixels wide and notice the painterly effect this gives the image. I ended up using 3 pixels. The mode should still be set to Lighten, so you will see more color detail with these thicker lines.

STEP 13: The Dog Edges B&W Fat layer combined using Lighten with the Orig Image channel.

STEP 14: The Dog Edges layer turned on again with Difference and Opacity of 20%. Here the dog is revealed as is from the Orig Dog layer.

STEP 14: Turn on the Dog Edges layer again and see how its different Blend modes affect the composite. Most of the effects created with this layer at 100% opacity are too radical to be very interesting. Try lowering the opacity of the Dog Edges layer, and you will notice the effects getting more subtle and interesting. The one I like best is setting the Blend mode of this Dog Edges layer to Difference and the opacity to 20%. To see the effect any particular layer is having on the final composite, just turn the Eye icon for the layer on and off and notice the difference.

STEP 15: Let's say you like this effect but you really want to see the dog as it was in the Orig Dog layer and only have the effect apply to the image around the dog. To do this, with Dog Edges as the Active layer, you need to Command-click on the DogMaskRail mask in the Channels palette to load it as a selection. Now Option-click on add the Layer Mask icon at the bottom left of the Layers palette to add a layer mask that will keep everything visible in this layer except the selected area. Now click the Dog Edges B&W Fat layer to activate it, reload the DogMaskRail selection, and then Option-click on the add Layer Mask icon again to create the same layer mask for this layer. Now the Dog is removed from the two effects layers so you see the original dog coming through from the Orig Dog layer at the bottom.

STEP 16: Let's assume that we want to selectively burn and dodge the dog a bit to add some contrast and definition. We want to do this in such a way that we can change it or undo it later. Option-click on the New Layer icon and name this layer 50% Gray. The new layer should be at the top of all the other layers. Choose Shift-Delete to Fill this layer with 50% Gray using the 50% Gray option in the Fill dialog box. Now your whole window will turn gray until you change the Blend mode on this layer to Soft Light. In

STEP 16: The Paris Dog layers as they should look at the end of step 16.

STEP 16: The same image as above after dodging and burning with the 50% Gray layer in Softlight mode.

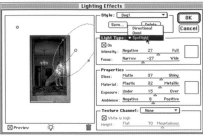

STEP 17: The different light types in the Lighting Effects filter.

STEP 17: The Spotlight.

STEP 17: The Directional light and Texture Channel set to Lines Thin.

STEP 17: The Lighting Effects filter with texture created by the Lines Thin pattern.

Soft Light mode, 50% gray does nothing to the layers underneath, but if you paint with darker than 50% gray, the image underneath will be darkened; painting with lighter than 50% gray will lighten the image. Now type J to get the Airbrush and set its pressure to 5%. If you did a double take there, Airbrush used to be A but was changed to J in Photoshop 5. Type a D to get the default colors of black and white and then, using a soft brush. Paint with black where you want to darken the dog and white where you want to brighten the dog. Because you are using the Airbrush, you can hold down the mouse button and paint to get more darkness or lightness. The great thing about burning and dodging this way is that you can undo the entire effect by just turning this layer on or off. You can also lessen the effect by changing the opacity of this gray layer. Now try changing the Blend mode to Overlay or Hard Light and notice that these also do nothing at 50% Gray. In Softlight mode, the effects are more subtle and you won't actually get full black or full white in your underlying image, even if you paint them in the gray layer. Overlay and Hardlight are more radical in their effects using the same gray layer, but you can always lower the opacity of the layer to lessen these effects. I often use this technique with Softlight mode to add highlights or burn or dodge. It's great when working with a client because you can show them different effects by just turning on one or the other 50% Gray layer, and you can always undo any part of any gray layer by just refilling that part with 50% gray again.

LIGHTING EFFECTS

STEP 17: Click on the Dog Edges B&W layer, go into the Channels palette, and make a copy of its Red channel using the New Channel icon at the bottom of the Channels palette. Name this copy Lines Thin. We are going to use this as a pattern in the Lighting Effects filter. In the Layers palette, make another copy of the Orig Dog layer right on top of that layer and call it Dog Pattern. Option-click on its Eye icon to turn off all the other layers for now.

Choose Filter/Render/Lighting Effects and notice the many options in this filter that allow you to add lighting with different types of lights to your image. The Photoshop manual has a good description of this filter, which you should read if you want to understand all of its features. We are going to try some of them here. Set the light type to Default, and click on the white circle over the dog preview in the dialog box. This is the original light. Drag it and place it on the dog's shoulder. Click on the other end of the line that is leading out of the white spot, and move it around so it ends up above and to the right of the dog's head. This is a spotlight pointing at the dog and coming from above and to the right of the dog. Set its intensity and width as shown here. You change the width by clicking on the sides of the oval and then dragging to make the oval wider or thinner.

Now add a new light by clicking on the Lightbulb icon at the bottom of the dialog box and dragging a new light to the desired location in the preview window. Set its light type to Directional and place it at the top left of the image near where the chandelier meets the ceiling. Drag the line coming out of the spot far above and a little to the right. This creates a light coming from above at a subtle angle. Set its parameters as shown in the dialog box. Click on OK to see the effects of these lights in more detail. Choose Command-Z to undo these effects. Type Command-Option-F to bring up the Lighting Effects filter again and change its options. Go down to the Texture Channel pop-up and select the Lines Thin channel you created at the beginning of this example. Set the parameters as in the illustration here. Now choose OK

STEP 18: The lighting Effects filter with texture created by the Dog Pattern pattern.

STEP 18: The Dog Pattern Lighting Effects layer seen to the left combined with Orig Dog using Soft Light mode at 70% Opacity.

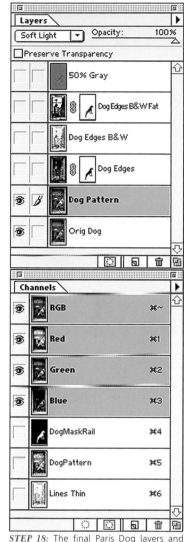

STEP 18: The final Paris Dog layers and channels after Step 18.

from the Lighting Effects filter, and you will see a texture formed around the line edges.

STEP 18: Choose Command Z to undo the previous incantation of Lighting Effects and Command-Option-F to go back into the filter. Change the Texture Channel to Dog Pattern and set the parameters as shown. Click on the OK button. Now turn on the Eye icon for the Orig Dog layer underneath. With Dog Pattern as the active layer, set the mode to Soft Light and the opacity to 70% to see the final effect pictured on the previous page. You should try the Lighting Effects filter with some of the textures in the Textures for Lighting Effects folder that come on the Photoshop CD-ROM within the Other Goodies folder. You can also create your own textures by scanning a textured object or material with a flat bed scanner.

STEP 18: The setup for the Texture Channel and Dog Pattern.

DISPLACEMENT MAPS

STEP 19: Now let's play with displacement maps. Click on the New Channel icon in the Channels palette to create a new channel. Type D to get the default colors; then use the Linear Gradient tool to do a linear gradient clicking down first with white at the top and dragging down to black at the bottom. Use Command-M to enter Curves, click on the Load button, and load the Displace Curve from the folder for this exercise. This will create a displacement map that is black in the center and white at the top and bottom. Using this as a displacement map will cause any value that is less than 128 to displace in a negative direction and any value that is greater than 128 to displace in a positive direction. Use the Duplicate Channel Channels palette menu item to copy this channel to a separate, new destination file and save it in Photoshop format. Name this new file Left/Right Flop. Any Photoshop file can be

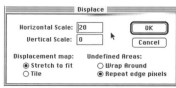

STEP 19: The settings for Displace.

STEP 19: The Left/Right Flop displacement map created with a gradient and curves.

STEP 19: The dog after being displaced by 20 horizontally.

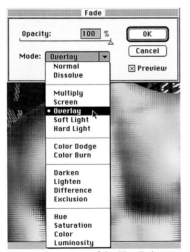

Displace

Horizontal Scale: 10   OK

Vertical Scale: 10   Cancel

Displacement map: Undefined Areas:
○ Stretch to fit   ○ Wrap Around
◉ Tile   ◉ Repeat edge pixels

STEP 20: The Displace settings for the Chain Displacement map.

Fade

Opacity: 100 %   OK

Mode: Overlay ▼   Cancel

Normal   ☒ Preview
Dissolve

Multiply
Screen
• Overlay
Soft Light
Hard Light

Color Dodge
Color Burn

Darken
Lighten
Difference
Exclusion

Hue
Saturation
Color
Luminosity

Here are the options of the Filter/Fade command that you can run right after using a filter. For the most flexibility, run the filter in a layer instead.

a displacement map. Make the Orig Dog layer alone active or make a copy of it; then choose Filter/Distort/Displace and set the parameters to displace as shown here. Make sure Stretch to fit and Repeat Edge pixels are turned on. When asked for a displacement map, open the file you just saved, Left/Right Flop. Notice that the pixels in the image whose corresponding pixels were less than 128, in the displacement map, moved to the right, and those that were more than 128 moved to the left. Use Command-Z to undo this. Now, try Displace again, but this time use –20 as the horizontal value. That causes the image to flop in the opposite direction.

STEP 20: Again, use Command-Z to undo the last Displace. Now use the Rectangular Marquee to select the right-most small chain hanging down to the bottom left of the window. Also select a little of the gray around the chain. Edit/Copy this, do Command-N and OK for a new file, and then paste this section of chain in the new file. Flatten this and then save it as ChainMap in Photoshop format. Now choose Filter/Distort/Displace again, but this time, change the settings to 10 in each of the horizontal and vertical directions and turn on the Tile setting. This will cause the same displacement map to be repeated over and over again until the image is covered. Choose the ChainMap for your displacement map, and you will get the image shown here. Try some other patterns for a displacement map. When there are two or more channels in the displacement map, the first channel is used to displace in the horizontal direction, and the second channel is used to displace in the vertical direction. Displace is a very powerful and fun filter that can be used for a lot of great effects. You just need to create the displacement map that is appropriate for your needs!

STEP 20: The dog after being displaced by the Chain Displacement map.

THE FILTER/FADE COMMAND

When you run a filter in Photoshop, you have the option of using Filter/Fade after running the filter to change the effect of the filter before it is made permanent. Using Fade is sort of like running a filter on the image in a separate layer above the image. If you do that, you can always go back and change the Opacity or Blend mode of that layer to blend the filter with the original image underneath. Doing this with layers is a great approach, and we used it a lot earlier in this chapter. The Filter/Fade command is like running the filter in this other layer, but if you don't adjust it before you do something else, it gets merged with the layer below. The feature says: "Let's give them one more chance to tweak this filter by changing the Opacity or Blend Mode; then we'll make the effect permanent on the layer that was active when you ran the filter."

To use Filter/Fade, just select it after running a filter and you will get the Fade dialog box shown here. You can switch the Blend mode or Opacity, but there is no Layer Options or Layer Mask. You can then Undo and Redo the Fade, but when you do anything else that changes the Undo buffer, the ability to further change the Fade goes away except by using the History Brush or Fill from History.

If you really want flexibility, just make a copy of the layer you were going to run the filter on, put that copy on top of the current layer, and then run the filter on the copy. Because this is a separate layer, you have all the capabilities of Fade, plus you have Layer Options, plus you can change it or undo it at any time just by changing the Eye icon, Opacity, Blend mode, or Layer Options. Even when you save the file and quit, you will later have these same options upon reopening the file. Maybe people will use Fade when making quick comps or if they don't have the memory to save the layer. I haven't used it much so far.

THE FILTERS ADDED SINCE PHOTOSHOP 3

For Photoshop 4, Adobe added a bunch of filters to Photoshop but they were not really new to the world. The Aldus Gallery Effects filters were tuned up and added to Photoshop. I guess this was a side effect of Adobe purchasing Aldus a few years ago. All these same filters are in Photoshop 5, and there are a few additions and changes for Photoshop 5.

These filters do seem to fall into several groups, as far as basic layout and functionality, and a particular group doesn't always go into the same submenu. There are the three option filters. All of them have the same size dialog box and they all have three options. The options have different names depending on the filter, but some of the names and functionality are shared among several of them. Another group is the Texture filters. They have a Texture section, at the bottom of their dialog boxes, that allows for an adjustment in the scale of the texture pattern, the intensity of the texture pattern, called Relief, and the direction of lighting on the texture. You can then choose the texture pattern from a small list of choices in an included pop-up menu or you can load a texture from a Photoshop file. The Photoshop 5 CD comes with a bunch of textures you can load from the Textures for Lighting Effects folder in the Other Goodies folder. These are not automatically installed with Photoshop, but you will find them on the same CD as the Installer. These textures work well with this set of filters as well as with lighting effects.

If you are browsing the Filter submenus, the filters in the Noise, Pixelate, Sharpen, Render, and Video menus are the same as they were in Photoshop 3 and 4

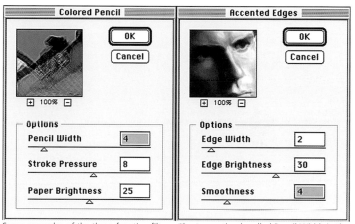

Some examples of the three-function filters. The top option is called Pencil Width in the Colored Pencil filter, but a somewhat similar option in the Accented Edges filter is called Edge Width. We have Edge Brightness in one, and then Paper Brightness in another. Smoothness and Stroke Pressure seem to actually be different options. If you use filters a lot, you should play with each of these and decide which ones are worthwhile for you.

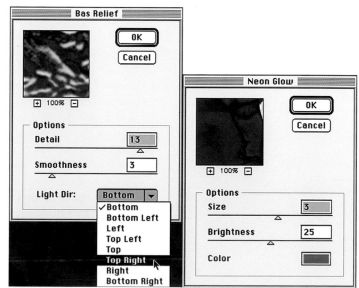

These are further variations of the three-function filter set. Some of them allow you to pick a lighting direction, and Neon Glow allows you to pick the color of the glow. Some of the other filters in this new set just use the foreground color as the filter's color. Notice that Smoothness and Brightness appear here as in some of the other new filters.

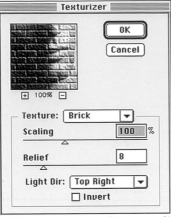

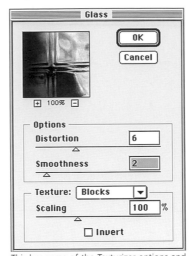

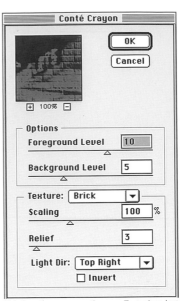

This is the basic variation of the Texture filter group I just mentioned. Here you can pick one of several built-in textures, or you can load a texture from a file. This also allows you to choose the lighting direction and even invert the lighting. Scaling scales the texture pattern and Relief controls how much the texture creates a 3D appearance.

This has some of the Texturizer options and a different set of other options. This filter is fun to play with. Increasing the Distortion makes the glass further distort the image underneath. The Smoothness controls the blending of the edges.

This has the same options as Texturizer but here they have added Foreground Level and Background Level.

except Photoshop 5 did add the 3D Transform filter to the Render menu. This new filter can produce some cool effects if you take the time to figure it out. The Artistic, Brush Strokes, Sketch, Digimarc, and Texture menus were added for Photoshop 4 and are the same for Photoshop 5. Smart Blur was added to the Blur menu; Diffuse Glow, Glass, and Ocean Ripple were added to the Distort menu; and Glowing Edges was added to Stylize all for Photoshop 4—and they are still there in Photoshop 5.

The Digimarc filters allow you to embed a watermark into your image for copyright protection. To get your own watermark, you need to register with the Digimarc people. I have not tried this myself, but recommend that you test the survival of their watermarks through the different types of JPEG compression, printing, and other digital contortions you will be doing before you assume it is a bulletproof solution to your particular copyright problems. There is more information about Digimarc in the Photoshop 5 manuals.

Doing an exhaustive explanation of each of the Photoshop filters is not the main focus of this book. Throughout the examples in this book, we show you how to use the ones that we feel are most useful to everyone that is doing digital photography and digital imaging. Many of the other filters are very useful for specific types of illustrations and effects and they are all really fun to play with. Check out Chapter 35: South Africa in Focus, Chapter 37: Bike Ride in the Sky, and Chapter 38: Posterize, Bitmaps, Textures, and Patterns for some other useful examples of filter and effects creation.

As we mentioned at the beginning of this chapter, the best way to learn about the filters is to play with them and combine them using layers and the Blend modes. Have fun!

Chapter 39: Filters and Effects

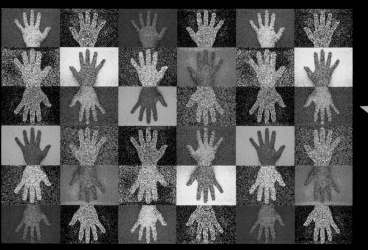

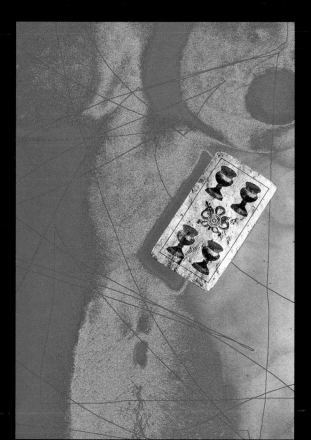

Create an image from components for a specified canvas size, a magazine ad; work with drop shadows, knock-outs, the Pen tool, and linked layers for high-quality output.

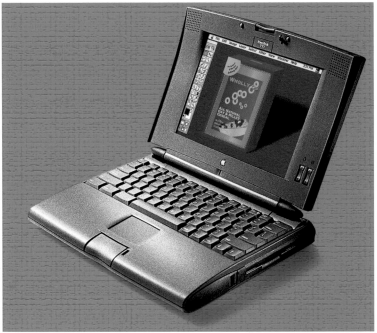

The final composite portable image. This is the image you will produce in this example from the components to the below.

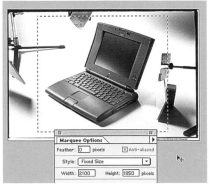

STEP 1: Here is the original portable grayscale image with the setup to crop it to its final size.

STEP 1: The Wholly O's cereal box.

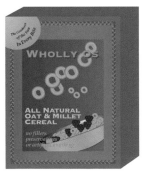

STEP 1: The menu bar.

STEP 1:
The Tool
palette.

SETTING UP THE PORTABLE IMAGE

STEP 1: Open the file Original Portable from the CD folder for this chapter. We want to use this to create an ad for a new computer brochure. The ad needs to be 6 inches wide by 5.3 inches high for a 175-line screen print job. That means we need to have an image that is 2,100 pixels wide by 1,850 pixels high. Type M for marquee and choose Fixed Size; then enter these dimensions. When you click down on the Original Portable image with the marquee, a selection will form that is exactly this size. With the mouse button down, move the selection around until you have a good crop. Now choose Image/Crop to crop the Portable to this size.

CREATING A NEW BACKGROUND FOR THE PORTABLE

STEP 2: We want this to be a color ad so choose Image/Mode/RGB to convert the Portable into an RGB image. We need to create an image to go on the screen of the portable as well as a background for it to sit on. First let's work on creating a background for the Portable to sit on. This black-and-white photo of the Portable still contains shooting setup objects around the actual computer. Use the Pen tool to make a Path of the outside edge of the Portable. When this Path is finished, name it Computer. Now drag a copy of this Path to the Copy icon at the bottom of the Paths palette. Call this copy Computer&Shadow and modify the points on the well at the bottom and right side of the Portable. Make a third path of the inside edge of the screen area on the Portable and call this path Screen. If you need help with the Pen tool, check out Chapter 30: Bob Goes To...

STEP 3: Now create a background color for the Portable image. Double-click the Background layer and rename it Portable. Choose New Layer from the Layers palette and call the new layer Green Background. Use Edit/Fill to fill it with a green color. Move this new layer below the Portable layer. Turn the Computer path into a selection by dragging it to the Create Selection icon, third from left, at the bottom of the Paths palette. With the Portable layer active, click the Add Layer Mask icon at the bottom-left area of the Layers palette to turn this selection into a layer mask that drops out the background around the Portable. The Portable should now be sitting against a green background.

STEP 4: Here we make a selection of the area to blur in the layer mask for the shadow.

Fixing the Portable's Shadow

STEP 4: Click the Portable Layer thumbnail and Option-drag it to the New Layer icon calling this copy of it Shadow. Throw out the layer mask on this copy and don't apply it on the way out. Drag the Shadow layer to below the Portable layer. Turn the Computer&Shadow path into a selection and then turn that selection into a layer mask for this new Shadow layer. Set the Opacity of this layer to about 55 percent and change its Blend mode to Multiply. You will notice that this tends to blend the shadow into the Green Background layer. Option-click this layer's layer mask thumbnail to look at just the mask. Set the feather on the Lasso to around 5; then use the Lasso tool to make a selection around the mask that is very wide around the bottom edges of the shadow area. Use Filter/Blur/Gaussian Blur to blur the shadow in this layer mask by about 25, and this softens the shadow in this Shadow layer. Take a look at my mask in the PortableLayers file in the Extra Info Files folder if you have any questions about how this mask should look. Choose Select/Deselect to remove the selection.

Adding Texture to the Background

STEP 5: Click the Green Background layer and run the Filter/Texture/Craquelure filter to give the background some texture. If you want to try out some other colors for the background without losing this texture, you can place a solid colored layer below this now textured Green Background layer. Now pick up the color of the layer below while still maintaining the Craquelure pattern by changing the Blend mode of this Green Background layer to Luminosity. Try it!

Adding Color to the Portable

STEP 6: Now we'll add some color to the Portable computer. Click the Portable layer to make it active; then choose New Adjustment Layer from the Layers palette menu to create a Grouped Adjustment layer of Type Hue/Saturation and call this layer Computer Hue/Saturation. Click OK to get to the Hue/Saturation dialog; then turn on the Colorize option. Move the Hue slider to the right and the Saturation slider to the left until you get a subtle bluish-gray color for the Portable. Grouping this layer with the previous Portable layer will only add color to the Portable itself.

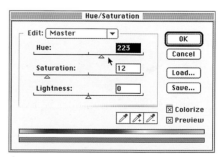

STEP 6: Here are the Hue/Saturation settings we used to Colorize the Portable.

Creating the Image for the Portable Monitor

STEP 7: Now we need to create the image that will go within the screen area of this Portable computer. Because the portable is sitting at a strange angle, it would be better to create the image to go on its screen first in a separate document and then place it within the screen using Free Transform. We are going to create the image for the screen so it has several possible main images. One of them will be a picture of some flowers, and the second will be a cereal box created in Adobe Illustrator.

STEP 7: Here we see the Portable's screen before adding the composite image.

Besides the image on the computer screen, we will also add the Photoshop Tool palette and the Photoshop menu to the Portable's screen. Open the file called FlowersYellow from the Folder for this exercise on the CD. This file is about the correct size for the screen area on the portable. It is actually a bit bigger than needed but it is better to have too much data than not enough. Crop the copyright information from the bottom of the file and then do a File/Save As and call this ScreenLayers. You can use the screen grabs we created of the Photoshop Tool palette and menu bar or you can create your own by doing Command-Shift-3 on the Mac or the Print Scrn key using Windows. Command-Shift-3 grabs the entire screen, and then you need to crop out the areas you want. You can also use Command-Shift-4, with System 8, and this allows you to draw a box of the area you want to grab, but you will lose your current cursor within the grab if you choose this options. In either case, on the Mac, this creates a pict file on your boot drive called Picture 1, Picture 2, and so on. These can be opened into Photoshop, cropped and saved as TIFF or some other format. The two included on the CD were scaled to 200% in Image/Image Size using the Nearest Neighbor algorithm that produced a sharper upsize for these mostly line drawings than the default Bicubic did in this case. Open the Tool Palette and MenuBar images from the CD, or create your own and add them to the left side and top of the Yellow Flowers image, each within its own layer.

STEP 8: Using File/Place to bring in the Wholly Os image from Illustrator. You want to do any required scaling here before pressing Return after the place. You can use the Free Transform commands to position and scale this image.

Setting Up the Wholly Os Image

STEP 8: Yellow flowers is the base image for this Portable ad, but we are going to provide the client with another image choice as well, and this image has been partially created in Adobe Illustrator. Choose File/Place to place the Wholly Os Outlines file on top of the Flowers layer and below the Tool Palette and MenuBar layers. When you Place a file, you are given a scale box on top of the image that represents the unrasterized postcript version of the Illustrator image. You then scale that to the size you like and press Return to rasterize the postscript. You should scale with the Shift key down in one of the corners, to hold proportions. Make sure you have the size correct before pressing Return because any further scaling after this will not be as accurate because it won't be coming from PostScript, the mathematical description of the Illustrator file. This cereal box will come in with its own layer having the same name as its Illustrator file.

THE CEREAL BOX BACKGROUND

STEP 9: Create a background color for the cereal box by choosing New Layer from the Layers palette and then filling that layer with a color. I added some texture to my Red Background using Filter/Texture/Texturizer and then choosing Load Texture and loading the Bumpy Leather texture in the Textures folder within the Goodies folder installed with Photoshop 5. There are also a lot of other textures in the Other Goodies folder on the Photoshop 5 CD.

ADDING TEXTURE TO THE CEREAL BOX

STEP 10: You might notice that my Wholly Os box also has some texture on it. This was created in three steps, corresponding to my Front, Side, and Top layers at the bottom of my screen layers file that you can find on the CD. I use the Texturizer filter with the Canvas texture added to each of these areas. Click on the Wholly Os Orig layer to make it active. First I selected the front of the box with the Pen tool and then turned that into a selection and finally a layer using Layer/New/Layer Via Copy. I ran the texture on this layer and then changed its opacity to combine it with the original cereal box below to get the effect I wanted. I did a similar thing to the Top layer but used a different opacity. For the Side layer, I needed the pattern to go in a different direction so I used the Measure tool to measure the angle of the side of the box. To do this, I chose the Measure tool and then dragged a line that was parallel with the top of the box.

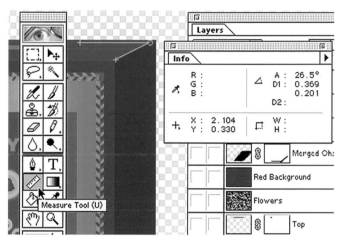

STEP 10: Measuring the angle to rotate the Cereal box side before adding texture.

Holding down the Option key, I dragged a second line that represented the angle with that top line that I wanted to measure. The angle shows up in the Info palette as you can see in the illustration. Now you use Edit/Transform/Numeric to Rotate the Side layer by that exact angle before running the Texture filter on the side of the box. After running the Texture filter, use Edit/Transform/Numeric again to Rotate the Side layer back to the same angle but in the opposite direction. The Side layer will now be back where it started but will have the texture in a believable angle for the perspective of the image. You can now play with the Opacity and Blend mode of each of these texture layers to combine them with the box layer underneath and create the texture effect you want. If you look at my ScreenLayers file, you notice that I added a layer mask to the Top layer and the Wholly Os Orig layer to remove a small portion of the top-left side of the box so the perspective looks a bit better.

STEP 11: Here are the Cereal box layers and the setup to use Merge Visible to merge them together.

MERGING THE CEREAL BOX LAYERS

STEP 11: When your cereal box is set up correctly and looking good, activate the Top layer in the group of layers that creates the cereal box and then Option-click the New Layer icon to create a new layer called Merged Cereal that will be on the top of the others. Turn off the Eye icons for all other layers except those that are used to create the cereal box and this new Merged layer on top. Hold down the Option key and keep it down while Photoshop is thinking as you choose Merged Visible from the Layers palette menu. This merges the effect of all the cereal box layers into this one Merged layer. Move the other cereal box layers below the Flowers layer leaving just this one Merged layer in their place. You can turn off the Eye icons of the other cereal box layers. Looking at this Merged layer, I noticed that the corners of the box looked too artificially sharp. To make them look more realistic, I made selections from my Front, Top, and Side paths, still in my Paths palette from

STEP 11: The layer setup after the Wholly Os layers are merged together and rearranged.

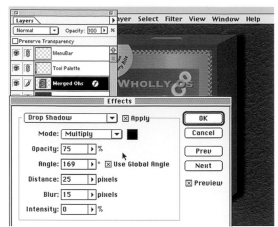

STEP 12: The Layer Effects settings for the Drop Shadow.

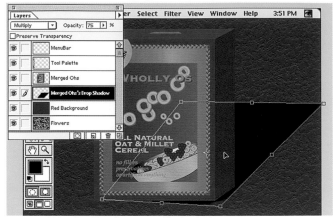

STEP 12: Using Free Transform to modify the shadow.

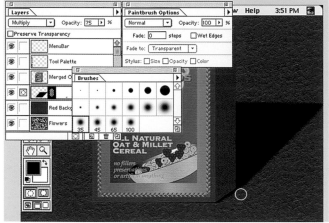

STEP 12: Editing the Shadow's layer mask with the Paintbrush.

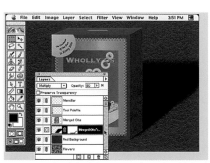

STEP 13: The linked layers as they should look before moving them to the Portable Layers image.

step 10, and used Select/Modify/Border to create a two-pixel border around each of those selections. I then did Select/Feather of one on each of those borders and then used Gaussian Blur (Shift F4) to blur the borders very slightly by about .5 pixels. Because the edges of some of these selections overlap, you need to deselect the border area here and there to make sure you don't blur any border more than once.

ADDING A DROP SHADOW TO THE CEREAL BOX

STEP 12: Make sure the Merged layer is active and then choose Layer/Effects/Drop Shadow to create a shadow for the cereal box. Use settings similar to the ones shown here or settings that you think will work for your image. Choose OK when you have a good looking shadow, realizing that we are going to transform the shadow to make it at a sharper angle behind the box. Now choose Layer/Effects/Create Layer to split this shadow off from the Merged Cereal layer into its own layer so you can modify it with Transform and other tools. With the new Merged Cereal Drop Shadow as the active layer, choose Edit/Free Transform (Command-T) to transform this shadow. And with the Command key down, which allows you to distort the edges, adjust the shadow so it looks similar to the one in the diagram here. Press Return when you are happy with your shadow transformation. Now click the Add Layer Mask icon at the bottom-left area of the Layers palette to add a layer mask to this shadow layer. Type a B to go to the Paintbrush tool, then D for default colors, and X so you are painting with black. Using a soft brush, paint in the layer mask with black to remove any parts of the shadow that appear below and in front of the box or to the right side of the box that don't look correct for this shadow. You should now have your final shadow image; you may want to adjust the opacity to make it look as realistic as it can.

LINKING LAYERS TO PREPARE FOR MOVING AND TRANSFORMATION

STEP 13: Make the Flowers layer active; then click in the linking layers middle column of the Red Background, Merged Os Shadow, Merged Os, Tool Palette and MenuBar layers above the Flowers layer to link all those layers to the Flowers layer.

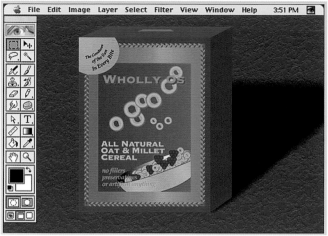

STEP 13: The final Screen Layers image before moving it to the Portable Layers image and transforming it into the Portable's screen area.

Linking them together allows you to use the Move tool to drag them all over to the Portable document. Save this document and then you will move it over to the Portable document.

STEP 14: Switch back to the PortableLayers document and click the top-most layer to activate it. Go back to the ScreenLayers document and put it in Normal screen mode so you can see the PortableLayers document also on the desktop. Activate the Flowers layer and use the Move tool to drag the Flowers layer and all the layers linked to it over to the PortableLayers document. They should now be added above the Computer Hue/Saturation layer.

STEP 13: The final Screen Layers image showing the Flowers version.

FINALIZING THE PORTABLE MONITOR IMAGE

STEP 15: Bring up the Paths palette and choose the Screen path; then turn it into a selection with a feather of zero. Click the Flowers layer and then choose Layer/Add Layer Mask/Reveal Selection. Option-click the line between the Red Background and the Flowers layer to group the Red Background layer with the Flowers layer. Now Option-click the line between Red Background and Wholly Os Drop Shadow, then Wholly Os, then Tool Palette, and finally MenuBar grouping all of these with the bottommost Flowers layer that contains the screen layer mask. You should now see only these layers within the Portable's monitor window.

STEP 16: Zoom out so there is lots of space around the edge of the Portable monitor area so we can easily Free Transform the bigger Screen layers image into the monitor space. Choose Edit/Free Transform (Command-T) and, with the Command key down, click each corner of the grouped Screen layers and drag that corner to the appropriate corner of the Portable monitor screen area. Now zoom in to 100% (Command-Option-0) and use the Command key again to exactly move the Screen layers group into the correct place so the menu bar lines up along the top of the screen area,

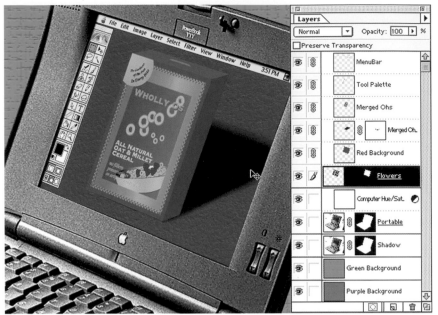

STEP 18: Here is the final Layers palette and composite image.

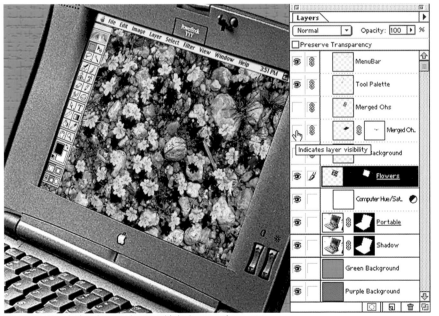

STEP 18: Here is the alternate image with its Layers palette setup.

just inside the shadow, and the Tool palette lines up along the left side, also just inside the shadow. Press Return to end the transform of this group of layers when they are lined up correctly.

Blending the Menu Bar and Tool Palette into the Shadow

STEP 17: Now click the layer mask of the Flowers layer and make a Lasso selection that is a wide selection including all of the left side and the top of the screen area. This is where the shadows are. While watching the effect on the blending of the shadow over the menu bar and the Tool palette, use Filter/Blur/Gaussian Blur to blur the Flowers layer's layer mask to soften the shadows along those edges.

STEP 18: Your composite should now be complete. You can view either the Flowers image or the Wholly Os image in the Portable's window by turning on or off the Red Background, Wholly Os Drop Shadow, and Wholly Os layers. You can change the color of the Portable computer by readjusting the Computer Hue/Saturation layer, and you can change the color of the background behind the computer between green and purple by changing the Blend mode of the Green Background layer between Normal, to see the Green Background, and Luminosity, to see the Purple background.

HANDS-ON SESSION: Creating Shadows

Different techniques to create and refine drop shadows and cast shadows, including objects that cast shadows with irregular shapes.

Here are a variety of techniques to add shadows to objects. This can be done in many different ways and people need to do it a lot. A particular technique may work better for a certain image so we are showing you many. We believe at least one of these techniques will meet your needs. You should also check out the technique for preserving shadows we use in Chapter 40: The Portable Computer Ad and also the technique for doing automatic knock-outs using Difference in Chapter 36: Blend Modes, Calculations, and Apply Image.

STEP 1: Open the file Reflection from the Shadows folder on the CD. This is a photo I took in Miami of the reflection of the sunrise in a lighting fixture. I removed the original background and added this new pink background; now all I have to do is add a shadow to combine these images. There are many ways to do this, all of which would work for this image. The technique you choose when creating your shadows will depend on the image and the type of shadow you need to create.

STEP 1: The original Layers palette for the new Reflection shadows file.

THE PHOTOSHOP 5 EFFECTS SHADOW

STEP 2: Drag the Original Reflection layer to the New Layer icon and name the copy Photoshop 5 Shadow. Turn off the Eye icon for the Original Reflection layer. Choose Layer/Effects/Drop Shadow and set up the options as shown here in the illustration. Play with the options a bit until you understand what each does. You can always double-click on this layer and change any of these options so long as you keep it as a separate layer. Using this built-

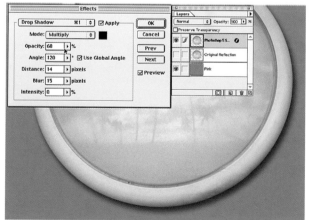

STEP 2: The setup for creating the shadow with the new built-in Drop Shadow Effect.

in option and keeping open the possibility of changing the settings on-the-fly doesn't allow you to change the shape of the shadow or make it darker or lighter in a particular place. If you do want to edit a shadow or effect created with layer effects, you need to first choose Layer/Effects/Create Layer. This will create a separate layer with the shadow or effect in it by itself. You can then go in and edit that layer to further refine it. After

STEP 2: The separate shadow layer created by Layer/Effects/Create Layer.

If you want a CMYK shadow to be only on the black printing plate, force the color of the shadow to 0,0,0,100 by clicking on the foreground color square and entering those CMYK values. The default black is a mixture of the four process inks. When you have a black shadow, sometimes creating it only on the black plate will avoid gradient color blending problems associated with using a combination of four inks. This is especially helpful when creating a shadow against a colored background. If you are using the 0, 0, 0, 100% black color for your shadows, you will want to set the Blend mode for the Shadow layer to Multiply when this shadow is against a nonwhite background; otherwise, it will seem washed out.

doing that here, Photoshop creates a new layer below the Photoshop 5 Shadow layer called Photoshop 5 Shadow's Drop Shadow. This can now be distorted with Free Transform or edited with the Airbrush or a layer mask for further refinements.

DROP SHADOW USING LAYER COPY

STEP 3: Before the new built-in Layer Shadow Effects, this next technique was the most generic and often used drop shadow technique and is similar to the Drop Shad Actions that can be accessed from ArtistKeys. Make another copy of the Original Reflection layer and name it Reflection for Copy. Now make another copy and name it Copy Shadow.

STEP 4: Go to Edit/Fill (Shift-Delete) and make sure that you turn on the Preserve Transparency option in the Fill dialog box. Fill this layer with 100% black or any other color that you wish to use as your shadow.

STEP 5: Click and drag the Copy Shadow layer in the Layers palette to move your Shadow layer below the Reflection for Copy layer. Now offset this layer in the desired direction of the shadow using either the Move tool (V) or the Filter/Other/Offset filter.

STEP 6: Make sure that Preserve Transparency is off in the Layers palette. When you have your shadow in position, use Filter/Blur/Gaussian Blur (Shift-F4) to soften the edges of the shadow. The amount of blur depends on how far from the original object you place your shadow—the farther away, the softer the shadow. With the Preview button on in the Gaussian Blur filter, you see the shadow form and change with different amounts of blur.

STEP 7: Finally, change the opacity of the Shadow layer. Once again, this depends on how close the shadow is to the object. A short, sharp shadow will be darker than a shadow cast from a distant light source.

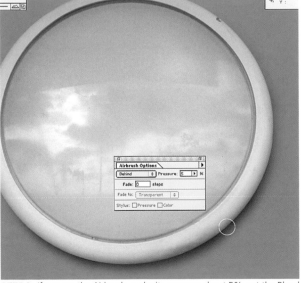

STEP 9: If you use the Airbrush, make its pressure about 5%, set the Blend Mode to Behind, and then slowly build up shadow density.

DROP SHADOW AIRBRUSH

STEP 8: Make another copy of the Original Reflection layer by Option-dragging it to the New Layer icon at the bottom of the Layers palette. Call this new layer Reflection for Airbrush and drag it to the top of the Layers palette. Turn off the Eye icons for the other layers except for the pink background. Use the Airbrush tool and choose a large soft brush. The hardness should be set to 0 to give you the absolute softest edge. Now choose the color for your shadow, set the pressure of the Airbrush at about 5%, and set the painting mode to Behind.

STEP 9: Use the Airbrush tool to paint your shadow. I prefer the Airbrush tool for its softer, more diffuse edge and for the ability to build up density as you go. Begin inside the object that you want to add the shadow to. Paint freehand with the mouse button down or click with the Painting tool for fine control. If you can draw the shadow with one stroke, you can undo it in one step if you don't like the effect. The Photoshop 5 History palette allows you to

Chapter 41: Creating Shadows

undo up to 100 steps so this should give you much more control than you had before for creating shadows this way. You can also paint from any previous undo state with the History Brush if you need to return part of the shadow to a previous state and yet you want to keep most of the current state. If you don't like your shadow, you can also just throw the whole layer away and start again by making another copy of the original object without the shadow. When hand painting, it is always a good idea to do your work on a copy of the layer and then only integrate it when you are happy with it. With a little practice you can create quick, cheap drop shadows at will.

Drop Shadow Path

STEP 10: Make another copy of the Original Reflection layer, call it Reflection for Path, and put it on top. Turn off the other layers underneath. Go to Window/Show Paths to bring up the Paths palette; then type P to get the Pen tool. Now make a path along the edge of the object where you want your shadow. Double-click on the Work Path name in the Paths palette and name this path Shadow Path.

STEP 11: Create a new Layer, call it Shadow Path, and place that new layer directly under the Reflection for Path layer. Select the Paintbrush tool with a large soft brush and set the Opacity to 100% and the Blend mode to Normal. Type a D to make sure the foreground color is black, or set the foreground color if you want something other than a black shadow.

STEP 12: Go back to the Paths palette and drag your path down to the Stroke Path icon at the bottom of the Paths palette. If you are unhappy with the size or location of your shadow, Edit/Undo the stroke (Command-Z) and change the shape of your path or the size of your brush. Now do the Stroke again until you are happy with the size and location of the shadow. To change the Opacity, just use the Opacity slider in the Shadow Path layer. By initially painting this in at 100% Opacity, you can always lower the opacity to be whatever you want.

Cast Shadow One

STEP 1: Open the Ball file from the Creating Shadows folder. Click on the Ball layer to make it active. Use Edit/Transform/Rotate to rotate the ball until the light source comes from above; then press Return or Enter to end the rotate.

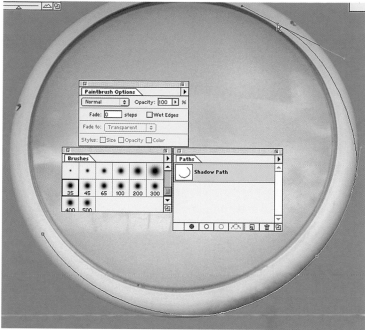

STEP 11: The setup for using the Pen tool to create your path and then stroking it with the Paintbrush to create the shadow.

STEP 12: The Drop Shadow using a stroked path.

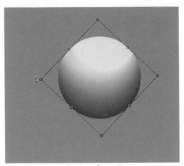

STEP 1: Use Edit/Transform/Rotate to rotate the ball so light comes from above.

STEP 2: Make a copy of the Ball layer by Option-dragging it to the New Layer icon at the bottom of the Layers palette, and then name it Shadow.

STEP 3: Shift-Delete to Fill the Shadow layer with 100% Black (or other shadow color). Make sure that you turn on the Preserve Transparency option in the Fill dialog box. Next, use Edit/Free Transform (Command-T) to flatten and widen the shape of the ball's shadow. Click down and drag in the top middle handle to flatten; then Command-Option-Shift-click in the top right and bottom right handles and drag to shrink the perspective on top and widen it on the bottom. Press Return or Enter to finish the transformation.

STEP 3: Use Edit/Free Transform to flatten the shape and add perspective.

STEP 4: Now move this layer down in the Layers palette between the ball and the background. Filter/Blur/Gaussian Blur (Shift-F4) the Shadow layer by about 8 pixels, and then change its opacity to about 60%.

STEP 5: Use the Move tool to position the shadow. Remember, the farther away from the shadow the object is positioned, the larger and softer the cast shadow. An item farther away from its shadow is also farther from the plane on which the shadow is cast. Therefore, an item that casts a large soft shadow, which does not touch the shadow itself, indicates that the item "floats" away from the projection plane. Experiment with moving the shadow closer or farther from the ball to see how this affects the depth perception of the object to its shadow. Save the file as Shadow Above.

STEP 5: Experiment with the placement, opacity, and softness of the shadow to achieve the effect of distance from the background and closeness of the light source.

CAST SHADOW TWO

STEP 6: Reopen the Ball file. Here we have an object lit from the upper right. Therefore, we will have a cast shadow that goes down and to the left at an opposite angle. Make a new layer of the ball by Option-dragging it to the New Layer icon at the bottom of the Layers palette and calling it Shadow. Press Shift-Delete to fill this layer with black, making sure Preserve Transparency is on. Use Edit/Free Transform (Command-T) to change the shape of the shadow to match the light source. You may have to try this transformation several times. Photoshop only gives you a rectangular shape to use as the basis for your distort, and it's difficult to get an accurate read on what your distorted shape will actually look like.

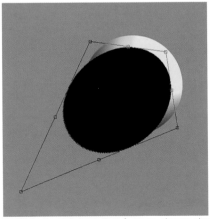

STEP 6: Use Edit/Free Transform to change the shape of the shadow.

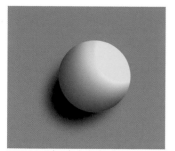

STEP 7: A hard, dark shadow seems to place the ball directly against the background.

STEP 7: A soft shadow with more off-set gives the appearance of the ball floating above the background.

With the Command key down to get the distort function, I brought the upper-right point inside the shape of the ball, the upper-left and lower-right points in on a diagonal but still outside the shape of the ball, and the lower-left point out and down in a diagonal in the opposite direction of the light source.

STEP 7: When you get a shape that you're happy with, move the shadow layer below the ball in the Layers palette. Filter/Blur/ Gaussian Blur the shadow layer; then use the Opacity slider to change the opacity and the Move tool to position the shadow. Remember that the distance from the object dictates how soft the shadow should be. The closer the shadow, the sharper the shadow. If the rotation of the shadow doesn't match the direction of the light, use Edit/Transform/Rotate to get the angle that matches. Use File/Save As and name the file Ball Cast Shadow.

CAST SHADOW THREE

This technique is similar to Cast Shadow Two but incorporates a fade from the front of the shadow to the back.

STEP 8: Make a copy of the shadow you just made in the Ball Cast Shadow file you were just working on and call the copied layer Shadow2. Reset the Opacity of this copy to 100%. Turn off the Eye icon of the first shadow layer. Use Edit/Free Transform to change the shadow shape to make it wider and longer than your last cast shadow.

STEP 9: Click in the add Layer Mask icon at the bottom left of the Layers palette to add a new layer mask to this Shadow2 layer. Type G to access the Gradient tool, Return to bring up the Options dialog, and Shift-G until the Options dialog says Radial Gradient Options in the tab at the top. Now set the options to Normal, 100%, Foreground to Background. Type a D for default colors, and then do a blend from slightly inside the shape of the ball and outward in the direction of the distort and beyond the bottom-left end of the distorted shadow. You should get a shadow that is soft on all sides but has a more pronounced fade at the tail. You may want to experiment with starting and ending your blend at different points as well as further distortion of the shadow layer to soften or enlarge your shadow.

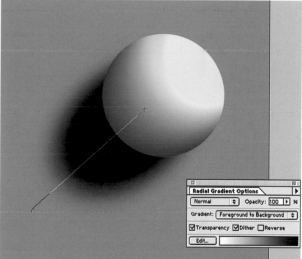

STEP 9: Try your Gradient Blend in the Shadow2 Layer Mask from this position and with these options.

STEP 9: Here is the faded shadow after the Radial Gradient Blend.

325

PHOTOSHOP 5.5 & IMAGEREADY 2,

NEW PHOTOSHOP 5.5 & IMAGEREADY 2 FEATURES

WHEN TO USE PHOTOSHOP VS IMAGEREADY

WHEN TO CHOOSE GIF, JPEG, OR PNG

ANIMATIONS, SLICES, AND ROLLOVERS

4-UP DIALOGS TO OPTIMIZE WEB IMAGES

WEB IMAGE GALLERIES AND PICTURE PACKAGES

IMAGES FOR THE WEB AND MULTIMEDIA

This photograph was shot with a 4 x 5 camera on Fuji Velvia film, the scan was done with a Tango drum scanner, with color correction in Photoshop.

42 DIFFERENCES IN CREATING FOR THE WEB AND 8-BIT COLOR

What is different about the Web and
determining which viewers are most important.

WHY ARE THE WEB AND MULTIMEDIA DIFFERENT?

When I first started working with digital images in 1988, I was in the "Hypermedia Group" at Apple. We used to have the most fun in our weekly meetings, daydreaming about futures like digital virtual reality environments, sending color images over high-speed ISDN networks, computers that actually had built-in CD players as well as accelerated image compression and decompression, digital video and video conferencing, experiences like QuickTime VR, and many other things that were not possible at the time with our slow Mac IIx computers. The only thing that was just barely possible then was full-color, printed output from a Mac or PC. I could actually make color prints on Apple's Dupont 4Cast dye-sub printer! All the 8-bit color stuff seemed of low quality and of little interest to me. There was no Web, as we know it today, back in 1988.

Now, in 2000, most of the things we dreamed about back then have happened and are old news. Now we have the Web and multimedia applications, where JPEG compression and 8-bit color are important in seeing the best quality digital images. Even for photographers, who like seeing all the minute detail in a photograph, the current reality is that we often have to transmit digital comps to clients who want both print and Web versions of their images, and we probably want to create a Web site to advertise our own work. In making Web images for myself and my clients, I have realized that there is a real art to creating quality images for the Web and multimedia. Many of the techniques are the same that we use in creating images for print, but some very important differences can help you to make the transition between mediocre Web images and great Web images.

The Web is a rapidly changing environment. With constantly new features and possibilities on the Web, you don't have to wait for a new book to be published or worry about the distribution channels to get the latest product. What I am telling you here in this book is based on what I know today and, in the world of the Web, that may easily change tomorrow or next week or a few months from now as new features appear. If you need to always know the latest about the Web, the best place to find that out is the Web because it can be updated any time. We've included some tips at the end of this chapter from our friend Ed Velandria, a true Web wizard. He gives you a couple of sites to visit to help you out. Our Web site is www.maxart.com, and we place updated information, like these chapter updates for Photoshop 5.5, there all the time, so check it frequently. You can send Wendy and me email at wendy@maxart.com or barry@maxart.com. We always enjoy hearing from our readers and try to answer questions when we can. By the way, our four-year-old son's name is Max!

WHY IS 8-BIT COLOR IMPORTANT AND WHAT IS IT?

Eight-bit color is important for two reasons. First, some computer users have computers that can see only 8-bit color on their monitors. Second, 8-bit color images take up less space to store than 24-bit color images of the same monitor display size. In most cases, this makes them faster to transmit over the Web and also allows you to store more of them on a multimedia CD. They are also faster to read from a CD and put up on the screen.

To display color on a computer screen, you need a 24-bit digital value. Eight bits of Red plus 8 bits of Green plus 8 bits of Blue specify the exact color value of each pixel on a computer monitor. A 24-bit video card that places that color on the screen needs enough memory to store one 24-bit value for each pixel on the screen. The 24-bit color values from your 24-bit color image get placed in the video card's memory buffer to display the part of the image you are currently seeing on the screen. This allows each pixel on your screen to be any one of 16,777,216 colors (256 ° 256 ° 256). Until recently, computer memory was quite expensive, so many computer models were shipped with the cheaper 8-bit color instead. With 8-bit color, you can only see a total of 256 different colors on your entire computer screen at one time. Out of the possible 16,777,216 colors, you can see only 256, but you can pick any 256 of these 16,777,216 colors. Images that are 8-bit color store only 8 bits of information for each pixel in that image. Because of this, 8-bit digital images can have a total of only 256 distinct colors, but each 8-bit image can pick the 256 colors it will have out of the set of 16,777,216 colors. The particular set of colors that is chosen is called the Color palette for that image. A Color palette is a table of 256 24-bit digital values.

When an 8-bit image is displayed on an 8-bit monitor, the 8-bit values of each pixel in the image are used as an index into a table of 256 24-bit color values to drive the monitor. The monitor itself still gets 24-bit values from the 8-bit video card; it just gets only 256 different values at a time. When that 8-bit image is first displayed on the screen, this table is loaded from the Color palette of that image. There are 256 24-bit values in a Color palette, and the index number (0–255) that represents each pixel in an 8-bit image is used to tell the video card which of those 256 24-bit values in the table to display for that pixel. If the pixel's value is 0, the first entry in the table will be used. If the pixel's value is 5, the fifth entry will be used, and so on. This table lookup and display of the color pixels on the screen generally happens at least 60 times per second for each pixel on the screen. This is just one of the many things the computer has to always do while you are just sitting there looking at it.

Eight-bit color files can be faster to load from a CD, or to transfer over the Web, because there are only 8 bits per pixel, versus 24, to load or transfer. One reason 8-bit video cards are cheaper is because they require only enough memory for 8 bits per pixel on the screen, plus the 256 entry 24-bit table, versus 24 bits per pixel on the screen. Now you know why the older computers with color monitors have had only 8-bit color. They were cheaper to produce! In the last

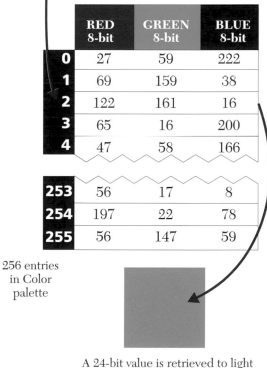

8-bit image with one byte (8 bits) for each pixel

2	2	99	99	82	81
2	17	137	122	17	17
17	2	36	38	36	2
36	137	126	122	17	17
245	27	65	33	89	88
55	84	56	24	17	12

8-bit value is used as an index (lookup number) into the Color palette table

	RED 8-bit	GREEN 8-bit	BLUE 8-bit
0	27	59	222
1	69	159	38
2	122	161	16
3	65	16	200
4	47	58	166
253	56	17	8
254	197	22	78
255	56	147	59

256 entries in Color palette

A 24-bit value is retrieved to light that pixel onscreen

few years, though, memory has become much cheaper, and most new video cards support 24 bit color.

ABOUT JPEG, GIF, AND PNG FILES

JPEG, GIF, and PNG file formats are all used in compressing images. The GIF and PNG-8 formats assume you start with an 8-bit image (or 7, 6, 5, or whatever). The trouble is that for photographs, a lot of loss occurs in converting from a 24-bit image to an 8-bit or lower format. After you have the 8-bit format, creating a GIF or PNG-8 will compress that, but the user will get the same 8-bit file when decompressed on the other end. No further loss will occur, but the main loss in a photograph has already occurred in converting from 24-bit to 8-bit. For graphic images that have fewer than 256 colors in them to start with, GIF is great because the image can decompress back to the original with all its colors.

The JPEG and PNG-24 formats start with a 24-bit image and compresses it to make it smaller on the disk or for Web transfers. When the user opens it on the other end, they will also get a 24-bit image of the same opened size as the original, but the quality will may be less than the original, with JPEG, due to the compression. The more compression you choose when you make the JPEG, the smaller the compressed file but the lower the quality when reopened again. The PNG-24 format has lossless compression but the files are considerably larger than JPEG compressed files. For more information on the JPEG and GIF file formats, see Chapter 6: File Formats and Image Compression. JPEG is generally best for compressing 24-bit color photographs, and GIF is generally best for compressing graphics. When you JPEG-compress graphics, the decompressed file will often not be as sharp as the original. PNG-24 is what you would have to use if you wanted a full 256 level transparency effect. This would allow an image that slowly fades into a background to slowly fade into any background that is on the current Web page. Not all browsers support this feature, however.

We sometimes end up compressing photographs using the GIF format because GIF gives you the option of having a transparent area surrounding a knocked-out photograph. This transparent GIF format, when displayed on a Web page, shows the background of the Web page in all the transparent areas. This allows transparent GIF images to be placed on any background and still, in theory, look fine. For this to work in practice, as we will show you, you need to be careful how you make your transparent GIF. Subtle gradient fades and drop shadow fades into different Web backgrounds can be tricky and may not give you what you'd like. Another advantage of the GIF and PNG-8 formats is that they also support images that require even less than 8 bits of information per pixel. Many of the images I have created for commercial sites, like the Netscape online catalog, were GIF files that required only 5 bits per pixel. These files can be made very small and can also be transparent GIFs.

DESIGNING FOR THE VIEWERS YOU CARE ABOUT THE MOST

When you, or your client, create a Web site or multimedia CD, it is important to consider who will be viewing it and what type of equipment those viewers might have. There is also the most important subset of those viewers, called "the ones you really care about." Those are the ones you want to design the site/CD for. In creating your Web/multimedia images, you want them to look best for these viewers, the ones you really care about. In creating the images for your project, you have to choose whether to use all 8-bit images, all 24-bit images, some of each, save your

---

WHAT ABOUT PNG?

The PNG format uses lossless compression that can sometimes give you smaller files than GIF. It interlaces two dimensionally for faster loading, and can be stored at 8, 24, or 32-bits. PNG-24 supports alpha channel transparency, up to 256 levels of transparency, it is cross-platform, and it tags files with color space information, allowing viewing software to compensate for different monitor settings. Photoshop 5.5 and ImageReady 2 support PNG, but some browsers don't support all of PNG-24's features. Try it out and compare it to GIF for your images. Just make sure the browsers you care about support its features.

Chapter 42: Differences in Creating for the Web and 8-Bit Color

images in JPEG, GIF, PNG, PICT, Targa, or some other format, or variations on each of these choices. Let's discuss how to simplify these decisions.

The average American who is browsing the Web may have a browser that uses a cheaper computer, or even his or her TV set, as the monitor environment (these are both 8-bit color) and a modem that is 28,800 kilobits/second in speed. Even with a 56 kb modem, many local phone systems actually transmit at a slower speed. I found this out when I moved from Silicon Valley to Corvallis, Oregon. At 28 kb, it takes about one-half second to download 1K (1,024 bytes) of information. The extra bits are taken up by software overhead, and the speed you actually get depends on a lot of issues, especially the performance of your Internet provider and the number of other people who are also trying to access information on that same site at the same time. If you create a 14K file, it will take these average Americans about seven seconds to download and view that image. If you are creating a site for the average American, say, the site for the Sears catalog, you can assume some of these people have 8-bit color. For them, you will want color photographs and graphics to be mostly 8-bit GIF files, which will look better on their 8-bit screens than 24-bit JPEG files. Eight-bit files generally look better on 8-bit monitors.

For our Web site, we make a different set of assumptions. We assume that the users we care most about are photographers, art directors, designers, and digital artists. These are the people who will be most interested in our books and services, and almost all of them have 24-bit color systems, 28.8 or faster modems, ISDN access, cable modems or even T1 lines, and they are interested in seeing the best-quality images. For our site, we save most images that started out as photographs in JPEG format. Anything that is a photograph of nature or people, or a commercial composite example, is saved in JPEG format so it opens up in 24-bit color on the viewer's screen. We are more concerned about showing the users a high-quality image on their screens than creating an image that opens a few seconds faster. We may even show them small, lower-quality versions and give them the option of waiting a little longer to see a higher-quality version. The only time we use a GIF is for a graphic or illustration that started with less than 256 different colors or for a small image that requires a transparent background. Our set of assumptions about the viewers we care most about are different than if we were creating a site for the average American Web surfer. When creating images for your site, or that of your client, you need to know the type of user who is most important for that site and design for the lowest common denominator of your target audience. Make your images look best for that user.

To let your viewer see the highest quality images no matter what type of system they have, you might want to provide a choice on your home page to either view a site for users with 8-bit systems or a site for users with 24-bit systems. You can then optimize the images on each separate branch of your main site to make each type of user happy.

43 HANDS-ON SESSION: USING PHOTOSHOP 5.5 AND IMAGEREADY 2 TO OPTIMIZE WEB IMAGES

Using the Photoshop 5.5 and ImageReady 2 4-Up Dialogs or using Photoshop 5 to create GIF, JPEG, and PNG files.

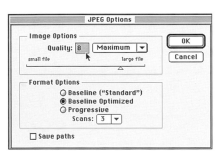

STEP 2: Using Photoshop 5 to choose the JPEG format with 8.3 name reflecting what you are saving.

STEP 2: Using Photoshop 5 to set the Quality to 8 for the Maximum quality setting. Also, make sure that Baseline Optimized is on and Save paths is off.

STEP 2: Different files sizes in Photoshop versus JPEG format.

USING THE 8.3 FILE NAMING CONVENTION.

We will be working on the files gc.psd, redac.psd, and macn.psd within the GIF JPEG and Color Palettes folder on your CD. The names of these files are abbreviations for Grand Canyon in Photoshop format, Red Acura in Photoshop format, and McNamaras in Photoshop format, respectively. When you are creating images to use on the Web, it's a good idea to use filenames that will work on any computer system. The names of your files will also be embedded in your HTML code for your Web pages, and that code needs to work on any system. Older DOS Windows systems can't read files with names longer than eight characters, and most Windows systems use the three-character suffix at the end of the filename to decide what type of file it is. If you use filenames with a maximum of eight characters and a three-character suffix, they will work on all Macs and all PCs. We will call this the 8.3 filename format. On UNIX systems, it can be even more complicated, because they see a difference between upper- and lowercase letters in filenames. If you specify a filename in your HTML code that was both upper- and lowercase but the file on the UNIX volume was all in lowercase, when you run that code on a UNIX server, the HTML code may not find your file. To be safe when creating images and HTML for the Web, make all your filenames lowercase and all the names in your HTML code also lowercase. That way, the code and the files will work together correctly, no matter what type of server your Web pages end up on.

GIFS VS JPEGS IN PHOTOSHOP 5

STEP 1: If you now have Photoshop 5.5 and ImageReady 2, you could skip ahead 4 pages to learn about creating Web images in their great 4-Up dialogs. You probably should read the next 4 pages anyhow, though, as there is lots of useful information within them. For Photoshop 5 and 5.02 users, you should start here. Open the files gc.psd, redac.psd, and macn.psd from within their respective folders located within the GIF JPEG and Color Palettes folder on your CD.

STEP 2: If you have Photoshop 5, then for each of these three open files, choose File/Save A Copy (Command-Option-S) and save one Maximum quality JPEG version and one Medium quality JPEG version. Set the Quality number on the Maximum to 8 and the Quality number on the Medium to 3. Give each an 8.3 format filename that reflects what you are doing in each file. For example, redacmed.jpg and redacmax.jpg are the names I used for the Red Acura file. Open all six of these files into Photoshop and compare them at 100% zoom factor to the original three files that are on the screen. Viewers of a Web site or a multimedia application are going

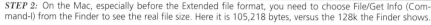

to be seeing the images at 100%. You will notice that all of these, even the medium-quality JPEG ones, look pretty good at 100%. Now compare each to its original when zoomed in to 200%. The Acura emblem in the center of the hood really breaks down in the medium-quality JPEG version. You will also notice more posterization in the faces of the McNamaras as the JPEG quality gets

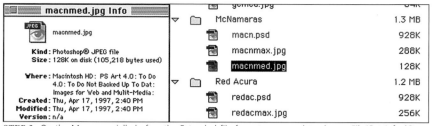

STEP 2: On the Mac, especially before the Extended file format, you need to choose File/Get Info (Command-I) from the Finder to see the real file size. Here it is 105,218 bytes, versus the 128k the Finder shows.

lower. The Grand Canyon image just looks a bit softer and more posterized at 200%. But hey, at 100% these JPEG mediums look pretty good and they are much smaller than the originals. When I am working on a commercial file for a client, I often send the client a digital comp over the Net by first resampling a copy of my image to about 5Mb in size, and then saving that as a medium-quality JPEG. This is usually a file, about 200–400K in size, that will quickly transfer with a 28.8 modem and then open up on a client's screen to a nice screen comp about 5Mb in size.

These three images each started out with a pixel resolution of exactly 640x480. When you open them back up from JPEG compression, they will still be 640x480 pixels; their file size just gets smaller for saving on the disk and transmitting over the network. The amount of compression you get depends on the contents of each individual image. The more complex it is, the less compression you get; the more areas of flat color or repeated patterns, the better the compression. To see the real size of any file, the size that will actually get transferred across the Net, you need to first click that file in the Finder; then choose File/Get Info (Command-I) to bring up the Info dialog box for that file. The right-most part of the Size line will have the actual bytes used in parentheses. You want to set File/Preferences/Saving Files to Never Save Image Previews, and then the size displayed by "bytes used" in the Get Info box will be correct. With Windows and DOS, the file sizes displayed are quite close to the actual file sizes. If you use Mac OS 8.1 or later and reformat your drives first using the Mac Extended drive format, you will also get a more accurate display of Finder file sizes.

STEP 3: Now we are going to create GIF versions of all these images and compare them to the JPEG versions you still have on your screen. See in a few pages how you can do this on the fly using the 4-Up dialog in Photoshop 5.5 or ImageReady 2. For each of the three images, use the Window menu to bring up the version saved in Photoshop format. Its filename will end in .psd. Choose Image/Duplicate (F5) to make a copy of the image; then choose Image/Mode/Index Color and convert it to Index Color using Adaptive Palette, 8 bits/pixel Color Depth, Diffusion Dither, and Best Color Matching. Now choose File/Save As and save this file with the Format set to CompuServe GIF. Give it a filename that shows this; for the McNamaras, we used macn8mi.gif. Macn tells us it's the McNamaras, 8 tells us it's 8 bits per pixel, mi tells us we used Mode/Index to do the conversion, and .gif tells us it's a GIF_file. Now click back on your original Photoshop version of the file and choose File/Export/GIF89a Export (F3) and set things up as shown in the dialog box to the right, to make an 8-bit GIF file using this better filter. The filename we used here was macn889.gif. The 89 before the .gif shows us that we used the GIF89a Export plug-in to generate the file. Open this file and you will notice that it looks just as good as the other 8-bit file on the screen, but if you look at its file size, you will notice that

STEP 3: The Photoshop 5 settings to create an 8-bit Index Color image using Image/Mode/Index Color. To save this as a GIF file, you then need to choose File/Save As and set the Format to CompuServe GIF. You can use the Color Depth pop-up to create 7-bit, 6-bit, or smaller index color images. Setting Dither to None will make the file smaller but it might not look as good. Best Color Matching takes longer to process than Faster, but images generally look less contrasty. Preserve Exact Colors prevents dithering of any colors that are in the current palette and can help keep fine lines and text from breaking up on the Web. File size remains much the same whether you choose Faster, Best, or either option with Preserve Exact Colors. Test your own images to see which settings look best.

STEP 3: In Photoshop 5, pattern Dither is only available when you are using Web or System palettes. It uses a sort of halftone screen to dither.

STEP 3: Here are the PS 5 settings to create an 8-bit GIF file using File/Export/Gif89a Export. This is a one-step process to convert your 24-bit RGB file directly into a GIF file on the disk, and you can choose the number of Colors while you are at it. 128 colors = 7-bit, 64 colors = 6-bit, 32 colors = 5-bit, and so on.

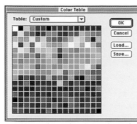

STEP 4: The Adaptive palette for the Red Acura image.

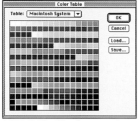

STEP 4: The Adaptive palette for the Grand Canyon image.

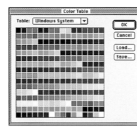

STEP 4: The Adaptive palette for the McNamaras image.

it is smaller than the file you created by choosing Save As. Now go back to the original Photoshop file one more time and again choose File/Export/GIF89a (F3), but this time, set the Colors to 32 instead of 256. Name this file macn589.gif. The 5 tells us it's a 5-bit image, using 5 bits of color information for each pixel. Open up this smaller 5-bit image and compare it to the others. In most cases, you will prefer the medium-quality JPEG-compressed file to any of the 8-bit images and certainly to the 5-bit image on a 24-bit color monitor. The 8-bit GIF file might look a bit sharper in some cases than the Medium JPEG-compressed version. Now look at the file sizes again. The Medium JPEG is always a lot smaller than any of the GIF versions, even the 5-bit GIF version. Even the Maximum quality JPEG is about the same size as the 8-bit GIF files and certainly a lot better quality on a 24-bit monitor. So if the intended client has a 24-bit monitor and the image is a continuous tone photograph, the file format of choice is JPEG. The only exception to this right now would be if you are going to create transparent GIF images as you will in the next chapter.

DISPLAYING IMAGES ON AN 8-BIT MONITOR

STEP 4: Now switch your monitor to 8-bit color. To do this on the Mac, choose Control Panels/Monitors from the Apple menu, and then choose the 256 Colors option in the Monitors dialog box. On most Macs, you can also use the control strip at the side of your screen. Different video card software and different Mac systems have other alternative ways to do this, but you should be able to do it on the fly in Photoshop. On Windows 95 or NT, you do this by accessing Display properties with your right mouse button on the Desktop, and sometimes you have to quit Photoshop and restart the program for the change to take effect. Go through and look at all the files we have created on the screen in 8-bit color mode. You will notice that the 8-bit images look better than the 24-bit ones when viewed on an 8-bit screen. To see an image properly on an 8-bit screen, you need to click on its window to activate it. This loads the Adaptive palette for that particular image. This makes that image look good because we are displaying it using a palette that was optimized for it. Notice, however, that the other images on the screen will not look so good. When looking at the 8-bit version of the Red Acura file, the Grand Canyon and the McNamaras files will not look as good. This is true for each of these images because everything on the

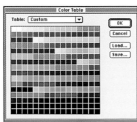

STEP 5: The Mac System palette.

STEP 5: The Windows System palette.

STEP 5: The Web palette.

STEP 5: Built-in Photoshop 5 palette choices.

screen needs to be displayed using the palette for the active window. Each time you activate a different image, the entire screen is viewed using its palette. To the left are the Adaptive Color palettes created by the GIF89a Export filter for each of these images. If you need to display more than one 8-bit image on an 8-bit monitor at a time, which you will often need to do for a Web page or in a multimedia application, you need to use the same palette for both images; otherwise, one of them will look bad. The palette also controls the colors used to display the menu bar and other system items or items from the application. By the way, you can display multiple 8-bit images on a 24-bit monitor and they will all look their best because all the palettes can be seen at the same time in 24-bit color. This makes it easier on a 24-bit monitor to compare several 8-bit images.

Chapter 43: Using Photoshop 5.5 and ImageReady 2 to Optimize Web Images

CHOOSING BETWEEN SYSTEM PALETTES AND CUSTOM ADAPTIVE PALETTES

STEP 5: There is a palette, called the System palette, that was created to deal with the differences between Adaptive palettes of images that need to be displayed on the same page of an 8-bit monitor. A System palette contains a

STEP 6: Here you see the three images pasted together in one so you can create a common Adaptive palette. When this is done, you can separate each image again.

broad range of colors from all over the spectrum so that you can display any image and it will look okay. It won't usually look as good as it would with its own Adaptive palette, but using the System palette, you can display many different images at the same time with reasonable results. The problem for Web developers is that the Mac and Windows OSs each have different colors in their System palettes. Fortunately, there are 216 colors in common between the two palettes. The palette with these common colors is called the Web palette. Photoshop 5 allows you to choose any of these palettes when creating 8-bit images using Image/Mode/Index Color. Creating images using the Web palette allows them to display well in 8-bit color on the Mac and on the PC when using Netscape or Internet Explorer to browse your images.

STEP 6: When creating images for a multimedia CD where you have absolute control over your palettes, you can also create a custom palette for each group of images that would be on the screen at one time. To do this from Photoshop 5, with these three images, choose one of the three original 24-bit images (let's do the Grand Canyon), type D, for default colors, and then go into Image/Canvas Size (Command-F8). The width of each of these images is almost nine inches, so make the new width 27 inches and choose OK. Put this image into Full Screen mode (F); then choose one of the other original RGB images from the Window menu. Press V to switch to the Move tool; then drag and drop this image on top of the new wider one below. Move it to one end or the other and then use the Window menu again to find the third image. Drag and drop the image on the other end of your new wider image and then choose Flatten Image from the Layers Palette menu. Your image should now look like the figure at the top of this page. It doesn't really matter which of the three images is in which position. Choose Image/Mode/Index Color and pick the same Adaptive, 8 bits Per Pixel, 256 Color, Diffusion Dither options you chose the last time you used this dialog box to create an adaptive palette. Choose OK to convert to 8-bit color, this has now created the common palette for all three images. Type C to get the Crop tool, and crop this composite back to the same Grand Canyon image you started with. Save this as gcall3.gif in CompuServe GIF format. Switch to one of the other two original 24-bit images and choose Image/Mode/Index Color, but this time, set the Palette type to Previous. This will use the same palette we created when all three images were together. Save this with another appropriate "all3" name like macall3.gif and then do the same thing with the third image. You now have all three images created with the same adaptive palette that was custom-developed for just these three images. You'll notice that, in 8-bit color monitor mode, you can switch back and forth between these three images with no flashing. That's because the Color palette is the same for each. Go into Image/Mode/Color Palette and look at this common palette. It is a mixture of the three you saw on the last page. Click the Save button and save this palette as All3Palette. Now you can load this palette from the Color Palette dialog box and also from the GIF89a Export plug-in. Now you know some palette

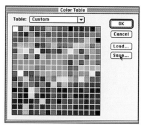

STEP 6: The All3Palette that works for all three of these images. Click the Save button; then you can later Load this into the GIF89a export.

When creating an Adaptive palette in Photoshop 5, to bias the color table toward particular colors in an image, make a selection of those color areas before you do the Index Color mode conversion. The color table will be more weighted to the selected area.

magic! If you need to make a lot of common palette images, create an action to do it to all the files in a folder, or better yet, read on to learn about the great Master Palette features in ImageReady 2 that automate this entire process and make it much easier and more powerful.

THE PHOTOSHOP 5.5 AND IMAGEREADY 2 4-UP DIALOGS

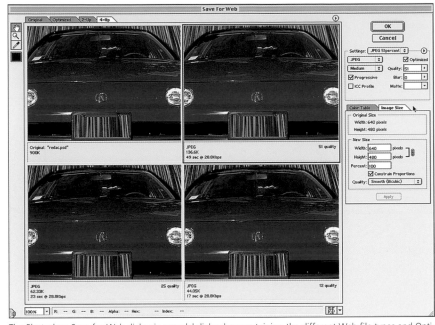

The Photoshop Save for Web dialog is a modal dialog box containing the different Web file types and Optimize options in the upper right corner, the Image Size and Color Table information below that to the right side and the 4 views when looking at it in 4-Up mode. In Photoshop, you can only save one image at a time without re-entering this dialog and you can only see one Photoshop image within this dialog at a time.

STEP 1: If you have Photoshop 5.5 and ImageReady 2, open the file redac.psd from the GIF JPEG and Color Palettes folder on your CD. Open each of these files in both Photoshop 5.5 and ImageReady 2, and then type F, for Full Screen Mode, in each of the programs. We will use this file as we explore the new ways to make GIF, JPEG and PNG files with Photoshop 5.5 or ImageReady 2.0.

In Photoshop, choose File/Save for Web (Command-Option-Shift-S) to open the Save for Web 4-Up dialog. Click on the 4-Up tab to choose the 4-Up view. This allows you to look at 4 different versions of the proposed Web file at the same time. Now switch to ImageReady 2, and you will notice that the different optimize options (Original, Optimized, 2-up, 4-Up) are available all the time without going into the Save for Web modal dialog. That gives ImageReady the option of saving any version of an optimized image any time without entering and then leaving the Save for Web modal dialog, as Photoshop 5.5 irritatingly does each time you choose OK to save from this dialog.

ORIGINAL, OPTIMIZED, 2-UP, 4-UP

STEP 2: In either application, clicking on the Original tab will allow you to use the entire window space to look at the original image without any Web optimizations. Clicking on the Optimized tab allows you to use the entire window to look at the one Optimized version. The 2-Up view allows you to compare the Original to one optimization or to look at two optimizations at a time. The 4-Up view gives you the most options because it allows you to compare four versions of an image at a time, so we will start there. Click on the 4-Up option in ImageReady; then click on the top left version of the red Acura image. Now switch back to Photoshop and click on the top left version of the red Acura image. Choose Original from the Settings pop-up in the top right of the window. This will continue to show you the original image in the top left window. Now click in the top, right window; then change the settings to JPEG High to look at a JPEG version of the image. Photoshop will now create the JPEG version with the High quality setting and display it on the screen. Notice that below this top right subwindow on the left you also see the file size of this version and how long it will take to transfer over the Web using a certain speed of modem. You can

STEP 2: The Preview menu in Photoshop's Save for Web dialog allows you to choose the color space used for image display within the dialog and also the speed of the model used to calculate Web file download times.

Chapter 43: Using Photoshop 5.5 and ImageReady 2 to Optimize Web Images

use the Preview pop-up menu at the top right of this Save for Web dialog to change the speed of the modem for these calculations and to also change the way Web images are displayed in Photoshop. We will explain the other settings in this Preview pop-up later. To change the modem speed display calculations in ImageReady, you use the pop-up menus on the bottom left of the window.

MAKING YOUR OWN OPTIMIZE SETTINGS

STEP 3: When you pick one of the Settings choices in either application, you are just choosing a predefined set for creating the Web image in this window. You can then optimize that choice by changing any of the options like Quality, Blur and Matt that you see here. Photoshop and ImageReady come with some predefined settings choices, but you can also create your own settings files once you have discovered which Web options work best for your most common images. To create your own settings file, just choose Save Settings from the Optimize Pop-up menu to the right of the Settings menu. You need to save these settings within the Adobe Photoshop 5.5/Adobe Photoshop 5.5 Settings/Optimize folder on your hard disk. Now click in the bottom left window; then change the Quality slider to 51%. Choose the Save Settings pop-up and save this as "JPEG 51percent" within the above mentioned folder. This setting will now be available to Photoshop and to make it available to ImageReady, you need to quit and then restart ImageReady

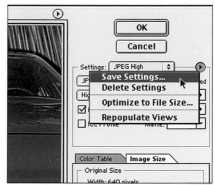

Step 3: Choosing Save Settings from Photoshop's Save for Web dialog to save a particular set of JPEG file options. You need to save these settings within the "Adobe Photoshop 5.5/Adobe Photoshop 5.5 Settings/Optimize" folder on your hard disk.

PHOTOSHOP VERSUS IMAGEREADY WEB-OPTIMIZE LAYOUT

STEP 4: Notice that in this Photoshop Save for Web dialog, you have all the Optimize settings options built into the top right corner, and then below that there is an Image Size section and a Color Table section. You can use the Image Size section, while in Save for Web, to actually resample the file just for a smaller (or larger) Web image of any dimension. That may seem convient, but actually it works better if you sharpen an image after it is resampled and before converting it to JPEG or GIF. Doing the resample within the Save for Web dialog doesn't give you that option. In ImageReady, on the other hand, you have to use the Image/Image Size command to resample each image before you choose its Web optimization. This is probably better because you can then sharpen it before converting it to JPEG or GIF. You can do it the same way in Photoshop; you just need to remember to resample and sharpen the image before bringing up the Save for Web dialog. That means that for the sharpest Web images, you probably won't use the Image Size section of Save for Web. The Color Table section of Save for Web is only used when you are making 8-bit or fewer GIF or PNG-8 files that will be using a color table. To see the Color Table in ImageReady,

This is the ImageReady 4-Up view of the current file. In ImageReady, to see a 4-Up view of any file, all you have to do is switch to that file and then click on the 4 Up tab. Here in ImageReady, you can save as many variations as you want from any open file since the 4-Up choice is always there. To get the Optimize options or the Color Table in ImageReady, you need to choose Window/Show Optimize or Window/Show Color Table. To change the Image Size in ImageReady, you need to choose Image/Image Size, which is really a better way to do it than using the built-in Image Size option in Photoshop's Save for Web dialog since you will probably want to sharpen the image after resizing it and before saving it in a Web format.

Adobe ImageReady

The document "redac.psd" is open in Adobe Photoshop with unsaved changes. Would you like to switch to Adobe Photoshop to save the changes?

Cancel   Switch

When switching back and forth between Photoshop 5.5 and ImageReady 2, you can get this message from either application when you try to open a file that is already open and has been modified within the other app. If you choose cancel, the app you are in just opens the original unmodified file. Choosing Switch allows you to switch to the other app and save the file first. If you turn on the Auto Update option in the General Preferences of either app, it will automatically update an open file before switching to the other app.

choose Window/Show Color Table. It looks like Adobe just took some of the ImageReady features and squeezed them into this Save for Web dialog. I wish they would have had time to add all the ImageReady features to Photoshop, but it is certainly good to have the most important ones in Photoshop and the rest in ImageReady.

Switch to ImageReady, and here you will need use Window/Show Optimize to bring up the Optimize palette. Choose Original from its Settings menu so that top left view of the image shows you the original Red Acura. Click on the top right view and choose JPEG-High from the Optimize palette's setting menu to set it to the High quality JPEG option. Now change the Quality slider to 51, which I think is the best JPEG compromise for this image between image size and image quality. Choose File Save Optimized As... and save this file as redacIR51.jpg so you can look at it later. To do this from the Photoshop Save for Web dialog, you would have to choose OK at the top right of the dialog while a subwindow with these options was selected. That would then put you out of Save for Web without the option of trying and saving further optimizations. To do more, you would have to then re-enter Save for Web, which takes extra time.

COMPARING GIF TO JPEG

STEP 5: Now click in the bottom left view for the red Acura within ImageReady. Choose GIF 128 Dithered from the settings menu in the Optimize dialog. You are now comparing the Original to a JPEG at quality 51 to a 128-color GIF file. Notice that the GIF file is very sharp, but the fine color transitions in the hood of the car look pixelated. Do Command-Spacebar-Click to zoom into the Acura emblem and the color transitions on the hood of the car. Notice that all 4 windows zoom in to the same place within the image for comparison. This is very cool, and the Save for Web dialog in Photoshop does it, too. Change the Palette options in the Optimize palette between Perceptual, Adaptive and Selective, and notice how the Color Table changes, within the Color Table palette. Notice how the Acura's pixelated hood changes, too. You can use this to get the best palette for each image. I think the Adaptive looks best here. If you need to scroll, just hold the Space-bar down; then scroll with the mouse just as you would within Photoshop. Change the Colors pop-up down to 64 and notice that the GIF file is still bigger than the 51 quality JPEG; you have to go down to 32 colors to make the GIF smaller, and by then it looks pretty bad. Choose File/Save Optimized As... to save this 32-color GIF just for fun. Now go up to 256 colors and the GIF looks great but, man, it is now almost twice as big as the 51 JPEG. Move Colors back to 32 and the GIF is smaller, but then click on the bottom right window, choose JPEG

Save For Web

STEP 5: With this screen grab graphics file, the PNG-8 format produces the smallest result followed closely by GIF, but the JPEG format is well over twice the size of either of these 8 bit formats and still doesn't look quite as good. This is the type of image you'll want to use an 8-bit format on even for display on a full 24-bit monitor.

Chapter 43: Using Photoshop 5.5 and ImageReady 2 to Optimize Web Images

and set the Quality to 25. Now this JPEG is twice as small as that very small and very ugly 32 GIF in the bottom left window. With the exception of what happens to the Acura emblem below the 51 quality setting, JPEG does a much better job than GIF in size versus quality with this image.

Where PNG-8 Beats GIF and GIF Beats JPEG

I was looking for a good example of the type of image where GIF does a better job compressing than JPEG and I found a great example! You can see with the 4-Up dialog of the Optimize to File Size screen grab below that a good-looking GIF file is over twice as small as an acceptable JPEG and that the PNG-8 version is actually even smaller than the GIF for this image. Images containing solid colors, straight lines, text and graphics are a great place to use the 8-bit GIF and PNG-8 formats even when these 8-bit files will be displayed on a 24-bit, full-color display.

I think you are getting the idea about the power of using the 4-Up dialog within ImageReady and also within Photoshop. ImageReady just has the edge of letting you do multiple saves while you are working. If you only save one image most of the time, then you can do all of your work, of this type, within Photoshop and you don't need ImageReady to make JPEG, GIF or PNG files. When you pick a particular set of options in either program, it appears that you get the same size and quality of image.

Optimize to File Size

STEP 6: Another feature you might find useful sometimes is the Optimize to File Size feature that is found in the Optimize palette pop-up in ImageReady and within the Optimize pop-up menu to the right of the Settings menu in Photoshop's Save for Web dialog. With that feature you choose a desired file size and the application will use either JPEG or GIF to create a file with that size. You can force it to choose one or the other format by being in that format when you enter the Optimize to File Size menu option, choosing Current Settings when you get there. If you don't care whether a GIF or JPEG is used, then choose Auto Select GIF/JPEG.

Setting Preferences for the 4-Up Dialogs

STEP 7: With ImageReady you can use File/Preferences/Optimization to set up your preferences as to which choices you initially get when you enter the different Optimization dialogs. You can see the dialog here with the preferences set to show different levels of JPEG quality. I use something like this as a starting point for a JPEG image; then I tweak the quality slider until I get the quality I want at the size I need. You have to be careful not to completely rely on the optimization preferences because the current settings within the Optimize palette may override the preference settings for the preview window that is currently active. If that happens, just use the Settings menu to put that window back where you want it. In Photoshop you will notice that if you set the top right optimize view to a certain setting, like JPEG High, quality 60, Photoshop will automatically repopulate the bottom left and bottom right views with JPEG settings that are 1/2 that quality, 30, and 1/4 that quality, 15. Photoshop will then use that same set of quality settings for the next image that you open. In fact, it seems that Photoshop just uses the last settings you had in the Optimize part of the Save for Web dialog as the settings for the top right view and then repopulates the lower views with settings that are 1/2 and 1/4 of that top right setting. That seems to be the default behavior for the Photoshop 4-Up window, so you don't have the same amount of control here as in ImageReady.

STEP 6: Choose the Optimize to File Size menu from either Photoshop or ImageReady to get this dialog and have the application choose the GIF or JPEG settings to get the file size you need. Current Settings will leave the format (GIF or JPEG) as you have it and just change the options of that format to try to get your desired size.

STEP 6: You get this menu from the Optimize dialog in ImageReady and from the rightmost Optimize pop-up menu in Photoshop Save for Web dialog.

STEP 7: In ImageReady, you can use File/Preferences/Optimization to tell ImageReady the default settings you want for Default Optimization, the 2-Up and 4-Up settings. If you set the Top-Left one to Original; then the next one has to be set to Current. You can set the other two to the ones you want.

Understanding the Other Options for Modifying Web Images

There are various options available for either JPEG, GIF or PNG that have some similarities and also some very important differences. To see all the options within the ImageReady Optimize palette, choose Show Options from the palette's pop-up menu. That section of the Save for Web dialog in Photoshop always shows you all options. We will now explain the other JPEG options (Optimized, Progressive, ICC Profile, Blur and Matt) and the other GIF Options (Lossy, Color Reduction Algorithum, Dither, Transparency, Interlaced, Matte and Web Snap). PNG-8 files have the same options as GIF but there is no Lossy option. Using the Lossy option can allow you to make a GIF file smaller than the corresponding PNG-8, but also of lower quality.

The Other JPEG Options

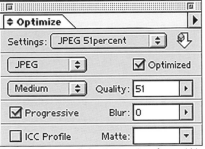

STEP 8: Here are all the JPEG options from within the ImageReady Optimize palette. Make sure you choose Show Options from the palette's pop-up menu to always see all the options for each format.

Optimized, Progressive, and ICC Profile

STEP 8: One of the other JPEG options here that we have not explored is Optimized, which creates a JPEG image with a little better compression than when Optimized is off. I have been using Optimized for quite a while with my JPEGs of photographs, and I'm very happy with the results. When you choose the next option, Progressive, then Optimized is automatically turned on. Progressive gives you a JPEG file that first quickly shows up on a Web page as a low-quality image that progressively gets better over time as the rest of the data downloads. Progressive is the default for Photoshop 5.5, but you can turn it off by clicking in the Progressive box. Make sure you are in ImageReady and then choose File/Open to open the file macn.psd on the CD within the McNamaras folder within the GIF JPEG and Color Palettes folder. Set the top right view to JPEG quality 60, the bottom left view to JPEG quality 51 and the bottom right view to JPEG quality 25. Notice for each of these JPEG versions that when you turn Progressive off, the file size actually gets a little bigger; when you also turn Optimized off, it gets bigger still. Having Progressive on doesn't usually make the file much larger and, as you can see here, it can actually make the file smaller. Your choice of having Progressive on for an image should be based on the overall design of the Web page that image will sit within and needs to consider the time it will take for the full quality image to load. I personally don't like the initially blurry progressive images and would only use them where I expected a blank image box to sit there for a long time otherwise. I always leave Optimized on though.

The ICC Profile choice, if on, will embed in the JPEG file an ICC profile for the color space the image was created in. This will make the image a very small amount larger but is a good choice if you really care about the way images look on a viewer's screen. If I were going to use a JPEG as a comp to send to an art director or an art dealer, I would turn ICC profile on. If you think there will be enough people looking at your site with calibrated monitors and browsers that make use of profiles, then turn ICC profile on.

Blur and Matte

STEP 9: The Blur option blurs the file with a Gaussian Blur of between 0 and 2 to minimize the artifacts caused by the lower-quality JPEG settings. This also blurs the entire image, however, so I usually don't use this option much for photographs. You might try it on problem text or graphics, like the Acura emblem in the redac image, to see if it can help more than damage the result. Blur settings below .5 are probably what you will want. Use the Window menu in ImageReady to switch back to the redac image and set the quality slider on both the top and bottom right views to 25. Make sure all the settings are the same. Now change the Blur setting on the bottom right image to .3, and you will notice as you compare the blurred bottom right to the unblurred top right that the size of the final JPEG gets smaller. This is another possible use of Blur. The noise around the Acura emblem lessens a bit, but the entire image also blurs a bit, too. Another feature that is there for you to play with!

Finally, the Matte option allows you to choose a Matte color to fill transparent areas of an image. You would only use this option if the image you were trying to compress a transparent area that you wanted to fill with the background color of a Web page. The JPEG format, unlike GIF or PNG, doesn't allow for a transparent area that will later be filled with a Web site's background color. With JPEG, though, you can choose this Matte setting and then fill a transparent area with the Web site's background color ahead of time. You need to know the site's background color ahead of time to do this. The JPEG matte will even give you soft shadows and nice things that you can't get with GIF transparency, but the catch is that if you later change the site's background color, you will have to re-create your JPEG files. That might be fine if you are generating your Web pages and their JPEG files automatically from a database using scripts and actions, like we often do. For more info about Transparency and Matte, see the discussion about these issues in a few pages at the end of the next GIF Options section.

THE GIF OPTIONS

STEP 10: In ImageReady, use the Window menu to switch back to the macn.psd file and use the Settings menu in the Optimize palette to set the top left view to Original, the top right view to JPEG Medium, the bottom left view to GIF 128 Dithered and the bottom right view to GIF 64 Dithered. One of the advantages of ImageReady over Photoshop is that you can look at 4-Up versions of more than one image at a time and just switch between them using the Window menu. Because Photoshop's 4-Up capabilites are within the Save for Web modal dialog, you don't have this capability in Photoshop. When you are in Photoshop 5.5's Save for Web modal dialog, you can't do anything else within Photoshop until you either exit the dialog using Cancel or make an optimization choice then save the Web file by exiting the dialog using OK. That's why we'll play with the GIF options using ImageReady.

STEP 9: Here are all the GIF options from within the Photoshop Save for Web dialog. In this dialog you always see all the options for each format.

Notice that for this file, the Medium 30 quality JPEG looks pretty good because it doesn't have a graphic like the Acura emblem in the redac image. Let's play with the GIF Options and see if we can use them to reduce the size. For this image, the GIF 64 Dithered version in the bottom right view doesn't look that bad. Click on the bottom left view and also set it to GIF 64 Dithered. Now click back into the bottom right view, and we'll play with the options and see how the file gets smaller and degrades as we work. When you convert an image into GIF (or PNG-8) format, it goes from having potentially millions of different possible colors down to having 256 or fewer colors. In this case we have chosen 64 colors to reduce the size of the file. When you do the conversion to 256 or fewer colors, you lose information, but the GIF (or PNG-8) format will give you the best rendition of the image with that number of colors; either format will compress that fewer color image, and that compression is lossless from that point of what you already lost reducing the number of colors.

LOSSY AND COLOR REDUCTION

With the GIF format, you have the additional option of turning on the Lossy option, which allows some further loss in image quality with the gain of making the image smaller. Changing the Lossy factor here to 80 will actually make this GIF version of the image about the same size as the JPEG 30, but it looks pretty bad. Setting the Lossy option to 25% here doesn't appear to do much damage to the image, and it does reduce its size from 186.6k down to 159k. When you are using these numeric options with the sliders, ImageReady sometimes starts to regenerate the image as you are sliding the slider and before you are finished. Looks like Adobe needs to work the bugs out of this, at least on the initial 5.5 release. It seems to work better if you double click on the number within the slider window, type in a new number, and then press Return/Enter on your keyboard to cause ImageReady to regenerate the image.

As you are making these adjustments, you'll notice that if you use Spacebar-Command-Click to zoom into 200% that many Web images look bad at that zoom factor. When I'm working on a high-quality art image that is not for the Web, I often zoom into 200% or higher to see all the details of what I'm doing. With Web images, I've found it is often better to do your final comparisons at 100% because that is what the user will see on the Web page. At 200% or higher, you often see a lot of problems that don't show up at 100% and so probably won't matter to the viewer of the Web site.

The second pop-up menu on the left, Color Reduction Algorithm, controls how the image is converted from 24 bit into 8 bit and specifically how the palette is made. The default option for the Gif 64 Dithered setting is Selective, which we still see in the bottom left veiw. Try Perceptual and Adaptive in the bottom right view to see which one of the three works best. Perceptual gives priority to the colors the human eye is more sensitive to, Selective favors large areas of color and including more Web colors and it is the default, and Adaptive gives priority to the colors appearing most within the image. For this image, it is hard for me to tell the difference between them, but if you zoom into 200%, you can see pixels change as you switch between them. Adaptive seems to take up an extra k of image space but somehow, maybe just because I'm used to using it, I like it better here. If you choose Custom at this point, from this same pop-up menu, that option will preserve the current selective, perceptual, or adaptive color table as a fixed palette and that palette will not change after you make further changes to the image. This may allow you to preserve a higher quality set of colors in the palette as you then go on and further refine the image to make it smaller. Choosing Mac OS gives you the standard Mac OS palette, Windows gives you the default Windows palette and Web gives you the Web palette, which contains the 216 colors that are common to both the Mac OS and Windows palette. Choosing Web avoids the possibility that a browser may dither your image when it's displayed on an 8-bit monitor.

THE DITHERING OPTIONS

I've left the Color Reduction Algorithm set to Custom and moved down the pop-ups on the left side to the Dither Algorithm pop-up. The file seems to be the smallest, leaving the setting at Diffusion with both the Pattern and Noise choices making a much bigger file without a noticeable difference at 100% viewing. Setting Dither Algorithm to No Dither does shave about 9k off the file size, but it also makes color transitions, especially on some of the shirts, clump up a bit. If you leave the Dither Algorithm at other than No Dither, you can also change the numeric Dither box to the right of this pop-up from the default 88% setting to a lesser amount of dithering. I tried turning Diffusion Dither back on and found that I needed a setting of about 50% before I noticed a difference between that and No Dither. I've just decided to choose No Dither with this image in the quest for a smaller file. Try these same settings with the redac image, with its subtle color gradations on the car hood, and notice how bad the hood looks when you swich from 88% diffusion dither to No Dither.

TRANSPARENCY AND MATTE

STEP 11: The Transparency and Matte options have to do with what will happen to images that contain transparent areas within their original RGB format. These options are also used in the next chapter, "Creating Small, Transparent GIF Composites". You'll notice that turning either option on or off while working on this macn image makes no difference in the size or appearance because this image contains no transparent areas. For images that contain no transparent areas, just leave Transparency off and leave Matte set to None.

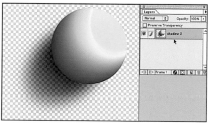

STEP 10: Here is how the Ball Cast Shadow file should look after you are finished initially setting it up as per the instructions to the left.

To learn more about Transparency and Matte, switch to ImageReady and open the file Ball Cast Shadow from the Extra Info Files folder within the Creating Shadows folder on the Photoshop 5 Artistry CD. Use Window/Show Layers to bring up the Layers palette, and click on the top Ball layer to activate it. Now choose Merge Down from the Layers palette menu to merge the Ball layer with the shadow 2 layer below it. Now drag the two layers below that, shadow and Layer 0, to the Trash icon at the bottom right of the Layers palette. Type C, for crop, and make the file a bit smaller so you are looking at the ball and its complete shadow. The file and Layers palette should now look like the one pictured here. Choose File/Save As and save this file on your hard disk while you work with it here. We will use this file to explore the Transparency and Matte options within all the file formats.

STEP 12: Type D to get the default colors and F for Full Screen mode; then close the Tool palette and any other palettes that are on the screen. Use Window/Show Optimize to bring up the Optimize palette. Make show you have chosen to see all the options by choosing Show Options, the top Optimize palette menu choice. Make sure that Auto Regenerate, in this same menu, is also turned on with a check mark next to it. Click on the 4-Up tab and then click on the top left view and set it to Original using the Settings menu within the Optimize palette. Now click on the top right view and set the Settings to JPEG High. Notice that the default for JPEG is to fill the transparent area, the checkerboard pattern, with the background color, white. JPEG format doesn't have a Transparency option, but it does allow you to fill the transparent parts of an image with a Matte color. If you choose the background color of your Web site as the Matte color, shadows within the JPEG file will look great, like they have 256 levels of transparency. You would have to re-create your JPEG file, however, each time you changed the background color on your Web site. Click in the white box next to word Matte at the bottom right of the Optimize palette. This will allow you to choose a color for the JPEG Matte. Type in FF66FF at the bottom right of the Color Picker dialog to insert this purple color as your Matte color. This is what

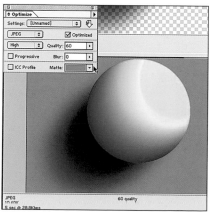

STEP 11: Here is the JPEG version of the ball after we have set the Matte color to FF66FF. This file looks pretty good and is quite small in JPEG format.

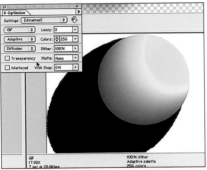

STEP 13: With Transparency off and Matte set to None, this is what we get when creating a GIF file.

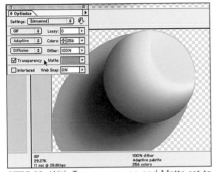

STEP 13: With Transparency on and Matte set to FF66FF, this is what we get when creating a GIF file.

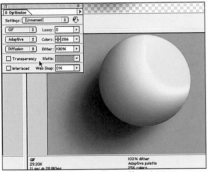

STEP 13: With Transparency off and Matte set to FF66FF, this is what we get when creating a GIF file.

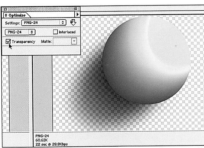

STEP 14: With the PNG-24 format, and a correctly set up browser, the shadow should correctly blend with either the current solid color or pattern background on your Web site.

we would do to create a JPEG version of this image to sit on a Web page that had this purple background color.

STEP 13: Now click in the bottom left veiw area and change the Settings for that view to GIF 128 Dithered. This setting starts out with the Matte color set to white and Transparency on. When Transparency is on with a GIF file and a Matte color is chosen, only the pixels that are 100% transparent will show the background of your Web page. Areas that are partially opaque, like the ball's

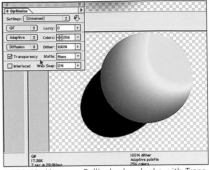

STEP 12: How our Ball's shadow looks with Transparency on and Matte set to None. This will not look to good on our Web page!

shadow, will be blended with the Matte color, which is now white. Click on the pop-up menu to the right of the Matte option and set the Matte to None. Now, with the Matte option off, opaque areas that are less than 50% opaque show up as transparent, and you will see your Web site's background in those areas. Areas that are more than 50% opaque, the darker shadow areas, now show up as black. There is no blending with GIF transparency!

STEP 14: Now turn Transparency off and you will get an even bigger black area. With Transparency off and no matte color, areas that are totally transparent in the original are filled with white and areas that are partially Opaque are filled with black. This is also of no help to our Web pages. Now turn Transparency back on; then click in the white box next to Matte and set the Matte color to FF66FF. With these settings, the totally transparent areas of the image will be replaced by your site's background color or pattern, and the partially Opaque areas will be blended with the Matte color. If we finally now turn Transparency off, the Matte color will blend with the shadow to give a natural look, but as with JPEG, you will need this Matte color to be the same as the background color of your Web page. To lessen the stepping of the ball's gradations and of the shadow as it blends into the purple background, set Colors to 256 and set the Color Reduction Algorithm to Adaptive. You might also want to set the Dither percentage up to 100%. Now your GIF file is almost three times as big as the JPEG version. If you want any random background pattern or color on your Web site to seamlessly blend with a soft shadow in your Web image, neither GIF, PNG-8 nor JPEG format will work for you.

STEP 15: Now click in the bottom right view and choose PNG-24 from the Settings menu. With Transparency on, the PNG-24 format will correctly show your 256 levels of shadow transparency onto any Web background color or pattern. Notice that the size of this file is twice as big as the GIF and about 6 times bigger than the JPEG. The advantage of this extra size, though, is that the ball and its shadow will be decompressed losslessly onto your Web page. The problem with using PNG-24, besides the larger file, is that not all browsers support the format and especially not its 256 levels of transparency--unless you have a PNG-24 plug-in installed. Check out the performance of PNG-24 images within the default versions of browsers you care about before you assume this Web image type will work for your site.

The Transparency and Matte options are also used in different ways within the next chapter, "Creating Small, Transparent GIF Composites." It's a good idea to check that out also.

Chapter 43: Using Photoshop 5.5 and ImageReady 2 to Optimize Web Images

INTERLACED AND WEB SNAP

STEP 16: Use the Window menu to switch back to the macn image within ImageReady. Turning on the Interlaced option, as in the Progressive JPEG option, make the GIF image download in multiple passes from a poorer, low-res version to a later, higher quality version. Unlike the Progressive JPEG option, however, turning on Interlaced with GIF increases the file size considerably, so I'm leaving it off here. Changing the Web Snap option doesn't change the file size, but it does switch colors in your current color palette to colors within the Web palette based on the tolerence factor you choose. With Web Snap set to 0, you'll notice here that none of the colors in this image's palette are common to the Web palette. When we change Web Snap to 50%, you'll see that some of the palette's colors have been changed to match similar Web palette colors. The purpose for doing this is to make the image look better on 256-color systems where the browser is currently using the Web palette. For this image I found that increasing the Web Snap to above 50% degraded the appearance of the image too much. One would more likely use the Web Snap option for a Web site that is likely to be viewed by a lot of users who only have 8-bit systems. I doubt I'll use it for my Web site.

STEP 15: Here we see the GIF Color Table and Optimize options within ImageReady with Web Snap set to 0.

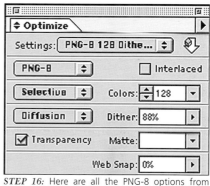

STEP 15: When we increase Web Snap to 50%, the colors in the Color Table that have been converted to Web colors have small white circles in them.

THE PNG-8 FORMAT

STEP 17: Within ImageReady using the macn image, click back on the top right view and choose PNG-8 128 Dithered from the Settings menu in the Optimize palette. Now change the Colors to 64 and you'll notice that the PNG-8 file is slightly smaller than the original GIF 64 Dithered in the bottom left view. You'll see that PNG-8 has the same options as GIF except PNG-8 doesn't have the Lossy option. With this image, the PNG-8 file seems to stay very slightly smaller than the GIF with the same settings, but when you turn on the 25% Lossy option in the GIF file, that makes the GIF significantly smaller. Be careful if you use the PNG-8 format because it is not supported by all browsers. Before you use it, be sure the versions of each browser you care about support this feature.

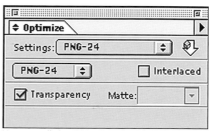

STEP 16: Here are all the PNG-8 options from within the ImageReady Optimize palette. Make sure you choose Show Options from the palette's pop-up menu to always see all the options for each format.

ABOUT THE PNG-24 FORMAT

PNG-24 files only have the Interlaced, Transparency and Matte options. The PNG-24 format creates a lossless, 24-bit compressed image and has the capability to create an image with 256 levels of transparency, like you can have with a Photoshop mask channel. Using 256 transparency levels allows transition images, like subtle soft shadows, to seamlessly blend into any Web background. As you will see with GIF transparency in the next chapter, you cannot get seamless blends of soft transitions into various random Web backgrounds. PNG-24 images are also generally a lot larger than JPEG images, which are also in 24 bit, so usually the only reason you would create a PNG-24 image would be if you need a lossless 24-bit image or if you need to have 256 levels of transparency. If you need one of those features, then check out PNG-24; otherwise, you'll probably want to use JPEG, GIF, or PNG-8. Be careful if you use the PNG-24 format because it and all its features, like 256 level transparency, are not supported by all browsers. Before you use it, be sure the versions of each browser you care about support it and the features you are using.

Here are all the PNG-24 options from within the ImageReady Optimize palette.

44 HANDS-ON SESSION: Creating Small, Transparent GIF Composites

I've used these techniques while creating commercial images for the Web sites of Netscape and FootWise.

STEP 1: Set the Crop tool to Fixed Target Size with these dimensions.

STEP 1: The initial crop before color correction.

STEP 1: The initial Collar crop.

One of my first experiences creating images for the Web was to create some advertising images for Netscape's General Store Bazaar. The specs for these images called for a final size of 180 pixels high by 144 pixels wide. They wanted noninterlaced transparent GIF files. Here, using some similar images, is how I would produce those GIF files today. The images in this example were shot by Frank Bevans Photography, 2164 Old Middlefield Way, Mountain View, CA 94043, 530-333-2274. Even though images for the Web end up small, it is still important to start out with a high-quality photo. Frank is the best!

First of all, if you have ever tried to do a scan that is 180 pixels by 144 pixels, you know that most scanners don't do a great job scanning something that small. You are better off doing a bigger scan and then resampling down to the small size after color correcting, compositing, and sharpening the image. In this example, we shot a model, me, wearing a jacket. The jacket was the item that ended up in the catalog, but we shot it with a person in it because the client wanted that "invisible man" look—that is, the jacket filled out as though an invisible man were wearing it. I have not figured out how to make myself invisible yet, so we shot a second shot of the collar without anyone in it. It was composited with the jacket; my head, hands, and body were removed.

THE SCANS, CROPS, AND COLOR

STEP 1: Do some bigger scans of each image. This project was shot with 35mm because that gives plenty of detail for the creation of Web images. I've also used a digital camera to easily capture and quickly turn around images for FootWise.com, a great Birkenstock store. If you have to shoot a lot of images for the Web, as they have to shoot many shoes, many of today's digital cameras, some costing less than $1,000 will work fine. For this jacket project, though, each image was scanned using a Nikon Super Cool scanner (the LS 1000), which is a great scanner for this type of project. I actually did the original scans at full size, full frame, without any resampling by the scanner. This scanner does the full-size 26Mb scans very quickly with interpolation turned off. Photo CD scans also work great for this type of project, and I have used them many times to save time and money. To do this project, open the Jacket and JacketCollar files from the Small Transparent GIFs folder on the CD. Type C to get to the Crop tool, and then press Return/Enter to bring up its options. In the options, turn on Fixed Target Size, and set the Height to 720 pixels, the Width to 576 pixels, and the dpi to 72. This is four times the final required pixel dimensions of 180x144. Doing all your work at this larger size and then resampling down at the end gives better results than trying to work with a 180x144 image. Crop the image as tightly as you can on the jacket without actually cutting out any of the jacket. Do a similar crop on the collar image, the same size but tighter around the collar area. Type V to get the Move tool; then Shift-drag and drop the collar on top of the Jacket image. The Shift key forces the collar layer to be centered. Name this new layer Collar; then double-click the Background layer and name it Jacket. Drag the Collar down underneath the Jacket layer in the Layers palette.

STEP 1: The initial layer setup with the Jacket and Collar.

STEP 2: You now want to do the Basic Overall Color Correction on the Jacket layer. (Review "The Grand Canyon" session if you don't know how to do this.) The background is actually white here and the Jacket is a neutral gray, so both of these need to be close to balanced in RGB to look correct. I found that exactly balancing them makes things look too yellow. Anyhow, you can load my Levels settings (JacketLevels) from the CD if you like. I ran these levels settings and increased the Saturation by 10% in Hue/Saturation. For Web images where I composite two images of the same object, I find that the color balance on the collar, after correcting the Jacket, will get pretty close by clicking the Collar layer and then doing Command-Option-L to run the same Levels settings in the Collar as I ran on the Jacket. I did the same thing with the Hue/Saturation settings on the Collar. You could also use Adjustment layers here for more color control.

STEP 3: The Layers setup for cleaning up of the jacket.

MAKING THE KNOCK-OUT

STEP 3: Now we want to create a knock-out of the jacket from the background because this composite is going to become a transparent GIF. It will help automate this process better if we first sharpen the image. We want to sharpen it before downsampling because there will not be enough pixels after downsampling to do a complete sharpen without it looking too pixelated. Click back on the Jacket layer to make it active; then choose Filter/Sharpen/Unsharp Mask (F4). I did a sharpen of 100% Amount, 1.0 Radius, and 0 Threshold. Click the Collar layer and press Command-F to sharpen it by the same amount. Now press Command-Shift-S (File/Save As) and save this file as JacketLayers. Click back on the Jacket layer; then bring up the Channels palette (Shift-F10) and look at each of the Red, Green, and Blue channels to select the one with the most contrast between the Jacket and the rest of the image. I picked the Red one because it had better contrast between my hands and the jacket than the others did. Click that channel and drag it to the New Channel icon at the bottom of the Channels palette. This makes a copy of it in Channel #4, named Alpha 1. Choose Image/Adjust/Threshold (Shift-F7) and adjust the threshold slider until you have the best edges on the jacket mask, at about 100, and then click OK. When

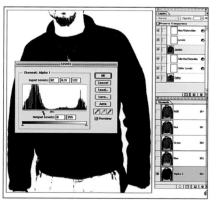

STEP 3: Using Levels to start a Jacket Knock-Out. I used the values 82, .31 and 122.

347

STEP 3: The jacket after the mask clean up.

STEP 4: The Layers setup for the final Jacket composite.

STEP 4: Using Free Transform to scale and rotate the collar so it fits behind the jacket.

you do this with Threshold, you get an absolute black or white with no anti-aliased edges. If you use Levels instead, you can get a similar effect but with a soft anti-aliased edge, if you want a soft edge that is. Press L to get the Lasso tool, and use it to clean up your mask by either filling holes with black or areas on the outside with white. You can also use the PaintBrush (B) and the larger 100% hardness brushes to edit the mask with white or black. The more I use Photoshop, the more I use the Paintbrush for this type of work. (For a review of using Threshold and Levels to make masks, see Chapter 31: Bob and the Kestrel or Chapter 29: Bryce Stone Woman or Chapter 30: Bob Goes To...) Option-click the New Layer icon in the Layers palette to create a new layer and name it Red. Use the Color Picker to pick a bright red as the foreground color; then use Edit/Fill (Shift-Delete) to fill this new layer with 100%, Normal of this Foreground color. Drag the Red layer to below the Jacket layer but above the Collar layer. Now Command-click Channel #4, Alpha 1, in the Channels palette to load a selection of the mask you just made. Click on the Jacket layer to make it active; then Option-click the New Layer Mask icon, the leftmost icon at the bottom of the Layers palette, to make a new layer mask with the selected area removed from the Jacket layer. You should now see a Jacket with a red background. Use Shift-F4 to Gaussian Blur the mask by about 0.7 to 1 pixels. This blends the edges of the jacket with the background. Type D for default colors, B for PaintBrush, and 0 for 100% Opacity on your brush. Use the left and right bracket keys ([and]) to scroll through the brushes until you find a medium-sized hard edge brush. Shift-[gets you to the top-left brush, and then a few]s will get you to a brush that will work here. Use the brush to clean up the edges of your mask. Painting with white adds more of the Jacket layer, and painting with black deletes from the Jacket layer, revealing more of the Red layer underneath. You can type X to eXchange between white and black. I tried making this mask with the new Photoshop 5.5 Extract command, but feel the way I'm showing you here actually works better because you can see the mask being made and look at the details of the edges as you work with them. Once you learn to mask this way, I believe you'll find it faster and more exact than Extract.

BLENDING THE JACKET AND COLLAR

STEP 4: When your Jacket mask is clean, click the Red layer and drag it to the bottom underneath the Collar. You will now see the collar behind the jacket. Click the Collar layer to make it active and then choose Edit/Free Transform (Command-T) to scale the collar. Shift-click and drag the corner handles to scale the Collar layer proportionally. Click in the middle of the handles and drag to move the scaled down collar up where it belongs behind the jacket. Continue to scale and move this until it seems to be in the right place; then press Return/Enter to finish your transform. Command-click the New Layer icon to create a new Adjustment layer of type Curves that is Grouped with the previous Collar layer. Use the curves to adjust the contrast and color of the Collar layer to best match that of the Jacket layer. Choose OK when it is as close as possible. Because this is an Adjustment layer, we can tweak it again later with no quality penalty. Now click back on the Collar layer and then click the Layer Mask icon, the leftmost icon at the bottom of the Layers palette, to add a new layer mask to the Collar layer. Use the Paintbrush again within the Collar's Layer Mask to remove the parts of the collar you don't want to see. Remember that the Collar is behind the Jacket, so you don't have to be too careful in areas that the Jacket layer is going to hide anyhow. You will now have to switch back and forth between painting in the Jacket layer mask and the Collar layer mask to blend these two layers

Chapter 44: Creating Small, Transparent GIF Composites

properly. You will also have to use a soft brush and less than 100% Opacity to seamlessly blend the edges between the two. I also used the Rubber Stamp tool to add a
little to the right side of the inside of the Collar layer where I needed a little more
blue ribbon and gray inside of the jacket. Check out my JacketLayers file on the CD
if you are having problems getting this to look right. Press Command-S to save this
version.

SCALING DOWN AND SHARPENING THE IMAGE

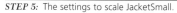

STEP 5: Now we are going to downsize the Jacket. The trick here is to get the smaller
version, when looking at it at 100%, to look similar to the big version. This jacket is
harder than most because it has that soft, fuzzy texture. The first step is to choose
Image/Duplicate (F5) to make a copy of the image; call the copy JacketSmall. You
want to copy all the layers, so don't check Merged Layers Only. Now go into
Image/Image Size (F7) to scale the image by 25%. Change either the Width or
Height Print Size setting to read as a percent and then type in the value 25. Because
Proportions is locked, both dimensions will scale the same and you should see the
"144 x 180 pixels" at the top in the Pixel Dimensions section. This is the final size we
want. You notice that the image now looks really blurry. While viewing it at 100%,
choose Filter/Sharpen/Unsharp Mask (F4) to sharpen first the Jacket layer and then
the Collar layer by the same amount. To get the look I wanted, I sharpened the layers by 100, 1.0, and 0 again before resampling them down and then sharpened each
of them by 200, 1.0, and 0. After downsampling, you might also try the Unsharp
Mask setting with the radius set to smaller than 1.0, I often use a 0.5 radius for Web
images. Most images don't require as much sharpening as this one, but to get the
fuzzy jacket look, that is what I did here. It really won't look right unless you are
viewing at 100% while doing this. Zooming in to 200% won't help you here because
you are used to looking at sharpening for print and this look is entirely different. Just
sharpen it so it will look the best at 100%; that's what people will see on the Web site.
If you are using Photoshop 5.5 or ImageReady, use File/SaveAs to save this small
sharpened file as JacketSmall then skip to step 10.

STEP 5: The settings to scale JacketSmall.

MAKING TRANSPARENT GIFS USING PHOTOSHOP 5

STEP 6: Because this will be a transparent GIF file, the Red background you see here
will actually be replaced by whatever background the Web page has. It helps if you
know the background color that is intended. However, if that background color is
likely to change, you should test out different ones now. Option-drag the Red layer
to the New Layer icon and make a copy called Gray. Pick a gray from the Color
Picker, Netscape Gray is 192, 192, 192; then use Shift-Delete to Fill this new layer
with that gray. You will now see that background instead of the Red, but you can turn
off the Eye icon on this Gray layer and the Red background will reappear. You can
test out as many background colors as you want using this process.

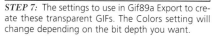

STEP 7: The settings to use in Gif89a Export to create these transparent GIFs. The Colors setting will
change depending on the bit depth you want.

USING THE GIF89A EXPORT FILTER

STEP 7: Turn off the Eye icons for all your background color layers. The image and
the Layers palette should match the illustration here. Whatever is transparent now
will be transparent in your transparent GIF file. Choose File/Export/GIF89a Export
(F3) to create the GIF. We want this file to be as small as possible, so we are going
to try 128, 64, and 32 Colors for our Adaptive palettes. Turn off the Interlaced option
and set the Colors to 128 with the Palette set at Adaptive. Click the OK button and

STEP 7: Here is how the image and the Layers
palette should look in preparation to make the
transparent GIFs.

Making Transparent GIFs Using Photoshop 5

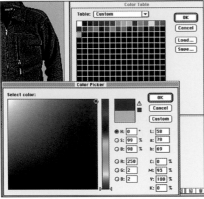

STEP 8: Editing the Color Table to test a background color with your GIF file.

STEP 9: The correct setup for doing the Merge Visible.

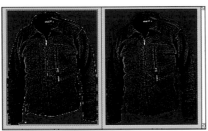

STEP 9: jack32.gif on the left, before the edges are fixed. The fixed version is on the right.

call this file jack128.gif. Use the export again (F3) with the same settings, but this time set the Colors to 64 and call it jack64.gif. One more time with Colors set to 32 and call it jack32.gif. Use File/Open to open all of these images in Photoshop. You will probably notice that the 32-color version doesn't look that different from the 128-color version. Look at the file sizes on each one (use Get Info on the Mac). You'll see that the 32-color one is a lot smaller. I got about 10k for the 32 colors, 13k for the 64 colors, and 16k for the 128 colors. The 128 colors is not worth the extra six seconds a Web surfer would have to wait to see it, but if this image had more variety of colors you may need 64 or 128 colors to make it look good.

TESTING AND FIXING THE BACKGROUND WITH PHOTOSHOP 5

STEP 8: Now we want to test out the actual background color you are going to have on the Web page. This is the secret to getting these to look the best. If you are developing your Web site on your system, you can just bring the image up in your browser and see how it looks. In Photoshop, though, there is an easy way to preview any solid color background. Let's use the jack32.gif image, but you can do the same procedure with any of them. While in the jack32.gif image, choose Image/Mode/Color Table (Shift-F3) and click the one gray color by itself at the bottom-left row. The color at the left in the bottom row is always the transparent background color. This color will be replaced by the background of your Web page. When you click it, that brings up the Color Picker, which allows you to pick any other color for that color. Pick a very bright red color; then choose OK to the Color Picker and OK to the Palette Editor (Return, Return). You will now see the image as it would appear against a bright red background. You might notice some white edges around the jacket and also around the edge of your image. These didn't show up against a gray background, and probably wouldn't show up against a white background, but they glare at you from a red background. To make a more perfect GIF file that will work against any background, you need to get rid of these.

STEP 9: If you see white edges around the jacket, they could have been caused by your layer masks not being perfect or as the result of the Gaussian Blur you did on the layer mask in the JacketLayers image. When working for print, Gaussian Blur of a mask edge is a good way to blend the edge with the new background and get rid of the jaggies. Because every pixel counts, and shows, on the Web, blurring the edge of a mask will only get rid of the edge jaggies if the background color for your site is similar to your original background color. With a totally different background color, it might be better to have masks that are not blurred, or not anti-aliased, on the edge. You might also notice that the very border of your image area, one or two pixels around the border, is not a solid red background color. To solve both of these types of problems, go back to the JacketSmall image. Turn on the Eye icons for the top three layers only, make sure Jacket is the active layer, and then choose Merge Visible from the Layers Palette menu. This will merge the Jacket, Collar, collar color correction, and their layer masks into one layer, called Jacket, with a transparent background. Choose Select/Load Selection of Jacket Transparency as a New Selection. Now click the New Layer Mask icon at the bottom-left area of the Layers palette. This will add the transparency as a layer mask that we can modify while looking at the results. Now turn on the Eye icon for the Red layer, and then choose Image/Adjust/Threshold (Shift-F7) to adjust the threshold of this new layer mask. With the Preview option on in Threshold, you will notice that when you move the slider to the right, the mask will cut away a few pixels from the edge of the jacket. Using Threshold will also force the mask to be either completely white or completely

Chapter 44: Creating Small, Transparent GIF Composites

black. It will remove any gray values from the edge of the jacket area and from the edge of the image. I found that moving the Threshold slider slightly to the right solved the problem for me.

You might want to Option-click the layer mask thumbnail, to just see the mask, and then do Command-Z over and over again to see the difference Threshold has made to your mask. Click back on the Jacket layer thumbnail so it is active and turn off the Eye icons for all your background layers. Now you are ready to try the GIF89a Export again. Use File/Export/GIF89a Export (F3) and re-create the 32-color image, calling it jack32f.gif (the fixed version) this time. Open this image and again choose Image/Mode/Color Table (Shift-F3) to bring up the Color Table and change the background color. If you made the right modifications to the mask, your improvements should look similar to the illustration on this page. All my versions of the files are on the CD in the area for this chapter. I resaved the fixed versions, calling them JacketSmallFixed, jack32f.gif, jack64f.gif, and jack128f.gif. For more information about creating images for the Web, see Lynda Weinman's *Designing Web Graphics.3* published by New Riders. Also, check out the bibliography of *Photoshop 5&5.5 Artistry* for information on some more great Web books and Web sites.

USING PHOTOSHOP 5.5 OR IMAGEREADY 2 TO MAKE THE FINAL IMAGE

STEP 10: After saving the JacketSmall file at the end of Step 5, close that file from Photoshop 5.5 and switch to ImageReady 2.0; then Open JacketSmall from inside ImageReady 2. You can also open the JacketSmall file from the Small Transparent GIFs chapter on the CD. Type D for default colors, then F for Full Screen Mode, and then click on the 4-Up tab. Make sure the top left view is set to Original; then click on the top right view and choose GIF 32 Dithered from the Settings menu in the Optimize palette. You'll notice that with only 32 colors, the Jacket still looks pretty good at 100%. Use Command-Spacebar-Click to zoom into 200% and look at how the Jacket edges blend with the transparent pattern. Notice that Transparency is on and Matte is actually set to White. Choose File/Save Optimized As and save this file as GIF32TonMWhite.gif. Click in the bottom left view and again choose GIF 32 Dithered from the Settings menu. Go down to the pop-up menu to the right of the Matte option and set this to None. It is hard to see any difference here between the display of these two images, but there is a difference, which we will show you when we open the file. Choose File/Save Optimized As and save this version as GIF32TonMNone.gif. Finally, click on the bottom right view and again choose GIF 32 Dithered from the Settings menu for this view. Now click on the white box next to the Matte word, and this will bring up the Color Picker. Click in the box and choose the bright red color at the top right of the box or just type in FF0000 at the bottom right of the dialog to enter that color; then choose OK. This view should look like the one to the right. Choose File/Save Optimized again and save this version as GIF32TonMRed.gif.

STEP 10: How the bottom right view should look in ImageReady when you set the Matte to Red.

STEP 11: Switch to Photoshop 5.5 and open all three of the GIF files you created within ImageReady. Use Command-Spacebar-Click to zoom each image to 200% and arrange the window on each so you can see the entire image and also so you can see all three of them next to each other. Although you can use File/PreviewIn from ImageReady to preview any image within a browser, I find that comparing them this way is a little more exact. Notice that the edges of the Jacket on the second image,

Using Photoshop 5.5 or ImageReady 2 to Make the Final Image

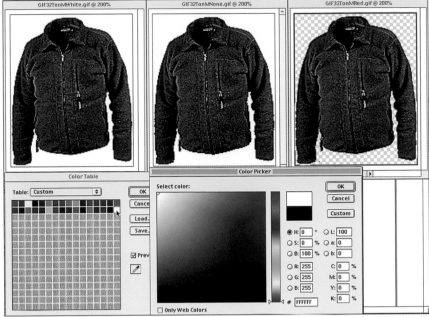

STEP 11: Here we are in Photoshop 5.5 with all three images open on the screen and we are setting the Color Table of the middle, GIF32TonMNone.gif, image to white. Notice how the edges where the jacket blend with the background are so jagged here. That is because then Transparency is on and there is no Matte; all pixels that are not 100% opaque become transparent; there is no edge blending. The GIF32Ton-MNone.gif image to the left had a white Matte setting so the semi-transparent pixels along the edge now blend with this white background very nicely and also softly. Since the Matte for the rightmost GIF32Ton-Mred.gif file was set to Red, that file will not blend very well with a white background. The red outline around the outside edge of this file indicates that that outside edge was not totally transparent within the original Photoshop file before we made the GIF. Photoshop's default checkerboard transparent display makes this hard to see within the Photoshop file.

STEP 12: Here we have changed the background color on all three images to the red. When you actually do this exercise on your screen, you'll be able to see in more detail the differences between the three images.

GIF32TonMNone, are a little more jagged than on the first, GIF32Ton-MWhite, version. We can go into the color table for each and change the transparent color so we can see in detail what will happen when that transparent color is replaced by a Web background color or pattern. Click on the GIF32TonMWhite image to make it active; then choose Image/Mode/Color Table to bring up its color table. Click on the transparent color swatch and change its color to white, FFFFFF. Do the same thing for the GIF32TonMNone image and notice how there is a subtle blending of the edges into the white on the GIF32TonMWhite image where the edges are jaggy on the GIF32TonM-None image. The initial white Matte in the GIF32TonMWhite GIF file settings replaced any areas that were neither totally transparent nor totally opaque with the white color using the opacity of the transparency of each pixel. That causes the edges to blend. Now use the Color Table to change the transparent color within the GIF32TonMRed.gif file and notice that the red outlines stay there. Only the totally transparent area are changed to Red.

STEP 12: Now go back into the Color Table of each of the three images (try using Shift-F3 if you have ArtistKeys installed) and set the transparent color to Red, FF0000. You will notice that the GIF32TonMRed.gif file on the right looks the best with the Red background color because those semi-transparent areas are blended. The middle file, GIF32TonMNone.gif, even though the edges are a bit jagged, still looks OK with the Red background. The leftmost file, GIF32TonMWhite.gif, looks really bad with a Red background. The moral to the story is that if you want to create a GIF (or PNG-8) and have the edges blend with any background color or pattern on your Web site, then Transparency must be on and Matte set to None. If you want the edges to softly blend with a particular background color, then you can set the Matte to that color, but if you later change the background color on your Web site, you could get a halo effect around the edges of your GIF, especially if that new Web site background color is quite different.

Chapter 44: Creating Small, Transparent GIF Composites

45 HANDS-ON SESSION: New Photoshop 5.5 and ImageReady 2 Features

A variety of new and improved Photoshop 5.5 and ImageReady 2 features are discussed here

JUMPING BETWEEN_PHOTOSHOP & IMAGEREADY

Even though Photoshop 5.5 and ImageReady 2 are bundled together in the same package, they are still separate programs. They both share a nearly identical interface, and many common tools, features and keyboard shortcuts. It's sort of like two neighborhood houses that were built from the same set of plans: the layout of the kitchen and the rooms are all very similar, there's just different things in the cupboards. With Photoshop and ImageReady, if you are already familar with one, this similarity should make it easier to get a running start learning the other. Adobe has also provided an easy way to switch from one program to the other, which preserves the changes in your file and opens it in the second application where you can apply further modifications. Although ImageReady shares many of Photoshop's features and tools, it's main strength is primarily as a program for creating and preparing images, rollovers and animations for the Web. If your main interest in Photoshop doesn't include Web graphics, you don't need to worry too much about jumping back and forth between the two programs. If you do need to move an image between the two, however, the process is very easy.

From Photoshop, use the Jump To button at the bottom of the Tool palette to switch between applications. This button appears in both programs. Using it in Photoshop will take you to ImageReady, and from ImageReady it will take you back to Photoshop. Jumping between applications requires that your file be saved before moving to the other program. If you have not already done this, then you will be prompted to save the file first. The keyboard shortcut for jumping between the two programs is Cmd-Shift-M (Mac) or Ctrl-Shift-M (Windows). If ImageReady is not already running, the program will launch and your file will be opened, ready for you to do further editing in ImageReady.

You can also switch between applications by means other than the Jump To button, such as by clicking on the document window of the file in the other program, or by using the Finder on a Mac or the Alt-Tab shortcut or taskbar on a Windows machine. If you have modified the file and have not saved it, you will be asked if you want to return to the application where the file was modified to save the file. The other option at this point is Cancel, which lets you continue on to the other application without saving the file.

In the Preferences for both programs (File/Preferences/General), there is an Auto-Update Files option. When this is checked and you modify a file in one program, the document will automatically be updated in the other program when the

The Jump To button at the bottom of the Tool palette in both Photoshop and ImageReady will prompt you to save your file and then open it in the program you wish to switch to.

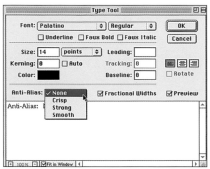

The Photoshop History palette with history states showing that the file was updated after being modified in ImageReady.

The new anti-alias options in the Photoshop Type dialog box.

Type Created at 72ppi

Anti-Alias: None (14 pt)

Anti-Alias: Crisp (14 pt)

Anti-Alias: **Strong (14 pt)**

Anti-Alias: Smooth (14 pt)

**Type Created at 150ppi,
sized down to 72ppi**

Anti-Alias: None (14 pt)

Anti-Alias: Crisp (14 pt)

Sample type created using the different anti-aliasing options avaiable in the Photoshop Type dialog. The top example was created at 72ppi, and the lower one was created at 150ppi and then resized down to 72ppi using the Image Size command.

file is saved. If this option is not selected, you will be asked if you want to update the file before switching programs. When the file is updated, a history state will be added to the History palette showing the update. This updating of the History palette occurs in both programs.

NEW TYPE FEATURES IN PHOTOSHOP & IMAGEREADY

Photoshop 5.5 intoduces some improvements to the Type dialog box and address issues that were not included, or implemented less than perfectly, in version 5.0. This is not to say that Photoshop's type capabilities approach the level found in professional page layout programs, but it represents a definite improvement, particularly in type that is destined for screen display on the Web. For those who are picky about their digital typesetting, the Type tool in this new version gives you much more control in the fine art of finessing your type to make it look just right.

For designing type for the Web, the new feature of note is the capability to specify the amount of anti-aliasing that is applied when the program rasterizes text. This is particulary useful when dealing with small type. There are four anti-aliasing levels that can be chosen: None, Crisp, Strong and Smooth. The effects of no anti-aliasing are self evident, resulting in text that lacks smooth curves and looks more pixelated. This is not necessarily a bad thing, however, and for certain on-screen small type it could be the appropriate choice. The Strong option adds weight to the text, making it stand out more, although not as much as you would see when choosing a bold typeface. The Crisp and Smooth options are very simliar, and we didn't notice much difference between them.

Because it's a common practice to create Web graphics at a larger size and then re-sample the image down to the specified size for the Web version, we created text at 72 and 150ppi. The 150ppi version was then re-sampled down to match the size of the 72ppi image, and the text was compared. The verdict: if you are making small text for Web display, the results will be better if you create the text at 72ppi and make use of Photoshop's type anti-aliasing controls than if you start at a higher resolution and sample down. In addition to the anti-aliasing options, another feature that will help you in setting good-looking type is the ability to specify fractional widths. Most letters are not an even number of pixels wide and using fractional widths can improve the overall letter spacing of your type.

Photoshop 5.5 also marks the return of generic italic, bold and underline options. This feature had been present in earlier releases of the program, but when Adobe introduced editable type layers in version 5.0, it had been removed and the only way you could create bold or italicized text in Photoshop was if you had the actual bold and italic version of a typeface installed on your system. The Type tool in 5.5 now has options for Underline, Faux Bold, and Faux Italic.

ImageReady 2 shares all of Photoshop's type features, but its implementation of type layers and the type palette has more in common with Illustrator, and this difference could cause some initial confusion to those users who are not familar with that program. As with Photoshop, type exists on separate, editable layers but it does not have the Type tool dialog that is familar to Photoshop users. Instead, when you select the Type tool and click in the image, a cursor appears allowing you to enter the text directly into the image as you would with a page layout or illustration program. Choosing a typeface and point size and accessing tracking and kerning controls is done through the Type palette, which is nearly identical to the Type palette in Illustrator. To edit the text, simply highlight it and make the necessary changes. In the ImageReady layers palette, a type layer is identified the same as in Photoshop, with an uppercase T, but when a type layer is active, the text in the image is underlined just as it is in Illustrator. Given the fact that Adobe is designing their graphics programs to have very similar interfaces and standard keyboard shortcuts, this difference between Photoshop and ImageReady's implementation of type controls seems strange. Because the ImageReady/Illustrator approach to the Type palette and the ability to edit type directly in the image seems a superior method, it would not be surprising to see a future version of Photoshop where the current, oversized Type dialog box is replaced by the more compact Type palette.

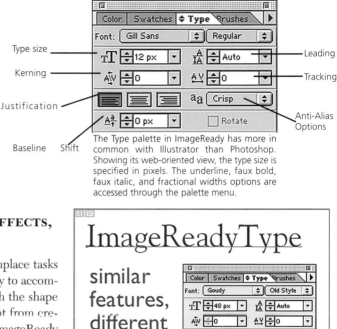

The Type palette in ImageReady has more in common with Illustrator than Photoshop. Showing its web-oriented view, the type size is specified in pixels. The underline, faux bold, faux italic, and fractional widths options are accessed through the palette menu.

USING IMAGEREADY'S SHAPE TOOLS, _LAYER EFFECTS, AND LAYER STYLES

Creating navigational buttons is one of the more commonplace tasks faced by Web designers, and ImageReady provides an easy way to accomplish this with its shape tools. Essentially, creating buttons with the shape tools, a rectangle, rounded rectangle and a circle is no different from creating a selection and filling it with the foreground color. The ImageReady approach simply streamlines the process by automatically filling the shape with the foreground color and creating it on a separate layer. In the Options palette for this tool, you can uncheck the separate layer box if you want the shape to be created on an existing layer. You can also specify a fixed pixel size and the blending mode that will be applied to the shape.

With layer effects it's easy to apply a three-dimensional look to your buttons by adding bevels, drop shadows and gradient and pattern fills. In ImageReady the layer effects can be accessed through the main Layers menu or from the icon at the bottom of the Layers palette. If you use a gradient/pattern layer effect, note that this effect is not supported by Photoshop 5.5. If you switch to that application, you will see the Layer Effect icon in the Layers palette combined with a triangle. This tells you that there is a layer effect that Photoshop cannot display, but it is still a part of that layer and when you return to ImageReady, it will be visible again.

Another way to customize the look of buttons or text, and to ensure that the same look can be recalled for future work, is the Layer Styles palette. Styles are noth-

In ImageReady, type is entered directly into the image, rather than through a type dialog box as in Photoshop. An active type layer is indicated with a colored line beneath the type. To make a change, simply select the Type tool and highlight the text.

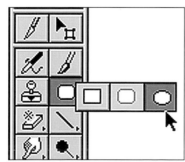

The Shape tools in ImageReady are ideal for the quick and easy creation of Web buttons.

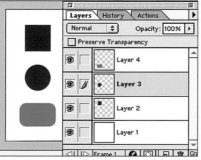

Shapes created with the ImageReady shape tools. The default setting always creates a shape on a new layer, making it very easy to then apply a layer effect and save as a transparent GIF.

Accessing the Layer Effects from the bottom of the Layers palette.

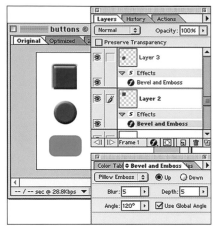

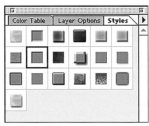

The same shapes with Layer Effects applied to add a three-dimensional look. In ImageReady, Layer Effects are accessed from the italic *f* in the black circle at the bottom of the Layers palette, or from the main Layers menu. Once a specific effect has been chosen, you can fine tune it with the controls in the Layer Effects palette.

The Layer Styles palette.

Evolution of a Pattern: First, random strokes were made with the Pencil tool. The Wave filter was applied, then a Gaussian Blur, and lastly, the Wave filter was applied one more time.

ing more than a set of layer effects that have been saved and named, allowing you to use them again and again with predictable results. ImageReady ships with several styles ready for you to use, or you can create your own. To apply a style to a layer, make sure that the target layer is selected and simply double click on the style in the Style palette, or drag the style onto the layer in the Layers palette, or directly onto the image. Applying a style will replace any previous layer effects you may have added to a layer. To create a new style based on a set of layer effects you have applied to a layer, make sure that the layer is active, and from the Palette menu on the Styles palette, choose New Style and name the style in the dialog that appears. Your new style now shows up in the Styles palette and can be easily accessed for future projects. This is a great way of ensuring that all of the buttons for a particular site have the same look thoughout, especially if more than one person is creating graphics.

CREATING A CUSTOM PATTERN FOR A LAYER STYLE

It's easy to use Photoshop or ImageReady to create custom patterns that can be applied as a layer style. In this way, you can move beyond the pre-fab choices that are installed with the program and personalize your work. For this example, a simple pattern was created entirely in ImageReady. First, a new file of 100x100 pixels was created. Using the Pencil tool, irregular black diagonal lines were added and then blurred using the Gaussian Blur filter. The Wave filter was appled to give the lines a swirling appearance. Finally, the edges of the pattern were blended using the Tilemaker filter (Filter/Other/Tilemaker). This filter helps to disguise any areas where the edges of the pattern may show up in the image. The file was saved as marble.psd and then accessed through the Gradient/Pattern palette by clicking on the pop-up menu of pre-defined patterns and choosing Other. After navigating to where the file was saved, it was applied to the image. If you want your custom pattern to show up in the pattern library, you need to save it to the same location where ImageReady stores these files and then restart the program. On both Mac and Windows platforms, these can be found in the Patterns folder, which is located in the Photoshop 5.5 Settings folder.

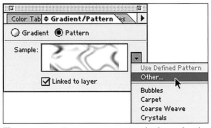

The new pattern was accessed through the Gradient/Pattern palette.

The new custom pattern, marble.psd, applied as a style to text in ImageReady.

AUTOMATED CONTACT SHEETS

Version 5.5 improves upon the Contact Sheet feature that first made its appearance in the 5.0 release. Like its predecessor, the new Contact Sheet II is also found in the Automate section under the File menu (File/Automate/Contact Sheet II). As the name suggests, this command automates the creation of multi-image layouts whose analog equivalents are the standard contact sheets that photographers are familiar with. You can specify a source folder of images and any subdirectories within that folder. Next, you tell the program what the document size should be, its resolution and color mode. Finally, you can customize the arrangment of the thumbnail images and whether or not to use the file name as a caption. An abbreviated list of fonts is available for you to use should you choose to include captions. Once you have made your selections, click OK and Photoshop will commence creating your contact sheet, opening each image in turn, resizing it and placing it in position in the layout. If there are more images than the number of thumbnails on your page will allow, then a second page is begun and the process continues until all thumbnails are placed. When the procedure is finished, you are presented with a layered file with the thumbnail images surrounded by transparency over a white background. At this point you can flatten the image or replace the white background with another of your choosing. If you have images that are tagged with RGB color profiles different from your current Photoshop RGB workspace, you might want to temporarily set the Profile Mismatch Handling to Ignore within File/Color Settings/Profile Setup, or you'll get an error that will halt the process. A better choice might be to temporarily change your RGB Setup to match the files that will be in the contact sheet; this will then tag them correctly when saved.

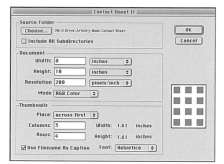

The Contact Sheet II dialog box.

The contact sheet is a great time-saving feature that automates a very useful process that any image maker will appreciate. Doing the same thing manually would take much longer and would be a bit tedious, especially if you had to do a lot of them. One feature that is conspicuously absent that would make a lot of sense, however, is the ability to enter a point size for the captions. The current implementation leaves the font size up to the program, and this is influenced by how many thumbnail images are being placed in the layout. The fewer the images, the larger the captions are, to the point of being disproportionately large in some cases. Including the file names as captions will also reduce the size of the individual thumbnails. You can get an idea of how much space the thumbnails will occupy by watching the layout preview as you add rows and columns, or switch on the captions options. Another feature that could be added that would improve the resulting contact sheets is a sharpening pass once the thumbnails have been resized. We found that running the Sharpen filter on the images, after the sheet was finished, helped with the overall appearence of the thumbnails.

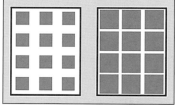

The size of the thumbnail images will vary greatly depending on whether or not you use captions. At left are thumbnails with captions, and at right without captions.

A finished contact sheet without captions.

Two contact sheets showing how fewer images increase the size of the captions. On the left, a sheet of six images, and on the right, a sheet containing twelve images. Unfortunately, you are unable to specify a point size for the captions.

PICTURE PACKAGES

A close cousin to the Contact Sheet feature is File/Automate/Picture Package, which allows you to create printed sheets of different sized prints from the same image. This is the Photoshop version of what portrait studios have been offering for years. Unlike the contact sheet, which allows you to choose many images to arrange on a single file, the Picture Package asks you to specify a single image that will be duplicated in one of several predetermined "packages" of prints. The packages offered are all traditional sizes that you would expect to find in a commercial portrait studio with the measurement unit in inches. There is no way to specify a page size, however, as the resulting package is always 8x10 inches at whatever resolution you enter. This, again, is conforming to the traditional model of picture packages being offered on an 8x10 sheet. You can either choose from an image file stored on disk or the frontmost file open in Photoshop.

As convenient as this feature may seem, however, it is important to note that it doesn't give you the exact size prints that were promised by the chosen package arrangement. One reason for this could be that your source image has an aspect ratio

The Picture Package dialog gives you a choice of eleven packages to choose from.

You can choose an image on disk, or the frontmost document that is open in Photoshop. Resolution and color mode can also be specified. The selected package is previewed at the right.

The finished picture package. Blue guides have been added to show the apparent addition of white borders. It appears that these borders are calculated into the final size of the package prints that are created.

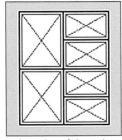

A closer view of the package preview is the only hint that borders will be added to the images.

different from the sizes in the chosen package and, since Photoshop does not crop the image to fit entirely into the chosen size, you could end up with odd-sized picture packages. In the example of the Buckminster Fuller portrait, the picture package was supposed to be (2) 4x5s and (4) 3.5x2.5s, but in the resulting layout the 4x5s were actually 3.71x4.64, and the wallet prints were 2.78x2.21. When the image of Mr. Fuller was measured, it was determined that it was originally an exact 4x5 proportion, yet the finished print size was clearly short on both sides.

The reason for this imprecise sizing seems to be that Photoshop is adding a white border around the image. The preview graphic showing the arrangement of the packages seems to show this border. Adobe's Photoshop 5.5 User Guide Supplement is not much help in this matter; its coverage of the feature is very brief and there is no indication that white borders will be caculated into the final print size. This is definitely something to be aware of before you begin using this feature in a high volume production environment. A better implementation of this concept would allow for controlling whether or not borders or a chosen color were added, and also allow the user to specify a general crop (center, left or right) for images where you want the program to crop the source image to fill the resulting package sizes entirely. That's an improvement we can hope for in the next version of Photoshop, but for now, if your picture package needs dictate that the image fill the desired print size with no borders, you're probably still going to have to do some of that work the old-fashioned way, by copying and re-positioning layers, or perhaps resizing your finished packages by a few percentage points. It would also be possible for you to write an action or two that would create picture packages, of your particular design, automatically from files that are within a folder. See chapter 4: Automating with Actions, to learn how to do this type of project. Actions are fun to work with, and they can give you the flexibitily that built in features don't allow.

CREATING IMAGE BACKGROUNDS WITH IMAGEREADY

ImageReady provides a very simple way to save a picture so that it will be used as the background image for a Web page. When it saves the image, it also creates an HTML file with the necessary code to accomplish this effect. Once the HTML file has been created, you can then use it as a base to add more elements to, or you can open it in an HTML editor or Web design program such as Dreamweaver or GoLive and continue building your page there. For those who already have some experience with Web layout applications or HTML, this ImageReady feature will not be too exciting, as the string of code used to generate a background image is one of the more basic steps in HTML. If you're just getting started with Web work, however, some of ImageReady's automatic HTML features may prove quite useful and serve as a good introduction into understanding how it all works.

To create a background, you need to have an image open on-screen. If you plan to have much text appearing over the background, you should probably choose something that is not too busy, as this can interfere with the readability of the type. From the File menu, choose HTML Background. In the dialog that appears, you can specify whether the image will be displayed as an Image or a Background. If you choose Image, you can then select either a background color or a background image that will be tiled across the entire page. Using this approach, the resulting HTML file places your main image in the upper left corner of the page with either a color or a tiled background behind it.

The Background option will create a tiled mosaic from your source image that will fill the entire Web page. When this method is selected, you can specify what color will appear as the image is loading. For this example, a file was created in ImageReady of some wooden planks. In the HTML Background dialog, Background was selected and a color similar to the image was chosen. The final step is to save the image using Save Optimized or Save Optimized As, both of which can be found in the File menu. Before you do this, however, you should double check the Optimized views of your image to verify if the correct settings are being applied. The Save Optimized method allows you to save a companion HTML file along with your image file that will contain the necessary code to properly display your background images. Once the HTML file has been saved, you can preview the results in a Web browser. Although ImageReady has a Preview In command (File/Preview In) that allows you to choose a Web browser to jump to, it seems to be intended for previewing animations, and in this instance it displayed just the single image that was still open on-screen and not the tiled background. The way around this is to open the HTML file from within your browser. The file will have been saved in the same location and with the same name as your image file. Make sure you open the HTML version and not the GIF or JPEG.

To assist in the creation of tiled backgrounds that blend together more seamlessly, ImageReady has a Tile Maker filter (Filter/Other/Tile maker) that allows you to blend the edges, or use a kaleidoscope effect to create an abstract design. The Tile Maker filter is also helpful when creating custom patterns as the blend edges feature helps disguise the edges of the pattern, resulting in a smoother transition as the pattern is distributed across the image. With the Kaleidoscope option you can take any image and transform it into stylish abstract that you can then save as a tiling HTML background. Even images that you might not at first consider for this effect become entirely new when viewed through the kaleidoscope. Although wild, colorful kaleidoscopic backgrounds may seem like a great thing to use on a Web page, it's always a good idea to keep in mind the audience who will be viewing your site. Specifically, does your background interfere with any text, making it difficult to read? If the main purpose of your Web page is the presentation of information, then a background should remain in the background, and not be competing with or overpowering the main content.

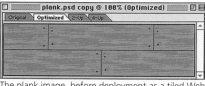

The plank image, before deployment as a tiled Web page background.

The HTML Background dialog in ImageReady. A color similar to the plank image is chosen. In a browser, this color will display first, before the plank GIF file is tiled.

Saving the optimized image. The checkmark by the Save HTML File box indicates that the appropriate code will be generated to display the image as a tiled background in a Web browser

```
<HTML>
<BODY BGCOLOR=#CC9966 BACKGROUND="plank1.gif">
</BODY>
</HTML>
```

The HTML code generated by ImageReady for the tiled background.

The kaleidoscope option in the Tile Maker filter transformed the Paris dog into an abstract pattern.

The kaleidoscope background of the Paris dog, as seen in a Web browser.

The tiled plank background, previewed in a Web browser.

CREATING WEB PHOTO GALLERIES

Have you always wanted to have a Web site showcasing some of your best images, but lacked the HTML savvy or Web design application necessary to put such a presentation together? Well, the time has come to start getting those favorite pictures ready because Photoshop 5.5 now boasts a cool feature that will do most of the work for you. The Web Photo Gallery command (File/Automate/Web Photo Gallery) will take all of the images in a specified folder, resize them, create smaller thumb-

The Web Photo Gallery dialog.

A finished thumbnail page viewed in a browser.

The main Packard image viewed in a browser. The left and right arrows take you to the previous and next image in the gallery; the up arrow returns you to the thumbnail index.

nails and generate the HTML code and the underlying directory structure needed to display a main thumbnail page as well as a page for each individual image. HTML purists and Web designers who use more advanced tools for building their sites may look down at such a push-button automated feature, but for those who don't have the time or need to learn HTML and can't justify investing in a Web authoring program, having Photoshop create your Web gallery is a very useful and convenient alternative.

The first step to the creation of a Web photo gallery is to put all the images for the gallery into a folder. From the File menu in Photoshop, choose Automate, Web Photo Gallery. In the dialog that appears, you can specify the source directory, whether to include any subdirectories, and the destination folder. The Site section lets you give your gallery a name, identify the photographer and enter a date. For the size of the thumbnail images, you can choose small, medium or large. This size classification is somewhat vague, but it translates into 50 pixels for small, 75 pixels for medium, and 100 pixels for large. This indicates the length of the longest side of the thumbnail. If your image is taller than it is wide, for example, then the medium-sized thumbnail will be 75 pixels high.Finally, you can choose the size of the main images for the gallery: 25% (small), 50% (medium) and 75% (large). You can also enter a custom size percentage, or choose to not resize them at all by unchecking the Resize Gallery Images checkbox. One thing to keep in mind about the size of your images is whether or not the source files have comparable dimensions. If not, then some of the final images could be much larger or smaller than anything else in your gallery. If you suspect that this may be the case with your files, then you might want to resize them all beforehand so that they will yield similarly sized gallery images. The final choice in this dialog controls the quality level of the finished JPEG file.

When you say OK to your settings, Photoshop begins opening the files, resizing them and creating the thumbnail images. The HTML code is generated in the background. When the process is completed, the gallery is automatically opened in a Web browser. When you click on the thumnail links, you are taken to the appropriate page showcasing that image. Arrow icons above the image allow you to navigate to the next image, previous image or back to the thumbnail index.

As you look at the thumbnails and the main images in your Web gallery, you may notice that they don't seem very sharp. When Photoshop creates the thumbnails and gallery versions of your images, it does not apply any sharpening, and this omission is often noticable in the finished product. A final touch that you can apply yourself would be to open each thumbnail and gallery image and determine the appropriate amount of sharpening necessary for each one. It might be as simple as the Sharpen filter, or you may want to assign specific values with the Unsharp Mask filter, but your images will look much better if you take the time to sharpen them after they have been resampled down for Web display. Once you know the sharpening values that work best for each size of image, you can create an action to do the sharpening and then use File/Automate/Batch to apply the action to all the images in your gallery.

If you are comfortable with basic HTML editing, you can easily customize your gallery pages by making a few simple modifications to the source code such as changing the background color, or perhaps adding a tiled background image. Even if you do most of your Web design work in a professional authoring program and create a very stylized layout for your main gallery, Photoshop's Web Gallery feature is great for making archive galleries, or Web-based stock image galleries, where a customized design is not needed.

A closeup of a Web gallery image (medium size, high quality) before and after sharpening with the Unsharp mask filter. The Web gallery feature does not apply sharpening, so you will have to do this manually after the images are created if you decide they are not sharp enough.

The HTML source code that Photoshop generated for the Packard page, viewed in a Web authoring program. If you are comfortable with basic HTML, you can customize your Web gallery by changing the background color, or adding a tiled background.

When making a Web photo gallery, Photoshop creates a directory structure for the image and HTML files. If you upload your gallery to a Web server, you need to be sure and preserve the relationship of the directories or the links and display of the images may not function correctly.

THE NEW PHOTOSHOP ERASER TOOLS & EXTRACT IMAGE COMMAND

In compositing work, isolating part of an image from its background is one of the most common tasks that a digital artist is called upon to do. Fortunately, Photoshop provides several methods for accomplishing this, whether it is by using the traditional selection tools such as the marquees, lassos and Magic Wand, the Pen tool for creating custom paths, or by more complex procedures involving the manipulation of channel data. With the 5.5 release of Photoshop, a trio of new features has been added to the digital imaging workbench: the Background Eraser, the Magic Eraser, and the Extract Image command. As interesting and useful as these new tools are, however, they do not represent the quantum leap forward in selection/masking techniques that some might be hoping for. Each has its specific strengths and limitations, and, as is often the case, the ideal way to select or mask part of a complicated image rarely involves just one tool, but rather a combination of various tools and procedures.

The two new eraser tools: the Background Eraser (with scissors icon) and the Magic Eraser.

THE MAGIC ERASER

Of the two new eraser tools, the least useful for photographic images is the Magic Eraser. It functions much like the Bucket tool but clears an area to transparency instead of filling it with color. Another way to achieve the same effect would be to click with the Magic Wand and then delete the resulting selection. Like the Wand and the Bucket tools, it has a tolerance setting to determine the range of pixels that are deleted, as well as anti-alias and contiguous options. The Magic Eraser is useful mainly on images where there is a clear difference between what you want to delete and what you want to keep. And, true to its name, it erases pixel information, leaving you with transparency. If all you're after is a quick way to generate a transparent GIF from a logo or get rid of an unwanted background, then this might suit your needs fine, but if you're using it on photographs, be sure to inspect the edges of what is left behind closely, or you may find that the Magic Eraser has been a bit clumsy in its deletion process. If you want to use this tool as shortcut to jumpstart the creation of a better mask, then you'll need to first duplicate the original image layer onto a separate layer, the Magic Eraser copy. That way, you still have the original in case important edge detail is acci-

The Magic Eraser works well on images where there is a distinct tonal or color difference between the foreground and background.

After clicking on the background with the Magic Eraser with a Tolerance setting of 45, most of the background has been deleted. Subsequent clicks on the remaining areas will clear the rest of the background.

Closer inspection of the final Magic Eraser results shows that parts of the pant's edge were deleted along with the background.

dentally sacrificed by the Magic Eraser. Once you have deleted the appropriate areas in the copy layer with the Magic Eraser, you can then Command-Click on the Magic Eraser copy Layer to load the layer transparency as a selection and either save it as an alpha channel or apply it to the original layer as a layer mask. In this way you can preserve all image data and have the option to further improve the mask using selection tools or brushes in the likely event that it is not perfect the first time.

THE BACKGROUND ERASER

Unlike the Magic Eraser, the Background Eraser is a much more refined tool that you will find more useful in helping to separate part of an image from the background. To those who have used Extensis MaskPro, the Background Eraser will be very familiar. The main deficiency of this tool, however, is that, like the Magic Eraser, it deletes image information and relaces it with transparency. If you want to ensure that necessary pixel information is not being thrown away, you need to duplicate the image onto a new layer, as described above, so that the Background Eraser performs its deletion on the copy layer and not the original image (be sure to turn the eye icon off for the original, so that you can see the effect of the tool). This working method preserves a back-up copy of all of your image data in case you need to fill in any areas where the eraser's choices were less than satisfactory. The downside of this is that, in making a duplicate layer of the entire image, you are effectively doubling your file size which results in more memory and disk space requirements, and on large image files, can cause Photoshop to run slower.

The Options palette for the Background Eraser.

The Options palette for the Background Eraser has three main settings that affect how it performs it pixel deletion. Discontiguous will erase the sampled color wherever it occurs in the layer; Contiguous will erase areas that contain the sampled color and are connected to one another; and Find Edges will erase the sampled color in contiguous areas, but do a better job at preserving the sharpness of object edges. From the Sampling options, you can choose Continuous to sample colors continuosly as you drag through the image. This option is best for erasing adjoining areas that are different in color. The Once option will only erase areas containing the color you first click. This is best for deleting a solid-colored area. The Background Swatch option will erase only areas containing the current background color. Finally, you set a Tolerance value much as with the Magic Wand tool. A low tolerance erases areas that are very simliar to the sampled color, and a high tolerance erases a broader range of colors.

To test this new tool, as well as the Extract Image command, we chose the Versailles image from chapter. Because that lesson requires the creation of a mask to replace the sky, we decided to try and make the knockout using the Background Eraser and see if it was any better than the masking techniques used in that chapter.

Here, the combination of a large brush and too high a tolerance setting has inadvertently introduced transparency into the edges of the buildings. Zooming in for a close view is advisable when using the Background Eraser, so you can watch for errors such as this.

When you select the Background Eraser and position it over the image, you'll notice that (if your cursor is displayed in brush size mode) it is represented by a circle with a crosshair in the center. The circle indicates your brush size (use the left and right bracket keys to cycle through smaller or larger brushes) and the crosshair is the hotspot

The Background Eraser in action. Tracing along the edge of the buildings, with the crosshair sampling from the sky, causes the sky pixels to be deleted.

where the tool is sampling the pixels as you drag through the image. Sampled pixels are compared with the tolerance setting, and any pixels within the specified range are deleted. To delete the background around an image, simply hold the mouse button down and move the tool, straddling the edge between what you want to keep and what you want to delete with the crosshair always in the area you want to delete. If you touch the area to be preserved with the crosshair, it will assume that you want to erase those pixels. Because this tool gives you live feedback, it's easy to tell if it's doing a good job or not. Beware of subtle hints of transparency that are sometimes added to edges you wish to keep, and, if there is not much tonal or color difference between the foreground and background, use the number keypad to decrease the tolerence setting as you are working with the tool.

After erasing the sky where it intersected with the buildings, the layer transparency was loaded as a selection and the bottom half containing the buildings was subtracted from the selection. The remaining sky area was then deleted from the layer, and a new layer was added underneath it and filled with white in order to proof the quality of the edges. As you can see from the illustration, the white layer reveals a trail of semi-transparent pixels that were not removed by the Background Eraser. Clearly, more work was needed to polish up the sky transparency, so the regular Eraser was used to eliminate the main pixel trail, and the Background Eraser was employed in areas of the image that were closer to the edges of the building.

After cleaning up the stray pixels on the working layer, a new sky was created for the image with the Gradient tool. This was done to gauge how effective the knockout was when combined with a different sky. We then loaded the layer transparency as a selection and saved the selection as a mask channel so we could compare it with the sky mask that was created for the Versailles exercise in chapter 32. The mask in that lesson was made using a technique called threshold masking, combined with touch-ups using the lasso tool, paintbrush, and Gaussian Blur filter. In comparing the two masks, both were very simliar. Although the one created from the results of the Background Eraser revealed places where slight amounts of transparency had been introduced into the building edges, this was not readily apparent when viewed as a composite with the new sky. With a different background, however, these deficiencies might be more noticable.

When the two methods of replacing the sky are compared, using the Background Eraser was not necessarily faster or more efficient than creating a layer mask using the Threshold command combined with other tools. Furthermore, its initial result was not perfect and required additional work to remove the trail of pixel debris left behind by the first pass. Although it doesn't supercede the techniques that are available using tradtional masks, it is good at removing background color contamina-

After erasing the sky where it intersected with the buildings, the layer transparency was loaded as a selection and then the lower part (the buildings) was subtracted from the selection.With only the sky area selected, it was then deleted from the layer, leaving us with an apparently satisfactory removal of the sky pixels.

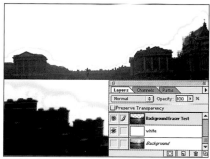

A white layer was added beneath the deleted sky, revealing a halo of pixel debris that had been left behind by the Background Eraser. Zooming in to at least 100%, the regular Eraser was employed on the main pixel trail, and the Background Eraser was used in areas closer to the building detail.

After the stray pixels have been cleaned up. A new sky is created with the Gradient tool. The effect is convincing and the edges look pretty good, but this method was not necessarily any faster or more efficient than using the Threshold masking techniques described in chapter 32.

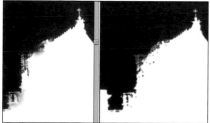

Two masks compared. On the left is the mask derived from the results of the Background Eraser tool, and on the right is the mask created for the Versailles exercise in Chapter 32. Both are very similiar, although the mask from the Background Eraser is a bit imprecise in the scaffolding on the chapel.

The results of the two masks when viewed in the final composites. On the left is the result of the Background Eraser tool, and on the right, the image from chapter 32. Since the scaffold is silhouetted against a similar colored sky, the imperfections from the Background Eraser tool are not very noticable.

tion from pixels along an edge, and its straightforward approach will undoubtedly have appeal for those who are intimidated by any procedure which involves channel masks. For those who already have some experience in creating digital masks, this is a tool to explore and determine how it can best be put to use in helping you refine a mask or a selection. And for those who are still mystified by the whole concept of masking, don't let the apparent ease of use of the Background Eraser keep you away from learning the techniques for modifying an image's color channels to help in the creation of a mask.

THE EXTRACT IMAGE TOOL

This tool is found at the bottom of the Image menu, and its interface and behavior is similar to third-party masking plug-ins such as Extensis MaskPro. Unlike MaskPro, however, you are unable to generate a mask directly from Extract as Extract actually removes pixels from your image. This means that you need to use this feature on a duplicate layer in order to have a back-up copy of your image data. It's also a good idea to use the History palette to create a snapshot just before you use Extract, in case you need to use the History Brush to touch up areas where necessary edge pixels were inadvertently removed. Just remember to create the snapshot after you have made the duplicate layer because the History features may not function if the number of layers in your image does not match those of the snapshot.

When you choose Image/Extract Image, you are presented with a large dialog/preview window that takes up most of the available screen space. Standard keyboard shortcuts that you use to zoom in and out and drag through the image elsewhere in Photoshop will also work for you here. The first step is to define the edge where this tool will be making its decisions on what to keep and what to delete. This is done by using the Highlighter tool to paint along the edge so that the color strokes a border that includes a bit of the foreground and some of the background. If you make a slight mistake in painting the highlight, you'll have to switch to the Eraser tool to correct it since the standard Undo key command (Cmd/Ctrl-Z) does not work in the Extract dialog. If the element you are trying to extract is surrounded by other image data, your highlight stroke should completely enclose it. If the object you are extracting extends to the borders of the image, you can simply extend your stroke to the edge of the picture as we did in the Versailles image. If you already have an alpha channel that would work for selecting the edge of the image, you can load that as a highlight by choosing Load Highlight in the lower right section of the dialog and choosing the appropriate channel.

Once the image border has been highlighted, the next step is to designate the interior area that is to be protetced from any pixel erasure. To do this, switch to the Bucket tool (keyboard shortcut K) and click inside the area you wish to keep, filling it with the selected fill color. If you accidentally click in the wrong section, simply click there again and the fill will be removed. To preview how good of a job the Extract tool will do on your image, click on the Preview button and wait for an extracted preview to generate. Once the preview is done, it's a good idea to zoom in and scroll around the image to inspect the edges for any errors that would yield an inferior extraction. You can also evaluate the preview using different colored mattes in place of the transparent areas. This is often very useful for determining if there is leftover pixel debris or areas where transparency has been accidentally added by the extraction process. In the Preview section in the lower right corner of the Extract dialog, open the Show menu and choose from a black, gray, white or custom color

The Extract Image dialog/preview contains a proxy of your image for you to work on. The mini-toolbar on the left contains an Edge Highlighter for defining an edge, a Bucket for specifying the interior of the image, an Eraser for removing areas of highlight or fill, an Eyedropper, and the Zoom and Hand tools for navigating within the preview window. Tool options, extraction and preview controls are on the right.

STEP 1: The first step in extracting an image is to define an edge with the highlighter tool. Although the icon for the tool looks like a felt tip pen, the keyboard shortcut is the same as the Brush tool, (B). As with the regular brush, you can increase or decrease the size of the brush by using the left and right bracket keys, or by using the brush size control. Three colors are available for the highlight: red, green or blue.

STEP 2: Once you have defined the edge where the extract tool is to do most of its work, you need to specify the area of the image to be preserved by filling it with the Bucket tool. If your image element is surrounded by the background, you need to completely enclose it with the edge highlight. In an image such as this, you only need to highlight to where the object touches the image boundaries. Clicking with the Bucket in an area that has already been filled will remove the fill.

STEP 3: When you are finished with the highlight and fill, choose Preview to see how well the Extract tool accomplishes its mission. You can zoom in using standard keyboard commands to inspect the edges. If you notice problem areas, choose View: Original and Show Highlight from the Preview section of the dialog box. Using the Eraser, you can make changes to your highlight and then paint in a new section. Once you have re-filled the image with the Bucket, you can generate a new preview. When you are satisfied, choose OK.

matte. If you choose custom, the Photo-shop Color Picker appears for you to select a new color.

In this same menu, one of the more interesting and useful options is the ability to preview the extraction as a mask, with black representing fully transparent aras, white fully opaque, preserved areas, and gray showing edge regions where some amount of transparency has been added. If you are already comfortable with the black-and-white representation of image masks, you will probably find this option to be very useful. The frustrating thing about being able to see the preview shown as a mask is that it amounts to nothing more than a tease since you can't actually save the extraction as a mask. Now that would be a truly useful function! Much more flexible and open-ended than just giving you transparency with large areas of deleted pixels. Adobe obviously realized the importance of being able to preview the extraction as a mask, yet they didn't follow that through to the next logical step of providing a way to save it as a mask. This is one of the reasons that the Extract Image tool seems to be a work in progress, and I expect that we'll see improvements to its interface and funtionality in future releases.

After closely inspecting the preview of the extraction, if you are satisfied with the results you can go ahead and click OK to apply the procedure to the actual image. I would still recommend further border patrol just to ensure that there are no surprises. If you find areas that need touching up, you can make use of the History Brush to restore those pixels that may have suffered in the image extraction. The Background Eraser is also handy if you need to remove any straggler pixels that were overlooked. And even though this operation has resulted in erasing image data to transparency, you can still generate a mask from it by simply loading the layer transparency as a selection and then either saving it as a channel or loading it into a layer mask by clicking on the Layer Mask icon while on an original layer of the image as it was before the extraction happened.

Although the Extract Image tool certainly will make some selection tasks easier in Photoshop, it is not a one-click wonder that will always present you with perfect results, and it doesn't do away with the need for more advanced third-party masking plug-ins that have been on the market awhile. The more complex the extraction, the more difficulties it will have in keeping and deleting the appropriate image data, and the more you will have to rely on additional tools to refine the initial extraction. It does do a very good job at decontaminating edge pixels from background color spill.

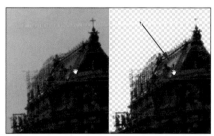

In the preview of an image extraction, it is advisable to zoom into the image and use the grabber hand to scroll around and inspect the edges of the image. In the Preview section in the lower right corner of the dialog, you can view the Original image or the current Extraction, and this will often show problem areas. In the example above, while the scaffolding has fared well, it is clear that transparency has been added to part of the roof of the chapel.

Viewing the extraction with the White Matte option also reveals the flaws in the area of the chapel roof, where some of the pixels are now partially transparent. The History Brush is very helpful for dealing with minor imperfections in the image extractions.

The Extract Image Tool

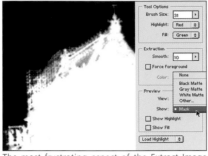

The most frustrating aspect of the Extract Image tool is that it allows you to preview the extraction as a mask, yet doesn't give you the ability to save it as a mask. This would be infinitely more flexible than the wholsale erasing of pixels that the tool currently produces.

If you are doing your work on a Macintosh, you can go into Image/Adjust/Gamma and choose Macintosh to Windows, and the image is actually adjusted to be lighter, on your Mac screen, to compensate for the fact that it will look darker when displayed on a Windows screen.

If you are doing your work on a Windows system, you can go into Image/Adjust/Gamma and choose Windows to Macintosh, and the image is actually adjusted to be darker, on your Windows screen, to compensate for the fact that it will look lighter when displayed on a Mac screen.

For certain images, where there is a more obvious separation between the foreground and the background, you may find that the Extract Image tool does quite well. Images with wispy hair are also good candidates for this feature, although if there is enough contrast between the subject and the background, exisiting channel masking techniques such as using Levels, Curves, or Threshold to modify a channel can work just as well.

PHOTOSHOP 5.5 AND IMAGEREADY COLOR MANAGEMENT AND IMAGE DISPLAY

This book goes to great length to explain how to display your color accurately within Photoshop 5 and 5.5. In ImageReady the default is to not compensate the screen display at all. That default is the Uncompensated Color choice of the View Preview command. This is what Photoshop 4 and earlier versions of Photoshop did. If you are using ColorSync on the Mac or ICM on the PC and you have profiles embedded within your Photoshop 5 or 5.5 created files, then for them to display correctly in ImageReady, you need to choose the Preview/Photoshop Compensation choice. This choice is only available for files that contain an ICC profile so if you want this color control you need to initially create your files in Photoshop 5 or 5.5. If you are working on a Mac or a Windows system and you want to see how a file will look on the typical Mac, then choose Standard Macintosh Color; to see how the file will work on a typical Windows system, choose Standard Windows Color. Using View New it would be possible to actually have three views of your image. Your original Color Managed View, where you do most of your work, could be viewed with Photoshop Compensation on. This is the default state within Photoshop 5 or 5.5. You could then choose View/New View to get another window on the same image and set its Preview state to Standard Macintosh Color and finally choose View/New View again and set its Preview state to Standard Windows Color. Now you can see all three potential color spaces: your Photoshop space (Adobe RGB for exam-

When you are working within ImageReady, the default is to display your images in Uncompensated Color. This is the color space of your Monitor and is how Photoshop 4 and older versions of Photoshop used to display your images. If you have an image that was saved from Photoshop 5 or 5.5 with an embedded color profile, then you can use Photoshop Compensation to display the image and it will display in the same way Photoshop 5 or 5.5 would display the image with RGB Setup set correctly for that image. The Standard Macintosh Color choice will display the image with a gamma of 1.8 as it will look on a typical Mac. The Standard Windows Color choice will display the image with a Gamma of 2.2 as it will look on a typical PC. If you are picky about color and want your images to display in ImageReady the same way they do in Photoshop with their color profiles working correctly, then you should set Preview to Photoshop Compensation.

ple), the Standard Mac space and the Standard Windows space. You can do this same thing within Photoshop 5.5 using the View/New View and View/Preview commands; just remember that in Photoshop 5 and 5.5 that Photoshop Compensation, for your RGB Setup space, is the default view. I just discovered, as I tried to open a LAB format file in ImageReady, that ImageReady does not support the LAB color space so you cannot open the files. You would have to open the file into Photoshop 5 or 5.5, then convert it to some other space, like Adobe RGB or ColorMatch RGB, then resave the file in that space to be able to open it into ImageReady. In the illustratons above of the Photoshop versus ImageReady displays of the Bruce Stone Woman

Here you see an image on the left displayed correctly in Photoshop 5.5 within the Adobe RGB colorspace. The same image was then opened into ImageReady and Viewed using Uncompensated Color. Big Difference!

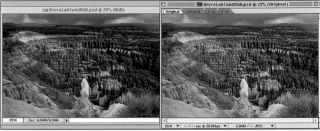

Here you see an image on the left displayed correctly in Photoshop 5.5 within the Adobe RGB colorspace. The same image was then opened into ImageReady and Viewed using Standard Macintosh Color using a Gamma of 1.8. This is quite different than Adobe RGB, which has a Gamma of 2.2.

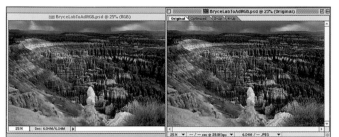

Here you see an image on the left displayed correctly in Photoshop 5.5 within the Adobe RGB colorspace. The same image was then opened into ImageReady and viewed using Standard Windows Color using a Gamma of 2.2. Although this is the same Gamma as Adobe RGB, notice that the color gamut is much smaller.

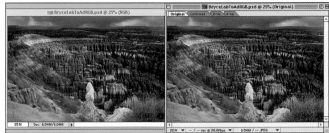

Here you see an image on the left displayed correctly in Photoshop 5.5 within the Adobe RGB colorspace. The same image was then opened into ImageReady and Viewed using Photoshop Compensation. Ahhhh...much better!

image, I originally opened the BryceLab image from the Bryce Stone Woman folder on the Photoshop 5 Artistry CD into Photoshop 5.5 with my RGB Setup set to Adobe RGB. I then did Image/Mode/RGB to convert the file from Lab into Adobe RGB space, then saved the file so I could open it into ImageReady. You can try this experiment yourself and I think you will see, on your screen more clearly than in the book, why you will want to view your images correctly within ImageReady and probably also save your JPEG compressed versions with ICC Profiles attached. Another thing you might want to note is that in the 2-Up or 4-Up ImageReady dialogs, you can choose the Preview state for each subview separately.

OPENING QUICKTIME MOVIES AS ANIMATIONS

With ImageReady 2 you can use File/Open to open QuickTime Movies. The movies are opened into ImageReady with each frame in the movie being a frame in the ImageReady Animation palette. Each frame in the Movie is also a separte layer within the Layers palette, and you'll notice that only the Eye icon changes, turning on the appropriate layer as you move through the frames. Opening QuickTime movies can use up a lot of space within ImageReady so you might want to consider using the Selected Range Only option, when opening a file, to open only a sub-range of the frames within the original movie. You can also open every 20th frame, for example, by turning on Limit to Every and entering the number 20.

Once the movie is converted to an animation within ImageReady, you can copy and paste frames, delete frames,

When you use File/Open to open a QuickTime movie into ImageReady, you can choose From Beginning to End, which will bring in the entire movie or Selected Range Only, chosen here, which will only open the range of frames from where you started the slider to where the slider ends up while you have the Shift key down. In Either case, you can use Limit to Every to only grab every 5th frame, every 10th frame, or whatever number you type in.

367

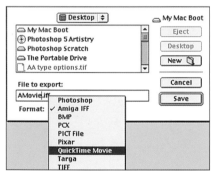

and use all of ImageReady's and Photoshop's commands on any frame because each frame is actually a layer. This allows you movie editing capabilities, although this application is certainly not Adobe Premiere. To make working with movies, and also large animations, quicker within ImageReady, use the Palette Options for each of the Animation and Layers palettes to set the size of the frame and layer icons to be as small as possible. This give ImageReady less work redisplaying these when you make changes.

When you are finished editing your movie, you can save it as a GIF animation by first setting the Optimize palette to the GIF options that work best for this animation and then choosing Save Optimized As and saving the HTML and GIF animation files. You can also choose File/Export Original to export your edited movie as another QuickTime Movie. You could also take an animation that your created within ImageReady and use Export Original to create a QuickTime movie from it. These digital movie editing features give ImageReady yet another scope of possible things you can do with it.

You have all these frame options available when editing a QuickTime movie that has been opened into ImageReady. You could also use any ImageReady or Photoshop operation on any layer (frame).

CREATING IMAGE MAPS WITH IMAGEREADY

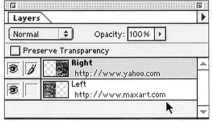

When you turn a layer into an image map, the URL shows up in the Layers palette.

An image map is similar to a slice except that image maps don't have to be rectangular. You will learn all about slices within the next chapter but the issue about slices to compare with image maps is that they both can be hot spots on the screen where you can click and be transferred to a different URL. Image maps allow you to link areas that are shaped as circles, polygons and also rectangles. Slices have the advantage over image maps of allowing you to apply different optimization settings to each slice as well as rollover states. To create an image map, you would use a different layer with a different Opaque area for each hot spot in your map area. The Opaque area of each layer will be used to define its hot spot, and the hot spot will fit as closely as possible into either a Rectangle, Circle or Polygon

When you choose File/Export Original, you get these choices of file formats for exporting your animation or movie.

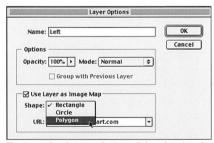

The ImageReady Layer Options dialog showing the choices for the shape of your image map. You type the URL into the text box at the bottom of the dialog.

depending on the choice you make when defining the image map. You define an image map by double clicking on a layer in the Layers palette and then turning on the Use Layer as image map choice at the bottom of the Layer dialog. You then choose Rectangle, Circle or Polygon as the shape of your map and enter the URL to go to when one clicks on/within the Opaque area of that layer. After turning a layer into an image map, the URL shows up within the Layers palette below the layer name.

CREATING AND USING MASTER PALETTES

When you have a group of images that need to be converted into 8-bit color and you want all those images to share the same color palette, you can use the new ImageReady Master Palette feature to easily make that special palette. To build a Master Palette, start out by choosing Image/Master Palette/Clear Master Palette to clear any colors that are left over from a previous project. Then open each image whose colors need to be added to the palette and while that image is the active window, choose Image/Master Palette/Add to Master Palette. That could be done as a Batch for all the images within an Action script. When you have added all the colors from all the images you need to consider, choose Image/Master Palette/Build Master Palette. Once you have built a Master Palette, if you save it in the right place (inside Adobe Photoshop 5.5/Adobe Photoshop 5.5 Settings/Color Tables), the Saved Master Palette becomes available as a choice within the Color Reduction Algorithm pop-up of the Photoshop and ImageReady Optimize palette. You can then use this palette to convert any future image to 8-bit color.

When you want to build a Master Palette, start out by choosing Clear Master Palette to clear any colors that are left over from a previous project. Then open each image whose colors need to be added to the palette, and while that image is the active window, choose Add to Master Palette. When you have all the colors from all the images you need to consider, choose Build Master Palette. One you have built a Master Palette, if you save it in the right plae, the Saved Master Palette becomes available as a choice within the Color Reduction Algorithm pop-up of the Optimize palette.

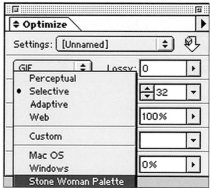

Here is where you should save your Master Palettes if you want them to be available to other parts of ImageReady and Photoshop.

Now my Stone Woman palette shows up within the ImageReady and Photoshop Optimize palette.

HANDS-ON SESSION: Creating Animations, Slices, and Rollovers in ImageReady 2

46

We'll learn these features as we go through the process of making a page on our Web site, www.maxart.com, that is now there to demonstrate the new Web features.

MAKING A WEB PAGE USING IMAGEREADY

While playing with ImageReady for the last few weeks and coming up with this example, I've learned a few things about creating a somewhat complex Web page with animations, rollovers, etc. First of all, once you start creating a lot of animations, it is hard to make major changes in the design of the Web page. It is best to figure out the basic, and even detailed, design first and lay out all the fairly stationary elements, then add the rollover effects to those stationary elements, and finally add the animations at the end. Each frame of each animation contains a list of all the layers that are turned on, as well as the position and effects state for each of those, for the display of that one frame. After you have created a lot of animations, it can be more work than you want to suddenly start moving lots of those layers around or changing them in a major way.

Animations of photographs take up a lot of space and, therefore, make your site load more slowly. I had to downsize both the dimensions and number of frames in my animations several times before their size became acceptable. Creating an animation on a Web page IS different from working with a QuickTime movie that is stored on your hard disk. Say this to yourself many times so you don't make something that is too big! This is really hard for me, because I'm used to looking at really large and very detailed photographic prints and also digital images on my screen. My natural instinct is that bigger and more details are better. That may be so, but after you wait many times, a long time each time, for ImageReady to create your Optimized Web page to Preview in Netscape, smaller starts looking better all the time. When you are doing most of your work in ImageReady and just using Photoshop from time to time, and the images you are working on are small Web images anyhow, change your memory allocation to give more memory to ImageReady than to Photoshop. It's amazing how quickly Photoshop, even with little memory, can open a complex ImageReady document that ImageReady takes much time to do almost anything with. Of course, ImageReady needs to keep track of a lot more about that document, including slices, animations, rollovers, etc., that Photoshop doesn't currently look at. It seems that ImageReady 2 sometimes gets slower over time while working on a document. Sometimes I save a document and quit ImageReady, and then start ImageReady again and reopen the document to find ImageReady much faster with the same document. ImageReady 2 may have some internal memory allocation bugs to work out. If so, these will hopefully be fixed with a bug fix version from Adobe or whenever Adobe comes out with Photoshop 6. In the meantime, quitting ImageReady and then restarting it from time to time may help.

We're going to create a Web page (see my version of this within www.maxart.com) that demonstrates how to use the various important features of ImageReady while also illustrating, to some small extent anyhow, the six different sections of the *Photoshop 5 & 5.5 Artistry* book. The intention here is to teach us how to use ImageReady so some of the book illustrations are much more trivial than they would need to be if this was a serious add for our book. But hey, let's have some fun doing this!

SETTING UP YOUR PAGE AND GUIDES

STEP 1: Within ImageReady, type D for default colors, then X to exchange the colors, and set the background color to black. Choose File/New to creat a new file that is 500 pixels by 375 pixels in size with Background Color selected to make it black. Just for fun and also usefulness, let's set up our Swatches and Color palettes so they display colors from the Web palette only. Then the colors will still show up when they are displayed on a system with an 8-bit monitor. Choose Window/Show Color; then choose Web Color Sliders and Make Ramp Web Safe from the Color palette's pop-up menu. Now bring up your Swatches palette, Window/Show Swatches, and choose Replace swatches from its menu. Load the Web colors in the Swatches palette by choosing Adobe Photoshop 5.5/Goodies/Color Swatches/Web Hues.aco.

Press TAB to get rid of your palettes, F for Full Screen Mode, then Command-Option-0 to zoom into 100%, and finally Command-R to bring up the Rulers. It's nice that many of these keyboard shortcuts work the same way in both ImageReady and Photoshop. Beware that not all of them do, however, and the most irritating one for old-time Photoshop users is that Command-Z in ImageReady does not toggle back and forth between Undo and Redo like Photoshop always has and still does in version 5.5. In ImageReady, repeated Command-Zs march back up the History palette, undoing state after state as they go. If this happens to you, as it did to me, just bring up the History palette and click back to where you wanted to be in the Undo state. In this brave new ImageReady world, Undo is still Command-Z but Redo is now Command-Shift-Z, and if you want to continue to toggle back and forth between Undo and Redo, that is now Command-Option-Z. This toggling seems to happen much slower than the old, Command-Z, Command-Z, Command-Z, etc. in Photoshop.

STEP 2: Choose View/Show Guides and also View/Snap to Guides. Choose Window/Show Info. We are going to add some guides that will help us line things up. Using the Move tool (V), click in the vertical ruler and drag out to the right until your first guide lines up at X value 8. You can see the location of the guide in the Info window as you move the guide. Go back to the vertical ruler again, click down and drag out another guide, then place it at X position 168. This creates an 8-pixel border area on the left edge, then another area that is 160 pixels wide. We'll now create a 2-pixel border between this 160-pixel column and the next, so drag the next guide to position 170. The fourth guide goes at X value 170 + 160 = 330, and then put the fifth one at 332. Now put the final guide at 332+160 = 492. Now we'll place some horizontal guides. Click in the top horizontal ruler and drag down until you reach Y value 40; then release to place a horizontal guide there. Drag the next horizontal guide down to Y value 200, and then drag one down to Y value 202 and then another to 362. If you want to make sure your guides are in the right place, you can use Com-

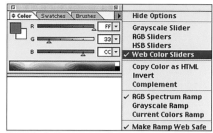

STEP 1: Setting up your Color palette for Web safe colors.

STEP 1: Setting up your Swatches palette for Web safe colors. Use Replace Swatches from the Swatches palette pop-up menu; then choose the file Web Hues.aco.

STEP 1: Creating the new 500 by 375 pixel document with a black background.

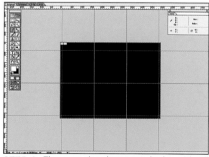

STEP 2: The way the document looks with all guides in place.

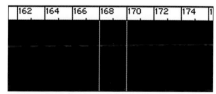

STEP 2: Zooming in on rulers to double check the guide locations.

371

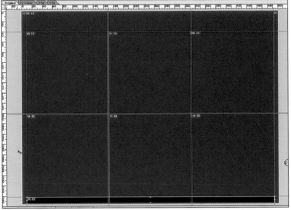

STEP 3: The document with all slices in place. Notice how when you are in Full Screen Mode you see the status bar at the bottom of your screen. Make sure you don't cover that with a palette during a Save, Save Optimized or Preview In Browser. Without seeing progress within that lower progress bar, you may actually think ImageReady has crashed. That blue strip progressing, sometimes very slowly, from left to right is the only sign that ImageReady has not crashed. We need better feedback from this program, Adobe, during its long calculations, or whatever it is doing!

STEP 3: The Slice Tool in the Tool palette.

STEP 4: The Rectangle tool in the Tool palette.

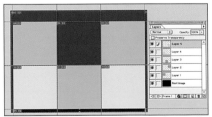

STEP 4: Your document and Layers palette at the end of Step 4.

mand-Spacebar-Click and drag to zoom up on the rulers at a high magnification and check the locations of the guides against the edges of the rulers.

CREATING YOUR SLICES

STEP 3: Choose the Slice tool from the Tool palette (it looks like an Exacto knife). You will use it to divide this image into 15 slices. Slices are areas on this, or any, Web page that each have a different purpose and can also each be Optimized in its own way. Each slice may contain a rollover or animation, or just some text or an image. A slice can also be a No Image slice like the borders will be. With the Slice tool, click in the top left corner and drag a skinny vertical slice down to the bottom left corner but over 8 pixels to that first vertical guide. This will be slice 1. You will notice that ImageReady has already positioned the starting place for slice 2 at the top to the right of slice 1. Click at the top just to the right of that first vertical guide and drag down and to the right until you reach the corner where the first horizontal guide and last vertical guide meet. This should be X value 492, Y value 40 (492,40). This is the bottom right of slice 2. Slice 3 will be the long vertical strip going from top to bottom of the image on the right side. Go ahead and create slice 3. Now slice 4 should be positioned at the top left corner at 8,40. Drag slice 4 down to the bottom right of this 160x160 box with its bottom right corner at 168,200. Slice 5 goes from a top left of 168,40 down to a bottom right of 170,200. Slice 6 coordinates are top left of 170,40 and bottom right of 330,200. Slice 7 is 330,40..332,200. Slice 8 is 332,40..492,200. Slice 9 is a long skinny horizontal slice from 8,200..492,202. Now slice 10 starts the bottom row of bigger boxes with positions 8,202..168,362. Slice 11 is 168,202..170,362. Slice 12 is 170,202..330,362, and slice 13 is 330,202..332,362. Slice 14 is 332,202..492,362 and, finally, slice 15, along the bottom is, 8,362..492,375.

STEP 4: Choose File/Save As and save this document as ImageReadyDemo on one of your local hard disks. Use Window/Show Layers to bring up the Layers palette and double click on the initial layer to rename it to Root Image. ImageReady doesn't have a *Background* layer; all layers are normal Photoshop style layers! Far Out!!! In the Tool palette, choose the Rectangle tool (U); then click on the foreground color and use the Hexadecimal box at the bottom right of the ImageReady Color Picker to enter the color 6699CC, a darker blue. Now use the guides to create a blue box, which will actually be a separate layer exactly within the area of slice 4, the top left, large 160-pixel square box. Make a similar box exactly inside slice 8 on the top right and another inside slice 12 at the bottom in the middle. Each of these areas will represent a different main section of my *Photoshop 5 & 5.5 Artistry* book. Click on the foreground color, or use Window/Show Color to bring up the Color palette; then choose 99CCFF,

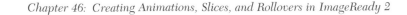

STEP 5: The ImageReady Type palette. The controls from top left are: Type Size, Leading, Kerning, Tracking and Baseline Shift at the bottom left. Notice the anti-aliasing options, aa, at the bottom right. You have the choise of None, Crisp, Strong and Smooth, but we'll leave it at the default, Crisp, for now.

Chapter 46: Creating Animations, Slices, and Rollovers in ImageReady 2

which is a lighter blue. Use the same Rectangle tool to draw similar light blue squares in slices 10 and 14.

ADDING THE TEXT INFORMATION

STEP 5: Click on the foreground color and set it to 6699CC. Type a T to choose the Type tool, Click the cursor over the top left blue box, then type the words "Things You Need to Know", the name of the first section of Photoshop 5 & 5.5 Artistry. Use Window/Show Type to bring up the Type palette and then select all the type you just entered by dragging across it. I chose 30 px (pixel) Orbon ITC Bold as the font, but you may not have that font so choose something similar. Notice how you can now modify the Leading, Tracking and Kerning using the pop-ups within the Type palette. Choose Show Options from the Type palette menu, and you can also modify the Baseline Shift. I set the Leading to 30 and the Tracking to 10. Use Window/Show Layers to bring up the Layers palette and notice that you now have a layer for each of the blue boxes, and then on top there is a type layer called Things You Need to Know. Choose Layer/Effects/Outer Glow and set the Opacity and Intensity values in the Outer Glow palette each to 75 and the Blur value to 5. Click on the Color box and set the color of this glow to FFFF00, a bright yellow. Now turn off the Eye icon to the left of this effect within the Layers palette. That will turn off the effect for the Normal Rollover state, we will use it later in the Over RollOver effect.

STEP 6: The Demo after all the main type is added.

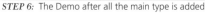

STEP 6: The Slice Select tool (A).

We just added it to this type layer for now so it will also be in all the copied type layers we are now going to make. For each of the other four blue boxes, you now need to copy this type layer by dragging it down to the New Layer icon at the bottom of the Layers palette. Then use the Move tool (V) to drag that copy over the top of the perspective blue box on the screen, and use the Type tool to select and change the actual type displayed over each box. Once you have changed the type, double click on its layer and also change the name of that layer to be the same as the type. When you are finished, your screen should look like the illustration here and you should now have a Layers palette like the one pictured here. Use the illustration at the right to see what type needs to be added over each box. Actually, we still need to add a few type items in step 6 that are pictured on these screens, but they will give you the idea.

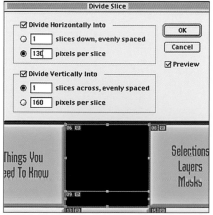

STEP 6: Dividing Slice 6 into two slices. Choose the pixels per slice option; then type 130 which will be the size of the top slice.

STEP 6: Click in the foreground color and change it to FF0000, a bright red. Now click down with the Type tool at the top center of the screen, within Slice 2, and type the words "Photoshop 5&5.5 Artistry". Now select all this type with the Type tool and use the Type palette to change its size to 34 px and its tracking to 30. Select the 5&5.5 part and change its tracking to -10. Select just the & character and change its size to 17 px and its Baseline Shift to 6. To access Baseline Shift in the Type palette, choose Show Options from it's menu. Now choose the Slice Select Tool and click on the top

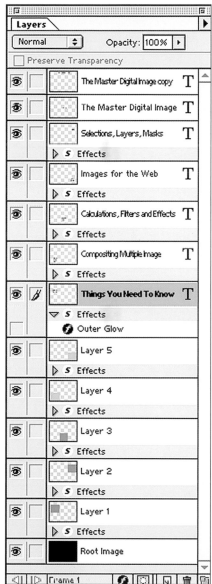

STEP 6: The Layers palette after all the blue boxes and the type are added.

373

middle 160x160 slice, slice number 6, which is the box that is still black. Choose Slices/Divide Slice from the main menu bar and choose the Divide Horizontally Into option and choose pixels per slice under that. Type 130 into the box to the left of the words pixels per slice. This will make the top slice, still number 6, be 130 pixels high and will create a new 30-pixel-high slice, now number 9, below the now shorter slice 6. Slices with numbers greater than 9 now get renumbered. Click in the foreground color and set it to FF6633, a bright orange. Go back to the type tool (T) and click down in the middle of the area of this new slice number 9. Set the type size to 24 px (or a size that allows your text to stay within this slice) with the tracking set to 10. Type the words "The Master Digital Image", which will represent the animation that will appear within slice 6 above. You have now entered all the text that will appear on the screen during all the non-rollover states.

STEP 7: Choose File/Save As and save your document as ImageReadyDemo1. After doing that, turn off the Eye icons in the Layers palette for all the text layers. The Eye icons should now be on for just the five blue boxes and also the Root Image layer. Click on the Root Image layer, at the bottom of the palette, to make it the active layer and then choose Merge Visible from the Layers palette pop-up menu. We do this to simplify the layer setup now, before we start to add rollover effects and animations to the demo. This will limit the number of layers that each animation frame and rollover needs to keep track of, and it will also simplify the Layers palette for us. After doing that, turn on the Eye icons again for all the rest of the layers; then do a File/Save As again and save this as ImageReadyDemo2. That way if you make a mistake when compressing layers, you can always go back to that earlier version and start over will all your layers still intact.

CREATING THE FIRST ANIMATION

STEP 8: Switch to Photoshop 5.5 and open the file GrandCanyonPCDRaw.psd from the Photoshop 5 Artistry CD folder 19. Crop only the copyright info from the bottom of the file; do not crop anything from the top or sides of the image. Now open GrandCanAfterLevels from inside the Extra Info Files folder within folder 19. Type a V to get the Move tool and then with the Shift key down the entire time, drag and drop this image on top of the original image in the first file. Make sure you release the mouse button before releasing the Shift key. This will add the image after the Levels adjustments that were applied as a second layer above the original scan below. The Shift key will center this new file, which should line it up correctly with the original. To check to see whether the two files are lined up, type Command-I to invert the top layer; then type a 5 to set the opacity to 50%. You should see a gray image on your screen with no embossed edges. Since you are still in the Move tool, pressing on an arrow key will move the top layer by one pixel and you should now see an embossed look, showing you that the two layers are not lined up. If you initially see the embossed look, then your layers were not lined up to start with and you should move that top layer with the arrow keys one pixel at a time until the embossed look goes away. At that point the two layers will be exactly aligned and you can type a zero to set the opacity of the top layer back to 100%, then Command-I to reinvert it to a positive. That is a great technique for lining up any two scans of the same original or two different shots of the same scene. Now open the file GrandCanAfterLev&HS and add it to the top of the previous two. Use the same technique to make sure it is correctly lined up with the layer below. Now open and add GrandCanAfter-LevHS&Curves at the very top and also make sure it is aligned.

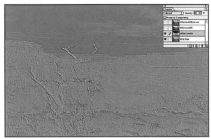

STEP 8: If the two layers are not lined up, they will look embossed like this after setting the top layer at 50% Opacity and Inverting it.

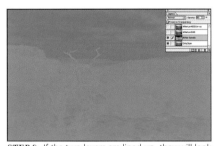

STEP 8: If the two layers are lined up, they will look smooth like this after setting the top layer at 50% Opacity and Inverting it.

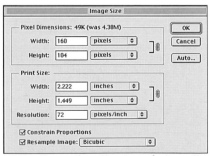
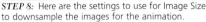

STEP 8: Here are the settings to use for Image Size to downsample the images for the animation.

We are going to make an animation showing how this image progresses as we color correct it. Choose File/Save As and save this file as GrandCanyonSandwich in case we have to go back to it later. Type an M to switch to the Marquee tool, so you don't accidentally move any of the layers with the Move tool. I hope Photoshop 6 adds a feature to lock each layer so you can't accidentally move it! Now go to Image/Image Size (F7) and resample this image so the pixel width is 160 and the dpi is 72. Use Filter/Sharpen/Unsharp mask to sharpen the top layer by 200,.5,0. You want to sharpen each layer to compensate for sampling the file down but not so much that it looks like the final sharpening. Now click on each of the three layers below; then type Command-F, which will sharpen that layer the same amount. Now click back on the top layer and make a copy of it, calling the copy AfterFinalSharpen. Sharpen that top layer by an additional 120,.5,3. Make sure the layers in this file are named, from bottom to top, Orig Scan, After Levels, AfterLev&HS, AfterLevHS&Curves and AfterFinalSharpen. Now we have the files that will be the source for our animation, so save this resampled and sharpened file as GrandCanSandSmall.psd.

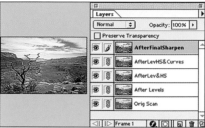

STEP 9: All the small Grand Canyon layers after linking them together.

STEP 9: Close this file from Photoshop, and then go back to ImageReady and choose View/Show Guides to make sure your guides are up. Use Command-SpaceBar-Click to zoom into 200% centered on slice 6, then choose Hide Slices from the Slices menu if the Slices are currently visible. You are going to create an animation within this slice. Click on the top layer in the Layers palette to make sure it is now active. Now choose File/Open and open the GrandCanSandSmall.psd file you just created within Photoshop. Click on the middle column within each layer in the Layers palette to link all the layers. Now use the Move tool (V) to drag and drop all these layers from this document onto your ImageReadyDemo2 document. Just click down on top of the GrandCanyon image area; then hold, drag and release when the cursor is on top of the ImageReadyDemo2 image area. You should see all five of the Grand-Canyon layers added to the top of your ImageReady2 Layer palette. Use the Move tool to drag the grandcanyon layers so their top left corner is exactly in the top left corner of slice 6. Having the Guides visible and also having Snap to Guides turned on will make lining this up correctly quite easy. The grandcanyon layers should be exactly the 160-pixel width of this slice. Now you can go back to the Grand-CanSandSmall file and close it (Command-W).

STEP 10: ImageReady Layers palette and screen after adding the "The Original Scan" text layer.

STEP 10: ImageReady Layers palette and screen after adding all the grand canyon animation text layers.

ADDING TEXT TITLES TO THE ANIMATION

STEP 10: Type an F to make sure you are in Full screen mode, then turn off the Eye Icons of the top 4 GrandCanyon layers, and then click on the Orig Scan layer within the Layers palette. Type a D for default colors, then an X to exchange the colors, and make the Foreground color white. Set the type size in the Type dialog to 20 px with the tracking set to 10; then click down on the image in the black area in the center below the grand canyon photo and above the orange "The Master Digital Image" on the screen and type the words "The Original Scan". Use the Move tool to center this text and notice that it has created a new layer above the Orig Scan layer in the Layers palette. Now click on the After Levels layer above that to make it visible and active; then turn off the Eye icon on The Original Scan type layer you just created. Now use the Type tool again to create another text layer above the After Levels layer saying "After Levels Adjustments". Use the Move tool again to line that up correctly. Repeat this process adding a "Adding Hue & Saturation" text layer above the After Lev&HS layer, then adding a "A Curve to Pop Greens" text layer above the After-LevHS&Curves layer and finally adding a "After Final Sharpening" text layer above the AfterFinalSharpen layer. For each one of these new layers, it is actually faster

375

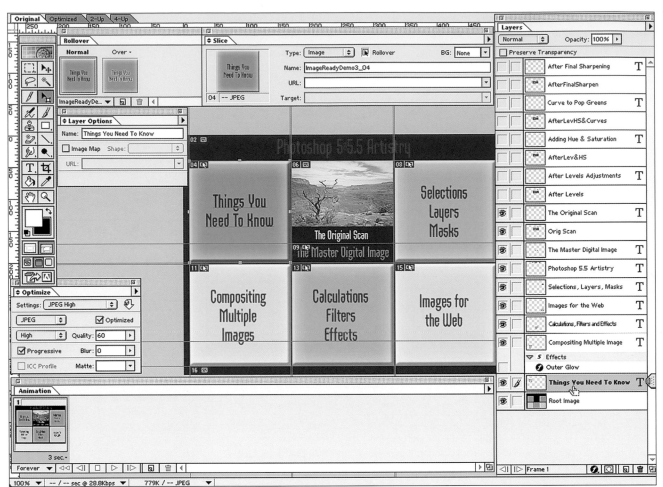

STEP 11: This palette layout worked well for me when working with the Animation, Rollover, Slices and Layers palettes all at the same time and also trying to see the Web page I'm working on. I typed F, for Full Screen Mode, which centered my image on the screen, and also used Command-Option-0 (Zero) to zoom the page into 100%.

and more accurate if you just copy the previous text layer and turn the Eye icon off for that previous layer, drag the new layer up one layer in the Layers palette, and then select and rename the text on that new layer. You then have to double click on the layer itself, within the Layers palette, and give it the correct name. Doing it this way keeps all the text layers aligned and centered correctly and keeps the font info and text color the same. Do a File/Save to save this file and all the progress you have made so far. Now do a File/Save As ImageReady3.psd to save the file again with a different name. Future progress on this project will now continue using the ImageReadyDemo3.psd version of the file so that way if we mess this file up, we can go back to the ImageReady2.psd version and we don't have to start over from the beginning.

ADDING ROLLOVER STATES TO THE TEXT AREAS

STEP 11: Now we'll go ahead and make the rollover states for the text on each of the five blue box slice areas. Use Window/Show Slice to bring up the Slices palette and Window/Show Rollover to bring up the Rollover palette. Choose the Slice Select tool (A) from the Tool palette; then Click on slice 4 in the the top left corner and then also click on the Things You Need to Know layer in the Layers palette to activate that

Chapter 46: Creating Animations, Slices, and Rollovers in ImageReady 2

layer. You may want to arrange your file and palettes as you see them in the illustration here so you can see what is happening in each all the time. In the Rollover palette, choose New State from the pop-up menu or just click on the new Rollover icon to the left of the Trash icon at the bottom of the palette. This will create a new Rollover state of type Over, which will cause the image within this slice, and anywhere else on the screen for that matter, to change so you can see the currently visible layers in the Layers palette whenever the mouse cursor is moved over this slice. Go to Layer/Effects Outer Glow and set the Opacity and Intensity of the glow to 75, set the color to FFFF00, a bright yellow, and the Blur to 5. The Blend Mode should be set to Screen. If this Outer Glow effect is still available below your text layer, you can just turn its Eye icon back on. Notice that this effect highlights the text slightly after adding it to the Things You Need to Know Text layer. Choose Layer/Effects/Copy Effect to copy this effect; then click back on the Normal state for this slice within the Rollover palette. You want to return this slice to the Normal state so that when you set the Over state for one of the other slices, this slice appears normal within that other slice's Over state. Now click on slice 11, called Compositing Multiple Images, below this one and also click on the Compositing Multiple Images layer in the Layers palette. Use the Rollover palette to add an Over state to that slice; then choose Layer/Effects/Paste Effects to add the same highlight effect to this text or just turn the effects Eye icon back on if it is still there from earlier. Remember to click back on the Normal state within the Rollover palette; then go on to add this same Over effect to the correct layer for each of slices 8, 13 and 15. When you have finished, click on slice 9, create an Over state for it; then choose Layer/Effects/Color Fill and change the color within the Color Fill palette to FF0000, a bright red. This text will now glow bright red when the cursor comes over the top of it. Remember to click on the Normal state for this slice before moving on to the next step.

STEP 12: Choose File/HTML Background and set the color to black. This just sets the background color of HTML files your create. Notice that the HTML Background dialog also allows you to choose an Image as the background for your HTML files. We won't use that feature this time. Now go to File/Preview/choose whatever browser you use. I'm currently using Netscape Communicator 4.51, so my menu will say File/Preview/Netscape Communicator. You should now check out the functionality of ImageReadyDemo3 within your browser and then go back and fix any problems you find within this ImageReady document. As you move the cursor over each blue box area, the text on that box should go into the highlighted Over state until you move the cursor off that area again. Once you have your Rollover states working correctly, we'll turn the Grand Canyon sequence into an animation.

STEP 12: Here we see the state of all the palettes after the 5 main animation frames are created.

Click on slice 6 with the Slice Select Tool (A). Click on the Orig Scan layer in the Layers palette to activate it and make sure that the Eye icon is also on for the "The Original Scan" text layer above it. The rest of the slices should appear in their Normal state at this time. This will be frame 1 of your animation. Use the little Frame Delay pop-up menu, in the bottom right of this frame's icon in the Animation palette, to set the frame delay time for this frame to 3 seconds. Now choose New Frame from the Animation palette pop-up or click the New Frame icon at the bottom of the Animation palette. This will create a second frame to the right of the first, and it will start out being a copy of the first frame. We now need to turn on the layers that will be visible during this second frame. Turn off the Eye icons for the Orig Scan layer and also for the "The Original Scan" text layer; then turn on the Eye icons for the After Levels layer and the "After Levels Adjustment" text layer. That is what is different about the appearance of frame 2 in this animation. Now create a third frame by clicking on the New Frame icon in the Animation palette and for this frame turn off the Eye icons for the After Levels layer and the "After Levels Adjustment" text layer. Turn on the Eye icons for the AfterLev&HS layer and the "Adding Hue & Saturation" text layer. Notice that the second and third frames already have their Frame Delay times set to 3 seconds because they were initially copies of the first frame. Now make a fourth frame in the same way, turn off the Eye icons for the AfterLev&HS layer and the "Adding Hue & Saturation" text layer, and turn on the Eye icons for the AfterLevHS&Curve layer and for the "Add Curve to Pop Greens" text layer. Finally add a fifth animation frame, turn off the Eye icons for the After-LevHS&Curve layer and the "Add Curve to Pop Greens" text layer, and turn on the Eye icons for the After Final Sharpen layer and the "After Final Sharpen" text layer. You now have the five main frames of your animation, but it won't be very animated because each of those frames will play for 3 seconds before moving on to the next.

TWEENING FRAMES INTO THE ANIMATION

STEP 13: Using the Slice Selection tool, click on slice 6 to make sure it is the current slice. Now click in frame 1, the leftmost frame, in the Animation palette. The Rollover palette should be in the Normal state for this slice. Click on the Orig Scan layer in the Layers palette to make sure it is the active layer within this frame. Now click on frame 2, to the right of frame 1, in the Animation palette and make the After Levels layer the active layer for this frame. Click back on frame 1 in the Animation palette; then choose Tween from the Animation palette pop-up menu. Tweening will allow you to automatically create frames between the existing frame 1 and frame 2 that will animate the state change between those two frames. Within the Tween dialog, choose All Layers, because you want to transition all the layers of each existing state, and also choose to tween the Opacity and Effects but not the Position. This will blend the way the two images look but not the location of the two images because they are actually already aligned. Set frames to add to 3, which will add three frames between the current frame 1 and frame 2, and you are going to Tween with the Next Frame. Choose OK and notice the added frames. Now click back into frame 1; then click on the right arrow with the vertical bar to the left of it, the Select Next Frame icon, at the bottom of the Animation palette. This will advance to the next frame. Advance through the sequence and notice how the image slowly transforms from looking like frame 1 into looking like frame 5, which is the original frame 2. Notice, though, that frames 2-4 are dull looking compared with either frame 1 or 5. This is not what we want.

STEP 14: Let's click on frame 2 and see what the Tween actually did. With frame 2 active, notice that the Opacity of the Orig Scan layer has been changed to 75% and the Opacity of the Levels Adjustment layer has been changed to 25%. I noticed that if I changed the Opacity of the Orig Scan Layer back to 100% that the effect worked better because then the new colors look more like they are being added to what was already there. In the Layers palette, change the Opacity of the Orig Scan layer back to 100%, just type a 0, and also turn off the Eye icon for The Orig Scan text layer so we no longer see this text in frame 2. Both the Levels Adjustment layer and the After Levels Adjustment text layer should still be set to 25% Opacity. Use the frame delay

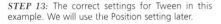

STEP 13: The correct settings for Tween in this example. We will use the Position setting later.

Chapter 46: Creating Animations, Slices, and Rollovers in ImageReady 2

time pop-up at the bottom right of the frame 2 area to set the delay time for this frame to .2 seconds. Now move on to frame 3 and in that frame, turn off the Eye icon for the The Orig Scan text layer, set the opacity for the Orig Scan layer to 100% and set the frame delay time to .2 seconds. Now move to frame 4, turn the Eye Icon off for the The Orig Scan text layer and set the opacity for the Orig Scan layer to 100% and set the delay time for this frame to .2 seconds.

STEP 15: Now click on frame 5 in the Animation palette. We are going to tween it with frame 6. Select Tween from the Animation palette and choose the same settings you did before. Set the Frame Delay time in each of the new frames 6, 7 & 8 to .2 seconds and also turn off the Eye icon for the After Levels Adjustment text layer and set the Opacity for the Levels Adjustment layer to 100% within each of those three frames. Now click on frame 9 and add a similar 3 frames between frames 9 and 10 except this time you will be turning off the Adding Hue & Saturation text layer and setting the Opacity of the After Lev&HS layer to 100%. Now click on frame 13 and Tween it with frame 14. In the new tweened frames 14, 15 & 16 you'll be setting the Opacity of the AfterLevHS&Curve layer to 100%, turning the Eye icon off for the Curve to Pop Greens text layer and setting each frame's delay time to .2 seconds. You should now have a total of 17 frames in your animation.

OPTIMIZING EACH SLICE WITHIN YOUR PAGE

STEP 16: Press the TAB key to get rid of most of your palettes; then bring up the Optimize palette and set it to GIF, 128 colors, Adaptive palette, Lossy at 25 and Diffusion Dither at 100%. Now click on the 2-Up tab at the top of the screen to see the Original image on the left and the optimized one on the right. You'll notice, by looking at the bottom left corner of the rightmost optimized area that with these settings it will take about 149k to compress this entire animation. If you play with the GIF settings, you'll notice that this size value, and the quality of the image, changes as you go. These settings seemed to make the image look good, but this animation is still larger than I would like. Using the Slice Selection tool, you can click on each slice and give it the Optimization settings you think will make it look the best and also compress that slice the most. This slice 6 has to be a GIF because

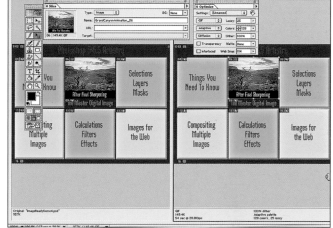

STEP 16: With the 2-Up view, you can see the original image on the left and compare that with the optimized version on the right. Adjust the Optimization settings for each slice until the size of that slice, at the bottom left of the righthand Optimize view, seems good and the slice also looks good on the screen. The Slice palette allows you to name the slice if you want, enter a HTML tag in the URL box if you want to jump to a URL when the slice is clicked, set a background color for the slice, and also set the Type to No Image if that slice doesn't contain an image.

it contains an animation. Bring up the Slices palette and notice that you can give each slice a Name and also enter a HTML address for each slice if you want to link a click on that slice with a jump to another Web page. In the Animation palette, return to frame 1 by clicking on frame 1. After doing that, go to each slice, set its Optimization settings and also give that slice a name if you would like. Each Slice has one possible Optimization setting for the entire slice, not one for each rollover state of each slice. Within the Slice palette, set the Slice Type on slices 1, 3, 5, 7, 10, 12, 14 and 16 to No Image, because those slices are just fillers. Set their Optimize settings to GIF, 2 Colors, No Dither, Adaptive palette. For slice 2, the title at the top of the Web page, the GIF 32 Dithered choice from the Settings menu seems to work well. For slices 4, 8, 11, 13 & 15, set Optimization to GIF 64 Dithered, because GIF 32 Dithered for those slices doesn't provide enough color variation to do the shading on the blue buttons without a noticeable stepping in the colors. Note that you can select multiple slices by holding down the Shift key when using the Slice Select tool.

CLEANING UP THE ANIMATION AND ROLLOVER INTERACTIONS

STEP 17: The idea for this page is that each of the six sections, representing the six major parts of my book, will have something to demonstrate what you learn in that part. The Master Digital Image part, the top middle section, is an animation of color correction that I want to play all the time. When you move the cursor over one of the other five sections, the text should highlight while the animation in the top middle section (call this the Master Image section) continues to play, and that text should stay highlighted as long as the cursor stays over that section. You will probably notice that the highlighting of the text in the other five sections is not currently working correctly. You will also notice that when you put the cursor over one of those five sections, the animation in the Master Image section goes back to the starting point. We need to fix these problems. Using the Slice Selection tool, click on the Master Image section, slice 6. Go to the Animation palette and choose Select All Frames from the palette's pop-up menu. Now choose Copy Frames from that same menu. Now choose the Things You Need to Know slice, slice 4 at the top left. In the Rollover palette, click on the Over state to select that state; then go back to the Animation palette and choose Paste Frames. This will paste the entire animation of the Master Image slice into the Over state of the Things You Need to Know slice. We want that animation to continue until we actually click down on the Things You Need to Know slice. Notice that doing the Paste Frames has caused a copy of the Things You Need to Know text layer to be placed at the top of the Layers palette. That is because the Animation we just pasted would have caused that layer to be hidden during parts of the animation, which would make your text highlight in this slice go away. When I did this though, the text effect that caused the highlight was not copied by ImageReady into this new layer. Click on the Things You Need to Know Text layer toward the bottom of the Layers palette; then go to Layer/Effects/Copy effects to copy the Outer Glow Effect from that original layer. Click back on the new Things You Need to Know Text layer that was added at the top of the Layers palette, to make it active; then choose Layer/Effects/Paste Effects to copy the effect up there also. Now go to the Animation palette and choose Match Layer Across Frames, from the palette's pop-up menu, to add the text highlight across all the frames of this version of the animation. After finishing this, click back in the Normal state within the Rollover palette so the change to the next slice will happen with this slice looking normal.

When you are working with this type of project, you have to be very careful what state you leave slice A in before you go and modify slice B; otherwise, slice A looks wrong when you are operating within the rollover state of slice B. Now click on the Compostiing Multiple Images slice to make the analogous changes there. First click into the Over state in the Rollover palette and then choose Paste Frames in the Animation palette; the Frames should still be available. Next, click on the new copy of the Compositing Multiple Images text layer in the Layers palette and do Layer/Effects/Paste Effects to copy the text highlight effect, which should also still be in the copy buffer. Now choose Match Layer Across Frames to copy that highlight effect across all the frames in this rollover state. Now click on the Normal rollover state in the Rollover palette. Go ahead and do these same steps for the other three blue box slices. Do a File/Save As ImageReadyDemo4. Do a File/Save Optimized as ImageReadyDemo4.html and click on the Saving Files Options; then within that, choose Put Images In Subfolder and name the folder IRD4-Images. This will save your document as an HTML file along with a folder containing all the required images. You can now open that HTML file into your browser (I use Open/Page In Navigator with Netscape) to check it out. This does a similar thing as File/Preview

In, but the files are left on your hard disk for your inspection after your browser is finished with them. You can look at the animations and images and see exactly what gets generated. You can also then edit the HTML file to add your own customizations.

ADDING A SECOND ANIMATION TO ANIMATE POSITION

STEP 18: Now we are going to add a different animation to the Things You Need to Know slice. Go into Photoshop 5.5 and make screen grabs of the Tool palette, the File/Color Settings/RBG Setup dialog, the Actions palette, the File/Color Settings/Profile Setup dialog, and the New Adjustment Layer dialog. These represent some of the things you learn about in the Things You Need To Know part of my book. On the Mac you can do a screen grab of a palette by choosing Command-Shift 4 and then drawing a box around the palette. Command-Shift-3 on the Mac does a screen grab of the entire screen, including the cursor. These are saved in PICT file format on your boot drive as Picture 1, Picture 2, etc. These files can then be opened into Photoshop, but you want to either drag them onto a Photoshop alias icon on your desktop or open them using the File/Open dialog within Photoshop. If you double click on one of these Picts, it may open into Simpletext. If you are using Windows, you use the PrintScreen key to get a screen grab of the current screen. On my Windows keyboard, there is actually a button, to the right of the main keyboard buttons at the top, called PrintScreen. The PrintScreen on my WindowsNT puts the screen grab into the copy buffer, so to get it into Photoshop on Windows, you can just do a Paste. Choosing File/New will give you the correct dimensions for the grab, since it's in the copy buffer; Return (or Enter) followed by Paste then gives you the screen grab within a new file.

STEP 19: Open all your screen grabs into Photoshop 5.5; then go to File/New and make a new file that is 160 pixels wide by 160 pixels high at 72 dpi. Type an F to put this file into Full Screen Mode. Click on the foreground color and use the HEX color entry box at the bottom right of the Color Picker to set it to C0C0C0, a neutral gray. Now choose Edit/Fill (Shift-Delete) and fill the layer with that color. Double click on the *Background* layer and name it gray. Use File/Save As to save this file as ThingsYouNeedToKnow.psd. Now use the Move tool (V) to drag and drop the screen grab of the Tool palette onto the file you just saved. This will create a new layer on top of the Gray layer. Double click on this layer and name it All Grabs. We are actually going to put all the screen grabs within this one layer on top of another vertically. With the Move tool, drag the Tool palette down within this layer until the top of the Tool palette is just below the visible part of the layer, i.e. below the window. The layer is now filled

STEP 19: If the Canvas of the All Grabs layer were bigger, the layer would look like this.

STEP 19: This is the way the ThingsYouNeedTo-Know file should look when you are done with it and save it. When you drag down on the All Grabs layer at this point, or use the downarrow key, all the grabs should slowly scroll by as partially illustrated by the image below.

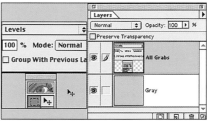

STEP 19: Here we see the All Grabs layer after its position has been moved down a bit by the Move tool. The next grab, of the Adjustment Layer dialog, is right on top of the Tool palette grab and on top of that will be the next grab, etc. I hope you can see what is supposed to happen with this file.

with transparency but the Tool palette is still there outside the visible area. If you did a Select All and then a Crop, the Tool palette would be entirely cropped out. Don't do that! Now drag and drop the next screen grab, for example the Adjustment Layer dialog, onto this document. It will come in as a new layer above the All Grabs layer. Use the Move tool to move this grab so that the bottom of it sits at the bottom of the visible area in the window. Now choose Merge Down from the Layers palette to Merge this down into the All Grabs layer. Use the Move tool to again Move this palette down so the top of it is just below the visible area, like you did with the Tool palette before. They are now both in this layer with the Tool palette vertically below the Adjustment Layer dialog. Now drag a third screen grab onto this document. Use the Move tool to align its bottom edge at the bottom of the viewable area; then do another Merge Down to integrate this into that same layer. Continue this process until this All Grabs layer contains all the screen grabs stacked one on top of another. Now take the Move tool and drag the layer up until the visible part of the layer again shows the Tool palette and actually the bottom part of the Tool palette. You'll be able to see the gray area in the Layer below on either side of the Tool palette. With the All Grabs layer active and while you are in the Move tool (V), you should now be able to hold down the down arrow key on you keyboard and see all the screen grabs scroll by as the Move tool moves the layer across the visible part of the window. Holding the Shift key down along with the down arrow makes this happen more quickly. This is similar to the effect we are now going to achieve with the animation of this slice. It would be a good idea to save the file at this point!

STEP 20: Switch back to ImageReady and click on slice 4, with the Slice Select tool. This is the Things You Need To Know slice, and we are going to add an animation to it that will happen when you click down on this slice. Click on the New State icon at the bottom of the Rollover palette or choose New State from its pop-up menu. Because you already have a Normal and Over rollover state, this new state will automatically be set to Down. You could change that with the pop-up where you see Down, but don't. Now switch to the Animation palette and choose Delete Animation from its menu to delete the animation that is already there in this state. This animation was just copied from the Normal state when you created a new state. In the Layers palette, click on the topmost layer to make it active. Use File/Open to open the ThingsYouNeedToKnow.psd file, which you just made in Photoshop, into ImageReady. Click on the All Grabs layer to make it active; then click on the linking column of the Gray layer, the middle column in the Layers palette, to link the two layers. Use the Move tool (V) to drag and drop these two layers onto your ImageReadyDemo4 document. They should show up at the top of the Layers palette. Choose View/Show Guides to turn on your guides and make sure View/Snap to Guides is turned on. Now drag the two layers, within the document window, until they line up exactly over the ThingsYouNeeToKnow slice, slice 4. When you get it into place, the Tool palette will be bleeding out the top of your view area, because this document has a larger canvas than the ThingsYouNeedToKnow.psd file did. Choose Select/Create Selection from Slice to get a selection exactly around the edge of this slice. Now choose Layer/Add Layer Mask/Reveal Selection from the main Layer

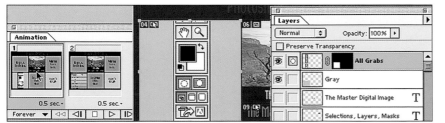

STEP 20: Here we see everything as it should look when Frame 1 of the animation is complete. Notice that we have now unlinked the Gray layer with the All Grabs layer so we can now move one without the other. In this Layer palette, we have not yet unlinked the All Grabs layer from the All Grabs layer mask, and actually, the Layer Mask is currently active.

Chapter 46: Creating Animations, Slices, and Rollovers in ImageReady 2

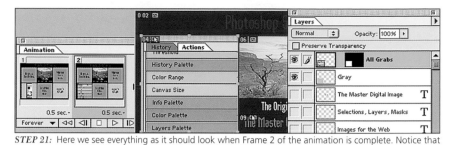

menu to add a layer mask to the All Grabs layer, which will only reveal the part within slice 4. This will now be frame 1 of your animation. Set the frame delay time to .5 seconds using the pop-up at the bottom right of the frame.

DOING THE POSITION TWEEN

STEP 21: In the Animation palette, click on the New Frame button to make frame 2 of your animation. In the Layers palette, click on the Layer thumbnail, the leftmost one, of the All Grabs layer. Now turn off the link, the icon between the Layer thumbnail and the Layer Mask thumbnail, between the layer and its mask. This will allow you to move the layer without moving the mask. Now click on the linking icon to the left of the Gray layer to unlink it so you can move the All Grabs layer without also moving the Gray layer. With the Move tool (V), drag the All Grabs layer down until you reach the top of all the screen grabs within that layer. This went faster on my machine after doing View/Hide Guides and also doing Slice/Hide Slices. I redid Slice/Show Slices when I was finished. We are now going to do a Tween between these two animation frames, so choose Tween from the Animation palette pop-up. Tween with the Previous Frame using Position only, adding 10 frames. See the Tween dialog settings here to the right. It may take ImageReady a while to add these frames depending on the amount of memory you give it and the speed of your processor. This type of project is obviously one that will encourage me to get a G4. I'm writing this on my Mac power PC 8600/300 and running Photoshop 5.5, ImageReady 2, Netscape, and QuarkXPress all at the same time. I've given ImageReady 125 megs or so of RAM, and it is slowing down quite a bit right now. I'll have to try this on my 550 Mhz AMD Athlon PC or my 350 Mhz G3 and see how it compares. More memory to ImageReady is probably the best solution. As I mentioned earlier, saving the document, quitting and then restarting ImageReady, and finally reopening the document may make things a lot faster with a fresh copy of ImageReady. I did that at the end of this step in the example, and the speed improvement was quite dramatic. When the new frames have been added, click back on the Normal state within the Rollover palette and then do a File/Save As ImageReadyDemo5.psd. If everything in the example works correctly within your browser at this point, you are really good at following directions and my directions pretty good, too. If something doesn't work properly, just remember that it is really easy to leave one of these palettes in the wrong state at some stage of the process and then you may get a different result. If that happens, look at what is happening on the screen of your browser and think about what state each slice needs to be in at that moment to get the behavior you desire. This will usually give you a hunch about what may be wrong and you can go back to ImageReady and find the problem.

OTHER THINGS ABOUT IMAGEREADY

STEP 22: Several Animation preference items can be important to set when working with ImageReady. One that may be important to set for a particular effect is the Frame Disposal Method. This decides if you should throw out the current frame in an animation before displaying the next frame. To set this for a particular frame in an animation, Control-Click on that frame within the Animation palette. The Restore to Background option will completely toss the current frame before displaying the

STEP 21: Here we see everything as it should look when Frame 2 of the animation is complete. Notice that we have now unlinked the Gray layer with the All Grabs layer so we can now move one without the other. We have now also unlinked the All Grabs layer mask with the All Grabs layer so we can move the layer without moving the mask. The layer and not the mask is now active.

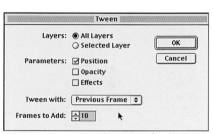

STEP 21: Here we see the settings for the Tween function choosing All Layers, Position, Previous Frame and the addition of 10 frames.

Other Things About ImageReady

next one. This will stop the current frame from appearing through any transparent areas of the next frame. If you use Restore to Background, you will see white, or the current background color, through those transparent areas. The Do Not Dispose option will leave the current frame visible as the next one is displayed so you will see the current frame through the transparent areas of the next frame. The Automatic option will automatically choose a method for each frame transition. Automatic will discard the current frame if the next frame contains any transparency; otherwise it won't do the discard. Within this example, I left the Frame Disposal Method set to Automatic.

Another thing to know about ImageReady is that Adjustment Layers can only be added in Photoshop, but they will remain when you open the file in ImageReady. For additional information about ImageReady, read the User Guide Supplement that comes with Adobe Photoshop 5.5 and ImageReady 2.0. It mentions most of the features, although it doesn't provide examples of all the ways each feature can be used. ImageReady, and Photoshop 5.5, also have an online help system that you can access from the Help menu. There are also demos, training sequences and further information that come on the Photoshop 5.5 CDs but don't all get installed when you install Photoshop 5.5 and ImageReady 2.0. Check our Web site, www.maxart.com, for additional and new update information about Photoshop, ImageReady and digital photography.

Chapter 46: Creating Animations, Slices, and Rollovers in ImageReady 2

Years of Print Display Before Noticeable Fading Occurs

For Members of the International Association of Fine Art Digital Printmakers
Distributed at the March 5–7, 1998 IAFADP Meeting in New York – Updated August 6, 1998

©1998 by Wilhelm Imaging Research, Inc.
Grinnell, Iowa 50112

(Inks and papers in this column are for use with Iris inkjet printers)

Iris Graphics Equipoise Ink Set

Arches Cold Press	32–36 years
Somerset Velvet Paper	20–24 years
Bulldog UG Canvas (Digital Pulse, Inc.)	18–22 years
Iris Canvas	16–18 years
Arches for Iris Paper	13–15 years
Liege Inkjet Fine Art Paper	2–3 years

Lyson Fine Arts Ink Set (FA-II M; ID C; FA-I Y+B)

Arches Cold Press	32–36 years
Somerset Velvet Paper	20–24 years
Arches for Iris Paper	20–24 years
Iris Canvas	10–12 years
Liege Inkjet Fine Art Paper	2–3 years

Lyson Fine Arts Inks with Prototype High-Stability Yellow

Arches Cold Press	(tests in preparation)
Somerset Velvet Paper	65–75 years
Arches for Iris Paper	(tests in preparation)
Iris Canvas	(tests in preparation)

ConeTech Wide Gamut Fine Art Ink Set

Somerset Velvet Paper	20–24 years

American Ink Jet Corp. "NE" Inks (C+M; Lyson FA-I Y+B)

Somerset Velvet Paper	4–6 years

American Ink Jet Corp. "NE" Inks (C+M; Iris ID Y+B)

Somerset Velvet Paper	3–5 years

Iris Graphics Industrial Design (ID) Ink Set

Arches Cold Press Paper	2–3 years [tentative]

Iris Equipoise Black Ink (Only) in Monochrome Prints

Arches Cold Press Paper	(tests continuing)	>100 years
Somerset Velvet Paper	(tests continuing)	>100 years
Arches for Iris Paper	(tests continuing)	>100 years
Iris Canvas	(tests continuing)	>100 years

ENCAD GO Ink Set (pigment-based inks)

ENCAD QIS Photo Glossy Paper	(tests continuing)	>100 years
ENCAD QIS Canvas	(tests continuing)	>100 years

ENCAD GA Ink Set (dye-based inks)

ENCAD QIS Photo Glossy Paper	
ENCAD QIS Canvas	1–2 years

ENCAD GS Ink Set (dye-based inks)

ENCAD QIS Photo Glossy Paper	1–2 years

Ilford Archiva Inks for ENCAD Printers (dye-based inks)

Ilford Ilfojet Photo Glossy Paper	70–80 years

Epson Stylus 3000 17x22-inch Printer (standard Epson inks)

Fuji Super Photo Grade Inkjet Paper	4–5 years
Epson Photo Quality Glossy White Film	2–3 years
Epson Photo Quality Glossy Paper	2 years
Epson Photo Quality Ink Jet Paper [matte]	1–2 years
Kodak Inkjet Photographic Quality Paper [new]	(being tested)
Kodak Photo Weight Premium Glossy Paper	6 months

Lysonic Inks for Epson Stylus 3000 Printer (prototype inks)

Various types of fine art & other media	(tests in preparation)

Current Photographic Color Negative Prints

Fujicolor Crystal Archive Paper	60 years*
Kodak Ektacolor Edge 7 and Royal VII Papers	18 years
Kodak Ektacolor Portra III Professional Paper	14 years
Konica Color QA Paper Type A7	14 years*
Agfacolor Paper Type 10	13 years

*Predictions integrated with manufacturer's Arrhenius dark storage data

Ilford Ilfochrome Silver Dye-Bleach Photographic Prints

Ilford Ilfochrome Classic Deluxe polyester-base	29 years**
Ilford Ilfochrome RC-base prints	29 years**

**Data based on tests completed in 1992 with Ilford Cibachrome (the former name of Ilfochrome) prints

Note: The display-life predictions given here were derived from accelerated glass-filtered fluorescent light fading tests conducted at 75°F and 60% RH and are based on the "standard" indoor display condition of 450 lux for 12 hours per day employed by Wilhelm Imaging Research, Inc. Illumination conditions in homes, offices, and galleries do vary, however, and color images will last longer when displayed under lower light levels; likewise, the life of prints will be shortened when displayed under illumination that is more intense than 450 lux. The predictions given here are the years of display required for specified, easily noticeable fading, changes in color balance, and/or staining to occur. These display-life predictions apply only to the specific ink and paper combinations listed. Print coatings tested to date have shown little if any benefit in terms of prolonging the display life of Iris inkjet prints (also known as Giclée prints); with some ink/paper/coating combinations, the coatings have even proven to be harmful to image stability. ©1998 by Wilhelm Imaging Research, Inc. All rights reserved. Wilhelm Imaging Research, Inc., 713 State Street, Grinnell, Iowa 50112 U.S.A. • Telephone: 515-236-4284 • Fax: 515-236-4222 • www.wilhelm-research.com

BIBLIOGRAPHY

PUBLICATIONS

Adams, Ansel with Mary Street Alinder. *Ansel Adams: An Autobiography*. Boston, MA: New York Graphic Society Books, 1985.

Adams, Ansel with Robert Baker. *Ansel Adams: The Camera*. Boston, MA: New York Graphic Society Books, 1980.

Adams, Ansel with Robert Baker. *Ansel Adams: The Negative*. Boston, MA: New York Graphic Society Books, 1981.

Adams, Ansel with Robert Baker. *Ansel Adams: The Print*. Boston, MA: New York Graphic Society Books, 1983.

Blatner, David, and Bruce Fraser. *Real World Photoshop 4: Industrial Strength Production Techniques*. Berkeley, CA: Peachpit Press, 1997.

Blatner, David, Phillip Gaskill, and Eric Taub. *QuarkXPress Tips & Tricks: Industrial-Strength Techniques, 2nd Edition*. Berkeley, CA: Peachpit Press, 1994.

Booth, Sara, ed. *Step-by-Step Electronic Design*. Peoria, IL: Step-by-Step Publishing.

Burns, Diane and Sharyn Venit. *The Official QuarkXPress Handbook, Macintosh 3.2 Edition*. New York, NY: Random House Electronic Publishing, 1994.

Cohen, Luanne Seymour, Russell Brown, Lisa Jeans, and Tanya Wendling. *Design Essentials*. Mountain View, CA: Adobe Press, 1992.

Cohen, Luanne Seymour, Russell Brown, and Tanya Wendling. *Imaging Essentials*. Mountain View, CA: Adobe Press, 1993.

Dayton, Linnea and Jack Davis. *The Photoshop Wow! Book*. Berkeley, CA: Peachpit Press, 1993.

Hamlin, J. Scott. *Photoshop Web Techniques*. Indianapolis, IN: New Riders Publishing, 1997.

Lawler, Brian P. *Photo CD Companion*. Rochester, NY: Eastman Kodak Company

McClelland, Deke. *Macworld Photoshop 4 Bible*. Foster City, CA: IDG Books Worldwide, 1997.

Rich, Jim and Sandy Bozek. *Photoshop 5 in Black-and-White: An Illustrated Guide to Producing Black-and-White Images Using Adobe Photoshop*. Berkeley, CA: Peachpit Press, 1998.

Tapscott, Diane, Lisa Jeans, Pat Soberanis, Rita Amladi, and Jim Ryan. *Production Essentials*. Mountain View, CA: Adobe Press, 1994.

White, Minor, Richard Zakia, and Peter Lorenz. *The New Zone System Manual*. Dobbs Ferry, NY: Morgan Press, Inc., 1976.

Weinman, Lynda, and John Warren Lentz. *Deconstructing Web Graphics.2*. Indianapolis, IN: New Riders Publishing, 1998.

Weinman, Lynda. *Designing Web Graphics.3*. Indianapolis, IN: New Riders Publishing, 1998.

Weinman, Lynda, and Bruce Heavin. *Coloring Web Graphics*. Indianapolis, IN: New Riders Publishing, 1996.

Wilhelm, Henry with Carol Brower. *The Permanence and Care of Color Photographs: Traditional and Digital Color Prints, Color Negatives, Slides, and Motion Pictures*. Grinnell, IA: Preservation Publishing Company, 1993.

WEB SITES (SEE WWW.MAXART.COM FOR FREE UPGRADES AND INFO RELATING TO *Photoshop 5 Artistry*)

Atkinson,Bill. *www.Natureimages.com*. Bill Atkinson Photography

Haynes, Barry and Wendy Crumpler. *www.Maxart.com*. Imaging consultants and *Photoshop 5 Artistry* authors.

Lawler, Brian P. *www.Callamer.com/BPLawler*. Graphic Arts Consultant

Palmer, John. *www.palmerdigital.com*. Photo CD scans and LightJet 5000 Fine Art Prints

Velandria, Ed. *http://dijon.nais.com/~espace*. Award-winning Web designer and creative director at Wavelength 21.

Weinman, Lynda. *www.Lynda.com*. Web books and information.

White, Nancy and René White, *www.lizmar.com*. Media designers for video, multimedia and the Web.

Wilhelm, Henry. *www.wilhelm-research.com*. Color permanence information.

INDEX

Blend modes, 50, 270-271, 274, 278-279
  accessing, 51
  Add, 282
  Apply Image command, 270-273
  Behind, 275
  Calculations command, 270-273
  Clear, 276
  Color, 283-284
  Color Burn, 284
  Color Dodge, 284
  Darken, 280
  Difference, 281-282
  Dissolve, 275
  Exclusion, 282
  Fill command, 270-271, 274
  Gradient tool, 58
  Hard Light, 279-280
  Hue, 283-284
  layers, 85
  Layers palette, 270-272
  Lighten, 280
  Luminosity, 283-284
  Multiply, 276, 279
    combining images, 287-288
  Normal, 275
  Overlay, 279-280
  painting tools, 270-271
  Saturation, 283-284
  Screen, 276, 279
  Soft Light, 277-279
  Subtract, 282
  text effects, creating, 288-289
blending
  images, 238-240
    color correction, 240-245
    removing picture elements, 239-240
  layers, 206, 348
Blur filters
  Gaussian Blur filter, 315
  Motion Blur, 304
  Radial Blur, 304
Blur Mask channel, 303
Blur option (Save for Web dialog box), 340-341
Blur tool, 54-55
blurring
  bitmaps to add gray values, 300-301
  shadows, 315
Bob & Kestrel folder (CD-ROM), 225
Bob Goes To folder (CD-ROM), 216
brightening images, 194-196
  contrast, adjusting, 195
  level adjustments, 195
  snapshots, 195
brightness
  adjusting
    color correction, 204
    master images, 141
  setting, 151
Brightness range, measuring, 98-99

Brightness/Contrast tool, 72
broadband ISDN, xxxviii
Brushes palette, 49
Buckminster Fuller folder (CD-ROM), 194
building Master Palettes, 369
built-in calibrators, 118
built-in Shadow/Edge effects, xxiv
built-in spot color support, xxiv
Burn tool, 55
  shortcut keys, xxix
  burning, 176-177, 197
Burnley Graveyard folder (CD-ROM), 162
buttons
  creating, 355
  transforming square buttons, 134-137
bytes, 122

C

Calculations command (Blend modes), 270-273
calibrating
  color management systems, 113-114
  duotones, 164
  imagesetters, 115
  monitors, 117-120
    built-in calibrators, 118
    CMYK soft proofs, 121
    Gamma utility, 119
    ICC profiles, creating, 117-120
  output devices, 114-117
    CMYK output devices, 116-117
    CMYK test files, 115
    RGB output devices, 116-117
Calibration folder, 115
Canon copiers, xxxvi
capturing images, xxxiii-xxxiv
  direct digital method, xxxiv
  Kodak Photo CD system, xxxiii-xxxiv
  scanners, xxxiii
case sensitivity, filenames, 332
cast shadows, creating
  Cast Shadow One technique, 323-324
  Cast Shadow Three technique, 325
  Cast Shadow Two technique, 324
casts (color casts), correcting for, 159-160
CD-ROM (included), 2
  Bike Ride in the Sky folder, 286
  Bob & Kestrel folder, 225
  Bob Goes To folder, 216
  Buckminster Fuller folder, 194
  Burnley Graveyard folder, 162
  Calibration folder, 115
  Color Correcting Al folder, 204
  content, 4-5
  demo software, 5
  Filters and Effects folder, 303
  folders, 4-5

Grand Canyon folder, 147
  images, 5
    copyright infringement, 5-6
  KansasRawPhotoCD file, 158-159
  McNamaras folder, 247
  Shadow folder, 321
  troubleshooting, 6
  Versailles folder, 229
CDs, Photo CD (color correcting), 138-145
Chain Displacement map, 309-310
Channel Mixer, 71
  oversaturation, fixing, 205-206
channels, 76
  16-bit channel support, xxvi
  Blur Mask channel, 303
  color casts, correcting for, 159-160
  color correction, compositing images, 240-242
  combining
    Apply Image command, 272-273
    Calculations command, 273
  copying, 79
  deleting, 78
  highlights, setting, 158-159
  layers, 81
  mask channels, 77
    editing, 78-80
    layer mask channels, 86
    loading as selections, 78
    saving selections, 170
    saving selections as, 77
    see also selections
  moving, 79
  shadows, setting, 159
  text effects, creating, 288
Channels palette
  Eye icons, 79
  layer masks, 85
  shortcut keys, xxix
characterizing (color gamuts)
  digital printers, 104-106
  monitors, 104
  scanners, 104
CIE xy chromaticity diagrams, 103
Clear mode (Blend modes), 276
CMY colors, 71
  RGB to CMY relationship, 73
CMYK
  color space, 62
    black ink, 63
    converting RGB to CMYK, 63
  Composites preference, 23-24
  Display mode, 192
  files, previewing, 111-112
  format, xxxv
  images
    channels, 76
    converting RGB images to CMYK, 187

COLOPHON

This book was produced almost entirely by the authors on two machines: first, a Mac Power PC 8600/300 with 4Gb internal, an external ProMax disk array (for Photoshop Scratch Disk), 160Mb RAM, built-in Video with an Apple Colorsync 17 display, Bernoulli 230Mb and ZIP transportable drives, and second, a Mac Power PC 9500/132 with 2Gb internal, 128Mb RAM, Radius Thunder 30/1152 video board and PressView 21 SR monitor, Bernoulli 230Mb and ZIP transportable drives. CD backups were burned using a Micronet Master CD Plus 2x4 CD burner, and tape backups were made to a Micronet DAT tape drive using Retrospect.

Each chapter of this book was set up as a separate document in QuarkXPress. The text was input directly into Quark using a template document with Master pages and style sheets. Charts were done in Adobe Illustrator and color correction and separation was done, of course, from Photoshop 4 and 5 using the methods and settings described in this book.

Screen captures were done with Screenshot™, and the Mac's Command-Shift-3 command. Low-res RGB captures were placed in the original documents and sized in Quark. After design decisions were made as to final size and position, the resolution was changed to 350 dpi and photos were resampled, sharpened, separated, and saved as CMYK TIFFs in Photoshop. They were then reimported into Quark at 100%.

Most photographs in this book are from Photo CD or Pro Photo CD scans from 35mm slides done primarily by Palmer Photographic in Mountain View, CA. Several, including the cover, were from scans done by Bill Atkinson Photography on a Tango drum scanner and the McNamaras scans came from a Leafscan-45.

Most pages were output at 2400 dpi using a 175-line screen. Critical color proofing was done using Kodak Approval proofs and less critical color was proofed with Fuji First Look proofs. We used the techniques explained in this book, as well as our GTI Soft-View D5000 Transparency/Print Viewer, to calibrate Photoshop 5 separations on our Apple Colorsync 17 and our PressView 21 SR monitors to color proofs for critical color pages and the cover.

Transfer of files was done primarily using CDs and Iomega ZIP disks which were sent via Airborne Express between the authors and the printer. Files were sent as Quark documents with high-res photos in position. We sent a FileMaker Pro document which delineated the names of each chapter, and the page start and length of the document. Film was set in signatures of 16 pages starting with the most color critical signatures first. In time-critical instances, images and Quark files were sent via internet between the authors and the publisher.

Printing was done by GAC Shepard Poorman in Indianapolis, direct to plate with a Creo platesetter, then printed on Heidelberg Speed Master sheet fed presses. The book is printed on 80lb Productolith Dull and the cover is 12pt C1s with a lay-flat gloss laminate.

Typefaces are New Caledonia, New Caledonia SC&OSF, and Frutiger from Adobe and, on the cover, ITC Orbon from International Typeface Corporation.

PHOTO AND ILLUSTRATION CREDITS

USE YOUR INFLUENCE

Have you ever said, "If only there were a book that…" or "I'd like like to have a book that told me how to…" If so, we want to hear from you.

Our next book is:

PHOTOSHOP, PAINTER, ILLUSTATOR: SIDE BY SIDE. This book is a comparative guide to help you learn Illustrator or Painter if you already know Photoshop. It will focus on the strengths of each program and explore why some of the tasks you are trying to accomplish in one could be more easily handled by another. This book will be out first quarter of 2000.

If you have projects you think should be included, want to talk about how you are currently working in all three programs, or need us to help you accomplish work that requires all three programs, contact us at wendy@maxart.com.

We have scheduled a new week long course in our studio, starting in 2000, that will help you create in all three programs. Check www.maxart.com for course dates.

LET US KNOW WHAT YOU WANT!

MAX ART

Please let me know when you ship:

☐ **PHOTOSHOP, PAINTER, ILLUSTRATOR: SIDE BY SIDE**

Actually, I'm more interested in a book about _____

_____

and I'd like to be on you course mailing list. Here's my important information:

Name _____

Address _____

City _____ *State* _____ *Zip* _____

Phone _____ *Fax* _____ *E-mail* _____

Courses We Currently Offer:
(for details see www.maxart.com)

Barry Haynes & Wendy Crumpler have small custom Photoshop, Illustrator and Painter workshops in their studio. Workshops for four students at a time!

Check www.maxart.com for course descriptions and the latest schedules.

Check www.maxart.com for Photoshop, calibration and printing tips, book errata, and information about new versions of Photoshop.

If you want to be on our mailing list, please send your e-mail address to barry@maxart.com with a request to be on the mailing list.

www.maxart.com or call us at 541-754-2219

The 5-day/4-evening courses:
- Printmaking for Photographers (Photoshop 5 or 5.5)
- The Photoshop, Painter, Illustrator Connection

The 3-day/2-evening courses:
- Advanced Photoshop for Color Correction and Calibration
- Advanced Photoshop for Compositing and Effects

In the 5-day courses, Barry or Wendy help you with your projects or questions during the day, then you solidify new techniques during the evening studio time. The 3-day courses combine instruction using examples from our books during the day with evening time for you to work on your own projects. Each class has a minimum of two students and maximum of four. A creative place with small class size that encourages student-student-instructor interactions. We want you to learn the most in the least amount of time and enjoy the process.

Stamp
Please

Barry Haynes and Wendy Crumpler
2222 NW Brownly Hts. Dr.
Corvallis, OR 97330

Hey, I'd also like to know more about

☐ THE PRINTMAKING FOR PHOTOGRAPHERS COURSE

☐ THE PROJECTS FOR DIGITAL ARTISTS COURSE

☐ BARRY'S UPCOMING "MAKING THE DIGITAL PRINT" BOOK

Check our Web site at www.maxart.com for detailed course descriptions, schedules and locations.

Fold this side up first, staple or tape the edge, and send it on!

Quotes from Photoshop Instructors:

"Simply put *Photoshop 5 Artistry* is the only book out there that does Photoshop the way it should be done. Real stuff for real users! I hope you can keep offering updates; your texts have been the core of all our courses that have anything to do with images and the computer environment. I would be lost with out *Photoshop 5 Artistry*!"
After version 4 came out: "The newest version is even better than the first! The students' reactions are even more positive than ever. The WEB chapters were especially helpful in clearing up confusion about color palettes and 8-bit color versus JPEG."
Before version 5: "I am looking forward to the next version of *Photoshop Artistry*. It has helped educated multitudes of future imagers and greatly enhanced and excited the classroom environment."

Bill Woolston, Professor of Photography, School of Communication, University of Idaho, woolston@uidaho.edu

"Hi, Barry and Wendy. We are using *Photoshop 5 Artistry* for our digital class here at Northern Kentucky University. It is a fountain of information that will serve students well long after the class is finished...I basically learned Photoshop via your first book; I don't think it's an exaggeration to say I couldn't have done it without you. Thanks."

Barry Andersen, Professor of Art, Northern Kentucky University, andersen@nku.edu

"Dear Barry, Just a line to say thanks and congratulations on the *Photoshop 4 Artistry* book. A couple of years ago, I hit an extended period of ill health, which limited my mobility for a time. I turned to digital imaging to keep my mind active, bought a copy of your book (just about the only one anyone really needs) and have enjoyed hundreds of hours of fun ever since. I've recently had some images published in a number of British magazines—which is largely thanks to the excellent examples in *Artistry* ... I've just gotten *Photoshop 5 Artistry* (and congratulations, it's even better than the PS4 version) ... I have a fairly large personal library of Photoshop books and, for what it's worth, I think *Photoshop 5 Artistry* is one of the two best books currently available on the subject —anywhere!...You should be proud to have created such a superb product and such things do take a phenomenal effort."

With great appreciation,
Kindest regards, Bob Rowe ARPS

"Just getting used to the new text version 4 and find it much improved. Thanks for your work! I don't know how I would teach my class without it...I would hate not to have your text available for my classes."

Jan Peterson Roddy, Associate Professor, Dept. Cinema & Photography #6610, Southern Illinois University, Carbondale 62901, jroddy@siu.edu

"Barry, we are anxiously awaiting *Photoshop 5 Artistry*! When will it be available? We use it as the primary text in our Intro to Digital Imaging course and love it. When I began using Photoshop 5, I went through each chapter to see if we would need to make any changes from procedures in the *Photoshop 4 Artistry* book....Thanx again to you and Wendy for the great book."

Stan Shire, Chair, Department of Photographic Imaging, Community College of Philadelphia, sshire@ccp.cc.pa.us

Quotes from Photographers:

"Simply, *Photoshop Artistry* is a book that will open the full potential of Photoshop to the user. There are theoretical sections, but the book is mainly concerned with a series of hands-on tutorials that will take you right around Photoshop and make you a competent user; the book is always there for reference if you should need it!"

With Regards, Ahmno "Himalaya CyberLink", bazra@mos.com.np
Ahmno shoots in Khatmando, India and other interesting places, and mentioned that a Buddist monastery in Khatmando he was helping out had our book!

"Hi Barry and Wendy. I just wanted to send you both a very big 'Thank you' across the ocean for the wonderful book *Photoshop 4 Artistry*. I found the book in a Barnes & Noble bookstore in Poughkeepsie, NY, while on a vacation trip. I immediately fell in love with your book and could barely wait to return to my home in Germany. In the meantime, I started studying it and worked through most of the hands-on examples. No trouble so far; everything is nicely explained. And I have had so much fun and learned so much about Photoshop in such a short time."

Joachim Hoegner, Sindelfingen Germany
JHOEGNER@compuserve.com

"Barry, yours is by far the best of the Photoshop adjunct books...Wish I could come to your workshops. I continue to use your book to refresh basics...We missed meeting in Camden, Maine. Kodak invited me as an artist-in-residence and suggested that I take your Photoshop offering. I was using an Amiga at the time. Had a one-person show at the Neikrug with some of those images. Am really a photojournalist (past stringer for *Life*, *People*, *Time*, etc.)....Look forward to many of your future books."

Judith Gefter, a few credentials: Life member of ASMP, listed in 15 Who's Who's including WW in American Art.

"Did you ever pick up a book and hear the author's voice behind your ear and know you know the voice? Well that about describes how I met you two. I was looking for something beyond the classroom edition I had already worked through (*Photoshop Artistry 4*), and to be honest, for some days now, I secretly hoped to meet some people to share this new adventure with. Well ,there you were. Not just writing on the page, but a real voice actually talking to me. I've started reading, and I just needed to say how pleased I am. Just a few details: I'm a computer professional, system architect, and have been doing serious nature photography for five years. (I have a background in film editing in a former life.) I recently decided to extend my photo activities through a digital darkroom. I greatly enjoyed visiting your site; it transpires the same warmth and good feeling I found in your book."

Milicska Jalbert, Montreal, Quebec, miljal@sympatico.ca

"Dear Barry and Wendy, I rate your *Photoshop 5 Artistry* the best Photoshop book I have seen. Indeed it is kept beside my bed for every evening reading so good it is!"

Best regards, Richard Kenward ABIPP, Richard Kenward Digital Imaging, kenward@photoimaging.demon.co.uk